WORKBOOK

STECK-VAUGHN *Second Edition*

Reasoning Through

LANGUAGE ARTS

TEST PREPARATION for the GED® Test

▶ Reading Informational Texts and Literary Texts

▶ Writing an Extended Response

▶ Using Standard English Grammar, Usage, and Conventions

CONTENT
GED
TESTING SERVICE®
ALIGNED

Aztec Paxen
Publishing

Printed in the U.S.A.

ISBN   978-1-954456-01-3

1 2 3 4 5 6 7 8 9 10   PX2030   30 29 28 27 26 25 24 23

A B C D E

Acknowledgments

For each of the selections and images listed below, grateful acknowledgment is made for permission to excerpt and/or reprint original or copyrighted material, as follows:

Credits

From The New York Times. "Some Progress on Kids and Jails" © 2008 The New York Times Company. All rights reserved. Used under license. **9** The Perils of Indifference by Elie Wiesel. Copyright © 1999 by Elie Wiesel. Reprinted by permission of Georges Borchardt, Inc., on behalf of the author's estate. **__** From CNN.com. "Holiday shoppers share tips for buying American" by Grinberg, Emanuella © 2012 Turner Broadcasting Systems, Inc. All rights reserved. Used under license. **19** From CNN.com. "Holiday shoppers share tips for buying American" by Grinberg, Emanuella © 2012 Turner Broadcasting Systems, Inc. All rights reserved. Used under license. **21** From The New York Times. "The Claim: Violent Video Games Make Young People Aggressive" by Connor, Anahad © 2005 The New York Times Company. All rights reserved. Used under license. **25** From reuters.com. "Organic food no more nutritious than non-organic: study finds" by Pittman, Genevra © 2012 reuters.com. All rights reserved. Used under license. **31** From DECLARATION OF CONSCIENCE by Margaret Chase Smith, 1950. Reprinted by permission of Margaret Chase Smith Library. **32** From The New York Times. "The Back-Door Physicians" © 1981 The New York Times Company. All rights reserved. Used under license. **33** From The New York Times. "A Stay of Execution for the Wolves" © 2008 The New York Times Company. All rights reserved. Used under license. **36** From NOBEL PRIZE ACCEPTANCE SPEECH by Gore, © 2007. Albert A. Gore's Nobel Lecture © The Nobel Foundation (Oslo, December 10, 2007). **37** From SPEECH ACCEPTING THE NOBEL PRIZE IN LITERATURE by William Faulkner, © 1950. William Faulkner's Nobel Lecture © The Nobel Foundation (Oslo, December 10, 1950) **38** From the DEMOCRATIC NATIONAL CONVENTION KEYNOTE ADDRESS by Barbara Jordan, © 1976. Reprinted by the permission of Texas Southern University. **__** Excerpt from "The Rorschach Chronicles" by Margaret Talbot, first published in THE NEW YORK TIMES. Copyright © 1999, used by permission of The Wylie Agency LLC. **46** From Forbes. "Failure to Launch: Adult Children Moving Back Home" by Dunn, Alan © 2012 Forbes. All rights reserved. Used under license. **48** From Newsweek's article RETHINKING FATHERS' RIGHTS by Dahlia Lithwick, © 2008. Reprinted by permission of Newsweek. **49** From The New York Times. "School Vs. Education" by Baker, Russell © 1975 The New York Times Company. All rights reserved. Used under license. **63** From MIAMI-NEW YORK by Martha Gellhorn, © 1948. Used with the permission of the Estate of Martha Gellhorn. **95** Excerpt(s) from THE TIGER IN THE GRASS: STORIES AND OTHER INVENTIONS by Harriet Doerr, copyright © 1995 by Harriet Doerr. Used by permission of Viking Books, an imprint of Penguin Publishing Group, a division of Penguin Random House LLC. All rights reserved. **97** "Pie Dance" from Rough Translations by Mollie Giles. Originally published by The University of Georgia Press © 1985. **103** Excerpt from "The Legacy" from A HAUNTED HOUSE AND OTHER SHORT STORIES by Virginia Woolf. Copyright © 1944, and renewed 1972 by Houghon Mifflin Harcourt Publishing Company. Reprinted by permission of Houghton Mifflin Harcourt Publishing Company. All rights reserved. **105** "In the Gloaming" by Alice Elliott Dark, The New Yorker © 1993 Alice Elliott Dark. Reprinted with permission by Dunow, Carlson and Lerner Literary Agency. **107** From THE PRICE OF TEA IN CHINA by Eileen Goudge, © 1998. Used with the permission of Eileen Goudge. **131** Excerpt from SEGREGATION NOW, SEGREGATION FOREVER: INAUGURAL ADDRESS by George Wallace, 1963. Reprinted with permission of Alabama Department of Archives and History. **132** From madeintheusaforever.com, "Top Ten Reasons To Buy American," by Todd Lipscomb, accessed 2013. Reprinted by permission of MadeinUSAForever.com. **137** From the filmpreservation.org article WHY PRESERVE FILM?, accessed 2013 reprinted with permission from the National Film Preservation Foundation. **141** From The Sacramento Bee. "Death penalty deters murders? Evidence doesn't bear that out" by The Sacramento Bee Editorial Board © 2012 McClatchy. All rights reserved. Used under license. **154** From the Massachusetts Historical Society's Thomas Jefferson Papers: An Electronic Archive: Garden Book, 1766–1824, by Thomas Jefferson, © 2003. Reprinted with permission Massachusetts Historical Society. **166** Excerpt from the article IDENTIFYING WHOLE GRAIN PRODUCTS, accessed 2013. Courtesy of Oldways Whole Grains Council, www.wholegrainscouncil.org. **170** Clemmit, M. "Social Media Explosion." CQ Researcher Vol. 23 (4). Copyright © 2013 by CQ Press. Reprinted by permission of SAGE Publications, Inc. **171** Clemmit, M. "Social Media Explosion." CQ Researcher Vol. 23 (4). Copyright © 2013 by CQ Press. Reprinted by permission of SAGE Publications, Inc. **172** Clemmit, M. "Social Media Explosion." CQ Researcher Vol. 23 (4). Copyright © 2013 by CQ Press. Reprinted by permission of SAGE Publications, Inc. **295–297** Excerpt from Assessment Guide for Educators, published by GED Testing Service LLC. Text copyright © 2014 by GED Testing Service LLC. GED® and GED Testing Service® are registered trademarks of the American Council on Education (ACE). They may not be used or reproduced without the express written permission of ACE or GED Testing Service. The GED® and GED Testing Service® brands are administered by GED Testing Service LLC under license from the American Council on Education. Reprinted by permission of GED Testing Service LLC.

Images

Cover (l) iStock.com/ihsanyildizli, **Cover (r)** iStock.com/BlackJack3D, **127** Photograph by Dorothea Lange, National Archives at College Park

Reasoning Through Language Arts

Workbook

Table of Contents

About the GED® Test

Today's GED® test is very different from the one your grandparents may have taken. Today's GED® test is aligned to the Common Core State Standards and other rigorous content standards. The GED® test serves both as a means to earn a high school equivalency credential and as a predictor of college and career readiness. The GED® test features four subject areas: Reasoning Through Language Arts (RLA), Mathematical Reasoning, Science, and Social Studies.

Each subject area is delivered via a computer-based format and includes multiple-choice items as well as an array of technology-enhanced item types as noted in the table.

Subject Area Test	Content Areas	Item Types	Time
Reasoning Through Language Arts	Informational texts—75% Literary texts—25%	multiple choice, drop-down, drag-and-drop, extended response	150 minutes
Mathematical Reasoning	Algebraic Problem Solving—55% Quantitative Problem Solving—45%	multiple choice, drop-down, fill-in-the-blank, drag-and-drop, hot spot	115 minutes
Science	Life Science—40% Physical Science—40% Earth and Space Science—20%	multiple choice, drop-down, fill-in-the-blank, drag-and-drop, hot spot, short answer	90 minutes
Social Studies	Civics and Government—50% U.S. History—20% Economics—15% Geography and the World—15%	multiple choice, drop-down, fill-in-the-blank, drag-and-drop, hot spot	70 minutes

Items on each subject-area exam connect to three factors:

- **Content Topics/Assessment Targets:** These topics and targets describe and detail the content on the GED® test.
- **Content Practices:** These practices describe the types of reasoning and modes of thinking required to answer specific items on the GED® test.
- **Depth of Knowledge (DOK):** The Depth of Knowledge model details the level of cognitive complexity and steps required to arrive at a correct answer on the test. For the GED® test, there are three levels of DOK complexity:
  - **Level 1:** Test takers must recall, observe, question, or represent facts or simple skills. Typically, they must exhibit only a surface understanding of text.
  - **Level 2:** Test takers must process information beyond simple recall and observation to include summarizing, ordering, classifying, identifying patterns and relationships, and connecting ideas. Test takers must scrutinize text.
  - **Level 3:** Test takers must explain, generalize, and connect ideas by inferring, elaborating, and predicting. Test takers must summarize from multiple sources, synthesize information, or express their thoughts in written responses.

Approximately 80 percent of items across all four content areas will be written to DOK Levels 2 and 3, with the remainder at Level 1. The extended response item in Reasoning Through Language Arts (45 minutes) is considered a DOK Level 3 item.

About the GED® Reasoning Through Language Arts Test

The GED® Reasoning Through Language Arts test assesses more than your knowledge of words. In fact, it reflects an attempt to increase the rigor of the GED® test to meet the demands of a 21st-century economy. To that end, the GED® Reasoning Through Language Arts test features an array of technology-enhanced question types. All questions are delivered via computer and reflect the knowledge, skills, and abilities that a learner would master in an equivalent high school experience.

Multiple-choice questions remain the majority of items on the GED® Reasoning Through Language Arts test. However, a number of technology-enhanced items, including, drag-and-drop, drop-down, and extended response questions, will challenge you to master and convey knowledge in deeper, fuller ways.

- Multiple-choice items assess virtually every content standard. Multiple-choice items include four answer options, structured in an A./B./C./D. format.
- Drag-and-drop items involve interactive tasks that require you to move words, phrases, or short sentences into designated drop zones on a computer screen. You may use drag-and-drop options to classify and sequence information, analyze an author's arguments, and edit to re-order sentences within a paragraph.
- Drop-down items include pull-down menus of response choices directly embedded within the text. You may use drop-down items to demonstrate mastery of language skills, such as conventions of Edited American English and standard usage and punctuation. Such items are designed to mirror the editing process.
- An extended response item on the GED® Reasoning Through Language Arts test is a 45-minute task that requires you to analyze one or more source texts in order to produce a writing sample. The source text will not exceed 650 words. Extended response items will be scored according to how well you fulfill three key traits:
    - analyzing arguments and gathering evidence found in source texts,
    - organizing and developing your writing, and
    - demonstrating fluency with conventions of Edited American English.

You will have a total of 150 minutes (including a 10-minute break) in which to answer about 54 items and write an extended response. A total of 75 percent of texts on the exam will be drawn from informational sources (including nonfiction passages from science, social studies, and workplace contexts). The remaining 25 percent will come from literature. All told, 75 percent of the items on the GED® Reasoning Through Language Arts test will be written at Depth of Knowledge Levels 2 and 3.

GED® Test on Computer

The GED® test is available on computer and only at approved Pearson VUE Testing Centers. You will need content knowledge and the ability to read, think, and write critically, and you must perform basic computer functions—clicking, scrolling, and typing—to succeed on the test. The screen below closely resembles a screen that you will experience on the GED® test.

The **HIGHLIGHT** button allows you to highlight text on the screen. Here, by clicking the Highlight button, you would display color choices for highlighting text. On the Mathematical Reasoning exam, similar buttons for **FORMULA SHEET** and **CALCULATOR REFERENCE** provide information that will help you answer items that require use of formulas or the TI-30XS calculator.

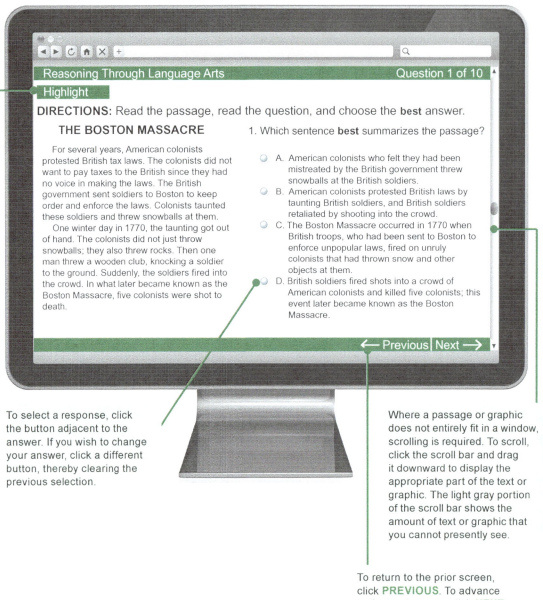

Reasoning Through Language Arts
Question 1 of 10

Highlight

DIRECTIONS: Read the passage, read the question, and choose the **best** answer.

THE BOSTON MASSACRE

For several years, American colonists protested British tax laws. The colonists did not want to pay taxes to the British since they had no voice in making the laws. The British government sent soldiers to Boston to keep order and enforce the laws. Colonists taunted these soldiers and threw snowballs at them.

One winter day in 1770, the taunting got out of hand. The colonists did not just throw snowballs; they also threw rocks. Then one man threw a wooden club, knocking a soldier to the ground. Suddenly, the soldiers fired into the crowd. In what later became known as the Boston Massacre, five colonists were shot to death.

1. Which sentence **best** summarizes the passage?

A. American colonists who felt they had been mistreated by the British government threw snowballs at the British soldiers.

B. American colonists protested British laws by taunting British soldiers, and British soldiers retaliated by shooting into the crowd.

C. The Boston Massacre occurred in 1770 when British troops, who had been sent to Boston to enforce unpopular laws, fired on unruly colonists that had thrown snow and other objects at them.

D. British soldiers fired shots into a crowd of American colonists and killed five colonists; this event later became known as the Boston Massacre.

← Previous | Next →

To select a response, click the button adjacent to the answer. If you wish to change your answer, click a different button, thereby clearing the previous selection.

Where a passage or graphic does not entirely fit in a window, scrolling is required. To scroll, click the scroll bar and drag it downward to display the appropriate part of the text or graphic. The light gray portion of the scroll bar shows the amount of text or graphic that you cannot presently see.

To return to the prior screen, click **PREVIOUS**. To advance to the next screen, click **NEXT**.

Some items on the GED® test, such as fill-in-the-blank, short answer, and extended response questions, will require you to type answers into an entry box. In some cases, the directions may specify the range of typing the system will accept. For example, a fill-in-the-blank item may allow you to type a number from 0 to 9, along with a decimal point or a slash, but nothing else. The system also will tell you keys to avoid pressing in certain situations. The annotated computer screen and keyboard below provide strategies for entering text and data for fill-in-the-blank, short answer, and extended response items.

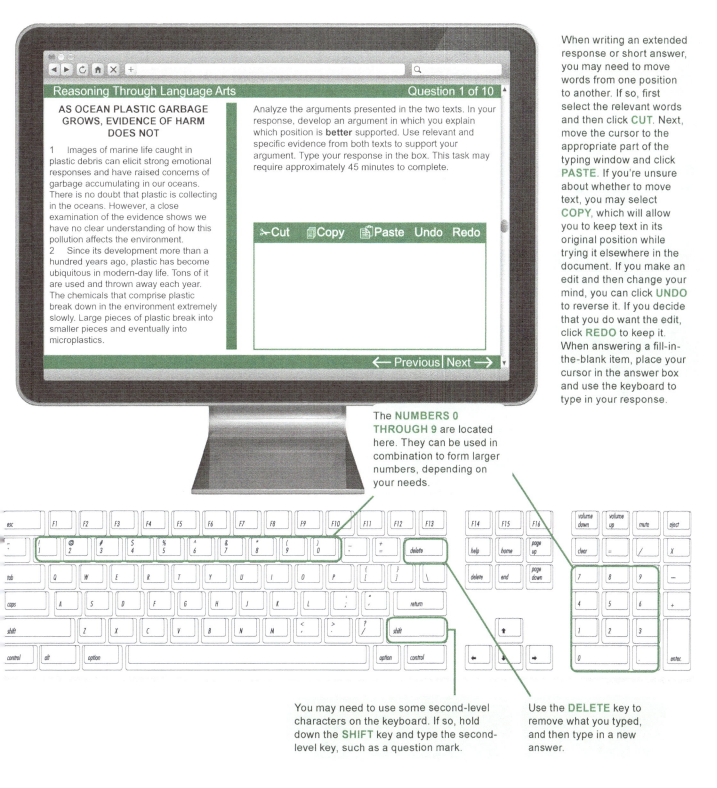

When writing an extended response or short answer, you may need to move words from one position to another. If so, first select the relevant words and then click **CUT**. Next, move the cursor to the appropriate part of the typing window and click **PASTE**. If you're unsure about whether to move text, you may select **COPY**, which will allow you to keep text in its original position while trying it elsewhere in the document. If you make an edit and then change your mind, you can click **UNDO** to reverse it. If you decide that you do want the edit, click **REDO** to keep it. When answering a fill-in-the-blank item, place your cursor in the answer box and use the keyboard to type in your response.

The **NUMBERS 0 THROUGH 9** are located here. They can be used in combination to form larger numbers, depending on your needs.

You may need to use some second-level characters on the keyboard. If so, hold down the **SHIFT** key and type the second-level key, such as a question mark.

Use the **DELETE** key to remove what you typed, and then type in a new answer.

About *Steck-Vaughn Test Preparation for the GED® Test, Second Edition*

The *Steck-Vaughn Test Preparation for the GED® test* as series focuses on on the acquisition of key reading and thinking concepts to help equip you with the skills and strategies to succeed on the GED® test.

Steck-Vaughn's Preparation Program for the GED® Test consists of a Student Book and companion Workbook for each subject area. To help learners develop a deeper understanding of content, the Workbook lessons cover the same skills as the corresponding Student Book lessons but explain concepts differently and provide twice as much practice. As in the Student Books, each Workbook lesson provides guided-practice items, callouts, and testing tips to aid in the development of critical skills. In addition, two-page *High Impact Lessons* address High Impact Indicators identified by the GED Testing Service as critical thinking skills that can help learners improve their performance on the GED® Test. Found throughout the units, *Spotlighted Item* features correspond to one of the technology-enhanced item types that appear on the GED® test

The **REVIEW THE SKILL** section reteaches the skill.

Each lesson includes correlations to **ASSESSMENT TARGETS** that will help focus your studies.

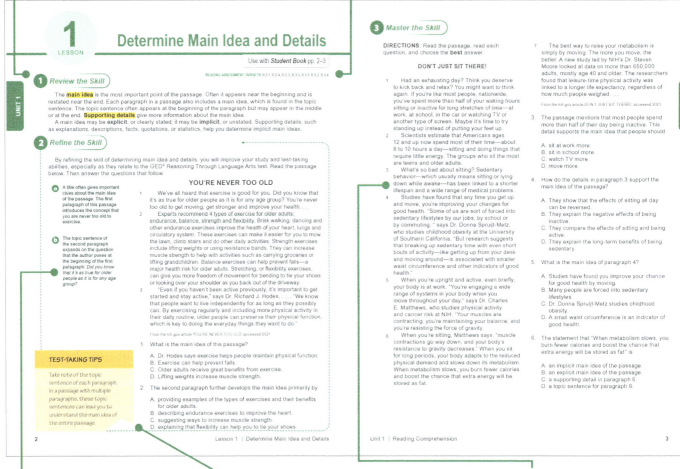

CALLOUTS provide strategies and information that you may use to understand and interpret various passages or graphics.

TEST-TAKING TIPS and other types of notes, such as **USING LOGIC**, offer specific support for succeeding on the GED® test.

PASSAGES, BRIEF TEXTS, AND COLOR VISUALS provide you with an experience similar to that which you can expect on the GED® test.

The *At Work* features at the end of units include practice items reflecting workplace contexts for the skills addressed. *At Work* items target specific career clusters relevant to language arts.

A highly detailed answer key provides correct answers and the rationale behind the answers so that learners know exactly why an answer is correct.

AT WORK items focus on the content covered in each unit.

Grouped by career clusters, **AT WORK** items provide real-world context and application of the skills.

Reading Comprehension at Work

MARKETING, SALES, AND SERVICE

DIRECTIONS: Read the passage, read each question, and choose the **best** answer.

You are a newly hired parts sales associate at GRIP Wholesale Auto Parts. Part of your training includes reading these instructions about sales receipts.

1   Sales receipts are an essential part of the sales process. Sales receipts serve several functions. Sales receipts confirm the payment for a product and provide proof of ownership. They are used by businesses to itemize expenses for tax purposes. They also provide contact information for items that need to be returned. GRIP Wholesale Auto Parts expects all employees to treat sales receipts as an important part of their job.

2   Every sale requires a sales receipt. The GRIP Wholesale Auto Parts store's point-of-sale system is designed to automatically create sales receipts for each purchase. When this system fails to generate a sales receipt, sales associates are expected to complete a sale receipt form and fill in the information by hand. Employees who fail to appropriately complete sales receipts may face disciplinary action, including termination.

3   The GRIP Wholesale Auto Parts sales receipt form has five components. All components must be legible.

   1. **Sales associate's name and employee number.** Be sure to legibly write your name and employee number.
   2. **Date of sale.** Record the month, day, and year.
   3. **Customer information.** Record the customer's name and account number.
   4. **Items.** Record each item, quantity sold, unit price, and total price. Be sure all math calculations are done accurately.
   5. **Payment.** Check the correct box for whether the sale was purchased using cash, check, or credit card.

4   Sales associates should become familiar with the standard GRIP Wholesale Auto Parts sales receipt form. Sales associates should be prepared to complete the form when necessary. For additional information, or if you have any questions or concerns regarding this policy, please contact your GRIP Wholesale Auto Parts store manager.

110

1. In paragraph 1, the author writes, "Sales receipts confirm the payment for a product and provide proof of ownership." Which main idea does this detail support?

    A. "Sales receipts are an essential part of the sales process."
    B. "They also provide contact information for items that need to be returned."
    C. "They are used by businesses to itemize expenses for tax purposes."
    D. "GRIP Wholesale Auto Parts expects all employees to treat sales receipts as an important part of their job."

2. What is the main idea of paragraph 2?

    A. Employees who fail to complete a sales receipt for a sale may be fired.
    B. The GRIP Wholesale Auto Parts store's point-of-sale system automatically creates sales receipts.
    C. A sales receipt is required for every sale.
    D. GRIP Wholesale Auto Parts sales associates need to fill out a sales receipt form for every sale.

3. What is the **most** logical conclusion to draw on the basis of the information in paragraph 3?

    A. Sales associates should know all customer account numbers.
    B. Sales associates need to complete all five of the components listed.
    C. Sales associates only need to worry about listing the items and the total price.
    D. Sales associates only need to complete sales receipts for items bought with cash.

4. How would the meaning of the first sentence of paragraph 4 change if the author had used the word **memorize** instead of the phrase **become familiar with**?

    A. The sentence would imply that sales receipts were optional.
    B. The sentence would imply that forgetting a sales receipt might lead to getting fired.
    C. The sentence would imply that remembering every detail of the sales receipt was not important.
    D. The sentence would imply that it was necessary to remember every detail of the sales receipt process.

HEALTH SCIENCE

DIRECTIONS: Read the passage, read each question, and choose the **best** answer.

You are a student who wants to become a dental hygienist. This excerpt is from a text discussing dental equipment.

INTRODUCTION TO ASPIRATION SYSTEMS

1   Dental aspiration systems are an essential part of all clinics and dental practices. The oral cavity inside a human mouth contains saliva, bacteria, and possibly viruses. The aspirator is a tube that suctions saliva that collects in the oral cavity.

2   Aspiration systems reduce or eliminate cross contamination between patients and dental professionals. When used properly, aspiration systems decrease the microbial cloud expelled from the oral cavity to a radius of less than 30 centimeters. This is less than the average distance between a patient and a dental professional.

3   Aspiration systems comprise the dental equipment (those parts that come into contact with the patients) and the engine room (or motor, which creates the suction). Systems that separate the liquid from the air in the engine room are called wet suction. Systems that separate the liquid in the dental equipment are called dry suction. Both wet and dry suction devices offer different advantages and disadvantages, including the amount of suction they create and the amount of water needed to function properly.

4   Because they are designed to collect bacteria, aspiration systems require constant cleaning and maintenance. Depending on the volume of patients, the systems should be disinfected every day to avoid unpleasant odors and prevent system clogs. This involves disassembling, or taking apart, certain sections of the system.

5. According to clues in the passage, **cross contamination** is

    A. the microbial cloud expelled from the oral cavity.
    B. the collection of saliva, bacteria, and viruses from the oral cavity.
    C. the elimination of bacteria between patients and dental professionals.
    D. the transfer of bacteria between patients and dental professionals.

6. How does the author categorize the types of aspiration systems?

    A. saliva, bacteria, and viruses
    B. dental equipment and engine room
    C. wet suction and dry suction
    D. cleaning and maintenance

7. How does the word **Because** function in paragraph 4?

    A. It introduces a cause-and-effect relationship between the collection of bacteria and the need to clean the equipment.
    B. It creates a contrast between the types of equipment in paragraph 3 and the need to clean the equipment in paragraph 4.
    C. It signals the continuing sequence of events started in paragraph 2.
    D. It reinforces the information in paragraph 3 by introducing an example.

8. What is the **most** logical conclusion to draw on the basis of the information in the last paragraph?

    A. Increasing the volume of patients will prevent system clogs.
    B. The equipment should be disinfected every day to disassemble certain sections.
    C. After certain sections of the equipment are disassembled, they collect bacteria.
    D. After certain sections of the equipment are disassembled, they are cleaned with disinfectant.

Reading Comprehension   111

4. D; DOK Level: 2; Reading Assessment Target: R.4.2. The word *memorize* means to commit to memory, which has a much stronger connotation than the phrase *become familiar with*. Because of this stronger connotation, answers A and C are incorrect. Also, although paragraph 2 states that failing to complete a sales receipt might result in disciplinary action, there is no reason to believe that forgetting to complete a sales receipt would lead to getting fired. Therefore, answer D is incorrect.

To convey meaning and facilitate understanding, **EXTENDED ANNOTATED RESPONSES** from the answer key provide you with the correct response and its rationale. In many cases, the key also explains why the incorrect answers are wrong.

Test-Taking Tips

The GED® test includes more than 160 items across the four subject-area exams of Reasoning Through Language Arts, Mathematical Reasoning, Science, and Social Studies. The four subject-area exams represent a total test time of a little over seven hours. Most items are multiple-choice questions, but a number are technology-enhanced items. These include drop-down, fill-in-the-blank, drag-and-drop, hot spot, short answer, and extended response items.

Throughout this book and others in the series, we help you build, develop, and apply core reading comprehension and thinking skills critical to success on the GED® test. As part of an overall strategy, we suggest that you use the test-taking tips presented here and throughout the book to improve your performance on the GED® test.

> **Always read directions thoroughly so that you know exactly what to do.** As we've noted, the GED® test is computer-based and includes a variety of technology-enhanced items. If you are unclear of what to do or how to proceed, ask the test provider whether directions can be explained.

> **Read each question carefully so that you fully understand what it is asking.** For example, some passages and graphics may present information beyond what is necessary to correctly answer a specific question. Other questions may use boldfaced words for emphasis (for example, "Which statement **best** states the main idea of the passage?").

> **Manage your time with each question.** Because the GED® test is a series of timed exams, you want to spend enough time with each question, but not *too* much time. For example, on the GED® Reasoning Through Language Arts test, you have 95 minutes in which to answer approximately 51 questions, or an average of about two minutes per question. The Reasoning Through Language Arts test also includes a 45-minute writing task. Obviously, some items will require more time and others will require less, but you should remain aware of the overall number of items and amount of testing time. The GED® test interface may help you manage your time. It includes an on-screen clock in the upper right corner that provides the remaining time in which to complete a test. Also, you may monitor your progress by viewing the **Question** line, which will give you the current question number, followed by the total number of questions on that subject-area exam.

> **Answer all questions**, **regardless of whether you know the answer or are guessing.** There is no benefit in leaving questions unanswered on the GED® test. Keep in mind the time that you have for each test, and manage it accordingly. If you wish to review a specific item at the end of a test, click **Flag for Review** to mark the question. When you do, the flag will display in yellow. At the end of a test, you may have time to review questions you've marked.

> **Skim and scan.** You may save time by first reading each question and its answer options before reading or studying an accompanying passage or graphic. Once you understand what the question is asking, review the passage or visual for the appropriate information.

> **Note any unfamiliar words in questions.** First, attempt to re-read the question by omitting any unfamiliar word. Next, try to use other words around the unfamiliar word to determine its meaning.

> **Narrow answer options by re-reading each question and re-examining the text or graphic that goes with it.** Although four answers are *possible* on multiple-choice items, keep in mind that only one is *correct*. You may be able to eliminate one answer immediately; you may need to take more time or use logic or make assumptions to eliminate others. In some cases, you may need to make your best guess between two options.

> **Go with your instinct when answering questions.** If your first instinct is to choose *A* in response to a question, it's best to stick with that answer unless you determine that it is incorrect. Usually, the first answer someone chooses is the correct one.

Study Skills

4 weeks out ...

➤ **Set a study schedule for the GED® test.** Choose times in which you are most alert and places, such as a library, that provide the best study environment.

➤ **Thoroughly review all material in *Steck-Vaughn Test Preparation for the GED® Test: Reasoning Through Language Arts.*** Use the *Reasoning Through Language Arts* workbook to extend understanding of concepts in the *Reasoning Through Language Arts* student book.

➤ **Keep a notebook for each subject area that you are studying.** Folders with pockets are useful for storing loose papers.

➤ **When taking notes, restate thoughts or ideas in your own words rather than copy them directly from a book.** You can phrase these notes as complete sentences, as questions (with answers), or as fragments, provided you understand them.

2 weeks out ...

➤ **Review your performance on the unit reviews in the student book, noting any troublesome subject areas.** Focus your remaining study around those areas. For additional test practice, you may also wish to take the GED Ready™ practice tests.

The days before ...

➤ **Map out the route to the test center, and visit it a day or two before your scheduled exam.** If you plan to drive to the test center on the day of the test, find out where you will need to park.

➤ **Get a good night's sleep the night before the GED® test.** Studies have shown that learners with sufficient rest perform better in testing situations.

The day of ...

➤ **Eat a hearty breakfast high in protein.** As with the rest of your body, your brain needs ample energy to perform well.

➤ **Arrive 30 minutes early to the testing center.** Arriving early will allow sufficient time in the event of a room change.

➤ **Pack a sizeable lunch.** A hearty lunch is especially important if you plan to be at the testing center most of the day.

➤ **Remember to relax.** You've come this far and spent weeks preparing and studying for the GED® test. Now it's your time to shine!

UNIT 1

1 Review the Skill

The **main idea** is the most important point of the passage. Often it appears near the beginning and is restated near the end. Each paragraph in a passage also includes a main idea, which is found in the topic sentence. The topic sentence often appears at the beginning of the paragraph but may appear in the middle or at the end. **Supporting details** give more information about the main idea.

A main idea may be **explicit**, or clearly stated; it may be **implicit**, or unstated. Supporting details, such as explanations, descriptions, facts, quotations, or statistics, help you determine implicit main ideas.

2 Refine the Skill

By refining the skill of determining main idea and details, you will improve your study and test-taking abilities, especially as they relate to the GED® Reasoning Through Language Arts test. Read the passage below. Then answer the questions that follow.

a A title often gives important clues about the main idea of the passage. The first paragraph of this passage introduces the concept that you are never too old to exercise.

b The topic sentence of the second paragraph expands on the question that the author poses at the beginning of the first paragraph: "Did you know that it's as true for older people as it is for any age group?"

a **YOU'RE NEVER TOO OLD**

1   We've all heard that exercise is good for you. Did you know that it's as true for older people as it is for any age group? You're never too old to get moving, get stronger and improve your health. . . .

2   Experts recommend 4 types of exercise for older adults: endurance, balance, strength and flexibility. Brisk walking, dancing and other endurance exercises improve the health of your heart, lungs and circulatory system. These exercises can make it easier for you to mow the lawn, climb stairs and do other daily activities. Strength exercises include lifting weights or using resistance bands. They can increase muscle strength to help with activities such as carrying groceries or lifting grandchildren. Balance exercises can help prevent falls—a major health risk for older adults. Stretching, or flexibility exercises, can give you more freedom of movement for bending to tie your shoes or looking over your shoulder as you back out of the driveway.

3   "Even if you haven't been active previously, it's important to get started and stay active," says Dr. Richard J. Hodes, ... "We know that people want to live independently for as long as they possibly can. By exercising regularly and including more physical activity in their daily routine, older people can preserve their physical function, which is key to doing the everyday things they want to do."

From the nih.gov article YOU'RE NEVER TOO OLD, accessed 2021

1. What is the main idea of this passage?

    A. Dr. Hodes says exercise helps people maintain physical function.
    B. Exercise can help prevent falls.
    C. Older adults receive great benefits from exercise.
    D. Lifting weights increase muscle strength.

2. Paragraph 2 further develops the main idea primarily by

    A. providing examples of exercises and their benefits.
    B. describing endurance exercises to improve the heart.
    C. suggesting ways to increase muscle strength.
    D. explaining that flexibility can help you to tie your shoes.

TEST-TAKING TIPS

Take note of the topic sentence of each paragraph. In a passage with multiple paragraphs, these topic sentences can lead you to understand the main idea of the entire passage.

DIRECTIONS: Read the passage, read each question, and choose the **best** answer.

DON'T JUST SIT THERE!

1   Had an exhausting day? Think you deserve to kick back and relax? You might want to think again. If you're like most people, nationwide, you've spent more than half of your waking hours sitting or inactive for long stretches of time—at work, at school, in the car or watching TV or another type of screen. Maybe it's time to try standing up instead of putting your feet up.

2   Scientists estimate that Americans ages 12 and up now spend most of their time—about 8 to 10 hours a day—sitting and doing things that require little energy. The groups who sit the most are teens and older adults.

3   What's so bad about sitting? Sedentary behavior—which usually means sitting or lying down while awake—has been linked to a shorter lifespan and a wide range of medical problems.

4   Studies have found that any time you get up and move, you're improving your chances for good health. "Some of us are sort of forced into sedentary lifestyles by our jobs, by school or by commuting," says Dr. Donna Spruijt-Metz, who studies childhood obesity at the University of Southern California. "But research suggests that breaking up sedentary time with even short bouts of activity—like getting up from your desk and moving around—is associated with smaller waist circumference and other indicators of good health."

5   When you're upright and active, even briefly, your body is at work. "You're engaging a wide range of systems in your body when you move throughout your day," says Dr. Charles E. Matthews, who studies physical activity and cancer risk at NIH. "Your muscles are contracting, you're maintaining your balance, and you're resisting the force of gravity."

6   When you're sitting, Matthews says, "muscle contractions go way down, and your body's resistance to gravity decreases." When you sit for long periods, your body adapts to the reduced physical demand and slows down its metabolism. When metabolism slows, you burn fewer calories and boost the chance that extra energy will be stored as fat.

7   The best way to raise your metabolism is simply by moving. The more you move, the better. A new study led by NIH's Dr. Steven Moore looked at data on more than 650,000 adults, mostly age 40 and older. The researchers found that leisure-time physical activity was linked to a longer life expectancy, regardless of how much people weighed. . . .

From the nih.gov article DON'T JUST SIT THERE!, accessed 2021

3. The passage mentions that most people spend more than half of their day being inactive. This detail supports the main idea that people should

    A. sit at work more.
    B. sit in school more.
    C. watch TV more.
    D. move more.

4. How do the details in paragraph 3 support the main idea of the passage?

    A. They show that the effects of sitting all day can be reversed.
    B. They explain the negative effects of being inactive.
    C. They compare the effects of sitting and being active.
    D. They explain the long-term benefits of being sedentary.

5. What is the main idea of paragraph 4?

    A. Studies have found you improve your chance for good health by moving.
    B. Many people are forced into sedentary lifestyles.
    C. Dr. Donna Spruijt-Metz studies childhood obesity.
    D. A small waist circumference is an indicator of good health.

6. The statement that "When metabolism slows, you burn fewer calories and boost the chance that extra energy will be stored as fat" is

    A. an implicit main idea of the passage.
    B. an explicit main idea of the passage.
    C. a supporting detail in paragraph 6.
    D. a topic sentence for paragraph 6.

3 Master the Skill

DIRECTIONS: Read the letter, read each question, and choose the **best** answer.

ENDANGERED BIRDS

1 My dear Mr. Chapman:

2   I need hardly say how heartily I sympathize with the purposes of the Audubon Society. I would like to see all harmless wild things, but especially all birds, protected in every way. I do not understand how any man or woman who really loves nature can fail to try to exert all influence in support of such objects as those of the Audubon Society.

3   Spring would not be spring without bird songs, any more than it would be spring without buds and flowers, and I only wish that besides protecting the songsters, the birds of the grove, the orchard, the garden and the meadow, we could also protect the birds of the sea shore and of the wilderness. The loon ought to be, and, under wise legislation, could be a feature of every Adirondack lake; ospreys, as everyone knows, can be made the tamest of the tame; and terns should be as plentiful along our shores as swallows around our barns. A tanager or a cardinal makes a point of glowing beauty in the green woods, and the cardinal among the white snows.

4   When the bluebirds were so nearly destroyed by the severe winter a few seasons ago, the loss was like the loss of an old friend, or at least like the burning down of a familiar and dearly loved house. How immensely it would add to our forests if only the great logcock were still found among them! The destruction of the wild pigeon and the Carolina paraquet has meant a loss as severe as if the Catskills or the Palisades were taken away. When I hear of the destruction of a species I feel just as if all the works of some great writer had perished; as if we had lost all instead of only part of Polybius or Livy.

    Very truly yours,
    Theodore Roosevelt

LETTER TO FRANK MICHLER CHAPMAN by Theodore Roosevelt, 1899

7 What is the main idea of this letter?

A. People who love nature should protect it.
B. The seasons would not seem right without the appropriate songs of birds.
C. All harmless wildlife, especially birds, should be protected.
D. Legislation should protect song birds as well as other kinds of birds.

8. What is the main idea of paragraph 3?

A. Birds belong to the cycle of the seasons.
B. Laws must be made to protect all birds.
C. Sea birds are in greater danger than meadow and garden birds.
D. Winter birds and spring birds are equally colorful.

9. Which detail in paragraph 3 **best** supports the main idea of the paragraph?

A. "Spring would not be spring without bird songs, any more than it would be spring without buds and flowers,"
B. "and I only wish that besides protecting the songsters, the birds of the grove, the orchard the garden and the meadow, we could also protect the birds of the sea shore and of the wilderness."
C. "The loon ought to be, and, under wise legislation, could be a feature of every Adirondack lake;"
D. "A tanager or a cardinal makes a point of glowing beauty in the green woods, and the cardinal among the white snows."

10. How does the author's comparison of the loss of the pigeon with the loss of the Catskill Mountains support the main idea of the letter?

A. Both pigeons and the Catskill Mountains are endangered.
B. Birds are just as important to the environment as larger and grander things like mountains.
C. Neither pigeons nor the Catskill Mountains can protect themselves.
D. Both pigeons and the Catskill Mountains are wild things.

11. Which sentence states the **implicit** main idea of paragraph 4?

A. The destruction of a species is like the loss of family, environment, and culture.
B. Birds such as the great logcock have added to the beauty of American forests.
C. The destruction of a species is like the destruction of the works of a great writer.
D. Some species, such as the wild pigeon and great logcock, already have been destroyed.

DIRECTIONS: Read the passage, read each question, and choose the **best** answer.

BROWN V. BOARD OF EDUCATION

1   Today, education is perhaps the most important function of state and local governments. . . .[I]t is a principal instrument in awakening the child to cultural values, in preparing him for later professional training, and in helping him to adjust normally to his environment. In these days, it is doubtful that any child may reasonably be expected to succeed in life if he is denied the opportunity of an education. Such an opportunity, where the state has undertaken to provide it, is a right which must be made available to all on equal terms.

2   We come then to the question presented: Does segregation of children in public schools solely on the basis of race, even though the physical facilities and other "tangible" factors may be equal, deprive the children of the minority group of equal educational opportunities? We believe that it does. . . .

3   To separate [some students] from others of similar age and qualification solely because of their race generates a feeling of inferiority as to their status in the community that may affect their hearts and minds in a way unlikely ever to be undone. The effect of this separation on their educational opportunities was well stated [in a previous case]:

4   "Segregation of white and colored children in public schools has a detrimental effect upon the colored children. The impact is greater when it has the sanction of the law; for the policy of separating the races is usually interpreted as denoting the inferiority of the negro group. A sense of inferiority affects the motivation of a child to learn. Segregation with the sanction of law, therefore, has a tendency to [retard] the educational and mental development of negro children and to deprive them of some of the benefits they would receive in a racial[ly] integrated school system."

5   We conclude that in the field of public education the doctrine of "separate but equal" has no place. Separate educational facilities are inherently unequal.

From the U.S. Supreme Court majority opinion BROWN V. BOARD OF EDUCATION, 1954

12. Which statement **best** states the main idea of the passage?

A. Every child needs a good education to succeed.
B. Facilities in segregated black schools are inferior to facilities in white schools.
C. Segregation deprives minority children of an equal chance for a good education.
D. Education is the most important function of state and local governments.

13. How do the details in paragraph 3 support the main idea of the passage?

A. They explain that separating black children because of their race harms their self-esteem.
B. They show that most white people want to send their children to segregated schools.
C. They describe the effects of separate school facilities on the ability of white children to learn.
D. They explain that the effect of segregation on children of either race is not known.

14. Which detail **best** supports the idea that separating children by race is rooted in racial prejudice? The decision states that

A. "a sense of inferiority affects the motivation of a child to learn."
B. "the impact [of the policy] is greater when it has the sanction of law."
C. segregation deprives children of some of the "benefits they would receive in a[n] . . . integrated school."
D. it is "usually interpreted as denoting the inferiority of the negro group."

15. Paragraph 4 states "A sense of inferiority affects the motivation of a child to learn." How does this statement support the main idea of the passage?

A. Children who lack motivation have less of a chance to obtain a good education.
B. White children do not learn as well in segregated schools.
C. Children with a sense of inferiority always drop out of school.
D. All children have less of a sense of inferiority in segregated schools.

Summarize

UNIT 1

1 Review the Skill

A **summary** briefly highlights the main points and important details of a text. The summary should restate the ideas of the text in your own words. Summaries should not contain your own opinions, beliefs, or judgments.

You might have summarized a story to a friend or summarized your work history to a possible employer. Think about your summary. You probably included only the most important information and told it in the simplest terms. These elements are key to a good summary.

2 Refine the Skill

By refining the skill of summarizing, you will improve your study and test-taking abilities, especially as they relate to the GED® Reasoning Through Language Arts test. Read the passage below. Then answer the questions that follow.

THE FOOD CHAIN

a This paragraph summarizes key details of what makes an organism a consumer. The first sentence gives the overall main idea of the paragraph and then the author uses the words *primary*, *secondary*, and *tertiary* to explain the levels of consumer.

b Understanding the main idea of the passage will help you summarize it. This section gives the reader an explicit example to explain the main idea.

All living things need energy to carry out life processes. Organisms that get energy from sunlight through photosynthesis are called producers. All green plants, such as grasses and seaweeds, are producers.

Organisms that eat other organisms in order to obtain energy are called consumers. Primary consumers, such as rabbits and sea urchins, eat producers to obtain energy. Secondary consumers, such as foxes and seals, eat primary consumers to obtain energy. Sometimes, there are tertiary (third-level) consumers, such as owls and killer whales, that eat secondary consumers.

For example, a food chain for a fox would show energy flow from the sun to the grass (producer) to a rabbit (primary consumer) to the fox (secondary consumer). A food chain shows how energy can flow from producers to consumers.

USING LOGIC

A good summary must capture the main idea of the paragraph, section, or whole passage, not just specific details of it. When choosing the best summary, eliminate answers that do not state the main idea.

1. Which statement **best** summarizes the passage?

A. Secondary consumers feed on primary consumers for energy.
B. Tertiary consumers feed on secondary consumers.
C. In a food chain, energy flows from the sun to producers and then to consumers.
D. All green plants are producers.

2. What is the function of the last sentence of the passage?

A. It provides additional information about consumers.
B. It provides additional information about producers.
C. It summarizes the second paragraph.
D. It summarizes the entire passage.

DIRECTIONS: Read the passage, read each question, and choose the **best** answer.

CONCERNS ABOUT JUVENILE OFFENDERS

1   The number of minors being held in adult jails and prisons in this country has dropped substantially, according to a new study based on federal data. That's welcome news. Criminologists warn that juvenile offenders who are thrown in with adult prisoners are exposed to social pressures and develop personal contacts that make it far more likely that they will become career criminals than those held in juvenile facilities.

2   The study ... shows that the number of minors being held in adult facilities has decreased by 38 percent since 1999. Because of reductions in juvenile crime and arrests, among other factors, the number of children held in juvenile facilities also fell.

3   Congress can consolidate these gains by using aid to impose a clear federal standard: To qualify for federal juvenile-justice funds, states should have to certify that people under 18 are not being jailed as adults, except in cases involving heinous crimes like rape and murder.

4   Unfortunately, not all of the new data is encouraging. States still seem to be holding in juvenile facilities a great many children who should instead be treated in therapeutic programs near their homes and families. Children with drug or alcohol problems should be in treatment programs, not juvenile lockups. Therapeutic programs can turn young lives around and reduce crime. ...

5   The data also show that too many children are still being confined for minor offenses like truancy, which should be dealt with through community-based programs. Putting truants into juvenile facilities makes it more likely that they will repeatedly return to custody and become permanently entangled in the system. Congress, which tried to end this practice with the Juvenile Justice and Delinquency Prevention Act of 1974, should close the loophole that allows states to continue ... confining truants.

6   Another cause for concern is the significant racial and ethnic disparities that show up in juvenile justice data. The decline in the juvenile custody rate was significantly greater for whites than for African-Americans, who account for less than 15 percent of the youth population but nearly 40 percent of those in confinement.

From *The New York Times's* editorial, SOME PROGRESS ON KIDS AND JAILS, © 2008

3. Which sentence **best** summarizes the results of the study?

    A. Less juvenile crime has caused fewer minors to be placed into the adult prison population.
    B. Fewer minors are being held in both juvenile and adult detention facilities.
    C. The number of minors held in adult detention facilities has decreased by 38 percent since 1999.
    D. Juvenile offenders thrown in with adult prisoners are likely to become career criminals.

4. Which sentence **best** summarizes the information in paragraph 4?

    A. Not all the results of the study were positive, but I disagree with them.
    B. Many youthful offenders need therapy rather than time in juvenile lockups.
    C. Children with drug or alcohol problems should be in facilities near their homes.
    D. Therapy can help reduce crime by helping young offenders find work.

5. Which sentence **best** states the main idea of paragraph 5?

    A. The study shows that too many minors are being held for truancy.
    B. Congress should close the loophole that allows states to hold minors for truancy.
    C. Truancy is a major cause for minors to be confined as juvenile offenders.
    D. Community-based organizations should deal with children's minor offenses.

6. How is paragraph 6 related to the rest of the passage?

    A. It summarizes the results of the study.
    B. It focuses on a detail of the summary in paragraph 5.
    C. It adds more information about the results of the study.
    D. It summarizes the one negative result of the study.

DIRECTIONS: Read the passage, read each question, and choose the **best** answer.

LET US CONTINUE

1   For 32 years Capitol Hill has been my home. I have shared many moments of pride with you, pride in the ability of the Congress of the United States to act, to meet any crisis, to distill from our differences strong programs of national action. An assassin's bullet has thrust upon me the awesome burden of the Presidency. I am here today to say I need your help. I cannot bear this burden alone. I need the help of all Americans, and all America.

2   This nation has experienced a profound shock, and in this critical moment, it is our duty, yours and mine, as the Government of the United States, to do away with uncertainty and doubt and delay, and to show that we are capable of decisive action; that from the brutal loss of our leader we will derive not weakness, but strength; that we can and will act and act now.

3   From this chamber of representative government, let all the world know and none misunderstand that I rededicate this Government to the unswerving support of the United Nations, to the honorable and determined execution of our commitments to our allies, to the maintenance of military strength second to none, to the defense of the strength and the stability of the dollar, to the expansion of our foreign trade, to the reinforcement of our programs of mutual assistance and cooperation in Asia and Africa, and to our Alliance for Progress in this hemisphere.

4   On the 20th day of January, in 19 and 61, John F. Kennedy told his countrymen that our national work would not be finished "in the first thousand days, nor in the life of this administration, nor even perhaps in our lifetime on this planet." "But," he said, "let us begin."

5   Today in this moment of new resolve, I would say to all my fellow Americans, let us continue.

From LET US CONTINUE by Lyndon Baines Johnson, 1963

7.   Which sentence **best** summarizes Johnson's message in paragraph 1?

   A. Capitol Hill has been his home for 32 years.
   B. He cannot bear his burden alone during a critical moment.
   C. He feels great pride in Congress and in the country.
   D. He needs Americans' support at this critical time.

8.   Which sentence **best** summarizes the information in paragraph 2?

   A. The assassination of John F. Kennedy was a terrible event for the nation.
   B. The nation must act with strength and determination despite the death of its leader.
   C. The unwillingness of Congress to take action has left the country paralyzed.
   D. The Government has a duty to act without further delays.

9.   What purpose does paragraph 3 serve in this speech?

   A. It summarizes the programs and policies for which Johnson seeks support.
   B. It summarizes major changes in American policy for which Johnson is responsible.
   C. It summarizes Kennedy's major achievements as President.
   D. It summarizes Johnson's past achievements as Vice President.

10.   How do the final words of the speech, "let us continue," summarize the overall message? The final words

   A. express Johnson's hope that Kennedy will not be forgotten.
   B. emphasize Johnson's point that he cannot bear the burden of the presidency without support.
   C. refer to the need for following the policies and programs that Kennedy began.
   D. express the need for starting over as a nation.

Lesson 2 | Summariz

DIRECTIONS: Read the passage, read each question, and choose the **best** answer.

INDIFFERENCE

1   Over there, behind the black gates of Auschwitz, the most tragic of all prisoners were the "Muselmanner," as they were called. Wrapped in their torn blankets, they would sit or lie on the ground, staring vacantly into space, unaware of who or where they were—strangers to their surroundings. They no longer felt pain, hunger, thirst. They feared nothing. They felt nothing. They were dead and did not know it.

2   Rooted in our tradition, some of us felt that to be abandoned by humanity then was not the ultimate. We felt that to be abandoned by God was worse than to be punished by Him. . . .

3   In a way, to be indifferent to that suffering is what makes the human being inhuman. Indifference, after all, is more dangerous than anger and hatred. Anger can at times be creative. One writes a great poem, a great symphony. One does something special for the sake of humanity because one is angry at the injustice that one witnesses. But indifference is never creative. Even hatred at times may elicit a response. You fight it. You denounce it. You disarm it.

4   Indifference elicits no response. Indifference is not a response. Indifference is not a beginning; it is an end. And, therefore, indifference is always the friend of the enemy, for it benefits the aggressor—never his victim, whose pain is magnified when he or she feels forgotten. The political prisoner in his cell, the hungry children, the homeless refugees—not to respond to their plight, not to relieve their solitude by offering them a spark of hope is to exile them from human memory. And in denying their humanity, we betray our own.

5   Indifference, then, is not only a sin, it is a punishment.

6   And this is one of the most important lessons of this outgoing century's wide-ranging experiments in good and evil.

From THE PERILS OF INDIFFERENCE by Elie Wiesel, © 1999

11. The author's main idea in paragraph 1 is that the Muselmanner are tragic because they

A. are prisoners in Auschwitz.
B. are about to die.
C. feel hunger, thirst, and pain.
D. have lost their connection with life.

12. Which statement **best** summarizes why the author believes indifference is more dangerous than anger or hatred?

A. No creativity or response comes from indifference.
B. Anger and hatred go away quickly.
C. Indifference can lead to creative actions.
D. Anger and hatred are simpler emotions than indifference.

13. Which statement **best** summarizes what the author means by saying that indifference is an "end"?

A. Indifference occurs after anger and hatred.
B. Indifference is the last step before death.
C. Indifference does not lead to action or result in a response to suffering.
D. Indifference is the goal of people who aim to hurt others.

14. Which sentence is the **best** summary of the author's view of indifference?

A. Indifference punishes people by denying them their humanity.
B. Indifference can be good as well as evil.
C. Indifference is equal to hatred because both hurt people.
D. Indifference is something that must be fought by aggressors.

15. How do the words in paragraph 5 support the overall argument of the passage?

A. The author believes that indifference should be a criminal offence, punishable by the law.
B. The author believes that the consequences of indifference punishes others more than the indifferent.
C. The author believes that we mush fight indifference with all we have.
D. The author believes that the consequences of indifference are so severe that in addition to being destructive to others, they are destructive to the self.

Determine Sequence

LESSON 3

READING ASSESSMENT TARGETS: R.3.1, R.3.2, R.5

UNIT 1

1 *Review the Skill*

Knowing the **sequence**, or order of events, when you are reading a text can help you understand how events are related. Look for key words like *first, next, later, after,* and *finally*. These words identify the order in which the events or steps take place. Sequence is important in understanding the progression of the text. Sometimes the progression is not straightforward, so understanding how to find the sequence of events can help you understand what you read.

2 *Refine the Skill*

By refining the skill of determining sequence, you will improve your study and test-taking abilities, especially as they relate to the GED® Reasoning Through Language Arts test. Read the passage below. Then answer the question that follows.

FBI'S FIRST WANTED POSTER

On December 2, 1919, a 23-year-old soldier named William N. Bishop slipped out of the stockade at Camp A. A. Humphreys— today's Fort Belvoir—in northern Virginia.

Shortly after Bishop's getaway, the Military Intelligence Division of the Army requested the Bureaus' help in finding him. One early assistant director, Frank Burke, responded by sending a letter to "All Special Agents, Special Employees and Local Officers" asking them to "make every effort" to capture Bishop. . . .

a Knowing the order of events can help you understand how events are related. The passage states that the letter was written "eleven years into its history," which means the FBI was created in 1908.

Burke labeled that document—dated December 15, 1919—"Identification Order No. 1." In essence, it was the Bureau's first wanted poster, and it put the organization squarely in the fugitive-catching business just eleven years into its history. It has been at it ever since.

b Phrases such as *by the 1920s* and *by the 1930s* indicate a step forward in the "timeline" of a text. This phrase indicates an approximate time gap, which is common in social studies text.

Within a few years, the identification order—or what soon became known throughout law enforcement as an "IO"—had become a staple of crime fighting. By the late 1920s, these wanted flyers were circulating not only throughout the U.S. but also Canada and Europe (and later worldwide). . . . By the 1930s, IOs were sent to police stations around the nation, enlisting the eyes of the public in the search for fugitives. In 1950, building on the "wanted posters" concept, the FBI created its "Ten Most Wanted Fugitives" list.

Adapted from the fbi.gov article A BRIEF HISTORY, accessed 2021.

USING LOGIC

Authors may include exact dates or use transitional language, such as *two years later*, to indicate a gap in time. You can determine the time between events based on dates or the transitional language.

Based on the passage, how much time passed between the first Identification Order and the creation of the "Ten Most Wanted Fugitives" list?

A. 42 years
B. 31 years
C. 22 years
D. 11 years

★ Spotlighted Item: **DRAG-AND-DROP**

DIRECTIONS: Read the passage and the question. Then use the drag-and-drop options to complete the chart.

COLIN L. POWELL

1   Colin L. Powell was appointed Secretary of State by George W. Bush on January 20, 2001, after being unanimously confirmed by the U.S. Senate. He served for four years, leaving the position on January 26, 2005. He was the first African American to serve as Secretary of State.

Rise to Prominence

2   Powell was born on April 5, 1937, in the New York City neighborhood of Harlem. The son of two Jamaican immigrants, he was raised in the South Bronx. He attended City College of New York, and it was there that he began his military service, joining the Reserve Officer Training Corps (ROTC). After his graduation in 1958, Powell was commissioned a second lieutenant in the U.S. Army. During his 35 years in the Army he served two tours in Vietnam, was stationed in West Germany and South Korea, and acted as President Ronald Reagan's National Security Advisor from 1987 until 1989. In 1989 he was promoted to the rank of general and was appointed by President George H.W. Bush to the position of Chairman of the Joint Chiefs of Staff. In the four years Powell served in that capacity, he oversaw 28 crises, including Operation Desert Storm in 1991. After his retirement in 1993, he founded America's Promise, an organization that helps at-risk children. He was nominated for Secretary of State by President George W. Bush on December 16, 2000.

Influence on U.S. Diplomacy

3   At the beginning of his term, Powell placed an emphasis on reaffirming diplomatic alliances throughout the world, supporting a national missile defense system, working towards peace in the Middle East, and prioritizing sanctions instead of force in potential hot spots such as Iraq. He also focused on reinvigorating U.S. diplomacy through reforms in the Department of State's

organizational culture and an infusion of resources for personnel, information technology, security, and facilities. Powell's term, however, was soon dominated by the challenges the Bush Administration faced after the September 11, 2001, terrorist attacks.

From the state.gov series BIOGRAPHIES OF THE SECRETARIES OF STATE: COLIN L. POWELL, accessed 2021

2. Drag and drop the events into the chart to show the order in which they occurred.

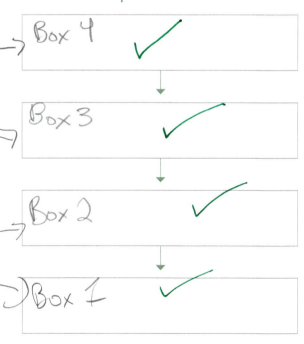

Sequence of Events

Box 4 ✓

Box 3 ✓

Box 2 ✓

Box 1 ✓

George W. Bush appoints Powell as Secretary of State. *1*	Powell founds America's Promise. *2*
Powell serves as Chairman of Joint Chiefs of Staff. *3*	Powell serves as National Security Advisor. *4*

★ Spotlighted Item: **DRAG-AND-DROP**

DIRECTIONS: Read the passage and the question. Then use the drag-and-drop options to complete the timeline.

WASHINGTON AT VALLEY FORGE

1   Dr. Albigence Waldo was born in Pomfret, Connecticut, in 1750. He became surgeon of the First Connecticut Infantry Regiment on January 1, 1777. In September 1777, the regiment was ordered to join the army in Pennsylvania. He resigned from service on October 1, 1779, and died on January 20, 1794.

2   While serving at Valley Forge during the winter of 1777-1778, Dr. Waldo kept a diary of the events of that time, in which he described men camped in cold, uncomfortable huts with little food. In the diary, he also lamented about "Poor food—hard lodging—Cold Weather—fatigue—Nasty Clothes—nasty Cookery" and general dismal conditions.

3   His journal at Valley Forge begins on November 10, 1777, and his entry for that day ends with "No salt to eat dinner with." On December 8, his regiment, along with sixteen others, was called to gather in front of the Washington barracks under the command of Sullivan and Wayne. At about one o'clock, the news arrived that the enemy had made a hasty retreat to the city of Philadelphia. On December 18, after illness and much personal suffering, Dr. Waldo wrote: "The Army are poorly supplied with Provision, occasioned it is said by the Neglect of the Commissary of Purchases. ... The Congress have not made their Commissions valuable Enough. Heaven avert the bad consequences of these things!" His last diary entry on January 8, 1778, notes: "Unexpectedly got a Furlow. Set out for home."

3.   Drag and drop the events into the timeline to show the order in which they occur in the passage.

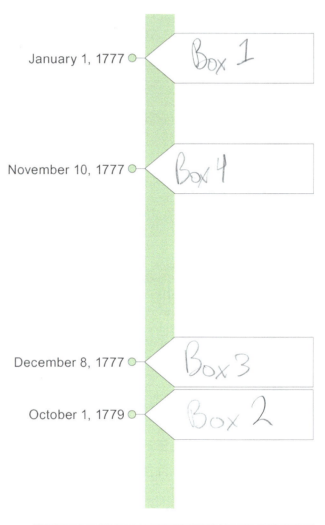

January 1, 1777	Box 1
November 10, 1777	Box 4
December 8, 1777	Box 3
October 1, 1779	Box 2

Dr. Waldo joins the First Connecticut Infantry Regiment.	1	Dr. Waldo's regiment is called to gather in front of the Washington barracks.	3
Dr. Waldo resigns from service.	2	Dr. Waldo begins journaling at Valley Forge.	4

DIRECTIONS: Read the passage and the question. Then use the drag and drop options to complete the chart.

HOW A BILL ORIGINATING IN THE HOUSE OF REPRESENTATIVES BECOMES A LAW

1   A bill is the form used for most legislation, whether permanent or temporary, general or special, public or private. The bill is assigned its legislative number by the clerk and referred to the appropriate committee.

2   It is during committee action that the most intense consideration is given to the proposed measures; this is also the time when the people are given the opportunity to be heard. Each piece of legislation is referred to the committee that has jurisdiction over the area affected by the measure.

3   After hearings are completed, the bill is considered in a session that is popularly known as the "mark-up" session. Members of the committee study the viewpoints presented in detail. Amendments may be offered to the bill, and the committee members vote to accept or reject these changes.

4   At the conclusion of deliberation, a vote of committee or subcommittee members is taken to determine what action to take on the measure. If the committee votes to report a bill, the Committee Report is written. This report describes the purpose and scope of the measure and the reasons for recommended approval.

5   [The full House then debates the bill.] After all debate is concluded and amendments decided upon, the House is ready to vote on final passage.

6   After a measure passes in the House, it goes to the Senate for consideration. After a measure has been passed in identical form by both the House and Senate, it is considered "enrolled." It is sent to the president who may sign the measure into law, veto it and return it to Congress, let it become law without signature, or at the end of a session, pocket-veto it.

From the house.gov article THE LEGISLATIVE PROCESS, accessed 2013

4.   Drag and drop the steps into the chart to show the order in which they occur in the process of a bill becoming a law.

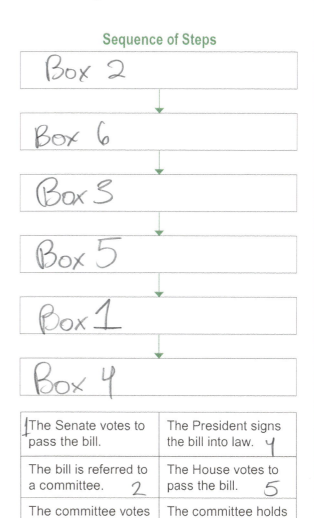

High Impact Lesson: Sequence of Events

Use with **Student Book** pp. 8–11

UNIT 1

1 Review the Skill

The order in which events take place is the **sequence** of events. Some informational texts will be in chronological order, which means the events take place in time order—first event, second event, third event, and so on. Some informational texts may use a nonchronological order, which means that events do not take place in time order. The writer may flashback to a previous time, flash-forward to a later time, or skip around in time order.

Signal Words

When reading informational texts, signal words can help you understand both the order of events and how events are related. Instructional, procedural, and scientific texts often explain how to do a task or how something works. These types of text will often include signal words such as *first, second, third, after, before,* and *finally*. Biographical passages and history texts generally include specific dates that events occur, such as March 3, 1914. These texts may also include references to other give dates or events, such as *Three years later* or *Before being elected*.

When informational texts do not use chronological order, authors will still include signal words that help readers identify how events are related to one another in time, such as *at, by, during, while,* and *until*.

On the GED® Reasoning Through Language Arts test, you will be expected to show you understand sequence of events. You may encounter questions that ask you to locate a specific event in a text, identify order of events in a text, describe how one event leads to the next, order non-chronological events in chronological order, or order chronological events in a different way.

2 Refine the Skill

ⓐ Notice in the last sentence of the first paragraph, the text tells readers it will explain how web servers work. This shows it will present a process, or sequence of events.

ⓑ The information is presented here as a numbered list. The numbers help readers understand the order of the sequence.

Scan the list for key words *assembles* and *content.* They are found in Step 3. What occurs the step before this? The correct answer is **C**.

HOW WEB SERVERS WORK

Servers make the Internet work. Servers are computers designed to provide data to other computers. Some operate e-mail systems, organize and manage data files, or provide secure financial transactions. There are many different types of servers. One of the most common is the web server. These are designed to provide access to websites. Web servers work like this:

1. Your computer sends a request through the Internet to a web server.
2. The server receives the request and interprets it.
3. The server then assembles all of the content needed to show the site, including text, images, video, and even content from other servers.
4. The server transmits the information in tiny chunks of data back through the Internet to your browser.
5. Your computer's web browser interprets the data it receives from the web server and presents it.

1. What step needs to happen before a web server assembles the content necessary to show a web site?

   A. The server provides secure financial transactions.
   B. The server finds text, images, and videos related to the web site.
   C. The server receives the request and interprets it.
   D. The web browser interprets data from the server.

DIRECTIONS: Read the passage, read each question, and choose the **best** answer.

HOW VINYL RECORDS ARE MADE

Vinyl records are more than relics of a bygone era. They are tangible artifacts, physical representations of the music people love. And although vinyl has largely been replaced with what some consider the superior quality of digital music files, a number of companies continue to make records. Here is how they do it.

Step 1: Make the music. Musicians work with producers and engineers to record the music. Studio equipment is used to add or remove vocals, instruments, and other elements. Their volumes are adjusted.

Step 2: Cut the master disc. The sound vibrations from the music are transferred to a master disc through a cutting tool, or lathe. The lathe cuts grooves into an aluminum disc, which is called the master.

Step 3: Create the stamper. The master disc is coated in chemicals and placed in a tank of liquid with dissolved nickel. Electricity is run through the liquid, causing the nickel to fuse with the chemical coating in a process called electroplating. The metal layer creates a positive image of the master disc's grooves. Since records have two sides, separate stampers are needed for both.

Step 4: Prepare the labels. Adhesive labels, which appear on the final products, are printed separately.

Step 5: Press the records. The metal stampers are placed in record presses. Polyvinyl chloride (PVC) pellets are loaded into a hopper. From there, the plastic is funneled through pipes and heated. At the other end is an extruder, which squeezes and shapes the PVC into small circles, called biscuits. Labels are placed on the biscuit, and it is moved into the press. The metal stamper is pressed into the hot vinyl, leaving impressions of the grooves that reproduce the music. The records are cooled, trimmed, and packaged.

2. When during the process are the music's volume levels adjusted?

   A. After the music tracks are recorded, but before the master disc is cut.
   B. After the master disc is cut, but before it is coated in chemicals.
   C. After the master disc is coated in chemicals, but before the stamper is made.
   D. After the stamper is made, but before the vinyl biscuits are produced.

3. Why is an aluminum disc put into the lathe?

   A. The lathe is used to add or remove vocals, instruments, and other elements.
   B. The lathe creates adhesive labels that appear on the final products.
   C. The lathe uses electroplating to create a stamper.
   D. The lathe cuts grooves into the aluminum disc.

4. According to the passage, the chemical coating on the master disc is needed for which step?

   A. The music editing process that adds or removes tracks.
   B. The electroplating process that fuses the nickel to the silver.
   C. The lathing process that cuts grooves into the master disc.
   D. The extruding process that squeezes the vinyl into biscuits.

5. According to the passage, when is it too late to create the adhesive labels?

   A. After the music is recorded and mixed in the studio.
   B. After the metal stamper is created using electroplating.
   C. After the PVC pellets are loaded into the hopper.
   D. After the metal stamper presses the biscuits into finished records.

6. What is the final step that needs to occur before the records are packaged?

   A. The adhesive labels need to be created.
   B. The biscuits need to be pressed.
   C. The records need to be trimmed.
   D. The PVC pellets need to be put in the hopper.

4 Categorize

LESSON

Use with **Student Book** pp. 12–13

READING ASSESSMENT TARGETS: R.2.1, R.2.3, R.2.4, R.2.5, R.2.7, R.2.8, R.5.1, R.5.2, R.5.3, R.5

UNIT 1

1 Review the Skill

Most people **categorize**, or organize, different types of objects or ideas every day. They might organize a shopping list by supermarket sections, such as meat, dairy, or cereal, or they might put various kinds of tools, such as hammers, wrenches, and nails, together in a particular place. Categorizing is a helpful reading skill because it allows you to group information by main ideas and to summarize a text.

2 Refine the Skill

By refining the skill of categorizing, you will improve your study and test-taking abilities, especially as they relate to the GED® Reasoning Through Language Arts test. Read the passage below. Then answer the questions that follow.

VOTING TRENDS IN THE UNITED STATES

a The author's main idea often identifies the key categories being described or compared. Here the author refers to **older** and **younger** citizens.

→ The Census Bureau, as well as private polls and studies, tracks voting trends in the United States. One discovery—not at all surprising—is that older citizens, particularly those over 65, vote more regularly than younger citizens in the 18–29 age range. One reason is mobility—or, conversely, stability. Voter registration in the United States is tied to voter residence. Because older voters change residences less frequently than younger voters do, voter registration for older citizens remains the same. They are permanently registered at the same address and do not have to think about registering before an election.

b The first sentence, which is the topic sentence and contains the signal phrase *on the other hand*, tells you to expect contrast. Here, the author provides important information about younger voters.

→ Younger voters, on the other hand, tend to move more often. Whether they join the military, go away to college, move to another election district or to another state, they tend not to remain in one place as long as older voters do. Therefore, younger voters must think about obtaining absentee ballots or registering in their new place of residence. If the state does not have election-day registration, then new residents may not register within the appropriate time frame and thus not register at all. When attributing causes of low election-day turnout among younger voters, researchers and pollsters should consider that residence-based voter registration system is in some part responsible for this situation.

1. To which other category is the age of a voter related?

   A. interest in politics
   B. mobility
   C. free time
   D. place of residence

2. How does the second paragraph relate to the first paragraph? In the second paragraph, the author

   A. provides exact details about the registration process.
   B. gives examples of other categories of voters.
   C. explains the situations of voters categorized as younger.
   D. defines the category of voter age.

TEST-TAKING TIPS

A question may ask how one paragraph supports or relates to another. Identifying the main idea of the first paragraph will help you choose the correct answer.

★ Spotlighted Item: **DRAG-AND-DROP**

DIRECTIONS: Read the passage and the question. Then use the drag-and-drop options to complete the web.

MORE NUTRITOUS RICE

1   American researchers have discovered varieties of rice that appear to have higher calcium content and other varieties that prevent germinating grains from becoming contaminated with arsenic. These discoveries could undoubtedly benefit rice farmers and consumers around the world.

2   Calcium is an important mineral for human bone structure and may even increase resistance to diseases such as cancer and diabetes. Arsenic is a mineral present in grains but, consumed in excess, it can be harmful to human health. Fortunately, there are groups of researchers who are looking for genes that affect the way rice varieties capture or store one or more of the 16 essential minerals, such as iron and zinc. Additionally, they seek to find the factors that can prevent arsenic from contaminating the food chain.

3   The study aims to provide growers with the knowledge they need to develop new varieties of rice with higher nutritional value. Considering that conventional genetic improvement does not require engineering, this is acceptable for many consumers.

4   Rice provides more than 40 percent of daily calories to the world's population, is low in fat, and easily digestible. This grain could, undoubtedly, be the main source of protein in certain parts of the world where rice is a staple of the diet.

UNIT 1

3.   Drag and drop the four minerals into the web.

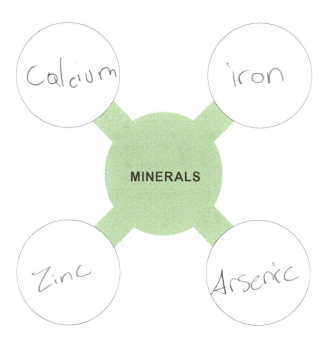

calcium	zinc
rice	grains
~~arsenic~~	~~iron~~

DIRECTIONS: Read the passage, read each question, and choose the **best** answer.

BUYING AMERICAN-MADE PRODUCTS

1   Sarah Wagner's interest in American manufacturing began with a family road trip. She and her husband loaded up their motor home in summer 2011 and visited small towns across the country whose fate seemed to be tied to the presence of industry.

2   Where plants and factories had closed down, they found empty main streets with boarded-up storefronts. In other places, such as Forest City, Iowa, home to the Winnebago factory, they found vibrant communities where they could tour manufacturing facilities and witness the pride employees took in their work.

3   When the trip was over, she started a Twitter account to share resources for all things made stateside. As USA Love List has evolved into a website, Wagner has learned that even though she can find plenty of goods made in the United States, it's impossible to live off them.

4   But she said the holiday season is the perfect time to experiment with how far she can go. For the second year in a row, Wagner has pledged to buy as many gifts as possible made in the United States. Knowing where to start can be a challenge, but Wagner and others for whom conscious consumerism means buying American say there are many places to check out, from craft fairs, Etsy and specialty boutiques to e-commerce.

5   "Gift-giving creates the perfect opportunity to try to buy American. You have extra time to research, and you have flexibility in what you choose to buy," said the married mother of two from Philadelphia.

6   "I'm a realist. I know that it's impossible to buy entirely American-made products year-round, but I also know there [are] a lot of wonderful American-made products, made by proud Americans, and it's worth my time to look for them."

From the cnn.com article HOLIDAY SHOPPERS SHARE TIPS FOR BUYING AMERICAN by Emanuella Grinberg, © 2012

4.   In paragraph 2, Sarah Wagner describes a type of American town with empty main streets. What do these towns have in common?

   A. They are in or near Iowa.
   B. They are vibrant communities.
   C. They have strong ties to farming.
   D. They have lost manufacturing jobs.

5.   Into which category of town does the author place Forest City, Iowa?

   A. a town with an active community and a successful industry
   B. a town with an active community and a strong service industry
   C. a vibrant town that thrives on the tourism industry
   D. a thriving community similar to other such communities in Iowa

6.   According to this passage, who would **best** fit into the category of "conscious consumer"?

   A. a person who shops on e-commerce sites
   B. a person who cares about how and where a product is made
   C. a person who is flexible in what he or she buys
   D. a person who knows where to buy American goods

7.   According to the passage, how can we support American-made products?

   A. buying American-made gifts
   B. buying American-made cars
   C. buying American-made technology
   D. buying American-grown produce

8.   Which statement **best** describes the category of "realist" in this passage?

   A. people who try to buy American-made products when they can
   B. people who claim that American-made products are superior to imported products
   C. people who buy American-made products no matter how expensive they may be
   D. people who have the time and commitment to look for American-made products

DIRECTIONS: Read the passage, read each question, and choose the **best** answer.

NEW POPULARITY FOR AMERICAN-MADE PRODUCTS

1 Motivated by a desire to boost the domestic economy or doubts over outsourcing, some Americans are making an effort to shop local for holiday gifts this year. It's a niche market, but it's one that has been growing in recent few years, and brands are starting to take notice.

2 A growing number of small companies have been catering to the desire for American-made clothing and accessories, fueled in large part by style blogs touting the benefits of heritage brands.

3 On a larger scale, Apple announced . . . that it would shift some of its production back to the United States, citing customer demand for American-made products. Though some have characterized the announcement as a publicity ploy that won't do much to alter Apple's manufacturing operations, it follows a continuing pattern of American companies bringing manufacturing back home due to rising labor, supply and production costs in China.

4 Some say buying American is a drop in the bucket when it comes to boosting the domestic economy, but experts agree that every bit counts. Manufacturing has the highest multiplier effect of any industry, meaning that it benefits other sectors that support its operations.

5 "Anytime something is manufactured in the United States it's going to have greater gains in terms of jobs than something made overseas," said Chad Moutray, chief economist for the National Association of Manufacturers. . . .

6 Electronics and appliances made in the United States are hard to come by, but jewelry, clothing, accessories, beauty products, even holiday decorations are easier to find than you might think, [Sarah Wagner] said.

7 Buying American for the holidays hasn't changed her budget significantly, she said. She'll spend about $700 on family, friends and white elephant gifts, about the same as in recent years. The only difference is that she spends a bit more time searching.

From the cnn.com article HOLIDAY SHOPPERS SHARE TIPS FOR BUYING AMERICAN by Emanuella Grinberg, © 2012

9. According to this passage, which product **best** fits into the category of a "heritage brand"?

   A. a computer manufactured in China and used in the United States
   B. a sweater made in the United States by a long-standing American company
   C. a shirt made in Italy and sold by an American company in American stores
   D. a popular brand of jeans worn throughout the United States

10. Which statement **best** explains how paragraph 1 and paragraph 3 are related?

   A. Paragraph 1 explains the concept of a "niche market" as it relates to American-made goods.
   B. The example of Apple in paragraph 3 contradicts the ideas of boosting the domestic economy mentioned in paragraph 1.
   C. Both paragraph 1 and paragraph 3 explain growing trends in style blogs.
   D. Paragraph 3 supports paragraph 1 by using Apple as an example of an industry heeding customer demand for American-made goods.

11. The author claims that manufacturing is the category of industry that has the greatest impact on creating American jobs. Which detail in the passage **best** supports this claim?

   A. Manufacturing benefits other sectors of the economy that support its operations.
   B. Apple is shifting some production back to the United States.
   C. Labor, supply, and production costs are rising in China.
   D. A growing number of small companies have been catering to the desire for American-made clothing and accessories.

12. According to the passage, which American-made product would be hardest to find?

   A. a silver bracelet
   B. a pair of cowboy boots
   C. a digital camera
   D. a wool scarf

Identify Cause and Effect

UNIT 1

1 *Review the Skill*

A **cause** is the event or condition that makes something happen. An **effect** is what happens. One cause may have several effects, and one effect may have several causes. A cause may be explicitly, or clearly, stated: *The house fire was caused by a burning candle.* Sometimes, however, a cause is implied, or not directly stated: *A house fire last night left three people without a home. They had been burning candles.* In both examples, the burning candle is the cause, and the house fire is the effect.

2 *Refine the Skill*

By refining the skill of identifying cause and effect, you will improve your study and test-taking abilities, especially as they relate to the GED® Reasoning Through Language Arts test. Read the passage below. Then answer the questions that follow.

a This passage is about the carbon cycle, which includes photosynthesis, respiration, and decomposition. As you read, look for clues that can guide you in understanding why there is carbon all over the earth.

b You can make an assumption about how humans affect the carbon cycle. Based on the passage, think about how the destruction of rainforests and subsequent decrease in the number of plants that absorb carbon dioxide from the atmosphere would affect this natural cycle and climate change.

CARBON CYCLE

Carbon moves through the environment in a process called the carbon cycle. Part of the carbon cycle is a short-term cycle in which plants, algae, and certain bacteria convert carbon dioxide from the atmosphere or ocean into sugars and starches through a process called photosynthesis. Plants use these substances for energy, releasing carbon dioxide into the air. Other organisms eat the plants to get the carbon. Like plants, the organisms break down sugars for energy through a process called respiration and release some of the carbon back into the air. When animals and plants die, their remains contain carbon. When left on the ground, these remains become a source of energy for microbes in soil. As these microbes break down carbon in a process called decomposition, they release carbon back into the atmosphere or soil.

In contrast, the long-term cycle moves carbon through Earth's system over very long periods. The remains of some animals and plants are buried on land or sink to the bottom of the ocean where they are safe from microbes. Over millions of years, these buried remains are compressed within the earth. Tissues and bones are eventually destroyed, but carbon persists and forms hydrocarbons. Hydrocarbons are the main components of fossil fuels.

1. When animals and plants die, why do they become a source of energy for microbes?

   A. because they convert carbon dioxide into sugars
   B. because they convert sugar into carbon dioxide
   C. because they are compressed and form hydrocarbons
   D. because they are on the ground and contain carbon

2. According to the passage, how does the compression of animal remains within the earth affect tissue and bones?

   A. Tissue and bones become infected with microbes.
   B. Tissue and bones are destroyed.
   C. Tissue and bones sink to the bottom of the ocean.
   D. Tissue and bones are released into the atmosphere.

CLOSER LOOK AT ITEMS

Questions about cause- and-effect relationships often begin with the word **why**. The word **result** in a question indicates an effect. The verb **affect** means "influence" and asks a question about an effect.

DIRECTIONS: Read the passage, read each question, and choose the **best** answer.

VIOLENT VIDEO GAMES

1   Republicans and Democrats alike screamed government waste last March when a group of senators suggested spending $90 million to study how video games "and other electronic media" influenced children's behavior. Surely an important question, critics of the plan said, but $90 million?

2   Some believe that, in any case, the verdict is already in. This month, the American Psychological Association called for a reduction of violence in all video games, saying the evidence from 20 years of research on the subject was clear. They based their conclusion largely on the work of Kevin M. Kieffer, a psychologist at St. Leo University near Tampa, Fla., who prepared an analysis of dozens of relevant studies.

3   He found that, in general, children exposed to virtual bloodshed showed greater "short-term" increases in hostility toward peers and authority figures than those exposed to more benign games. And many of the studies included in the analysis were randomized, rebutting the notion that aggressive people are simply drawn to violent games, Dr. Kieffer found. . . .

4   In the end, the study's findings may be more in line with public opinion. On the day its findings were announced, a jury in Alabama reached a guilty verdict in the case of Devin Moore, who killed three people when he was 18 and as his defense blamed the video game "Grand Theft Auto."

5   Studies generally show that violent video games can have short-term, or momentary, effects on children, but there is little evidence of long-term changes.

From *The New York Times*'s article THE CLAIM: VIOLENT VIDEO GAMES MAKE YOUNG PEOPLE AGGRESSIVE by Anahad O'Connor, © 2005

3. Why did Republicans and Democrats not want to spend $90 million on a video game study? They agreed that

    A. it was too much money to spend on such a study.
    B. a solution had already been found.
    C. the subject of violent video games did not merit further study.
    D. a study of electronic media, but not video games, would be worth the money.

4. The passage states, "[The American Psychological Association] based their conclusion largely on the work of Kevin M. Kieffer, a psychologist at St. Leo University near Tampa, Fla., who prepared an analysis of dozens of relevant studies" (paragraph 2). The results of these studies showed

    A. no connection between violent video games and hostility in children.
    B. increased "short-term" and "long-term" hostility in children exposed to violent video games.
    C. increased "short-term" hostility in children exposed to violent video games.
    D. no change in "short-term" hostility among all children.

5. How does the verdict in the court case support the study's conclusion about the effects of viewing violent video games?

    A. The jury agreed that watching violent videos had long-term effects and was a defense for murder.
    B. The jury agreed that the murder could not have been caused by the short-term effects of watching violent videos.
    C. The jury agreed that the short-term effects of violent videos were to blame because the murder happened immediately after the defendant watched a violent video.
    D. The jury agreed that violent videos affected children only, so the defendant was found guilty because he was not a child.

UNIT 1

★ Spotlighted Item: DRAG-AND-DROP

DIRECTIONS: Read the passage and the question. Then use the drag-and-drop options to complete the organizer.

KEEPING YOUR COOL

1   Many people love the warm summer months. But hot and humid days can sometimes be dangerous. It's not good for the body to be too hot for too long. Too much heat can damage your brain and other organs. It's important to keep your cool when the days are hot.

2   Your body has its own natural cooling system. Sweating is key to cooling when hot weather or exercise causes your body temperature to climb. When sweat dries, it carries heat away from your body's surface and lowers your temperature. When sweating isn't enough to help you cool down, you're at risk for a heat-related illness called hyperthermia.

3   Hyperthermia can happen to anyone. Older people, infants and young children, and people who are ill, obese or on certain medications are especially at risk. These people may be more sensitive to the effects of extreme heat and less likely to sense or respond to changes in temperature.

4   "High temperatures can cause various organs within the body not to function optimally," says Dr. Marie Bernard, deputy director of NIH's National Institute on Aging. Excess body heat can stress the heart and harm the brain. It might even lead to a coma.

5   Hyperthermia can cause several heat-related illnesses, ranging from mild to serious. These include heat cramps, heat edema, heat exhaustion and heat stroke. . . .

    Air conditioning is the best way to protect against hyperthermia. If you don't have air conditioning, go to places that are cool on hot and humid days. Try community centers, shopping malls, movie theaters, libraries or the homes of friends and family.

6   Heat-related illness is preventable. Still, hundreds of deaths from extreme heat events occur in the United States each year. It's important to be aware of who's at greatest risk so you can take steps to help beat the heat.

From the nih.gov article STAY COOL: GETTING TOO HOT CAN BE DANGEROUS, accessed 2021

6. Drag and drop into the boxes each possible effect of hyperthermia.

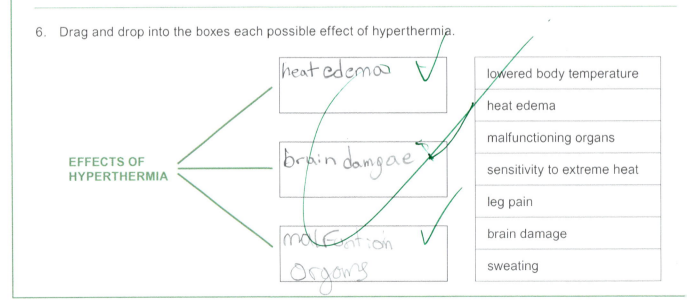

DIRECTIONS: Read the passage, read each question, and choose the **best** answer.

ABOUT POISON IVY

1   Every year, poison ivy affects adults and children alike. The somewhat jagged leaves of the poison ivy plant grow in groups of three and may appear anywhere in wooded areas or even in your own backyard.

2   The poison ivy rash is an allergic reaction to urushiol (u-Roo-shee-ole), an oily substance in the poison ivy plant. Not everyone is allergic to poison ivy; in fact, many people experience no reaction at all. However, those who are susceptible to poison ivy can suffer great discomfort from an itchy skin rash.

3   People usually contact poison ivy by touching part of the plant itself; however, because the sticky urushiol in the plant is the cause of the reaction, contact with anything that has urushiol on it—such as clothing, accessories, tools, machinery, animal fur—can cause the reaction.

4   The rash may begin as a series of small blisters that appear in a straight line. The reason for this appearance is that the plant may have brushed against the skin in a linear pattern. The rash then may appear on other areas of the skin, causing some swelling, redness, and blisters. Generally, the more urushiol on the skin, the more serious the rash. No special treatment is needed for most cases of poison ivy, although some over-the-counter medications are available to relieve the painful and sometimes constant itching. Serious cases, however, may require the use of a corticosteroid.

5   If someone with poison ivy scratches the rash and blisters break, bacteria under the fingernails may cause the skin to become infected. A doctor probably will prescribe antibiotics if such infection occurs.

6   Poison ivy is neither contagious nor spread by open blisters. It is spread by contact with the urushiol, so touching anything with urushiol and then touching another part of the body can cause the rash to spread. Despite the discomfort of the poison ivy rash, more serious than direct physical contact with urushiol is breathing its fumes. If the plant is burned, inhaled smoke can affect the lungs.

7. What causes the poison ivy rash?

   A. direct contact with three-leafed plants
   B. urushiol from the poison ivy plant
   C. blisters that cause urushiol to spread
   D. inhaling smoke from burning plants

8. A large amount of urushiol on the skin may cause

   A. effective protection from poison ivy.
   B. less susceptibility to bacterial infection.
   C. more blisters but less redness and swelling.
   D. more severe cases of poison ivy.

9. What causes the poison ivy rash to spread to other parts of the body?

   A. pus from broken blisters
   B. brushing against a cat or dog
   C. touching items contaminated by urushiol
   D. direct contact with a person who has poison ivy

10. According to the text, what causes blisters to appear in a straight line?

   A. The reaction from poison ivy contact is a rash in a straight line.
   B. The plant brushed against the skin in a line.
   C. The skin reacts to contact by any allergen with a series of blisters in a straight line.
   D. The only way to come in contact with poison ivy is to brush it on the skin in a straight line.

11. What is one possible effect of scratching a poison ivy rash?

   A. Blisters can burst and spread from one area to another.
   B. Skin can become infected from bacteria.
   C. Urushiol can spread, causing fever and swelling.
   D. Lungs and nasal passages may become irritated.

12. On the basis of what causes poison ivy, washing thoroughly immediately after contact with the poison ivy plant might help

   A. get rid of urushiol on the skin.
   B. prevent the spread of infection.
   C. keep the skin clean.
   D. lubricate areas of dry skin.

6 LESSON

Compare and Contrast

Use with **Student Book** pp. 16–17

READING ASSESSMENT TARGETS: R.2.1, R.2.2, R.2.3, R.2.4, R.2.5, R.2.7, R.2
R.3.2, R.3.4, R.3.5, R.5.1, R.5.2, R.5.3

UNIT 1

1 Review the Skill

When you **compare** things, you look for ways in which they are similar. When you **contrast** things, you look for ways in which they are different. Certain key words can indicate when two things are being compared or contrasted. Comparison key words include *like*, *such as*, *in addition to*, *similarly*, and *likewise*. Contrast key words include *unlike*, *whereas*, *however*, *on the other hand*, *but*, *yet*, and *in contrast*.

2 Refine the Skill

By refining the skill of comparing and contrasting, you will improve your study and test-taking abilities, especially as they relate to the GED® Reasoning Through Language Arts test. Read the passage below. Then answer the questions that follow.

a Authors often use the structure of a text to organize the details they supply to compare and contrast. Here the author discusses President Lincoln's plan in paragraph 1 and then the Radical Republican's plan in paragraph 2.

b Phrases such as *on the other hand* signal contrast—in this case, how the views of Radical Republicans in Congress differed from Lincoln's views.

REBUILDING A NATION

1   As the Civil War came to a close, President Abraham Lincoln began to consider how the United States should be rebuilt. In his second inaugural address, he summed up the ideas on which he based his plan, saying ". . . let us strive on to finish the work we are in; to bind up the nation's wounds. . . ." He hoped to heal the nation with as little animosity as possible between the North and the South. In his plan, former Confederates who agreed to support the Constitution and the United States would be offered pardons. Confederate states could rejoin the Union if they established anti-slavery governments. Moreover, after rejoining, southern states would be allowed to elect former Confederates to Congress.

2   Radical Republicans in Congress, on the other hand, had a different view. In an explanation of the Radical Republicans' stance, Congressman Thaddeus Stevens stated, "Our fathers . . . proclaimed the equality of men before the law. Upon that they created a revolution and built the Nation. It is our duty to complete their work." Under their plan, former Confederates would be banned from Congress, and southern states placed under military rule. The Radical Republicans also expected states to allow former slaves some rights afforded white citizens.

1.   The Reconstruction plans of Lincoln and the Radical Republicans

   A. aimed to rebuild the nation as quickly as possible.
   B. featured different objectives for the process of Reconstruction.
   C. delegated much responsibility for Reconstruction to the states.
   D. imposed similarly harsh penalties on the Confederacy.

2.   In contrast to the Radical Republicans' plan for Reconstruction, how is Lincoln's plan **best** described?

   A. forgiving
   B. harsh
   C. bold
   D. ambitious

TEST-TAKING TIPS

When answering a question, you may find information all together in one place or in different places in a text. Here you need to read different parts of the text to determine ways in which the plans are alike and different.

DIRECTIONS: Read the passage, read each question, and choose the **best** answer.

CHOOSING ORGANIC OR CONVENTIONAL FOOD

1   "People choose to buy organic foods for many different reasons. One of them is perceived health benefits," said Dr. Crystal Smith-Spangler. . . .

2   "Our patients, our families ask about, 'Well, are there health reasons to choose organic food in terms of nutritional content or human health outcomes?'"

3   To try to answer that question, she and her colleagues reviewed over 200 studies that compared either the health of people who ate organic or conventional foods or, more commonly, nutrient and contaminant levels in the foods themselves.

4   Those included organic and non-organic fruits, vegetables, grains, meat, poultry, eggs and milk. . . .

5   According to United States Department of Agriculture standards, organic farms have to avoid the use of synthetic pesticides and fertilizers, hormones and antibiotics. Organic livestock must also have access to pastures during grazing season.

6   Many conventional farms in the U.S., in contrast, use pesticides to ward off bugs and raise animals in crowded indoor conditions with antibiotics in their feed to promote growth and ward off disease. The Food and Drug Administration has been examining that type of antibiotic use and its contribution to drug-resistant disease in humans.

7   Smith-Spangler and her colleagues found there was no difference in the amount of vitamins in plant or animal products produced organically and conventionally—and the only nutrient difference was slightly more phosphorus in the organic products. . . .

8   There were more significant differences by growing practice in the amount of pesticides and antibiotic-resistant bacteria in food.

9   More than one-third of conventional produce had detectable pesticide residues, compared to seven percent of organic produce samples. And organic chicken and pork w[ere] 33 percent less likely to carry bacteria resistant to three or more antibiotics than conventionally produced meat.

From the reuters.com article ORGANIC FOOD NO MORE NUTRITIOUS THAN NON-ORGANIC, STUDY FINDS, © 2012

3. How does the information in paragraphs 3 and 4 **best** relate to the main idea of the passage?

    A. It explains the reason that people choose organic food.
    B. It introduces the elements being compared in the study.
    C. It explains the quotations in the first and second paragraphs.
    D. It shows that no significant difference exists between organic and non-organic foods.

4. Which statement **best** explains an important difference between organic farms and conventional farms?

    A. Conventional farms treat animals better than organic farms do.
    B. Conventional farms use fertilizers, but organic farms do not.
    C. Organic farms give antibiotics to animals, but conventional farms give growth hormones.
    D. Organic farms must avoid synthetic products, but conventional farms may use them.

5. What did Smith-Spangler find that organic and non-organic products had in common?

    A. Plant and animal products had the same vitamin content.
    B. Food had the same taste when prepared the same way.
    C. Animals showed the same levels of antibiotic-resistant bacteria.
    D. Plant products had the same levels of phosphorus.

6. Which statement **best** supports the conclusion that organic food may be healthier than non-organic food?

    A. Conventional farms are more careful to use pesticides to ward off bugs.
    B. Pesticide levels in non-organic produce were considerably higher.
    C. Organic meats contained no antibiotic-resistant bacteria.
    D. The nutrient level in organic products was higher.

★ Spotlighted Item: **DRAG-AND-DROP**

DIRECTIONS: Read the passage and the question. Then use the drag-and-drop options to complete the Venn diagram.

HEALTHY FATS

1   Fat is an essential nutrient for our bodies. It provides energy. It helps our guts absorb certain vitamins from foods. But what types of fat should you be eating? Are there any you should avoid?

2   Recommendations about dietary fat have shifted over the last two decades. From the 1970s through the 1990s, nutrition researchers emphasized eating a low-fat diet.

3   This was largely because of concerns about saturated fats, explains Dr. Alice H. Lichtenstein, who studies diet and heart health at Tufts University. Saturated fat that's in the bloodstream raises the levels of LDL cholesterol—the "bad" cholesterol. This in turn raises the risk of heart disease.

4   "There's still this misconception that eating fat—any kind of fat—is bad. That it will lead to heart attacks, or weight gain. That's not true. People really should be encouraged to eat healthy fats," says Dr. Frank Sacks, a nutrition expert at Harvard University.

5   Research has shown that unsaturated fats are good for you. These fats come mostly from plant sources. Cooking oils that are liquid at room temperature, such as canola, peanut, safflower, soybean, and olive oil, contain mostly unsaturated fat. Nuts, seeds, and avocados are also good sources. Fatty fish—such as salmon, sardines, and herring—are rich in unsaturated fats, too.

6   Large studies have found that replacing saturated fats in your diet with unsaturated fats can reduce your risk of heart disease by about the same amount as cholesterol-lowering drugs.

7   People should actively make unsaturated fats a part of their diet, Sacks says. You don't need to avoid healthy fats to lose weight, he adds.

From the nih.gov article THE SKINNY ON FAT, accessed 2020

---

7.   Drag and drop each phrase into the correct place in the Venn diagram.

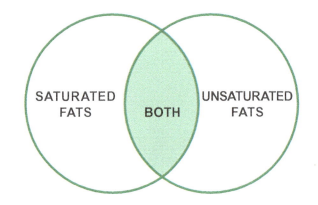

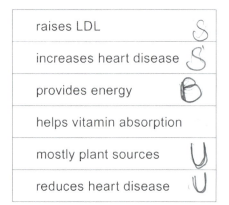

raises LDL	S
increases heart disease	S
provides energy	B
helps vitamin absorption	
mostly plant sources	U
reduces heart disease	U

DIRECTIONS: Read the passage, read each question, and choose the **best** answer.

THE ARTICLES OF CONFEDERATION AND THE U.S. CONSTITUTION

1   After declaring independence from Britain, the American colonies set forth to govern themselves. In 1776 and 1777, colonial leaders wrote the Articles of Confederation, designed to limit the national government's power to make and enforce laws. The Articles were adopted by Congress on November 15, 1777, and fully ratified by all states on March 1, 1781.

2   Although some important achievements occurred under the Articles, including a plan for new states in the Northwest Ordinance of 1787, the weak central government made it difficult for the states to function as one nation. In particular, the national government was unable to tax or regulate trade between states.

3   Therefore, in the summer of 1787, a group of 55 delegates attended the Constitutional Convention in Philadelphia to draft a more effective governing document. The Constitution they submitted for ratification in September established a strong national government, with a president, a bicameral instead of a unicameral legislature, and a supreme court, which could settle disputes between states. The legislature was a mixture of equal and proportional representation. All three branches of government were powerful but checked one another.

4   Other differences between the Articles of Confederation and the U.S. Constitution involved levying taxes, admitting new states, adding amendments, and coining money. Under the Articles, the states collected taxes, but under the Constitution, only the national government collected taxes. Under the Articles, new states were admitted by agreement of at least nine states. Under the Constitution, new states were admitted through agreement by Congress. The Articles could be amended only by agreement of all states; the Constitution could be amended by agreement of three fourths of the states. The Constitution removed the states' power to coin money.

5   At the time of ratification, the U.S. Constitution had no provisions protecting personal freedoms. Although states were concerned about a strong national government that did not secure freedoms, the U.S. Constitution became law when ratified by nine states in 1788. The Bill of Rights was added in 1791.

8. According to the passage, both the Articles of Confederation and the U.S. Constitution were

    A. ratified by all states.
    B. signed by 55 representatives.
    C. written to govern the original states.
    D. amendments to the Northwest Ordinance.

9. Unlike the U.S. Constitution, the Articles of Confederation

    A. created a plan for admitting new states.
    B. gave states more power than the national government.
    C. established three branches of government.
    D. contained a Bill of Rights to protect individual freedoms.

10. One difference between the legislative branch in the Articles of Confederation and the U.S. Constitution is that the Articles

    A. provided for two houses of Congress, but the Constitution provided for one.
    B. established the presidency, but the Constitution provided for a supreme court.
    C. had three legislative branches, but the Constitution had a single legislative branch.
    D. had a single legislature, but the Constitution provided for two legislative houses.

11. Which act would have been possible under the Articles of Confederation only?

    A. Members of the Senate levied a tax.
    B. Ten states ratified a constitutional amendment.
    C. Pennsylvania elected two representatives more than Virginia.
    D. The state of New Hampshire collected taxes.

12. A major difference between the Articles of Confederation and the U.S. Constitution is that the Articles of Confederation

    A. listed individual rights and responsibilities, but the Constitution added the Bill of Rights later.
    B. enabled the states to function more as individual nations, but the Constitution enabled them to function as a single union.
    C. modeled French government, but the Constitution modeled British government.
    D. protected against the power of the British monarchy, but the Constitution protected against strong national government.

1 Review the Skill

Authors use **transitional language** and **signal words** to show how ideas are related. Transitional language may appear at the beginning of a sentence, in the middle, or at the end. Some of the most frequently used signal words include *after, also, and, because, but, first, however, like, next,* and *then.* When reading informational texts, you can use signal words to help you determine how ideas are connected.

Authors connect ideas in different ways. Comparing ideas shows how they are similar, or alike. Contrasting ideas shows how they are different. Transitional language and signal words can be used to add information, provide examples, or organize ideas—either by presenting a sequence or by showing cause and effect.

On the GED® Reasoning Through Language Arts test, you will be expected to show you understand transitional language and signal words. You may encounter questions that ask you to identify transitional language and its function in a text. Some questions may ask you to explain how transitional language conveys meaning by connecting ideas. Other questions may ask you to explain how transitional language helps you understand a text or how it supports the author's purpose or main idea.

2 Refine the Skill

BUSINESS CLUSTERS

1   A business cluster is a concentration of companies that are connected to each other and that are located in the same area. It might comprise businesses that are part of the same manufacturing and supply chain or are in the same industry. Notable clusters include Silicon Valley in California, the financial districts in New York City and London, and the auto industry in Detroit. However, on a local level, clusters can be seen at shopping malls or busy intersections.

a The word *however* contrasts the notable, or well-known, clusters with clusters "on a local level."

2   Clusters occur when there is an advantage created from shared resources. For example, technology companies in Silicon Valley share a pool of educated workers. The auto industry in Detroit is part of a supply chain of parts and materials. And the stores at the local shopping mall share consumers. Although businesses in a cluster often compete against each other, the benefits of shared resources more than make up for this added competition.

b The phrase *For example* makes it clear that the next idea is an example of how these businesses share resources.

Scan paragraph 2 for the word *Although.* It is in the last sentence. Re-read the sentence and determine what kind of relationship the word creates. The correct answer is **C**.

1.   How does the word **Although** function in paragraph 2?

A. It links the cause of a benefit with its effect.
B. It provides an example of a benefit.
C. It contrasts benefits of clusters with drawbacks of clusters.
D. It compares benefits of clusters.

DIRECTIONS: Read the passage, read each question, and choose the **best** answer.

NUTRITION AND HEALTH ARE CLOSELY RELATED

1   Over the past century, malnourishment has dramatically decreased. Many infectious diseases have been conquered. Most Americans can now expect a long and productive life. However, as infectious disease rates have dropped, the rates of noncommunicable diseases—specifically, chronic diet-related diseases—have risen. This is due in part to changes in lifestyle behaviors.

2   A history of poor eating and physical activity patterns has increased with time. These behaviors also contribute to significant health challenges that now face the U.S. population. About half of all American adults—117 million individuals—have one or more preventable chronic diseases, many of which are related to poor-quality eating patterns and physical inactivity. These include cardiovascular disease, high blood pressure, type 2 diabetes, some cancers, and poor bone health.

3   More than two-thirds of adults and nearly one-third of children and youth are overweight or obese. These high rates of overweight and obesity, and the chronic disease linked to these conditions, have persisted for more than two decades. The results have been increased health risks, not to mention high financial costs.

4   In 2017, the total estimated cost of diagnosed diabetes was $327 billion. This includes $237 billion in direct medical costs and $90 billion in decreased productivity.

Adapted from a health.gov article NUTRITION AND HEALTH ARE CLOSELY RELATED, accessed 2020

2. In paragraph 1, which contrast does the word **However** signal?

   A. Chronic diet-related illnesses have increased as infectious diseases have decreased.
   B. Chronic diet-related illnesses and infectious diseases have both decreased.
   C. Infectious diseases have increased as chronic diet-related illnesses have decreased.
   D. Infectious diseases and chronic diet-related illnesses have both increased.

3. In paragraph 1, how does the phrase **due in part to** function in the passage?

   A. It introduces an example of a chronic diet-related disease.
   B. It makes a comparison between chronic diet-related diseases and lifestyle behaviors.
   C. It relates how lifestyle changes are partly the cause of chronic diet-related diseases.
   D. It reinforces a contrast between lifestyle behaviors and chronic diet-related diseases.

4. In paragraph 2, the word **also** adds information about

   A. chronic diet-related diseases.
   B. significant health challenges that people face.
   C. patterns that have increased with time.
   D. poor eating and physical activity.

5. How is the last sentence in paragraph 2 related to the previous sentence?

   A. The phrase "many of which" in the previous sentence shows a comparison with the last sentence.
   B. The phrase "many of which" in the previous sentence creates a chronological sequence with the last sentence.
   C. The phrase "These include" creates a contrast with "poor quality eating patterns and physical activity."
   D. The phrase "These include" signals a list of examples of "preventable chronic diseases" mentioned in the previous sentence.

6. What is the function of the phrase **not to mention** in paragraph 3?

   A. It links the results of these conditions to their cause.
   B. It adds more information about the results of these conditions.
   C. It contrasts the results of these conditions with their benefits.
   D. It compares the different results of these conditions.

Determine Author's Point of View

Use with *Student Book* pp. 22–23

READING ASSESSMENT TARGETS: R.2.3, R.2.7, R.3.4, R.3.5, R.4.3/L.4.3, R.5
R.5.2, R.6.1, R.6.2, R.6.3, R.6.4

UNIT 1

1 Review the Skill

An author's <mark>point of view</mark> usually has an impact on how he or she approaches writing about a subject. Readers can figure out an author's point of view according to the type of text, the topic, certain details offered from the text, and the words the author uses to describe events or situations. Look for words and ideas that evoke positive or negative feelings. Look also at titles and at the newspaper, magazine, or Internet site for an idea of an author's point of view.

2 Refine the Skill

By refining the skill of determining an author's point of view, you will improve your study and test-taking abilities, especially as they relate to the GED® Reasoning Through Language Arts test. Read the passage below. Then answer the questions that follow.

b **STATEMENT OF MICHAEL CONAWAY, U.S. REPRESENTATIVE, TEXAS**

I noticed recently when the price of oil collapsed in March, some of the anti-oil folks were gleeful about that. The truth of the matter is, they really should want really high oil prices, really high gasoline prices because it makes all of these other alternatives competitive against the current system. Whatever that utopia looks like out there that doesn't use fossil fuels—and maybe that is centuries from now—we will get there. But in the meantime, we have to afford it. We have to be able to live. We have to be able to sustain it, keep our families alive, and those kinds of things. As we go up about these projects, figuring out who pays for it, where that cost gets ultimately settled is really a key to making this thing work.

From HOUSE HEARING 116–35 ON-FARM ENERGY PRODUCTION: IMPACTS ON FARM INCOME AND RURAL COMMUNITIES, July 23, 2020

a The author uses examples that have strong emotional meaning, including *we have to be able to live* and *keep our families alive.*

b An author's background may help you determine his or her point of view. The author of this statement represented a district in West Texas, an area known for producing oil.

1. What is the author's point of view about alternative sources of energy?

   A. Alternative sources of energy will only gain widespread use when their cost is competitive with existing sources of energy.
   B. Fossil fuels will always be more cost effective than alternative forms of energy.
   C. Alternative sources of energy will be in common use within a few centuries.
   D. The federal government should pay for projects that help people adopt alternative sources of fuel.

2. A *utopia* is an imagined place where everything is perfect. How does the author use the word *utopia* to advance his point of view?

   A. to emphasize that widespread use of alternative fuels will never be a reality
   B. to question the value of researching alternative sources of energy
   C. to emphasize that widespread use of alternative energy does not reflect our current reality or energy needs
   D. to question the need for alternative energy sources

USING LOGIC

Evaluate the source of the passage. If the passage comes from an editorial or opinion piece, the author may use strong language to show his or her thoughts or feelings.

★ Spotlighted Item: **DRAG-AND-DROP**

DIRECTIONS: Read the passage and the question. Then use the drag-and-drop options to complete the chart.

DECLARATION OF CONSCIENCE

Senator Margaret Chase Smith, from Maine, gave this speech before the Senate to express her strong opposition to the tactics of the House Committee on Un-American Activities. Smith was one of the first to speak against the Committee and its leader, Senator Joseph McCarthy.

1   I speak as a Republican. I speak as a woman. I speak as a United States Senator. I speak as an American.

2   The United States Senate has long enjoyed worldwide respect as the greatest deliberative body in the world. But recently that deliberative character has too often been debased to the level of a forum of hate and character assassination sheltered by the shield of congressional immunity. . . .

3   It is strange that we can verbally attack anyone else without restraint and with full protection and yet we hold ourselves above the same type of criticism here on the Senate Floor. Surely the United States Senate is big enough to take self-criticism and self-appraisal. Surely we should be able to take the same kind of character attacks that we dish out to outsiders.

4   I think that it is high time for the United States Senate and its members to do some soul searching—for us to weigh our consciences—on the manner in which we are performing our duty to the people of America—on the manner in which we are using or abusing our individual powers and privileges. . . .

5   Whether it be a criminal prosecution in court or a character prosecution in the Senate, there is little practical distinction when the life of a person has been ruined.

6   Those of us who shout the loudest about Americanism in making character assassinations are all too frequently those who, by our own words and acts, ignore some of the basic principles of Americanism—

7   The right to criticize;

8   The right to hold unpopular beliefs;

9   The right to protest;

10   The right of independent thought.

11   The exercise of these rights should not cost one single American citizen his reputation or his right to a livelihood nor should he be in danger of losing his reputation or livelihood merely because he happens to know someone who holds unpopular beliefs. Who of us doesn't? Otherwise none of us could call our souls our own. Otherwise thought control would have set in.

From DECLARATION OF CONSCIENCE by Margaret Chase Smith, 1950

3.   Drag and drop the phrases into the appropriate places in the chart.

Smith supports	Smith opposes

special treatment for political leaders.	traditional American ideals.
freedom of speech.	thought control.
making unsupported claims.	thoughtful political debate.

DIRECTIONS: Read the passage, read each question, and choose the **best** answer.

THROUGH THE BACK DOOR

1   Thousands of students rejected by American medical schools are attending second-rate schools abroad and then returning for further clinical training and eventually a license to practice medicine in the United States. The situation has stirred bitter controversy. Parents of the overseas students are pressing to facilitate their return while American medical schools are resisting.

2   Now the battle is joined in New York State. The Board of Regents recently proposed to rate some of the foreign schools and to admit some of their students for clinical training (the third and fourth years of medical school) in New York teaching hospitals. The Association of American Medical Colleges protests that this would produce inferior physicians. So far, neither side has a fully persuasive case.

3   Medical educators make some telling points against the Regents' plan. The foreign schools probably cannot be rated reliably by questionnaire, as is planned in most cases. And a flood of students with mediocre preparation could well lower the quality of care given patients in teaching hospitals. Moreover, since slots for students in the best hospitals are oversubscribed, the returning students would be apt to wind up in hospitals with weak teaching programs and supervision.

4   Worse yet, once New York welcomes back these students, it would only encourage more aspiring physicians to enroll for questionable two-year training periods abroad. Some 10,000 to 11,000 American students already attend foreign medical schools, mostly in Mexico, the Caribbean and Europe. Now that American medical schools and Federal authorities feel that the country is already producing enough doctors, why should the applicants that those schools rejected be encouraged to enter the profession by the back door?

From *The New York Times*'s editorial BACK DOOR PHYSICIANS, © 1981

4.   In paragraph 1, what is the author's point of view about overseas medical schools? The author thinks that overseas medical schools

   A. are not as good as medical schools in the United States.
   B. train their students as well as medical schools in the United States do.
   C. have an edge over medical schools in the United States.
   D. far surpass medical schools in the United States.

5.   Which statement **best** explains the author's viewpoint regarding the Board of Regents proposal?

   A. The proposal will benefit students receiving overseas medical education.
   B. The proposal offers a good compromise.
   C. The proposal has flaws, as pointed out by the Association of Medical Colleges.
   D. The proposal lacks solid reasoning.

6.   How does the proposal by the Board of Regents reflect the point of view of parents of medical students studying in foreign medical schools? The proposal

   A. ignores the parents' point of view about returning students.
   B. addresses some parents' concerns about returning students.
   C. agrees fully with parents' concerns about returning students.
   D. disagrees with parents' concerns about returning students.

7.   With which group's point of view does the author agree?

   A. the New York Board of Regents
   B. parents of students training in foreign medical schools
   C. students training in foreign medical schools
   D. the Association of American Medical Colleges

DIRECTIONS: Read the passage, read each question, and choose the **best** answer.

SAVING THE GRAY WOLVES

1   A federal judge in Missoula, Mont., has given Rocky Mountain gray wolves a well-deserved reprieve. In February, the federal Fish and Wildlife Service had effectively sentenced hundreds of wolves to death by lifting the protections provided by the Endangered Species Act. Since then, because of far weaker state protections in Wyoming, Montana and Idaho, more than 100 wolves out of a total population of 1,500 have been killed. As many as 500 more were doomed to die in state-authorized hunts this fall.

2   Judge Donald Molloy issued a preliminary injunction last week restoring federal protections. That ends the slaughter, at least for now. And while the case is far from settled, the dozen conservation groups that brought the suit are hopeful that his injunction will survive further court tests and that the Fish and Wildlife Service will be forced to provide a better plan to protect the wolves.

3   The centerpiece of Judge Molloy's decision was his finding that the Fish and Wildlife Service had failed to meet its own criteria for removing the wolf from the endangered species list. Before stripping the wolves of federal protection, the agency was required to show that wolf subpopulations across the area were interbreeding—a genetic necessity for healthy, sustainable numbers. The judge found that the agency had offered no such evidence.

4   Judge Molloy also found that this fall's hunts could irreparably damage the species. He seemed particularly annoyed at the agency's failure to explain why it had "flip-flopped" on Wyoming's plan, which allows unregulated hunting on most state lands. The agency had previously rejected it as insufficiently protective. . . .

5   This deep-set hostility has only a little to do with ranching. It is really driven by the competition between human hunters and wolves for the same game animals: elk and deer. And underneath it all is a false myth—the wolf as a kind of ferocious coward and an indiscriminate killer—that says less about the true nature of wolves than it does about human fear.

From *The New York Times's* editorial A STAY OF EXECUTION FOR THE WOLVES, © 2008

8. Which statement **best** explains the author's background as reflected in the passage?

    A. The author has little knowledge about the problem.
    B. The author has always disagreed with the judge's opinion.
    C. The author has researched the topic.
    D. The author has a strong bias against hunters.

9. Which statement from the text **best** supports the idea that the author strongly supports protecting gray wolves?

    A. ". . . more than 100 wolves out of a total population of 1,500 have been killed."
    B. "Judge Donald Molloy issued a preliminary injunction last week restoring federal protections."
    C. "That ends the slaughter, at least for now."
    D. "The judge found that the agency had offered no such evidence."

10. In paragraph 4, the author describes the judge's point of view as

    A. pleased with the Fish and Wildlife service.
    B. irritated with the Fish and Wildlife service.
    C. indifferent toward the entire case.
    D. unfamiliar with the Fish and Wildlife Service.

11. Which sentence **best** states the author's point of view?

    A. The author believes that people should be informed about laws concerning wildlife.
    B. The author favors elk and deer over wolves.
    C. The author agrees with the states of Wyoming, Montana, and Idaho regarding the disposal of wolves.
    D. The author disagrees with the states about wolf hunting and believes the animals should be protected.

12. What statement **best** reflects the Fish and Wildlife Service's point of view about gray wolves?

    A. Gray wolves no longer need the protection of the Endangered Species Act.
    B. Laws protecting gray wolves in Wyoming, Montana, and Idaho are not strict enough.
    C. Better plans must be made to protect gray wolves.
    D. State lands must be off limits for unregulated hunting.

Make Inferences

LESSON **8**

Use with *Student Book* pp. 16–17

1 Review the Skill

READING ASSESSMENT TARGETS: R.2.3, R.2.4, R.2.5, R.3.5, R.4.1/L.4
R.4.3/L.4.3, R.5.1, R.5.4, R.6.1, R.6.3, R.6.4

As you learned in Lesson 1, some main ideas and details may be implied, or not directly stated. When an author does not directly state ideas, you must **make inferences** to figure out what important information the author wants to communicate. Combined with your prior knowledge, an author's suggestions, clues, facts, language, and tone can help you make inferences.

2 Refine the Skill

By refining the skill of making inferences, you will improve your study and test-taking abilities, especially as they relate to the GED® Reasoning Through Language Arts test. Read the passage below. Then answer the question that follows.

a You can infer that after you meet the $50 per family deductible, you will have to pay the remaining 10 percent of the covered charges.

b Notice the author gives specific details of the rules that apply to coverage. It gives you clues as to how you can best use your coverage.

EYECARE VISION PLAN BENEFITS

The plan requires the payment of a $50 yearly deductible per family, after which the network pays 90 percent of the covered charges. In order to receive the 90 percent co-insurance provision, employees must use the ophthalmologists, optometrists, or opticians who participate in the EyeCare network. Employees who elect to use nonparticipating eyecare professionals will be reimbursed at a 75 percent rate.

Under the plan, lens replacement (eyeglasses or contact lenses) is allowed every 12 months, but only if necessary due to a change in prescription or damage to the lenses. Frames may be replaced every 24 months. Laser surgery for purely cosmetic purposes is not covered under the plan. Please contact Human Resources for an enrollment form, a description of benefits, and a list of participating vision professionals.

1. What can you infer about benefits under the plan?

   A. Designer frames will incur a higher co-pay.
   B. Laser surgery that is medically necessary will probably be covered.
   C. An enrollee can switch from eyeglasses to contact lenses after 12 months if they want to.
   D. The Human Resources department will assign an eye doctor to each employee.

TEST-TAKING TIPS

You may be asked to make inferences about people, ideas, situations, actions, or meanings of words. Remember that information directly stated in the passage is not an inference.

DIRECTIONS: Read the passage, read each question, and choose the **best** answer.

THOUGHTS ABOUT MUSKETAQUID LAND

1   When I walk in the fields of Concord and meditate on the destiny of this prosperous slip of the Saxon family—the unexhausted energies of this new country—I forget that this which is now Concord was once Musketaquid and that the American race has had its destiny also. Everywhere in the fields—in the corn and grain land—the earth is strewn with the relics of a race which has vanished as completely as if trodden in with the earth.

2   I find it good to remember the eternity behind me as well as the eternity before. Where ever I go I tread in the tracks of the Indian—I pick up the bolt which has but just dropped at my feet. And if I consider destiny I am on his trail. I scatter his hearth stones with my feet, and pick out of the embers of his fire the simple but enduring implements of the wigwam and the chase—In planting my corn in the same furrow which yielded its increase to support so long—I displace some memorial of him. . . .

3   Nature has her russet[1] hues as well as green—Indeed our eye splits on every object, and we can as well take one path as the other—If I consider its history it is old—if [I consider] its destiny it is new—I may see a part of an object or the whole—I will not be imposed on and think nature is old, because the season is advanced. I will study the botany of the mosses and fungi on the decayed—and remember that decayed wood is not old, but has just begun to be what it is. I need not think of the pine almond or the acorn and sapling when I meet the fallen pine or oak—more than of the generations of pines and oaks which have fed the young tree."

[1]russet—reddish brown

From JOURNALS by Henry David Thoreau

2. Based on the first sentence of this passage, what inference can be made about the author?

    A. He is lamenting that the land he stands on used to belong to another group.
    B. He is thinking about how we perceive time and place based on our experiences.
    C. He is thinking about how Musketaquid became Concord.
    D. He is celebrating the history of his location.

3. On the basis of the information in paragraph 1, of whom is Thoreau speaking when he refers to "relics of a race which has vanished"?

    A. his deceased family members
    B. settlers who worked the land before him
    C. neighbors who moved far away from his cabin
    D. Native Americans who first lived on the land

4. What does the author imply when he writes "In planting my corn in the same furrow which yielded its increase to support so long—I displace some memorial of him" (paragraph 2)?

    A. He has planted corn in the same place as his ancestors.
    B. As he plants his own corn, he is taking away traces of Native Americans.
    C. He is acknowledging that others have planted in this spot before him.
    D. He is claiming the land as his own through his planting ritual.

5. What is the **most** logical inference to make about the meaning of the statement "decayed wood is not old" (paragraph 3)?

    A. There are much older forms of wood than decayed wood.
    B. Decay is a natural process.
    C. Decayed wood is the start of a new cycle of life.
    D. Decayed wood is young compared with mosses and fungi.

6. Based on the first sentence of paragraph 3, the author would most likely agree

    A. that plants were important to his ancestors.
    B. that people can understand their place in the world by studying plant life.
    C. that how we view nature depends on our mood and experience.
    D. that death is inevitable.

UNIT 1

UNIT 1

DIRECTIONS: Read the passage, read each question, and choose the **best** answser.

THE AUTHOR'S QUEST

1   Sometimes, without warning, the future knocks on our door with a precious and painful vision of what might be. One hundred and nineteen years ago, a wealthy inventor read his own obituary, mistakenly published years before his death. Wrongly believing the inventor had just died, a newspaper printed a harsh judgment of his life's work, unfairly labeling him "The Merchant of Death" because of his invention— dynamite. Shaken by this condemnation, the inventor made a fateful choice to serve the cause of peace. Seven years later, Alfred Nobel created this prize and the others that bear his name.

2   Seven years ago tomorrow, I read my own political obituary in a judgment that seemed to me harsh and mistaken—if not premature. But that unwelcome verdict also brought a precious, if painful, gift: an opportunity to search for fresh new ways to serve my purpose. Unexpectedly, that quest has brought me here. Even though I fear my words cannot match this moment, I pray what I am feeling in my heart will be communicated clearly enough that those who hear me will say, "We must act. . . ."

3   We, the human species, are confronting a planetary emergency—a threat to the survival of our civilization that is gathering ominous and destructive potential even as we gather here. But there is hopeful news as well: we have the ability to solve this crisis and avoid the worst—though not all—of its consequences, if we act boldly, decisively, and quickly. . . .

4   So today, we dumped another 70 million tons of global-warming pollution into the thin shell of atmosphere surrounding our planet, as if it were an open sewer. And tomorrow, we will dump a slightly larger amount, with the cumulative concentrations now trapping more and more heat from the sun.

5   As a result, the earth has a fever. And the fever is rising. The experts have told us it is not a passing affliction that will heal by itself. We asked for a second opinion. And a third. And a fourth. And the consistent conclusion, restated with increasing distress, is that something basic is wrong. We are what is wrong, and we must make it right.

From NOBEL PEACE PRIZE LECTURE by Al Gore, © 2007

7. From the information in paragraph 1, which is th **most** logical inference to make? Nobel created the prize

    A. as a memorial to his accomplishments as an inventor.
    B. so people would remember him after his death.
    C. to continue his legacy and encourage others to invent things.
    D. because he did not want to be known as "The Merchant of Death."

8. To what event is the speaker **most likely** referrin at the beginning of paragraph 2?

    A. an event that occurred when he became Vice-President in 1992
    B. his loss in the 2000 presidential election
    C. the death of a friend who was involved in politics
    D. a mistaken report of his own death

9. What does the author imply when he says, "it is not a passing affliction that will heal by itself" (paragraph 5)?

    A. People must take action and make changes t fix the problem.
    B. Nothing can be done to fix the problem.
    C. People will not make changes unless they are forced.
    D. The problem will correct itself over time naturally.

10. Which statement **best** explains the meaning of the last sentence in paragraph 5?

    A. Many people are sick from the effects of global warming and must cure themselves.
    B. Humans have caused global warming and now must fix the damage it has caused.
    C. People who have done wrong things should be punished for them.
    D. People are reluctant to admit they are wrong.

DIRECTIONS: Read the passage, read each question, and choose the **best** answer.

A WRITER'S VIEW

1   Our tragedy today is a general and universal physical fear so long sustained by now that we can even bear it. There are no longer problems of the spirit. There is only the question: When will I be blown up? Because of this, the young man or woman writing today has forgotten the problems of the human heart in conflict with itself which alone can make good writing because only that is worth writing about, worth the agony and the sweat.

2   He must learn them again. He must teach himself that the basest of all things is to be afraid; and, teaching himself that, forget it forever, leaving no room in his workshop for anything but the old verities and truths of the heart, the old universal truths lacking which any story is ephemeral [short-lived] and doomed—love and honor and pity and pride and compassion and sacrifice. Until he does so, he labors under a curse. He writes not of love but of lust, of defeats in which nobody loses anything of value, of victories without hope and, worst of all, without pity or compassion. His griefs grieve on no universal bones, leaving no scars. He writes not of the heart but of the glands.

3   Until he relearns these things, he will write as though he stood among and watched the end of man. I decline to accept the end of man. It is easy enough to say that man is immortal simply because he will endure: that when the last ding-dong of doom has clanged and faded from the last worthless rock hanging tideless in the last red and dying evening, that even then there will still be one more sound: that of his puny inexhaustible voice, still talking. I refuse to accept this. I believe that man will not merely endure: he will prevail. He is immortal, not because he alone among creatures has an inexhaustible voice, but because he has a soul, a spirit capable of compassion and sacrifice and endurance.

4   The poet's, the writer's, duty is to write about these things. It is his privilege to help man endure by lifting his heart, by reminding him of the courage and honor and hope and pride and compassion and pity and sacrifice which have been the glory of his past. The poet's voice need not merely be the record of man, it can be one of the props, the pillars to help him endure and prevail.

From SPEECH ACCEPTING THE NOBEL PRIZE IN LITERATURE by William Faulkner, © 1950

11. On the basis of the information in the passage, the author thinks that young writers of his time are lacking

   A. fearlessness.
   B. endurance.
   C. devastation.
   D. victories.

12. In paragraph 1, the author says that young writers have "forgotten the problems of the human heart in conflict with itself which alone can make good writing." Which is the **best** inference to make about this statement?

   A. Young writers are more concerned with publishing than with writing.
   B. Good writing usually contains tragic elements.
   C. Readers are no longer interested in love stories.
   D. Writers are not focusing on human emotions.

13. In paragraph 2, Faulkner implies that young writers are creating works that are

   A. violent.
   B. passionate.
   C. superficial.
   D. difficult.

14. In paragraph 3, what does the author imply about humanity?

   A. The human spirit gives us the ability to transcend.
   B. Every human surely will die.
   C. New writers will perish just as a human perishes.
   D. Humans have no spirits or souls.

15. In paragraph 4, what is the **most** logical inference to make about how Faulkner views poets and writers? He sees them as

   A. messengers of human emotions.
   B. potential supporters of society.
   C. providers of important facts.
   D. intelligent and respected entertainers.

Analyze Style and Tone

Use with *Student Book* pp. 26–27

READING ASSESSMENT TARGETS: R.3.4, R.4.1/L.4.1, R.4.2/L.4.2, R.4.3/L.4
R.5.1, R.5.2, R.5.4

UNIT 1

1 Review the Skill

An author writes in a specific **style** that best fits the topic, audience, and purpose. An author's style is made up of the words and structures of sentences and paragraphs within the text. For example, a style may be formal, informal, direct, poetic, comic, earnest, or a combination of these and other ways of expression.

An author's **tone** is directly related to the author's style. Tone shows the reader how the author thinks or feels about the topic. Try to determine the author's tone by analyzing the words chosen for the piece. Determine whether the words have emotion or feeling behind them and whether they have positive or negative connotations, or meanings that go beyond the literal ones.

2 Refine the Skill

By refining the skill of analyzing style and tone, you will improve your study and test-taking abilities, especially as they relate to the GED® Reasoning Through Language Arts test. Read the passage below. Then answer the questions that follow.

PUBLIC SERVANTS MUST SET AN EXAMPLE

a The author uses the words *participate* and *suffer* to appeal to the audience's sense of responsibility and patriotism. These words are an example of the author's style and tone in this speech.

b The author is employing a certain style by putting quotation marks around the words *public servants*. This treatment indicates that she will focus on what the idea of "public servants" means to her.

A nation is formed by the willingness of each of us to share in the responsibility for upholding the common good. A government is invigorated when each one of us is willing to participate in shaping the future of this nation. In this election year, we must define the "common good" and begin again to shape a common future. Let each person do his or her part. If one citizen is unwilling to participate, all of us are going to suffer. For the American idea, though it is shared by all of us, is realized in each one of us.

And now, what are those of us who are elected public officials supposed to do? We call ourselves "public servants" but I'll tell you this: We as public servants must set an example for the rest of the nation. It is hypocritical for the public official to admonish and exhort the people to uphold the common good if we are derelict in upholding the common good. ... We must hold ourselves strictly accountable. We must provide the people with a vision of the future.

From the DEMOCRATIC NATIONAL CONVENTION KEYNOTE ADDRESS by Barbara Jordan, © 1976

1. By using the term **public servants** instead of **politicians,** the author makes "public servants" seem

   A. more interested in winning elections than in serving the public.
   B. less concerned with the present than with a vision of the future.
   C. more dedicated to the public than to politics.
   D. less interested in accountability than in politics.

2. Which word **best** describes the tone of this passage?

   A. passionate
   B. uncaring
   C. upbeat
   D. sarcastic

TEST-TAKING TIPS

Remember that a writer's tone often is connected closely to the style. If a question asks you to identify the author's purpose, or reason for writing, you can look at the style and tone for clues.

INAUGURAL ADDRESS

1   This is America's day. This is democracy's day. A day of history and hope. Of renewal and resolve. Through a crucible for the ages, America has been tested anew and America has risen to the challenge. Today, we celebrate the triumph not of a candidate, but of a cause, the cause of democracy. The will of the people has been heard and the will of the people has been heeded. We have learned again that democracy is precious. Democracy is fragile. And at this hour, my friends, democracy has prevailed.

2   So now, on this hallowed ground where just days ago violence sought to shake this Capitol's very foundation, we come together as one nation, under God, indivisible, to carry out the peaceful transfer of power as we have for more than two centuries. We look ahead in our uniquely American way—restless, bold, optimistic—and set our sights on the nation we know we can be and we must be.

3   I thank my predecessors of both parties for their presence here. I thank them from the bottom of my heart. You know the resilience of our Constitution and the strength of our nation. . . .

4   I have just taken the sacred oath each of these patriots took—an oath first sworn by George Washington. But the American story depends not on any one of us, not on some of us, but on all of us. On "We the People" who seek a more perfect Union.

5   This is a great nation and we are a good people. Over the centuries through storm and strife, in peace and in war, we have come so far. But we still have far to go. We will press forward with speed and urgency, for we have much to do in this winter of peril and possibility. Much to repair. Much to restore. Much to heal. Much to build. And much to gain.

6   Few periods in our nation's history have been more challenging or difficult than the one we're in now. A once-in-a-century virus silently stalks the country. It's taken as many lives in one year as America lost in all of World War II. Millions of jobs have been lost. Hundreds of thousands of businesses closed. A cry for racial justice some 400 years in the making moves us. The dream of justice for all will be deferred no longer. A cry for survival comes from the planet itself. A cry that can't be any more desperate or any more clear. And now, a rise in political extremism, white supremacy, domestic terrorism that we must confront and we will defeat.

7   To overcome these challenges—to restore the soul and to secure the future of America—requires more than words. It requires that most elusive of things in a democracy: Unity.

8   In another January in Washington, on New Year's Day 1863, Abraham Lincoln signed the Emancipation Proclamation. When he put pen to paper, the President said, "If my name ever goes down into history it will be for this act and my whole soul is in it." My whole soul is in it.

9   Today, on this January day, my whole soul is in this: Bringing America together. Uniting our people. And uniting our nation.

From INAUGURAL ADDRESS by President Biden, 2021

3.   What is the tone of paragraph 1?

   A. professional detachment
   B. hope and triumph
   C. determination and hostility
   D. judgmental irony

4.   How does the style of paragraph 7 differ from the style of paragraph 6? Paragraph 6

   A. uses complete sentences to describe challenges the nation faces, but paragraph 7 uses fragments to describe a solution.
   B. uses a mix of complete sentence and fragments to describe challenges the nation faces, but paragraph 7 uses complete sentences to describe a solution.
   C. uses a mix of complete sentences and fragments to describe challenges, but paragraph 7 uses only fragments to describe a solution.
   D. uses only fragments to describe challenges the nation faces, but paragraph 7 uses a mix of complete sentences and fragments to describe a solution.

5.   Based on the words spoken in paragraph 3 and 4, which word **best** describes the author?

   A. humble
   B. vain
   C. self-conscious
   D. arrogant

★ Spotlighted Item: **DRAG-AND-DROP**

DIRECTIONS: Read the passage and the question. Then use the drag-and-drop options to complete the web.

PERSONALITY TESTING

1   Modern personality testing—which encompasses everything from artsy interpretative exercises like the Rorschach inkblot to exhaustive questionnaires like the Minnesota Multiphasic Personality Inventory (M.M.P.I.)—is a child of 20th-century research psychology, born of the dream that we can crack the code of human behavior if only we can devise the right set of questions. These tests grew up with the help of modern bureaucracies, like corporations and the military, that needed an efficient means of categorizing people by temperament, the better to predict their on-the-job behavior.

From *The New York Times's* article THE RORSCHACH CHRONICLES by Margaret Talbot, © 1999

6.   Drag and drop into the web the three words that **most strongly** contribute to the tone of the paragraph.

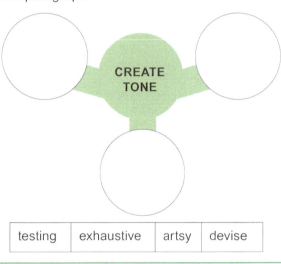

testing	exhaustive	artsy	devise

DIRECTIONS: Read the passage, read the question, and choose the **best** answer.

HOOKED ON TESTING

1   Psychologists have been happy to oblige in this quest, for it has allowed them to indulge in a fantasy of their own: that personality assessment may someday attain the authority and respect of more objective medical tests, helping, in turn, to endow psychology with some of the status of the hard sciences. Indeed, from the 1920's on, the inventors of such tests have resorted to a favorite telltale metaphor from the world of medicine. "As a rule," wrote Henry Murray, the Harvard psychologist who invented the TAT [a psychological test in which a person looks at pictures and tells a story about them] in the early 1940's, "the subject leaves the test happily unaware that he has presented the psychologist with what amounts to an X-ray of his inner self.". . .

2   For all that, though, personality testing is here to stay—not only because of the many institutions now hooked on it but also because of the deep human curiosity it promises, however teasingly, to satisfy. Long before scientific testing, we tried to classify temperament and character based on the shapes of people's skulls or the color of their humors. Before the

Rorschach, a popular 19th-century parlor game called Blotto invited players to assess one another's creativity on the basis of their interpretations of inkblots. Leonardo da Vinci used a similar method to judge the imaginative potential of his students.

From *The New York Times's* article THE RORSCHACH CHRONICLE by Margaret Talbot, © 1999

7.   In paragraph 1, the author compares psychology with the "hard" sciences. What connotation does **hard** have in this passage?

A. It suggests that these sciences are rigid.
B. It suggests that these sciences are more difficult to understand than psychology.
C. It suggests that these sciences are based more in reality than psychology is.
D. It suggests that these sciences are older than psychology.

8.   Which statement **best** applies to paragraph 2?

A. The examples support the author's viewpoint.
B. The author changes her mind about testing.
C. The tone becomes more emotional.
D. The author makes more personal judgments.

DIRECTIONS: Read the passage, read each question, and choose the **best** answer.

LESSONS LEARNED

1   I am a scientist. I am often wrong, and that's okay.

2   You may have heard about major errors in science and engineering that made the news headlines, like the collapse of the Tacoma Narrows Bridge, aka "Galloping Gertie," or the 1999 crash of the Mars Climate Orbiter. Or maybe you've seen the recent video from SpaceX, "How Not to Land an Orbital Rocket Booster." You may not realize how often scientists are wrong, but being wrong is actually part of the process of doing science. The trick is to catch errors before they leave the lab, and certainly before they make the front-page news, though, obviously, that doesn't always happen. . . .

3   I have had many moments of being wrong in my scientific career. One of my most memorable moments was during a hands-on exam in school when I was given equipment to observe and measure the radioactive decay of a certain isotope. . . . I had incorrectly assumed that this experiment would have the same property as most science experiments: that the results (in this case, the decay rate) wouldn't change over time. . . .

4   Looking back, this experience taught me several lessons. First, I learned that science can be humbling. I shouldn't be overly confident in my conclusions because there's always a chance I might be wrong, . . . More importantly, though, the experience taught me that it's okay to be wrong if you are willing to accept that possibility and make corrections. . . .

5   In my current work, I often follow the same basic framework. I have a hypothesis that I want to test. I do experiments and analyze the data to look for evidence that will confirm or disprove that hypothesis. Many times, the trend I find does not match my expectations, so I go back and re-examine my hypothesis and/or check whether I'm doing the experiment correctly. Problems with an experiment are common because it's easy to overlook factors like the temperature stability or uniformity inside an oven, or the alignment of a laser in the experimental setup. A lot of effort in the laboratory is spent troubleshooting and repeating experiments before arriving at a conclusion. . . .

6   Thinking like a scientist involves recognizing that you will occasionally (or more than occasionally) be wrong and knowing how to find out why. Science is a journey, and part of that journey is making errors and being empowered to make changes based on lessons learned.

7   Even the news-making science errors have had lasting, positive impacts. From the Tacoma Narrows bridge collapse, scientists learned the importance of wind and aerodynamics for bridges. After the Mars orbiter crash, NASA made changes that enabled the success of the two Mars rovers, Spirit and Opportunity. Making errors in science is just part of the process and allows scientists to learn and broaden what we know. It's only by being wrong that we ever learn what's right.

8   So, to all you scientists and non-scientists, go forth and be wrong! You'll probably discover something new on your journey.

From the nist.gov article IT'S ALL RIGHT TO BE WRONG IN SCIENCE by Paulina Kuo, 2018

9. Which word **best** describes the author's style in this passage?

    A. emotional
    B. argumentative
    C. anecdotal
    D. mysterious

10. The author says, "I am often wrong, and that's okay." What does this statement indicate about the author's attitude?

    A. The author sees herself as below the people she is addressing.
    B. The author has little experience with the subject matter.
    C. The author displays a nervous attitude and is uneasy about her topic.
    D. The author displays a sense of humility, honesty, and openness.

11. In paragraph 4, the author says that she learned that "science can be **humbling**." How would the tone of the paragraph change if she had substituted the word **demeaning** for **humbling**?

    A. The paragraph would emphasize the lesson learned rather than the mistake.
    B. The paragraph would emphasize the mistake rather than the lesson learned.
    C. The tone would be more sarcastic.
    D. The tone would be less formal.

Draw Conclusions

LESSON 10

Use with *Student Book* pp. 28–29

READING ASSESSMENT TARGETS: R.2.4, R.2.5, R.2.8, R.3.2, R.3.3, R.3. R.3.5, R.4.3/L.4.3, R.5.1, R.6.3

1 Review the Skill

When you **draw conclusions**, you make judgments based on information provided in the text or from inferences. Remember that an inference is an educated guess based on facts or evidence and on your own prior knowledge. Identify the important details of a passage, and then use those details to make inferences and draw conclusions. You may find that different facts support different conclusions but that these conclusions can lead you to a larger conclusion about the whole text.

2 Refine the Skill

By refining the skill of drawing conclusions, you will improve your study and test-taking abilities, especially as they relate to the GED® Reasoning Through Language Arts test. Read the passage below. Then answer the questions that follow.

a Notice in the last sentence of paragraph 1 the use of the word *limits*. What can readers infer about the other 47 states where very little sugarcane is produced?

b Notice the second paragraph tells readers which state produces the most sugarcane. Then it provides a description of the state. What conclusion can be drawn from these two facts?

SUGARCANE PRODUCTION IN THE UNITED STATES

1   One of the primary sources of raw material for manufactured sugar is sugarcane. The sugarcane plant is a form of tall grass that grows in warm, rainy climates. This limits sugarcane plantations in the United States, the world's 10th largest producer of sugarcane, mostly to Florida, Louisiana, and Texas.

2   Florida is the country's largest sugarcane grower. The southern part of the state has rich soil and long growing seasons. Production in Florida expanded significantly following the U.S.'s 1960 ban on importing Cuban sugar. In Louisiana, sugarcane production occurs mostly along the Mississippi Delta. In Texas, sugarcane is grown in the lower Rio Grande Valley.

USING LOGIC

To draw conclusions, you must make assumptions, or educated guesses. If a topic or an author's purpose is unclear, read the text carefully, and make logical assumptions based on what you read and on prior knowledge.

1. Based on the passage, the **most** logical conclusion to draw about sugarcane farming is that it

    A. benefits from rich soil and long growing seasons.
    B. benefits from climates with four distinct seasons.
    C. does not grow well along river systems.
    D. does not employ many people in the United States.

2. What logical conclusion is supported by this passage?

    A. Sugarcane farming employs people throughout the country.
    B. Sugarcane is one of the country's most important crops.
    C. The United States is forced to import large amounts of sugarcane.
    D. The United States is largely unsuitable for growing sugarcane.

UNIT 1

⭐ Spotlighted Item: **DRAG-AND-DROP**

DIRECTIONS: Read the passage and the question. Then use the drag-and-drop options to complete the chart.

THE NEW WORK-FROM-HOME ECONOMY

1   As the COVID-19 pandemic spread from the Northeast and West Coast to the South and Midwest, people were told to stay home. And many people did. Restaurants, gyms, retail stores, beauty salons, and schools shut their doors. Millions of people were left unemployed.

2   But millions more were able to work from home. Studies differ, but data suggests more than half of the U.S. labor force worked remotely during the summer of 2020. Even as restrictions eased, many Americans continued to work from their make-shift offices. Although safety concerns sparked the changes, businesses may find many reasons to continue this trend.

3   Companies can benefit from attracting workers from many locations. This is particularly useful for businesses not located in major cities with large labor pools.

4   Employees often benefit from more flexible work hours and decreased commuting. Sure, you still need to call in for the daily team meeting. But you don't need to suffer through a long drive through heavy traffic. And when the meeting is over, you can handle home-related issues.

5   The decreased dependence on location and flexible working hours allow companies to promote more inclusive hiring practices. Many more working parents and skilled employees from different demographics can bring diversity to a company's work force.

6   Less commuting means employees spend less money on gas and parking. In addition, less time in a central office decreases other employee expenses, such as wardrobe and eating out at restaurants. Businesses can spend less money on office space. These cost savings combined with happier employees means increased productivity.

7   Finally, reduced commuter traffic reduces vehicle-related pollution, which benefits the environment.

8   These benefits do not come without some challenges. For example, not everyone has a reliable Internet connection or a dedicated work space. While many advances in technology make remote working possible, remote working may be problematic for some businesses and their employees.

3.   Drag and drop the phrases into the appropriate places in the chart.

Benefits of Work-from-Home Economy

Challenges of Work-from-Home Economy

Attract workers from many locations	Inclusive hiring practices
Flexible work hours	Some people do not have reliable Internet
Decreased commuting	Lack of dedicated work space

DIRECTIONS: Read the passage, read each question, and choose the **best** answer.

CLOSE THE STEM GENDER GAP

1   The number of women graduating with college degrees related to STEM (**s**cience, **t**echnology, **e**ngineering, and **m**ath) has increased over the past two decades. However, the number of men earning these degrees has also gone up. This means the gap between women and men in STEM-related careers has remained persistent. Although women comprise half the population, they account for less than 30 percent of the jobs in these fields. This gap is even more pronounced among Black and Hispanic women, who account for about 5 percent of STEM jobs.

2   Women in STEM are paid approximately 10 percent less than men, and women are found in far fewer leadership positions. For example, data shows women comprise less than 15 percent of the boards of information technology companies.

3   Experts offer different solutions to close this gap. A number of programs across the country are designed to encourage young women to pursue STEM-related educations and careers. These organizations provide resources to help women overcome social obstacles and gain confidence. Many of these programs also advocate for women who face workplace discrimination and hostility.

4   Another important part of closing the gap is highlighting the work women have made in science, technology, engineering, and math. Albert Einstein, Steve Jobs, and many other men are household names for their work in STEM. Donna Strickland, Frances Arnold, and Tu Youyou earned Nobel Prizes in physics, chemistry, and medicine, respectively. They should all be more widely known for their accomplishments.

5   Finally, advocates for more women in STEM say an important factor that needs to be better developed is mentorships and peer networks. Women who have succeeded in these fields need to form stronger ties with each other and provide greater support for up-and-comers. Resource groups in companies and at universities increase women's standing in these organizations and decrease the sense of isolation many women feel.

4. From the information in paragraph 1, what is the **best** conclusion to draw about the gender gap in STEM-related careers?

    A. Women are getting better grades than men in STEM courses.
    B. Fewer STEM degrees are being earned by both women and men.
    C. The number of women entering STEM careers has not been enough to close the gap.
    D. The gender gap in STEM-related careers is difficult to measure.

5. Which statement **best** explains the author's conclusion about the gender gap in STEM-related careers?

    A. The gap persists because fewer men are deciding to pursue these careers.
    B. The gap persists for a number of societal issues, including discrimination.
    C. The gap is not important enough to address.
    D. The gap can only be eliminated by women who already work in these fields.

6. According to the passage, what conclusion can you draw about how the author feels about resource groups for women?

    A. They provide necessary support for women who are starting in STEM careers.
    B. They are not helpful to women who are already in leadership positions.
    C. They do not help reduce the gender gap in STEM fields.
    D. They are the reason many women feel isolated in their careers.

7. What is the **most** logical conclusion to draw about the author's overall point of view in this passage? The author believes that

    A. women already make significant contributions in STEM-related careers.
    B. the gender gap in STEM-related careers will never close.
    C. workplace discrimination and hostility are the main causes of the gender gap.
    D. there should be more women succeeding in STEM-related careers.

DIRECTIONS: Read the passage, read each question, and choose the **best** answer.

THE SPEAKER'S SUCCESS

1   When I arose to speak, there was considerable cheering, especially from the coloured people. As I remember it now, the thing that was uppermost in my mind was the desire to say something that would cement the friendship of the races and bring about hearty cooperation between them. So far as my outward surroundings were concerned, the only thing that I recall distinctly now is that when I got up, I saw thousands of eyes looking intently into my face. . . .

2   The first thing that I remember, after I had finished speaking, was that Governor Bullock rushed across the platform and took me by the hand, and that others did the same. I received so many and such hearty congratulations that I found it difficult to get out of the building. I did not appreciate to any degree, however, the impression which my address seemed to have made, until the next morning, when I went into the business part of the city. As soon as I was recognized, I was surprised to find myself pointed out and surrounded by a crowd of men who wished to shake hands with me. This was kept up on every street on to which I went, to an extent which embarrassed me so much that I went back to my boarding-place. The next morning I returned to Tuskegee. At the station in Atlanta, and at almost all of the stations at which the train stopped between the city and Tuskegee, I found a crowd of people anxious to shake hands with me. . . .

3   I very soon began receiving all kinds of propositions from lecture bureaus, and editors of magazines and papers, to take the lecture platform, and to write articles.

From UP FROM SLAVERY by Booker T. Washington

8. On the basis of the content in paragraph 1, what is the **best** conclusion to draw about the background for the author's desire to "cement the friendship of the races"?

    A. The author is happy that race relations seem to be improving.
    B. The author is offended that the audience is segregated.
    C. The author is unconcerned about race relations.
    D. The author is satisfied that he was able to bring about cooperation between the races.

9. On the basis of the information in the passage, what is the **best** conclusion to draw about the author's character? The author is a person who is

    A. forgetful.
    B. pessimistic.
    C. humble.
    D. arrogant.

10. Which statement from the passage **best** supports the conclusion about the author's character?

    A. "When I arose to speak, there was considerable cheering. . . ."
    B. "The first thing that I remember, after I had finished speaking, was that Governor Bullock rushed across the platform and took me by the hand, and that others did the same."
    C. "I received so many and such hearty congratulations that I found it difficult to get out of the building."
    D. "As soon as I was recognized, I was surprised to find myself pointed out and surrounded by a crowd of men who wished to shake hands with me."

11. Which is the **most** logical conclusion to draw about why the author received invitations from "lecture bureaus, and editors of magazines and papers"?

    A. His speech was amusing.
    B. His speech was successful.
    C. His speech caused debate.
    D. His speech created racial unrest.

11
LESSON

Make Generalizations

Use with **Student Book** pp. 30–31

READING ASSESSMENT TARGETS: R.2.4, R.2.5, R.2.7, R.2.8, R.3.5, R.5.2, R.

UNIT 1

1 Review the Skill

A **generalization** is a broad statement that applies to principles, ideas, people, places, and events. Key words such as *all, everyone, few, none, some,* or *usually* can act as indicators when you look for or make your own generalizations. Generalizations may be valid or invalid. Valid generalizations are supported by sufficient and credible facts, but invalid ones are not. Stereotypes are often invalid, oversimplified generalizations.

2 Refine the Skill

By refining the skill of making generalizations, you will improve your study and test-taking abilities, especially as they apply to the GED® Reasoning Through Language Arts test. Read the passage below. Then answer the questions that follow.

RETURNING HOME CAN BE A SMART DECISION

a The author makes a broad statement about people living at home with their parents. The key word *majority* indicates a generalization about this group of people.

There's a flip side to the debate about adult children returning home. Depending on the situation, moving back in with mom and dad can actually be the wisest choice a person can make. The majority of people living at home with their parents continue to work full-time or part-time jobs, allowing them to pool their resources with other family members. This increases the overall income of the household and helps reduce stress on any individual family member.

b Generalizations may serve to support the author's point of view. The author claims that people can save a **substantial** amount of money by living back home.

Living back home also enables [young people] to reduce their expenses and focus on saving money. Rather than struggling to make ends meet, they can put money aside in savings accounts or investments and begin growing a nest egg. Considering the high cost of living throughout the nation, a substantial amount of money can be saved if the individual does not have to foot the entire cost alone.

From *Forbes*'s article FAILURE TO LAUNCH: ADULT CHILDREN MOVING BACK HOME by Alan Dunn, © 2012

USING LOGIC

Sometimes an author may over-generalize by making a broad assertion without supplying enough support. Use logic to ask yourself whether a writer's generalization is always valid or only sometimes valid.

1. On the basis of this passage, which is the **best** generalization to make about why moving back home is a wise choice?

   A. It encourages people to earn more money.
   B. It allows people to work part-time and pursue interests.
   C. It reduces expenses and helps people save money.
   D. It allows parents to take on more of the expenses.

2. What information would add to the validity of the author's generalization about the cost of living?

   A. support for the fact that it is high throughout the nation
   B. support for the fact that it has regional differences
   C. a definition of the term *cost of living*
   D. an example of what something costs

DIRECTIONS: Read the passage, read each question, and choose the **best** answer.

DISCRIMINATION IN THE WORKPLACE

1   There are federal laws prohibiting employment discrimination. Employment discrimination is the unfavorable treatment of workers based on certain traits, such as race, sex, age, or medical-related issues. Discrimination occurs far too often because most employers do not understand what behaviors are prohibited.

2   Racial discrimination in the workplace remains far too common. Some companies may hire people of color to maintain an appearance of equal opportunity employment practices. But once hired, these employees may not receive the same opportunities and support as other workers, or worse, they may face physical or emotional abuse.

3   Similarly, women have historically faced discrimination, including mistreatment, lack of support, or lack of opportunities. Although not as common, men in the workplace also report discrimination because of their gender, only to find their claims are not taken seriously because they are men. Sex-related discrimination also extends to employees who are treated unfairly because of their sexual preference or gender identity.

4   The most commonly reported employment discrimination is based on retaliation. This type of discrimination happens when a business or some other organization takes illegal action against workers because they engaged in a protected activity. For example, employees who participate in an investigation or file discrimination charges against the company are afforded some protections. It is unlawful for employers to retaliate against them.

5   Because employment discrimination is a legal issue, it is important for workers who feel they have been targeted to consult someone with expertise in the area. Employees should at the very least become familiar with the state and federal laws that govern workplace discrimination.

6   It is also important to document and report events. Make detailed notes about incidents as soon as it is safe to do so. Then determine who to report the matter to, whether it is within the company or to an outside agency.

3. In paragraph 1, what generalization does the author make?

    A. There are federal laws prohibiting employment discrimination.
    B. Employment discrimination is the unfavorable treatment of workers.
    C. Discrimination can occur based on race, sex, age, or other traits.
    D. Most employers do not understand what behaviors are prohibited.

4. How is paragraph 3 related to the previous paragraph?

    A. It provides additional examples of stereotyping that may occur in the workplace.
    B. It makes a generalization about women in the workplace.
    C. It makes a generalization about men in the workplace.
    D. It explains that sex-related discrimination does not include sexual preference or gender identity issues.

5. Based on the passage, which is the **most** accurate generalization to make about employees who face workplace discrimination?

    A. Every employee is protected from employment discrimination by laws.
    B. Gender-based discrimination occurs far more than racial discrimination.
    C. Companies and their employees do not need to be familiar with discrimination laws.
    D. Reporting discrimination will result in retaliation by the employer.

6. According to the information in the passage, which is the **best** generalization to make about why employees who feel they have been targeted by discrimination should consult an expert?

    A. Experts are better at documenting and reporting events.
    B. Employers may not know they are discriminating, and an expert can provide training.
    C. Discrimination is emotionally damaging, and an expert can help employees better understand their feelings.
    D. Legal issues can be complicated, and an expert in the area may know how to proceed.

DIRECTIONS: Read the passage, read each question, and choose the **best** answer.

MEN, WOMEN, AND CHILD CUSTODY

1   Every few years, some father who believes he's been wronged by the family court system grabs headlines and draws attention to the flawed ways in which we split up families. Custody proceedings are often brutal and adversarial. Otherwise fit parents can be drawn into a bare-knuckle fight over who poses a greater danger to the children. . . .

2   Despite the fact that divorce is rarely triggered by violence or abuse, the incentives to allege that a man is abusive and out of control are undeniable. They tap into age-old stereotypes about men and ensure that Mom becomes the primary custodian. Even without abuse allegations, simple rules of physics (one child cannot be split into two and two cannot be split into four) make it likely that many good fathers will be downgraded from full-time dads to alternating-weekend carpool dads. They will be asked to pay at least a third of their salaries in child support for that privilege. Simple rules of modern life make it likely that an ex-wife will someday decide that a job or new husband demands a move to a faraway state. At which point the alternating-weekend-carpool dad is again demoted, to a Thanksgivings-if-you're-lucky dad.

3   I recognize the allure for some men of the man-pushed-until-he-snaps narrative. My husband rents those movies, too. But . . . there are dozens of nonviolent fathers who believe that the mere fact of their divorce should not result in an arrangement in which they pay for the right to see their kids on alternating Sundays. If the family-court system is ever going to improve, we need to hear their stories, not tales of kidnappings and murder. Much of what's wrong with family law today lies in warmed-over stereotypes of men as fundamentally unsuited to caring for children.

From *Newsweek*'s article RETHINKING FATHERS' RIGHTS by Dahlia Lithwick, © 2008

7. Based on the information in paragraph 1, what generalization does the author make about custody proceedings?

    A. They are generally amicable.
    B. They are generally combative.
    C. They are simple to resolve.
    D. They are extremely complex.

8. What generalization does the author make about which parent gets custody of the children after a divorce?

    A. Fathers almost always get full custody.
    B. Mothers almost always get primary custody.
    C. Mothers and fathers always split custody equally.
    D. Fathers never get custody.

9. According to the excerpt, which stereotype is associated with men after a divorce?

    A. Men are less likely than women to want custody of their children.
    B. Men are more interested in their careers than in their families.
    C. Men rarely fight for legal custody of their children.
    D. Men are assumed to be abusive because they are male.

10. The author mentions the allure of violent movies (paragraph 3). According to the passage, which statement is the **best** generalization to make about men and violent movies?

    A. Violent movies lead custodial fathers to violence.
    B. Fathers who enjoy violent movies should not have custody of their children.
    C. Violent movies probably have little effect on custodial fathers.
    D. Children exposed to violent movies act out frequently.

11. Which is the **most** logical generalization to make on the basis of the information in this passage?

    A. All custody arrangements should equally split the time children spend with both parents.
    B. Men can be good caregivers and are entitled to fair custody arrangements.
    C. Men are now considered better caregivers than women are.
    D. Men and women with children should remain married until the children are adults.

DIRECTIONS: Read the passage and the question. Then use the drag-and-drop options to complete the chart.

WHAT WE LEARN AT SCHOOL

1   By the age of six the average child will have completed the basic American education and be ready to enter school. If the child has been attentive in these preschool years, he or she will already have mastered many skills.

2   From television, the child will have learned how to pick a lock, commit a fairly elaborate bank holdup, prevent wetness all day long, get the laundry twice as white, and kill people with a variety of sophisticated armaments. . . .

3   During formal education, the child learns that life is for testing. This stage lasts twelve years, a period during which the child learns that success comes from telling testers what they want to hear.

4   Early in this stage, the child learns that he is either dumb or smart. If the teacher puts intelligent demands upon the child, the child learns he is smart. If the teacher expects little of the child, the child learns he is dumb and soon quits bothering to tell the testers what they want to hear. . . .

6   At this stage of education, a fresh question arises for everyone. If the point of lower education was to get into college, what is the point of college? The answer is soon learned. The point of college is to prepare the student—no longer a child now—to get into graduate school. In college the student learns that it is no longer enough simply to tell the testers what they want to hear. Many are tested for graduate school; few are admitted.

7   Those excluded may be denied valuable certificates to prosper in medicine, at the bar, in the corporate boardroom. The student learns that the race is to the cunning and often, alas, to the unprincipled.

8   Thus, the student learns the importance of destroying competitors and emerges richly prepared to play his role in the great simmering melodrama of American life.

9   Afterward, the former student's destiny fulfilled, his life rich with Oriental carpets, rare porcelain, and full bank accounts, he may one day find himself with the leisure and the inclination to open a book with a curious mind, and start to become educated.

From *The New York Times's* article SCHOOL VS. EDUCATION by Russell Baker, © 1975

12. Drag and drop each generalization into the correct position on the chart, according to the phase of American education.

Stage of Education	Generalization
Preschool Years	
The Twelve Years of Formal Education	
College	
Graduate School	

Students are labeled by test scores, which determine their formal education.
Students impress teachers to move to the next level of education.
Students must be shrewd and do what it takes to achieve more than their classmates.
This group learns a great deal from exposure to media.

Synthesize Information

READING ASSESSMENT TARGETS: R.2.7, R.2.8, R.3.4, R.3.5, R.4.3/L.4.3, R.6.4, R.9.1/R.7.1, R.

1 Review the Skill

When you **synthesize** information, you combine ideas from one or more sources to form a new idea. Synthesizing allows you to extend ideas by applying them to new situations. You can draw conclusions and make generalizations about the ideas you read. You can also draw conclusions and make generalizations about new ideas related to those you read.

2 Refine the Skill

By refining the skill of synthesizing information, you will improve your study and test-taking abilities, especially as they relate to the GED® Reasoning Through Language Arts test. Read the passages below. Then answer the question that follows.

LINCOLN'S "A HOUSE DIVIDED" SPEECH

"A house divided against itself cannot stand." I believe this government cannot endure, permanently, half slave and half free. I do not expect the Union to be dissolved; I do not expect the house to fall; but I do expect it will cease to be divided. It will become all one thing, or all the other. Either the opponents of slavery will arrest the further spread of it and place it where the public mind shall rest in the belief that it is in the course of ultimate extinction, or its advocates will push it forward till it shall become alike lawful in all the states, old as well as new, North as well as South.

From A HOUSE DIVIDED by Abraham Lincoln, 1858

a Lincoln uses the analogy of a "house divided against itself" to describe the status of the country. The idea is restated in more literal language in the final sentence.

JOHNSON'S GETTYSBURG SPEECH

In this hour, it is not our respective races which are at stake—it is our nation. Let those who care for their country come forward, North and South, white and Negro, to lead the way through this moment of challenge and decision. . . .

Until justice is blind to color, until education is unaware of race, until opportunity is unconcerned with color of men's skins, emancipation will be a proclamation but not a fact. To the extent that the proclamation of emancipation is not fulfilled in fact, to that extent we shall have fallen short of assuring freedom to the free.

From SPEECH AT GETTYSBURG by Lyndon Baines Johnson, 1963

b Johnson made this speech to mark the anniversary of the Emancipation Proclamation, which ended slavery in the United States. His speech is a reflection on the status of civil rights for African Americans 100 years later.

TEST-TAKING TIPS

When answering a test question that asks you to identify information or language that applies to two passages, start by eliminating answer choices that apply to only one of the passages.

1. Which comparison **best** describes the situation in **both** passages?

   A. a person waking up in the morning
   B. a bridge stopping halfway across a river
   C. a person who is blind regaining sight
   D. a telephone call remaining unanswered

DIRECTIONS: Read the passage, read each question, and choose the **best** answer.

H1N1 FLU PANDEMIC

1   On April 15, 2009, it was discovered that a new influenza A virus had infected a 10-year-old boy in California.

2   Two days after CDC confirmed the first case, laboratory testing confirmed a second infection with the same virus in another patient. On April 21, CDC requested that state public health laboratories send to CDC all influenza A positive specimens that could not be subtyped. Within three days, additional specimens from patients with the new virus infection arrived at CDC for testing. CDC's Influenza Division laboratory testing confirmed that these samples also were positive for the virus that would come to be called "2009 H1N1." On April 22, 2009, the CDC activated its Emergency Operations Center.

3   The new virus spread quickly through the spring and summer. Within weeks, new cases were reported across the United States and the world. On June 11, 2009, the World Health Organization (WHO) declared a global influenza pandemic.

4   CDC's response lasted nearly a year. Over those many months, CDC remained at the forefront of the global response—sharing laboratory reagents for diagnostic testing with states and ministries of health; using gene sequencing; estimating U.S. cases, hospitalizations, and deaths from the pandemic every month; and working to implement a domestic vaccination program, increase antiviral drug use, and ensure clear guidance on personal protective equipment.

5   As with previous pandemics, the scientific community, including experts at CDC, took away learned lessons that influence how we prepare and monitor for future pandemics.

6   The Influenza Risk Assessment Tool (IRAT) is one example. The IRAT assesses the potential pandemic risk posed by influenza A viruses currently circulating in animals. The IRAT evaluates animal-origin flu viruses based on their risk of emergence and their potential public health impact. It does not forecast pandemics. Influenza viruses are too unpredictable.

7   CDC scientists also developed a tool to assess the severity of a future pandemic—the Pandemic Severity Assessment Framework (PSAF). Once a novel influenza A virus is identified and is spreading from person-to-person in a sustained manner, public health officials use the PSAF to help determine the impact of the pandemic, make timely and informed decisions, and take appropriate actions.

8   Influenza pandemics are uncommon; only three have occurred since the 1918 pandemic. Yet, influenza pandemics are one of the world's greatest public health threats because of their potential to overwhelm public health and healthcare systems, and cause widespread illness, death, and social disruption.

Adapted from the cdc.gov article 10 YEARS LATER: THE LASTING IMPACT OF THE H1N1 FLU PANDEMIC RESPONSE, 2019

2. Which statement represents the **most** logical conclusion about the importance of confirming the spread of a new virus strand?

   A. Confirming a new virus is spreading speeds up the process of creating a vaccine.
   B. Confirming the spread of a new virus strand lessens the infection rate.
   C. Confirming the spread of a new virus strand prevents healthcare systems from being overwhelmed.
   D. Confirming the spread of a new virus strand is necessary before declaring a global pandemic.

3. Based on paragraph 6, you can conclude that

   A. animal flu viruses can spread to humans.
   B. animal flu viruses are responsible for the last three flu pandemics.
   C. animal flu viruses are more contagious than human flu viruses.
   D. animal flu viruses are more predictable than human flu viruses.

4. Which of the following pandemic responses would cause the **most** social disruption?

   A. People may worry about contracting the virus.
   B. People may be asked to wear masks and wash hands.
   C. National, state, and local governments may use shelter-in-place orders to prevent spread of the virus.
   D. People may be encouraged to get vaccinated.

UNIT 1

DIRECTIONS: Read the passage, read each question, and choose the **best** answer.

WATCH OUT FOR ELECTRIC RICKSHAWS

1   It is possible that when you hear the word *rickshaw* you imagine a person pulling a two-wheeled carriage through crowded streets in India. Modern rickshaws now use pedal power or, for longer trips, diesel engines that provide far greater speed and endurance than their human-powered precursors. Modern rickshaws are ubiquitous in India's major cities.

2   Innovations in electric technology and investments by one of the world's largest multinational corporations may result in a boost to electric rickshaws.

3   Electric rickshaws have been available for several years. They use electric engines and rely on rechargeable batteries. Proponents assert they are better for the environment. Studies estimate that air pollution causes more than 1 million premature deaths in India. However, critics note they have not been as affordable as diesel rickshaws, and that electric vehicles may be impractical in cities with unreliable electrical infrastructure.

4   Manufacturers, such as Altigreen and Saarthi, have announced new models of electric rickshaws. Even though the initial cost may be more than a diesel rickshaw, the daily cost for fuel is much lower. Data suggests that a vehicle that may spend $4.70-$5.40 per day on diesel fuel could be replaced with a rickshaw that spends 90 cents to cover the same distance. This is a substantial difference in a country where rickshaw drivers might earn $8-9 per day.

5   These new vehicles may benefit from a plan by the Indian government what would require that all two- and three-wheeled vehicles be electric by the year 2025.

6   Following the government's announcement, Amazon, one of the world's largest multinational corporations, said it would rollout 10,000 new electric 3- and 4-wheel vehicles for its delivery fleet. The company said this is part of its greater initiative to reduce its carbon emissions.

5. Which statement **best** explains why rickshaw drivers prefer diesel rickshaws?

    A. Electric rickshaws create less air pollution.
    B. Diesel rickshaws are more affordable to buy.
    C. Diesel rickshaws are more affordable to fuel.
    D. Electric rickshaws are ubiquitous in major cities.

6. How would a change in the cost of diesel fuel **most likely** affect the sale of electric rickshaws?

    A. An increase in diesel fuel costs would likely have no effect on the sale of electric rickshaws.
    B. A decrease in diesel fuel costs would likely lead to an increase in electric rickshaw sales.
    C. An increase in diesel fuel costs would likely lead to an increase in electric rickshaw sales.
    D. A decrease in diesel fuel costs would likely have no effect on the sale of electric rickshaws.

7. What will be necessary to implement the Indian government's plan for 2025?

    A. A more reliable electrical infrastructure to fuel to electric rickshaws.
    B. More fuel-efficient diesel engines to reduce the air pollution they create.
    C. More spending on fixing and building roads to accommodate the new rickshaws.
    D. More spending on education programs to remind everyone that diesel rickshaws are illegal.

8. What is the **most likely** relationship between the Indian government's plan regarding electric rickshaws and Amazon's rollout of electric delivery vehicles?

    A. Amazon's decision was probably not affected by the government's plan.
    B. The government's plan was a factor in Amazon's decision to rollout its electric fleet in India.
    C. The government announced its plan because of Amazon's decision.
    D. The government likely discouraged Amazon from rolling out its electric fleet.

DIRECTIONS: Read the passages, read each question, and choose the **best** answer.

THE BRAIN AND THE SENSE OF SMELL

1   Recent studies in rodents have established that the same sectors of the brain that process our senses are also responsible, at least partially, for storing emotional memories. For example, the smell of roast turkey could make a person smile and remember a joyous Thanksgiving dinner from their childhood.

2   Smell has another special feature. In all the other senses (sight, hearing, taste, touch), information travels from the sensory organs (eyes, ears, skin, tongue) towards a brain structure called the thalamus. The thalamus is a kind of portal to our consciousness. If we focus in one sense (for example, on vision while reading), we can block information from other senses, (for example, not listening to those who speak to us while we read). However, olfactory information bypasses the thalamus, so smells are processed more quickly than other sensory information. Because olfactory information is independent of the thalamus, we cannot block the act of smelling.

3   In addition, according to some research, studies show that being in the presence of an odor intensifies the memory each time you smell the same scent. Scents are undoubtedly linked to memories.

SMELL TRIGGERS EMOTIONS

1   Smells can take you back to powerful and emotional memories of the past. The stronger the emotional event, the more closely you will link it and the sensation of odors you were exposed to.

2   In one study of 985 people, approximately 80 percent said odors gave them a longing for things, persons, or situations from their childhood. The smell of freshly baked goods brought about the most memories. However, the smells and their memories varied depending on where participants grew up. For those who grew up on farms, the smell of the animals they raised brought back memories. For older adults, the smell of rain or freshly cut grass sent them reeling back to the past. The smells of favorite candies and jet fuel evoked pleasant memories in young people.

9. According to the information provided in both passages, which generalization is **most** accurate?

    A. Smells create less of an emotional response as people age.
    B. Repeated exposure to scents can be used to desensitize a person from an emotional response.
    C. The emotions associated with a smell tend to change as a person associates the smell with new experiences.
    D. A smell can create a powerful response before a person even places what the smell is.

10. According to both passages, which experience is **most likely** to trigger the quickest emotional response?

    A. a photo of a person's first love
    B. the smell of the cologne worn by a person's first love
    C. a fragrant flower that a person smells for the first time
    D. the first notes of a person's favorite song

11. According to the information in both passages, which type of positive memory would **most likely** be triggered by the smell of chlorine?

    A. the memory of looking at a photograph of a beautiful swimming pool in a magazine
    B. the memory of hearing a friend's story about an exciting trip to the water park
    C. the memory of enjoying childhood summer days at the local swimming pool
    D. the memory of the smell of bleach used as a disinfectant to disguise hospital odors

12. The **most likely** explanation for the smell of jet fuel triggering an instantaneous memory is that

    A. the smell of jet fuel is stronger than the smell of other fuels.
    B. smells are not processed by the thalamus and are thus experienced very quickly.
    C. families traveling by air may experience long airport delays.
    D. the brain processes smells more accurately than other sensory perceptions.

Use Context Clues

Use with **Student Book** pp. 34–35

READING ASSESSMENT TARGETS: R.4.1/L.4.1, R.4.2/L.4.2, R.4.3/L.4

1 **Review the Skill**

Readers can use **context clues** to make informed guesses about the meanings of unfamiliar words by examining the surrounding details in a sentence or paragraph. Other words, phrases, or explanations may help readers understand the unfamiliar word or expression.

Writers often use words that have **connotations**. These words have meanings that go beyond their definitions. Connotations may be positive or negative. For example, a person who tells others what to do may be described as "bossy" (negative) or as "showing leadership" (positive).

2 **Refine the Skill**

By refining the skill of using context clues, you will improve your study and test-taking abilities, especially as they relate to the GED® Reasoning Through Language Arts test. Read the passage below. Then answer the questions that follow.

AN OASIS IN LONDON

It lies not far from the Temple-Bar.

Going to it, by the usual way, is like stealing from a heated plain into some cool, deep glen, shady among harboring hills.

Sick with the din and soiled with the mud of Fleet Street—where the Benedick tradesmen are hurrying by, with ledger-lines ruled along their brows, thinking upon rise of bread and fall of babies—you adroitly turn a mystic corner—not a street—and glide down a dim, monastic way, flanked by dark, sedate, and solemn piles, and still wending on, give the whole care-worn world the slip, and disentangling, stand beneath the quiet cloisters of the Paradise of Bachelors.

Sweet are the oases in Sahara; charming the isle-groves of August prairies . . . but sweeter, still more charming, most delectable the dreamy Paradise of Bachelors, found in the heart of stunning London.

From THE PARADISE OF BACHELORS by Herman Melville

a The word *glen* might be unfamiliar, but the context indicates that it is a kind of valley.

b You might not know the word *wending*, but the context describes a way of walking.

1. The author contrasts a noisy place with a quiet place. Which word **best** indicates the presence of noise?

   A. din
   B. muddy
   C. sedate
   D. cloisters

2. Which places could **best** be described as oases?

   A. busy streets in English cities
   B. dusty fields in dry climates
   C. shaded gardens in crowded cities
   D. low ground beneath high hills

CLOSER LOOK AT ITEMS

Read test questions for clues. Question 1 gives a clue about noise. Notice in the passage that *din* is used to describe a noisy street. The other choices do not refer to noise.

UNIT 1

DIRECTIONS: Read the passage, read each question, and choose the **best** answer.

AN AFTERNOON SCARE

1   One day my teacher and I were returning from a long ramble. The morning had been fine, but it was growing warm and sultry when at last we turned our faces homeward. Two or three times we stopped to rest under a tree by the wayside. Our last halt was under a wild cherry tree a short distance from the house. The shade was grateful, and the tree was so easy to climb that with my teacher's assistance I was able to scramble to a seat in the branches. It was so cool up in the tree that Miss Sullivan proposed that we have our luncheon there. I promised to keep still while she went to the house to fetch it.

2   Suddenly a change passed over the tree. All the sun's warmth left the air. I knew the sky was black, because all the heat, which meant light to me, had died out of the atmosphere. A strange odour came up from the earth. I knew it, it was the odour that always precedes a thunderstorm, and a nameless fear clutched at my heart. I felt absolutely alone, cut off from my friends and the firm earth. The immense, the unknown, enfolded me. I remained still and expectant; a chilling terror crept over me. I longed for my teacher's return; but above all things I wanted to get down from that tree.

3   There was a moment of sinister silence, then a multitudinous stirring of the leaves. A shiver ran through the tree, and the wind sent forth a blast that would have knocked me off had I not clung to the branch with might and main. The tree swayed and strained. The small twigs snapped and fell about me in showers. A wild impulse to jump seized me, but terror held me fast. I crouched down in the fork of the tree. The branches lashed about me. I felt the intermittent jarring that came now and then, as if something heavy had fallen and the shock had traveled up till it reached the limb I sat on. It worked my suspense up to the highest point, and just as I was thinking the tree and I should fall together, my teacher seized my hand and helped me down. I clung to her, trembling with joy to feel the earth under my feet once more. I had learned a new lesson—that nature "wages open war against her children, and under softest touch hides treacherous claws."

From THE STORY OF MY LIFE by Helen Keller

3. In paragraph 1, the narrator says that they were "returning from a long ramble." What does the word **ramble** mean in this sentence?

    A. a vacation in a faraway place
    B. a long-winded argument
    C. an aimless story
    D. a leisurely walk

4. In paragraph 1, the author describes the weather as "warm and sultry." What does the use of the word **sultry** suggest about the weather?

    A. It is stormy and frightening.
    B. It is humid and unpleasant.
    C. It is breezy and pleasant.
    D. It is bright and invigorating.

5. In the first sentence of paragraph 3, the narrator describes the silence as "sinister." How would the meaning of the sentence change if the author had used the word **worrisome** instead of **sinister**?

    A. It would lessen the threatening tone of the sentence.
    B. It would increase the threatening tone of the sentence.
    C. It would change the threatening tone to a humorous tone.
    D. It would change the humorous tone to a threatening tone.

6. In paragraph 3, the narrator says "A shiver ran through the tree." In this context, what does the word **shiver** reinforce about the narrator's feelings?

    A. that the narrator is lonely
    B. that the narrator is excited
    C. that the narrator is cold
    D. that the narrator is afraid

③ *Master the Skill*

DIRECTIONS: Read the passage, read each question, and choose the **best** answer.

IN THE GARDEN

1   While Giovanni stood at the window, he heard a rustling behind a screen of leaves, and became aware that a person was at work in the garden. His figure soon emerged into view, and showed itself to be that of no common laborer, but a tall, emaciated, sallow, and sickly looking man, dressed in a scholar's garb of black. He was beyond the middle term of life, with gray hair, a thin gray beard, and a face singularly marked with intellect and cultivation, but which could never, even in his more youthful days, have expressed much warmth of heart. . . .

2   The distrustful gardener, while plucking away the dead leaves or pruning the too luxuriant growth of the shrubs, defended his hands with a pair of thick gloves. Nor were these his only armor. When, in his walk through the garden, he came to the magnificent plant that hung its purple gems beside the marble fountain, he placed a kind of mask over his mouth and nostrils, as if all this beauty did but conceal a deadlier malice; but, finding his task still too dangerous, he drew back, removed the mask, and called loudly, but in the infirm voice of a person affected with inward disease, "Beatrice! Beatrice!"

3   Soon there emerged from under a sculptured portal the figure of a young girl, arrayed with as much richness of taste as the most splendid of the flowers, beautiful as the day, and with a bloom so deep and vivid that one shade more would have been too much. She looked redundant with life, health, and energy. . . . Yet Giovanni's fancy must have grown morbid, while he looked down into the garden; for the impression which the fair stranger made upon him was as if here were another flower, the human sister of those vegetable ones, as beautiful as they—more beautiful than the richest of them—but still to be touched only with a glove, nor to be approached without a mask. As Beatrice came down the garden-path, it was observable that she handled and inhaled the odor of several of the plants which her father had most sedulously avoided. . . .

From RAPPACCINI'S DAUGHTER by Nathaniel Hawthorne

7. The narrator uses the word **emaciated** to describe the gardener. If the narrator had used **slender** instead of **emaciated** in the description, how would the meaning change?

    A. The gardener would have appeared to be fit and well-groomed.
    B. The gardener would have appeared to be healthy and full of energy.
    C. The gardener would have appeared to be suffering from a recent or mild illness.
    D. The gardener would have appeared to be in the final stages of his illness and near death.

8. In the context of the excerpt, what does the expression **beyond the middle term of life** mean?

    A. He looked younger than his actual age.
    B. He looked older than his actual age.
    C. He was younger than middle age.
    D. He was older than middle age.

9. Based on the context, what does the phrase **redundant with life** mean?

    A. bored with life
    B. full of life
    C. afraid of life
    D. amused by life

10. As Giovanni watches the girl, the narrator says that his "fancy must have grown morbid." According to the context of the passage, what does the expression imply?

    A. His imagination makes the scene seem disturbing, and he feels as though he should avoid the girl.
    B. His imagination makes the scene seem joyful, and he feels as though he should join the girl in the garden.
    C. His imagination makes the scene seem deadly, and the girl seems threatening.
    D. His imagination makes the scene seem eerie, and the girl seems ghostly.

DIRECTIONS: Read the passage, read each question, and choose the **best** answer.

THE NARRATOR DESCRIBES ZELIG

1   Old Zelig was eyed askance by his brethren. No one deigned to call him "Reb" Zelig, nor to prefix to his name the American equivalent— "Mr." "The old one is a barrel with a stave missing," knowingly declared his neighbors. "He never spends a cent; and he belongs nowheres." For "to belong," on New York's East Side, is of no slight importance. . . .

2   In the cloakshop where Zelig worked he stood daily, brandishing his heavy iron on the sizzling cloth, hardly ever glancing about him. The workmen despised him, for during a strike he returned to work after two days' absence. He could not be idle, and thought with dread of the Saturday that would bring him no pay envelope.

3   His very appearance seemed alien to his brethren. His figure was tall, and of cast-iron mold. When he stared stupidly at something, he looked like a blind Samson. His gray hair was long, and it fell in disheveled curls on gigantic shoulders somewhat inclined to stoop. His shabby clothes hung loosely on him; and, both summer and winter, the same old cap covered his massive head. . . .

4   In the shop where he found a job at last, the workmen feared him at first; but, ultimately finding him a harmless giant, they more than once hurled their sarcasms at his head. . . .

5   But Zelig paid little heed to what was said about him. He dedicated his existence to the saving of his earnings, and only feared that he might be compelled to spend some of them. More than once his wife would be appalled in the dark of night by the silhouette of old Zelig in nightdress, sitting up in bed and counting a bundle of bank notes which he always replaced under his pillow. She frequently upbraided him for his miserly nature, for his warding off all requests outside the pittance for household expense. She pleaded, exhorted, wailed. He invariably answered: "I haven't a cent by my soul." She pointed to the bare walls, the broken furniture, their beggarly attire.

From ZELIG by Benjamin Rosenblatt

11. The narrator says that neighbors never call the main character "Reb" Zelig. Not using this title indicates their feelings toward him. The term **Reb**

    A. is the equivalent of *brother*.
    B. is the equivalent of *Mister*.
    C. is a title for a blacksmith.
    D. is a title for a tailor.

12. Zelig's neighbors describe him as "a barrel with a stave missing." What idiomatic expression is close in meaning to this phrase?

    A. not a mean bone in his body
    B. sharp as a tack
    C. not all there
    D. larger than life

13. Zelig's appearance is described as seeming "alien" to other people. In this context, what does **alien** mean?

    A. different or strange
    B. foreign or interesting
    C. from another planet
    D. scary or menacing

14. Zelig is described as "of cast-iron mold." In this context, what does this description imply about Zelig?

    A. He is quick to lose his temper.
    B. He is stubborn and unyielding.
    C. He is loud and opinionated.
    D. He is strong and sturdy.

15. The state of Zelig's hair and clothing is described as "disheveled." Which of the following words is a synonym for **disheveled**?

    A. large
    B. messy
    C. neat
    D. clumsy

High Impact Lesson: Connotative Meanings

1 Review the Skill

All words have denotations and connotations. **Denotation** is the word's definition or basic meaning. **Connotation** is the idea or feeling associated with a word and adds a layer of meaning beyond its denotation. A word's connotative meaning is different than its denotative, or literal meaning. Authors use **connotative meanings** to create associations that are positive, negative, or neutral. Understanding connotative meaning can help readers understand an author's purpose or intention.

The denotative meanings of words and phrases can often be determined using **context clues** from the sentence or passage. Context clues can include synonyms, antonyms, explanations, or examples. These clues may appear in the same sentence as the word you are trying to understand, or they may appear elsewhere in the text. Although determining a word's connotation can be more difficult because connotation often depends on cultural context, context clues can also be used to determine a word's connotative meaning.

On the GED® Reasoning Through Language Arts test, you will be expected to show you understand connotative meanings. You may encounter questions that ask you to identify what a word means specifically in the context of a sentence, distinguish between a word's denotative, or literal, meaning and its connotative meaning, and explain how the context of the sentence affects a word's meaning.

2 Refine the Skill

a Notice the first sentence describes two contrasting ideas: "a series of strategically significant victories" and "a staggering initial reversal." Understanding the connotations of these descriptions helps readers understand the passage.

Scan the first sentence for the word *staggering*. Re-read the sentence, substituting the different answer choices. The correct answer is **A**.

WAR PLANS

Behind the decision to go into Leyte lay a series of strategically significant victories, which had followed a staggering initial reverse. American prewar plans for the Pacific had originally been based on the assumption that only the United States and Japan would be at war and that the U.S. Pacific Fleet would be in existence. But the destruction of the fleet at Pearl Harbor and the entrance of Germany and Italy into the war nullified these plans. The strategy of the Joint Chiefs of Staff in early 1942, therefore, was concerned chiefly with trying to limit the rapid advance of the Japanese and with keeping the line of communications to Australia open. The Pacific Theater was divided into command areas—the Southwest Pacific Area, with General Douglas MacArthur as Supreme Commander (he referred to himself, however, as Commander in Chief), and the Pacific Ocean Area (which included the Central Pacific), with Admiral Chester W. Nimitz as Commander in Chief.

From LEYTE: THE RETURN TO THE PHILIPPINES by M. Hamlin Cannon

1. Which definition **best** matches the use of the word **staggering** in the first sentence?

   A. extremely overwhelming
   B. reeling from side to side
   C. causing doubt or hesitation
   D. alternating in a pattern

DIRECTIONS: Read the passage, read each question, and choose the **best** answer.

SEEKING ANSWERS

1   The first thing about his American teachers that struck David Rudinsky was the fact that they were women, and the second was that they did not get angry if somebody asked questions. This phenomenon subverted his previous experience. When he went to heder (Hebrew school), in Russia, his teachers were always men, and they did not like to be interrupted with questions that were not in the lesson. Everything was different in America, and David liked the difference.

2   The American teachers, on their part, also made comparisons. They said David was not like other children. It was not merely that his mind worked like lightning; those neglected Russian waifs were almost always quick to learn, perhaps because they had to make up for lost time. The quality of his interest, more than the rapidity of his progress, excited comment. Miss Ralston, David's teacher in the sixth grade, which he reached in his second year at school, said of him that he never let go of a lesson till he had got the soul of the matter. 'I don't think grammar is grammar to him,' she said, 'or fractions mere arithmetic. I'm not satisfied with the way I teach these things since I've had David. I feel that if he were on the platform instead of me, geography and grammar would be spliced to the core of the universe.'

3   One difficulty David's teachers encountered, and that was his extreme reserve. In private conversation it was hard to get anything out of him except 'yes, ma'am' and 'no, ma'am,' or, 'I don't understand, please.' In the classroom he did not seem to be aware of the existence of anybody besides Teacher and himself. He asked questions as fast as he could formulate them, and Teacher had to exercise much tact in order to satisfy him without slighting the rest of her pupils. To advances of a personal sort he did not respond, as if friendship were not among the things he hungered for.

From THE LIE by Mary Antin

2. Which definition **best** matches the use of the word **struck** in paragraph 1?

    A. closed
    B. occurred to
    C. punched
    D. deleted

3. In paragraph 1, the author uses the word **phenomenon**. How would the meaning of the sentence change if the author had used the word **fact** instead?

    A. It would suggest that David did not see the point in asking questions.
    B. It would suggest that David did not believe the teachers were sincere.
    C. It would suggest that David was amazed by the difference.
    D. It would suggest that David noticed the difference but did not find it significant.

4. In paragraph 2, the author states David's mind "worked like lightning." The connotations of the phrase **worked like lightning** instead of the neutral description **smart** suggests the author

    A. is emphasizing David's ability to learn quickly.
    B. is suggesting David has supernatural powers.
    C. is implying that David's intelligence frightens his teachers.
    D. is suggesting David's behavior is temperamental.

5. Which of the following **best** matches the connotation of the word **spliced** in paragraph 2?

    A. combined permanently
    B. explained in a confusing way
    C. united for better understanding
    D. divided between science and art

6. Which of the following **most nearly** matches the meaning of the word **formulate** in paragraph 3?

    A. to put into words without care and thought
    B. to put into words with care or thought
    C. to express ideas in an insulting way
    D. to express ideas in a meek way

14 LESSON

Identify Cause and Effect in Fiction

READING ASSESSMENT TARGETS: R.2.1, R.2.5, R.2.7, R.2.8, R.3.2, R.3.3, R.3.4, R.3 R.4.3/L.4.3, R.5.1, R.5.3

1 Review the Skill

The actions, thoughts, and conversations of people in stories have consequences that affect, or influence, events as the story progresses. These actions, thoughts, and conversations are **causes** that lead to other actions or situations, called **effects**. One cause can create more than one effect, and one effect may have more than one cause. These causes and effects shape the developments of a story.

2 Refine the Skill

By refining the skill of identifying cause and effect in fiction, you will improve your study and test-taking abilities, especially as they relate to the GED® Reasoning Through Language Arts test. Read the passage below. Then answer the questions that follow.

THE NARRATOR FEELS UNWELL

a The description of John has a clear cause-and-effect structure, with a cause given first and a series of effects following.

b The narrator gives "one reason" for not getting well faster. The word *reason* signals a cause. In this case, the reason, surprisingly, is that her husband is a physician.

John laughs at me, of course, but one expects that in marriage.

John is practical in the extreme. He has no patience with faith, an intense horror of superstition, and he scoffs openly at any talk of things not to be felt and seen and put down in figures.

John is a physician, and perhaps—(I would not say it to a living soul, of course, but this is dead paper and a great relief to my mind)—perhaps that is one reason I do not get well faster.

You see he does not believe I am sick!

And what can one do?

If a physician of high standing, and one's own husband, assures friends and relatives that there is really nothing the matter with one but temporary nervous depression—a slight hysterical tendency—what is one to do?

My brother is also a physician, and also of high standing, and he says the same thing.

From THE YELLOW WALLPAPER by Charlotte Perkins Gilman

1. What causes John to want things to be "put down in figures"?

    A. John has no patience with faith.
    B. John has a horror of superstition.
    C. John is practical in the extreme.
    D. John is a physician.

2. Why does the narrator feel powerless?

    A. She knows that nothing is wrong with her.
    B. Her husband and brother do not believe she is sick.
    C. She has a temporary nervous depression.
    D. She is not getting well despite her husband's treatment.

TEST-TAKING TIPS

When looking for cause-and-effect relationships, complete this statement: "Because of _[cause]_, _[effect]_ happened." One event leads to the next. Look for connections, other than simply time sequence.

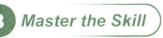

★ Spotlighted Item: **DRAG-AND-DROP**

DIRECTIONS: Read the passage and the question. Then use the drag-and-drop options to complete the chart.

AN INVITATION TO A BALL

1   Mathilde Loisel was one of those pretty and charming young creatures who sometimes are born, as if by a slip of fate, into a family of clerks. She had no dowry, no expectations of being married by any rich and distinguished man, so she married a clerk of the Ministry of Public Instruction.

2   Mathilde suffered ceaselessly, feeling herself born to enjoy all delicacies and all luxuries. She was distressed at the poverty of her dwelling, at the bareness of the walls, at the shabby chairs, the ugliness of the curtains. All those things, of which another woman of her rank would never even have been conscious, tortured her and made her angry. She had no gowns, no jewels, nothing. And she loved nothing but that. She felt made for that. She would have liked so much to be envied and sought after. She had a wealthy friend named Jeanne Forestier whom she did not like to visit anymore because she felt so sad when she came home.

3   One evening her husband came home with a triumphant air and holding a large envelope in his hand. "There is something for you," he said. *The Minister of Public Instruction and Mrs. George Ramponneau request the honor of Mr. and Mrs. Loisel's company at the Ministry ball on Monday evening, January 18th.*

4   Instead of being delighted, as her husband had hoped, his wife threw the invitation on the table crossly. Wiping her wet cheeks, she said, "I have no gown and therefore can't go to this ball." Her husband, who had saved some money for his own purpose, assured her she could purchase a pretty gown with that money.

5   The day of the ball drew near and Madame Loisel seemed sad and anxious even though her dress was ready. Her husband asked, "What is the matter?"

6   And she answered, "It annoys me not to have a single piece of jewelry. I shall look poverty-stricken."

7   "Look up your friend Jeanne," her husband said. "Ask her to lend you some jewelry."

8   The next day she went to her friend and told her of her distress. Jeanne took out a large jewel box and told Mathilde to choose. Mathilde chose a superb diamond necklace.

Adapted from THE DIAMOND NECKLACE by Guy de Maupassant

3.   Drag and drop the **most likely** cause or effect into the correct location in the chart.

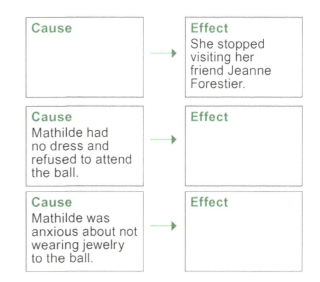

| Mathilde had no dowry. |
| Mathilde was unhappy with her lack of wealth. |
| Mathilde's husband brought home an invitation to a ball. |
| Mathilde's husband gave her money to buy a dress. |
| Mathilde borrowed a necklace from Jeanne Forestier. |

DIRECTIONS: Read the passage, read each question, and choose the **best** answer.

THE GUEST WANTS INFORMATION

1 "Sylvy, Sylvy!" called the busy old grandmother again and again, but nobody answered, and the small husk bed was empty and Sylvia had disappeared.

2 The guest waked from a dream, and remembering his day's pleasure hurried to dress himself that it might sooner begin. He was sure from the way the shy little girl looked once or twice yesterday that she had at least seen the white heron, and now she must really be made to tell. Here she comes now, paler than ever, and her worn old frock is torn and tattered, and smeared with pine pitch. The grandmother and the sportsman stand in the door together and question her, and the splendid moment has come to speak of the dead hemlock-tree by the green marsh.

3 But Sylvia does not speak after all, though the old grandmother fretfully rebukes her, and the young man's kind, appealing eyes are looking straight in her own. He can make them rich with money; he has promised it, and they are poor now. He is so well worth making happy, and he waits to hear the story she can tell.

4 No, she must keep silence! What is it that suddenly forbids her and makes her dumb? Has she been nine years growing and now, when the great world for the first time puts out a hand to her, must she thrust it aside for a bird's sake? Sylvia cannot speak; she cannot tell the heron's secret and give its life away. The murmur of the pine's green branches is in her ears, she remembers how the white heron came flying through the golden air and how they watched the sea and the morning together, and Sylvia cannot speak; she cannot tell the heron's secret and give its life away.

From A WHITE HERON by Sarah Orne Jewett

4. Because Sylvia does not tell her grandmother and the guest what they want to know,

   A. the guest pays the grandmother for his lodging and leaves.
   B. Sylvia's grandmother encourages Sylvia to be more outgoing.
   C. Sylvia's grandmother scolds her for not sharing the location of the heron.
   D. the guest attempts to hunt the heron on his own.

5. What leads the guest to think Sylvia has seen the white heron?

   A. Sylvia's inability to speak
   B. Sylvia's torn dress
   C. the grandmother's confession
   D. the way Sylvia looks

6. Why does the grandmother want Sylvia to tell the guest about the white heron?

   A. Sylvia likes to entertain guests with stories.
   B. The guest has offered them money.
   C. The grandmother wants to find out about the white heron.
   D. Sylvia knows a great deal about local birds.

7. Why does the author describe Sylvia's memories of the heron in paragraph 4?

   A. Sylvia is trying to think of where the heron might have gone so she can help her grandmother.
   B. Sylvia has warm memories of her time with the heron and wants it to remain free.
   C. Sylvia wants to send the sportsman to the wrong place.
   D. Sylvia believes the sportsman knows of these places and will likely check there next.

8. Why does Sylvia keep silent?

   A. She is unsure of the heron's location.
   B. She has trouble speaking to strangers.
   C. She wants her grandmother to ask for more money.
   D. She fears the guest will harm the heron.

9. What **most likely** happens because Sylvia keeps her secret?

   A. Sylvia's grandmother becomes rich.
   B. The guest finds the white heron.
   C. The white heron escapes capture.
   D. Sylvia's grandmother praises her.

DIRECTIONS: Read the passage, read each question, and choose the **best** answer.

A FLIGHT FROM MIAMI

1   A woman who had traveled a great deal in planes, and had never trusted them because she understood nothing about them, sat in the double front seat behind the magazine rack. This was the best seat, as she knew, because there was enough room to stretch your legs. Also you could see well from here, if you wanted to see. Now, for a moment she looked out the window and saw that the few palm trees at the far edge of the field were blowing out in heavy plumes against the sky. There was something so wrong about Miami that even a beautiful night, sharp with stars, only seemed a real-estate advertisement. The woman pulled off her earrings and put them carelessly in her coat pocket. She ran her hands through her very short dark upcurling hair, deliberately making herself untidy for the night ahead. She hunched her shoulders to ease the tired stiffness in her neck and slouched down in the chair. She had just leaned her head against the chair back and was thinking of nothing when the man's voice said, Is this place taken? No, she said without looking at him. She moved nearer to the window. Anyhow, she said to herself, only eight or ten hours or whatever it is to New York; even if he snores, he can't snore all the time.

From MIAMI-NEW YORK by Martha Gellhorn, © 1948

10. Because the woman is an experienced traveler, she knows

    A. to arrive at the airport on time.
    B which seat is most comfortable.
    C. not to be bothered by delays.
    D. how long the trip will take.

11. Why does the narrator describe Miami as "so wrong"?

    A. Miami is not as beautiful as other cities.
    B. The woman in the story dislikes Miami.
    C. Miami is in a dangerous tropical location, prone to hurricanes.
    D. Miami looks more like a real-estate advertisement than a city.

12. The woman speaks to the man and then moves nearer the window. The **most likely** reason for her change of position is to

    A. hear the man's conversation.
    B. be rude to the man.
    C. make room for the man.
    D. see better from the window.

13. Later in the story, the man tries to talk to the woman after the plane lifts off. On the basis of the woman's behavior in this passage, what is the **most likely** effect the man's attempts at conversation will have on the woman?

    A. She will try to ignore the man.
    B. She will have a long conversation with him.
    C. She will begin to snore.
    D. She immediately will ask to change her seat.

14. Travelers might behave as the woman in the story does because they

    A. want to meet other travelers.
    B. want to be left alone.
    C. enjoy looking at scenery.
    D. do not enjoy traveling.

15. What conclusion can be drawn about the woman in the story based on the behaviors described by the author?

    A. Because of her experience flying, she had a plan for how she wanted to experience the flight. The man taking the seat next to her was not part of that plan, but she would adjust.
    B. She had set her plan for the flight, told the flight attendants she wanted to be left alone, and her body language discouraged anyone from taking the seat next to her until the man insisted on taking the open seat.
    C. She was looking forward to a quiet flight to New York, but welcomed the company, as travel could be lonely.
    D. She had spread her belongings out on the seat to discourage others from taking it, pretending to be asleep to avoid having to share space with other travelers.

Compare and Contrast in Fiction

READING ASSESSMENT TARGETS: R.2.1, R.2.2, R.2.5, R.2.6, R.2.7, R.2.8, R.3. R.3.3, R.3.4, R.3.5, R.4.3/L.4.3, R.5.1, R.5.3, R.6.1

1 Review the Skill

Comparing is showing how two or more elements are similar. **Contrasting** is showing how these elements are different. In stories, authors may compare and contrast characters, settings, or points of view. The author compares or contrasts to help readers understand more about a particular part of the story.

2 Refine the Skill

By refining the skill of comparing and contrasting in fiction, you will improve your study and test-taking abilities, especially as they relate to the GED® Reasoning Through Language Arts test. Read the passage below. Then answer the questions that follow.

MARGARET, JO, BETH, AND AMY

a The narrator uses adjectives and images to describe the appearance of the sisters.

b Taking into account the detailed description of the appearance of each of the sisters, you will be able to find similarities and differences between them.

Margaret, the eldest of the four, was sixteen, and very pretty, being plump and fair, with large eyes, plenty of soft brown hair, a sweet mouth and white hands, of which she was rather vain. Fifteen-year-old Jo was very tall, thin, and brown, and reminded one of a colt, for she never seemed to know what to do with her long limbs, which were very much in her way. She had a decided mouth, a comical nose, and sharp, gray eyes, which appeared to see everything, and were by turns fierce, funny, or thoughtful. Her long, thick hair was her one beauty, but it was usually bundled into a net, to be out of her way. Round shoulders had Jo, big hands and feet, a flyaway look to her clothes, and the uncomfortable appearance of a girl who was rapidly shooting up into a woman and didn't like it. Elizabeth, or Beth, as everyone called her, was a rosy, smooth-haired, bright-eyed girl of thirteen, with a shy manner, a timid voice, and a peaceful expression which was seldom disturbed. . . . Amy, though the youngest, was a most important person, in her own opinion at least. A regular snow maiden, with blue eyes, and yellow hair curling on her shoulders, pale and slender, and always carrying herself like a young lady mindful of her manners.

From LITTLE WOMEN by Louisa May Alcott

MAKE ASSUMPTIONS

Authors compare and contrast to differentiate characters. When a story has several main characters, pay attention to descriptions that show how the characters are similar and different. Assume that emphasized similarities or difference are significant.

1. By comparing Jo to a colt, the narrator highlights that

   A. Jo has long hair and is very graceful.
   B. Jo has long arms and legs and is not very graceful.
   C. Jo has large eyes that seem to notice everything.
   D. Jo is very tall and has beautiful hair.

2. How does Margaret's description contrast with Jo's description?

   A. Margaret and Jo are both beautiful, but Jo is more vain.
   B. Margaret is pretty and a bit vain, and Jo is not as pretty and a bit awkward.
   C. Margaret is sixteen and sweet, while Jo is fifteen and shy.
   D. Margaret is fair with brown eyes, while Jo is pale with blue eyes.

DIRECTIONS: Read the passage, read each question, and choose the **best** answer.

THE KELVEY GIRLS ARE SHUNNED

1   Playtime came and Isabel was surrounded. The girls of her class nearly fought to put their arms round her, to walk away with her, to beam flatteringly, to be her special friend. She held quite a court under the huge pine trees at the side of the playground. Nudging, giggling together, the little girls pressed up close. And the only two who stayed outside the ring were the two who were always outside, the little Kelveys. They knew better than to come anywhere near the Burnells.

2   For the fact was, the school the Burnell children went to was not at all the kind of place their parents would have chosen if there had been any choice. But there was none. It was the only school for miles. And the consequence was all the children in the neighborhood, the judge's little girls, the doctor's daughters, the store-keeper's children, the milkman's, were forced to mix together. . . . But the line had to be drawn somewhere. It was drawn at the Kelveys. Many of the children, including the Burnells, were not allowed even to speak to them. They walked past the Kelveys with their heads in the air, and as they set the fashion in all matters of behaviour, the Kelveys were shunned by everybody. Even the teacher had a special voice for them, and a special smile for the other children when Lil Kelvey came up to her desk with a bunch of dreadfully common-looking flowers.

3   They were the daughters of a spry, hardworking little washerwoman, who went about from house to house by the day. This was awful enough. But where was Mr. Kelvey? Nobody knew for certain. But everybody said he was in prison. So they were the daughters of a washerwoman and a jailbird. Very nice company for other people's children! And they looked it. Why Mrs. Kelvey made them so conspicuous was hard to understand. The truth was they were dressed in "bits" given to her by the people for whom she worked.

From THE DOLL'S HOUSE by Katherine Mansfield

3. What do the Kelveys and the Burnells have in common?

   A. They attend the same school.
   B. They play with the same girls.
   C. They both like wildflowers.
   D. They are both shunned by others.

4. In paragraph 1, the narrator contrasts the children who are inside Isabel's ring with those who are outside it in order to

   A. show the difference in status.
   B. indicate a difference in ages.
   C. emphasize a difference in size.
   D. reveal that not all children like Isabel.

5. The narrator says that the school is not at all the kind of place that the Burnell parents "would have chosen." How would a school of their choosing differ from the school in the passage?

   A. It would provide a better education.
   B. It would be closer to their home.
   C. It would not accept poor children.
   D. It would abolish social class distinction.

6. What does the narrator imply about the children who do not speak to the Kelveys?

   A. Their families are more concerned with fashion than the Kelveys are.
   B. Their families are better off than the Kelveys are.
   C. The Kelveys have more social status than those families do.
   D. The Kelveys are more educated than those families are.

7. In paragraph 2, the narrator states "Even the teacher had a special voice" for the Kelvey children. What does the signal word **even** reveal about the teacher's attitude toward the children?

   A. She is always equally fair to all children.
   B. She feels sorry for the Kelvey girls.
   C. She, unlike others, is kind to the Kelvey children.
   D. She, like others, would shun the Kelvey girls.

DIRECTIONS: Read the passage, read each question, and choose the **best** answer.

TWO FRIENDS ATTEND A BALL

1   Mr. Bingley was good-looking and gentlemanlike; he had a pleasant countenance, and easy, unaffected manners. His sisters were fine women, with an air of decided fashion. His brother-in-law, Mr. Hurst, merely looked the gentleman; but his friend Mr. Darcy soon drew the attention of the room by his fine, tall person, handsome features, noble mien, and the report which was in general circulation within five minutes after his entrance, of his having ten thousand a year. The gentlemen pronounced him to be a fine figure of a man, the ladies declared he was much handsomer than Mr. Bingley, and he was looked at with great admiration for about half the evening, till his manners gave a disgust which turned the tide of his popularity; for he was discovered to be proud; to be above his company, and above being pleased; and not all his large estate in Derbyshire could then save him from having a most forbidding, disagreeable countenance, and being unworthy to be compared with his friend.

2   Mr. Bingley had soon made himself acquainted with all the principal people in the room; he was lively and unreserved, danced every dance, was angry that the ball closed so early, and talked of giving one himself at Netherfield. Such amiable qualities must speak for themselves. What a contrast between him and his friend! Mr. Darcy danced only once with Mrs. Hurst and once with Miss Bingley, declined being introduced to any other lady, and spent the rest of the evening in walking about the room, speaking occasionally to one of his own party. His character was decided. He was the proudest, most disagreeable man in the world, and everybody hoped that he would never come there again. Amongst the most violent against him was Mrs. Bennet, whose dislike of his general behavior was sharpened into particular resentment by his having slighted one of her daughters.

3   Elizabeth Bennet had been obliged, by the scarcity of gentlemen, to sit down for two dances; and during part of that time, Mr. Darcy had been standing near enough for her to hear a conversation between him and Mr. Bingley, who came from the dance for a few minutes, to press his friend to join it.

4   "Come, Darcy," said he, "I must have you dance. I hate to see you standing about by yourself in this stupid manner. . . ."

5   "I certainly shall not. You know how I detest it, unless I am particularly acquainted with my partner . . . and there is not another woman in the room whom it would not be a punishment to me to stand up with."

6   "I would not be so fastidious as you are," cried Mr. Bingley, "for a kingdom! Upon my honor, I never met with so many pleasant girls in my life as I have this evening; and there are several of them you see uncommonly pretty. . . ."

7   "Which do you mean?" and turning round he looked for a moment at Elizabeth, till catching her eye, he withdrew his own and coldly said: "She is tolerable, but not handsome enough to tempt me; I am in no humor at present to give consequence to young ladies who are slighted by other men. You had better return to your partner and enjoy her smiles, for you are wasting your time with me."

From PRIDE AND PREJUDICE by Jane Austen

8.   Which statement **best** describes Mr. Bingley and Mr. Darcy?

   A. Mr. Bingley is intense and standoffish, and Mr. Darcy is lively and friendly.
   B. Mr. Bingley enjoys meeting new people, and Mr. Darcy is shy and reserved.
   C. Mr. Bingley and Mr. Darcy are both handsome, but Mr. Bingley is more friendly and good-natured than Mr. Darcy.
   D. Mr. Bingley and Mr. Darcy are both admired gentlemen, but Mr. Darcy is more popular because he is rich.

9.   How does the conversation Elizabeth overhears relate to the narrator's description of Mr. Bingley and Mr. Darcy?

   A. The conversation confirms the narrator's assessment of Mr. Darcy but contradicts the narrator's assessment of Mr. Bingley.
   B. The conversation confirms the narrator's assessment of Mr. Bingley but contradicts the narrator's assessment of Mr. Darcy.
   C. The conversation contradicts the narrator's assessment of both characters.
   D. The conversation confirms the narrator's assessment of both characters.

DIRECTIONS: Read the passage, read each question, and choose the **best** answer.

A SOLDIER'S QUEST

1   Sometimes they of the infantry looked down at a fair little meadow which spread at their feet. Its long, green grass was rippling gently in a breeze. Beyond it was the grey form of a house half torn to pieces by shells and by the busy axes of soldiers who had pursued firewood. The line of an old fence was now dimly marked by long weeds and by an occasional post. A shell had blown the well-house to fragments. . . .

2   Collins, of A Company, said: "I wisht I had a drink. I bet there's water in that there ol' well yonder!"

3   "Yes; but how you goin' to git it?"

4   For the little meadow which intervened was now suffering a terrible onslaught of shells. Its green and beautiful calm had vanished utterly. Brown earth was being flung in monstrous handfuls. And there was a massacre of the young blades of grass. They were being torn, burned, obliterated. . . .

5   There was a quarrel in A Company. Collins was shaking his fist in the faces of some laughing comrades. "Dern yeh! I ain't afraid t' go. If yeh say much, I will go!"

6   "Of course, yeh will! You'll run through that there medder, won't yeh?"

7   Collins said, in a terrible voice: "You see now!" At this ominous threat his comrades broke into renewed jeers.

8   Collins gave them a dark scowl, and went to find his captain. The latter was conversing with the colonel of the regiment.

9   "Captain," said Collins, saluting and standing at attention—in those days all trousers bagged at the knees—"Captain, I want t' get permission to go git some water from that there well over yonder!"

10   The colonel and the captain swung about simultaneously and stared across the meadow. The captain laughed. "You must be pretty thirsty, Collins?"

11   "Yes, sir, I am."

12   "Well—ah," said the captain. After a moment, he asked, "Can't you wait?"

13   "No, sir."

14   The colonel was watching Collins's face. "Look here, my lad," he said, in a pious sort of a voice—"Look here, my lad"—Collins was not a lad—"don't you think that's taking pretty big risks for a little drink of water."

15   "I dunno," said Collins uncomfortably.

From A MYSTERY OF HEROISM by Stephen Crane

10. Which detail **best** emphasizes the implicit contrast between pre-war and post-war conditions?

 A. Someone's home is torn apart from the wartime fighting.
 B. The well might contain water for the soldiers to drink.
 C. The soldiers bicker as if they have known one another a long time.
 D. The captain and the colonel consult each other rather than consult the soldiers.

11. How are Collins and the soldiers with whom he is bickering similar?

 A. Every soldier is concerned with the welfare of the other soldiers.
 B. Collins and the other soldiers resent the captain and the colonel.
 C. Collins's and the other soldiers' manner of speaking makes them seem uneducated.
 D. All the soldiers are willing to take big risks during the war.

12. How is Collins different from the captain and the colonel?

 A. Collins is hopeful; the captain and the colonel are without hope.
 B. Collins is naïve and impulsive; the captain and the colonel are experienced and cautious.
 C. Collins is brave and fearless; the captain and the colonel are anxious and self-doubting.
 D. Collins is cunning; the captain and the colonel are straightforward.

13. How does the contrast between the natural landscape and the wartime activity enhance the story?

 A. The contrast between the natural landscape setting and devastating wartime activity emphasizes the beauty and power of nature.
 B. The peaceful natural setting emphasizes that the wartime activity will end soon.
 C. The simple natural setting contrasts with and emphasizes the complex tactics required during wartime.
 D. The contrast between the tranquil natural setting and the violent wartime activity emphasizes the destructive nature of war.

High Impact Lesson: Transitional Language and Signal Words in Fiction

Use with **Student Book** pp. 44–47

1 Review the Skill

READING ASSESSMENT TARGET: R.5

In fiction, **transitional language** and **signal words** can help readers keep track of different times, locations, or points of view. Stories rarely happen during a single time frame or within a single location. When authors change time frame or location between segments, they can create an easy transition by using transitional language or signal words. These segments may involve scenes, chapters (or subsections within a chapter), acts, or whatever designation the author wishes to use.

Story scenes in fiction detail actions and dialogue that transpire within a short period of time. When the scene is done, authors use transitional language or signal words to show that time has elapsed. Sometimes this is mere moments; sometimes it may be years. Often, scene changes move the action to different locations.

Authors also use transitional language or signal words to indicate when a scene is told from a different point of view. For example, one chapter may be from the main character's point of view and the next chapter may be from a supporting character's point of view. Changes in point of view often occur at section, scene, or chapter changes, but authors may also use transitional language or signal words to signal a change.

On the GED® Reasoning Through Language Arts test, you will be expected to show you understand transitional language and signal words. You may encounter questions that ask you to identify transitional language and signal words, explain how they function in a story, or explain how they convey meaning or make a story easier to understand.

2 Refine the Skill

(a) The passage starts with the narrator telling readers this is the "present." This provides clear information about the scene's time frame.

Scan the paragraph for the words or phrases from the answer choices. Think about how each word or phrase is used in the paragraph. The transitional word *first* shows the beginning of a sequence. The correct answer is **D**.

A FURIOUS DEPARTURE

1 <u>My present situation</u> was one in which all voluntary thought was swallowed up and lost. I was hurried away by fury; revenge alone endowed me with strength and composure; it molded my feelings and allowed me to be calculating and calm at periods when otherwise delirium or death would have been my portion.

2 My first resolution was to quit Geneva for ever; my country, which, when I was happy and beloved, was dear to me, now, in my adversity, became hateful. I provided myself with a sum of money, together with a few jewels which had belonged to my mother, and departed.

From FRANKENSTEIN by Mary Shelley

1. How does transitional language in paragraph 2 help the author move the plot forward?

   A. The word *together* shows that the narrator collected all of his belongings.
   B. The word *now* indicates that action takes place outside of Geneva.
   C. The phrase *when I was happy and beloved* begins a flashback.
   D. The phrase *My first resolution* shows the beginning of a sequence of actions.

DIRECTIONS: Read the passage, read each question, and choose the **best** answer.

NIGHTIME RAID

1   Breakfast eaten and the slim camp-outfit lashed to the sled, the men turned their backs on the cheery fire and launched out into the darkness. At once began to rise the cries that were fiercely sad—cries that called through the darkness and cold to one another and answered back. Conversation ceased. Daylight came at nine o'clock. At midday the sky to the south warmed to rose-color, and marked where the bulge of the earth intervened between the meridian sun and the northern world. But the rose-color swiftly faded. The grey light of day that remained lasted until three o'clock, when it, too, faded, and the pall of the Arctic night descended upon the lone and silent land.

2   As darkness came on, the hunting-cries to right and left and rear drew closer—so close that more than once they sent surges of fear through the toiling dogs, throwing them into short-lived panics.

3   At the conclusion of one such panic, when he and Henry had got the dogs back in the traces, Bill said:

4   "I wisht they'd strike game somewheres, an' go away an' leave us alone."

5   "They do get on the nerves horrible," Henry sympathized.

6   They spoke no more until camp was made.

7   Henry was bending over and adding ice to the babbling pot of beans when he was startled by the sound of a blow, an exclamation from Bill, and a sharp snarling cry of pain from among the dogs. He straightened up in time to see a dim form disappearing across the snow into the shelter of the dark. Then he saw Bill, standing amid the dogs, half triumphant, half crestfallen, in one hand a stout club, in the other the tail and part of the body of a sun-cured salmon.

From WHITE FANG by Jack London

2. Based on the transitional language used in paragraph 1, how much time has elapsed from the beginning of the paragraph to the end?

    A. one year
    B. one day
    C. three months
    D. three days

3. "At midday the sky to the south warmed to rose-color, and marked where the bulge of the earth intervened between the meridian sun and the northern world." Which of the following **best** describes how this sentence functions in the passage?

    A. It indicates that time has elapsed.
    B. It indicates that the weather has changed.
    C. It indicates the location has changed.
    D. It indicates a shift in point of view.

4. How does transitional language in paragraph 2 help the author move the plot forward?

    A. The phrase *As darkness came on* marks the end of a flashback.
    B. The phrase *As darkness came on* shows the passage of time and builds tension.
    C. The phrase *to the right and left and rear* shows that the men have split up.
    D. The phrase *to the right and left and rear* shows that the men are huddled together.

5. Which transitional language in paragraph 7 shows both an unexpected turn of events and builds tension?

    A. "when he was startled"
    B. "in time to see"
    C. "across the snow"
    D. "Then he saw"

16 LESSON

Analyze Plot Elements

Use with *Student Book* pp. 48–49

READING ASSESSMENT TARGETS: R.2.7, R.2.8, R.3.2, R.3
R.3.4, R.3.5, R.5.1, R.5.4

UNIT 1

1 Review the Skill

The plot of a story is made up of a series of events. **Plot elements** include **exposition**, **rising action**, **complications** (also called conflicts), **climax**, **falling action**, and **resolution**. The exposition provides a story's background and sets up the events to come. Rising action includes events leading to the climax. During rising action, characters face complications, which are difficulties that characters try to overcome. Complications are often the result of conflict between characters or within one person. The climax is the point of highest tension in the story. Falling action includes events leading to the resolution. The resolution is the er of a story, where loose ends are tied up.

2 Refine the Skill

By refining the skill of analyzing plot elements, you will improve your study and test-taking abilities, especially as they relate to the GED® Reasoning Through Language Arts test. Read the passage below. Then answer the questions that follow.

a The exposition reveals the speaker's sadness. She worries that people she knew and remembers will never be remembered after she is gone.

b The second speaker, Anna, offers a solution to the conflict facing her aunt. This offer marks the story's climax.

THE PROBLEM IS RESOLVED

"There's all those poor dear lasses there's nobody but me left to remember, and soon there'll not be even that. Sometimes they seem to be pleading not just to be forgotten, so I have to be keeping them alive in my head. . . . My grief! That I'll have to be leaving them! They'll die now, for no man lives who can remember them anymore."

Anna . . . leaned forward with girlish eagerness. "Auntie Margaret," she breathed, with new tenderness, "there's many a day left you yet. I'll be sitting here aside of you every evening at twilight just, and you can be showing me the lasses you have in mind. . . . I'll see them just as clear as yourself, for I've a place in my head where pictures come as thick and sharp as stars on a frosty night, when I get thinking. Then, with me ever calling them up, they'll be dancing and stravaging about till doomsday."

So the old woman had her heart's desire.

From LITTLE SELVES by Mary Lerner

1. What is the aunt's conflict?

   A. She wishes to regain her youth.
   B. She wants her niece to help write her memories.
   C. She fears dying alone.
   D. She fears no one will remember her memories.

2. The aunt is happy about the resolution because

   A. her past will remain a secret.
   B. she is comforted by her niece's offer.
   C. she and Anna will create photo albums.
   D. her niece will move in with her.

CONTENT TOPICS

There are several types of conflict. The most common conflicts are character versus self, character versus character, character versus nature, and character versus society.

DIRECTIONS: Read the passage, read each question, and choose the **best** answer.

THE CANARY PROVIDES A CLUE

1   When the two women were alone in Minnie Wright's kitchen, Martha Hale said low and slowly, "She liked the bird. She was going to bury it in that pretty box."

2   Mrs. Hale's eyes made a slow sweep of the room, as if seeing what that kitchen had meant through all the years. "No, Wright wouldn't like the bird," she said after that— "a thing that sang. She used to sing. He killed that too." Her voice tightened.

3   Mrs. Peters, the sheriff's wife, moved uneasily and replied, "Of course we don't know who killed the bird."

4   "I knew John Wright," was Mrs. Hale's answer.

5   "It was an awful thing was done in this house that night, Mrs. Hale," said the sheriff's wife. "Killing a man while he slept—slipping a thing round his neck that choked the life out of him."

6   Mrs. Hale had not moved. "If there had been years and years of—nothing, then a bird to sing to you, it would be awful—still—after the bird was still."

7   They stopped and busied themselves as they heard the sound of the men coming back down the stairs. They waited until the sheriff had followed the county attorney through the kitchen and into the other room. Then, the two women were alone in that kitchen for one final moment.

8   Martha Hale sprang up, her hands tight together, looking at that other woman, with whom it rested. Slowly, unwillingly, Mrs. Peters turned her head until their eyes met. There was a moment when they held each other in a steady, burning look in which there was no evasion nor flinching. Then Martha Hale's eyes pointed the way to the basket in which was hidden the thing that would make certain the conviction of Minnie Wright—that woman who was not there and yet who had been there with them all through that hour.

9   For a moment Mrs. Peters did not move. And then she did it. With a rush forward, she threw back the quilt pieces, got the box, tried to put it in her hand-bag. It was too big. Desperately she opened it, started to take the bird out. But there she broke—she could not touch the bird. She stood there helpless, foolish.

10   There was the sound of a knob turning in the inner door. Martha Hale snatched the box from the sheriff's wife, and got it in the pocket of her big coat just as the sheriff and the county attorney came back into the kitchen.

11   Mrs. Hale's hand was against the pocket of her coat.

Adapted from A JURY OF HER PEERS by Susan Glaspell

3. According to the women's actions, which complication **most likely** arose before the beginning of this excerpt?

    A. The women stole a canary from a friend.
    B. The sheriff arrested Mr. Peters.
    C. The sheriff and county attorney questioned the women.
    D. The women found a dead canary in a box.

4. The women hear "the sound of a knob turning in the inner door" (paragraph 10). This event could **best** be described as

    A. a complication.
    B. the exposition.
    C. the falling action.
    D. the resolution.

5. What is the climax of this passage?

    A. Mrs. Peters stands helpless.
    B. Martha Hale's hand hides the box in the pocket of her coat.
    C. Martha Hale snatches the box from Mrs. Peters and puts it in her pocket.
    D. The men enter the kitchen.

6. On the basis of this passage, which is the **most likely** resolution?

    A. Mrs. Hale will tell the sheriff and county attorney about the canary.
    B. The sheriff and county attorney will remain unaware of the canary.
    C. Mrs. Peters will tell the sheriff and county attorney that Mrs. Hale is hiding the canary.
    D. The sheriff and county attorney will notice the box in Mrs. Hale's pocket.

DIRECTIONS: Read the passage, read each question, and choose the **best** answer.

MARY RECEIVES SURPRISING NEWS

1   Again there was a quick peal upon the street-door. Fearing that her sister would also be disturbed, Mary wrapped herself in a cloak and hood, took the lamp from the hearth, and hastened to the window. By some accident, it had been left unfastened, and yielded easily to her hand.

2   "Who's there?" asked Mary, trembling as she looked forth.

3   The storm was over, and the moon was up; it shone upon broken clouds above, and below upon houses black with moisture. A young man in sailor's dress, wet as if he had come out of the depths of the sea, stood alone under the window. Mary recognized him as one whose livelihood was gained by short voyages along the coast; nor did she forget that, previous to her marriage, he had been an unsuccessful wooer of her own.

4   "What do you seek here, Stephen?" said she.

5   "Cheer up, Mary, for I seek to comfort you," answered the rejected lover. "You must know I got home not ten minutes ago, and the first thing my good mother told me was the news about your husband. So, without saying a word to the old woman, I clapped on my hat, and ran out of the house. I could not have slept a wink before speaking to you, Mary, for the sake of old times."

6   "Stephen, I thought better of you!" exclaimed the widow, preparing to close the lattice.

7   "But stop, and hear my story out," cried the young sailor. "I tell you we spoke a brig yesterday afternoon, bound in from Old England. And who do you think I saw standing on deck, well and hearty, only a bit thinner than he was five months ago?"

8   Mary leaned from the window, but could not speak. "Why, it was your husband himself," continued the generous seaman. "He and three others saved themselves on a spar, when the Blessing turned bottom upwards. The brig will beat into the bay by daylight, with this wind, and you'll see him here tomorrow. There's the comfort I bring you, Mary, and so good night."

9   He hurried away, while Mary watched him with a doubt of waking reality, that seemed stronger or weaker as he alternately entered the shade of the houses, or emerged into the broad streaks of moonlight. Gradually, however, a blessed flood of conviction swelled into her heart, in strength enough to overwhelm her, had its increase been more abrupt.

Adapted from THE WIVES OF THE DEAD by Nathaniel Hawthorne

7.   The passage states that Stephen was Mary's "unsuccessful wooer" (paragraph 3). This information about Mary and Stephen's past is part of the story's

   A. exposition.
   B. conflict.
   C. climax.
   D. resolution.

8.   According to the details in the passage, what is the **most likely** source of Mary's conflict?

   A. She still loves Stephen.
   B. Stephen has disappointed her.
   C. She believes her husband has died.
   D. Stephen's mother has gossiped about Mary.

9.   A complication in the passage is that at first Mary doubts Stephen's reasons for visiting her. By saying, "I thought better of you" (paragraph 6), what does Mary mean?

   A. Mary thinks Stephen is there to tell her more news of her husband.
   B. Mary thinks Stephen should have waited until a better time to visit her.
   C. Mary thinks Stephen has come to console her and has romantic intentions.
   D. Mary disapproves of the way Stephen refers to his mother.

10. On the basis of the details in the passage, what is the **most likely** ending?

   A. Stephen will ask Mary to marry him.
   B. Mary's husband will come home.
   C. Mary will leave her husband.
   D. Stephen will rescue Mary's husband.

DIRECTIONS: Read the passage, read each question, and choose the **best** answer.

THE STORY OF AN HOUR

1   Because it was known that Mrs. Mallard had heart trouble, great care was taken to break to her as gently as possible the news of her husband's death. It was her sister Josephine who told her; veiled hints that revealed in half concealing. Her husband's friend Richards was there too, near her. It was he who had been in the newspaper office when intelligence of the railroad disaster was received, with Brently Mallard's name leading the list of "killed."

2   She wept at once, with sudden, wild abandonment, in her sister's arms. When the storm of grief had spent itself she went away to her room alone. She sank into an armchair pressed down by a physical exhaustion that haunted her body and seemed to reach into her soul. She sat quite motionless, except when a sob came up into her throat and shook her. She was young, with a fair, calm face, whose lines bespoke repression and even a certain strength. But now there was a dull stare in her eyes.

3   There was something coming to her and she was waiting for it, fearfully. What was it? She was beginning to recognize this thing that was approaching, and she was striving to beat it back with her will. When she abandoned herself a little whispered word escaped her lips. She said it over and over under her breath: "free, free, free!" The vacant stare and the look of terror that had followed it went from her eyes. They stayed keen and bright.

4   She knew that she would weep again when she saw the face that had never looked save with love upon her, fixed and gray and dead. But she saw beyond that bitter moment a long procession of years to come that would belong to her absolutely. There would be no one to live for; she would live for herself. She had loved him—sometimes. Often she had not. What did it matter!

5   She arose at length and opened the door. There was a feverish triumph in her eyes, and she carried herself like a goddess of Victory. She descended the stairs. Richards stood waiting for them at the bottom.

6   Some one was opening the front door with a key. It was Brently Mallard who entered, a little travel-stained, carrying his grip-sack and umbrella. He had been far from the scene of accident, and did not even know there had been one. He stood amazed at Josephine's piercing cry; at Richards's quick motion to screen him from the view of his wife.

7   But Richards was too late.

8   When the doctors came they said she had died of heart disease—of joy that kills.

Adapted from THE STORY OF AN HOUR by Kate Chopin

11. In the opening line, the narrator says that "Mrs. Mallard had heart trouble." This information is part of the story's

    A. resolution.
    B. climax.
    C. conflict.
    D. exposition.

12. Which of the following represents the climax of the story?

    A. "It was her sister Josephine who told her; veiled hints that revealed in half concealing."
    B. "She sat quite motionless, except when a sob came up into her throat and shook her."
    C. "She said it over and over under her breath: 'free, free, free!'"
    D. "She knew that she would weep again when she saw the face that had never looked save with love upon her, fixed and gray and dead."

13. Do the events in paragraphs 3, 4, and 5 support or contradict the ending statement?

    A. contradict; Mrs. Mallard was happy to be free of her husband, so she was not happy to see him alive.
    B. contradict; Mrs. Mallard was scared of her husband, so she was not happy to see him alive.
    C. support; Mrs. Mallard was terrified of being alone, so she was happy to see him alive.
    D. support; Mrs. Mallard was saddened by the loss of her husband, so she was happy to see him alive.

High Impact Lesson: Sequence and Plot

Use with *Student Book* pp. 50–53

1 Review the Skill

A chronological order of events creates a **sequence**. **Plot** is the arrangement of events and scenes in fiction that make up the story. However, plot events are not always presented in chronological order. Authors sometimes organize events out of sequence to support a theme or main idea or to influence readers' emotional states.

Plot has five stages: exposition, rising action, climax, falling action, and resolution. The exposition presents the story's main characters, setting, theme, and conflict. During the rising action, protagonists face obstacles as the conflict increases. During the climax, the conflict reaches its greatest intensity when the protagonist faces and overcomes the most difficult obstacle. During the falling action, any minor conflicts that remain are resolved. The resolution is the conclusion or end of the story.

Authors may create stories out of chronological order to build tension. Authors do this using backstory, flashbacks, and parallel plots. Backstory describe previous events often through internal or external dialogue. Flashbacks show previous events through narration. Parallel plots involve the weaving of different story lines from different time periods.

On the GED® Reasoning Through Language Arts test, you will be expected to show you understand sequence and plot. You may encounter questions that ask you to locate a specific event in a text, identify order of events in a text, describe how one event leads to the next, order non-chronological events in chronological order, or order chronological events in a different way.

2 Refine the Skill

a The first sentence shows a cause-and-effect relationship between two events: the prince being pursued and persecuted and then being deserted and left to himself.

b Notice in the second sentence information that is not in chronological order. It provides details as to why the mob left the prince alone.

Scan the paragraph for key words from the answer choices: *silent, weary, left to himself.* The second sentence notes "weariness finally forced him to be silent." How does that relate to the other events in the answer choices? The correct answer is **B**.

DESERTED

After hours of persistent pursuit and persecution, the little prince was at last deserted by the rabble and left to himself. As long as he had been able to rage against the mob, and threaten it royally, and royally utter commands that were good stuff to laugh at, he was very entertaining; but when weariness finally forced him to be silent, he was no longer of use to his tormentors, and they sought amusement elsewhere. He looked about him, now, but could not recognize the locality. He was within the city of London—that was all he knew. He moved on, aimlessly, and in a little while the houses thinned, and the passers-by were infrequent. He bathed his bleeding feet in the brook which flowed then where Farringdon Street now is; rested a few moments, then passed on, and presently came upon a great space with only a few scattered houses in it, and a prodigious church. He recognized this church.

From THE PRINCE AND THE PAUPER by Mark Twain

1. Which statement **best** describes the relationship between two events in this excerpt?

A. After the prince fell silent, he grew weary.
B. After the prince fell silent, the mob left the prince to himself.
C. After the mob left the prince to himself, he fell silent.
D. After the mob left the prince to himself, he uttered commands.

DIRECTIONS: Read the passage, read each question, and choose the **best** answer.

MOTHER AND SON

1   Robert talked a good deal about himself. He was very young, and did not know any better. Mrs. Pontellier talked a little about herself for the same reason. Each was interested in what the other said. Robert spoke of his intention to go to Mexico in the autumn, where fortune awaited him. He was always intending to go to Mexico, but some way never got there. Meanwhile he held on to his modest position in a mercantile house in New Orleans, where an equal familiarity with English, French, and Spanish gave him no small value as a clerk and correspondent.

2   He was spending his summer vacation, as he always did, with his mother at Grand Isle. In former times, before Robert could remember, "the house" had been a summer luxury of the Lebruns. Now, flanked by its dozen or more cottages, which were always filled with exclusive visitors from the "Quartier Francais," it enabled Madame Lebrun to maintain the easy and comfortable existence which appeared to be her birthright.

3   Mrs. Pontellier talked about her father's Mississippi plantation and her girlhood home in the old Kentucky bluegrass country. She was an American woman, with a small infusion of French which seemed to have been lost in dilution. She read a letter from her sister, who was away in the East, and who had engaged herself to be married. Robert was interested, and wanted to know what manner of girls the sisters were, what the father was like, and how long the mother had been dead.

4   When Mrs. Pontellier folded the letter it was time for her to dress for the early dinner.

5   "I see Leonce isn't coming back," she said, with a glance in the direction whence her husband had disappeared. Robert supposed he was not, as there were a good many New Orleans club men over at Klein's.

From THE AWAKENING by Kate Chopin

2. What is the first action described in this passage?

    A. Mrs. Pontellier talked a little bit about herself.
    B. Mrs. Pontellier talked about growing up in old Kentucky bluegrass country.
    C. Robert traveled to Mexico to seek his fortune.
    D. Robert talked about himself.

3. In paragraph 2, which phrase **best** shows that information is shown in non-chronological order?

    A. *with his mother*
    B. *In former times*
    C. *which were always filled*
    D. *appeared to be her birthright*

4. In paragraph 3, what does Mrs. Pontellier reading a letter lead to?

    A. Robert wanted to know more about Mrs. Pontellier and her sister.
    B. Robert explained why he moved away to the East.
    C. Mrs. Pontellier talked about her father's Mississippi plantation.
    D. Mrs. Pontellier was engaged to be married.

5. Which statement is the **best** explanation for Mrs. Pontellier putting away the letter?

    A. Her sister was engaged to be married.
    B. Robert had wanted to know about Mrs. Pontellier and her sister.
    C. It was time for her to dress for the early dinner.
    D. Her husband, Leonce, was not coming back.

6. Which answer presents a correct chronological order of two events described in this passage?

    A. Leonce disappeared. He returned in time for the early dinner.
    B. Robert went to Mexico. He held a position in a mercantile house.
    C. Madame Lebrun maintained a comfortable existence. She talked about her father's plantation.
    D. Mrs. Pontellier talked a little about herself. She read a letter from her sister.

Analyze Character

READING ASSESSMENT TARGETS: R.3.2, R.3.3, R.3.4, R.3.5, R.4.3/L.4

UNIT 1

1 Review the Skill

Characters are the fictional people that make stories interesting and often memorable. Readers who analyze character behaviors can better understand the plot and action of stories. Analyzing characters involves noticing not only what they say and do, but also how they look and behave and what others say or think about them. Even a small detail about a character's appearance or a gesture can provide clues about what he or she is thinking and feeling.

2 Refine the Skill

By refining the skill of analyzing characters, you will improve your study and test-taking abilities, especially as they relate to the GED® Reasoning Through Language Arts test. Read the passage below. Then answer the questions that follow.

a Phrases such as "dressed with due clerical neatness" and "stooping … as is customary with abstracted men" indicate that Mr. Hooper is tidy, methodical, and absorbed in thought.

b The way that one character responds to another provides insight into both characters. The parishioners hardly return Mr. Hooper's greeting because they are taken aback by his appearance.

THE REVEREND MR. HOOPER

The cause of so much amazement may appear sufficiently slight. Mr. Hooper, a gentlemanly person of about thirty, though still a bachelor, was dressed with due clerical neatness, as if a careful wife had starched his band and brushed the weekly dust from his Sunday's garb. There was but one thing remarkable in his appearance. Swathed about his forehead and hanging down over his face, so low as to be shaken by his breath, Mr. Hooper had on a black veil. On a nearer view it seemed to consist of two folds of crape, which entirely concealed his features except the mouth and chin, but probably did not intercept his sight further than to give a darkened aspect to all living and inanimate things. With this gloomy shade before him good Mr. Hooper walked onward at a slow and quiet pace, stooping somewhat and looking on the ground, as is customary with abstracted men, yet nodding kindly to those of his parishioners who still waited on the meeting-house steps. But so wonder-struck were they that his greeting hardly met with a return.

From THE MINISTER'S BLACK VEIL by Nathaniel Hawthorne

1. According to the description of the way Mr. Hooper dresses and walks, he seems

   A. awkward and strange.
   B. neat and reserved.
   C. self-conscious and shy.
   D. troubled and unfriendly.

2. Which statement **best** confirms that Mr. Hooper's veil has a chilling effect on his appearance?

   A. He looks down at the ground as he walks.
   B. The veil completely conceals his eyes.
   C. Parishioners do not return his greeting.
   D. The veil is the only remarkable thing about him.

MAKING ASSUMPTIONS

People make assumptions about someone who walks into a room. The person's hair, clothes, poise, and style influence a first impression. Characters can make similar impressions.

★ Spotlighted Item: **DRAG-AND-DROP**

DIRECTIONS: Read the passage and the question. Then use the drag-and-drop options to complete the web.

THE APPEAL OF NICK

1   It is difficult to convey in words the charm that Nick possessed. Seeing him, you beheld merely a medium-sized young mechanic in reasonably grimed garage clothes when working; and in tight pants, tight coat, silk shirt, long-visored green cap when at leisure. A rather pallid skin due to the nature of his work. Large deft hands, a good deal like the hands of a surgeon, square, blunt-fingered, spatulate. Indeed, as you saw him at work, a wire-netted electric bulb held in one hand, the other plunged deep into the vitals of the car on which he was engaged, you thought of a surgeon performing a major operation. . . .

2   All this, of course, could not serve to endear him to the girls. On the contrary, you would have thought that his hands alone, from which he could never quite free the grease and grit, would have caused some feeling of repugnance among the lily-fingered. But they, somehow, seemed always to be finding an excuse to touch him: his tie, his hair, his coat sleeve. They seemed even to derive a vicarious thrill from holding his hat or cap when on an outing. They brushed imaginary bits of lint from his coat lapel. . . .

3   No; it can't be classified, this powerful draw he had for them. His conversation furnished no clue. It was commonplace conversation, limited, even dull. . . .

4   His unconcern should have infuriated them, but it served to pique. He wasn't actually as unconcerned as he appeared, but he had early learned that effort in their direction was unnecessary. Nick had little imagination; a gorgeous selfishness; a tolerantly contemptuous liking for the sex. Naturally, however, his attitude toward them had been somewhat embittered by being obliged to watch their method of driving a car in and out of the Ideal Garage doorway. His own manipulation of the wheel was nothing short of wizardry.

From THE AFTERNOON OF A FAUN by Edna Ferber

3. Drag and drop into the web the traits that **most likely** contribute to Nick's appeal to women.

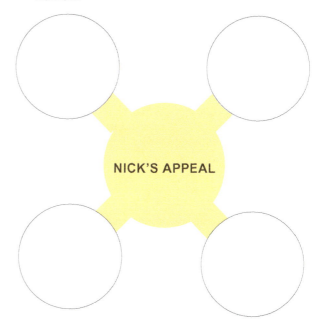

He looks like a surgeon when he works.
He is a wizard at driving.
His complexion is pale.
His behavior is selfish.
He makes no effort with women.
He has little imagination.

DIRECTIONS: Read the passage, read each question, and choose the **best** answer.

A VISIT FROM THE POLICE

1   As the bell sounded the hour, there came a knocking at the street door. I went down to open it with a light heart—for what had I now to fear? There entered three men, who introduced themselves, with perfect suavity, as officers of the police. A shriek had been heard by a neighbor during the night; suspicion of foul play had been aroused; information had been lodged at the police office, and they (the officers) had been deputed to search the premises.

2   I smiled—for what had I to fear? I bade the gentlemen welcome. The shriek, I said, was my own in a dream. The old man, I mentioned, was absent in the country. I took my visitors all over the house. I bade them search—search well. I led them, at length, to his chamber. I showed them his treasures, secure, undisturbed. In the enthusiasm of my confidence, I brought chairs into the room, and desired them here to rest from their fatigues, while I myself, in the wild audacity of my perfect triumph, placed my own seat upon the very spot beneath which reposed the corpse of the victim.

3   The officers were satisfied. My manner had convinced them. I was singularly at ease. They sat, and while I answered cheerily, they chatted of familiar things. But, ere long, I felt myself getting pale and wished them gone. My head ached, and I fancied a ringing in my ears: but still they sat and still chatted. The ringing became more distinct—It continued and became more distinct: I talked more freely to get rid of the feeling: but it continued and gained definiteness—until, at length, I found that the noise was not within my ears. . . .

4   "Villains!" I shrieked, "dissemble no more! I admit the deed!—tear up the planks! here, here!—It is the beating of his hideous heart!"

From THE TELL-TALE HEART by Edgar Allan Poe

4. On the basis of details in paragraph 1, which word **best** describes the narrator's mood when the doorbell rang?

    A. frightened
    B. hesitant
    C. confident
    D. excited

5. The narrator suggests that he felt no fear when the police officers arrived. Which statement by the narrator implies that he felt more fear than he claimed?

    A. "The shriek, I said, was my own in a dream. The old man, I mentioned, was absent in the country."
    B. "I bade them search—search well. I led them, at length, to his chamber. I showed them his treasures, secure, undisturbed."
    C. "In the enthusiasm of my confidence, I brought chairs into the room, and desired them here to rest from their fatigues. . ."
    D. "The officers were satisfied. My manner had convinced them. I was singularly at ease."

6. The police officers rest and chat of familiar things. What do these actions **most likely** reveal about the police officers?

    A. They are unsuspecting.
    B. They are distrustful.
    C. They are apologetic.
    D. They are thorough.

7. On the basis of the details in paragraph 3, which word **best** describes how the narrator feels after he has been sitting for a while with the officers?

    A. murderous
    B. guilty
    C. confident
    D. cheerful

8. When the narrator hears the noise, the police officers sit and continue to chat. The police officers **most likely**

    A. wonder about the narrator's headache.
    B. are annoyed by the narrator's talkativeness.
    C. do not hear the noise that the narrator does.
    D. are still trying to obtain evidence of foul play.

9. The narrator is motivated to confess **most likely** because he believes that the

    A. house is alive.
    B. officers are criminals.
    C. officers are tricking him.
    D. old man's heart is beating.

UNIT 1

MATTIE

1   He had always been more sensitive than the people about him to the appeal of natural beauty. His unfinished studies had given form to this sensibility and even in his unhappiest moments field and sky spoke to him with a deep and powerful persuasion. But hitherto the emotion had remained in him as a silent ache, veiling with sadness the beauty that evoked it.

2   He did not even know whether anyone else in the world felt as he did, or whether he was the sole victim of this mournful privilege. Then he learned that one other spirit had trembled with the same touch of wonder: that at his side, living under his roof and eating his bread, was a creature to whom he could say: "That's Orion down yonder; the big fellow to the right is Aldebaran, and the bunch of little ones—like bees swarming—they're the Pleiades. . ." or whom he could hold entranced before a ledge of granite thrusting up through the fern while he unrolled the huge panorama of the ice age, and the long dim stretches of succeeding time.

3   The fact that admiration for his learning mingled with Mattie's wonder at what he taught was not the least part of his pleasure. And there were other sensations, less definable but more exquisite, which drew them together with a shock of silent joy: the cold red of sunset behind winter hills, the flight of cloud-flocks over slopes of golden stubble, or the intensely blue shadows of hemlocks on sunlit snow. When she said to him once: "It looks just as if it was painted!" it seemed to Ethan that the art of definition could go no farther, and that words had at last been found to utter his secret soul. . . .

From ETHAN FROME by Edith Wharton

10. The details in the first two sentences of paragraph 1 reveal that Ethan Frome was **most likely**

A. a tireless traveler.
B. a cheerful and sociable man.
C. a sensitive and lonely man.
D. a serious professional.

11. Based on the first sentence in paragraph 2, Ethan felt that his affinity to nature

A. was a unique characteristic that filled him with happiness.
B. was a characteristic that only he could enjoy.
C. was a characteristic that he shared with his friends.
D. was a heavy burden.

12. Which word **best** describes how Ethan feels about Mattie?

A. bitterness
B. fascination
C. annoyance
D. boredom

13. Based on the information in paragraph 3, Mattie is **most likely**

A. cunning and efficient.
B. serious and controlling.
C. enthusiastic and sensitive.
D. cheerful and jovial.

14. Based on the details in paragraph 3, Ethan will **most likely**

A. quickly get bored with Mattie.
B. look for ways to meet others and expand his social circle.
C. try to convince Mattie to start painting.
D. find himself increasingly drawn to Mattie.

15. Which statement by the narrator implies that Mattie had a profound effect on Ethan?

A. "He had always been more sensitive than the people about him to the appeal of natural beauty."
B. "But hitherto the emotion had remained in him as a silent ache, veiling with sadness the beauty that evoked it."
C. "He did not even know whether anyone else in the world felt as he did, or whether he was the sole victim of this mournful privilege."
D. "And there were other sensations, less definable but more exquisite, which drew them together with a shock of silent joy…"

16. The details in paragraph 3 reveal that at the moment in time described, Ethan Frome **most likely**

A. finally found happiness and contentment in Mattie's companionship.
B. was inspired to paint the images Mattie admired to entice her to like him.
C. did not have strong feelings or an emotional tie to the moments they spent together.
D. was afraid to get close to Mattie for fear of rejection, so he did not get close to her.

Analyze Setting

Use with **Student Book** pp. 56–57

READING ASSESSMENT TARGETS: R.2.1, R.2.7, R.3.2, R.3.3, R.3.4, R.3.5, R.4.1/4.1, R.4.3/L.

UNIT 1

1 Review the Skill

An author constructs a **setting** through the details that describe a place and time. The plants that grow in a particular spot or the ways in which characters speak, for example, help readers imagine where the story takes place. A setting can affect the way characters think and behave. Some characters are at ease in a setting, while others are not. A setting also affects a story's feeling, or mood. For instance, a place that appears barren or difficult to live in creates a different feeling from a setting that is lush and fertile.

2 Refine the Skill

By refining the skill of analyzing setting, you will improve your study and test-taking abilities, especially as they relate to the GED® Reasoning Through Language Arts test. Read the passage below. Then answer the questions that follow.

a The underlined sentence and phrases show the author's use of sensory details—details that appeal to the five human senses—to create the setting.

b During the 1800s and early 1900s, sugarcane plantations around the world relied on forced and cheap labor. Here the description contrasts the sweetness of the cane with the poverty of the workers.

SUGAR CANE LANDSCAPE

Up from the deep dusk of a cleared spot on the edge of the forest a mellow glow arose and spread fan-wise into the low-hanging heavens. And all around the air was heavy with the scent of boiling cane. A large pile of cane-stalks lay like ribboned shadows upon the ground. A mule, harnessed to a pole, trudged lazily round and round the pivot of the grinder. Beneath a swaying oil lamp, a Negro alternately whipped out at the mule, and fed cane-stalks to the grinder. A fat boy waddled pails of fresh ground juice between the grinder and the boiling stove. Steam came from the copper boiling pan. The scent of cane came from the copper pan and drenched the forest and the hill that sloped to factory town, beneath its fragrance. It drenched the men . . . seated around the stove.

From BLOOD-BURNING MOON by Jean Toomer

USING LOGIC

Note the author's use of phrases with similar connotations or reader associations: "low-hanging heavens," "air was heavy," and "ribboned shadows." These words provide clues about the setting.

1. The details of the setting reveal

   A. an oppressive environment.
   B. a modern farming operation.
   C. the sweetness of the land.
   D. the narrator's love of agriculture.

2. The description of the setting helps explain why the

   A. mule gets whipped.
   B. boy carries the pails.
   C. men feel trapped.
   D. mule trudges lazily.

3 Master the Skill

DIRECTIONS: Read the passage, read each question, and choose the **best** answer.

LIFE ON THE DIVIDE

1   Near Rattlesnake Creek, on the side of a little draw, stood Canute's shanty. North, east, south, stretched the level Nebraska plain of long rust-red grass that undulated constantly in the wind. To the west the ground was broken and rough, and a narrow strip of timber wound along the ... muddy little stream that had scarcely ambition enough to crawl over its black bottom. If it had not been for the few stunted cottonwoods and elms that grew along its banks, Canute would have shot himself years ago. The Norwegians are a timber-loving people, and if there is even a turtle pond with a few plum bushes around it they seem irresistibly drawn toward it. ...

2   As to the shanty itself, Canute had built it without aid of any kind, for when he first squatted along the banks of Rattlesnake Creek there was not a human being within twenty miles. It was built of logs split in halves, the chinks stopped with mud and plaster. The roof was covered with earth and was supported by one gigantic beam curved in the shape of a round arch.

From ON THE DIVIDE by Willa Cather

3.   Which statement **best** describes the view from Canute's house?

A. The house looks out on green plains.
B. Nothing but mud surrounds the house.
C. Canute can see the river on the eastern side.
D. The view in one direction is different from the others.

4.   Which statement **best** describes the effect of the setting on Canute?

A. Everything but the trees makes him deeply depressed.
B. He enjoys living a rugged outdoor life despite the wind.
C. His house gives him a sense of comfort and accomplishment.
D. The bare, treeless landscape makes him miss city life.

DIRECTIONS: Read the passage, read each question, and choose the **best** answer.

A CHILDHOOD REMEMBERED

1   A wigwam of weather-stained canvas stood at the base of some irregularly ascending hills. A footpath wound its way gently down the sloping land till it reached the broad river bottom; creeping through the long swamp grasses that bent over it on either side, it came out on the edge of the Missouri.

2   Here, morning, noon, and evening, my mother came to draw water from the muddy stream for our household use. Always, when my mother started for the river, I stopped my play to run along with her. . . .

3   I was a wild little girl of seven. Loosely clad in a slip of brown buckskin, and light-footed with a pair of soft moccasins on my feet, I was as free as the wind that blew my hair, and no less spirited than a bounding deer. These were my mother's pride—my wild freedom and overflowing spirits. She taught me no fear save that of intruding myself upon others.

From IMPRESSIONS OF AN INDIAN CHILDHOOD by Zitkala-Sa

5.   Which description **best** reflects the landscape?

A. hilly on the edge of a river
B. dry and flat with little water
C. rich, cultivated farmland
D. dense forests untouched by humans

6.   The girl's home and clothing reveal that she **most likely** lives

A. in a small river town in Missouri.
B. near a big Midwestern city in the 1880s.
C. in a rural Native American community.
D. in a windy area heavily populated by deer.

7.   How does the girl's behavior reflect the setting?

A. The girl has no interest in the outdoors and prefers reading.
B. The mother is worried that the girl is too free to wander in the woods.
C. The girl is a free spirit, like the wind and the deer.
D. The girl's actions reflect the gentle flow of the river.

UNIT 1

DIRECTIONS: Read the passage, read each question, and choose the **best** answer.

THE BREAD LINE

1   The street was very dark and absolutely deserted. It was a district on the "South Side," not far from the Chicago River, given up largely to wholesale stores, and after nightfall was empty of all life. The echoes slept but lightly hereabouts, and the slightest footfall, the faintest noise, woke them upon the instant and sent them clamoring up and down the length of the pavement between the iron-shuttered fronts. The only light visible came from the side door of a certain "Vienna" bakery, where at one o'clock in the morning loaves of bread were given away to any who should ask. Every evening about nine o'clock the outcasts began to gather about the side door. The stragglers came in rapidly, and the line—the "bread line" as it was called—began to form. By midnight it was usually some hundred yards in length, stretching almost the entire length of the block.

2   Toward ten in the evening, his collar turned up against the fine drizzle that pervaded the air, his hands in his pockets, his elbows gripping his sides, Sam Lewiston came up and silently took his place at the end of the line.

3   He stood now in the enfolding drizzle, sodden, stupefied with fatigue. Before and behind stretched the line. There was no talking. There was no sound. The street was empty. It was so still that the passing of a cable-car in the adjoining thoroughfare grated like prolonged rolling explosions, beginning and ending at immeasurable distances. The drizzle descended incessantly. After a long time midnight struck.

4   There was something ominous and gravely impressive in this interminable line of dark figures, close-pressed, soundless; a crowd, yet absolutely still; a close-packed, silent file, waiting, waiting in the vast deserted night-ridden street; waiting without a word, without a movement, there under the night and under the slow-moving mists of rain.

From A DEAL IN WHEAT by Frank Norris

8. Which phrase **best** describes the setting in this passage?

A. poor and rural
B. poor and urban
C. wealthy and cosmopolitan
D. middle-class and residential

9. "The echoes slept but lightly hereabouts, and the slightest footfall, the faintest noise, woke them upon the instant and sent them clamoring up and down the length of the pavement between the iron-shuttered fronts." How do the details in this description of the setting set the mood in paragraph 1?

A. The text gives the impression of extreme sadness, that nobody dares to move in this solemn place.
B. The text gives the impression of fear, that any noise will cause danger.
C. The text gives the impression of complete silence, that the slightest noise will be heard throughout the streets.
D. The text gives the impression of peaceful stillness, that any movement might disturb.

10. In this passage, how does the setting affect the feeling, or mood, of the story? The setting makes the mood

A. active and purposeful.
B. warm and inviting.
C. distant and other-worldly.
D. gloomy and forbidding.

11. To which location would a man in Sam Lewiston's condition be **most likely** to go?

A. a shelter
B. a park bench
C. a restaurant
D. another bakery

12. What can you conclude from the details about the South Side? The neighborhood is probably

A. a gritty business district.
B. an upscale warehouse district.
C. a suburban destination.
D. a performing arts district.

13. How does the description of the weather add to the overall effect of the passage?

A. It shows the gratitude of the men in line.
B. It heightens the difficulty of making the bread.
C. It emphasizes the discomfort of the characters.
D. It contrasts with the gloominess of the street.

DIRECTIONS: Read the passage, read each question, and choose the **best** answer.

THE BLACK VEIL

1   The appearance of the place through which he walked in the morning, was not calculated to raise the spirits of the young surgeon, or to dispel any feeling of anxiety or depression which the singular kind of visit he was about to make, had awakened. Striking off from the high road, his way lay across a marshy common, through irregular lanes, with here and there a ruinous and dismantled cottage fast falling to pieces with decay and neglect. A stunted tree, or pool of stagnant water, roused into a sluggish action by the heavy rain of the preceding night, skirted the path occasionally; and, now and then, a miserable patch of garden-ground, . . . and old palings imperfectly mended with stakes pilfered from the neighbouring hedges, bore testimony, at once to the poverty of the inhabitants, and the little scruple they entertained in appropriating the property of other people to their own use.

2   Occasionally, a filthy-looking woman would make her appearance from the door of a dirty house, to empty the contents of some cooking utensil into the gutter in front, or to scream after a little slip-shod girl, who had contrived to stagger a few yards from the door under the weight of a sallow infant almost as big as herself; but, scarcely anything was stirring around: and so much of the prospect as could be faintly traced through the cold damp mist which hung heavily over it, presented a lonely and dreary appearance perfectly in keeping with the objects we have described.

3   After plodding wearily through the mud and mire; making many inquiries for the place to which he had been directed; and receiving as many contradictory and unsatisfactory replies in return; the young man at length arrived before the house which had been pointed out to him as the object of his destination. It was a small low building, one story above the ground, with even a more desolate and unpromising exterior than any he had yet passed. An old yellow curtain was closely drawn across the window up-stairs, and the parlour shutters were closed, but not fastened. The house was detached from any other, and, as it stood at an angle of a narrow lane, there was no other habitation in sight.

From THE BLACK VEIL by Charles Dickens

14. The first sentence of paragraph 1 suggests that

    A. the protagonist was happy.
    B. the protagonist's mood improved upon leaving his house.
    C. the protagonist is afraid.
    D. the protagonist felt depressed.

15. The setting the author describes is **most likely**

    A. a place of wealthy people.
    B. the field.
    C. a poor suburb.
    D. an isolated place.

16. How does the description of the woman in paragraph 2 impact the setting?

    A. It demonstrates that the people in the town did not take care of themselves.
    B. It demonstrates that the woman has disdain for the girl carrying the young child.
    C. It demonstrates that the difficult life of the people contribute to the dreary setting.
    D. It demonstrates that despite difficult times, the town had a culture of caring for each other.

17. The first sentence of paragraph 3 suggests that

    A. the doctor found the house right away.
    B. the way to the house was unpleasant and complicated.
    C. the doctor never reached his destination.
    D. many people delayed him on his way.

18. The sensation that the protagonist **most likely** had when he saw the house was

    A. of happiness.
    B. of despair.
    C. of anger.
    D. of jealousy.

READING ASSESSMENT TARGETS: R.2.7, R.3.2, R.3.5, R.4.1/L.4.1, R.4.2/L.4.2, R.4.3/L.4.3, R.5.1, R.5

UNIT 1

1 Review the Skill

Authors use **figurative language** when they compare one thing with something very different in order to explain an idea or create a particular effect. **Similes** make comparisons using key words such as *like* or *as*. **Metaphors** make the same type of comparison but omit the key words. **Analogies** are longer, or extended, comparisons.

Authors use other kinds of figurative language as well. **Hyperbole** is extreme exaggeration. **Personification** gives human qualities to an animal, inanimate object, or element in nature. **Onomatopoeia** uses words that create the sounds they describe, such as *whish* or *buzz*.

2 Refine the Skill

By refining the skill of interpreting figurative language, you will improve your study and test-taking abilities, especially as they relate to the GED® Reasoning Through Language Arts test. Read the passage below. Then answer the questions that follow.

DENCOMBE'S ILLNESS

a In this description, objects are given human qualities. The **bench looked to the south**, and the **hill has a sloping shoulder**.

b Here, the *abyss of human illusion* is a metaphor meaning that the speaker's ability to fool himself is as great as the ocean's depths.

The April day was soft and bright, and poor Dencombe, happy in the conceit of reasserted strength, stood in the garden. . . . The sociable country postman, passing through the garden, had just given him a small parcel which he took out with him, leaving the hotel to the right and creeping to a bench he had already haunted, a safe recess in the cliff. It looked to the south, to the tinted walls of the Island, and was protected behind by the sloping shoulder of the down. He was tired enough when he reached it, and for a moment was disappointed; he was better, of course, but better, after all, than what? He should never again, as at one or two great moments of the past, be better than himself. The infinite of life was gone, and what remained of the dose a small glass scored like a thermometer by the apothecary. He sat and stared at the sea, which appeared all surface and twinkle, far shallower than the spirit of man. It was the abyss of human illusion that was the real, the tideless deep.

From THE MIDDLE YEARS by Henry James

1. The narrator compares Dencombe's remaining life to "the dose of a small glass scored like a thermometer by the apothecary" to

    A. indicate the brief time that Dencombe has left to live.
    B. reassure Dencombe that his medicine works.
    C. show that the sea is shallower than it appears to be.
    D. prove that the thermometer Dencombe uses is accurate.

2. The comparison of the spirit of man with the sea means that

    A. Dencombe has vast and deep thoughts about life.
    B. the human spirit is of depths greater than the depth of the ocean.
    C. Dencombe's ability to fool himself is shallower than the ocean.
    D. the human spirit is shallow and superficial.

CONTENT TOPICS

Figurative language is not limited to fiction. Much nonfiction writing contains similes, metaphors, and analogies to explain information, to describe places, or simply to make the writing more enjoyable.

DIRECTIONS: Read the passage, read each question, and choose the **best** answer.

A STORMY NIGHT

1   The bareness of Mrs. Pearce's front room was fully displayed at ten o'clock at night when a powerful oil lamp stood on the middle of the table. The harsh light fell on the garden; cut straight across the lawn; lit up a child's bucket and a purple aster and reached the hedge. Mrs. Flanders had left her sewing on the table. There were her large reels of white cotton and her steel spectacles; her needle-case; her brown wool wound round an old postcard. There were the bulrushes and the Strand magazines; and the linoleum sandy from the boys' boots. A daddy-long-legs shot from corner to corner and hit the lamp globe. The wind blew straight dashes of rain across the window, which flashed silver as they passed through the light. A single leaf tapped hurriedly, persistently, upon the glass. There was a hurricane out at sea.

2   Archer could not sleep.

3   Mrs. Flanders stooped over him. "Think of the fairies," said Betty Flanders. "Think of the lovely, lovely birds settling down on their nests. Now shut your eyes and see the old mother bird with a worm in her beak. Now turn and shut your eyes," she murmured, "and shut your eyes."

4   The lodging-house seemed full of gurgling and rushing; the cistern overflowing; water bubbling and squeaking and running along the pipes and streaming down the windows. . . .

5   "I thought he'd never get off—such a hurricane," she whispered to Rebecca, who was bending over a spirit-lamp in the small room next door. The wind rushed outside, but the small flame of the spirit-lamp burnt quietly, shaded from the cot by a book stood on edge.

6   "Did he take his bottle well?" Mrs. Flanders whispered, and Rebecca nodded and went to the cot and turned down the quilt, and Mrs. Flanders bent over and looked anxiously at the baby, asleep, but frowning. The window shook, and Rebecca stole like a cat and wedged it.

7   The two women murmured over the spirit-lamp, plotting the eternal conspiracy of hush and clean bottles while the wind raged and gave a sudden wrench at the cheap fastenings.

From JACOB'S ROOM by Virginia Woolf

3. In paragraph 1, a leaf "tapped hurriedly, persistently, upon the glass." This is an example of

   A. metaphor.
   B. hyperbole.
   C. personification.
   D. onomatopoeia.

4. Which sentence from the passage includes onomatopoeia?

   A. "Think of the lovely, lovely birds settling down on their nests."
   B. "The lodging-house seemed full of gurgling and rushing; the cistern overflowing; water bubbling and squeaking and running along the pipes and streaming down the windows."
   C. "The wind rushed outside, but the small flame of the spirit-lamp burnt quietly, shaded from the cot by a book stood on edge."
   D. ". . . Mrs. Flanders bent over and looked anxiously at the baby, asleep, but frowning."

5. In paragraph 6, "Rebecca stole like a cat" to the window. This simile implies that Rebecca

   A. moved loudly, unconcerned about waking the child.
   B. moved quickly and quietly, with care not to wake the child.
   C. moved to take someone's else spot.
   D. moved to gain attention.

6. Which sentence from the passage includes an example of personification?

   A. "The harsh light fell on the garden; cut straight across the lawn;"
   B. "A daddy-long-legs shot from corner to corner and hit the lamp globe."
   C. "The wind blew straight dashes of rain across the window, which flashed silver as they passed through the light."
   D. ". . . the wind raged and gave a sudden wrench at the cheap fastenings."

DIRECTIONS: Read the passages, read each question, and choose the **best** answer.

MEG'S WEDDING DAY

1   "You do look just like our own dear Meg, only so very sweet and lovely that I should hug you if it wouldn't crumple your dress," cried Amy, surveying her with delight when all was done.

2   "Then I am satisfied. But please hug and kiss me, everyone, and don't mind my dress. I want a great many crumples of this sort put into it today," and Meg opened her arms to her sisters, who clung about her . . . feeling that the new love had not changed the old.

3   "Now I'm going to tie John's cravat for him, and then to stay a few minutes with Father quietly in the study," and Meg ran down to perform these little ceremonies, and then to follow her mother wherever she went, conscious that in spite of the smiles on the motherly face, there was a secret sorrow hid in the motherly heart at the flight of the first bird from the nest. . . .

JO'S LIFE AT PLUMFIELD

4   It never was a fashionable school . . . but it was just what Jo intended it to be—"a happy, homelike place for boys, who needed teaching, care, and kindness." Every room in the big house was soon full. . . . She had boys enough now, and did not tire of them, though they were not angels, by any means, and some of them caused . . . trouble and anxiety. But her faith in the good spot which exists in the heart . . . gave her patience, skill, and in time success, for no mortal boy could hold out long with [the Professor] shining on him as benevolently as the sun, and [Jo] forgiving him seventy times seven. Very precious to Jo was the friendship of the lads. . . .

5   Yes, Jo was a very happy woman there, in spite of hard work, much anxiety, and a perpetual racket. She enjoyed it heartily and found the applause of her boys more satisfying than any praise of the world, for now she told no stories except to her flock of enthusiastic believers and admirers. As the years went on, two little lads of her own came to increase her happiness—Rob, named for Grandpa, and Teddy, a happy-go-lucky baby, who seemed to have inherited his papa's sunshiny temper as well as his mother's lively spirit. How they ever grew up alive in that whirlpool of boys was a mystery to their grandma and aunts, but they flourished like dandelions in spring. . . .

From LITTLE WOMEN by Louisa May Alcott

7. Meg's statement "I want a great many crumples of this sort put into it today" means that Meg

    A. does not care whether her dress gets wrinkled.
    B. cares more about love than about a wrinkled dress.
    C. is concerned because she looks different in her wedding dress.
    D. would rather stay with her sisters than get married.

8. The comparison in paragraph 3 indicates that Meg's mother

    A. smiles but secretly disapproves of the man Meg will marry.
    B. fears that Meg will not attend to the birds in the garden.
    C. worries about the family's finances after Meg marries.
    D. shows joy mixed with sorrow because her first child is leaving.

9. In paragraph 4, the narrator says, "no mortal boy could hold out long with [the Professor] shining on him as benevolently as the sun, and [Jo] forgiving him seventy times seven." Which statement **best** explains the hyperbole?

    A. The Professor and Jo treat the boys with a great deal of kindness and patience.
    B. Troubled boys do well at Plumfield because of its strict behavior standards and academic focus.
    C. Plumfield emphasizes permissiveness and shows little attention to academic standards.
    D. The Professor is providing little academic training, and Jo is losing patience.

10. What does the metaphor "whirlpool of boys" suggest?

    A. a group of boys at the beach
    B. boys studying the movement of water
    C. the boys' constant motion and activity
    D. the movement of a top or spinning toy

11. The comparison of the boys flourishing "like dandelions in spring" shows that the boys

    A. are growing fast and constantly.
    B. help keep the lawns under control.
    C. enjoy playing outdoors in the spring.
    D. prefer wildflowers to cultivated gardens.

DIRECTIONS: Read the passage, read each question, and choose the **best** answer.

SENTENCED TO DEATH

The narrator has been sentenced to death by the judges of the Inquisition.

1 I WAS sick—sick unto death with that long agony; and when they at length unbound me, and I was permitted to sit, I felt that my senses were leaving me. The sentence—the dread sentence of death—was the last of distinct accentuation which reached my ears. After that, the sound of the inquisitorial voices seemed merged in one dreamy indeterminate hum. It conveyed to my soul the idea of revolution— perhaps from its association . . . with the burr of a mill wheel. This only for a brief period; for presently I heard no more. Yet, for a while, I saw; but with how terrible an exaggeration! I saw the lips of the black-robed judges. They appeared to me white—whiter than the sheet [of paper] upon which I trace these words. . . . I saw them fashion the syllables of my name; and I shuddered because no sound succeeded. I saw, too, for a few moments of delirious horror, the soft and nearly imperceptible waving of the sable draperies which enwrapped the walls of the apartment. And then my vision fell upon the seven tall candles upon the table. At first they wore the aspect of charity, and seemed white and slender angels who would save me; but then, all at once, there came a most deadly nausea over my spirit, and I felt every fiber in my frame thrill as if I had touched the wire of a . . . battery, while the angel forms became meaningless specters, with heads of flame, and I saw that from them there would be no help. And then there stole into my fancy, like a rich musical note, the thought of what sweet rest there must be in the grave. The thought came gently and stealthily, and it seemed long before it attained full appreciation; but just as my spirit came at length properly to feel and entertain it, the figures of the judges vanished, as if magically, from before me; the tall candles sank into nothingness; their flames went out utterly; the blackness of darkness supervened; all sensations appeared swallowed up in a mad rushing descent as of the soul into Hades. Then silence, and stillness, night were the universe.

2 I had swooned. . . .

From THE PIT AND THE PENDULUM by Edgar Allan Poe

12. The onomatopoeic words **hum** and **burr** near the beginning of the passage help reveal that the narrator

   A. suffers from ringing in his ears.
   B. hears voices as musical notes.
   C. cannot distinguish individual sounds.
   D. is held captive in a mill.

13. Which feeling does the narrator's comparison of the candles with charitable angels **most likely** represent?

   A. warmth
   B. regret
   C. hope
   D. fear

14. When the narrator says that he felt every fiber in his frame thrill as if he had touched the wire of a battery, what does he **most likely** mean?

   A. His dread is causing him physical discomfort.
   B. He is excited to be alive.
   C. The judges have sentenced him to be electrocuted.
   D. His captors have finally unbound him.

15. The thought of death entering the narrator's mind "like a rich musical note" emphasizes that death seems something the narrator **most likely** would

   A. fight against.
   B. welcome with pleasure.
   C. find difficult to understand.
   D. consider a creative act.

16. As the narrator loses consciousness, he compares his fainting spell with a soul's descent into Hades. On the basis of other details in the passage, which sentence **best** describes the effect of this comparison?

   A. It confirms that the narrator deserves to be condemned.
   B. It emphasizes the narrator's hopeless situation.
   C. It foretells the narrator's fiery death.
   D. It suggests that the Inquisition judges are demons.

High Impact Lesson: Figurative Meanings

READING ASSESSMENT TARGET: R.4.1/L.

UNIT 1

1 Review the Skill

Authors use **figurative meanings** to communicate complicated or abstract ideas. **Figurative language** is the use of a word or phrase to represent something other than its denotative, or literal, meaning. A word's figurative meaning might also differ from any connotations, or emotional value, the word might have.

For example, *steel* is a form of metal made from iron and carbon. Depending on the context, the word *steel* can have connotations of being sturdy, strong, or unfeeling. When used figuratively, these connotations may b clearer: *Jordan had eyes of steel*. Jordan does not literally have eyes of steel. This figurative language means Jordan's eyes were steady and did not show emotion.

There are many different forms of figurative language. A **metaphor** directly compares two unlike things. A **simile** compares two unlike things using the words *like* or *as*. **Personification** is giving nonliving things huma feelings, characteristics, or qualities. **Onomatopoeia** is a word or phrase that approximates the sound of a thing. **Imagery** uses words that appeal to the reader's senses to describe something. A **symbol** represents both itself and something else with a deeper meaning. **Irony** uses words to express something that is differen and often the opposite, of its literal meaning. **Sarcasm** is a specific form of verbal irony that is intended to be satirical or hurtful. **Hyperbole** is the use of exaggeration to achieve an effect. **Understatement** is used to represent something as smaller or less intense to achieve an effect. **Idioms** are phrases with meanings that are unconnected to the underlying meaning of its component words. If a figurative meaning is unclear, you car look for context clues in the passage to help find its meaning.

On the GED® Reasoning Through Language Arts test, you will be expected to show you understand figurative meanings. You may encounter questions that ask you to distinguish between a word's figurative meaning and its denotative or connotative meanings.

2 Refine the Skill

a This passage uses figurative language in different ways. The first sentence states, "Jurgis talked lightly about work." The phrase *talked lightly* is an idiom that means he spoke of work without any seriousness.

b The second sentence contains another idiom: *make flesh creep*. For readers who are unfamiliar with its meaning, it is important to look at the rest of the sentence for context clues.

Scan the paragraph for the phrase. It is used to describe how people react to hearing these stories about "the breaking down of men." How might people react to these stories? The correct answer is **C**.

YOUNG AND STRONG

Jurgis talked lightly about work, because he was young. They told him stories about the breaking down of men, there in the stockyards of Chicago, and of what had happened to them afterward—stories to make your flesh creep, but Jurgis would only laugh. He had only been there four months, and he was young, and a giant besides. There was too much health in him. He could not even imagine how it would feel to be beaten. "That is well enough for men like you," he would say, "silpnas[1], puny fellows—but my back is broad."

[1] silpnas—Lithuanian for "weak"

From THE JUNGLE by Upton Sinclair

1. In the second sentence, the author uses the idiom **make your flesh creep**. Which definition **best** matches the figurative meaning of the phrase?

A. to freeze with anger
B. to shake uncontrollably with laughter
C. to shudder with disgust or fear
D. to wince or flinch with pain

DIRECTIONS: Read the passage, read each question, and choose the **best** answer.

ATLANTA

1 South of the North, yet north of the South, lies the City of a Hundred Hills, peering out from the shadows of the past into the promise of the future. I have seen her in the morning, when the first flush of day had half-roused her; she lay gray and still on the crimson soil of Georgia; then the blue smoke began to curl from her chimneys, the tinkle of bell and scream of whistle broke the silence, the rattle and roar of busy life slowly gathered and swelled, until the seething whirl of the city seemed a strange thing in a sleepy land.

2 Once, they say, even Atlanta slept dull and drowsy at the foot-hills of the Alleghanies, until the iron baptism of war awakened her with its sullen waters, aroused and maddened her, and left her listening to the sea. And the sea cried to the hills and the hills answered the sea, till the city rose like a widow and cast away her weeds, and toiled for her daily bread; toiled steadily, toiled cunningly,—perhaps with some bitterness, with a touch, of réclame[1],—and yet with real earnestness, and real sweat.

3 It is a hard thing to live haunted by the ghost of an untrue dream; to see the wide vision of empire fade into real ashes and dirt; to feel the pang of the conquered, and yet know that with all the Bad that fell on one black day, something was vanquished that deserved to live, something killed that in justice had not dared to die; to know that with the Right that triumphed, triumphed something of Wrong, something sordid and mean, something less than the broadest and best. All this is bitter hard; and many a man and city and people have found in it excuse for sulking, and brooding, and listless waiting.

4 Such are not men of the sturdier make; they of Atlanta turned resolutely toward the future; and that future held aloft vistas of purple and gold:— Atlanta, Queen of the cotton kingdom; Atlanta, Gateway to the Land of the Sun; Atlanta, the new Lachesis, spinner of web and woof for the world.

[1]réclame: dramatization

From THE SOULS OF BLACK FOLK by W.E.B. Du Bois

2. How does the use of personification in the passage support the author's purpose?

   A. Describing the city as "peering out" creates a sense of foreboding or fear.
   B. Attributing human-like qualities to Atlanta makes the complicated city easier to relate to.
   C. Describing the city as "a sleepy land" emphasizes that not much happens there.
   D. Comparing Atlanta to a queen implies that people who live there are wealthy and powerful.

3. In paragraph 1, the author writes **the tinkle of bell and scream of whistle**. How would the tone of this sentence change if he had used the phrase **noises broke the silence**?

   A. The tone would be less humorous.
   B. The tone would be more descriptive.
   C. The noisy tone would become quieter.
   D. The expressive tone would become plain.

4. In paragraph 2, the author uses the simile **the city rose like a widow**. Which statement **best** matches the figurative meaning of the phrase?

   A. The survivors continued their lives after the war.
   B. The survivors wore black clothing and mourned.
   C. The city increased its elevation.
   D. The city opened itself to outsiders.

5. In paragraph 3, the author uses the phrase **the ghost of an untrue dream**. Which of the following **best** matches the figurative meaning of the phrase?

   A. the survivors who were covered in ash
   B. the smoke from the buildings that were burned
   C. the spirits of soldiers who died in the war
   D. the memory of an idea that proved wrong

6. What does the use of the phrase **Such are not men of the sturdier make** in paragraph 4 reveal about the author's point of view about Atlanta's citizens?

   A. The author uses sarcasm to explain the people of Atlanta.
   B. The author accurately describes the men of Atlanta as unsteady.
   C. The author contrasts the imagery of weakness with the strength he sees in Atlanta.
   D. The author associates Atlanta losing the war with weakness.

Determine Narrative Point of View

Use with *Student Book* pp. 64–65

READING ASSESSMENT TARGETS: R.2.7, R.2.8, R.3.2, R.3.3, R.3.5, R.5.1, R.

UNIT 1

1 Review the Skill

Any story is shaped by the ==narrator,== or person who tells it. The narrator's ==point of view== determines the perspective readers will have on events. A **limited** third-person narrator can share only one character's thoughts and feelings. An ==omniscient== third-person narrator can share all or most of the characters' thoughts and feelings. A ==first-person== narrator provides only a partial view of events—the way he or she sees or interprets them. Analyzing the point of view of a story will help you identify who is telling a story and how the narrator's method of story-telling affects a tale.

2 Refine the Skill

By refining the skill of determining point of view in fiction, you will improve your study and test-taking abilities, especially as they relate to the GED® Reasoning Through Language Arts test. Read the passage below. Then answer the questions that follow.

ON THE GALLOWS

a The narrator's language is detached, describing the scene as an observer might. This objectivity is likely to indicate that the story is told by an omniscient narrator.

b A first-person narrator also could describe all the details, but they would be based on the narrator's perceptions of them.

A man stood upon a railroad bridge in northern Alabama, looking down into the swift water twenty feet below. The man's hands were tied behind his back, the wrists bound with a cord. A rope closely encircled his neck. It was attached to a stout cross-timber above his head and the slack fell to the level of his knees. Some loose boards laid upon the ties supporting the rails of the railway supplied a footing for him and his executioners—two private soldiers of the Federal army, directed by a sergeant who in civil life may have been a deputy sheriff. At a short remove [distance] upon the same temporary platform was an officer in the uniform of his rank, armed. He was a captain. A sentinel at each end of the bridge stood with his rifle in a position known as "support," that is to say, vertical in front of the left shoulder, the hammer resting on the forearm thrown straight across the chest—a formal and unnatural position, enforcing an erect carriage of the body. It did not appear to be the duty of these two men to know what was occurring at the center of the bridge; they merely blockaded the two ends of the foot planking that traversed it.

From AN OCCURRENCE AT OWL CREEK BRIDGE by Ambrose Bierce

1. In this passage, the narrator provides information about

   A. what characters think.
   B. how characters feel.
   C. why events are taking place.
   D. what the scene looks like.

2. If the man about to be executed were describing this scene, he **most likely** would include

   A. the sentinels' feelings about executions.
   B. his own thoughts and feelings about his situation.
   C. the executioners' feelings about their task.
   D. the captain's thoughts about the event.

TEST-TAKING TIPS

A first-person narrator uses the pronoun *I* to tell the story. A third-person narrator uses the pronouns *he, she,* and *they* to tell the story.

Master the Skill

DIRECTIONS: Read the passage, read each question, and choose the **best** answer.

THE GIRLS RECEIVE PRESENTS

1   Jo was the first to wake in the gray dawn of Christmas morning. No stockings hung at the fireplace, and for a moment she felt as much disappointed as she did long ago, when her little sock fell down because it was crammed so full of goodies. Then she remembered her mother's promise and, slipping her hand under her pillow, drew out a little crimson-covered book. She knew it very well, for it was that beautiful old story of the best life ever lived, and Jo felt that it was a true guidebook for any pilgrim going on a long journey. She woke Meg with a "Merry Christmas," and bade her see what was under her pillow. A green-covered book appeared, with the same picture inside, and a few words written by their mother, which made their one present very precious in their eyes. Presently Beth and Amy woke to rummage and find their little books also, one dove-colored, the other blue, and all sat looking at and talking about them, while the east grew rosy with the coming day.

2   In spite of her small vanities, Margaret had a sweet and pious nature, which unconsciously influenced her sisters, especially Jo, who loved her very tenderly, and obeyed her because her advice was so gently given.

3   "Girls," said Meg seriously, looking from the tumbled head beside her to the two little night-capped ones in the room beyond, "Mother wants us to read and love and mind these books, and we must begin at once. We must be faithful about it, but since Father went away and all this war trouble unsettled us, we have neglected many things. You can do as you please, but I shall keep my book on the table here and read a little every morning as soon as I wake, for I know it will do me good and help me through the day."

From LITTLE WOMEN by Louisa May Alcott

3. The narrator in the passage knows that Jo is disappointed about the lack of presents and that Meg [Margaret] has "a sweet and pious nature" (paragraph 2). The narrator in the story is

A. Jo.
B. Meg.
C. omniscient.
D. first-person.

4. Meg [Margaret] is described as having "small vanities" (paragraph 2). According to the passage, who has this perspective about Meg?

A. the narrator
B. Jo
C. Meg's mother
D. Beth

5. By using this point of view, the author **most likely** intended to

A. provide insight into the reading habits of girls in the 1800s.
B. analyze the girls' reactions to their Christmas gifts.
C. reveal Jo's despair at the family's lack of money.
D. present the thoughts of all the characters.

6. In the last line of the excerpt, Meg says, "I shall keep my book on the table here and read a little every morning . . . for I know it will do me good." How does this statement support the narrator's point of view about Meg?

A. Meg's statement shows that she has small vanities as the narrator has described.
B. Meg's statement shows that Meg is no longer disappointed.
C. Meg's statement shows that she is sweet and pious, as the narrator has described.
D. Meg's statement shows her feeling that the book is a true guidebook.

DEXTER AND THE GIRL

1 Dexter knew that there was something dismal about this Northern spring, just as he knew there was something gorgeous about the fall. Fall made him clinch his hands and tremble and repeat idiotic sentences to himself, and make brisk abrupt gestures of command to imaginary audiences and armies. October filled him with hope which November raised to a sort of ecstatic triumph, and in this mood the fleeting brilliant impressions of the summer at Sherry Island were ready grist to his mill. . . .

2 And one day it came to pass that Mr. Jones—himself and not his ghost—came up to Dexter with tears in his eyes and said that Dexter was the—best caddy in the club, and wouldn't he decide not to quit if Mr. Jones made it worth his while, because every other—caddy in the club lost one ball a hole for him—regularly.

3 "No, sir," said Dexter decisively, "I don't want to caddy any more." Then, after a pause: "I'm too old."

4 "You're not more than fourteen."

5 . . . The little girl who had done this was eleven—beautifully ugly as little girls are apt to be who are destined after a few years to be inexpressibly lovely and bring no end of misery to a great number of men. The spark, however, was perceptible. There was a general ungodliness in the way her lips twisted down at the corners when she smiled, and in the—Heaven help us!—in the almost passionate quality of her eyes. Vitality is born early in such women. It was utterly in evidence now, shining through her thin frame in a sort of glow.

6 She had come eagerly out onto the course at nine o'clock with a white linen nurse and five small new golf clubs in a white canvas bag which the nurse was carrying. When Dexter first saw her she was standing by the caddie house, rather ill at ease and trying to conceal the fact by engaging her nurse in an obviously unnatural conversation graced by startling and irrelevant grimaces from herself.

7 "Well, it's certainly a nice day, Hilda," Dexter heard her say. She drew down the corners of her mouth, smiled, and glanced furtively around. . . .

8 The smile again—radiant, blatantly artificial—convincing.

9 "I don't know what we're supposed to do now," said the nurse, looking nowhere in particular.

10 "Oh, that's all right. I'll fix it up."

11 Dexter stood perfectly still, his mouth slightly ajar. He knew that if he moved forward a step his stare would be in her line of vision—if he moved backward he would lose his full view of her face. For a moment he had not realized how young she was. Now he remembered having seen her several times the year before—in bloomers.

From WINTER DREAMS by F. Scott Fitzgerald

7. In this passage, the narrator provides information about

A. what Dexter thinks and feels.
B. what the girl thinks and feels.
C. what Hilda thinks and feels.
D. what Mr. Jones thinks and feels.

8. The little girl is described as "beautifully ugly as little girls are apt to be who are destined after a few years to be inexpressibly lovely and bring no end of misery to a great number of men." Who has this perspective about the little girl?

A. Hilda
B. Dexter
C. Mr. Jones
D. the narrator

9. In the excerpt, the little girl's smile is "radiant, blatantly artificial—convincing" (paragraph 8). This description indicates that the narrator

A. knows only the thoughts of the nurse.
B. knows the girl's thoughts.
C. can describe the girl's actions, not her feelings.
D. will describe the girl sympathetically.

10. If Dexter were the narrator of this passage, he would

A. be unable to overhear the girl talking.
B. use the pronouns *she* and *he* to describe the girl and himself.
C. use the pronoun *I* to describe his feelings.
D. be able to hear all of the conversation between the girl and the nurse.

DIRECTIONS: Read the passage, read each question, and choose the **best** answer.

A ROTTEN DRIVER

1   At first I was flattered to go places with [Jordan Baker], because she was a golf champion, and everyone knew her name. Then it was something more. I wasn't actually in love, but I felt a sort of tender curiosity. The bored haughty face that she turned to the world concealed something—most affectations conceal something eventually, even though they don't in the beginning—and one day I found what it was. When we were on a house-party together up in Warwick, she left a borrowed car out in the rain with the top down, and then lied about it—and suddenly I remembered the story about her that had eluded me that night at Daisy's. At her first big golf tournament there was a row that nearly reached the newspapers— a suggestion that she had moved her ball from a bad lie in the semifinal round. The thing approached the proportions of a scandal—then died away. A caddy retracted his statement, and the only other witness admitted that he might have been mistaken. The incident and the name had remained together in my mind.

2   Jordan Baker instinctively avoided clever, shrewd men, and now I saw that this was because she felt safer on a plane where any divergence from a code would be thought impossible. She was incurably dishonest. . . .

3   It was on that same house-party that we had a curious conversation about driving a car. It started because she passed so close to some workmen that our fender flicked a button on one man's coat.

4   "You're a rotten driver," I protested. "Either you ought to be more careful, or you oughtn't to drive at all."

5   "I am careful."

6   "No, you're not."

7   "Well, other people are," she said lightly.

8   "What's that got to do with it?"

9   "They'll keep out of my way," she insisted. "It takes two to make an accident."

10   "Suppose you met somebody just as careless as yourself."

11   "I hope I never will," she answered. "I hate careless people. That's why I like you."

12   Her grey, sun-strained eyes stared straight ahead, but she had deliberately shifted our relations, and for a moment I thought I loved her. But I am slow-thinking and full of interior rules that act as brakes on my desires, and I knew that first I had to get myself definitely out of that tangle back home. I'd been writing letters once a week and signing them: "Love, Nick," and all I could think of was how, when that certain girl played tennis, a faint mustache of perspiration appeared on her upper lip. Nevertheless there was a vague understanding that had to be tactfully broken off before I was free.

13   Everyone suspects himself of at least one of the cardinal virtues, and this is mine: I am one of the few honest people that I have ever known.

From THE GREAT GATSBY by F. Scott Fitzgerald

11. The story is told from a

A. first-person point of view.
B. second-person point of view.
C. limited third-person point of view.
D. omniscient third-person point of view.

12. Jordan Baker's thoughts and actions are revealed through

A. the other characters.
B. Jordan Baker herself.
C. Daisy.
D. the narrator.

13. Paragraph 12 includes the statement "But I am slow-thinking and full of interior rules that act as brakes on my desires . . ." What does this quotation reveal about Nick?

A. He expects others to follow rules.
B. He falls in and out of love quickly.
C. He does not like to lie to others.
D. He does not value honesty.

14. Which of the narrator's qualities does the point of view emphasize?

A. honesty
B. experience
C. cynicism
D. carelessness

Make Inferences in Fiction

Use with **Student Book** pp. 66–67

READING ASSESSMENT TARGETS: R.2.7, R.3.2, R.3.3, R.3.4, R.

UNIT 1

1 Review the Skill

Making **inferences** requires readers to look for suggestions, or small details, that provide clues about events, characters, or other elements in a story. These small details may give information about the story's setting, for example, or about a character's background or motives. By making inferences, you can better understand a character, situation, and other parts of the story that are not explicitly stated.

2 Refine the Skill

By refining the skill of making inferences in fiction, you will improve your study and test-taking abilities, especially as they relate to the GED® Reasoning Through Language Arts test. Read the passage below. Then answer the questions that follow.

a The details about Sarah Penn indicate that she has been obedient and accepting during her marriage. You can infer that she talks plainly now because she has lost patience.

b From Sarah's comments about the condition of the room and from her comparison with other people's homes, you can infer that Sarah has lost patience with her husband's stinginess.

MOTHER IS UPSET

"Now father, look here"—Sarah Penn had not sat down; she stood before her husband in the humble fashion of a Scripture woman—"I'm going to talk real plain to you; I never have sence I married you, but I'm goin' to now. I ain't never complained, an' I ain't goin' to complain now, but I'm goin' to talk plain. You see this room here, father, you look at it well. You see there ain't no carpet on the floor, an' you see the paper is all dirty and droppin' off the walls. We ain't had no new paper on it for ten year, an' then I put it on myself, an' it didn't cost you but nine-pence a roll. You see this room, father; it's all the one I've had to work in an' eat in an' sit in sence we was married. There ain't another woman in the whole town whose husband ain't got half the means you have but what's got better. It's all the room Nanny's got to have her company in, an' there ain't one of her mates but what's got better, an' their father's not so able as hers is. It's all the room she'll have to be married in. . . . Father, ain't you got nothin' to say?" said Mrs. Penn.

"I've got to go off after that load of gravel. I can't stan' here talkin' all day."

From THE REVOLT OF MOTHER by Mary E. Wilkins

1. What is the **most** logical inference to make about Sarah's eagerness to improve the condition of her home?

   A. Her daughter will be married in the room.
   B. Sarah feels cold without a carpet on the floor.
   C. Her husband will be more comfortable in improved surroundings.
   D. She has complained about it for years and wants to take action now.

2. The **most** logical inference about Sarah's husband is that he

   A. likes to entertain friends.
   B. is reluctant to spend money.
   C. earns barely enough to live on.
   D. is willing to discuss problems.

TEST-TAKING TIPS

Look for evidence of characters' references to events that occurred in the past. These clues often can help explain conflicts that take place in the present.

DIRECTIONS: Read the passage, read each question, and choose the **best** answer.

EDIE HAS TEA WITH THE CHILDREN

1   In the middle of an April night in 1919, a plain woman named Edith Fisk, lifted from England to California on a tide of world peace, arrived at the Ransom house to raise five half-orphaned children.

2   A few hours later, at seven in the morning, this Edith, more widely called Edie, invited the three eldest to her room for tea. They were James, seven; Eliza, six; and Jenny, four. Being handed cups of tea, no matter how reduced by milk, made them believe that they had grown up overnight.

3   "Have some sugar," said Edie, and spooned it in. Moments later she said. "Have another cup." But her h's went unspoken and became the first of hundreds, then thousands, which would accumulate in the corners of the house and thicken in the air like sighs.

4   In an adjoining room the twins, entirely responsible for their mother's death, had finished their bottles and fallen back into guiltless sleep. At the far end of the house, the widower, Thomas Ransom, who had spent the night aching for his truant wife, lay across his bed, half awake, half asleep, and dreaming.

From EDIE: A LIFE by Harriet Doerr, © 1995

3.   Which is the **most likely** inference to make about Edie?

   A. She is from England.
   B. She is from California.
   C. She dislikes tea.
   D. She dislikes children.

4.   Based on paragraph 2, what inference can be made about being invited to tea?

   A. The children were summoned to tea because there was trouble.
   B. The children felt an invitation to tea was a sign they were being treated like adults.
   C. The children did not enjoy tea, so milk was added to their cups.
   D. The children were nervous to meet Edie.

5.   On the basis of the information in the passage, what **most likely** has happened to Mrs. Ransom? She has

   A. moved to England.
   B. abandoned her children.
   C. died in childbirth.
   D. divorced her husband.

6.   From the description of Edie in the passage, which is the **best** inference about her character? Edie is

   A. desperate for attention.
   B. annoyed and bored.
   C. stricken with grief.
   D. kind and capable.

7.   What might Edie's relationship be to the Ransom family?

   A. She is most likely the children's aunt who has come to raise them.
   B. She is most likely the children's grandmother who has come to raise them.
   C. She is most likely a governess, or nanny, who has been hired to help raise the children.
   D. She is most likely Mr. Ransom's new wife.

8.   Which is the **most likely** inference to make about Mr. Ransom's emotional state?

   A. The five children exhaust him.
   B. He is stricken with grief.
   C. New responsibilities overwhelm him.
   D. His dreams comfort him.

9.   Which situation is **most** like the situation in this passage?

   A A mother-in-law arrives for a summer visit.
   B. A niece lives with her aunt while attending school.
   C. A grandfather teaches his grandchildren to play chess.
   D. A grandmother arrives to help care for a newborn.

DIRECTIONS: Read the passage, read each question, and choose the **best** answer.

A BRIEF FRIENDSHIP

1 ". . . No one living can remember seeing a Znaeym [Georg] and a von Gradwitz [Ulrich] talking to one another in friendship. And what peace there would be among the forester folk if we ended our feud tonight. And if we choose to make peace among our people, there is none other to interfere, no interlopers from outside. . . ."

2 For a space both men were silent, turning over in their minds the wonderful changes that this dramatic reconciliation would bring about. In the cold, gloomy forest, with the wind tearing in fitful gusts through the naked branches and whistling around the tree trunks, they lay and waited for the help that would now bring release and succor to both parties. . . .

3 "Let's shout for help," he [Ulrich] said; "in this lull our voices may carry a little way."

4 "They won't carry far through the trees and undergrowth," said Georg, "but we can try. Together, then."

5 The two raised their voices in a prolonged hunting call.

6 "Together again," said Ulrich a few minutes later, after listening in vain for an answer halloo.

7 "I heard something that time, I think," said Ulrich.

8 "I heard nothing but the pestilential wind," said Georg hoarsely.

9 There was silence again for some minutes, and then Ulrich gave a joyful cry. "I can see figures coming through the wood. They are following in the way I came down the hillside."

10 Both men raised their voices in as loud a shout as they could muster.

11 "They hear us! They've stopped. Now they see us. They're running down the hill towards us," cried Ulrich.

12 "How many of them are there?" asked Georg.

13 "I can't see distinctly," said Ulrich; "nine or ten."

14 "Then they are yours," said Georg; "I had only seven out with me."

15 "They are making all the speed they can, brave lads," said Ulrich gladly.

16 "Are they your men?" asked Georg. "Are they your men?"

17 "No," said Ulrich with a laugh, the idiotic chattering laugh of a man unstrung with hideous fear.

18 "Who are they?" asked Georg quickly, straining to see what the other would gladly not have seen.

19 "Wolves."

From THE INTERLOPERS by Saki

10. What is the **most** logical inference to make about the relationship between Ulrich and Georg?

   A. They have been good friends for many years.
   B. Their families have long been enemies.
   C. Their families have been business associates.
   D. They have been on many adventures together.

11. Ulrich and Georg do not leave the forest because they are probably

   A. cold.
   B. hunting.
   C. injured.
   D. feuding.

12. How do Ulrich and Georg feel about their situation before the wolves appear?

   A. annoyed with their men for lagging behind
   B. thankful for their newfound friendship
   C. angry about the continuing feud
   D. hopeful for a peaceful future

13. Georg tells Ulrich that "there is none other to interfere, no interlopers from outside" to stall the changes to come from their reconciliation. From the information in the passage, you can infer that Georg is incorrect because the men are likely to

   A. break their pact once rescued.
   B. be killed by wolves.
   C. feud with the forester folk.
   D. freeze to death in the forest.

14. Why does Ulrich's joy turn to fear?

   A. Ulrich sees wolves approaching him and Georg.
   B. Georg's men will soon threaten Ulrich.
   C. Ulrich realizes the danger of walking alone in the forest.
   D. Georg believes that they will not be rescued.

DIRECTIONS: Read the passage, read each question, and choose the **best** answer.

A VISIT FROM PAULINE

1   I don't know what to do about my husband's new wife. She won't come in. She sits on the front porch and smokes. She won't knock or ring the bell, and the only way I know she's there at all is because the dog points in the living room. The minute I see Stray standing with one paw up and his tail straight out I say, "Shhh. It's Pauline." I stroke his coarse fur and lean on the broom and we wait. We hear the creak of a board, the click of a purse, a cigarette being lit, a sad, tiny cough. At last I give up and open the door. "Pauline?" The afternoon light hurts my eyes. "Would you like to come in?"

2   "No," says Pauline.

3   Sometimes she sits on the stoop, picking at the paint, and sometimes she sits on the edge of an empty planter box. Today she's perched on the railing. She frowns when she sees me and lifts her small chin. She wears the same black velvet jacket she always wears, the same formal silk blouse, the same huge dark glasses. "Just passing by," she explains.

4   I nod. Pauline lives thirty miles to the east, in the city, with Konrad. "Passing by" would take her one toll bridge, one freeway, and two backcountry roads from their flat. But lies are the least of our problems, Pauline's and mine, so I nod again, bunch my bathrobe a little tighter around my waist, try to cover one bare foot with the other, and repeat my invitation. She shakes her head so vigorously the railing lurches. "Konrad," she says in her high young voice, "expects me. You know how he is."

From PIE DANCE by Molly Giles, © 1985

15. How does the narrator know that Pauline is on her porch?

   A. The narrator hears a creaking board on the porch.
   B. The narrator sees her dog "pointing" at the front door.
   C. The narrator smells the cigarette smoke.
   D. The narrator hears her coughing.

16. The narrator describes Pauline as having a "high young voice." What does this imply about Pauline?

   A. Pauline annoys the narrator.
   B. Pauline is lying to the narrator.
   C. Pauline is younger than the narrator.
   D. Pauline considers herself better than the narrator.

17. Based on the details in the passage, who is Konrad?

   A. the narrator's dog
   B. the narrator's brother
   C. the narrator's neighbor
   D. the narrator's ex-husband

18. Based on the narrator's tone and actions, what is the **most** logical inference about how the narrator feels about Pauline's visits?

   A. She is concerned about Pauline.
   B. She is jealous of Pauline.
   C. She is amused by Pauline.
   D. She is angry at Pauline.

19. Pauline says of Konrad, "You know how he is," and the narrator understands. The **most** logical inference to make from this statement is that

   A. Konrad is patient and understanding.
   B. Konrad is rich and hard-working.
   C. Konrad is loving and supportive.
   D. Konrad is demanding or difficult.

20. Based on the details in the passage, what can you infer about Pauline's visits?

   A. This is the first time Pauline has visited the narrator in the morning.
   B. This is the first time Pauline has visited the narrator.
   C. Pauline has visited the narrator more than once.
   D. Pauline visits the narrator every night.

22

Identify Theme

Use with **Student Book** pp. 68–69

READING ASSESSMENT TARGETS: R.2.6, R.2.7, R.3.3, R.3.5, R.4.3/L.4.3, R.5.1, R.

1 **Review the Skill**

The **theme** of a story is an idea about the world we live in or about life in general. Themes usually are not stated explicitly; they must be inferred from the details and clues included in the story. A story's theme usually can be expressed in a short statement.

Think of the story "The Ugly Duckling." A baby bird is left on its own and believes it is a duck, although other ducks see it as different and unappealing. At the end of the story, the "duckling" grows up to be a beautiful swan. The theme of this story could be stated as *Do not judge others on their appearances*.

2 **Refine the Skill**

By refining the skill of identifying a story's theme, you will improve your study and test-taking abilities, especially as they relate to the GED® Reasoning Through Language Arts test. Read the passage below. Then answer the questions that follow.

PLAYING IN WINTER

a At the beginning of the passage, the narrator describes the scene. The descriptions give readers a sense of how the children live.

b The narrator describes the children's activities and the different ways that the children play together, despite the cold weather.

When the short days of winter came dusk fell before we had well eaten our dinners. When we met in the street the houses had grown sombre. The space of sky above us was the colour of ever-changing violet and towards it the lamps of the street lifted their feeble lanterns. The cold air stung us and we played till our bodies glowed. Our shouts echoed in the silent street. The career of our play brought us through the dark muddy lanes behind the houses where we ran the gauntlet of the rough tribes from the cottages, to the back doors of the dark dripping gardens where odours arose from the ashpits, to the dark odorous stables where a coachman smoothed and combed the horse or shook music from the buckled harness. When we returned to the street light from the kitchen windows had filled the areas. If my uncle was seen turning the corner we hid in the shadow until we had seen him safely housed.

From ARABY by James Joyce

1. Which sentence **best** states the theme of the passage?

   A. Children are able to find ways to have fun in different situations.
   B. Cold winter air is bad for gardens.
   C. It is dangerous for children to hide from their relatives.
   D. The winter is bleak and unappealing to city dwellers.

2. Which sentence from the passage **best** supports the theme?

   A. "When the short days of winter came dusk fell before we had well eaten our dinners."
   B. "When we met in the street the houses had grown sombre."
   C. "The cold air stung us and we played till our bodies glowed."
   D. "If my uncle was seen turning the corner we hid in the shadow until we had seen him safely housed."

TEST-TAKING TIPS

Look for details that contribute to a larger idea. These details may be descriptions, actions, thoughts, or words. Narrators often reveal significant thematic clues.

UNIT 1

DIRECTIONS: Read the passage, read each question, and choose the **best** answer.

RAY'S THOUGHTS ABOUT UNFAIRNESS

1   The beauty of the country about Winesburg was too much for Ray on that fall evening. That is all there was to it. He could not stand it. All of a sudden he forgot all about being a quiet old farmhand and throwing off the torn overcoat began to run across the field. As he ran he shouted a protest against his life, against all life, against everything that makes life ugly. "There was no promise made," he cried into the empty spaces that lay about him. "I didn't promise my Minnie anything and Hal hasn't made any promise to Nell. I know he hasn't. She went into the woods with him because she wanted to go. What he wanted she wanted. Why should I pay? Why should Hal pay? Why should anyone pay? I don't want Hal to become old and worn out. I'll tell him. I won't let it go on. I'll catch Hal before he gets to town and I'll tell him. . . ."

2   Then as he ran he remembered his children and in fancy felt their hands clutching at him. All of his thoughts of himself were involved with the thoughts of Hal and he thought the children were clutching at the younger man also. "They are the accidents of life, Hal," he cried. "They are not mine or yours. I had nothing to do with them."

3   Darkness began to spread over the fields as Ray Pearson ran on and on. His breath came in little sobs. When he came to the fence at the edge of the road and confronted Hal Winters, all dressed up and smoking a pipe as he walked jauntily along, he could not have told what he thought or what he wanted. . . .

4   "You came to tell me, eh?" he said. "Well, never mind telling me anything. I'm not a coward and I've already made up my mind." He laughed again and jumped back across the ditch. "Nell ain't no fool," he said. "She didn't ask me to marry her. I want to marry her. I want to settle down and have kids."

From THE UNTOLD LIE by Sherwood Anderson

3. Which sentence **best** states the theme of the passage?

    A. Even in beautiful country, farm owners treat their employees unfairly.
    B. A hasty marriage often leads to tragedy.
    C. Disappointed people may try to stop others from making similar mistakes.
    D. Good friends will try to help each other when problems arise.

4. Ray asks "Why should I pay?" (paragraph 1). How is Ray's protest related to the theme of the passage? He is protesting against his

    A. responsibilities.
    B. job as a farmhand.
    C. torn overcoat.
    D. brief friendship with Hal.

5. Which detail about Ray **best** supports the theme?

    A. He throws off his torn overcoat.
    B. He runs to catch Hal before he does something with which Ray disagrees.
    C. He enjoys living in a beautiful, peaceful place like Winesburg.
    D. He is a quiet, old farmhand.

6. How is paragraph 1 connected thematically to paragraph 3?

    A. Paragraph 3 summarizes Ray's thoughts and feelings introduced in paragraph 1.
    B. Paragraph 3 describes the landscape of Winesburg.
    C. Paragraph 3 reveals that Ray will not share his thoughts.
    D. Paragraph 3 shows that Hal has fashionable clothing.

7. How does Hal saying that he has already made up his mind reflect the theme of the passage?

    A. While Ray is trying to keep Hal from repeating his mistakes, Hal has already decided not to heed Ray's advice.
    B. Hal has chosen to marry Nell with Ray's blessing.
    C. While Ray is trying to discourage Hal, he is doing so because he is jealous.
    D. Hal believes Ray is unhappy and therefore wants him to be unhappy, too.

DIRECTIONS: Read the passage, read each question, and choose the **best** answer.

AN UPRIGHT TOWN

1   It was many years ago. Hadleyburg was the most honest and upright town in all the region round about. It had kept that reputation unsmirched during three generations, and was prouder of it than of any other of its possessions. It was so proud of it, and so anxious to insure its perpetuation, that it began to teach the principles of honest dealing to its babies in the cradle, and made the like teachings the staple of their culture thenceforward through all the years devoted to their education. . . . The neighbouring towns were jealous of this honourable supremacy, and affected to sneer at Hadleyburg's pride in it and call it vanity; but all the same they were obliged to acknowledge that Hadleyburg was in reality an incorruptible town. . . .

2   But at last, in the drift of time, Hadleyburg had the ill luck to offend a passing stranger—possibly without knowing it, certainly without caring, for Hadleyburg was sufficient unto itself, and cared not a rap for strangers or their opinions. Still, it would have been well to make an exception in this one's case, for he was a bitter man, and revengeful. All through his wanderings during a whole year he kept his injury in mind, and gave all his leisure moments to trying to invent a compensating satisfaction for it. . . . At last he had a fortunate idea, and when it fell into his brain it lit up his whole head with an evil joy. He began to form a plan at once, saying to himself "That is the thing to do—I will corrupt the town."

3   Six months later he went to Hadleyburg, and arrived in a buggy at the house of the old cashier of the bank about ten at night. He got a sack out of the buggy, shouldered it, and staggered with it through the cottage yard, and knocked at the door. A woman's voice said, "Come in," and he entered, and set his sack behind the stove in the parlour, saying politely to the old lady who sat reading the "Missionary Herald" by the lamp:

4   "Pray keep your seat, madam, I will not disturb you. There—now it is pretty well concealed; one would hardly know it was there. . . . I merely wanted to leave that sack in [your husband's]

care, to be delivered to the rightful owner when he shall be found. I am a stranger; he does not know me; I am merely passing through the town to-night to discharge a matter which has been long in my mind. My errand is now completed, and I go pleased and a little proud, and you will never see me again. There is a paper attached to the sack which will explain everything. Good-night, madam."

5   The old lady was afraid of the mysterious big stranger, and was glad to see him go. But her curiosity was roused, and she went straight to the sack and brought away the paper. It began as follows:

6   "TO BE PUBLISHED, or, the right man sought out by private inquiry—either will answer. This sack contains gold coin weighing a hundred and sixty pounds four ounces—"

7   "Mercy on us, and the door not locked!"

From THE MAN THAT CORRUPTED HADLEYBURG by Mark Twain

8. Which sentence **best** states the theme of the passage?

   A. Pride leads to corruption.
   B. Swift revenge is best.
   C. Strangers often make poor judgments about a town.
   D. Honesty must be able to withstand challenges.

9. What does the last sentence imply about the town?

   A. The townspeople distrust all strangers.
   B. The townspeople may not be as honest or upright as claimed.
   C. The town does not have a proper bank.
   D. The town lacks proper funding to maintain buildings.

10. Why did the man seek revenge on Hadleyburg?

   A. He had been offended when passing through Hadleyburg at some time in the past.
   B. He was from a neighboring town and wanted to prove his town was better.
   C. Someone from the town had borrowed money from him and not paid it back.
   D. He grew up there and resented having to learn the principles of honesty.

DIRECTIONS: Read the passage, read each question, and choose the **best** answer.

THE TOY EXPERIMENT

1   "Harvey," said Eleanor Bope, handing her brother a cutting from a London morning paper of the 19th of March, "just read this about children's toys, please; it exactly carries out some of our ideas about influence and upbringing."

2   "At the Children's Welfare Exhibition, the Peace Council will make an alternative suggestion to parents in the shape of an exhibition of 'peace toys,' such as miniature civilians and ploughs."

3   "The idea is certainly an interesting and very well-meaning one," said Harvey; "whether it would succeed well in practice—"

4   "We must try," interrupted his sister; "you are coming down to us at Easter, and you always bring the boys some toys, so that will be an excellent opportunity for you to inaugurate the new experiment. I tire of the toy soldiers and constant battles." . . .

5   "Your uncle has brought you the newest thing in toys," Eleanor had said impressively.

6   "Here is a model of the Manchester branch of the Young Women's Christian Association. This is a municipal dust-bin," said Harvey hurriedly; "you see all the refuse and litter of a town is collected there, instead of lying about and injuring the health of the citizens. That," he said, "is a distinguished civilian, John Stuart Mill. He was an authority on political economy."

7   . . . Peeping in through the doorway, Harvey observed that the municipal dustbin had been pierced with holes to accommodate the muzzles of imaginary cannon, and now represented the principal fortified position in Manchester. . . .

8   "He bleeds dreadfully," exclaimed Bertie, splashing red ink liberally all over the façade of the Association building.

9   "The soldiers rush in and avenge his death with the utmost savagery. A hundred girls are killed . . . and the surviving five hundred are dragged off to the French ships."

10   Harvey stole away from the room and sought out his sister.

11   "Eleanor," he said, "the experiment—"

12   "Yes?"

13   "Has failed. We have begun too late."

Adapted from THE TOYS OF PEACE by Saki

11. How does Harvey feel about peace toys?

    A. He is completely in favor of them.
    B. He is not sure they will succeed.
    C. He thinks they are foolish.
    D. He thinks they will fail.

12. What do the boys do with the peace toys?

    A. They ignore them and play with their other toys.
    B. They eagerly use them as intended.
    C. They turn them into war toys.
    D. They give them away to friends.

13. How does Eleanor Bope feel about toys in general?

    A. She feels that toys should influence a child's ideas.
    B. She feels that toys should be given out only at holidays.
    C. She feels that toys are fun and frivolous.
    D. She feels that toys are a waste of money.

14. Which sentence **best** expresses the theme of the passage?

    A. Keeping up with the latest parenting trends ensures that children will learn important values.
    B. Children will use toys in accordance with their intended purpose.
    C. As children get older, parents are more successful in influencing them with gifts.
    D. Children's views and habits do not instantly change.

LESSON

Draw Conclusions in Fiction

Use with **Student Book** pp. 70–71

READING ASSESSMENT TARGETS: R.2.8, R.3.2, R.3.3, R.3.5, R.4.3/L.4.3, R.

UNIT 1

1 Review the Skill

To **draw conclusions** in fiction, pay attention to the details of the story. Often, you can combine details in a story with your own experience and make an important observation that will help you understand what happens in the story or what the author means. This observation is the conclusion.

2 Refine the Skill

By refining the skill of drawing conclusions in fiction, you will improve your study and test-taking abilities, especially as they relate to the GED® Reasoning Through Language Arts test. Read the passage below. Then answer the questions that follow.

RIP VAN WINKLE AND HIS WIFE

a From the description of Rip Van Winkle's attitude as *happy* and *foolish*, you can infer that he is a person who does not want complications in his life.

Rip Van Winkle, however, <u>was one of those happy mortals, of foolish, well-oiled dispositions, who take the world easy,</u> eat white bread or brown, whichever can be got with least thought or trouble, and would rather starve on a penny than work for a pound. If left to himself, he would have whistled life away in perfect contentment; but his wife kept continually dinning in his ears about his idleness, his carelessness, and the ruin he was bringing on his family. Morning, noon, and night, her tongue was incessantly going, and everything he said or did was sure to produce a torrent of household eloquence. Rip had but one way of replying to all lectures of the kind, and that, by frequent use, had grown into a habit. <u>He shrugged his shoulders, shook his head, cast up his eyes, but said nothing.</u> This, however, always provoked a fresh volley from his wife; so that he was fain to draw off his forces, and take to the outside of the house—the only side which, in truth, belongs to a hen-pecked husband.

b When reprimanded by his wife, Rip Van Winkle "… shrugged his shoulders, shook his head, cast up his eyes, but said nothing." His reaction shows that the criticisms bothered him, but he did not respond to them.

From RIP VAN WINKLE by Washington Irving

1. What is the **most** logical conclusion to draw from the passage?

   A. Rip Van Winkle and his wife have a happy marriage.
   B. Rip Van Winkle and his wife struggle financially.
   C. Rip Van Winkle and his wife have similar values.
   D. Rip Van Winkle and his wife are wealthy.

2. The **most** logical conclusion to be drawn about Rip Van Winkle is that

   A. he is a man with little motivation to work.
   B. he feels comfortable and relaxed at home.
   C. he enjoys arguing with his wife.
   D. he rarely leaves his house.

USE LOGIC

In this passage, you can take the description of Rip Van Winkle and his wife and add it to your own knowledge to draw conclusions about the couple's relationship.

DIRECTIONS: Read the passage, read each question, and choose the **best** answer.

ANGELA'S GIFTS

1   "For Sissy Miller." Gilbert Clandon, taking up the pearl brooch that lay among a litter of rings and brooches on a little table in his wife's drawing-room, read the inscription: "For Sissy Miller, with my love."

2   It was like Angela to have remembered even Sissy Miller, her secretary. Yet how strange it was, Gilbert Clandon thought once more, that she had left everything in such order—a little gift of some sort for every one of her friends. It was as if she had foreseen her death. Yet she had been in perfect health when she left the house that morning, six weeks ago; when she stepped off the kerb in Piccadilly and the car had killed her.

3   He was waiting for Sissy Miller. He had asked her to come; he owed her, he felt, after all the years she had been with them, this token of consideration. Yes, he went on, as he sat there waiting, it was strange that Angela had left everything in such order. Every friend had been left some little token of her affection. Every ring, every necklace, every little Chinese box—she had a passion for little boxes—had a name on it. And each had some memory for him. This he had given her; this—the enamel dolphin with the ruby eyes—she had pounced upon one day in a back street in Venice. He could remember her little cry of delight. To him, of course, she had left nothing in particular, unless it were her diary. Fifteen little volumes, bound in green leather, stood behind him on her writing table. Ever since they were married, she had kept a diary. Some of their very few—he could not call them quarrels, say tiffs—had been about that diary. When he came in and found her writing, she always shut it or put her hand over it. "No, no, no," he could hear her say, "After I'm dead—perhaps." So she had left it him, as her legacy. It was the only thing they had not shared when she was alive. But he had always taken it for granted that she would outlive him. If only she had stopped one moment, and had thought what she was doing, she would be alive now. But she had stepped straight off the kerb, the driver of the car had said at the inquest. She had given him no chance to pull up. . . .

From THE LEGACY by Virginia Woolf, © 1944

3. On the basis of the details in the passage, which is the **most** logical conclusion to draw about Angela?

    A. She treated Sissy Miller badly.
    B. She owned valuable jewelry.
    C. She was rich and famous.
    D. She was thoughtful and organized.

4. Although she died suddenly, Angela left "a little gift of some sort for every one of her friends" (paragraph 2). You can conclude from the facts surrounding her death that Angela

    A. told her secrets to Sissy Miller.
    B. forgot to leave her husband a gift.
    C. did not tell anyone of her illness.
    D. planned her own death.

5. The narrator says, "To him of course, she had left nothing in particular, unless it were her diary." From this statement and other details in the passage, the **most** logical conclusion to draw about Angela's diary is that it

    A. reveals problems in her marriage.
    B. includes love poems to her husband.
    C. will likely be published as a book.
    D. is the gift that her husband wanted most.

6. Angela's diary caused Gilbert Clandon and Angela to have "he would not call them quarrels, say tiffs" (paragraph 3). Which is the **most** logical conclusion to draw from this situation?

    A. Angela shared everything with Gilbert.
    B. Married couples are bound to have quarrels.
    C. Gilbert has tried to minimize marital problems.
    D. Diaries, like jewelry, cause marital problems.

7. The narrator says, "But he had always taken it for granted that she would outlive him." Based on this statement, what is the **most** logical conclusion to draw about Gilbert Clandon's feelings about the diary?

    A. The diary was something that he was never meant to read.
    B. The diary might contain insight into what had happened to Angela.
    C. The diary was filled with only joyful memories.
    D. The diary was meant to be published.

DIRECTIONS: Read the passage, read each question, and choose the **best** answer.

NEIGHBORS

1   Even after she had her foot on the doorstep, her hand on the knob, Martha Hale had a moment of feeling she could not cross that threshold. And the reason it seemed she couldn't cross it now was simply because she hadn't crossed it before. Time and time again it had been in her mind, "I ought to go over and see Minnie Foster"—she still thought of her as Minnie Foster, though for twenty years she had been Mrs. Wright. And then there was always something to do and Minnie Foster would go from her mind. But now she could come. . . .

2   The county attorney was looking around the kitchen. . . . He kicked his foot against some dirty pans under the sink.

3   "There's a great deal of work to be done on a farm," said Mrs. Hale stiffly.

4   "To be sure. And yet"—with a little bow to her—"I know there are some Dickson County farm-houses that do not have such roller towels." He gave it a pull to expose its full length again.

5   "Those towels get dirty awful quick. Men's hands aren't always as clean as they might be."

6   "Ah, loyal to your sex, I see," he laughed. He stopped and gave her a keen look. "But you and Mrs. Wright were neighbors. I suppose you were friends, too."

7   "I've seen little enough of her of late years. I've not been in this house—it's more than a year."

8   "And why was that? You didn't like her?"

9   "I liked her well enough," she replied with spirit. "Farmers' wives have their hands full, Mr. Henderson. And then—" She looked around the kitchen.

10   "Yes?" he encouraged.

11   "It never seemed a very cheerful place," said she, more to herself than to him.

12   "No," he agreed; "I don't think any one would call it cheerful. I shouldn't say she had the home-making instinct."

13   "Well, I don't know as Wright had, either," she muttered.

14   "You mean they didn't get on very well?" he was quick to ask.

15   "No' I don't mean anything," she answered, with decision. As she turned a little away from him, she added: "But I don't think a place would be any the cheerfuller for John Wright's bein' in it."

From A JURY OF HER PEERS by Susan Glaspell

8. What conclusion can you draw from the man's comments in paragraph 4?

    A. He thinks Mrs. Hale and other farmers' wives take better care of their kitchens.
    B. The man preferred hand towels to the roller type of towel.
    C. The man had never seen a roller towel before.
    D. The man thought that farmers' wives did not have much work to do.

9. The attorney seems to be **most** interested in learning

    A. if Mrs. Wright was cheerful.
    B. if Mrs. Wright was a good home-maker.
    C. if the Wrights got along.
    D. if Mrs. Hale is a good homemaker.

10. Mrs. Hale's comment about John Wright in paragraph 15 leads the reader to believe that

    A. Mr. Wright did not help his wife keep the house clean.
    B. Mrs. Wright caused her husband's unhappiness.
    C. Mr. Wright was a difficult person to live with.
    D. Mrs. Hale thinks that Mrs. Wright is guilty of something.

DIRECTIONS: Read the passage, read each question, and choose the **best** answer.

LAIRD TALKS WITH HIS MOTHER

1   "Dad ran off quickly," he said one night. She had been wondering when he would mention it.

2   "He had a phone call to make," she said automatically.

3   Laird looked directly in her eyes, his expression one of gentle reproach. He was letting her know he had caught her in the central lie of her life, which was that she understood Martin's obsession with his work. She averted her gaze. The truth was that she had never understood. Why couldn't he sit with her for half an hour after dinner, or, if not with her, why not with his dying son. . . .

4   "I don't think Dad can stand to be around me."

5   "That's not true." It was true.

6   "Poor Dad. He's always been a hypochondriac—we have that in common. He must hate this."

7   "He just wants you to get well."

8   "If that's what he wants, I'm afraid I'm going to disappoint him again. At least this will be the last time I let him down."

9   He said this merrily with the old, familiar light darting from his eyes. She allowed herself to be amused. He had always been fond of teasing, and held no subject sacred. As the de facto authority figure in the house—Martin hadn't been home enough to be the real disciplinarian—she had often been forced to reprimand Laird, but, in truth, she shared his sense of humor. She responded to it now by leaning over to cuff him on the arm. It was an automatic response, prompted by a burst of high spirits that took no notice of the circumstances. It was a mistake. Even through the thickness of his terrycloth robe, her knuckles knocked on bone. There was nothing left of him.

10   "It's his loss," she said, the shock of Laird's thinness making her serious again.

From IN THE GLOAMING by Alice Elliott Dark, © 1993

11. Which is the **most** logical conclusion to draw from Laird's conversation with his mother?

   A. Laird is angry with his mother.
   B. Laird uses humor to avoid talking about uncomfortable subjects.
   C. Laird is cautious about expressing his true feelings.
   D. Laird attempts to be open and honest with her.

12. Laird refers to his father, saying that "at least this will be the last time I let him down (paragraph 8). The **most** logical conclusion to draw from this statement and other details in the passage is that

   A. Martin is proud of Laird's accomplishments.
   B. Laird and Martin do not get along well.
   C. Martin has always encouraged Laird.
   D. Laird and his mother dislike Martin.

13. In the last paragraph, Laird's mother says that Martin's behavior is "his loss." Which is the **most** logical conclusion to draw about this statement, according to the details in the passage?

   A. She believes Martin is right to ignore Laird.
   B. She thinks Martin is missing out by ignoring Laird.
   C. She loves Martin more than she loves Laird.
   D. She wants Laird to be more respectful toward Martin.

14. On the basis of the information in the passage, which is the **most** logical conclusion to draw about Martin?

   A. Martin has always worked hard to support his wife and sickly son.
   B. Martin's strict discipline has caused Laird to turn against him.
   C. Martin has been distant and preoccupied before and during Laird's illness.
   D. Martin and his wife have shared equally in bringing up their son.

24 LESSON

Apply Ideas

Use with **Student Book** pp. 72–73

READING ASSESSMENT TARGETS: R.2.7, R.2.8, R.3.2, R.3.3, R.3.4, R.3.5, R.4.1/L.4.1, R.4.3/L.

1 Review the Skill

When you **apply ideas**, you can make predictions or generalizations based on your own knowledge and the details found in the story. When you apply ideas, you identify patterns and use logic to determine what a character might do or say in another situation. You also can make predictions about what might happen to the character or draw parallels between the character's situation and other circumstances.

2 Refine the Skill

By refining the skill of applying ideas, you will improve your study and test-taking abilities, especially as they relate to the GED® Reasoning Through Language Arts test. Read the passage below. Then answer the questions that follow.

PAUL LEAVES FOR NEW YORK

a Paul had been "sulking" the day before. This behavior indicates that he was likely upset about something before he took the money.

Yet it was but a day since he had been sulking in the traces; but yesterday afternoon that he had been sent to the bank with Denny & Carson's deposit, as usual—but this time he was instructed to leave the book to be balanced. There was above two thousand dollars in checks, and nearly a thousand in the bank notes which he had taken from the book and quietly transferred to his pocket. At the bank he had made out a new deposit slip. His nerves had been steady enough to permit of his returning to the office, where he had finished his work and asked for a full day's holiday tomorrow, Saturday, giving a perfectly reasonable pretext. The bankbook, he knew, would not be returned before Monday or Tuesday, and his father would be out of town for the next week. From the time he slipped the bank notes into his pocket until he boarded the night train for New York, he had not known a moment's hesitation. It was not the first time Paul had steered through treacherous waters.

b The narrator says that it was "not the first time Paul had steered through treacherous waters." Paul seems to be used to trouble and danger.

From PAUL'S CASE by Willa Cather

1. After Paul returned to work, his co-workers **most likely** noticed

   A. that he seemed particularly anxious.
   B. nothing unusual about his behavior.
   C. the unusual accuracy of his work.
   D. that his holiday request was excessive.

MAKING ASSUMPTIONS

You can make assumptions about characters from what you know about their past behavior. Unless an author explains that a character has changed, you can infer future behavior from past behavior.

2. Which is the **most** accurate prediction to make about how the situation will turn out for Paul?

   A. He will use the money to begin an honest life in New York.
   B. After enjoying his trip, he will return to his job.
   C. He will feel guilty and admit what he has done.
   D. Things likely will end badly when his crime is discovered.

DIRECTIONS: Read the passage, read each question, and choose the **best** answer.

THE AGING PROCESS

1   In the large Spanish-style house she and my father have shared for thirty-five of the nearly fifty years of marriage, a black-and-white Hollywood-style studio portrait of my mother as a wet-lipped ingénue, circa 1940, hangs framed on the stucco wall over the fireplace. Other than that, you would never guess what pride she once took in her beauty. No face lift or eye tuck for Margaret Pierce; at seventy-four, she would no sooner go under the knife for the sake of appearing five or six years younger than buy a dress simply because it was marked down. The same goes for reinforced undergarments, costly moisturizers holding out the promise of eternal youth, and hair rinses the various burnished hues of expensive luggage. "I'd rather look ancient," she'd sniff, "than pathetic."

2   Mother is a prime specimen of what most women claim to want even while desperately doing everything within their grasp to prevent it: growing old gracefully. Only traces remain of the ashy-lidded glamour queen over the fireplace that made a mockery of my own crabbed, self-conscious crawl toward womanhood. Her weathered beauty has taken on a kind of monolithic status more akin to Mount Rushmore than Rita Hayworth.

From THE PRICE OF TEA IN CHINA by Eileen Goudge, © 1998

3. From the information in the passage, what opinion would you expect the narrator to have about her mother's current appearance?

   A. She is embarrassed by her mother's current appearance.
   B. She is jealous of her mother's current appearance.
   C. She admires her mother's approach to aging.
   D. She disapproves of her mother's approach to aging.

4. Margaret states that she would "rather look ancient ... than pathetic" (paragraph 1). Which example **best** illustrates this statement?

   A. a new, custom-detailed sports car
   B. a car with hybrid technology
   C. a 1950s convertible restored to its original state
   D. a well-maintained, ten-year-old sedan

5. The narrator says that her mother is "growing old gracefully" (paragraph 2). On the basis of the tone of the passage, the narrator would **most probably** describe her mother as

   A. old-fashioned.
   B. practical.
   C. arrogant.
   D. pathetic.

6. On the basis of the narrator's description, Margaret is a person who **most likely**

   A. eats sensible, healthful meals.
   B. spends long hours at the gym.
   C. enjoys Hollywood social events.
   D. shops frequently for bargains.

7. The narrator says that her mother does not use expensive moisturizers or hair rinses. On the basis of her preferences, which response is Margaret **most likely** to make to a department store clerk offering free samples of beauty products?

   A. "This is just my color!"
   B. "I can't afford this."
   C. "No, but thank you."
   D. "Lovely! May I have another?"

8. When Margaret Pierce looks at the image over the fireplace, she **most likely** feels

   A. a nostalgia and longing for days past.
   B. a frustration at the changes that time has handed her.
   C. contentment with both the past and the present.
   D. a fear that her best days are behind her.

★ Spotlighted Item: **DRAG-AND-DROP**

DIRECTIONS: Read the passage and the question. Then use the drag-and-drop options to complete the chart.

ANOTHER TWIST

I had no drop again till the next day, for I was carried triumphantly through the following hours by my introduction to the younger of my pupils. The little girl who accompanied Mrs. Grose appeared to me on the spot a creature so charming as to make it a great fortune to have to do with her. She was the most beautiful child I had ever seen, and I afterward wondered that my employer had not told me more of her. . . .

But it was a comfort that there could be no uneasiness in a connection with anything so beatific as the radiant image of my little girl, the vision of whose angelic beauty had probably more than anything else to do with the restlessness that, before morning, made me several times rise and wander about my room to take in the whole picture and prospect; to watch, from my open window, the faint summer dawn, to look at such portions of the rest of the house as I could catch, and to listen, while, in the fading dusk, the first birds began to twitter, for the possible recurrence of a sound or two, less natural and not without, but within, that I had fancied I heard. There had been a moment when I believed I recognized, faint and far, the cry of a child; there had been another when I found myself just consciously starting as at the passage, before my door, of a light footstep. But these fancies were not marked enough not to be thrown off, and it is only in the light, or the gloom, I should rather say, of other and subsequent matters that they now come back to me. To watch, teach, "form" little Flora would too evidently be the making of a happy and useful life. It had been agreed between us downstairs that after this first occasion I should have her as a matter of course at night, her small white bed being already arranged, to that end, in my room. What I had undertaken was the whole care of her, and she had remained, just this last time, with Mrs. Grose only as an effect of our consideration for my inevitable strangeness and her natural timidity. In spite of this timidity . . . I feel quite sure she would presently like me.

From TURNING OF THE SCREW by Henry James

9. Drag and drop the possible actions of Flora's governess into the correct location in the chart

Flora's governess would

Flora's governess would not

neglect her duties
take great care of Flora
try to make Flora happy
resent having so much responsibility

DIRECTIONS: Read the passage, read each question, and choose the **best** answer.

PREPARING FOR THE PARTY

1   "Good morning," she said, copying her mother's voice. But that sounded so fearfully affected that she was ashamed, and stammered like a little girl, "Oh—er—have you come—is it about the marquee [sign]?"

2   His smile was so easy, so friendly that Laura recovered. . . . And now she looked at the others.

3   . . . "Cheer up, we won't bite," their smile seemed to say. How very nice workmen were! And what a beautiful morning! She mustn't mention the morning; she must be business-like. . . .

4   "Well, what about the lily-lawn? . . ."

5   "I don't fancy it," said he. "Not conspicuous enough. You see, with a thing like a marquee . . . you want to put it somewhere where it'll give you a bang slap in the eye, if you follow me."

6   Laura's upbringing made her wonder for a moment whether it was quite respectful of a workman to talk to her of bangs slap in the eye. But she did quite follow him.

7   "A corner of the tennis-court," she suggested. "But the band's going to be in one corner."

8   "H'm, going to have a band, are you?" said another of the workmen. He was pale. He had a haggard look as his dark eyes scanned the tennis-court. What was he thinking?

9   "Only a small band," said Laura gently. Perhaps he wouldn't mind so much if the band was quite small. But the tall fellow interrupted.

10   "Look here, miss, that's the place. Against those trees. Over there. That'll do fine."

11   Against the karakas. Then the karaka-trees would be hidden. And they were so lovely, with their broad, gleaming leaves, and their clusters of yellow fruit. They were like trees you imagined growing on a desert island, proud, solitary, lifting their leaves and fruits to the sun in a kind of silent splendour. Must they be hidden by a marquee?

12   They must. Already the men had shouldered their staves and were making for the place. Only the tall fellow was left. He bent down, pinched a sprig of lavender, put his thumb and forefinger to his nose and snuffed up the smell. When Laura saw that gesture she forgot all about the karakas in her wonder at him caring for things like that—caring for the smell of lavender. How many men that she knew would have done such a thing?

Oh, how extraordinarily nice workmen were, she thought. Why couldn't she have workmen for friends rather than the silly boys she danced with and who came to Sunday night supper? She would get on much better with men like these.

From THE GARDEN PARTY by Katherine Mansfield

10. Which situation is **most** similar to the workman's (paragraph 12)?

   A. While walking to the courtroom, a busy lawyer stops to watch an artist at work.
   B. A band manager has to decide where to put a sign promoting her band.
   C. While planting a new flower bed, a gardener sees a child pick one of the newly planted flowers.
   D. A factory worker spends his lunch hour walking in the park.

11. Laura **most likely** has spent leisure time

   A. in an office.
   B. working on a farm.
   C. at a country club.
   D. selling garden supplies.

12. Which statement is the **most likely** prediction of how Laura would react if the workmen did a poor job in completing their work?

   A. She would refuse to pay them.
   B. She would demand that they complete the job to her satisfaction.
   C. She would make excuses for them.
   D. She would be unlikely to notice.

13. On the basis of the information in the passage, which is the **most likely** prediction about the plot of this story? The plot will involve

   A. the band hired to play at the party.
   B. Laura's attraction to the workmen.
   C. Laura's mother's affectations.
   D. the boys with whom Laura dances.

Reading Comprehension at Work

MARKETING, SALES, AND SERVICE

DIRECTIONS: Read the passage, read each question, and choose the **best** answer.

You are a newly hired parts sales associate at GRIP Wholesale Auto Parts. Part of your training includes reading these instructions about sales receipts.

1   Sales receipts are an essential part of the sales process. Sales receipts serve several functions. Sales receipts confirm the payment for a product and provide proof of ownership. They are used by businesses to itemize expenses for tax purposes. They also provide contact information for items that need to be returned. GRIP Wholesale Auto Parts expects all employees to treat sales receipts as an important part of their job.

2   Every sale requires a sales receipt. The GRIP Wholesale Auto Parts store's point-of-sale system is designed to automatically create sales receipts for each purchase. When this system fails to generate a sales receipt, sales associates are expected to complete a sale receipt form and fill in the information by hand. Employees who fail to appropriately complete sales receipts may face disciplinary action, including termination.

3   The GRIP Wholesale Auto Parts sales receipt form has five components. All components must be legible.

1. **Sales associate's name and employee number.** Be sure to legibly write your name and employee number.
2. **Date of sale.** Record the month, day, and year.
3. **Customer information.** Record the customer's name and account number.
4. **Items.** Record each item, quantity sold, unit price, and total price. Be sure all math calculations are done accurately.
5. **Payment.** Check the correct box for whether the sale was purchased using cash, check, or credit card.

4   Sales associates should become familiar with the standard GRIP Wholesale Auto Parts sales receipt form. Sales associates should be prepared to complete the form when necessary. For additional information, or if you have any questions or concerns regarding this policy, please contact your GRIP Wholesale Auto Parts store manager.

1. In paragraph 1, the author writes, "Sales receipt confirm the payment for a product and provide proof of ownership." Which main idea does this detail support?

    A. "Sales receipts are an essential part of the sales process."
    B. "They also provide contact information for items that need to be returned."
    C. "They are used by businesses to itemize expenses for tax purposes."
    D. "GRIP Wholesale Auto Parts expects all employees to treat sales receipts as an important part of their job."

2. What is the main idea of paragraph 2?

    A. Employees who fail to complete a sales receipt for a sale may be fired.
    B. The GRIP Wholesale Auto Parts store's point of-sale system automatically creates sales receipts.
    C. A sales receipt is required for every sale.
    D. GRIP Wholesale Auto Parts sales associates need to fill out a sales receipt form for every sale

3. What is the **most** logical conclusion to draw on the basis of the information in paragraph 3?

    A. Sales associates should know all customer account numbers.
    B. Sales associates need to complete all five of the components listed.
    C. Sales associates only need to worry about listing the items and the total price.
    D. Sales associates only need to complete sales receipts for items bought with cash.

4. How would the meaning of the first sentence of paragraph 4 change if the author had used the word **memorize** instead of the phrase **become familiar with**?

    A. The sentence would imply that sales receipts were optional.
    B. The sentence would imply that forgetting a sales receipt might lead to getting fired.
    C. The sentence would imply that remembering every detail of the sales receipt was not important.
    D. The sentence would imply that it was necessary to remember every detail of the sales receipt process.

HEALTH SCIENCE

DIRECTIONS: Read the passage, read each question, and choose the **best** answer.

You are a student who wants to become a dental hygienist. This excerpt is from a text discussing dental equipment.

INTRODUCTION TO ASPIRATION SYSTEMS

1   Dental aspiration systems are an essential part of all clinics and dental practices. The oral cavity inside a human mouth contains saliva, bacteria, and possibly viruses. The aspirator is a tube that suctions saliva that collects in the oral cavity.

2   Aspiration systems reduce or eliminate cross contamination between patients and dental professionals. When used properly, aspiration systems decrease the microbial cloud expelled from the oral cavity to a radius of less than 30 centimeters. This is less than the average distance between a patient and a dental professional.

3   Aspiration systems comprise the dental equipment (those parts that come into contact with the patients) and the engine room (or motor, which creates the suction). Systems that separate the liquid from the air in the engine room are called wet suction. Systems that separate the liquid in the dental equipment are called dry suction. Both wet and dry suction devices offer different advantages and disadvantages, including the amount of suction they create and the amount of water needed to function properly.

4   Because they are designed to collect bacteria, aspiration systems require constant cleaning and maintenance. Depending on the volume of patients, the systems should be disinfected every day to avoid unpleasant odors and prevent system clogs. This involves disassembling, or taking apart, certain sections of the system.

5. According to clues in the passage, **cross contamination** is

   A. the microbial cloud expelled from the oral cavity.
   B. the collection of saliva, bacteria, and viruses from the oral cavity.
   C. the elimination of bacteria between patients and dental professionals.
   D. the transfer of bacteria between patients and dental professionals.

6. How does the author categorize the types of aspiration systems?

   A. saliva, bacteria, and viruses
   B. dental equipment and engine room
   C. wet suction and dry suction
   D. cleaning and maintenance

7. How does the word **Because** function in paragraph 4?

   A. It introduces a cause-and-effect relationship between the collection of bacteria and the need to clean the equipment.
   B. It creates a contrast between the types of equipment in paragraph 3 and the need to clean the equipment in paragraph 4.
   C. It signals the continuing sequence of events started in paragraph 2.
   D. It reinforces the information in paragraph 3 by introducing an example.

8. What is the **most** logical conclusion to draw on the basis of the information in the last paragraph?

   A. Increasing the volume of patients will prevent system clogs.
   B. The equipment should be disinfected every day to disassemble certain sections.
   C. After certain sections of the equipment are disassembled, they collect bacteria.
   D. After certain sections of the equipment are disassembled, they are cleaned with disinfectant.

Determine Author's Purpose

LESSON 1

Use with *Student Book* pp. 88–89

① Review the Skill

READING ASSESSMENT TARGETS: R.2.1, R.2.4, R.2.5, R.2.7, R.2.8, R.3.2, R.3 R.4.3/L.4.3, R.5.1, R.5.4, R.6.1, R.6.2, R.6.3, R.6.4, R.8.2

Identifying the intended ==audience== of a passage can help you understand the ==author's purpose==. An author writing to inform a general audience, for example, will include enough information for anyone to understand the topic. When writing specifically to persuade a particular group to do something or to think in a certain way, a writer might include details that would be especially persuasive to people in that group.

② Refine the Skill

By refining the skills of determining author's purpose and identifying audience, you will improve your study and test-taking abilities, especially as they relate to the GED® Reasoning Through Language Arts test. Read the passage below. Then answer the questions that follow.

UNIT 2

ⓐ The phrase "frequently asked questions" gives you a clue to the intended audience of this passage. The authors are likely writing for a general audience if they are answering frequently asked questions. The information should be fairly easy to understand.

ⓑ The format of the passage gives you clues to the authors' purpose. The passage is a series of questions and answers. Because the authors are answering questions, their purpose is likely to inform.

FREQUENTLY ASKED QUESTIONS: FLU

What's New this Flu Season?

1   For the 2019-2020 flu season, CDC recommends that vaccination be offered by the end of October and provided additional information on what might be considered vaccinating too early. "Vaccinating early—for example, in July or August—may lead to reduced protection against influenza later in the season, particularly among older adults."

How well-matched are 2019-2020 vaccine viruses to circulating flu viruses? How well is flu vaccine protecting against illness?

2   CDC does not have flu vaccine effectiveness estimates for this season yet. In the meantime, antigenic characterization data can provide some insight into how well vaccines might work.

3   During past seasons when vaccine viruses were antigenically "like" most circulating viruses, vaccine effectiveness in the range of 40% to 60% has been observed. This means that people who get vaccinated may still get sick, but they are about half as likely to get sick as someone who was not vaccinated. Another important thing to remember is that vaccination may make illness less severe in people who get vaccinated and still get sick. In general, people who get vaccinated are better off than people who do not get vaccinated.

Adapted from the cdc.gov article FREQUENTLY ASKED INFLUENZA (FLU) QUESTIONS: 2019-2020 SEASON, accessed 2020

TEST-TAKING TIPS

You may need to use prior knowledge to make an inference and answer a question. For example, in question 1, think about what you know about doctors and how they might differ from a general audience.

1. How might the passage differ if doctors were the intended audience?
   A. It might include more advanced medical vocabulary.
   B. It might tell a funny story about someone afraid of getting a shot.
   C. It might inform readers what to expect when getting a shot.
   D. It might answer a question about the cost of flu shots.

2. Which detail shows the author's purpose is also to persuade?
   A. The CDC is offering additional guidelines.
   B. The CDC does not have vaccine effectiveness data yet.
   C. The flu vaccine does not protect against illnesses other than flu.
   D. People who get vaccinated are better off than people who do not get vaccinated.

3 Master the Skill

DIRECTIONS: Read the passage, read each question, and choose the **best** answer.

STRATEGIC PLANS FOR ATLANTA

1   GENERAL [J.B. Hood, commanding Army of Tennessee, Confederate Army]: I have the honor to acknowledge the receipt of your letter of this date . . . consenting to the arrangements I had proposed to facilitate the removal south of the people of Atlanta, who prefer to go in that direction. I [e]nclose you a copy of my orders, which will, I am satisfied, accomplish my purpose perfectly.

2   You style the measures proposed "unprecedented," and appeal to the dark history of war for a parallel, as an act of "studied and ingenious cruelty." It is not unprecedented; for General Johnston himself very wisely and properly removed families all the way from Dalton down, and I see no reason why Atlanta should be excepted. Nor is it necessary to appeal to the dark history of war, when recent and modern examples are so handy. You yourself burned dwelling-houses along your parapet, and I have seen to-day fifty houses that you have rendered uninhabitable because they stood in the way of your forts and men. You defended Atlanta on a line so close to town that every cannon-shot and many musket-shots for our line of investment, that overshot their mark, went into the habitations of women and children. General Hardee did the same at Jonesboro', and General Johnston did the same, last summer, at Jackson, Mississippi. I have not accused you of heartless cruelty, but merely instance these cases of very recent occurrence, and could go on and enumerate hundreds of others, and challenge any fair man to judge which of us has the heart of pity for the families of a "brave people."

3   . . . In the name of common-sense, I ask you not to appeal to a just God in such a sacrilegious manner. You who, in the midst of peace and prosperity, have plunged a nation into war—dark and cruel war—who dared and badgered us to battle, insulted our flag, seized our arsenal and forts, . . . expelled Union families by the thousands, burned their houses, and declared, by an act of your Congress, the confiscation of all debts due Northern men for goods had and received!

4   If we must be enemies, let us be men, and fight it out as we propose to do, and not deal in such hypocritical appeals to God and humanity. God will judge us in due time, and he will pronounce whether it be more

humane to fight with a town full of women and the families of a brave people at our back or to remove them in time to places of safety among their own friends and people. I am, very respectfully, your obedient servant,

W.T. Sherman, Major-General commanding [Union Army]

From HEADQUARTERS MILITARY DIVISION OF THE MISSISSIPPI, IN THE FIELD, ATLANTA, GEORGIA by General William T. Sherman, September 10, 1864

3. This is an excerpt from a letter written during the Civil War. Which of the following identifies the author of the letter and the recipient of the letter?

A. The author is General Sherman, a general in the Union Army. The recipient is General Hood, a general in the Confederate Army.
B. The author is General Hood, a general in the Confederate Army. The recipient is General Sherman, a general in the Union Army.
C. The author is General Sherman, a general in the Union Army. The recipient is General Johnston, a general in the Confederate Army.
D. The author is General Johnston, a general in the Confederate Army. The recipient is General Sherman, a general in the Union Army.

4. Which of the following describes the explicit purpose of the letter?

A. to identify precedents for his plans
B. to accuse General Hood of cruelty
C. to confirm the plans for evacuating Atlanta
D. to acknowledge that war will involve casualties and destruction of property

5. Based on the information in paragraph 2, General Hood accused General Sherman of

A. pity
B. cruelty
C. bravery
D. hypocrisy

DIRECTIONS: Read the passage, read each question, and choose the **best** answer.

THE AMERICAN NEED FOR MORE

1   Many of us find that we seem to require more necessities than we can get the money to pay for. Our friends with more money are constantly showing how indispensably convenient these necessities are, and we keep buying them until we either outspend our incomes or miss the higher concerns of life. The saddest part of all is that it is in great measure an American development, and we Americans keep inventing new necessities. Of course it all belongs to "progress," and no one is quite willing to have it stop.

2   Take houses, for example. An ideal of earthly comfort is to get a house so big that it is burdensome to maintain and fill it up so full of extras that it is a constant occupation to keep it in order. However, when nature provides a house, that house fits the occupant. Animals, which build by instinct, build only what they need. But man's building instinct is boundless. Nature never tells him when he has finished. And perhaps it should not surprise us that in so many cases he doesn't know. He just goes ahead as long as the materials last.

3   If another man tries to oppress him, he understands this kind of tyranny. . . . He is ready to fight and sacrifice all he has, rather than submit to it. But the tyranny of things is so subtle, so gradual in its approach, and comes so masked with seeming benefits, that it has him hopelessly bound before he suspects. He says, "I will add thus to my house," "I will have one or two more horses," "I will make a little greenhouse in my garden," and so he goes on having things and imagining that he is richer for owning them. It is only over time that he begins to realize that it is the things that own him.

Adapted from THE TYRANNY OF THINGS by Edward Sanford Martin

6.   What is the author's **main** purpose?

   A. to tell a story about expanding a house
   B. to inform readers about animals' instincts
   C. to persuade readers to think about their real needs
   D. to describe the newest conveniences for the home

7.   How does paragraph 1 support the author's purpose?

   A. The author offers several examples of how and why people spend on items they do not need.
   B. The author berates people for spending on expenses they want.
   C. The author bemoans the spending habits of the wealthy.
   D. The author begs people to be more frugal by not purchasing the items they want.

8.   How does contrasting the tyranny of things with oppression by another person (paragraph 3) advance the author's purpose? The contrast shows that

   A. people are unaware of the way things come to rule them.
   B. people confuse what they want with what they need.
   C. oppression by a ruler is much more common.
   D. humans often destroy themselves needlessly or unknowingly.

9.   How might a reader respond if he or she finds the author's argument convincing?

   A. The reader might try to live without material possessions.
   B. The reader might seek to overthrow the government.
   C. The reader might buy fewer luxury or convenience items.
   D. The reader might try to study and learn from nature.

10. How does the structure of the last two sentences emphasize a key idea of the passage?

   A. The last sentence summarizes the quotations in the sentence before to emphasize that people do not have good instincts.
   B. The last sentence reverses the wording of the sentence before to emphasize that possessions can limit a person's freedom.
   C. The last sentence paraphrases the sentence before to emphasize that people are quick to respond to tyranny.
   D. The last sentence adds details to the sentence before to emphasize that people want to live lifestyles they cannot afford.

UNIT 2

DIRECTIONS: Read the passage, read each question, and choose the **best** answer.

THE HOME OFFICE TAX DEDUCTION

1   As part of ongoing efforts by the Administration to reduce paperwork burdens, the Internal Revenue Service (IRS) announced today that it is providing a new, simpler option for calculating the home office tax deduction, allowing small business owners and employees who work from home and who maintain a qualifying home office to deduct up to $1,500 per year.

2   The IRS also expects taxpayers to save more than 1.6 million hours per year in tax preparation time from this simpler calculation method.

3   The new option allows qualified taxpayers to deduct annually $5 per square foot of home office space on up to 300 square feet, for as much as $1,500 in deductions. To take advantage of the new option, taxpayers will complete a much simpler version of the current 43-line form.

4   The announcement builds on the President's commitment to streamline and simplify the tax code for small businesses and to reduce the burden for tax compliance. It is part of broader efforts to make interacting with the federal government easier and more efficient for businesses of all sizes.

5   These new rules help our tax code better reflect the needs of America's 21st Century workforce and especially small businesses, which play a vital role in our economy. Today, more than half of all working Americans own or work for a small business. An estimated 52 percent of small businesses are home-based, and many of these small businesses have home office space that would qualify for the deduction. And as technology improves, more businesses—large and small—are going virtual and recruiting employees from across the country, many of whom work from home offices.

From the treasury.gov article THE HOME OFFICE TAX DEDUCTION: SIMPLIFYING RULES AND HELPING SMALL BUSINESS OWNERS SUCCEED by Neal S. Wolin and Karen G. Mills, accessed 2021

11. What is the explicit purpose of the IRS announcement?

    A. to inform readers about the new home office tax deduction
    B. to persuade taxpayers to take the home office deduction
    C. to describe the size and layout of a home office
    D. to persuade taxpayers to work from home

12. What is the implicit purpose of the passage?

    A. to inform readers about which tax forms to file
    B. to persuade readers to support the current administration
    C. to explain proposed changes to the tax code
    D. to tell a story about a successful home-based business

13. Which piece of evidence **best** supports the claim that small businesses "play a vital role in our economy"?

    A. The government is trying to simplify the tax code for small businesses.
    B. Owners of small businesses could deduct up to $1,500 per year.
    C. More than half of all working Americans own or work for a small business.
    D. An estimated 52 percent of small businesses are home-based.

14. If the audience were limited only to owners of home businesses, what additional details or information might the passage include?

    A. an explanation of how the IRS determined the new calculation method
    B. an estimate of how many people failed to claim the old deduction
    C. a tax form showing a sample calculation of the deduction
    D. an address to which taxpayers can send comments about the tax code

15. In paragraph 5, the authors address their audience, which is "the 21st Century workforce." Which word **best** describes this group?

    A. flexible
    B. traditional
    C. organized
    D. loyal

Analyze Elements of Persuasion

Use with *Student Book* pp. 90–91

READING ASSESSMENT TARGETS: R.2.2, R.2.7, R.3.1, R.5.1, R.5.2, R.5.3, R.5
R.6.1, R.6.2, R.8.1, R.8.2, R.8.6

UNIT 2

1 Review the Skill

When writing to persuade, an author may begin by giving background information. Then the author may state the **claim**, or point he or she wants to make, provide **evidence**, and conclude by asking readers to think in a certain way or to do something. Authors may make assumptions about how much an audience knows about the topic.

A piece of persuasive writing may make more than one claim. When an author wants to persuade readers of several things or make several points, he or she might include **multiple claims**. An author may also include **counterclaims**, which argue against or explain differing views on the subject. As in any piece of persuasive writing, each claim should be supported by evidence and sound logic.

2 Refine the Skill

By refining the skill of analyzing elements of persuasion and argument, you will improve your study and test-taking abilities, especially as they relate to the GED® Reasoning Through Language Arts test. Read the passage below. Then answer the questions that follow.

THE IMPORTANCE OF RAIL IN THE NEXT DECADES

a Look for evidence supporting the multiple claims that rail is cost effective (economical), that it doesn't use a lot of oil, and that it is environmentally friendly.

By 2050, America's transportation network will have to move more than 100 million additional people and four billion more annual tons of freight. ... Long term, rail's efficiencies simply cannot be ignored. With service targeted to the market, it can be the most cost-effective, least oil reliant, most environmentally friendly mode of transportation.

One train can take approximately 100 trucks off the road. And, since the early 1980s, our freight rail network has managed the amazing feat of doubling its haul without increasing its total fuel consumption. Two railroad tracks can carry as many passengers per hour as 16 lanes of freeway.

b This statement might counter the claim that building rail lines costs more than building roads.

And, while the cost of building rail compares favorably with roads, rail right-of-way only consumes one-third of the land required by roadways.

From REMARKS FOR THE AMERICAN ASSOCIATION OF STATE HIGHWAY AND TRANSPORTATION OFFICIALS (AASHTO) by Joseph C. Szabo, 2012

1. The author states that freight rail has doubled "its haul without increasing its total fuel consumption" to support the claim that

   A. building railroads is economical.
   B. rail does not require a lot of oil.
   C. railroads need less land than roads.
   D. rail's efficiencies cannot be ignored.

2. To which group is the statement "One train can take approximately 100 trucks off the road" **most likely** to appeal?

   A. environmentalists
   B. politicians
   C. truck drivers
   D. police officers

COMPUTER TIPS

You will be able to use electronic highlighting on the GED® test. When you read persuasive passages, consider highlighting the author's claims and the evidence that supports the claims.

⭐ Spotlighted Item: **DRAG-AND-DROP**

DIRECTIONS: Read the passage and the question. Then use the drag-and-drop options to complete the graphic organizer.

WE ARE NOT YET FREE

1   It ought to be possible, in short, for every American to enjoy the privileges of being American without regard to his race or his color. In short, every American ought to have the right to be treated as he would wish to be treated, as one would wish his children to be treated. But this is not the case.

2   The Negro baby born in America today, regardless of the section of the Nation in which he is born, has about one-half as much chance of completing high school as a white baby born in the same place on the same day, one-third as much chance of completing college, one-third as much chance of becoming a professional man, twice as much chance of becoming unemployed, about one-seventh as much chance of earning $10,000 a year, a life expectancy which is 7 years shorter, and the prospects of earning only half as much.

3   This is not a sectional issue. Difficulties over segregation and discrimination exist in every city, in every State of the Union, producing in many cities a rising tide of discontent that threatens the public safety. Nor is this a partisan issue. In a time of domestic crisis men of good will and generosity should be able to unite regardless of party or politics. This is not even a legal or legislative issue alone. It is better to settle these matters in the courts than on the streets, and new laws are needed at every level, but law alone cannot make men see right. . . .

4   One hundred years of delay have passed since President Lincoln freed the slaves, yet their heirs, their grandsons, are not fully free. They are not yet freed from the bonds of injustice. They are not yet freed from social and economic oppression. And this Nation, for all its hopes and all its boasts, will not be fully free until all its citizens are free.

From ADDRESS ON CIVIL RIGHTS by John F. Kennedy, 1963

3.   Drag and drop each statement into the box that tells which part of the argument it is.

Claim

> [ ]

Evidence

> [ ]

Evidence

> [ ]

Evidence

> [ ]

Conclusion

> [ ]

Statements

> The Negro baby born in America today ... has about one-half as much chance of completing high school as a white baby.

> One hundred years of delay have passed since President Lincoln freed the slaves, yet their heirs, their grandsons, are not fully free.

> The Negro baby born in America today ... [has] twice as much chance of becoming unemployed.

> Difficulties over segregation and discrimination exist in every city, in every State of the Union.

> It ought to be possible, in short, for every American to enjoy the privileges of being American without regard to his race or his color.

UNIT 2

DIRECTIONS: Read the passage, read each question, and choose the **best** answer.

TO WIN THE FIGHT AGAINST AIDS, WE MUST FIRST DEFEAT TB

1   This week, tremendous and unprecedented progress in the fight against HIV/AIDS is being celebrated around the world by the HIV and AIDS community. The world has definitely made crushing AIDS a top priority and we've been able to accomplish what many would have said 15 years ago was impossible. But let's not forget that if the dream of making this the generation that defeats AIDS is to become reality, we must also tackle the leading killer of people with HIV—tuberculosis (TB).

2   The overlap of TB and HIV is a deadly combination with tragic consequences. TB is the leading killer of people with HIV, accounting for one in four HIV-related deaths. Globally, one-third of the 34 million people living with HIV is infected with TB, and if left unchecked and untreated, TB can kill a person with HIV/AIDS in a matter of weeks. Furthermore, the alarming increase in multi-drug resistant TB (MDR-TB) threatens to reverse progress made against HIV/AIDS despite our efforts to achieve the 2015 Millennium Development Goals related to TB.

3   Pressing public health challenges like this demand our collective and immediate attention. Today, the Global Fund is on the second and final day of its fourth Replenishment Conference in Washington, D.C. Hosted by the United States government, this meeting is a pivotal opportunity for donor countries to increase their pledges over the next three years to bring treatment and hope for HIV, TB and malaria to some of the world's most underserved and heavily disease-burdened populations.

4   In his remarks at the Global Fund Partnership Symposium yesterday, Secretary Kerry reminded global leaders that the goal of eliminating TB deaths in our lifetime is achievable if we make the commitment and stay the course—*"TB is curable, and make no mistake: With the right effort and the right focus, the right energy, we can eliminate it." (. . .)*

5   Simply put, we have a historic opportunity to turn the tide on an age-old killer that has plagued mankind for generations. By the global community banding together with resources and endorsements to meet the challenge, the goal of ending TB deaths in our lifetime is within our reach.

From the blog.usaid.gov article TO WIN THE BATTLE AGAINST AIDS, WE MUST ERADICATE TUBERCULOSIS FIRST by Cheri Vincent, 2013

4. What is the author's main purpose?

    A. to explain symptoms of HIV, tuberculosis, and malaria
    B. to inform readers about treatments for HIV
    C. to persuade readers that funding tuberculosis research is critical to fight AIDS
    D. to describe the purpose of the Global Fund Partnership Symposium

5. The author includes a quote by Secretary Kerry to support the claim that

    A. the world has definitely made crushing AIDS top priority.
    B. TB is the leading killer of people with HIV.
    C. the goal of ending TB deaths in our lifetime is within our reach.
    D. tremendous and unprecedented progress in the fight against HIV/AIDS is being celebrated around the world.

6. Which of the following is a claim the author makes?

    A. We should not celebrate progress in the fight against HIV/AIDS because there are still so many patients dying from the disease.
    B. Tuberculosis kills everyone who has the HIV virus.
    C. If the spread of multi-drug resistant tuberculosis is not controlled, all the gains made in the fight against HIV/AIDS could be lost.
    D. The Global Fund has not done enough to help the nations most affected by HIV/AIDS.

7. What evidence does the author provide to support the claim that "the overlap of TB and HIV is a deadly combination"?

    A. ". . . we have a historic opportunity to turn the tide on an age-old killer that has plagued mankind for generations."
    B. "Pressing public health challenges like this demand our collective and immediate attention."
    C. "TB is the leading killer of people with HIV, accounting for one in four HIV-related deaths."
    D. ". . . the alarming increase in multi-drug resistant TB (MDR-TB) threatens to reverse progress made against HIV/AIDS."

DIRECTIONS: Read the passage, read each question, and choose the **best** answer.

THE SUPREME COURT RULES ON THE AFFORDABLE CARE ACT

1   In 2012, the United States Supreme Court issued a ruling on the Patient Protection and Affordable Care Act. After the passage of the Affordable Care Act, as it is commonly called, several states sued the federal government. They argued that the individual mandate was beyond the scope of Congress's power. The "individual mandate," or the requirement that most Americans buy health insurance or pay a fine if they do not, is an important part of the act. The government argued that Congress passed the act under the powers granted to it by the Commerce Clause of the U.S. Constitution. This part of the Constitution states that Congress has the power to regulate interstate commerce, or business that crosses state boundaries.

2   Although the court finally upheld the individual mandate, Chief Justice John Roberts did find that passage of the individual mandate was unconstitutional. In the majority opinion [the document stating the court's ruling], Justice Roberts argued that Congress acted beyond the powers granted to it by the Commerce Clause.

3   In evaluating whether the individual mandate is constitutional, Justice Roberts found that the individual mandate does not regulate commerce that already exists. Instead, it compels, or forces, people into commerce by making them buy a product. Roberts noted that no historical precedents, or examples, exist of Congress's acting to compel people into commerce. He also noted that the language of the Constitution, which states that Congress may "regulate Commerce," assumes that the commerce already exists. The individual mandate would bring new people into the market; consequently, it would not be regulating commerce that already exists, but creating commerce.

4   Therefore, Roberts determined that the act reached beyond the scope of the power described in the Constitution. He wrote that understanding the Commerce Clause "to permit Congress to regulate individuals precisely because they are doing nothing would open a new and potentially vast domain to congressional authority."

Adapted from the United States Supreme Court's ruling on the AFFORDABLE CARE ACT, 2012

8. How does paragraph 1 relate to the rest of the passage?

    A. It explains the government's claim, which is supported by the rest of the passage.
    B. It provides background information to help readers understand Roberts's argument.
    C. It gives evidence to support Roberts's claim at the end of the passage.
    D. It states the viewpoint of those opposed to the act, which the rest of the passage counters.

9. Which transition word in paragraph 3 indicates a result?

    A. whether
    B. instead
    C. also
    D. consequently

10. How does the word **therefore** in paragraph 4 emphasize Roberts's purpose?

    A. It connects Roberts's understanding of the Commerce Clause to his decision.
    B. It indicates why the government believed the act was constitutional under the Commerce Clause.
    C. It indicates how the individual mandate results in business that crosses state boundaries.
    D. It connects states' reasons for suing with the requirements of the individual mandate.

11. Which statement **best** summarizes the steps in Roberts's argument?

    A. The Commerce Clause grants Congress certain powers. Congress passed the act under the Commerce Clause. The act is constitutional.
    B. The Supreme Court decides whether acts are constitutional. The individual mandate is part of an act. The Supreme Court can decide whether it is constitutional.
    C. The individual mandate creates commerce. The Commerce Clause allows Congress to regulate only existing commerce. The individual mandate is unconstitutional.
    D. Congress cannot pass acts that affect only one state. The Affordable Care Act crosses state boundaries. Congress can pass the act.

3 LESSON

Identify Evidence

Use with **Student Book** pp. 92–93

READING ASSESSMENT TARGETS: R.2.4, R.2.5, R.2.8, R.3.5, R.4.3/L.4.3, R.5.1, R.5 R.6.1, R.6.3, R.8.2, R.8.3, R.8.4

UNIT 2

1 Review the Skill

Claims are supported by **evidence**—reasons and information that show why readers should believe or agree with the claim. Claims are usually **opinions**, or judgments. Opinions cannot be proven, but they can be supported by strong, convincing evidence. **Facts**, on the other hand, can be proven true or untrue. Authors often use facts, as well as other evidence, to support their claims.

Writers may use appeals to **logic** (reason), appeals to **emotion** (feelings), and appeals to **ethics** (credibility) to persuade readers.

2 Refine the Skill

By refining the skill of identifying evidence, you will improve your study and test-taking abilities, especially as they relate to the GED® Reasoning Through Language Arts test. Read the passage below. Then answer the questions that follow.

KNOW THE RISKS

a The first paragraph contains facts. Details about the number of young adults using e-cigarettes can be proved correct or incorrect.

b The author uses strong words like *critical* and describes the **harm** caused by nicotine exposure. These words appeal to readers' emotions.

As of 2014, more than one-third of young adults had tried e-cigarettes. In 2018, more than 3.6 million U.S. youth, including 1 in 5 high school students and 1 in 20 middle school students, used e-cigarettes. E-cigarette use poses a significant—and avoidable—health risk to young people in the United States. Besides increasing the possibility of addiction and long-term harm to brain development and respiratory health, e-cigarette use is associated with the use of other tobacco products that can do even more damage to the body.

Nicotine exposure during adolescence, a critical period for brain development, can cause addiction and can harm the developing brain. Until about age 25, the brain is still growing. Each time a new memory is created or a new skill is learned, stronger connections—or synapses—are built between brain cells. Because addiction is a form of learning, adolescents can get addicted more easily than adults. Nicotine also changes the way synapses are formed, which can harm the parts of the brain that control attention and learning.

Adapted from the e-cigarettes.surgeongeneral.gov article KNOW THE RISKS, accessed 2021

CLOSER LOOK AT ITEMS

Drag-and-drop items (like those on the next page) may have more answer choices than places to move them or more available places than answer choices. Read and respond carefully.

1. In stating the claim, the authors use words such as **significant health risk** and **critical** to

   A. show readers that they are a credible source.
   B. mislead readers about the dangers of e-cigarettes.
   C. emphasize how e-cigarette use is increasing.
   D. make the dangers of e-cigarettes seem real and urgent.

2. What evidence would the authors use to add to an appeal to ethics?

   A. more data about the nicotine's impact on brain development
   B. a description of how e-cigarettes work
   C. a quotation by an expert on health risks related to e-cigarettes
   D. differing opinions about the threats of nicotine

★ Spotlighted Item: **DRAG-AND-DROP**

DIRECTIONS: Read the passage and the question. Then use the drag-and-drop options to complete the chart.

ABOLISHING THE ELECTORAL COLLEGE

1 I am pleased to be here today to express the League's [League of Women Voters] support for a constitutional amendment to abolish the electoral college. . . .

2 The electoral college system is fundamentally unfair to voters. In a nation where voting rights are grounded in the one person, one vote principle, the electoral college is a hopeless anachronism.

3 The current system is unfair for two reasons.

4 First, a citizen's individual vote has more weight if he or she lives in a state with a small population than if that citizen lives in a state with a large population.

5 For example, each electoral vote in Alaska is equivalent to approximately 112,000 people. Each electoral vote in New York is equivalent to approximately 404,000 eligible people (based on 1990 census data). And that's if everyone votes!

6 The system is also unfair because a citizen's individual vote has more weight if the percentage of voter participation in the state is low. For example, if only half of all people in Alaska vote, then each electoral vote is equivalent to roughly 56,000 people.

7 Moreover, the electoral vote does not reflect the volume of voter participation within a state. If only a few voters go to the polls, all the electoral votes of the state are still cast.

8 Finally, the electoral college system is flawed because the constitution does not bind presidential electors to vote for the candidates to whom they have been pledged. For example, in 1948, 1960, and 1976, individual electors pledged to the top two vote getters cast their votes for third place finishers and also-rans. Defecting electors in a close race could cause a crisis of confidence in our electoral system.

From TESTIMONY BEFORE THE U.S. HOUSE SUBCOMMITTEE ON THE CONSTITUTION: PROPOSALS FOR ELECTORAL COLLEGE REFORM by Becky Cain, 1997

3. Drag and drop each detail into the correct location in the chart.

Type of Appeal	Detail
Logical	
Emotional	
Ethical	

Details

I am pleased to be here today to express the League's support for a constitutional amendment.
Defecting electors in a close race could cause a crisis of confidence in our electoral system.
Each electoral vote in Alaska is equivalent to approximately 112,000 people. Each electoral vote in New York is equivalent to approximately 404,000 eligible people.
In a nation where voting rights are grounded in the one person, one vote principle, the electoral college is a hopeless anachronism [something outdated].

DIRECTIONS: Read the passage, read each question, and choose the **best** answer.

SAFE DRIVING

1 Driving a car can give you freedom. But it's also one of the riskiest things you do every day. More than 36,000 people died in car accidents in the U.S. in 2018. Millions more are injured each year. . . .

2 You've likely seen ads reminding you to keep your eyes on the road. With cell phones and screens everywhere, distracted driving has become a major problem.

3 "Because we're so phone driven, the tendency is when somebody calls us or texts us, we want to respond immediately," says Dr. Bruce Simons-Morton, an NIH [National Institutes of Health] expert on teen driving. To drive safely, we have to overcome that powerful impulse, he explains.

4 Texting can take your eyes off the road for seconds at a time. In just five seconds, you travel the entire length of a football field at 55 miles per hour.

5 Distraction isn't limited to phones. It's anything that takes attention away from driving the car. Eating, playing with the radio, and adjusting your navigation system all distract from safe driving.

6 "Reaching for objects is also a big problem," says Simons-Morton. You may take your eyes off the road when you reach for your sunglasses or something in the seat next to you.

7 People of any age can give in to distractions while driving. Many adults admit to texting, answering calls, and other dangerous behaviors. That's a problem because teens are modeling their parents' actions as they learn to drive.

8 Studies show that teen drivers are at greatest risk for crashes. Crashes are higher among 16- to 19-year-olds than any other age group. That's because some driving skills get better with experience. Teens are also prone to distraction, especially with friends in the car.

9 "The first six months of driving on their own is the most dangerous," says Dr. Ginger Yang, a teen driving expert at Nationwide Children's Hospital and The Ohio State University. The risk of getting in an accident remains high until at least their early 20s. . . .

10 "Parents need to be good role models, because teens are still watching and learning from how parents behave," Yang says. She is currently researching how parents can communicate with their teens to help improve their driving.

11 Her past studies suggest parents can make a difference. By motivating their teens to engage in safe driving behaviors early on, parents can help teens establish safe driving habits that they carry into adulthood.

From the newsinhealth.nih.gov article SAFE DRIVING, accessed 202

4. How do the authors appeal to **ethics** to support the claim that distracted driving is a problem?

   A. They quote an expert on teen driving.
   B. They cite the number of death caused by car accidents in 2018.
   C. They provide examples of distractions.
   D. They use strong language to emphasize the importance of keeping your eyes on the road.

5. In paragraph 7, the authors claim "That's a problem because teens are modeling their parents' actions as they learn to drive. " How is paragraph 10 related to this claim?

   A. It supports the claim with data from a study.
   B. It restates the claim in a quote from an expert
   C. It counters the claim with data from a study.
   D. It broadens the claim with anecdotal evidence

6. Which statement from the passage is an opinion

   A. Driving a car can give you freedom.
   B. "Many adults admit to texting, answering calls and other dangerous behaviors."
   C. "Crashes are higher among 16- to 19-year-olds than any other age group."
   D. "The risk of getting in an accident remains hig until at least their early 20s."

7. In paragraph 4, the authors state "In just five seconds, you travel the entire length of a football field at 55 miles per hour." This statement is an appeal to

   A. ethics
   B. emotion
   C. logic
   D. values

DIRECTIONS: Read the passage, read each question, and choose the **best** answer.

SAVING THE RED WOLF

1 **Why do red wolves matter?**

Living in a variety of habitats, red wolves help maintain the balance and health of ecosystems by removing old and sick animals. They eat white-tailed deer, raccoons, nutria, rabbits, and small rodents, and provide a benefit by eating small predators that prey on ground-nesting birds, such as quail and turkey. Red wolves have aesthetic value too. Outdoor enthusiasts, including many hunters, say they like being in an environment where the full natural diversity of wildlife still exists. The presence of red wolves contributes significantly to local economies from people wanting to see and learn more about this endangered species.

2 **Why do red wolves need help?**

Once a top predator throughout the southeastern United States, the red wolf nearly vanished due to loss of habitat and human persecution. As a result, a managed breeding program was established in 1973 at Point Defiance Zoo & Aquarium to conserve the remaining red wolves and increase their numbers. The success of the breeding program led to the reintroduction of red wolves in 1987 in the Alligator River National Wildlife Refuge, North Carolina. Red wolves now inhabit a five-county area in northeastern North Carolina, and although their numbers have grown, human-caused mortalities, such as gunshot and vehicle strikes, can threaten their survival. The red wolf is one of our planet's most endangered species.

3 **How you can help red wolves:**

- **Learn about red wolves and other wildlife. Teach others.**
- **Visit a place where red wolves live.**
- **Get involved.**
- **Express your concerns about wildlife.**
- **Protect natural areas.**
- **Reduce your carbon footprint.**

From the fws.gov brochure RED WOLF, 2011

8. Which **implicit** claim does the evidence in this passage support?

A. Red wolves are a danger to many small animals.
B. Red wolves maintain the balance and health of ecosystems.
C. Red wolves were reintroduced in North Carolina due to the success of a managed breeding program.
D. Red wolves need human intervention in order to survive.

9. What evidence **best** supports the opinion that the presence of red wolves contributes significantly to the local economies?

A. Those who want to see or learn more about red wolves will visit their habitats and the local communities.
B. Red wolf populations have grown since the inception of the 1973 breeding program.
C. Local communities can play a role in the protection of the red wolf through education and awareness.
D. The red wolf now inhabits a five-county area in North Carolina.

10. In paragraph 2, the brochure identifies the red wolf as "once a top predator" and goes on to describe the red wolf is still in danger of "human mortalities, such as gunshot and vehicle strikes." Which statement **best** describes this type of evidence?

A. an appeal to reason by providing data
B. an appeal to the emotion of preservation
C. a strong opinion supported by facts
D. an appeal to ethics by naming the source of the facts

11. Which claim lacks supporting evidence in the passage?

A. Education is key in supporting the successful return of the red wolf population.
B. The number of red wolves was diminished due to loss of habitat and human activities.
C. Efforts to protect the red wolf and preserve its population are expensive and can be unsuccessful.
D. The red wolf is important to the health of ecosystems and local economies surrounding its habitat.

High Impact Lesson: Premise of an Argument

Use with **Student Book** pp. 94–97

1 Review the Skill

When writers make arguments, they use **premises** to support their arguments' **conclusion**. Each premise is an assumption that the author makes, either explicitly or implicitly. **Explicit** premises **are claims and assumptions** written out in the text. **Implicit** premises are unstated, or implied, claims and assumptions.

To build convincing arguments, writers support each premise with **evidence**. Effective evidence does not leave out important information that would be important to the argument. Evidence should not be presented in an overly emotional way or show **bias**, a favorable or unfavorable prejudice toward one side or another.

On the GED® Reasoning Through Language Arts test, you will be expected to show you understand the premise of an argument. You may encounter questions that ask you to identify explicit and implicit premises that are part of an argument. You may encounter other questions that ask you to explain the author's biases and assumptions. You may also encounter questions that ask you to judge whether any of the premises of the argument are justified by the evidence in the text.

2 Refine the Skill

In this 1909 letter to the editor, the writer is making an argument in response to an editorial which argued women should not have the right to vote.

SHE IS THERE TO STAY, AND SHE NEEDS THE SUFFRAGE

a In paragraph 1, the writer states her conclusion—that women need the protection of the vote. She uses a premise that the editorial had used to make the opposite point.

1   In an editorial entitled "The Hardiness of Woman," you show by statistics that the entrance of women into industry has had a disastrous effect on their health and shortened their lives, and you draw the conclusion that women should not be burdened with the vote. The conclusion that I should draw from your premises would be that women apparently need the protection of the vote. . . .

b In paragraph 2, the writer gives evidence to support her premise. Rephrase the evidence and premise to check your understanding: Since legislators listen to those who elect them, one of the best ways to improve conditions for a group is to give them the vote.

2   Now, one of the best ways of improving the conditions under which any class works is to give that class the suffrage. Legislators make the laws regulating the conditions of work and hours in the factories, and legislators, naturally, pay most attention to the interests of those who elect them. If the workers are women and therefore in need of special legislation for the protection of their health one of the surest ways of securing that legislation is to make the legislators dependent on the votes of women as well as men for any continuance of office.

From *The New York Times* article SHE IS THERE TO STAY, AND SHE NEEDS THE SUFFRAGE; Tuesday, March 16, 1909

Implicit premises are not stated directly. Re-read the text and eliminate any answer choice that is stated in the text. The correct answer is **D**.

1.   Which is an implicit premise in the text?

A. Groups who are able to vote wield more political power.
B. Working outside the home has shortened women's lives.
C. Industry has a disastrous effect on women's health.
D. Women want better, healthier working conditions.

UNIT 2

DIRECTIONS: Read the passage, read each question, and choose the **best** answer.

This excerpt is from a newspaper article printed in 1903, when child labor was common.

CHILD LABOR AS A FACTOR IN THE INCREASE OF PAUPERISM

1   Each age has of course its own temptations, and above all its own peculiar industrial temptations. When we ask why it is that child labor has been given to us to discuss and to rectify rather than to the people who lived before us, we need only remember that for the first time in industrial history the labor of the little child has in many industries become as valuable as that of a man or woman. The old-fashioned weaver was obliged to possess skill and enough strength to pull his beam back and forth. With the invention of machinery the need of skill has been eliminated from many processes, and with the application of steam and electricity strength has also been largely eliminated, so that a little child may mend the thread in a textile mill almost as well and, in some respects, better than a strong and clumsy adult. This is true of many other industries, until it has come about that we are tempted as never before to use the labor of little children and that the temptation to exploit premature labor is peculiar to this industrial epoch.

2   What, then, are we doing about it? How deeply are we concerned that this labor shall not result to the detriment of the child, and what excuses are we making to ourselves for thus prematurely using up the strength of the child? . . .

3   We may trace a connection between child labor and pauperism, not only for the child and his own family, bringing on premature old age and laying aside able-bodied men and women in the noontide of their years, but also the grievous charge is true that it pauperizes the community itself. I should also add that it debauches our moral sentiment, it confuses our sense of values, so that we learn to think that a bale of cheap cotton is more to be prized than a child properly nourished, educated, and prepared to take his place in life. Let us stand up to the obligations of our own age. Let us watch that we do not discount the future and cripple the next generation because we were too indolent. I was going to say because we were too dull, to see all that it involves, when we use the labor of little children.

From *The New York Times* article CHILD LABOR AS A FACTOR IN THE INCREASE OF PAURPERISM by Jane Addams of Hull House, Chicago; Sunday, October 4, 1903

2. Which is an explicit premise in paragraph 1?

   A. Children's labor is valuable, and factories should employ them.
   B. Children's labor is in demand since work is easier because of machines.
   C. Children have always been able to work as skilled weavers.
   D. The Industrial Age is an improvement on previous eras.

3. What is an explicit premise in paragraph 3?

   A. We are obligated to work in factories instead of children.
   B. We are too lazy to fight child labor.
   C. Cheap cotton is more important than a child's development.
   D. Allowing child labor hurts the morals of communities.

4. What is an implicit premise in paragraph 3?

   A. Pauperism, or being poor, is something people want to avoid.
   B. Child labor causes premature old age for the workers.
   C. Child labor confuses the moral sentiments of those who allow it.
   D. Aging prematurely is worth it if children are steadily employed.

5. What answer **best** states the conclusion of Hull's argument?

   A. Machines make it easier for children to work.
   B. Child labor makes cotton cheaper.
   C. Child labor should be stopped.
   D. The current era is industrial.

6. What is the **best** example of emotional language?

   A. "The old-fashioned weaver was obliged to possess skill . . ."
   B. "With the invention of machinery the need of skill has been eliminated . . ."
   C. ". . . with the application of steam and electricity strength has also been largely eliminated . . ."
   D. ". . . also the grievous charge is true that it pauperizes the community itself."

4

LESSON

Analyze Visuals and Data

Use with *Student Book* pp. 98–99

READING ASSESSMENT TARGETS: R.2.8, R.3.5, R.6.1, R.6.2, R.6.3, R.7.2, R.7.4, R.█

UNIT 2

1 Review the Skill

Visuals allow authors to highlight important information and present data in different ways. For example, a graph can show how something changes over time. A chart can show comparisons among groups. Photographs and pictures can appeal to readers' emotions and help readers understand what a particular situation was or is like. Authors use **data** to inform readers and support logical arguments.

2 Refine the Skill

By refining the skill of analyzing visuals and data, you will improve your study and test-taking abilities, especially as they relate to the GED® Reasoning Through Language Arts test. Read the passage, and study the graph below. Then answer the questions that follow.

THE IMPORTANCE OF VACCINATION

The Centers for Disease Control and Prevention has found that groups opposed to vaccination may claim that some diseases began to disappear before vaccines were introduced. Better nutrition and cleanliness have certainly reduced disease. But vaccination remains an important part of keeping populations healthy.

The graph below shows that a dramatic decrease in incidence of measles began when the measles vaccine became widespread.

a The title of a graph or table indicates the information it shows. This graph shows the number of cases of measles in the United States between 1950 and 2001.

b This graph shows the numbers of cases on the vertical *y*-axis and years on the horizontal *x*-axis.

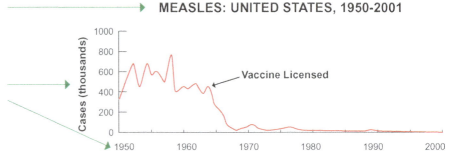

Source: Centers for Disease Control and Prevention

TEST-TAKING TIPS

Review visuals carefully. It is important to notice, for example, that the numbers on this graph's y-axis represent hundreds of thousands of cases. These numbers show how important the vaccine is.

1. How does the graph help the author respond to anti-vaccination viewpoints? The graph shows that

   A. vaccinations were more effective than cleanliness and nutrition.
   B. vaccines have been effective in eliminating many diseases.
   C. measles cases declined steeply after the vaccine was licensed.
   D. measles cases rose and fell consistently before the vaccine was introduced.

2. Why is the year the vaccine was licensed indicated on the graph?

   A. to confirm how quickly cases declined
   B. to indicate when the decline in cases began
   C. to prove that cleanliness is unimportant
   D. to explain why cases of measles declined

DIRECTIONS: Read the passage, and study the photograph. Then read each question, and choose the **best** answer.

PRESIDENT FORD'S PROCLAMATION ABOUT THE END OF JAPANESE INTERNMENT

1   During World War II, over 100,000 Japanese Americans were removed from their homes on the Pacific Coast of the United States. The Japanese Americans were allowed to return to their homes when World War II ended, but the order for their removal was not formally canceled. On February 19, 1976, President Gerald Ford issued a proclamation confirming the cancellation of the order.

2   President Ford noted that February 19 is the anniversary of a sad day in American history. On this date in 1942, the executive order for the removal of the Japanese Americans was issued. The War Relocation Authority did try to protect the welfare of the Japanese Americans. Nevertheless, the executive order represented a "fundamental setback of American principles."

3   President Ford stated that now the country knew what it did not know in 1942—that the Japanese Americans were loyal Americans. At home and in battle, they made great contributions and sacrifices. He called upon the American people to promise with him that the country had learned from the tragedy. He urged them to "treasure liberty and justice for each individual American" and to make sure that such an action never happened again.

Adapted from PROCLAMATION 4417 by Gerald R. Ford, 1976

3. Which implied claim do the passage and photograph support?

    A. Japanese Americans feared that the removal order could be reissued.
    B. The removal order violated the civil rights of Japanese Americans.
    C. Americans are likely to forget the contributions of Japanese American soldiers.
    D. The War Relocation Authority provided inadequate food for Japanese Americans.

Photograph by Dorothea Lange of Japanese Americans waiting to enter the mess hall at Tanforan Assembly Center, 1942

4. What information does the photograph provide that the passage does not? The photograph shows

    A. some of what life was like at Tanforan Assembly Center.
    B. the number of Japanese Americans who stayed at Tanforan Assembly Center.
    C. how Japanese Americans contributed on the battlefield.
    D. that Americans' views about World War II had changed by 1976.

5. Which statement **best** explains the purpose of the photograph?

    A. to teach readers about American history
    B. to prove that the camps existed
    C. to create sympathy for Japanese Americans
    D. to anger those who experienced removal

6. Which conclusion is **best** supported by the photograph?

    A. Japanese Americans at the camps faced uncomfortable conditions.
    B. President Ford believed the removal of Japanese Americans was unjust.
    C. Japanese Americans faced removal in Oregon, Washington, and California.
    D. Japanese Americans were separated from their friends and families at the camps.

DIRECTIONS: Read the passage, and study the graph. Then read each question, and choose the **best** answer.

FARMING EFFICIENCY

1   A competitive market requires efficiency. Efficiency means that the time, energy, and money put into a job results in more production with less waste. Over the years, American farmers have become fewer and more efficient. In the 1850s, about 50 percent of Americans were farmers. By the 1900s, the number of farms in the United States grew to more than 6,000. The number of farms started to decline rapidly in the 1950s. By 1970, there were fewer than 3,000 farms in the United States. Only 0.8 percent of Americans today make their living as farmers.

2   Farmers can produce more food because of technological advances in machinery and farming techniques. Today farmers use machines, special seeds, fertilizers, and weed killers. As a result, it takes fewer farmers to produce a larger food supply. In the 1850s, one farmer produced enough food to feed five people. Today, the average farmer feeds about 166 people.

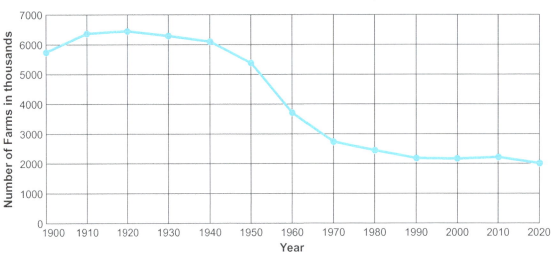

Number of Farms in the United States, 1900–2020

Source: U.S. Department of Agriculture

7. Which claim from the text is **not** supported by information in the graph?

    A. American farmers have become fewer and more efficient.
    B. The average farmer feeds about 166 people.
    C. By the 1900s, the number of farms in the United States grew to more than 6,000.
    D. There were fewer than 3,000 farms in the United States in 1970.

8. Which is the **most likely** conclusion to draw from information in both the text and the graph?

    A. Farming was more profitable in the 1900s.
    B. Advances in farming technology increased greatly between 1940 and 1980.
    C. Competition among farmers increased in the 1950s.
    D. Farming is a dying industry.

9. Which statement from the text **best** explains the overall purpose of the graph?

    A. "Today, the average farmer feeds about 166 people."
    B. "By the 1900s, the number of farms in the United States grew to more than 6,000."
    C. "A competitive market requires efficiency."
    D. "Over the years, American farmers have become fewer and more efficient."

10. Which of these claims does the graph help clarify?

    A. "The number of farms started to decline rapidly in the 1950s."
    B. "Only 0.8 percent of Americans today make their living as farmers."
    C. "About 50 percent of Americans were farmers in the 1850s."
    D. "In the 1850s, one farmer produced enough food to feed five people."

DIRECTIONS: Read the passage, and study the table. Then read each question, and choose the **best** answer.

IMPORTANCE OF STEM WORKERS

Over the past 10 years, growth in [science, technology, engineering, and mathematics (STEM)] jobs was three times as fast as growth in non-STEM jobs. STEM workers are also less likely to experience joblessness than their non-STEM counterparts. . . .

- In 2010, there were 7.6 million STEM workers in the United States, representing about 1 in 18 workers.
- STEM occupations are projected to grow by 17.0 percent from 2008 to 2018, compared to 9.8 percent growth for non-STEM occupations.

Workers in STEM occupations also earn more on average than their counterparts in other jobs, regardless of their educational attainment. . . . On average, [STEM workers with a high-school diploma or less] earned almost $25 per hour, $9 more per hour than those in other occupations in 2010. It should be noted, however, that only about 1 out of every 10 STEM workers has a high-school diploma or less. Those with graduate degrees in a STEM job earned more than $40 per hour, nearly $4.50 more per hour on average than those with non-STEM jobs.

AVERAGE HOURLY EARNINGS OF FULL-TIME STEM VS. NON-STEM WORKERS, 2010

	Average hourly earnings		Difference	
	STEM	Non-STEM	DOLLARS	PERCENT
High school diploma or less	$24.82	$15.55	$9.27	59.6%
Some college or associate degree	$26.63	$19.02	$7.61	40.0%
Bachelor's degree only	$35.81	$28.27	$7.54	26.7%
Graduate degree	$40.69	$36.22	$4.47	12.3%

From the esa.doc.gov article STEM: GOOD JOBS NOW AND FOR THE FUTURE by David Langdon, et al., July 2011, accessed 2021

11. How do the data reported about the projected growth of STEM occupations support the author's claim about STEM workers' job security?

A. STEM workers are 17% more likely to experience joblessness than their non-STEM counterparts.
B. STEM workers are 9.8% less likely to experience joblessness as their non-STEM counterparts.
C. STEM workers are more likely to experience joblessness than their non-STEM counterparts.
D. STEM workers are less likely to experience joblessness than their non-STEM counterparts.

12. The table lists average hourly earnings of STEM and non-STEM workers across several levels of education to show

A. that STEM workers earn less on average than non-STEM workers, regardless of their educational level.
B. that STEM workers earn more on average than non-STEM workers, regardless of their educational level.
C. that the largest difference in earnings occurs between STEM and non-STEM workers with a graduate degree.
D. that only 10% of STEM workers have a high-school diploma or less.

LESSON 5

Identify Faulty Evidence

Use with **Student Book** pp. 100–101

1 **Review the Skill**

To identify **faulty reasoning** as you read persuasive texts, consider several things. First, ask yourself whether the information is reliable and connects to the claim. Next, remember that although two events may happen one after the other, the first event does not necessarily cause the second. Also, consider whether the author acknowledges other points of view and presents an accurate picture of an issue.

To identify **faulty evidence**, consider whether the author relies only on emotion to support a claim. Ask yourself whether the author uses emotional language when facts and information would provide more effective support for a claim. Ask yourself whether the evidence is relevant and accurate.

UNIT 2

2 **Refine the Skill**

By refining the skill of identifying faulty reasoning and evidence, you will improve your study and test-taking abilities, especially as they relate to the GED® Reasoning Through Language Arts test. Read the passage below. Then answer the questions that follow.

a The detail that new diets spring up every year is irrelevant because other diets have no relevance to the effectiveness of gluten-free diets.

b The author considers celebrity testimonials unreliable. However, the author provides no evidence from experts who think gluten-free diets are ineffective.

IGNORE THE GLUTEN-FREE FAD

Gluten is a protein found in wheat flour, but these days, it seems as though gluten-free products are everywhere. Although some people do suffer from celiac disease and cannot eat foods containing gluten, there's no reason for others to change what they eat.

Every year seems to bring a new diet to change your life. But the only changes are in your wallet! Most people have no problems digesting gluten and should not compromise their nutrition by giving up something that occurs naturally in many foods.

Celebrities, always quick to jump on trends, have used social media to trumpet the benefits of going gluten-free. Now doctors and other experts are lining up against the musicians and movie stars. Wouldn't you rather join the ranks of those who form opinions on the basis of expert recommendations? The experts, by the way, agree that gluten-free diets are just a fad. If so, that may be the best thing about them—fads go quickly out of style.

1. Which statement **best** explains why the passage is not reliable?

   A. The author relies on testimonials from celebrities.
   B. The author uses strong language to frighten readers.
   C. The author presents only one side of the argument.
   D. The author uses a false cause-and-effect relationship.

2. Which detail makes an appeal to a reader's need to fit in?

   A. Some people cannot eat foods containing gluten.
   B. We should not compromise our own nutrition by giving up something that occurs naturally in so many foods.
   C. Wouldn't you rather join the ranks of those who form opinions on the basis of expert recommendations?
   D. The experts agree that gluten-free diets are just a fad.

CLOSER LOOK AT ITEMS

Most items on the test require you to demonstrate at least two skills. Usually these are reading and critical thinking. For example, to answer question 1, you must understand the passage, **and** you must evaluate its reliability.

DIRECTIONS: Read the passage, read each question, and choose the **best** answer.

This passage is an excerpt from the inaugural speech of George Wallace on his election as governor of Alabama in 1963. In the second part of the speech, Wallace responds to federal desegregation laws.

SEGREGATION NOW, SEGREGATION FOREVER

1   I have said to you that I would eliminate the liquor agents in this state and that the money saved would be returned to our citizens. . . . I am happy to report to you that the big-wheeling cocktail-party boys have gotten the word that their free whiskey and boat rides are over, that the farmer in the field, the worker in the factory, the businessman in his office, the housewife in her home, have decided that the money can be better spent to help our children's education and our older citizens, and they have put a man in office to see that it is done. It shall be done. Let me say one more time: no more liquor drinking in your governor's mansion. . . .

2   Today I have stood, where once Jefferson Davis stood, and took an oath to my people. It is very appropriate then that from this Cradle of the Confederacy, this very Heart of the Great Anglo-Saxon Southland, that today we sound the drum for freedom as have our generations of forebears before us done, time and time again through history. Let us rise to the call of freedom-loving blood that is in us and send our answer to the tyranny that clanks its chains upon the South. In the name of the greatest people that have ever trod this earth, I draw the line in the dust and toss the gauntlet before the feet of tyranny. And I say, segregation today, segregation tomorrow, segregation forever.

3   The Washington, D.C., school riot report is disgusting and revealing. We will not sacrifice our children to any such type school system—and you can write that down. The federal troops in Mississippi could be better used guarding the safety of the citizens of Washington, D.C., where it is even unsafe to walk or go to a ballgame— and that is the nation's capital. I was safer in a B-29 bomber over Japan during the war in an air raid, than the people of Washington are walking to the White House neighborhood. . . .

From SEGREGATION NOW, SEGREGATION FOREVER: INAUGURAL ADDRESS by George Wallace, 1963

3. How does the author show faulty reasoning in paragraph 1?

   A. He suggests a cause-and-effect relationship between his election and successful factories.
   B. He includes irrelevant information about liquor agents and the governor's mansion.
   C. He implies that the state can have either liquor agents or money for education and seniors.
   D. He suggests that voters should support his policies because they are popular.

4. The author states, "today we sound the drum for freedom as have our generations of forebears before us done, time and time again through history." This statement **most likely** made his audience of supporters feel

   A. patriotic and proud.
   B. angry and betrayed.
   C. satisfied and optimistic.
   D. disheartened and pessimistic.

5. Why does the author use inflammatory language to describe desegregation laws as "the tyranny that clanks its chains upon the South"?

   A. to appeal to the audience's sense of tolerance
   B. to arouse the audience's anger about desegregation
   C. to appeal to the audience's sense of shame
   D. to make the audience feel regret about segregation

6. In paragraph 3, the author makes the implied claim that desegregated schools are not safe. Which statement **best** explains how the author supports the claim?

   A. He uses exaggeration to make desegregation seem frightening and dangerous.
   B. He provides facts and data to prove the dangers of desegregation.
   C. He tells a personal story to illustrate what could happen during desegregation.
   D. He cites an example of how desegregation caused an increase in violence.

DIRECTIONS: Read the passage, read each question, and choose the **best** answer.

BUY AMERICAN!

1   "Buy American!" might sound like nothing more than a slogan advanced by American manufacturers to sell products made in the USA, but the truth is that there are many reasons to consider buying American-made clothing, American-made toys, and other US-manufactured goods . . . .

2   10) Foreign labor standards allow unsafe worker conditions in many countries. When you buy American you support not only American manufacturers but also American workers, safe working conditions, and child labor laws.

3   9) Jobs shipped abroad almost never return. When you buy goods made in the USA, you help keep the American economy growing.

4   8) US manufacturing processes are much cleaner for the environment than many other countries'; many brands sold here are produced in countries using dangerous, heavily polluting processes. When you purchase American-made products, you know that you're helping to keep the world a little cleaner for your children. . . .

5   6) The growing lack of USA ability to manufacture many products is strategically unsound. When you seek out American-made goods, you foster American independence. . . .

6   4) Foreign product safety standards are low. For example, poisonous levels of lead are in tens of millions of toys shipped to the USA. When you buy toys and other goods made in the USA, you can be confident that American consumer protection laws and safety standards are in place to protect your family. . . .

7   1) As the US manufacturing ability fades, future generations of US citizens will be unable to find relevant jobs. Buy American and help keep your friends and neighbors—and even yourself— earning a living wage.

From the madeintheusaforever.com article TOP TEN REASONS TO BUY AMERICAN by Todd Lipscomb, accessed 2013

7. How does the general tone of the passage support the author's claim?

A. The bullying tone makes readers feel guilty about buying foreign products.
B. The patriotic tone makes readers proud to buy American products.
C. The threatening tone makes readers fearful of buying American products.
D. The lighthearted tone makes readers think the source of products is unimportant.

8. Which detail would **most likely** make readers fearful of buying foreign goods?

A. Foreign labor standards allow unsafe worker conditions in many countries.
B. U.S. manufacturing processes are much cleaner for the environment than many other countries' processes.
C. Poisonous levels of lead are in tens of millions of toys shipped to the United States.
D. As U.S. manufacturing ability fades, future generations will be unable to find relevant jobs.

9. The author uses an inaccurate either/or situation by suggesting that if readers do not buy American products, then

A. the United States will fall behind technologically.
B. readers' children will be harmed by their toys.
C. conditions will never improve for foreign workers.
D. there will be far fewer jobs for Americans.

10. Which sentence from the passage appeals to readers' fears about the U.S. position of leadership among developed countries?

A. "When you buy American you support safe working conditions and child labor laws."
B. "Many brands sold here are produced in countries using dangerous, heavily polluting processes."
C. "The growing lack of American ability to manufacture products is strategically unsound."
D. "Buy American and help keep your friends and neighbors—and even yourself— earning a living wage."

DIRECTIONS: Read the passage, read each question, and choose the **best** answer.

REASONS WE OPPOSE VOTES FOR WOMEN

1   Because the basis of government is force—its stability rests upon its physical power to enforce its laws; therefore, it is inexpedient to give the vote to women. Immunity from service in executing the law would make most women irresponsible voters. . . .

2   Because it means simply doubling the vote, and especially the undesirable and corrupt vote of our large cities.

3   Because the great advance of women in the last century—moral, intellectual and economic—has been made without the vote; which goes to prove that it is not needed for their further advancement along the same lines. . . .

4   Because the ballot has not proved a cure-all for existing evils with men, and we find no reason to assume that it would be more effectual with women. . . .

5   Because our present duties fill up the whole measure of our time and ability, and are such as none but ourselves can perform. Our appreciation of their importance requires us to protest against all efforts to infringe upon our rights by imposing upon us those obligations which cannot be separated from suffrage, but which, as we think, cannot be performed by us without the sacrifice of the highest interests of our families and of society. . . .

6   We do, therefore, respectfully protest against the proposed Amendment to establish "woman suffrage" in our State. We believe that political equality will deprive us of special privileges hitherto accorded to us by law.

From the memory.loc.gov document SOME REASONS WHY WE OPPOSE VOTES FOR WOMEN by the National Association Opposed to Woman Suffrage, 1894, accessed 2021

11. How does the author show faulty reasoning in paragraph 1?

A. The author claims that the basis for government is the economy and women do not contribute equally to its growth.
B. The author claims that since women cannot serve in the armed forces they have not earned the right to vote.
C. The author claims women are not intelligent enough to vote.
D. The author claims that the basis of government is force and implies women lack the physical power to enforce laws.

12. In paragraph 3, the author states that because women have advanced morally, intellectually, and economically without suffrage, it "goes to prove that [suffrage] is not needed for their further advancement along the same lines." Why does this statement represent faulty reasoning?

A. Women do not want the vote in order to advance morally, intellectually, and economically.
B. The author bases the claim on threatening language rather than facts and information.
C. The author does not acknowledge the viewpoint that women or the United States could benefit from women's right to vote.
D. Women cannot vote, so it is impossible to know what would change if they could.

13. Why is the author's statement that "the ballot has not proved a cure-all for existing evils with men" an example of faulty reasoning?

A. The author dismisses any good that suffrage offers women because it has not fixed every problem men face.
B. The author uses words such as *evils* to make readers fear the results of women's suffrage.
C. The author appeals to readers' needs to fit in with those considered moral and admirable.
D. The author suggests a false cause-and-effect relationship between suffrage and immorality.

14. Which statement **best** explains why the evidence in this passage is faulty?

A. The author relies on personal stories rather than facts and statistics.
B. The author does not address specific reasons that women might want suffrage.
C. The author includes testimonials from celebrities in order to persuade readers.
D. The author uses patriotic language to inspire readers to oppose suffrage.

Classify Valid and Invalid Evidence

Use with **Student Book** pp. 102–103

READING ASSESSMENT TARGETS: R.2.8, R.4.3/L.4.3, R.5.1, R.5.4, R.6.3, R.6 R.8.2, R.8.3, R.8.4, R.8.5, R.8.6

1 Review the Skill

Evidence that an author uses to support a claim should be from a reliable source—that is, a source that is trustworthy, such as an expert on the topic. Evidence should be complete and accurately reflect both sides of an argument. Evidence should be relevant, or directly related to the claim. Evidence that is reliable, complete, and relevant is <mark>valid</mark>. Evidence that is unreliable, incomplete, or irrelevant is <mark>invalid</mark>.

2 Refine the Skill

By refining the skill of identifying faulty reasoning and evidence, you will improve your study and test-taking abilities, especially as they relate to the GED® Reasoning Through Language Arts test. Read the passage below. Then answer the questions that follow.

UNIT 2

WIND POWER IS A DAYDREAM

Environmentalists like to claim that wind power could replace traditional energy sources, but the drawbacks of wind power far outweigh any supposed benefits. American taxpayers should not be forced to pay for subsidies to support this immature technology.

Traditional power plants produce a steady supply of electricity. Wind turbines, however, produce electricity only when the wind is blowing. During windless periods, backup power plants must fill the gap to provide electricity.

a The New York Times is a major national newspaper. Information from this source can generally be considered reliable.

Furthermore, areas with the steadiest winds are usually far from the cities and communities that use electricity. _The New York Times_ notes that in Texas, the leading state for wind-power production, the wind is strongest hundreds of miles from big cities. Building lines to transmit the electricity from wind turbines to communities is an expensive endeavor. Wind farms off the coast are equally expensive. The construction of the Cape Wind Project near Cape Cod could cost one billion dollars. Until we find practical solutions to these problems, we should not devote any tax dollars to this daydream of environmental extremists.

b The author calls environmentalists **extremists** but provides no supporting evidence. The author is likely not presenting both sides of the issue fairly and may be considered biased.

1. Which detail is **valid** evidence that supports the author's claim?

   A. Environmentalists like to claim that wind power could replace traditional energy sources.
   B. Tax dollars support subsidies for development of wind power.
   C. Wind power is an immature technology.
   D. _The New York Times_ notes that in Texas the wind is strongest hundreds of miles from big cities.

2. Which type of evidence would **most** strengthen the claim that the drawbacks of wind power outweigh the benefits?

   A. examples of some of the benefits of wind power
   B. examples of how environmentalists can be extremists
   C. additional data about the cost of constructing wind farms
   D. stories from people who have to rely on unreliable wind power

TEST-TAKING TIPS

Question 1 asks you first to determine the author's claim and then to identify valid evidence. You must understand the claim **before** you can evaluate the evidence that supports it.

DIRECTIONS: Read the passage, read each question, and choose the **best** answer.

GIVE A GIFT OF LIFE

1   A gift with a major impact—one that will long be remembered with gratitude—takes just a bit of preparation. When you become an organ donor, you can save the lives of up to 8 people. And if you donate tissues like blood cells, bone or corneas, you can help even more.

2   Organ transplantation was once considered an experimental procedure with a low success rate. Many transplanted organs survived just a few days or weeks. But researchers have transformed transplant surgery from risky to routine. It's now the treatment of choice for patients with end-stage organ diseases. Each day about 80 Americans receive a lifesaving organ transplant.

3   "The outcomes of transplantation are really so good these days that it truly makes a difference for the people who receive organ transplants," says Dr. Sandy Feng, a transplant surgeon at the University of California, San Francisco. "The organs are clearly livesaving.". . .

4   You can donate some organs—like a kidney or part of your liver—while you're still alive. You have 2 kidneys but really need only one. And the liver can re-grow if part of it is removed. But donating these organs requires major surgery, which carries risks. That's why living donors are often family or friends of the transplant recipient.

5   Most organs, though, are donated after the donor has died. The organs must be recovered quickly after death to be usable. Many come from patients who've been hospitalized following an accident or stroke. Once all lifesaving efforts have failed and the patient is declared dead, then organ donation becomes a possibility.

6   "When a person dies, it can feel like a burden to a family to make decisions about organ donation," says Feng. "So it would be a real gift to a family to indicate your decision to be an organ donor while you're still alive, so they don't have to make the decision for you." . . .

7   You can help reduce the need for donated organs in the first place by living well. . . . Talk to your doctor about your weight, blood pressure and cholesterol. And while you're taking these healthy steps, be sure to sign up to be an organ donor so you can help others as well.

From the nih.gov article ORGAN DONATION: PASS IT ON, accessed 2021

3. What makes Dr. Feng a reliable source on this topic?

    A. She describes several surgeries.
    B. She includes statistics.
    C. She is a transplant surgeon.
    D. Her facts come from a variety of published sources.

4. Which detail from the passage **best** supports the claim that it is important to make a decision to be an organ donor when you are still alive?

    A. "You can help reduce the need for donated organs in the first place by living well."
    B. "So it would be a real gift to a family to indicate your decision to be an organ donor while you're still alive, so they don't have to make the decision for you."
    C. "You can donate some organs . . . while you're still alive."
    D. "That's why living donors are often family or friends of the transplant recipient."

5. The passage suggests that donating certain organs requires major surgery, which carries risks. What type of evidence would **best** strengthen this claim?

    A. quotations from researchers about family members applying to become organ donors
    B. information from reports about the length of major surgeries
    C. data showing the types of risks resulting from organ donor surgery and their survival rates
    D. stories from family members who donated organs to other family members

6. Which detail from the passages relies on emotional language to encourage organ donation?

    A. "And while you're taking these healthy steps, be sure to sign up to be an organ donor so you can help others as well."
    B. "Once all lifesaving efforts have failed and the patient is declared dead, then organ donation becomes a possibility."
    C. "Each day about 80 Americans receive a lifesaving organ transplant."
    D. "A gift with a major impact—one that will long be remembered with gratitude—takes just a bit of preparation."

DIRECTIONS: Read the passage, read each question, and choose the **best** answer.

IN FAVOR OF ROUNDABOUTS

1   Either as a driver or a passenger, everyone has been there: stuck at a traffic light, already running late to get somewhere. The light turns green, and then you rush forward, only to stop at another light.

2   Much of a roadway's capacity to allow traffic to flow depends on intersections. More intersections lead to more time waiting at red lights and stop signs.

3   The solution could lie in roundabouts. A roundabout is a type of intersection where 3–4 roads meet. It's a circular pattern in which traffic flows counterclockwise, but there are no lights or stop signs. To enter the roundabout from any lane, you must yield to anyone who is already driving in the roundabout. That means you only must worry about the car to your left (in addition to any crosswalks). This is an incredibly simple and safe system.

4   There are other aspects of roundabouts that make them safer than other types of intersections. Generally, these are only a couple hundred feet in diameter, and that small size means cars can't build up much speed. Most vehicles travel under 20 mph through them because you must slow down considerably just to enter, and possibly even wait for other cars. Roundabouts reduced injury crashes by 76% and fatal crashes by 90% when compared to conventional signal and stop sign controlled intersections, according to a study by the Insurance Institute for Highway Safety. The Federal Highway Administration identified roundabouts as a proven safety countermeasure.

5   Another benefit of roundabouts is that they are also more efficient. They improve traffic capacity by up to 50%. That means more cars can flow through the streets with less congestion. In addition, because roundabout decrease the amount of time cars idle, they also reduce fuel consumption and emissions. Roundabout reduce carbon monoxide emissions by 15-45% and carbon dioxide emissions by 23-34%. Plus, they're also cheaper to build and maintain than other intersections.

6   There seems to really be only one problem with roundabouts: expectations. Many city planners prefer them and find that the biggest deterrent is local drivers. It can be strange at first to drive straight through a place where you would expect to stop. But, over time, I feel certain that our local drivers will get used to it and even appreciate the change. They will especially appreciate fewer accidents. Because of all this, I want our city to consider implementing roundabouts in some of our most congested intersections. The next time you're sitting in traffic, you might consider their benefits, too!

7.   One reason the authors cite in favor of roundabouts is that "Roundabouts reduced injur crashes by 76% and fatal crashes by 90% when compared to conventional signal and stop sign controlled intersections, according to a study by the Insurance Institute for Highway Safety." This statement is an example of incomplete evidence because the evidence

   A. does not include data about the number of overall reduction in crashes compared to conventional intersections.
   B. is from a source unlikely to have knowledge about vehicular crashes.
   C. does not take into account the speed of vehicles in roundabouts.
   D. is not relevant to the claim that roundabouts are safer than other types of intersections.

8.   Which piece of evidence is irrelevant to the claim made in paragraph 5?

   A. "They improve traffic capacity by up to 50%."
   B. ". . . they also reduce fuel consumption and emissions."
   C. "Roundabout reduce carbon monoxide emissions by 15–45% and carbon dioxide emissions by 23–34%."
   D. ". . . they're also cheaper to build and maintai than other intersections."

9.   The author includes information from the Federa Highway Administration. Which claim does this information support?

   A. Some drivers are unfamiliar with roundabouts and prefer conventional intersections.
   B. Roundabouts are more efficient than other types of intersections.
   C. Roundabouts are safer than other types of intersections.
   D. Roundabouts are cheaper to build and maintain than other types of intersections.

DIRECTIONS: Read the passage, read each question, and choose the **best** answer.

THE FIGHT TO SAVE OUR FILMS

1   Movies have documented America for more than one hundred years. Since Thomas Edison introduced the movie camera in 1893, amateur and professional filmmakers have used motion pictures to tell stories, record communities, explain the work of business and government, and illustrate current events. They captured, with the immediacy unique to the moving image, how generations of Americans have lived, worked, and dreamed. By preserving these films, we save a century of history.

2   Unfortunately, movies are not made to last. Created on perishable plastic, film decays within years if not properly stored. Already the losses are high. The Library of Congress has documented that only 20% of U.S. feature films from the 1910 and 1920s survive in complete form in American archives; of the American features produced before 1950, about half still exist. For shorts, documentaries, and independently produced works, we have no way of knowing how much has been lost.

3   For Hollywood, the tide has turned. Commercial producers now invest heavily in the protection of their film libraries. With the development of television, home video, DVD, cable, and Internet exhibition, Hollywood sound films have become valuable assets and have many markets after their initial release.

4   Still at risk, however, are documentaries, silent-era films, anthropological footage, avant-garde works, newsreels, home movies, works made for ethnic communities, industrial films, and other independent productions. We call these orphan films because they fall outside the scope of commercial preservation programs. Orphan films may document viewpoints, traditions, and places not depicted in the mainstream media and have a cultural value that transcends their simple origins. They often survive as one-of-a-kind copies in archives, libraries, museums, universities and historical societies. These organizations are the first line of defense for saving American movies made outside of Hollywood. . . .

5   By investing in saving film on film and storing it properly, we make sure that movies will be here to be studied and enjoyed for years to come.

From the filmpreservation.org article WHY PRESERVE FILM?, accessed 2013.

10. Which claim is **best** supported by the evidence in this passage?

    A. Film is the most effective way to capture history.
    B. The need to preserve early films is urgent.
    C. Hollywood has contributed to the loss of films.
    D. Saving orphan films could bring financial rewards.

11. The statements in paragraph 1 support the claim that the preservation of film is an important task. Which statement **best** explains why some evidence in this paragraph is invalid?

    A. The evidence does not include accurate details about how film is used.
    B. The evidence does not acknowledge other viewpoints about film.
    C. The evidence includes the outdated testimonial of Thomas Edison.
    D. The evidence relies on appeals to readers' sense of patriotism and pride.

12. In paragraph 2, the authors note, "The Library of Congress has documented that only 20% of U.S. feature films from the 1910 and 1920s survive in complete form in American archives." Which statement **best** explains the purpose of this evidence?

    A. The evidence comes from a reliable source and supports the article's claim.
    B. The evidence acknowledges and responds to an opposing viewpoint.
    C. The evidence provides background information necessary for understanding the article's claim.
    D. The evidence is likely to have an emotional impact on readers.

13. In paragraph 4, the authors note that orphan films are in greater need of preservation than mainstream Hollywood movies. What additional evidence would improve support for this claim?

    A. data about how many orphan films are made each year
    B. a statement from a film-history professor about the importance of orphan films
    C. a chart comparing resources spent preserving Hollywood films versus orphan films
    D. descriptions of several orphan films that might be familiar to readers

High Impact Lesson: Evaluate Support and Evidence

Use with *Student Book* pp. 104–107

UNIT 2

1 Review the Skill

When writers make arguments, look carefully at the way they support their claims. Do they use relevant evidence or irrelevant evidence? **Relevant evidence** ties closely to an argument. **Irrelevant evidence** does not tie closely to an argument. A good argument will include relevant evidence.

Also look at whether the article provides **sufficient evidence**—enough evidence to justify the claim. If not enough evidence is provided, the article has **insufficient evidence**. When writers make arguments, they use evidence, or data, to support a claim. Writers also may include **explanations** that explain how evidence supports the claim or **reasoning** to explain why evidence supports the claim.

On the GED® Reasoning Through Language Arts test, you will be expected to show you understand evidence in an argument. You may encounter questions that ask you to distinguish between an idea that has sufficient evidence and one that does not or between an idea that has relevant evidence and one that does not. You may also encounter questions that ask you to distinguish between evidence and explanation, or between evidence and reasoning.

2 Refine the Skill

a Inhofe uses the word *hysteria* to describe global warming. Based on this paragraph, we see the senator is making the argument that climate change is unreal. A piece of evidence is the large snowstorm that year.

b While giving the speech, the senator actually took out a snowball and threw it to the president of the senate. Re-read the text and think about why Senator Inhofe does this.

Scan the text for the word *snowball*. Re-read the text and how the snowball relates to the issue of climate change. The correct answer is **D.**

SENATOR JAMES INHOFE'S COMMENTS ON CLIMATE CHANGE

Mr. President, I am reminiscent, with the snow on the ground, of 5 years ago. The Presiding Officer was not here at that time. He does not have the advantage of knowing the story of what is behind this. The story that is behind this is that back when they started all the hysteria on global warming, there happened to be another snowstorm that was unprecedented. It set a record that year. . . .

In case we have forgotten, because we keep hearing that 2014 has been the warmest year on record, I ask the Chair: Do you know what this is? It is a snowball. That is just from outside here. So it is very cold out, very unseasonable. So, Mr. President, catch this.

From CONGRESSIONAL RECORD VOL, 161, NO. 33, February 26, 2015

1. Which **best** describes the reason that the senator uses a snowball in his speech?

   A. The snowball is relevant evidence to support the argument that global warming is real.
   B. The snowball is relevant evidence to support the argument that global warming causes unprecedented snowstorms.
   C. The snowball is sufficient evidence to support the argument that global warming is based on hysteria.
   D. The snowball is insufficient evidence to support the argument that there is no global warming.

DIRECTIONS: Read the passage, read each question, and choose the **best** answer.

SENATOR JAMES INHOFE'S VIEW OF CLIMATE CHANGE

1   We hear the perpetual headline that 2014 has been the warmest year on record. Now the script has flipped. I think it is important, since we hear it over and over and over again on the floor of this Senate. Some outlets are referring to the recent cold temperatures as the ``Siberian Express,'' as we can see with the snowball out there. This is today. This is reality. . . .

2   Now, President Obama is using a similar tactic in order to scare Americans into supporting his extreme climate change agenda. In a recent interview, President Obama agreed that the media overstates the dangers of terrorism while downplaying the risks of climate change. His Press Secretary, Josh Earnest, later reiterated that President Obama believes climate change affects far more Americans than terrorists. . . .

3   According to the President, our biggest threat is not the continued threats made by extremists against the United States and its citizens. It is not the successful attacks carried out in the United States and other places such as New York, Boston, Fort Hood or potential attacks of lone wolves or sleeper cells against soft targets such as the Mall of America, which is the most recent subject of an ISIL threat. Even as these atrocities are taking place, President Obama is telling the world that climate change is a greater threat to our Nation than terrorists. This is just another illustration that this President and his administration are detached from the realities that we are facing today and into the future.

From CONGRESSIONAL RECORD VOL. 161, NO. 33, February 26, 2015

2. Why does Inhofe include the phrase "the Siberian Express"?

    A. to support the idea that current cold conditions show climate change is not real
    B. to support the idea that climate change causes surprising weather conditions
    C. to support the idea that outlets are trying to scare Americans with weather descriptions
    D. to support the idea that America is becoming too much like Russia

3. How does Inhofe's use of the phrase "extreme climate agenda" in paragraph 2 affect his argument?

    A. The persuasive language shows that the climate change critics are correct.
    B. The emotional language shows his views may be biased.
    C. The factual language appeals to the logic of his listeners.
    D. The ethical language appeals to the listeners' sense of justice.

4. What does Inhofe present as his strongest evidence that President Obama's views on climate change are unreasonable?

    A. He states that Obama is insufficiently worried about the climate change.
    B. He mentions several attacks against the U.S. carried out by terrorists.
    C. He states that Obama is detached from the realities Americans are facing.
    D. He states that Obama believes climate change is more of a risk than terrorism.

5. What is the **most likely** reason that Inhofe includes a list of attacks on the U.S.?

    A. to support the idea that terrorism is more dangerous than climate change
    B. to support the idea that climate change has increased terrorism worldwide
    C. to support the idea that Obama is correct in his beliefs about current dangers
    D. to support the idea that Obama is afraid of dealing with terrorist threats

6. What is the **best** evaluation of the list of attacks as evidence for Inhofe's main argument?

    A. The list of attacks is sufficient to prove that terrorism poses a grave threat to Americans.
    B. The list of attacks is insufficient to prove that terrorism is more of a threat to Americans than climate change.
    C. The list of attacks is relevant to the argument that President Obama is detached from realities.
    D. The list of attacks is irrelevant to the claim that terrorism poses a threat to Americans.

Analyze the Structure of Arguments

LESSON 7

Use with **Student Book** pp. 108–109

READING ASSESSMENT TARGETS: R.4.3/L.4.3, R.5.1, R.5.2, R.5.3, R.5.4, R.6.1 R.6.2, R.6.3, R.8.1, R.8.2, R.8.3, R.8.5

UNIT 2

1 Review the Skill

Structure refers to the organization, or arrangement, of ideas in a text. In persuasive writing, authors may use a specific structure that best supports their claims.

In a traditional "sandwich" structure, an author introduces the claim, presents evidence to support the claim, and ends with a conclusion. In a pro/con structure, an author explains the positives and negatives related to a claim or an idea. In a refutation/proof structure, an author presents information that shows why another claim is inaccurate or false. In an order-of-importance structure, an author lists evidence in order of effectiveness—either from weakest to strongest or from strongest to weakest.

2 Refine the Skill

By refining the skill of analyzing the structure of arguments, you will improve your study and test-taking abilities, especially as they relate to the GED® Reasoning Through Language Arts test. Read the passage below. Then answer the questions that follow.

PAYING STUDENTS TO LEARN

American students are falling behind their counterparts in other developed countries. Among the many strategies for improving student performance, few have yielded such promising, if mixed, results as paying students to learn.

a Whatever the structure of a passage, the author must include valid evidence. Roland Fryer, Jr., is a reliable source who is considered an expert in his field.

Students who are paid for behaviors in their control, such as reading or attendance, seem to do better on standardized tests. Harvard economist Roland Fryer, Jr. found that second-graders who were paid for each book they read performed better on reading tests at the end of the year. The gains also carried over to the following year when students were not getting paid.

There are drawbacks, however, to paying students. When the rewards are for results, such as grades, rather than behaviors, test scores do not improve. Critics also argue that payment systems teach students to value education for only short-term gains.

b The phrase *in sum* indicates that the author is stating a conclusion or summarizing the points in an argument.

In sum, evidence suggests that when applied in the right way, programs that pay students to learn do bring results.

1. The word **however** in the third paragraph signals a

   A. contrast between the benefits and drawbacks of paying students.
   B. cause-and-effect relationship between payment and test scores.
   C. result that contradicts the author's viewpoint about payment.
   D. strategy that could be an alternative to paying students.

2. Why is pro/con an effective structure for this argument?

   A. The conclusion includes a strong call to action.
   B. Particularly strong evidence appears at the beginning.
   C. The claim is a response to those opposed to paying students.
   D. There are positives and negatives to paying students.

DIRECTIONS: Read the passage, read each question, and choose the **best** answer.

THE DEATH PENALTY RE-EXAMINED

1   Ever since California added the death penalty to its penal code in the 1870s, supporters have argued that the threat of executions would make potential murderers think twice before committing heinous crimes.

2   *The* [*Sacramento*] *Bee* made that argument numerous times in its early years, and many politicians and prosecutors have offered it since. But does the evidence show that capital punishment deters murders, even when applied frequently and expeditiously? Research suggests it does not.

3   One obvious way to look at the problem is to compare the murder rates in states with executions and those without.

4   For example, compare the homicide rates in California, New York and Texas, as the National Research Council has done. From 1974 to 2009, the homicide rates in those three states tracked virtually identically—going up at the same time in the late 1970s and late 1980s and all declining dramatically since then.

5   Yet during that time Texas had 447 executions and New York had none; California had 13. Clearly, something other than executions has had an effect on declining murder rates. And that clearly is what we should focus on.

6   That pattern holds up in comparisons of Canada and the United States, too.

7   Murder rates in Canada have gone up and down in virtual lockstep with U.S. rates over the years. Yet Canada has had no executions since 1962. In fact, during the period just after the United States reinstated the death penalty in 1976, murder rates remained high in the United States while declining in Canada.

8   Murder rates in the United States began a real decline in the 1990s, and research suggests multiple factors are involved.

9   For example, crime experts attribute the steep decline in violent crime that began in 1993 to new police strategies such as targeted police patrols of gun-crime hot spots and effective enforcement of gun laws. The waning of the crack epidemic and the decline of the percentage of 18- to 24-year-olds in the population also played a role.

From *The Sacramento Bee*'s editorial DEATH PENALTY DETERS MURDERS? EVIDENCE DOESN'T BEAR THAT OUT, © 2012

3.   How does paragraph 4 relate to the author's purpose and structure of the editorial?

   A. It suggests that even respected organizations can be incorrect about some issues, thus contradicting the information presented.
   B. It indicates that the National Research Council conducts a wide range of studies, thus explaining the purpose of the organization.
   C. It shows readers that the evidence is from a reliable source, thus validating the example.
   D. It emphasizes that most research has been done by government organizations.

4.   How does the example of murder rates in Canada (paragraph 7) relate to the preceding examples?

   A. It helps explain how the United States differs from other countries in the use of the death penalty.
   B. It shows that the death penalty is unnecessary in Canada because murder rates are low.
   C. It clarifies the author's claim about the effectiveness of the death penalty.
   D. It provides further evidence that murder rates are not related to the use of the death penalty.

5.   How does paragraph 9 relate to the evidence presented earlier in the passage?

   A. It adds further evidence that the death penalty is ineffective.
   B. It provides an alternative explanation for why the murder rate has declined in recent years.
   C. It introduces a personal story to show readers the impact of the death penalty.
   D. It identifies the crime experts who provided the author with data.

6.   Why is a refutation/proof structure effective for this passage?

   A. The purpose of the argument is to show that the death penalty does not deter crime.
   B. The evidence shows the positives and negatives of enforcing the death penalty.
   C. Some evidence in favor of the death penalty is much stronger than other evidence.
   D. Readers need background information about the death penalty to understand the claim.

DIRECTIONS: Read the passage, read each question, and choose the **best** answer.

CITIZENSHIP AND THE RIGHT TO VOTE

In November 1872, Susan B. Anthony voted in a presidential election at her polling place in Rochester, New York. She was arrested, indicted, and put on trial for voting illegally. Before her trial in 1873, she gave this speech presenting the main argument in her defense.

1   I stand before you tonight under indictment for the alleged crime of having voted at the last presidential election, without having a lawful right to vote. . . . I not only committed no crime, but instead, simply exercised my citizen's rights, guaranteed to me and all United States citizens by the National Constitution, beyond the power of any state to deny.

2   The preamble of the Federal Constitution says: "We, the people of the United States, in order to form a more perfect union, establish justice, insure domestic tranquility, provide for the common defense, promote the general welfare, and secure the blessings of liberty to ourselves and our posterity, do ordain and establish this Constitution for the United States of America."

3   It was we, the people, not we . . . the male citizens; but we, the whole people, who formed the Union. And we formed it, not to give the blessings of liberty . . . to the half of ourselves and the half of our posterity, but to the whole people—women as well as men. And it is a downright mockery to talk to women of their enjoyment of the blessings of liberty while they are denied the use of the only means of securing them . . . the ballot. . . .

4   To . . . [women] this government has no just powers derived from the consent of the governed. To them this government is not a democracy. It is not a republic. It is an odious aristocracy, a hateful oligarchy of sex . . . which makes father, brothers, husband, sons, the oligarchs over the mother and sisters, the wife and daughters, of every household—which ordains all men sovereign, all women subjects, carries dissension, discord, and rebellion into every home of the nation.

5   Webster, Worcester, and Bouvier [dictionaries] all define a citizen to be a person in the United States, entitled to vote and hold office.

6   The only question left to be settled now is: Are women persons? And I hardly believe any of our opponents will have the hardihood to say they are not. Being persons, then, women are citizens, and no state has a right to make any law,

or to enforce any old law, that shall abridge their privileges. . . . Hence, every discrimination against women in the constitution and laws of the several states is today null and void, precisely a is every one against Negroes.

From WOMEN'S RIGHT TO VOTE by Susan B. Anthony, 1873

7. Which statement **best** describes the structure o the passage?

   A. It presents evidence in a refutation/proof structure to respond to the idea that women do not have the right to vote.
   B. It uses a pro/con structure to explain the positives and negatives of voting rights for women.
   C. It uses a traditional sandwich structure to present evidence supporting the claim that women have the right to vote.
   D. It engages readers by beginning with the strongest evidence showing that women have the right to vote.

8. How does the quoted excerpt from the preamble of the U.S. Constitution help support Anthony's argument?

   A. It suggests that the rights in the U.S. Constitution belong only to women.
   B. It explains the meaning of the U.S. Constitution.
   C. It explains why states cannot make laws abou the right to vote in federal elections.
   D. It helps establish that a citizen's rights flow from all of the people and are shared by all of them.

9. What is the purpose of paragraph 5?

   A. It explains why women are citizens of the United States.
   B. It sets up the next paragraph by establishing that a citizen is a person with the right to vote
   C. It sets up the next paragraph to contradict the definitions in Webster, Worcester, and Bouvier.
   D. It establishes that the U.S. Constitution gives women the right to vote and hold office.

DIRECTIONS: Read the passage, read each question, and choose the **best** answer.

PREVENTING ALCOHOL ABUSE AND ALCOHOLISM

1   Alcohol consumption can lead to alcohol dependence and abuse, contribute to a number of diseases and mental and behavioral disorders, and may lead to a range of injuries.

2   Drinking produces immense costs to society in terms of healthcare expenses, lost productivity, and lost years of lives. One of the most effective ways to lessen the costs associated with alcohol abuse and alcoholism is to prevent people from starting abusive drinking patterns. ...

What Is High-Risk Drinking?

3   Sometimes simply knowing what risky drinking is can help people to recognize and curb their unhealthy drinking patterns. Low-risk drinking is considered to be no more than 14 standard drinks per week (4 per day) for men and 7 standard drinks per week (3 per day) for women.

Targeted Prevention Approaches—What Works

4   When providing healthy-drinking guidelines is not enough to stop harmful drinking, a next step is to target specific groups with focused prevention messages. ...

Interventions in the Workplace

5   Because most adults are employed, workplace programs can potentially reach audiences and populations that otherwise would not have access to a prevention program. ...

6   Workplace prevention programs can help address some of the factors that may accompany abusive drinking. For example, lifestyle campaigns have shown promise in encouraging workers to ease stress, improve nutrition and exercise, and reduce risky behaviors such as drinking, smoking, and drug use.

Conclusion

7   Given the high costs of alcohol abuse and dependence to both people and society, evidenced-based approaches for preventing harmful alcohol are key. Communities, schools, and workplaces provide essential venues for reaching risky drinkers with prevention messages and strategies.

From ALCOHOL ALERT courtesy of National Institute on Alcohol and Abuse and Alcoholism

10. Which statement **best** explains the purpose of paragraphs 1 and 2?

A. to alert readers that the passage will present the health risks and benefits of drinking alcohol
B. to present background information about drinking alcohol in order to imply the author's point of view
C. to show evidence, appeal to reason, and state the author's claim
D. to share a personal story to draw readers into the passage and persuade them to agree with the author's viewpoint

11. What do the words **For example** indicate about the relationship between the two sentences in paragraph 6?

A. They indicate that the second sentence will present different information.
B. They indicate that the second sentence is a direct result of the first sentence.
C. They indicate that the second sentence acknowledges the negative side of an argument.
D. They indicate that the second sentence will provide specific evidence to support the first sentence.

12. Which statement **best** explains how the author has constructed the argument?

A. The author states a claim and presents the pros and cons related to it.
B. The author uses a traditional sandwich structure to introduce a claim and present evidence.
C. The author states the claim and presents evidence in order of strongest to weakest.
D. The author describes personal events in the order in which they happened.

Analyze Rhetorical Devices

Use with **Student Book** pp. 110–111

1 Review the Skill

Authors and speakers use **rhetorical devices** to achieve desired effects, usually to create rhythm and hold readers' attention. When using **enumeration**, the author lists details, which emphasize an idea and create a rhythm. When using **repetition**, the author repeats words and phrases to create rhythm and, sometimes, build to a climax. When using **parallelism**, the author repeats grammatically similar phrases.

Other rhetorical devices help clarify or emphasize. **Analogy**, for example, is the use of comparison to clarify an idea. A **qualifying statement** adds to or changes an earlier statement to clarify or highlight a point. Juxtaposition of opposites, or antithesis, places opposing ideas together to emphasize contrast. Rhetorical devices reflect an author's tone and are part of an author's style, as explained in Unit 1, Lesson 9.

2 Refine the Skill

By refining the skill of analyzing rhetorical devices, you will improve your study and test-taking abilities, especially as they relate to the GED® Reasoning Through Language Arts test. Read the passage below. Then answer the questions that follow.

LINCOLN'S GETTYSBURG ADDRESS

Fourscore and seven years ago our fathers brought forth on this continent a new nation, conceived in liberty and dedicated to the proposition that all men are created equal.

Now we are engaged in a great civil war, testing whether that nation or any nation so conceived and so dedicated can long endure. We are met on a great battlefield of that war. We have come to dedicate a portion of that field as a final resting-place for all those who here gave their lives that that nation might live. It is altogether fitting and proper that we should do this.

But in a larger sense, we cannot dedicate, we cannot consecrate, we cannot hallow this ground. The brave men, living and dead who struggled here have consecrated it ... It is rather for us to be here dedicated to the great task remaining before us ... that we here highly resolve that these dead shall not have died in vain, that this nation under God shall have a new birth of freedom, and that government of the people, by the people, for the people shall not perish from the earth.

From GETTYSBURG ADDRESS by Abraham Lincoln, 1863

a This expression is an example of **juxtaposition**: death and life.

b This sentence displays **parallelism**, which emphasizes that no memorial can match the sacrifice of the soldiers who died at Gettysburg.

1. What effect does the juxtaposition of opposites have in the phrase "those who here gave their lives that that nation might live"?

   A. It emphasizes the violence of the fighting.
   B. It emphasizes the sorrow of the soldiers' loved ones.
   C. It emphasizes the importance of the soldiers' sacrifices.
   D. It emphasizes the number of soldiers who died during the battle.

2. The parallelism at the end of the passage emphasizes Lincoln's

   A. determination to persevere through the war.
   B. sadness that so many people have died.
   C. anger at the injustice of slavery.
   D. respect for the U.S. Constitution.

COMPUTER TIPS

As you read during the test, you can use the highlighting function to highlight rhetorical devices. Highlighting will help you find the relevant text quickly if a question asks about a rhetorical device.

DIRECTIONS: Read the passage, read each question, and choose the **best** answer.

THE IMPORTANCE OF WOMEN'S RIGHTS

1   If there is one message that echoes forth from this conference, it is that human rights are women's rights. . . . And women's rights are human rights.

2   Let us not forget that among those rights are the right to speak freely. And the right to be heard.

3   Women must enjoy the right to participate fully in the social and political lives of their countries if we want freedom and democracy to thrive and endure.

4   It is indefensible that many women in non-governmental organizations who wished to participate in this conference have not been able to attend—or have been prohibited from fully taking part.

5   Let me be clear. Freedom means the right of people to assemble, organize, and debate openly. It means respecting the views of those who may disagree with the views of their governments. It means not taking citizens away from their loved ones and jailing them, mistreating them, or denying them their freedom or dignity because of the peaceful expression of their ideas and opinions.

6   In my country, we recently celebrated the 75th anniversary of women's suffrage. It took 150 years after the signing of our Declaration of Independence for women to win the right to vote. It took 72 years of organized struggle on the part of many courageous women and men.

7   It was one of America's most divisive philosophical wars. But it was also a bloodless war. Suffrage was achieved without a shot fired.

8   We have also been reminded, in V-J Day observances last weekend, of the good that comes when men and women join together to combat the forces of tyranny and build a better world.

9   We have seen peace prevail in most places for a half century. We have avoided another world war.

10   But we have not solved older, deeply rooted problems that continue to diminish the potential of half the world's population.

11   Now it is time to act on behalf of women everywhere.

From REMARKS FOR THE UNITED NATIONS FOURTH WORLD CONFERENCE ON WOMEN by Hillary Rodham Clinton, 1995

3.   In paragraph 1, the author states, "human rights are women's rights. . . . And women's rights are human rights." Reversing the order of the phrases **human rights** and **women's rights**

   A. shows that the author believes human rights are worth fighting for.
   B. shows that the author has deep respect for women's rights.
   C. suggests that most women are denied their human rights.
   D. stresses the closeness of women's rights and human rights.

4.   What is the purpose of the qualifying statement in paragraph 4?

   A. to celebrate that so many women were able to attend the conference
   B. to suggest that not letting women participate fully in the conference is as bad as not letting them attend
   C. to note that the conference is incomplete without more women in attendance
   D. to emphasize that some organizations overcame great challenges to send women to the conference

5.   In paragraph 5, the author defines freedom by enumerating, or listing, the conditions of freedom in order to

   A. compare the rights of women now and the rights of women years ago.
   B. show that she has studied the work of civil rights leaders.
   C. clarify that freedom should not differ depending on gender or place of residence.
   D. argue that most people do not understand what freedom really is.

6.   What rhetorical device does the author use in paragraph 8?

   A. analogy
   B. enumeration
   C. repetition
   D. parallelism

DIRECTIONS: Read the passage, read each question, and choose the **best** answer.

A SHIP LOST AT SEA

1   A ship lost at sea for many days suddenly sighted a friendly vessel. From the mast of the unfortunate vessel was seen a signal, "Water, water; we die of thirst!" The answer from the friendly vessel at once came back, "Cast down your bucket where you are." A second time the signal, "Water, water; send us water!" ran up from the distressed vessel, and was answered, "Cast down your bucket where you are." And a third and fourth signal for water was answered, "Cast down your bucket where you are." The captain of the distressed vessel, at last heeding the injunction, cast down his bucket, and it came up full of fresh, sparkling water from the mouth of the Amazon River. To those of my race who depend on bettering their condition in a foreign land or who underestimate the importance of cultivating friendly relations with the Southern white man, who is their next-door neighbor, I would say: "Cast down your bucket where you are"—cast it down in making friends in every manly way of the people of all races by whom we are surrounded.

2   Cast it down in agriculture, mechanics, in commerce, in domestic service, and in the professions. . . . Our greatest danger is that in the great leap from slavery to freedom we may overlook the fact that the masses of us are to live by the productions of our hands, and fail to keep in mind that we shall prosper in proportion as we learn to dignify and glorify common labour, and put brains and skill into the common occupations of life; we shall prosper in proportion as we learn to draw the line between the superficial and the substantial, the ornamental gewgaws of life and the useful. No race can prosper till it learns that there is as much dignity in tilling a field as in writing a poem. It is at the bottom of life we must begin, and not at the top. Nor should we permit our grievances to overshadow our opportunities.

From UP FROM SLAVERY: AN AUTOBIOGRAPHY by Booker T. Washington

7. The analogy in paragraph 1 suggests that

   A. African Americans are overlooking opportunities in their communities.
   B. African Americans should not be afraid to leave the South now that they have their freedom.
   C. Sea voyages can be dangerous for inexperienced sailors.
   D. Americans of different races should not befriend one another.

8. The author begins paragraph 2 by enumerating, or listing, the areas in which people work. How does this list relate to the rest of the passage?

   A. It contradicts the rest of the paragraph, which is about problems in the lives of African Americans.
   B. It creates a build-up of information to keep readers' attention.
   C. It continues and extends the comparison begun in paragraph 1.
   D. It introduces the topic of the paragraph, which is about work African Americans can pursue.

9. Which statement **best** explains why the author continues to repeat the phrase **cast down** after concluding the analogy?

   A. to extend the analogy to other occupations
   B. to connect the analogy with a call to action
   C. to use the analogy to dignify common labor
   D. to apply the analogy to future prosperity

10. In paragraph 2, the author states, "It is at the bottom of life we must begin, and not at the top." What does the author mean by this juxtaposition of opposites?

   A. Everyone must work his or her way up.
   B. Good fortune is not a substitute for hard work.
   C. Opportunities can come and go quickly.
   D. All people should have an equal start in life.

DIRECTIONS: Read the passage, read each question, and choose the **best** answer.

FROM PRESIDENT KENNEDY'S INAUGURAL ADDRESS

1 . . . [W]e observe today not a victory of party, but a celebration of freedom—symbolizing an end, as well as a beginning—signifying renewal, as well as change. For I have sworn before you and Almighty God the same solemn oath our forebears prescribed nearly a century and three quarters ago.

2 The world is very different now. For man holds in his mortal hands the power to abolish all forms of human poverty and all forms of human life. And yet the same revolutionary beliefs for which our forebears fought are still at issue around the globe—the belief that the rights of man come not from the generosity of the state, but from the hand of God.

3 We dare not forget today that we are the heirs of that first revolution. Let the word go forth from this time and place, to friend and foe alike, that the torch has been passed to a new generation of Americans—born in this century, tempered by war, disciplined by a hard and bitter peace, proud of our ancient heritage—and unwilling to witness or permit the slow undoing of those human rights to which this Nation has always been committed, and to which we are committed today at home and around the world.

4 Let every nation know, whether it wishes us well or ill, that we shall pay any price, bear any burden, meet any hardship, support any friend, oppose any foe, in order to assure the survival and the success of liberty.

5 This much we pledge—and more.

From INAUGURAL ADDRESS by John F. Kennedy, 1961

11. In paragraph 1, the author says, "We observe today not a victory of party, but a celebration of freedom—symbolizing an end, as well as a beginning—signifying renewal, as well as change." What rhetorical devise is used in this sentence?

   A. analogy
   B. enumeration
   C. repetition
   D. parallelism

12. In paragraph 2, the author states that humans can now "abolish all forms of human poverty and all forms of human life." The juxtaposition of the terms **human poverty** and **human life**

   A. illustrates how technologically advanced yet socially backward humans have become.
   B. suggests that there are problems beyond the scope of human inventiveness.
   C. emphasizes the best and worst parts of human resourcefulness.
   D. implies that the President is a man of the people but very powerful.

13. In paragraph 3, the author refers to the "first revolution"—also called the American Revolution—in order to make the audience feel

   A. proud and connected to history.
   B. afraid that liberty is threatened once again.
   C. disappointed that the country has not accomplished more.
   D. excited and optimistic about the future.

14. In paragraph 3, the author enumerates, or lists, the characteristics of "a new generation of Americans." What tone does this enumeration **best** reflect?

   A. hope
   B. sincerity
   C. fear
   D. doubt

15. In paragraph 4, the author uses parallel phrases with the word **any** to emphasize

   A. that the United States faces serious threats.
   B. the military victories of the United States.
   C. that the United States can overcome all challenges.
   D. the distance the United States has come in the past century.

Compare and Contrast Texts

9
LESSON

Use with *Student Book* pp. 112–113

UNIT 2

READING ASSESSMENT TARGETS: R.2.1, R.2.2, R.4.2/L.4.2, R.5.1, R.5.4, R.6 R.6.3, R.7.4, R.9.1/R.7.1, R.9.2

1 Review the Skill

Remember that when you **compare** and **contrast** two texts, you look for similarities and differences. Sometimes two texts written on similar topics or in similar genres, or forms of writing, may appear very similar. However, you need to dig deeper than what appears on the surface to find out whether they are as similar as they look.

In fact, you may uncover subtle differences. Authors might have a different point of view on a topic but may agree on some smaller points. Furthermore, you might find that authors engage readers in different ways or reveal differences in solutions to problems.

2 Refine the Skill

By refining the skill of comparing and contrasting texts that address similar topics or themes, you will improve your study and test-taking abilities, especially as they relate to the GED® Reasoning Through Language Arts test. Read the passages below. Then answer the question that follows.

PARENT OR SPECTATOR

Parents of children in sports toggle back and forth between being a spectator and being a Mom or Dad. For some, the transition is easy. These parents cheer for and support their child no matter what happens on the field. For others, the lines are blurred. They yell at coaches or referees and continue to mull over plays or calls even when the game is over. What effect do these parents have on the child? Some believe it forces the child out of the game.

Commentary by Coach Judith Freeman

a Freeman introduces the topic in an engaging way by including a question and an answer that lay groundwork for her viewpoint.

SPORTS PARENTS

When I'm at games, I avoid overzealous sports parents like I avoid sitting on sticky bleachers or behind spectators with large hats.

I've never been a big fan of overzealous sports parents. The ones who yell directions at their kids on the field and find fault in anything less than the perfect pass, the perfect block— well in anything less than perfection, really. The ones who tell their kids, "Put some effort into it" or "You're not giving 100% today." I feel that these types of parents suck the fun right out sports by putting too much pressure on their kids.

Commentary of Mike Torres

b Torres engages the reader as well but does so in a different way. He draws the reader in through humor.

TEST-TAKING TIPS

When identifying an author's perspective, look for strong words expressing the author's opinion or attitude. For example, think how the sentence would change if Torres had used **enthusiastic** or **passionate** instead of **overzealous**.

1. Which statement **best** explains the authors' views about sports parents?

   A. Freeman believes that overbearing sports parents are misunderstood, but Torres finds them entertaining.
   B. Both authors believe that for athletes to succeed, they need parents who are passionate about sports.
   C. Freeman believes that successful athletes have pushy sports parents, but Torres believes that pushy sports parents are rare.
   D. Both authors believe that overbearing sports parents can have a negative effect on children.

DIRECTIONS: Read the remainder of the passages, read each question, and choose the **best** answer.

PARENT OR SPECTATOR

1   As a coach and former youth athlete, I have seen the effects. I have seen passionate parents yell at me or players during countless games. These "all or nothing" parents could make it harder for their children to want to play. Staying off the field may be easier for children with these types of parents. Other well-meaning parents may have a different approach with the same effect. These "analyst" parents review how the game went, what happened, and what will be different next time well after the child has let it go. Just how many would-be athletes have left sports because of an over-bearing parent?

2   Reports claim that as many as 75 percent of those who play youth sports quit before age 14. There could be many reasons, including lack of talent or interest. Still, parents should be careful about being too involved with their child's sport activities. A parent's level of involvement just might determine who stays in the game or leaves the field for good.

Commentary by Coach Judith Freeman

2. What is the purpose of Freeman's text?

   A. to explain how and why even well-intentioned sports parents can have a negative effect on children
   B. to entertain with stories about parents who are passionate about sports
   C. to describe the problems on the way to becoming a college athlete
   D. to persuade student athletes to discuss their problems with their parents

3. How are the authors' perspectives similar? Both believe that

   A. coaches should limit parental involvement in youth sports.
   B. youth sports culture cannot change.
   C. as long as parents do not berate other people's children during games, no harm is done.
   D. attentive and concerned parents can become over-zealous and affect their children.

SPORTS PARENTS

1   I've always prided myself on promoting the fun aspects of sports—making new friends, being part of a team, and developing new skills and moves. Don't get me wrong. I take pride in my kids when they do well or display some winning moves. I certainly enjoy watching my kids' teams win more than I enjoy watching them lose, but I try to stay positive no matter the final score. My post-game comments are usually along the lines of "Looked like you were having fun out there. I enjoyed watching you play."

2   Some of my best memories are sports-related. I know I kicked a few lockers after losing a game, but I remember the fun and friendships more than I remember the disappointments. When my kids look back at their numerous team photos, I want them to smile because they remember the fun they had or the friends they made. I don't want to see them grimace because their team won only 2 games that season.

3   So, given my aversion to overzealous parents who focus on performance over fun, you can imagine my horror when I heard my own voice yell out some not-so-helpful advice to my child on the field, "Focus! You know you can do better than that!"

4   As soon as those words left my mouth and I saw my child's scowl, I knew I had let my own stressful day and high emotions get the better of me. I had to turn those words back on myself and promise to do better next time.

Commentary of Mike Torres

4. Which statement **best** explains the differences in the authors' styles?

   A. Freeman uses vivid, poetic descriptions, but Torres uses formal, academic language.
   B. Freeman uses logical reasoning, but Torres uses emotional appeals and tells a personal narrative.
   C. Freeman uses inspirational, emotional language, but Torres uses fact-based reasoning and a sophisticated vocabulary.
   D. Freeman uses engaging anecdotes, but Torres uses motivational terms.

UNIT 2

DIRECTIONS: Read the passages. Then choose the **best** answer to each question on the next page.

DO NOT CLOSE THE DOORS ON THE ARTS

Dear Members of the Board of Education:

1   I am writing in opposition to the proposed restructuring and moving (read closing) of Lowell High School of the Visual and Performing Arts. This institution has been the soul of downtown for 52 years and has seen many of its students go on to professional success, in large part because of the opportunities and flexibility it provides. Smaller and larger cities maintain similar schools that nurture talent and offer opportunities for gifted teens to develop at their own pace and to combine professional and academic responsibilities. Actors such as Jennifer Anniston, Al Pacino, and Robert DeNiro attended The High School of Performing Arts in New York, the model of Lowell High School, and Lowell graduates now work in film, theater, and design.

2   Imagine these celebrities and others as teenagers with special gifts that did not lend themselves to traditional classrooms. Such students need accommodation for special training, auditioning, rehearsing, and performing, in addition to academic subjects. To combine Lowell with a traditional suburban school is as much a disservice as moving it, limiting access to the downtown locations. Attending Lowell as it has been and where it has been has enabled student artists to connect with other artists, develop their skills, and realize their potentials not only as performers but as the people in our society who tell our stories, forge the connections between past and present, envision the future, and weave a sense of cultural identity.

3   Moreover, the closing of the school is a bad economic decision. Nearby restaurants, coffee shops, bookstores, and theaters benefit from their proximity to the school. Staff, students, residents, and visitors frequent these establishments and support the local economy. Without the school, a good part of downtown will die.

4   I urge you to reconsider your decision, not only to honor the school's cultural service and current economic value, but to preserve opportunities for future generations of artists.

Sincerely,
Mallory Riley
Parent and Local Business Owner

LET'S ALL CONTRIBUTE TO OUR THEATERS

Dear Editor:

1   Theater in the United States will never be as respected or successful as theater in Great Britain unless more of the public contributes to private theaters. In England, actors like David Oyelowo and Ian McKellan get training and experience in excellent repertory companies such as the Royal Shakespeare Company. Because of its long success, the Royal Shakespeare Company can afford to produce new work, such as Tim Minchin's *Matilda*. Theaters like the Royal Shakespeare Company inspire audiences and make them proud.

2   In the United States, on the other hand, many regional and community theaters struggle and are forced to mount safe productions of a very short list of plays in order to guarantee an audience. It is hard for the audiences to get excited about yet another production of *Annie* or *A Christmas Carol*. If more people contribute to theaters, the theaters will be able to afford to take more chances and choose new and innovative plays. This will help build an audience for contemporary plays, which may help the audience deal with timely issues. Importantly, the theaters themselves will be able to play a vital part in the economy of the community. Every community needs the arts and theater is communal. Thriving theaters will bring excitement and help nearby businesses.

3   Local businesses should contribute to theaters along with private donors. Others will feel good will for the businesses that contribute, since people value the arts. The contributions will also help the community, since neighborhoods with more arts venues are generally more pleasant places to live and work. If the businesses partner with the theaters on incentive programs for their employees, the employees will be able to attend productions more easily. That, in turn, will help inspire workers' creativity. Finally, the growing audience will help nearby restaurants, shops, and hotels succeed, and these are also important to a thriving community. Let's do as the British do and support our theaters!

Sincerely,
Koji Iyo
Theater Lover

5. What is Riley's perspective regarding the arts?

   A. The arts mirror popular views of life and stimulate dialogue.
   B. The arts are tied to periods of time and do not cross these boundaries.
   C. The arts create emotional bonds among generations of students.
   D. The arts connect the cultural past to the present and future.

6. Which is Iyo's perspective regarding the arts, especially theater?

   A. The arts are vital, despite the economic costs to a community.
   B. Nations with strong artistic programs are less likely to go to war.
   C. The arts help create strong, thriving communities.
   D. Focusing on the economic benefits of the arts diminishes the social benefits of the arts.

7. What is the explicit purpose of Riley's letter?

   A. to persuade the audience to protect the school
   B. to entertain the audience with biographical details
   C. to contrast traditional and alternative high schools
   D. to explain the role of a school in a neighborhood

8. What is the purpose of Iyo's letter?

   A. to describe well-known theater companies
   B. to persuade readers of the importance of contributing to the arts
   C. to entertain with stories about the Royal Shakespeare Company
   D. to inform readers about fundraising opportunities

9. Iyo addresses the idea that businesses that contribute to theaters should do so because of

   A. the economic as well as cultural benefits of the arts for the community.
   B. the artistic merits of the theater alone.
   C. the importance of charitable giving for any company.
   D. the benefits for the local governments, which can then organize fundraising for the arts.

10. How does paragraph 2 support the main idea of Riley's letter?

    A. Riley emphasizes that a combination of an alternative and traditional school is unacceptable.
    B. Riley explains that the needs of creative and professional students differ from those of traditional students.
    C. The parallel between the economic choices of students and staff emphasizes the writer's ethical appeals.
    D. The reference to local businesses provides solutions for the problem of how the school might be repurposed.

11. What do both authors believe about the arts and the economy?

    A. Supporting the visual and performing arts puts a drain on taxpayers.
    B. High prices of concert and theater tickets prevent many from attending.
    C. Active arts and cultural communities benefit the local economies.
    D. Support for the arts should come from public and private sources.

12. Which statement **best** explains why the authors mention specific artists? Riley mentions them to

    A. show that she knows them personally; Iyo mentions them to show pride in their unique heritage.
    B. prove that young artists should study techniques of famous artists; Iyo mentions them to show that new artists do not depend on older artists.
    C. inform readers that people do not appreciate young artists; Iyo mentions them as supporters of the Royal Shakespeare Company.
    D. serve as examples of successful professionals who attended a special high school; Iyo mentions them to show that they were able to build their craft in England's successful theaters.

13. Which word **best** describes the authors' attitude toward the arts?

    A. ironic
    B. negative
    C. resigned
    D. respectful

Compare Texts in Different Formats

LESSON 10

Use with **Student Book** pp. 114–115

1 Review the Skill

READING ASSESSMENT TARGETS: R.5.1, R.5.4, R.6.3, R.6.4, R.7.2, R.7.3, R.7 R.9.1/R.7.1

Information that appears in expository texts can appear in other formats as well. For example, a table, picture, diagram, or timeline can give you the same information about a topic as an article, editorial, or excerp from a book. As you **compare texts in different formats**, consider which format is more effective in deliverin a message. A table may offer a clearer presentation of information than an article, but an article may offer more of the author's thoughts, feelings, or arguments, as well as a deeper understanding of the topic.

2 Refine the Skill

By refining the skill of comparing and contrasting texts in different formats, you will improve your study and test-taking abilities, especially as they relate to the GED® Reasoning Through Language Arts test. Read the passages below. Then answer the question that follows.

THE MOON'S NATURAL RESOURCES

The moon has many natural resources that we could harvest during moon mining missions. What resources could we mine from the moon and for what purpose?

The minerals yttrium, lanthanum, and samarium are considered "rare Earth minerals." These minerals are used in the creation of technology products. The mineral titanium is more abundant on the moon, occurring over 100-times more in lunar rocks than those on Earth. Titanium could be mined for its effectiveness in retaining vital gases needed in space exploration. The moon's soil is also rich in helium-3. This element, also rare on earth, is highly prized for its use in nuclear fusion.

a The first text is an article, and the second is a table. The article offers more details, but the table is more direct and leads the reader to information faster.

WHAT'S ON THE MOON?

Mineral	Significance
Helium-3	a non-radioactive nuclear fusion fuel
Lunar water	could be split into hydrogen and oxygen for fuel cells
Yttrium, lanthanum, and samarium	rare Earth minerals increasingly critical in the making of high-tech products
Pink spinel	prized as a gemstone

b The article and table are written for different purposes. The article offers explanations and opinions; the table presents information in an easy-to-read format.

USING LOGIC

Look at the titles of the texts. The title of the article indicates additional and more complex information. The title of the table indicates that it will list and explain briefly what is on the moon.

1. Which perspectives do the texts share?

   A. Moon mining is more cost-efficient than mining on Earth.
   B. The moon contains minerals never found on Earth.
   C. Much has been achieved in moon mining over the last few years.
   D. The moon contains valuable and diverse resources.

★ Spotlighted Item: **DRAG-AND-DROP**

DIRECTIONS: Read the passage, and study the table. Then use the drag-and-drop options to answer the question.

REQUIREMENTS FOR PUBLIC OFFICE

The U.S. Constitution provides specific age and citizenship requirements for representatives, senators, and President of the United States. Article I focuses on the legislative branch of the government. It establishes the two houses of Congress: the Senate and the House of Representatives. Article II of the Constitution establishes the executive branch. The head of this branch is the President.

Article I Section 2 provides these specifications: The House of Representatives will be composed of members chosen every second year by the people of the states. To be a representative, a person must be at least 25 years old, a citizen of the United States for at least seven years, and, when elected, a resident of the state in which he or she is chosen.

Article I Section 3 specifies that the Senate of the United States will be composed of two senators from each state. To be a senator, a person must be at least 30 years old, a citizen of the United States for at least nine years, and, when elected, a resident of the state in which he or she is chosen. The Vice President of the United States is President of the Senate but has no vote unless the Senate is equally divided and the Vice President must break the tie vote.

Article II Section 2 sets the age, citizenship, and residency requirements for President of the United States. These requirements are as follows: No person except a natural-born citizen, or a citizen of the United States at the time of the adoption of this Constitution, is eligible to be President. To hold this office, a person must be at least 35 years old and a resident within the United States for at least 14 years.

REQUIREMENTS FOR HOLDING OFFICE

Office	Minimum Age	Citizenship
Representative	25 years old	U.S. citizen for at least 7 years
		Resident of state in which elected at time of election
Senator	30 years old	U.S. citizen for at least 9 years
		Resident of state in which elected at time of election
President of the United States	35 years old	Natural-born citizen
		Resident within United States for at least 14 years

2. Drag and drop each option to label each statement. Label the statement *Passage* if the information is found only in the passage. Label the statement *Table* if the information is found only in the table. Label the statement *Both* if the information is found in both.

	A senator must be at least 30 years old.

	There are two senators from each state.

	Representatives are elected for two-year terms.

Labels

Passage

Table

Both

UNIT 2

DIRECTIONS: Read the passages. Then choose the **best** answer to each question on the next page.

THOMAS JEFFERSON'S GARDEN

1   Thomas Jefferson is considered a "renaissance man" in the early days of this country. Best known as the author of the Declaration of Independence, the first Secretary of State, and the third President of the United States, Jefferson was also a lawyer, writer, statesman, architect, and scientist—among other things. And as if these were not enough, Jefferson was an avid gardener as well. Anyone who visits his Virginia plantation, Monticello, can still see today how much Jefferson enjoyed growing fruits, vegetables, and herbs for his own kitchen.

2   To Jefferson, his garden was a laboratory in which he could grow various plant species from around the world, many of which were uncommon and considered exotic in the United States at the time; tomatoes, chickpeas, and eggplant were quite unusual in the 1700s. For Jefferson, gardening was a passion, and he shared seeds and cuttings of those species with friends and neighbors, believing that the "greatest service which can be rendered any country is to add a useful plant to its culture."

3   In his garden notes, Jefferson provided precise information about his experiments. Jefferson described how he planted each species, how he spaced them out, and when the plants came to flower or bore fruit. Of course, not everything that Jefferson tried to grow in his garden proved "useful" or successful. In fact, he met with significant failure in his trials. From his garden book, we learn of pests, disease, drought, and poor soil. For example, we are told that his Hotspur peas were "killed by frost Oct. 23" and that his Windsor Beans were "killed by bug" on August 21.

4   However, one thing is also certain from his garden notes: he never let his failures stop him from continuing to plant, grow, and experiment. According to Jefferson, "[T]he failure of one thing is repaired by the success of another." If one plant in a hundred succeeded, he believed it well worth the endeavor.

JEFFERSON'S GARDEN NOTES

1766   **Shadwell**
Mar. 30   Purple hyacinth begins to bloom.

Apr. 6   Narcissus and Puckoon open.
13   Puckoon flowers fallen.
16   a bluish colored, funnel-formed flower in lowgrounds in bloom.
30   purple flag blooms. Hyacinth & Narcissus gone.

May 4   Wild honeysuckle in our woods open. — also the Dwarf flag & Violets
7   blue flower in lowgrounds vanished.
11   The purple flag, Dwarf flag, Violet & wild Honeysuckle still in bloom. went journey to Maryland, Pennsylva., New York. so observations cease. . . .

1774
May 4   the blue ridge of mountains covered with snow.
5   a frost which destroyed almost every thing. it killed the wheat, rye, corn, many tobacco plants, and even large saplings. the leaves of the trees were entirely killed. all the shoots of vines. at Monticello near half the fruit of every kind was killed; and before this no instance had ever occurred of any fruit killed here by the frost. in all other places in the neighborhood the destruction of fruit was total. this frost was general & equally destructive thro the whole country and the neighboring colonies.
14   cherries ripe.
16   first dish of peas from earliest patch.
26   a second patch of peas come to table.

June 4   Windsor beans come to table.
5   a third & fourth patch of peas come to table.
13   a fifth patch of peas come in.

From GARDEN BOOK, 1766–1824 manuscript by Thomas Jefferson

UNIT 2

3. The first paragraph of the article supports the author's views on Jefferson by

   A. noting Jefferson's talents and abilities.
   B. explaining the experimental nature of Jefferson's gardening.
   C. clarifying Jefferson's motives for gardening.
   D. supporting the idea that gardening can be difficult.

4. In paragraph 3, the author quotes Jefferson in order to

   A. entertain with an anecdote.
   B. bring Jefferson to life for readers.
   C. illustrate instances of failure.
   D. prove Jefferson's optimisim.

5. How does the statement in paragraph 2 that Jefferson viewed his garden as a laboratory connect to the purpose of Jefferson's Garden Notes?

   A. Jefferson's documenting of the progress of his garden in full detail demonstrates the scientific nature of his approach to gardening.
   B. Jefferson's garden notes were meant to be a diary from which he could draw peaceful recollections of his time in the garden.
   C. Jefferson's gardening involved a lot of experimentation with different hybrid techniques.
   D. Jefferson's approach to gardening, while methodical, was never meant to be a scientific record.

6. Which statement **best** suggests that the garden notes are journal entries?

   A. The writer breaks grammar or punctuation rules, and lists entries by date.
   B. The writer organizes ideas by order of importance and highlights ideas of special interest.
   C. The writer writes only of subjects of interest or consequence to himself.
   D. The writer breaks off his observations whenever he must travel away from home.

7. What makes the format of the garden notes effective for its purpose?

   A. The transitions between ideas highlight important information for easy access.
   B. Ideas are separated by headers, which guide the reader to necessary information.
   C. Consistent numbering corresponds to steps in a process.
   D. Each concise entry is noted by dates, helping the reader locate information quickly.

8. Which perspective do the article and the garden notes share?

   A. Note-taking is essential to growing a successful garden.
   B. Gardening can result in both failures and successes.
   C. Experimenting with "exotic" crops can be both exciting and frustrating.
   D. Adding useful plants to one's culture is a service to humankind.

9. How do the two texts differ in purpose?

   A. The article entertains with details about Jefferson's garden, but the notes explain how to keep a garden.
   B. The article explores why Jefferson was a successful gardener, but the notes merely list his successes.
   C. The article informs readers about Jefferson's experiments in gardening, but the notes list his observations.
   D. The article explains the challenges of gardening, but the notes show that Jefferson enjoyed tending his garden.

10. How do the article and the garden notes differ in audience?

   A. The article is for a general audience, but the garden notes were for Jefferson's own use.
   B. The article is for visitors to Jefferson's garden, but the garden notes are for a general audience.
   C. The article is for gardeners, but the garden notes are for historians.
   D. The article is for new experimental gardeners, but the garden notes are for people who want to follow Jefferson's methods.

11. On the basis of the information in both texts, the **most** logical conclusion to draw about Thomas Jefferson is that he

   A. had a great deal of leisure time.
   B. was organized, patient, and an avid learner.
   C. preferred gardening to being around others.
   D. was a keen observer but impractical.

Compare Texts in Similar Genres

LESSON 11

1 Review the Skill

READING ASSESSMENT TARGETS: R.2.7, R.4.3/L.4.3, R.5.1, R.5.2, R.5
R.6.1, R.6.2, R.6.3, R.6.4, R.9.1/R.7.1, R.9.2

By **comparing and contrasting**, you can gain a better understanding of texts, especially those in similar **genres**. To begin, ask questions to identify each author's **perspective** and **tone**. What does each author think or feel about the main topic?

Build from your answers to find out each **author's purpose**. Given the author's perspective or tone, what is he or she trying to achieve? Go even further to analyze how each author tries to achieve his or her purpose. What techniques does the author use? For example, does the author use a certain text **structure** or **style**? Finally, evaluate how the author's techniques help achieve his or her purpose.

2 Refine the Skill

By refining the skill of comparing and contrasting texts in similar genres, you will improve your study and test-taking abilities, especially as they relate to the GED® Reasoning Through Language Arts test. Read the passages below. Then answer the question that follows.

COMMENTS AT A CHARITY DINNER

. . . From 1949 until just before the Great Society got underway in 1964, the percentage of American families in poverty fell dramatically—from nearly 33 percent to only 18 percent. But by 1980, with the full impact of the Great Society's programs being felt, the trend had reversed itself, and there was an even higher proportion of people living in poverty than in 1969.

The simple truth is that low inflation and economic expansion in the years prior to the Great Society mean enormous social and economic progress for the poor of America. But after the gigantic increases in government spending and taxation, that economic progress slowed dramatically.

From REMARKS AT A FUNDRAISING DINNER HONORING FORMER REPRESENTATIVE JOHN M. ASHBROOK IN ASHLAND, OHIO by Ronald Reagan, 1983

a Reagan uses dates to create a comparison of the impact of government programs on poverty rates to build his persuasive argument.

THE GREAT SOCIETY

The Great Society is a place where every child can find knowledge to enrich his mind and to enlarge his talents. . . . It is a place where the city of man serves not only the needs of the body and the demands of commerce but the desire for beauty and the hunger for community. It is a place where man can renew contact with nature. It is a place which honors creation for its own sake and for what it adds to the understanding of the race.

From THE GREAT SOCIETY by Lyndon Baines Johnson, 1964

b Johnson uses the repetition of "It is a place" to emphasize his viewpoint about the Great Society he describes.

TEST-TAKING TIPS

When answering multiple-choice questions, use evidence in the passage(s) to eliminate or support answer choices. Ask yourself: *Which words in the passage prove this answer is correct? Which prove it is incorrect?*

1. Which statement **best** expresses each author's perspective about the term "Great Society"?

A. Reagan believes it represents an intrusive government, but Johnson believes it represents an engaged, supportive community.
B. Reagan believes it represents economic progress, but Johnson believes it represents the importance of small businesses.
C. Reagan believes it represents great American wealth, but Johnson believes it promotes self-reliance.
D. Reagan believes it represents the dangers of social progress, but Johnson believes it represents community pride.

DIRECTIONS: Read the remainder of the passages, read each question, and choose the **best** answer.

COMMENTS AT A CHARITY DINNER

1   With the coming of the Great Society, government began eating away at the underpinnings of the private enterprise system. The big taxers and big spenders in the Congress had started a binge that would slowly change the nature of our society and, even worse, it threatened the character of our people.

2   By the end of the decade, the situation seemed out of control. ... the Federal Budget tripled. And, to pay for all of this spending, the tax load increased until it was breaking the backs of working people, destroying incentive, and siphoning off resources needed in the private sector to provide new jobs and opportunity.

3   Inflation had jumped to double-digit levels. Unemployment was climbing. And interest rates shot through the roof. ... Perhaps the saddest part of the whole story is that much of this federal spending was done in the name of helping those it hurt the most, the disadvantaged. For the result of all that big spending and taxing is that, today, those at the lower end of the economic ladder are the hardest hit of all. ...

4   In 1980 the American people sent a message to Washington, D.C. They no longer believed that throwing tax money at a problem was acceptable, no matter how good the intentions of those doing the taxing and spending.

From REMARKS AT A NATIONAL BLACK REPUBLICAN COUNCIL DINNER by Ronald Reagan, 1982

2. What is the purpose of Reagan's speech?

    A. to inform his audience about basic economics
    B. to persuade his audience that more government oversight is needed
    C. to inform his audience about the Federal Budget
    D. to persuade his audience that government spending creates more problems than solutions

3. Paragraph 3 of Reagan's speech supports his purpose by

    A. providing an example of inflation.
    B. providing examples of problems created by too much taxing and spending.
    C. explaining how government policies reflect economic principles.
    D. explaining the difficulties that interest rates cause.

THE GREAT SOCIETY

1   But most of all, the Great Society is not a safe harbor, a resting place, a final objective, a finished work. It is a challenge constantly renewed, beckoning us toward a destiny where the meaning of our lives matches the marvelous products of our labor.

2   So I want to talk to you today about three places where we begin to build the Great Society—in our cities, in our countryside, and in our classrooms. ...

3   The solution to these problems does not rest on a massive program in Washington, nor can it rely solely on the strained resources of local authority. They require us to create new concepts of cooperation, a creative federalism, between the National Capital and the leaders of local communities.

From THE GREAT SOCIETY by Lyndon Baines Johnson, 1964

4. Paragraph 1 shows how Johnson's style helps achieve his purpose. Johnson uses

    A. figurative language to persuade.
    B. concrete examples to inform.
    C. simple, direct language to inform.
    D. informal language to persuade.

5. Which statement **best** reflects a difference in the authors' tones?

    A. Reagan's tone is sentimental, but Johnson's is joyful.
    B. Reagan's tone shows indifference, but Johnson's shows pride.
    C. Reagan's tone shows criticism, but Johnson's shows optimism.
    D. Reagan's tone is mournful, but Johnson's is ironic.

6. With which statement would both authors **most likely** agree?

    A. The private sector is more efficient than the government.
    B. Local government should take over most responsibilities of the federal government.
    C. The federal government should not regulate industry.
    D. Funding massive federal programs strains the American people.

UNIT 2

DIRECTIONS: Read the passages below. Then choose the **best** answer to each question on the next page.

OFF THE GRID

1   For many people, powering their homes or small businesses using a small renewable energy system that is not connected to the electricity grid—called a stand-alone system—makes economic sense and appeals to their environmental values.

2   In remote locations, stand-alone systems can be more cost-effective than extending a power line to the electricity grid (the cost of which can range from $15,000 to $50,000 per mile). But these systems are used also by people who live near the grid and wish to obtain independence from the power provider or demonstrate a commitment to non-polluting energy sources.

3   Successful stand-alone systems generally take advantage of a combination of techniques and technologies to generate reliable power, reduce costs, and minimize inconvenience. Some of these strategies include using fossil fuel or renewable hybrid systems and reducing the amount of electricity required to meet your needs.

4   In addition to purchasing photovoltaic panels, a wind turbine, or a small hydropower system, you will need to invest in some additional equipment (called "balance-of-system") to condition and safely transmit the electricity to the load that will use it. This equipment can include:

- Batteries
- Charge controller
- Power conditioning equipment
- Safety equipment
- Meters and instrumentation.

From the energy.gov article OFF-GRID OR STAND-ALONE RENEWABLE ENERGY SYSTEMS, accessed 2021

ON THE GRID

1   A grid-connected system allows you to power your home or small business with renewable energy during those periods (daily as well as seasonally) when the sun is shining, the water is running, or the wind is blowing. Any excess electricity you produce is fed back into the grid. When renewable resources are unavailable, electricity from the grid supplies your needs, eliminating the expense of electricity storage devices like batteries.

2   In addition, power providers (i.e., electric utilities) in most states allow net metering, an arrangement where the excess electricity generated by grid-connected renewable energy systems "turns back" your electricity meter as it is fed back into the grid. If you use more electricity than your system feeds into the grid during a given month, you pay your power provider only for the difference between what you used and what you produced.

3   Some of the things you need to know when thinking about connecting your home energy system to the electric grid include:

- Equipment required to connect your system to the grid
- Grid-connection requirements from your power provider
- State and community codes and requirements.

4   Aside from the major small renewable energy system components, you will need to purchase some additional equipment (called "balance-of-system") in order to safely transmit electricity to your loads and comply with your power provider's grid-connection requirements. You may need the following items:

- Power conditioning equipment
- Safety equipment
- Meters and instrumentation.

5   Because grid-connection requirements vary, you or your system supplier/installer should contact your power provider to learn about its specific grid-connection requirements before purchasing any part of your renewable energy system. . . .

From the energy.gov article GRID-CONNECTED RENEWABLE ENERGY SYSTEMS, accessed 2021

7. In paragraph 2 of the first passage, the signal word **But** indicates that the author

   A. is providing evidence that stand-alone renewable energy systems appeal also to those living near an energy grid.
   B. disagrees with the traditional practice of obtaining energy from a power provider.
   C. is suggesting that independence and environmental concerns are not cost effective.
   D. agrees that extending power lines to energy grids is too costly for average consumers.

8. What is the author's perspective in the first passage? The author believes that stand-alone renewable energy systems

   A. are costly and inconvenient.
   B. are underrated and should be used more.
   C. have potential but are still unreliable.
   D. can be beneficial to anyone.

9. What is the purpose of the first passage?

   A. to persuade readers to switch to stand-alone renewable energy systems
   B. to inform readers about stand-alone renewable energy systems
   C. to persuade readers in remote locations to extend power lines to energy grids
   D. to inform readers how to reduce energy costs and minimize inconvenience

10. What is the purpose of the second passage?

   A. to inform readers of the grid-connection requirements of most power providers
   B. to persuade readers to switch to grid-connected renewable energy systems
   C. to inform readers about grid-connected renewable energy systems
   D. to persuade readers to feed their energy from renewable energy systems back into the grid

11. How are both authors' perspectives similar?

   A. Both agree that consumers can switch by themselves to renewable energy systems.
   B. Both recognize the cost and inconvenience of switching to renewable energy systems.
   C. Both believe that stand-alone systems are better than grid-connected systems.
   D. Both agree that renewable energy systems help save energy, money, and the environment.

12. How do the passages differ from each other in scope?

   A. The second passage addresses energy systems that obtain power with and without a grid connection; the first passage does not.
   B. The first passage discusses energy systems that are environmentally friendly; the second passage does not.
   C. The second passage lists what consumers need to purchase for a renewable energy system; the first passage does not.
   D. The first passage explains when using the renewable energy system makes sense; the second passage does not.

13. Both authors achieve their overall impact in part by using

   A. an aggressive tone and cautionary language.
   B. straightforward language and logical evidence.
   C. emotional appeals and figurative language.
   D. relevant anecdotes about renewable energy.

14. Which is the **most likely** conclusion to draw about the authors of the passages?

   A. The authors have stand-alone renewable energy systems in their own homes and businesses.
   B. The authors are government contractors who design non-polluting energy systems.
   C. The authors would recommend a renewable energy system to the owner of a small business.
   D. The authors are technicians who install energy systems for power companies.

15. On the basis of the information in both passages, a grid-connected system would be the **best** choice for a homeowner who

   A. cares deeply about the environment.
   B. lives a great distance from a city or town.
   C. resents dealing with power companies.
   D. is frugal and experiences unpredictable seasons.

12 LESSON

Compare Texts in Different Genres

Use with **Student Book** pp. 118–119

READING ASSESSMENT TARGETS: R.2.7, R.2.8, R.4.3/L.4.3, R.5.1, R.5 R.5.4, R.6.1, R.6.3, R.7.3, R.7.4

1 Review the Skill

You will often need to ==compare== and ==contrast== texts with similar information in different ==genres==, or forms of writing. Often the author's purpose, audience, or the information itself determines which genre an author will use. For example, you might find similar information in a speech and an interview or in a magazine article and a recipe. On the other hand, you might find not only different information but also different writing styles, different audiences, and different purposes.

2 Refine the Skill

By refining the skill of comparing and contrasting texts in different genres, you will improve your study and test-taking abilities, especially as they relate to the GED® Reasoning Through Language Arts test. Read the passages below. Then answer the question that follows.

OBAMA HONORS ROSA PARKS

Mr. Speaker, . . . to the friends and family of Rosa Parks; to the distinguished guests who are gathered here today.

This morning, we celebrate a seamstress, slight in stature but mighty in courage. She defied the odds, and she defied injustice. She lived a life of activism, but also a life of dignity and grace. And in a single moment, with the simplest of gestures, she helped change America—and . . . the world.

From REMARKS BY THE PRESIDENT AT DEDICATION OF STATUE HONORING ROSA PARKS—U.S. CAPITOL by Barack Obama, 2013

a The first passage begins with President Obama addressing his audience directly. This introduction shows that the genre is a speech.

ROSA PARKS FAQ

How is Rosa Parks a pioneer of civil rights?
On December 1, 1955, Rosa Parks, a black seamstress, refused to give up her seat to a white passenger on a public bus in Montgomery, Alabama. She was arrested for violating the segregation laws and fined $10. Her action helped touch off the Civil Rights Movement. A 381-day bus boycott in Montgomery followed. The boycott led to a successful Supreme Court challenge to segregation on public buses.

What happened that day on the bus?
The seats for white passengers in the front of the bus were occupied by blacks when several white passengers boarded the bus. The bus driver asked Parks and three other black passengers to give up their seats in the middle of the bus for a white man who was left standing. Parks refused. The bus driver had Parks arrested.

b The second passage is written in an FAQ (Frequently Asked Questions) format. Answers are provided to typical questions that someone might ask about Rosa Parks.

TEST-TAKING TIPS

When answering questions about paired passages, remember that both parts of an answer choice must be correct. Read questions carefully and completely; reject answers that are correct for one passage only.

1. On the basis of the information in both passages, what is the **most** logical conclusion to draw about Parks's arrest?

   A. Parks's act of defiance helped others fight against inequality.
   B. Parks had caused other public disturbances before her arrest.
   C. Parks was already acting as part of an orchestrated protest.
   D. Parks's actions leading to her arrest were out of character.

★ Spotlighted Item: **DRAG-AND-DROP**

DIRECTIONS: Read the remainder of the passages. Then use the drag-and-drop options to complete the chart.

OBAMA HONORS ROSA PARKS

1   Rosa Parks tells us there's always something we can do. She tells us that we all have responsibilities, to ourselves and to one another. She reminds us that this is how change happens—not mainly through the exploits of the famous and the powerful, but through the countless acts of often anonymous courage and kindness and fellow feeling and responsibility that continually, stubbornly, expand our conception of justice—our conception of what is possible.

2   Rosa Parks's singular act of disobedience launched a movement. The tired feet of those who walked the dusty roads of Montgomery helped a nation see that to which it had once been blind. It is because of these men and women that I stand here today. It is because of them that our children grow up in a land more free and more fair; a land truer to its founding creed.

3   And that is why this statue belongs in this hall—to remind us, no matter how humble or lofty our positions, just what it is that leadership requires; just what it is that citizenship requires. Rosa Parks would have turned 100 years old this month. We do well by placing a statue of her here. But we can do no greater honor to her memory than to carry forward the power of her principle and a courage born of conviction.

From REMARKS BY THE PRESIDENT AT DEDICATION OF STATUE HONORING ROSA PARKS—U.S. CAPITOL by Barack Obama, 2013

ROSA PARKS FAQ

1   **Why did Rosa Parks refuse to give up her seat that day?**

2   Parks was tired of the humiliation of segregation laws that made blacks second-class citizens and treated them as lesser human beings. She decided to take a stand. At the time of her arrest, Parks was already involved in the National Association for the Advancement of Colored People (NAACP) and had participated in drives to encourage black people to register to vote. In fact, on the day of her arrest she was rushing home to send out notices about the group's coming election of officers. Although she did not plan on getting arrested, she understood the importance of her action and stood by it.

3   **How was Parks's action significant?**

4   Her act of civil disobedience helped people across the country see the injustice of the segregation laws. In Montgomery, her action touched off a boycott of the buses that lasted more than a year and helped change the segregation laws. A key figure in the boycott was a local 26-year-old preacher, Martin Luther King, Jr. He took up the fight against segregation and became a national civil rights leader.

5   **What did the Civil Rights Movement mean to Parks?**

6   She believed that people of all races are equal and should have equal opportunities. She believed in fighting oppression and continued her support for civil rights throughout her life.

2.   Drag and drop each statement into the correct column in the chart.

Obama Honors Rosa Parks	Rosa Parks FAQ

Statements

People should believe in themselves and their ideals.

An act of civil disobedience changed a nation.

All people deserve the same opportunities.

Courageous acts by ordinary people lead to change.

UNIT 2

DIRECTIONS: Read the passages below. Then choose the **best** answer to each question on the next page.

MY GREEK CHILDHOOD: A MEMOIR

1   When we kids were sick with fever, our grandmother would make us Greek chicken soup—the universal cure for everything from colds and flu to broken hearts. She swore by its healing powers, but we always laughed. After all, it was Chicago in the 1980s; even our European-born grandfather believed that remedies came from the pharmacy, not the kitchen. But Grandma was a woman who, despite a modern American upbringing and chic modern wardrobe, still subscribed to the "old ways."

2   Indeed, some of her superstitions were downright embarrassing to us. The worst was the *kako mati*, the "evil eye" charm she pinned to our clothing to protect us from envy. If one of us had a headache, she'd close her eyes and say the *vaskania*, a prayer to ward off the evil eye. I'll admit we usually felt better soon after, but the cure was probably the result of the acetaminophen my grandfather gave us. As Grandma sat in a corner chanting, Grandpa would roll his eyes, reach into the medicine cabinet, and, with a conspiratorial grin, hand us a pill.

3   Still, her chicken soup seemed to work better than any pharmaceutical in curing a cold or flu. The tasty warm liquid soothed our throats and the rich aroma seemed to clear nasal passages. The moment one of us caught a chill, Grandma would march to the stove, place a pot on the burner, and throw in a chicken carcass (from the ample supply in her freezer), a few eggs, some rice, and several squeezed lemons. She'd even include more bones and several feet (unusual for some but also in ample supply in her freezer), insisting that the marrow in the bones would conquer all illness.

4   We scoffed, discounting her theory as an old wives' tale, the idea of ingesting chicken marrow unappetizing, at best. We ate the soup because we liked it. It was tasty and soothing, probably the only appealing form of nourishment. However, the joke was on us. As it turns out—and modern science has proved this—chicken soup, especially the kind made with bones and feet, boosts the human immune system. Although I'm not sure about broken hearts and *kako mati*, the chicken soup remedy was indeed the real thing.

ELDERBERRY SYRUP RECIPE

1   This winter, you cold and flu sufferers are probably reaching for over-the-counter remedies to make you feel normal again. But did you know that many of these medications are not only ineffective but unsafe as well?

2   No need to worry. There's a natural effective remedy that's absolutely safe and tastes great! It's also fast and easy to make, using only four ingredients! Elderberry syrup, which contains the medicinal properties of the black elderberry tree, is rich in antioxidants, and recent studies have shown that it's a powerful antiviral as well. Consequently, it kills cold and flu bugs while it gives your immune system a natural boost!

3   To make elderberry syrup, you'll need
- 1 cup dried elderberries
- cheesecloth
- 1 cinnamon stick
- lidded pot
- 4 cups distilled water
- strainer
- 2 cups sugar
- measuring cup

1. Mix water, berries, and cinnamon in a pot. Cover and bring to a boil on medium high heat.
2. Reduce heat to a simmer, and raise the lid just enough to let out some steam.
3. Let the mixture reduce halfway, and let it cool. This step will take an hour or more.
4. Strain the mixture through a sieve lined with cheesecloth. With the berries wrapped in the cloth, wring to get out the remaining juice.
5. Measure the juice, which should come to 2 cups. If you have more than 2 cups, continue to simmer. If less, add water to reach 2 cups.
6. Return the mixture to the pot, and add 2 cups of sugar. Boil and stir until sugar is dissolved.
7. Let the mixture cool, pour your syrup into glass bottles, and refrigerate. This syrup should last a year.

4   Adults can take 1 tsp. per day to prevent illness or 1 tbs. three to five times per day as a cure. Check with a pediatrician or trained herbalist for children's dosing.

5   Caution: Use black elderberries only (Sambucus Nigra). Do NOT use red elderberries. They are toxic! Not to be snarky, but using them would defeat the purpose of this recipe! Enjoy and be well!

3. The purpose of the memoir is to

    A. persuade readers to make their own chicken soup.
    B. contrast homemade chicken soup with store-bought chicken soup.
    C. explain how to make the author's grandmother's chicken soup.
    D. entertain readers with a story about chicken soup.

4. How do the memoir and the recipe differ in structure?

    A. The memoir presents a list of steps in a process, but the recipe presents ideas in order of importance.
    B. The memoir is written in paragraph form, but the recipe is written primarily as a numbered list of steps.
    C. The memoir makes comparisons and contrasts, but the recipe presents a main idea and details.
    D. The memoir explains a series of causes and effects, but the recipe presents sequential order.

5. The word **consequently** in paragraph 2 of the recipe signals that the information following the word will

    A. contradict information in the paragraph.
    B. have no relation to the rest of the paragraph.
    C. result from information in the paragraph.
    D. show the sequence of steps in the paragraph.

6. How do the memoir and the recipe differ in scope?

    A. The recipe leaves gaps in information, but the memoir is detailed and informative.
    B. The recipe explains the process of making a home remedy, but the memoir is vague about process details.
    C. The memoir explains how the remedy was used, but the recipe focuses solely on preparation.
    D. The memoir introduces the remedy and then provides detailed instruction, but the recipe gives no introduction.

7. Which statement **best** describes the impact of both passages?

    A. The informal writing style makes both passages easy to read and the detailed recipe easy to follow.
    B. The gloomy tone emphasizing illness makes the remedies seem unpleasant and useless.
    C. The cautionary tone emphasizes the dangers of the syrup and the ineffectiveness of the chicken soup.
    D. The researched information encourages readers to use both remedies rather than over-the-counter medicines.

8. Although both passages are for general audiences, the author of the memoir assumes that readers **most likely**

    A. know how to make Greek chicken soup.
    B. are familiar with Greek culture.
    C. do not follow superstitions.
    D. treat colds and flu with chicken soup.

9. How do the passages differ in emphasis?

    A. The recipe does more than the memoir to stress why natural remedies are preferable to over-the-counter medicines.
    B. The memoir does more than the recipe to stress the ease of preparing the remedy.
    C. The memoir does more than the recipe to stress safety measures.
    D. The recipe does more than the memoir to stress the unusual ingredients in the remedy.

10. Which perspective do the two passages share?

    A. Anyone using natural remedies as well as over-the-counter medicines should consult a doctor.
    B. Natural remedies can be as effective as modern medications.
    C. Homemade remedies are of better quality than store-bought remedies.
    D. People should take great care in using over-the-counter medicines.

11. On the basis of the information in the passages, the grandmother in the memoir would **most likely** favor

    A. over-the-counter medications for a cold.
    B. home-made elderberry syrup to prevent flu.
    C. consulting a doctor for any illness.
    D. wearing the *kako mati* to ward off viruses.

Gain Information from Multiple Texts

Use with *Student Book* pp. 120–121

READING ASSESSMENT TARGETS: R.7.3, R.7.4, R.9.1/R.

1 Review the Skill

As you read different passages about similar topics, you will **synthesize** information by combining ideas from each text into one unifying idea. Synthesizing reflects your understanding of the texts and helps you gain new insights. Often, you also need to **draw conclusions**, or broad inferences, based on smaller inferences you make about the texts. When you **apply information** to other situations, you also show a deeper understanding. For example, applying information based on the texts may require you to predict what an author might do or feel in another situation.

2 Refine the Skill

By refining the skills of synthesizing, drawing conclusions, and applying information from multiple texts, you will improve your study and test-taking abilities, especially as they relate to the GED® Reasoning Through Language Arts test. Read the passages below. Then answer the question that follows.

BENEFITS OF PART-TIME JOBS

If you are unemployed and having trouble securing a full-time position, you should consider searching for a part-time job. With a part-time job, you can earn a regular, although reduced, paycheck and maintain ties to the workforce. Working a part-time job also allows you to avoid gaps in your work history, which are often viewed as a detriment on a résumé.

(a) The first text is an article explaining the benefits of taking a part-time job. The second is a job offer letter. As you read the letter, think how the first text might influence the recipient's decision.

JOB OFFER LETTER

Dear Mr. Osborne:

At ABC Books, we feel that your skills and prior publishing experience are an ideal fit for our editorial department. Therefore, we are pleased to offer you the part-time position of assistant editor on these terms:

- Your starting date will be May 15, and you will report to Supervising Editor Jim Mason.
- Initially, you will be paid an hourly rate of $15.00 on a biweekly basis. Direct deposit is available.
- As a part-time, temporary employee, you will not be eligible for insurance benefits or paid vacation.

(b) To synthesize ideas from both passages, think of ways in which the ideas in the first passage help explain why the job offer in the second passage is a good option.

MAKING ASSUMPTIONS

Before answering question 1, consider what you know about part-time jobs. Make an assumption about how the recipient of the letter most likely feels and what he would want.

1. According to the information in the passage, the recipient of the job offer letter should accept the position because it

A. offers a good benefits package while he continues his job search.
B. will help him gain experience in a new field so that he can build up his résumé.
C. will give him the chance to make up for the gaps in his résumé that extend over long periods.
D. offers the chance to continue working in his field while he searches for a permanent full-time position.

★ Spotlighted Item: **DRAG-AND-DROP**

DIRECTIONS: Read the remainder of the passages. Then use the drag-and-drop options to complete the chart.

BENEFITS OF PART-TIME JOBS

1   To make the most of a part-time job experience, look for a part-time job related to your current profession or field. This allows you to put your past experience to use, keep your skills up-to-date, provide references for future jobs, and network with people in your field. Having your supervisor write a letter of recommendation or endorse your skills on a professional networking website can help tip the scales in your favor when you seek out full-time employment. Networking can provide leads or referrals to open full-time positions that you may not have found on your own.

2   While not as advantageous, working part-time in an unrelated field still allows you to avoid employment gaps in your résumé, obtain recommendations or endorsement, and maintain your employment soft skills, such as time management, conflict resolution, and teamwork.

JOB OFFER LETTER

1   • While employed at ABC Books, you may engage in other employment as long as it does not compete with or create a conflict of interest with ABC Books. We ask you to sign a non-compete agreement upon hiring.

2   • Your employment with ABC Books is "at will"; therefore, you or the company may terminate your employment at any time and for any reason. Although your job title, duties, and compensation are subject to change, the "at will" nature of your employment is not.

3   Although we cannot offer you the full-time permanent position you seek now, we hope that accepting our offer will allow you to continue working in your field of interest.

4   We believe that you will be an asset to our editorial team as you expand your knowledge, skills, and experience. We hope that you accept our offer. If you do, please sign the enclosed forms and return them to me. Please let me know if you need additional information.

Sincerely,
Mikela Ealing
Director, Human Resources
ABC Books

2. Drag and drop the phrases that indicate what the offered part-time job provides and does not provide into the correct location on the chart.

Provides	Does Not Provide

Phrases

experience in desired field
insurance benefits
leads to letters of recommendation
acquisition of professional contacts
high pay
paid vacation

UNIT 2

DIRECTIONS: Read the passages below. Then choose the **best** answer to each question on the next page.

CONCERNS ABOUT FOOD LABELS

1   If you're like many consumers, you probably take little time to read food labels carefully. Yet even if you do read them, you may find them confusing. You are not alone. Sometimes it seems as though labels are meant to confuse consumers. For example, manufacturers use boldface type to highlight certain words on food packages—words that grab your attention and appeal to your desire to be healthy. Sometimes the labels are helpful; other times they are not. However, you should be aware that words such as *natural*, *multigrain*, and *organic* are often misleading or false, encouraging consumers to believe that a product is a healthier choice than it actually is.

2   Consider the term *organic*. Just because something is organic, it is not necessarily healthful. A granola bar made of organic ingredients may still be loaded with sugar, fat, and calories. Consumers should read the entire label before buying such a product.

3   *Natural* is another misleading term; it is neither defined legally nor regulated in most foods. *Natural* does not always mean "healthful." For example, many sugars occur in nature, so a food containing corn syrup can be considered *natural*. Also, foods labeled as *natural* may contain preservatives that are unhealthful, even when the main ingredient is indeed natural and healthful by itself. Consider, for example, the added sodium in pork or chicken. Added food dyes make food more appealing and healthful-looking, as is often the case with dark breads like rye and pumpernickel.

4   *Multigrain* is yet another term used liberally. Although the label makes the product seem nutritious, most multigrain breads and crackers consist mainly of refined flour, which has been depleted of the most nutritious properties of the whole grain. If you want to choose healthful and nutritious products, what you want are whole grains. Therefore, unless the first ingredient on the label is *100% whole grain*, the product is likely to contain refined grain and possibly sugar and chemicals. You can avoid these problems by preparing your own food with raw whole grains, such as wild rice, barley, oats, and corn. Or you can read labels carefully and understand what they mean, in addition to what they say.

WHOLE GRAIN LABELS

1   The Whole Grains Council has created an official packaging symbol called the Whole Grain Stamp that helps consumers find real whole grain products. . . .

2   Many whole grain products not yet using the Stamp will list the grams of whole grain somewhere on the package, or say something like "100% whole wheat." You can trust these statements. But be skeptical if you see the words "whole grain" without more details, such as "crackers made with whole grain." The product may contain only miniscule amounts of whole grains.

Words You May See on Packages	What They Mean
whole grain [name of grain]	
whole wheat	
whole [other grain]	
stoneground whole [grain]	YES—Contains all parts of the grain, so you're getting all the nutrients of the whole grain.
brown rice	
oats, oatmeal (including old-fashioned oatmeal, instant oatmeal)	
wheatberries	
wheat	
semolina	MAYBE—These words are accurate descriptions of the package contents, but because some parts of the grain MAY be missing, you are likely missing the benefits of whole grains. When in doubt, don't trust these words!
durum wheat	
organic flour	
stoneground	
multigrain (may describe several whole grains or several refined grains, or a mix of both)	
enriched flour	
wheat flour	
degerminated (on corn meal)	NO—These words never describe whole grains.
bran	
wheat germ	

Courtesy of Oldways Whole Grains Council, www. wholegrainscouncil.or

3. Based on information in both passages, which food is **most likely** to contain whole grain?

   A. cornbread
   B. organic chips
   C. wild rice
   D. crackers

4. Which purpose do the first passage and the table share?

   A. to persuade readers to grow some of their own food and buy organic products
   B. to inform readers of the truth about food labels and how to read them properly
   C. to entertain readers with anecdotes about healthful foods and misleading food labels
   D. to demonstrate how natural, whole foods are better than processed, refined foods

5. Both passages indicate that food labels

   A. are often misleading, confusing, and unreliable.
   B. are tightly regulated by state and federal laws.
   C. tell consumers what they need to know, but most people ignore them.
   D. provide honest information, but most people do not understand them.

6. In which way is the information in the first passage similar to the information in the table?

   A. Both dismiss the skepticism that consumers feel about food labels.
   B. Both emphasize that the Whole Grain Stamp helps consumers find whole grain products.
   C. Both explain the real meanings of terms used in food labels.
   D. Both explain how all natural-grain products are better than multigrain products.

7. Based on information in the first passage and the table, which item is the **most** healthful purchase?

   A. a package of dark rye rolls
   B. a loaf of organic whole grain bread
   C. a bag of pancake mix with enriched flour
   D. a box of low-fat wheat germ cereal

8. According to the first passage and the table, why are refined grains less healthful than whole grains?

   A. Refined grains contain preservatives or other unnatural substances.
   B. Refined grains may contain food dyes.
   C. Refined grains have lost beneficial nutrients.
   D. Refined grains are made with corn syrup.

9. Which is the **most likely** conclusion to draw about the authors of the passages? The author of the first passage

   A. writes for farmers growing organic wheat; the author of the second passage helped create the Whole Grain Stamp.
   B. is a nutritionist who knows about whole grain products; the author of the second passage is an organic farmer.
   C. is a retailer promoting whole grain products; the author of the second passage always chooses nutritious food products.
   D. is a journalist writing about health issues; the author of the second passage most likely belongs to the Whole Grains Council.

10. The **most** logical conclusion to draw about much of the food industry is that it

    A. is willing to use deception to get people to buy food that is not healthful.
    B. is tightly regulated in areas other than labeling.
    C. has a vested interest in consumers' health.
    D. disagrees with organic growers and whole-food advocates about the Whole Grain Stamp.

11. Based on information in both passages, the **most** healthful and nutritious breakfast dish would be

    A. a bowl of bran flakes.
    B. a bowl of oatmeal.
    C. two slices of multigrain toast.
    D. two slices of rye bread.

12. Which is the **most** logical conclusion to draw from reading these passages?

    A. Reading food labels will tell you exactly what you are getting.
    B. Labeling on whole grains may be deceptive, but other food labeling is more accurate.
    C. Food labels may not provide complete or accurate information.
    D. Natural and organic products are neither natural nor organic.

GED® Extended Response Prompt

Use with **Student Book** pp. 132–135

1 Understand the Prompt and Scoring

WRITING ASSESSMENT TARGETS: W.1, W.2, W.:

On the GED® Reasoning Through Language Arts test, you will have 45 minutes to respond to an extended response prompt. The prompt requires you to read and analyze one or two argumentative passages, or source texts, to determine which is better supported by evidence. Although the wording of prompts can vary, they typically look similar to this:

> Analyze the authors' positions in the two speeches. In your response, develop an argument in which you explain which position is **better** supported. Use relevant and specific evidence from both speeches to support your response.

> Remember, the better-argued position is not necessarily the position with which you agree. This task should take approximately 45 minutes to complete.

To respond to the prompt, you will need to do three things: Read, Plan, and Write.

1. **Read** and analyze the source texts. The source texts will appear on the left-hand side of the screen. As you read, note the evidence that the authors use to support their position on the topic.

2. **Plan** your response. Decide which position you think is better supported and has the stronger evidence, develop an argument to explain how one position is stronger, and choose the **text evidence** you will use to support your argument. You will need to incorporate text evidence into your response and **explain why** the evidence makes one position stronger than the other. Use your whiteboard to organize your ideas or plan out a rough outline.

3. **Write** by typing your response in the text box on the right-hand side of the screen. Your response should contain 4 to 7 paragraphs, each with 3 to 7 sentences. Be sure to leave a few minutes to rea over your response and make revisions or corrections.

It is important to understand how the GED® Extended Response is scored. Your response will be graded using three traits, or categories. You can earn up to 2 points for each trait, for a total of 6 points. (See detailed scoring rubrics on pages 292–294.)

Trait 1: Creation of Arguments and Use of Evidence (0–2 points)

This trait looks at how well your response demonstrates your understanding of the prompt and the source texts and your ability to analyze evidence. Ask yourself: *Does my response clearly identify which text is better supported? Does my response use evidence from the source texts to support my argument? Do I evaluate the effectiveness of the evidence in my response?*

Trait 2: Development of Ideas and Organizational Structure (0–2 points)

This trait looks at how well your response is organized and how well your ideas are developed. Ask yoursel*f Do I explain my ideas fully? Are my ideas presented in a logical way? Do I make clear connections between my main points and the details? Do I use clear language that is appropriate for my audience?*

Trait 3: Clarity and Command of Standard English Conventions (0–2 points)

This trait looks at your response's sentence structure and grammar. Ask yourself: *Are my sentences clear and grammatically correct? Do I use varied sentence structures? Do the sentences demonstrate correct punctuation and spelling? Are there any grammar or usage mistakes that make my response hard to understand?*

Practice and preparation are key to earning a passing score on the GED® Extended Response. Although it is a writing task, you will need to use reading comprehension, logic and organization, and time-management skills.

The first step is to practice how you will use your time. You will have 45 minutes to complete the writing task. It is important to finish all of the steps within that time. Practice responding to sample prompts using a 45-minute timer to help you become faster, more efficient, and more confident with your test-taking skills.

- **0–5 minutes: Read and analyze the source texts.** Read the passages. Identify the topic and the two sides that are being argued. Look for evidence, facts, and details that support each argument. Note which evidence is strongest.

- **6–10 minutes: Take a position and organize your ideas.** Identify which source text is better supported by evidence, without regard to your feelings on the topic. Write a brief outline to organize your ideas.

- **11–40 minutes: Write your response.** Start with an introduction that clearly states which source text is **better** supported. Move to the body paragraphs in which you present text evidence to support your position. Be sure to explain why the evidence supports your position. Write clearly as you explain your analysis. It is okay if some paragraphs are shorter than others. End with a conclusion.

- **41–45 minutes: Proofread your response.** Always leave enough time to read over your response and make revisions or corrections. Consider each sentence to make sure it is clear and makes sense. Look at whether the sentences connect with each other and flow from paragraph to paragraph. Fix any punctuation or spelling errors you notice.

Other Tips

- A complete response should have 300 to 500 words. This usually requires 4 to 7 paragraphs; each paragraph should have 3 to 7 sentences.

- As you read through the source texts, think about how the arguments are presented. Identify the claims for each side. Look at the evidence used to support each argument. Pay close attention to the strategies and organization used in the source texts.

- Explain how the position you chose is better supported than the other position. Include evidence from both source texts in your response. If you use an exact phrase or sentence from the source texts, use quotation marks to show it is a direct quote. You must provide commentary or analysis of cited evidence to receive a high score.

- Be thorough and organized. Pick two or three main points and explain them fully. Your main points should be clear and easy to understand.

- Connect your ideas, sentences, and paragraphs using transitional words and phrases.

- Choose your words carefully and maintain a formal tone. Using the right word with the right connotation can add clarity. However, do not take too much time trying to think of the "perfect" word.

- Use a mix of simple, compound, and complex sentences. Varying your sentence structure makes your response easier to read and understand.

- Take the time to check for spelling and grammatical errors. Your response does not have to be error free to receive a passing score, but too many spelling and grammatical errors can make your response confusing and difficult to understand.

Compare Opposing Arguments

LESSON 1

Use with *Student Book* pp. 136–137

READING ASSESSMENT TARGETS: R.5.1, R.5.3, R.5.4, R.6.1, R.6.2, R.6.4, R.9.2, R…

1 Review the Skill

A debatable topic is one that is open to different, and sometimes opposite, points of view. In such cases, authors present their differing claims about the topic and support those claims with reasons and evidence such as facts, statistics, quotations, or anecdotes. In some cases, different authors may even present the same evidence but emphasize or interpret it differently.

When asked to identify the **similarities and differences between two opposing views**, begin by identifying the main and supporting claims of each author. Then identify the reasons and evidence each author gives to support those claims. Consider the strategies each author uses to present the argument and to make it persuasive. On the basis of this analysis, you will decide which argument is stronger or more convincing.

2 Refine the Skill

By refining the skill of comparing opposing arguments, you will improve your study, writing, and test-taking abilities, especially as they relate to the GED® Reasoning Through Language Arts test. Read the passages below. Then answer the question that follows.

SOCIAL MEDIA BECOMING A DISTRACTION

The [appeal] of socializing online has created a nation of mobile-device [fans], many of whom can go barely 10 minutes without checking their smartphones. . . . Some believe that . . . social media . . . may already be [changing] how people think and learn. . . .

When electronic devices were first becoming [popular], some hoped they would teach a new generation how to multitask better than previous generations did.

From the cqpress.com article SOCIAL MEDIA EXPLOSION by Marcia Clemmitt, © 2013

a Clemmitt writes to advance a point of view about social media. She supports her position by addressing an opposing viewpoint and later in the passage cites evidence from research on multitasking.

TEXTING CAN IMPROVE LITERACY

You call your son, daughter, or spouse to dinner. "Just a minute!" he or she yells. In the distance, you see the glow of a small screen. A familiar annoyance builds. You respond, "Stop texting and get in here!" The next time you find yourself in this situation, you may decide to hold your tongue. Some studies have shown that texting improves communication skills.

Researchers at Coventry University have found that texting is about more than wasting precious time and annoying family members.

From TEXTING CAN IMPROVE LITERACY by Kristine Leung, © 2013

b Leung writes to advance a different point of view regarding social media. She supports her position by mentioning evidence from research on literacy.

TEST-TAKING TIPS

When authors acknowledge another point of view in their argument, they may follow it with their own response. Watch for these paired arguments in your reading.

1. On the basis of the passages, what are the opposing viewpoints?

   A. Clemmitt claims that social media have affected learning and thinking; Leung says that social media have positive effects on communication.
   B. Clemmitt claims that social media have positive effects on thinking; Leung says that they have negative effects on communication.
   C. Clemmitt claims that social media have positive effects on learning; Leung says that they annoy others.
   D. Clemmitt claims that social media have positive effects on communication; Leung says that they have negative effects on learning.

UNIT 3

DIRECTIONS: Read the remainder of the passages, read the questions, and choose the **best** answer.

SOCIAL MEDIA BECOMING A DISTRACTION

1 But research [shows] that people who grew up with electronic devices "really can't multitask" either, says . . . Larry Rosen, a professor of psychology at California State University, Dominguez Hills. . . . As a result, the typical technology-obsessed person now gives "continuous partial attention" to just about everything and full attention to almost nothing. "You never do anything in depth," he says.

2 "You're constantly interrupted, and you're self-interrupting," too, he says. The very nature of the brain seems to decree that, for many activities, people simply can't do two or more tasks at once. In addition, while the brain can switch rapidly from task to task, doing so takes more time to do the tasks. In addition, he says, "You simply don't do as thorough a job," and some tasks simply aren't amenable to being done in a shallow way. The repeated switching of attention also "adds to one's stress. . . ."

3 The sleep disruptions that [go along with] social technology may help account for [mental] changes, says . . . Kaveri Subrahmanyam, a professor of psychology at California State University, Los Angeles. . . . The "digital native" generation—teens and young 20-somethings who have grown up with these technologies—"sleep with the cell phone and get up in the middle of the night to respond to texts," she says. While the long-term effects of such behavior are unknown, research has shown that "frequent sleep interruptions make it harder for the brain to consolidate the day's learning and memories," she says.

From the cqpress.com article SOCIAL MEDIA EXPLOSION by Marcia Clemmitt, © 2013

2. Both authors cite research studies as evidence. Which sentence **best** states the authors' emphasis on research?

A. Both studies focus on mental processes.
B. One study focuses on mental processes, but the other study focuses on social interactions.
C. Both studies focus on social interactions.
D. One study focuses on emotions, but the other study focuses on anatomy.

TEXTING CAN IMPROVE LITERACY

1 In reality, texters may be improving their literacy skills. Dr. Beverly Plester says, "The more exposure you have to the written word the more literate you become and we tend to get better at things we do for fun." Recent criticisms that text language, including abbreviations and contractions, for example, may begin to appear in formal writing have not proven true. Dr. Plester concludes that text language follows the general rules of language and that people "have a sophisticated understanding of the appropriate use of words."

2 Furthermore, texting is a fast and convenient way to communicate with others. The practice has even made its way into the traditional classroom. Ms. Elsa Turner, a reading-language arts teacher, regularly uses a free educational Internet texting site to communicate with her students. She says, "I send reminders about homework assignments and notifications when I've updated online grades. The students love it because the information is short and relevant, and the texts help relieve stress over forgotten deadlines."

3 A study by the Pew Research Center found that on average, older teenagers send about 60 texts per day and use texting as their "dominant daily mode of communication." Their adult counterparts are not far behind in this rising trend. Perhaps the next time it's time to call the family to dinner, it might be more efficient to send a group text.

From TEXTING CAN IMPROVE LITERACY by Kristine Leung, © 2013

3. Both authors mention a connection between social media and stress. Which sentence **best** states the authors' interpretations of this connection?

A. Clemmitt and Leung agree that social media add to stress.
B. Leung cites evidence that social media add to stress, but Clemmitt cites evidence that social media relieve stress.
C. Clemmitt and Leung agree that social media relieve stress.
D. Clemmitt cites evidence that social media add to stress, but Leung cites evidence that social media relieve stress.

★ Spotlighted Item: **DRAG-AND-DROP**

DIRECTIONS: Read the information, and study the headings in the chart. Then drag and drop the excerpts into the correct locations on the chart.

SOCIAL MEDIA BECOMING A WORRISOME DISTRACTION

Author's Point of View	When electronic devices were first becoming [popular], some hoped they would teach a new generation how to multitask better than previous generations did. But research [shows] that people who grew up with electronic devices "really can't multitask" either, says . . . Larry Rosen, a professor of psychology at California State University, Dominguez Hills.
Acknowledgment and Response to Conflicting Viewpoint or Counterclaim	As a result, the typical technology-obsessed person now gives "continuous partial attention" to just about everything and full attention to almost nothing.
Rhetorical Strategy: Qualifying Statement	Some believe that . . . social media . . . may already be [changing] how people think and learn.
Supporting Reason or Key Idea	The sleep disruptions that [go along with] social technology may help account for [mental] changes, says . . . Kaveri Subrahmanyam, a professor of psychology at California State University, Los Angeles. . . .
Transitional Language or Signal Words that Indicate Relationships: Cause and Effect	While the long-term effects of such behavior are unknown, research has shown that "frequent sleep interruptions make it harder for the brain to consolidate the day's learning and memories," she says.

UNIT 3

DIRECTIONS: Read the information, and study the headings in the chart. Then drag and drop the excerpts into the correct locations on the chart.

TEXTING CAN IMPROVE LITERACY

Author's Point of View	Furthermore, texting is a fast and convenient way to communicate with others.
Acknowledgment and Response to Conflicting Viewpoint or Counterclaim	Recent criticisms that text language, including abbreviations and contractions, for example, may begin to appear in formal writing have not proven true. Dr. Plester concludes that text language follows the general rules of language and that people "have a sophisticated understanding of the appropriate use of words."
Rhetorical Strategy: Bandwagon	Some studies have shown that texting improves communication skills.
Supporting Reason or Key Idea	In reality, texters may be improving their literacy skills.
Transitional Language or Signal Words that Indicate Relationships: Addition	A study by the Pew Research Center found that on average, older teenagers send about 60 texts per day and use texting as their "dominant daily mode of communication." Their adult counterparts are not far behind in this rising trend. Perhaps the next time it's time to call the family to dinner, it might be more efficient to send a group text.

2 LESSON

Develop a Thesis

Use with **Student Book** pp. 138–139

READING ASSESSMENT TARGETS: R.5.3, R.6.2, R.6.4, R.8.1, R.8.2, R.8.3, R.9.2, R.
WRITING ASSESSMENT TARGETS: W.1, W.2

1 Review the Skill

To begin the writing task required by the extended response, you must first read the prompt carefully to determine your purpose and task. You must then read, analyze, and evaluate the source texts. Remember to reread the prompt when you have finished. This practice will help you focus your extended response.

The next step is to develop the claim or **thesis** that you will defend in your extended response. This thesis is based on your evaluation of the source texts. Often, you will be asked to determine whether an author makes an argument that is logical and persuasive. To make this determination, examine the elements of the author's argument: *Are the reasons and evidence logical and credible? Is the rhetoric convincing or misleading?*

2 Refine the Skill

By refining the skill of developing a claim or thesis, you will improve your study, writing, and test-taking abilities, especially as they relate to the GED® Reasoning Through Language Arts test. Read the information below. Then answer the question that follows.

EXTENDED RESPONSE PROMPT

While Clemmitt's article outlines some drawbacks of social media, Leung's article identifies some benefits of social media.

In your response, analyze both articles to determine which position is **better** supported. Use relevant and specific evidence from both sources to support your response.

CLAIM OR THESIS

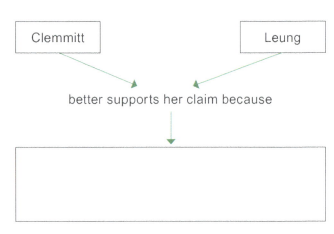

a The prompt asks you to determine which argument is better supported. Consider your initial reactions to the articles. *With whom do you agree? Does either change your thinking about the subject or make you consider a new point of view?*

b Fill in the blank box on the basis of the argumentative elements you identified in Unit 3, Lesson 1, such as point of view, response to counterarguments, rhetorical techniques, key ideas, or transitional language.

USING LOGIC

For example, you may complete the thesis frame as follows: Leung better supports her claim because she does not qualify her evidence as Clemmitt does.

1. Which thesis statement is the **best** response to the prompt above?

A. Clemmitt and Leung present equally strong arguments.
B. Clemmitt fails to address the benefits of social media.
C. Clemmitt and Leung present equally weak arguments.
D. Leung supports her argument better than Clemmitt does.

★ Spotlighted Item: **EXTENDED RESPONSE**

DIRECTIONS: Study and complete the graphic organizer. Then read the questions, and write your answers on the lines below.

SOCIAL MEDIA BECOMING A DISTRACTION

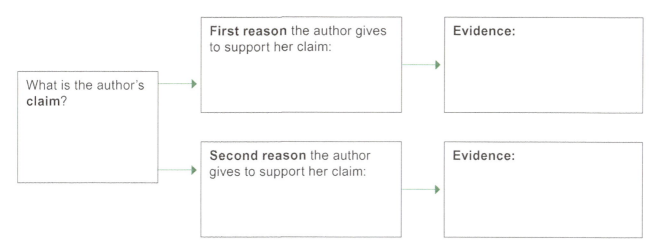

What is the author's **claim**?

First reason the author gives to support her claim:

Evidence:

Second reason the author gives to support her claim:

Evidence:

TEXTING CAN IMPROVE LITERACY

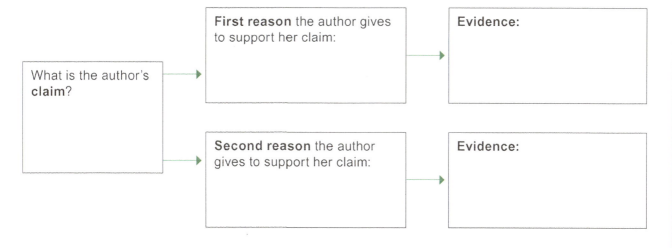

What is the author's **claim**?

First reason the author gives to support her claim:

Evidence:

Second reason the author gives to support her claim:

Evidence:

2. What are the strengths and weaknesses of Clemmitt's argument?

_____

_____

3. What are the strengths and weaknesses of Leung's argument?

_____

_____

UNIT 3

★ Spotlighted Item: **EXTENDED RESPONSE**

DIRECTIONS: Study the table. Then use the marking graphics noted in the chart to mark the texts in Unit 3, Lesson 1.

MARK THE TEXTS

Marking Graphic	Text Element	Example from Leung
[Bracket]	**Claim:** What is the author's claim or point of view?	[Texting improves communication skills.]
Circle and Number ^1, 2, 3	**Reason:** What reasons does the author offer in support of her claim?	Literacy ^1
Underline	**Evidence:** What evidence does the author offer in support of each reason—for example, facts, statistics, quotations, anecdotes, descriptions, definitions, or graphics?	"The more exposure you have to the written word the more literate you become . . ."
Box and Label	**Rhetorical Technique:** How does the author try to persuade readers—for example, analogies, enumerations, repetition and parallelism, juxtaposition of opposites, or qualifying statements?	Bandwagon Perhaps the next time it's time to call the family to dinner, it might be more efficient to send a group text.
Wavy Line	**Opposing Viewpoint:** Does the author acknowledge and respond to counterclaims?	Recent criticisms that text language . . . may begin to appear in formal writing have not proven true.
Triangle	**Relationship:** Does the author use transitional language or signal words to show the relationships among ideas?	Furthermore, texting is a fast and convenient way to communicate with others.

DIRECTIONS: Study and complete the graphic organizer. Write your answers on the lines provided. Then draw a star next to the thesis you plan to use.

WRITE A THESIS STATEMENT

_____

supports her argument better than

_____

supports her argument because

_____

_____.

_____

makes a stronger argument than

_____

because _____

_____.

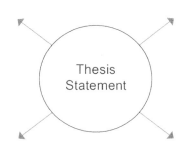

Thesis Statement

While _____

argues that _____,

_____ makes

a better argument in favor of/against

_____ because

_____

_____.

_____

best supports her claim because

_____

_____

_____

_____

_____.

UNIT 3

Define Points and Gather Evidence

Use with *Student Book* pp. 140–141

READING ASSESSMENT TARGETS: R.5.3, R.9.2, R.
WRITING ASSESSMENT TARGETS: W.1, W.2

1 Review the Skill

Before you write your extended response, you must determine what points you will use to support your thesis. Begin by rereading the passages and identifying points of similarity between them. For each point you define, **identify textual evidence from each passage**. Your extended response should include at least three points of comparison and at least one example from each passage per point.

For example, one point of similarity between the passages by Clemmitt and Leung is that they both address counterarguments. You may explain how each author acknowledges and responds to a specific counterargument. Then evaluate which author responds to counterarguments more effectively.

2 Refine the Skill

By refining the skills of defining points of comparison and gathering evidence, you will improve your study, writing, and test-taking abilities, especially as they relate to the GED® Reasoning Through Language Arts test. Study the diagram below. Then answer the question that follows.

a Use a Venn diagram to compare and contrast the passages. In the space where the circles overlap, write the points of similarity between the two passages.

b In the outer circles, note the differences. For example, on each side of the point **Counterargument**, write how each author responds to a counterargument.

VENN DIAGRAM

CLEMMITT — LEUNG

Claim/Point of View
Reasons
Evidence
Counterargument
Purpose
Rhetorical Technique
Tone

USING LOGIC

Start by brainstorming many points of comparison. Then choose the best three for your extended response. About which points do you have the most to say? Which points best support your thesis?

1. Which point of comparison **best** fits in the diagram above?

A. Transitional language
B. Multitasking
C. Literacy
D. Sleep disruption

UNIT 3

⭐ Spotlighted Item: **EXTENDED RESPONSE**

DIRECTIONS: Study and complete the graphic organizer. You may choose three of the points listed on the previous page, come up with points of your own, or use a combination of the two.

DEFINING POINTS AND GATHERING EVIDENCE

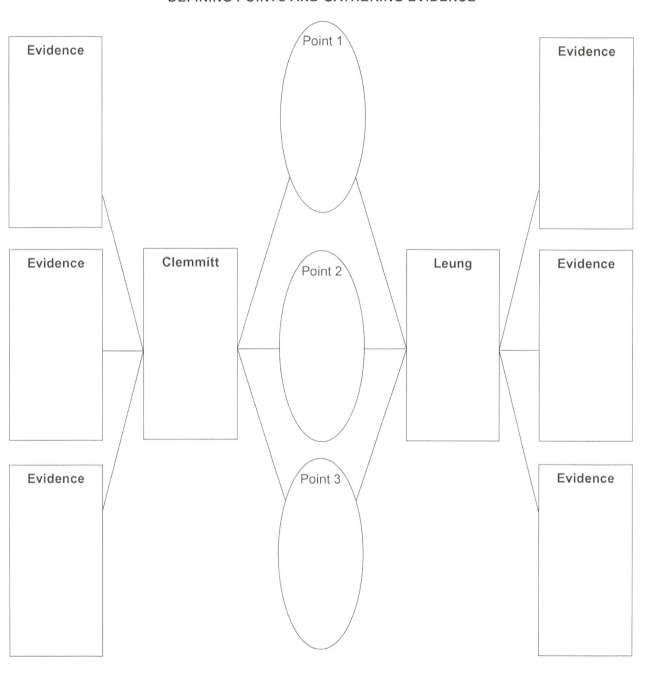

★ Spotlighted Item: **EXTENDED RESPONSE**

DIRECTIONS: Study and complete the graphic organizer. You may choose three of the points listed on the first page of this lesson, come up with points of your own, or use a combination of the two.

DEFINING POINTS AND GATHERING EVIDENCE

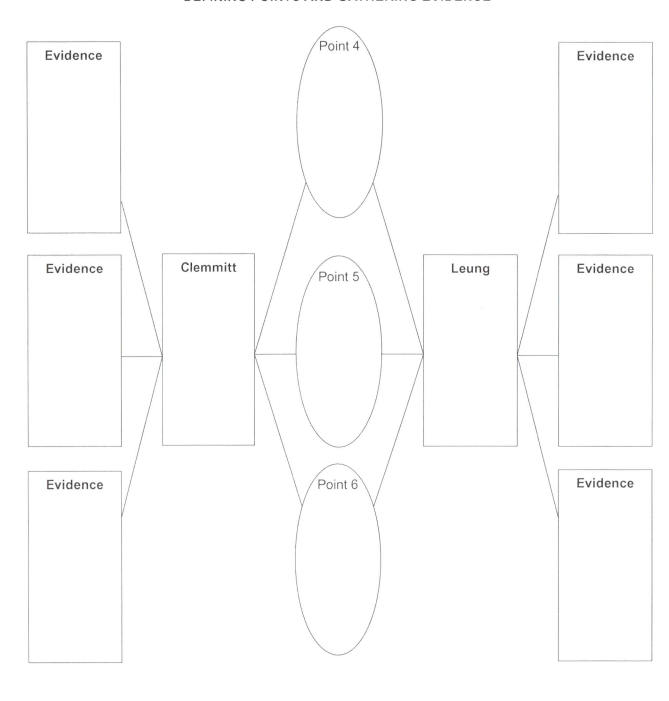

DIRECTIONS: Review the six points for which you have recorded text evidence. Draw a star next to the three points you will use for your extended response. Then read the questions, and write your answers on the lines below.

2. Which three points did you select for your extended response?

   In my extended response, I will focus on these three points of comparison:

   _____

   _____

   _____

3. Why did you choose these three points for your extended response?

   These three points **best** support my thesis statement because

   _____

   _____

   _____

   _____

   _____

4. Why did you eliminate the other three points?

   These three points do not support my thesis statement as well because

   _____

   _____

   _____

   _____

   _____

4
LESSON

Plan the Extended Response

Use with **Student Book** pp. 142–143

1 Review the Skill

In the same way that the human body is supported by a skeleton, an essay is built around an **organizational structure**. In comparison-and-contrast writing, this outline may take one of two commonly used forms. The first is **subject by subject**. In this form, you address one passage, or subject, and all related points before moving to the next subject. The second form is **point by point**. In this form, you address a single point common to both passages and then move to the next point.

With either structure, you must decide how to sequence the points. You may choose to start with the most important point and move toward the least important, or do the reverse. When choosing an organizational structure and sequence, think about what would make the most sense and be most convincing to readers.

2 Refine the Skill

By refining the skill of planning an extended response, you will improve your study, writing, and test-taking abilities, especially as they relate to the GED® Reasoning Through Language Arts test. Study the diagrams below. Then answer the question that follows.

SUBJECT BY SUBJECT

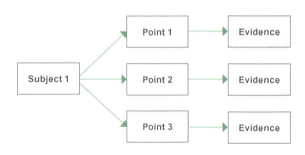

POINT BY POINT

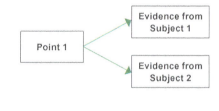

(a) Repeat this organizer for each subject. Consider using this structure when writing
• a short essay.
• in a timed situation.
• about topics unfamiliar to your audience.

(b) Repeat this organizer for each point. Consider using this structure when writing
• a long essay.
• in a timed situation.
• about topics familiar to your audience.

USING LOGIC

If the audience is opposed to your ideas, consider presenting the most convincing point first. If the audience agrees with you, consider presenting the most important point last.

1. In a subject-by-subject structure, which item would follow the first mention of a point about rhetorical strategy?

A. the introduction of a second point
B. evidence from the Clemmitt and Leung passages
C. evidence from the Clemmitt passage
D. explanation of a counterargument

⭐ Spotlighted Item: **EXTENDED RESPONSE**

DIRECTIONS: Study the diagram. Write in the three points of comparison or contrast that you defined in Unit 3, Lesson 3, and number them from most important to least important. Then read the questions, and write your answers on the lines below.

ORDER OF IMPORTANCE

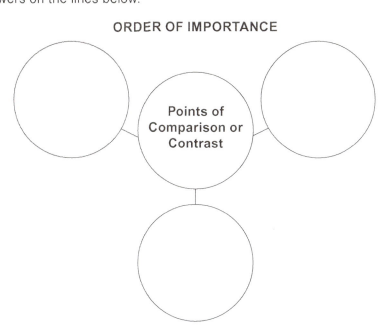

2. Point 1: _____

This point is **most** important because

_____

_____

3. Point 2: _____

This point is second in importance because

_____

4. Point 3:

This point is least important because

_____

_____

5. I will list my points in order from (circle one) most to least / least to most important because

_____

_____

UNIT 3

★ Spotlighted Item: **EXTENDED RESPONSE**

DIRECTIONS: Review the graphic organizers. Choose and complete either the Subject-by-Subject organizer on this page or the Point-by-Point organizer on the next page. Refer to the points you defined and the evidence you gathered in Unit 3, Lesson 3, if needed. If you are unsure about which structure to choose, complete both organizers. Then decide which makes more sense to use on the basis of logic and persuasiveness.

SUBJECT BY SUBJECT

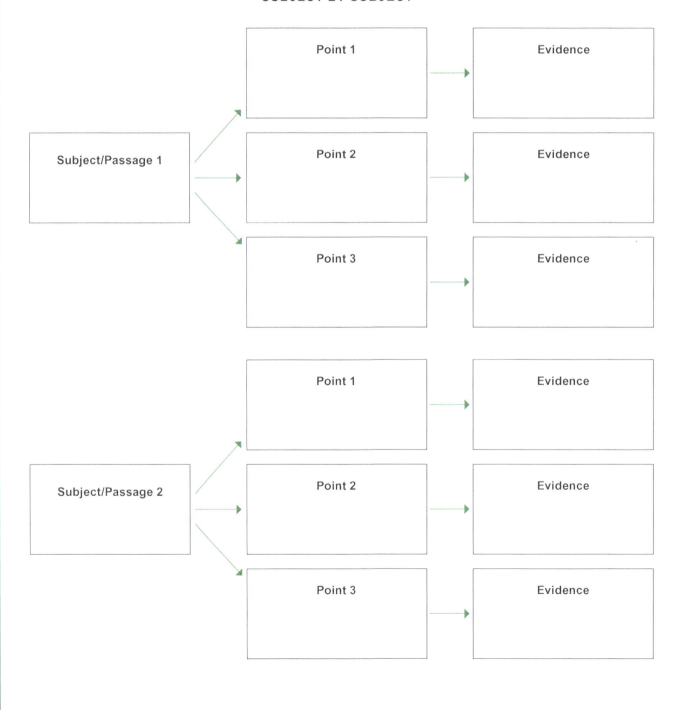

POINT BY POINT

	Evidence from Subject/Passage 1
Point 1	
	Evidence from Subject/Passage 2
	Evidence from Subject/Passage 1
Point 2	
	Evidence from Subject/Passage 2
	Evidence from Subject/Passage 1
Point 3	
	Evidence from Subject/Passage 2

5 Write an Introduction and Conclusion

LESSON

Use with **Student Book** pp. 144–145

READING ASSESSMENT TARGETS: R.5.1, R.5.
WRITING ASSESSMENT TARGETS: W.1, W.2, W
LANGUAGE ASSESSMENT TARGETS: L.1.9, L.

1 Review the Skill

The **introduction** of an essay is also called a lead because it guides readers into the essay's subject and thesis. The introduction has two functions: to get readers' attention and to introduce the thesis. You may accomplish these goals by using introductory strategies such as action, dialogue/quotation, or reaction and then transitioning to the thesis statement.

The closing section of an essay is the **conclusion**. Research suggests that the conclusion is the part of the essay that readers are most likely to remember. Therefore, it should restate the thesis and summarize the main points of the essay. However, it also must ask readers to think about the topic beyond the act of reading the essay. You may use strategies such as anecdotes, connections, or facts to leave readers with a strong, memorable concluding thought or call to action.

2 Refine the Skill

By refining the skill of writing an introduction and a conclusion for your extended response, you will improve your study, writing, and test-taking abilities, especially as they relate to the GED® Reasoning Through Language Arts test. Read the information and strategies below. Then answer the question that follows.

INTRODUCTION

You've grabbed five items for purchase in the grocery store. You're in a hurry to get home, so you choose the speedy checkout line. There are two customers ahead of you. The cashier finishes with the first person, but the second fails to move forward. He is texting! If this scenario seems familiar to you, you're not alone. People everywhere are multitasking and not doing it well. Although authors such as Kristine Leung sing the praises of social media, Marcia Clemmitt makes a stronger argument against social media in her article "Social Media Becoming a Distraction."

a This introduction illustrates the action strategy. The writer uses the active verb *grabbed* to describe a social media-related scenario from the reader's point of view. The writer then transitions to the thesis statement.

CONCLUSION

In conclusion, Clemmitt makes a stronger case against social media by citing credible scientific evidence from Rosen and Subrahmanyam about the disturbing effects of social media on the brain, including their disruption of sleep patterns and the brain's ability to focus. Leung's anecdotal evidence from a teacher pales in comparison. While people may be charmed by the convenience of social media, they must resist the technological dumbing down of modern culture while they still have the brain power to do so.

b This conclusion illustrates the connection strategy. The writer suggests that readers who fall for the charms of social media do so at the risk of limiting brain function.

USING LOGIC

Authors use transitions both within and between paragraphs. Note that in the introduction above, the writer moves from the specific to the general and uses the contrasting transition *although*.

1. Which statement is an example of a surprising concluding fact or statistic?

A. Next time, think about using a group text to call the family to dinner; the response may be quicker.

B. Teenagers send about 60 texts per day and use texting as their dominant means of communication.

C. During dinner time at the Martinez house, family members sit at the table and text friends and coworkers.

D. How many times per day do you text when you're supposed to be doing something else?

UNIT 3

★ Spotlighted Item: **DRAG-AND-DROP**

DIRECTIONS: Read the information and study the table. Then drag and drop the excerpts into the correct locations on the chart.

INTRODUCTIONS

Introduction Strategy	Example
Action	
Dialogue/Quotation	
Reaction	

INTRODUCTIONS

The [appeal] of socializing online has created a nation of mobile-device [fans], many of whom can go barely 10 minutes without checking their smartphones. . . .

You call your son, daughter, or spouse to dinner. "Just a minute!" he or she yells. In the distance, you hear the clicking of fingers on a keypad. A familiar annoyance builds. You respond, "Stop texting and get in here!"

"Right now, with social networks and other tools on the Internet, . . . 500 million people have a way to say what they're thinking and have their voice be heard," says Mark Zuckerberg, founder of Facebook.

CONCLUSIONS

Conclusion Strategy	Example
Anecdote	
Connection	
Fact/Statistic	

CONCLUSIONS

While the long-term effects of such behavior are unknown, research has shown that "frequent sleep interruptions make it harder for the brain to consolidate the day's learning and memories," she says.

Perhaps the next time it's time to call the family to dinner, it might be more efficient to send a group text.

During dinner time at the Martinez house, family members sit at the table and text friends and coworkers.

UNIT 3

★ Spotlighted Item: **EXTENDED RESPONSE**

DIRECTIONS: Read the questions below. Then write your answers on the lines provided. You may wish to begin by writing your thesis in item 6, then going back and brainstorming the leads.

INTRODUCTION

2. Write an action introduction for your thesis statement.

_____

_____

_____

_____

3. Write a dialogue/quotation introduction for your thesis statement.

_____

_____

_____

_____

4. Write a reaction introduction for your thesis statement.

_____

_____

_____

_____

5. Choose the **most** effective introduction from items 2–4 above, and circle it. Then write a transition from the lead you selected to your thesis.

_____

_____

6. Copy your thesis statement from Unit 3, Lesson 2, here.

_____

_____

_____

DIRECTIONS: Read the questions below. Then write your answers on the lines provided.

CONCLUSION

7. Select a concluding transition to open your conclusion.

_____

8. Write a summary of your thesis and the points and evidence you developed in Unit 3, Lessons 2–4.

_____

_____

_____

_____

9. Write a final thought that includes an anecdote.

_____

_____

_____

_____

10. Write a final thought that includes a connection with the reader.

_____

_____

_____

_____

11. Write a final thought that includes a surprising fact or statistic from one of the passages.

_____

_____

_____

_____

12. Choose the **most** effective final thought from items 9–11 above and circle it.

6 LESSON

Draft the Extended Response

Use with **Student Book** pp. 146–149

READING ASSESSMENT TARGET: R.5.3
WRITING ASSESSMENT TARGETS: W.1, W.2, W
LANGUAGE ASSESSMENT TARGET: L.1.9

1 Review the Skill

Up to this point, you have analyzed the source passages, developed a thesis, defined points of comparison and contrast, located supporting evidence, planned your outline, and prepared an introduction and a conclusion. Now it is time to write the **draft of your extended response** by putting these pieces together. In some cases, you also will have to develop your ideas further by writing complete sentences and explanations and adding transitions to show relationships among ideas.

As you work on your draft, stay focused on your purpose for writing, which is to persuade readers that your analysis of the passages is valid. It is also important to keep in mind your audience, who in this case are the test scorers who will use a rubric to assess your response.

2 Refine the Skill

By refining the skill of drafting an extended response, you will improve your study, writing, and test-taking abilities, especially as they relate to the GED® Reasoning Through Language Arts test. Read the outline and strategies below. Then answer the question that follows.

OUTLINE

I. Introduction and Thesis

II. First Point of Comparison or Contrast
    A. State and explain point.
    B. Provide example from passage 1.

III. Second Point of Comparison or Contrast
    A. State and explain point.
    B. Provide example from passage 1.

IV. Third Point of Comparison or Contrast
    A. State and explain point.
    B. Provide example from passage 1.

V. Restatement of First Point
    A. Provide example from passage 2.

VI. Restatement of Second Point
    A. Provide example from passage 2.

VII. Restatement of Third Point
    A. Provide example from passage 2.

VIII. Conclusion

a This is a subject-by-subject organizational structure. To organize by point, remove items **V–VII**, and move the evidence in **A** to items **II–IV**.

b Remember to use transitions to connect one paragraph to the next and to connect each paragraph to the thesis statement.

USING LOGIC

Use a frame to help you write body paragraphs:
For example: "[Author] states that [point 1]. She uses this strategy to [explanation of strategy]. For example, [author] notes that [example]."

1. Which transition sentence would make the **most** sense between items IV and V in the outline?

A. Clemmitt argues against social media, and Leung argues in favor of social media.
B. Clemmitt discusses dangers of social media. On the other hand, Leung focuses on their positive influence on communication.
C. In like manner, Clemmitt and Leung acknowledge the mental dangers and social triumphs of social media.
D. Clemmitt outlines the mental dangers of social media. In addition, Leung notes their positive influence on communication.

★ Spotlighted Item: **EXTENDED RESPONSE**

DIRECTIONS: Read the information below, and refer to the notes and planning organizers you completed in Unit 3, Lessons 1–5. Then write your extended response on the lines provided. If you chose a point-by-point organizational structure, you will need to adjust the frame. If you require additional space, you may continue your response on a separate sheet of paper.

EXTENDED RESPONSE

Introduction and Thesis: Copy the introduction you developed in Unit 3, Lesson 5, here. Finish with the thesis statement you developed in Unit 3, Lesson 2. Revise and edit for content, transitions, or word choice as necessary.

_____

_____

_____

_____

_____

Body: State and explain the first point of comparison or contrast here. Then add evidence from the Clemmitt article. Review your notes in Unit 3, Lessons 3 and 4, as needed. Revise and edit for content, transitions, or word choice as necessary.

_____

_____

_____

_____

_____

Body: State and explain the second point of comparison or contrast here. Then add evidence from the Clemmitt article. Review your notes in Unit 3, Lessons 3 and 4, as needed. Revise and edit for content, transitions, or word choice as necessary.

_____

_____

_____

_____

_____

_____

UNIT 3

★ Spotlighted Item: **EXTENDED RESPONSE**

EXTENDED RESPONSE (CONTINUED)

Body: State and explain the third point of comparison or contrast here. Then add evidence from the Clemmitt article. Review your notes in Unit 3, Lessons 3 and 4, as needed. Revise and edit for content, transitions, or word choice as necessary.

_____

_____

_____

_____

_____

Body: Restate and explain the first point of comparison or contrast here. Then add evidence from the Leung article. Review your notes in Unit 3, Lessons 3 and 4, as needed. Revise and edit for content, transitions, or word choice as necessary.

_____

_____

_____

_____

_____

Body: Restate and explain the second point of comparison or contrast here. Then add evidence from the Leung article. Review your notes in Unit 3, Lessons 3 and 4, as needed. Revise and edit for content, transitions, or word choice as necessary.

_____

_____

_____

_____

_____

EXTENDED RESPONSE (CONTINUED)

Body: Restate and explain the third point of comparison or contrast here. Then add evidence from the Leung article. Review your notes in Unit 3, Lessons 3 and 4, as needed. Revise and edit for content, transitions, or word choice as necessary.

Conclusion: Copy the conclusion you developed in Unit 3, Lesson 5, here. Revise and edit for content, transitions, or word choice as necessary.

UNIT 3

7 LESSON

Review the Extended Response

Use with **Student Book** pp. 150–151

WRITING ASSESSMENT TARGETS: W.1, W.2, W.3
LANGUAGE ASSESSMENT TARGETS: L.1.1, L.1.2, L.1.3, L.1.4, L.1.5, L.1.6, L.1
L.1.8, L.1.9, L.2.1, L.2.2, L.2.3, L.2.4

1 Review the Skill

Before submitting your extended response for scoring, use the remaining time to **review** your draft and **revise** as needed to correct errors or improve your writing. Replace generic language such as *thing* or *said* with more specific words such as *smartphone* or *shouted*. Make sure that every sentence contains both a subject and an action. Check that sentences contain transitions to connect ideas. Finally, review and correct errors in grammar, usage, punctuation, and spelling.

2 Refine the Skill

By refining the skill of reviewing the extended response, you will improve your study, writing, and test-taking abilities, especially as they relate to the GED® Reasoning Through Language Arts test. Review the diagram and strategies below. Then answer the question that follows.

WORD CHOICE

Your word choices and vocabulary must be purposeful, clear, logical, advanced, and formal. Consider these synonyms for *cell phone*. Which ones are appropriate for your extended response?

a The term *cell* may be too informal for academic writing. The word *phone* is vague, and could refer to cellular phones or landline phones.

b The terms *cellular phone*, *mobile phone*, or *smartphone* are specific and formal, making them more appropriate for academic writing.

cell

smartphone

mobile phone

CELL PHONE

cellular phone

phone

TEST-TAKING TIPS

Replace vague words in your writing with more specific language.
Vague Nouns: *everyone, men, people, stuff, things*
Vague Verbs: *come, go, is, say, want*
Vague Adjectives: *bad, good, nice, pretty, ugly*

1. "People are more likely to wean themselves from <u>bad things</u> when they understand the negative results. The time has come to wean ourselves from a diet of social distraction." Which is the **best** way to write the underlined portion of the sentences?

A. unhealthful things
B. foods and drinks
C. stuff that is harmful for them
D. soda, coffee, and high-fat foods

UNIT 3

★ Spotlighted Item: **EXTENDED RESPONSE**

DIRECTIONS: Study the chart. Choose examples for revision from your draft in Unit 3, Lesson 6, and record them in the chart. Then revise each example as directed. If you have trouble locating examples, ask an instructor or partner for help. Part of the chart has been filled in to help you get started.

REVIEW FOR WORDS

Review Category	Example from Draft	Revision
Usage: Words and forms should be appropriately formal. Avoid contractions and slang.	1. Subrahmanyam proposes that social media mess up sleep patterns and the brain's ability to process learning and memory. 2.	1. Subrahmanyam proposes that social media interrupt sleep patterns and compromise the brain's ability to process learning and memory. 2.
Words: Word choices must be clear, logical, and purposeful. Use advanced, specific vocabulary.	1.	1.
Wordiness: Ideas must be clear and concise.	1.	1.
Transitions: Transitional phrases must be strategic and effective.	1.	1.

★ Spotlighted Item: EXTENDED RESPONSE

DIRECTIONS: Study the chart. Choose examples for revision from your draft in Unit 3, Lesson 6, and record them in the chart. Then revise each example as directed. If you have trouble locating examples, ask an instructor or partner for help. Part of the chart has been filled in to help you get started.

REVIEW FOR SENTENCE STRUCTURE

Review Category	Example from Draft	Revision
Parallelism: Make words, phrases, or clauses in a series parallel by using the same structure for each.	1. Multiple distractions and interrupting by social media actually compromise a person's ability to do any one thing well. 2.	1. Multiple distractions and interruptions from social media actually compromise a person's ability to do any one thing well. 2.
Compound Sentences: Join two short sentences with an appropriate coordinating conjunction or conjunctive adverb, such as *or, and, but*, *however*, or *therefore*. Use commas and semicolons correctly to punctuate.	1.	1.
Complex Sentences: Join two short sentences with an appropriate subordinating conjunction, such as *although*, *because*, or *while*, using a comma if needed.	1.	1.
Run-On or Fused Sentences: Make run-on sentences into two sentences, or create a compound or complex sentence.	1.	1.
Sentence Fragments: Be sure that all sentences contain subjects and verbs and that subordinate clauses are connected to main clauses.	1.	1.

DIRECTIONS: Study the chart. Choose examples for revision from your draft in Unit 3, Lesson 6, and record them in the chart. Then revise each example as directed. If you have trouble locating examples, ask an instructor or partner for help. Part of the chart has been filled in to help you get started.

REVIEW FOR CONVENTIONS AND MECHANICS

Review Category	Example from Draft	Revision
Subject-Verb Agreement: Do singular subjects have singular verbs, and do plural subjects have plural verbs?	1. Finally, each author employ rhetorical strategies to convince readers. 2.	1. Finally, each author employs rhetorical strategies to convince readers. 2.
Frequently Confused Words: Watch out for words that sound the same but are spelled differently. For example, have you used *its* and *it's*, *your* and *you're*, and *there* and *their* correctly?	1.	1.
Pronoun Use: Do singular subjects have singular pronouns? Do pronouns refer clearly to antecedents? Are subject, object, and possessive pronouns used correctly?	1.	1.
Modifiers: Are modifiers placed correctly for clarity? Do all modifiers clearly describe another word or word group?	1.	1.
Capitalization: Have you correctly capitalized proper nouns, titles, and the beginnings of sentences?	1.	1.
Possessive Apostrophes: Have you used apostrophes correctly to show singular and plural possession?	1.	1.
Commas: Are commas used correctly? For example, have you used commas to separate items in a series, intervening elements, and clauses that should be separated by commas?	1.	1.
End Marks: Does every sentence end with a period, question mark, or exclamation point?	1.	1.

1 LESSON

Nouns

Use with **Student Book** pp. 162–163

LANGUAGE ASSESSMENT TARGET: L.
WRITING ASSESSMENT TARGET: W.3

1 Review the Skill

A **noun** names a person, place, idea, or thing. Nouns can be singular (one person, place, idea, or thing) or plural (more than one person, place, idea, or thing). If the noun names a specific person, place, or thing, it is a proper noun and should be capitalized. Some nouns refer to a group of people, animals, or things: an army, a family, a herd, or a set. These are called **collective nouns**.

2 Refine the Skill

By refining the skill of using nouns correctly, you will improve your writing and test-taking abilities, especially as they relate to the GED® Reasoning Through Language Arts test. Study the explanations and examples below. Then answer the questions that follow.

▶ Study these examples to review how to form the plurals of certain types of nouns.

a Be careful when forming the plural of words ending in ch, sh, o, or x. Most take −es. Some common examples are **watches, rashes, echoes,** and **boxes**.

Add −s at the end of the word.	Drop the f and add −ves.

The underlined employees stocked the shelves with fresh produce, such as tomatoes and cranberries.

Add −es at the end of the word.	Drop the y and add −ies.

b Collective nouns like **team** are singular when members act as a whole. For example, you write, "The team is ready," when all members are ready.

So far, my team has caught the most fish.

Collective noun is singular.	Spelling does not change when this noun is plural.

1. **The senators voted to build recycling centers in several countys across the state.** Which correction should be made to the sentence?

   A. Replace senators with Senators.
   B. Replace state with State.
   C. Replace centers with centeres.
   D. Replace countys with counties.

2. **Many calfs are born each spring.** Which correction should be made to the sentence?

   A. Change spring to springes.
   B. Change calfs to calves.
   C. Change spring to Spring.
   D. Change calfs to calfes.

CONTENT TOPICS

The plural form of some nouns does not end in −s. For example, the plural of man is men, the plural of woman is women, and the plural of child is children.

UNIT 4

★ Spotlighted Item: **DROP-DOWN**

DIRECTIONS: Read the passage. From the drop-down list, choose the answer that **best** completes the sentence.

MEMO: EMERGENCY NOTIFICATION SYSTEM

To: All Students

From: Registrar's Office

Subject: Emergency Notification System

As part of a statewide effort to inform different audiences about major safety-related emergency news, [3. Drop-down 1] plans to implement the new Emergency Notification System. Beginning next semester, students and staff members will receive alerts from the new system regarding emergencies on campus. The college defines emergencies as "situations that could pose immediate and significant harm to students and staff." These include, but are not limited to, extreme weather (such as hurricanes and [3. Drop-down 2]), fires, flooding, power outages, violent or criminal behavior, and unsafe physical conditions on campus.

The system uses multiple delivery methods, including e-mails, voice messages, and text messaging. Emergency information will also be posted on the campus Web site. Staff members have been registered and have chosen a preferred delivery method. The default method of notification for students will be through the college e-mail system. If [3. Drop-down 3] prefer to receive alerts as text or voice messages, they should e-mail the registrar's office.

Ten [3. Drop-down 4] are conducting tests of the new Emergency Notification System over the next several weeks. Communicating emergency information is very important to us, and we thank you for your support in this endeavor.

Drop-Down Answer Options

3.1 A. Warner college
B. warner college
C. warner College
D. Warner College

3.2 A. tornado's
B. tornadoies
C. tornadoes
D. tornadoses

3.3 A. student body members
B. student bodies
C. students bodys
D. student bodies members

3.4 A. Campus police officers
B. Campus police Officers
C. campus police officers
D. campus Police Officers

UNIT 4

★ Spotlighted Item: DROP-DOWN

DIRECTIONS: Read the passage. From the drop-down list, choose the answer that **best** completes the sentence.

MADISON COUNTY JURY SERVICES

SERVING ON A JURY

Serving on a jury is an important civic duty. Your service as a juror is one of the most valuable contributions you can make to the justice system. Serving on a jury allows you to see how the justice system works and gain a better understanding of how your

| 4. Drop-down 1 | works, in general.

The | 4. Drop-down 2 | guarantees citizens the right to a trial by a jury of one's peers. The | 4. Drop-down 3 | its decision based on the facts in a case. The jury's decision must be fair and impartial in order to protect the rights of the person on trial.

While serving on a jury, you will be asked to assume certain responsibilities. First, you should always be on time because a trial cannot proceed or end until all jury members are present. Second, you should not research the case you are deciding in any way. Finally, you should not discuss the case with anyone else, including your friends, relatives, spouse, or other jurors. After deliberations begin in the jury room, only the jury can discuss the case until the verdict is agreed upon.

You are required to serve on only one trial. The length of each trial varies by the case. The judge will inform you how long your case is expected to last. Many cases last less than a week. A juror receives $40 per day. For further information, contact

| 4. Drop-down 4 | at 123-555-1234.

Thank you in advance for your service!

Drop-Down Answer Options

4.1 A. government
    B. Government
    C. governmentes
    D. Governmentes

4.2 A. United states constitution
    B. United States Constitution
    C. United States constitution
    D. united states constitution

4.3 A. jury make
    B. juries makes
    C. jurys make
    D. jury makes

4.4 A. arthur collins
    B. Arthur collins
    C. Arthur Collins
    D. arthur Collins

DIRECTIONS: Read the passage. From the drop-down list, choose the answer that **best** completes the sentence.

MEMORANDUM

To: Food Smart Grocery Team

From: Ally Zeta, Manager

Subject: New Guidelines for Produce Section

As many of you know, sales in our produce department have declined over the last year. While competition from the new Freshway Organic Grocery has hurt most departments in the store, the produce department has particular problems. Not only are sales down, but we aren't selling what we have fast enough to prevent large [5. Drop-down 1] of fruit and vegetables from spoiling.

Although items in several store departments spoil quickly (for example, spoiled [5. Drop-down 2] are thrown out each day), waste in our produce section has increased by 50% in the last year. To increase profits in the department and better manage our inventory, we are implementing these changes:

- The amount of each type of fresh vegetable on display will be cut by 25%. We will train employees how to arrange [5. Drop-down 3] to maintain the appearance of a fully stocked department.

- We will no longer stock some exotic fruits and vegetables, including sunchokes and porcini mushrooms.

- The fresh herb section will be reduced to the most popular herbs, such as basil and parsley.

- Our stock of fruit will include major staples like bananas, oranges, and apples. However, our stock of more expensive or less popular types of fruit, such as [5. Drop-down 4] will vary by season.

Please keep me informed of any customer comments or complaints regarding these changes to the department.

Drop-Down Answer Options

5.1 A. quantitees
    B. quantitys
    C. quantities
    D. quantity

5.2 A. batches of fish
    B. batchs of fishies
    C. batchs of fishes
    D. batches of fishs

5.3 A. shelves and itemes
    B. shelfs and items
    C. shelfs and item
    D. shelves and items

5.4 A. peaches and strawberries
    B. peachs and strawberries
    C. peaches and strawberrys
    D. peachs and strawberrys

UNIT 4

2 Pronouns
LESSON

Use with **Student Book** pp. 164–165

LANGUAGE ASSESSMENT TARGET: L.

1 Review the Skill

A **pronoun** is a word that takes the place of a noun. The noun being replaced by the pronoun is called the antecedent. Writers use subject, object, and possessive pronouns to avoid repeating nouns and to improve the flow of text. Pronouns must agree in gender (male, female, neuter) and number (singular or plural) with the nouns they replace. This agreement is called **pronoun-antecedent agreement**.

2 Refine the Skill

By refining the skill of using pronouns correctly, you will improve your writing and test-taking abilities, especially as they relate to the GED® Reasoning Through Language Arts test. Read the explanations and examples below. Then answer the questions that follow.

▶ Remember these three types of pronouns. **Subject** pronouns replace the subject of a sentence. **Object** pronouns replace an object. **Possessive** pronouns show ownership.

ⓐ The possessive pronouns *mine, ours, yours, his, hers, its,* and *theirs* take the place of two nouns: both the subject that possesses and the thing that is possessed. For example, you can write "That is hers" rather than "That is Jana's book." *Hers* replaces *Jana's book*.

		Examples
Subject Pronouns	I, we, you, he, she, they, it	You did a great job on the test. They went to the movies.
Object Pronouns	me, us, you, him, her, them, it	Tommy helped us choose a computer for a good price. I told them not to come.
Possessive Pronouns	my, mine, our(s), your(s), his, her(s), their(s), its	The store offers good deals for its extended warranties. Is this book his or ours?

1. **After Tony and I watched the game, Tony and I went to the restaurant to meet some friends.** Which is the **best** way to write the underlined portion of the sentence?

   A. I and Tony
   B. us
   C. we
   D. me and Tony

2. **Jennifer and Luke used Jennifer's car.** Which is the **best** way to write the underlined portion of the sentence?

   A. hers
   B. she
   C. his
   D. her

USING LOGIC

Although the noun and the pronoun that replaces it usually appear in the same sentence, sometimes the noun appears in a previous sentence. As you read or write, be sure that you can trace each pronoun back to a noun.

UNIT 4

Master the Skill

★ Spotlighted Item: **DROP-DOWN**

DIRECTIONS: Read the passage. From the drop-down list, choose the answer that **best** completes the sentence.

THE PROBLEM WITH OUR CELEBRITY CULTURE

Dear Editor:

In today's high-tech world, mass media and globalization maintain our celebrity culture. Satellite communication, social media, communication apps, and the Internet allow information to be transmitted around the world. [3. Drop-down 1] make details about celebrities almost impossible to avoid. When a person turns on [3. Drop-down 2] television or goes online, there it is: the latest gossip about who has a new haircut or which couple is breaking up.

Although some famous people, such as actors or athletes, want desperately to keep their private lives private, the media seem to want to know everything about them. This frenzy of information is fueled by the people who buy magazines and newspapers or watch entertainment programs. They want to know everything there is to know about [3. Drop-down 3] favorite stars.

This intrusion into privacy sometimes causes negative reactions. Some superstars have physically attacked journalists or photographers who aggressively seek fresh information or try to get new pictures. Society needs to reexamine [3. Drop-down 4] priorities. Does society really need to know everything about famous people? Do we have a right to invade privacy just because someone is in the public eye?

Drop-Down Answer Options

3.1 A. They
B. It
C. Them
D. Us

3.2 A. he
B. their
C. him or her
D. his or her

3.3 A. your
B. them
C. us
D. their

3.4 A. it
B. its
C. their
D. it's

UNIT 4

⭐ Spotlighted Item: **DROP-DOWN**

DIRECTIONS: Read the passage. From the drop-down list, choose the answer that **best** completes the sentence.

MEMO

To: All McMahon Employees

From: Human Resources

Subject: Absentee Policy

Date: August 1, 2019

Coming to work when you are sick can be as hard on your co-workers as it is on you. [4. Drop-down 1] can spread disease and illness and cause others to miss work. Although we hope all employees will make every effort to come to work when they are well, we encourage employees who are ill to stay home when necessary. Therefore, McMahon Construction has implemented the following rules to help you know what to do if you are too ill to come to work.

- Call your supervisor as early in the day as possible. If you can't speak to [4. Drop-down 2] directly, leave a message.

- Leave a message for the HR department so that [4. Drop-down 3] absence can be noted in your employment record.

- If you miss more than three consecutive workdays, you must obtain a release from your doctor before returning to work.

- Employees are allowed five paid sick days per calendar year. Any additional sick days will be unpaid and the employee's status may be reviewed. Employees with excessive numbers of sick days may be asked to provide detailed information explaining the reasons for [4. Drop-down 4] absence from work.

Drop-Down Answer Options

4.1 A. You
 B. I
 C. We
 D. Them

4.2 A. she or he
 B. them
 C. us
 D. him or her

4.3 A. their
 B. you
 C. your
 D. its

4.4 A. his or her
 B. their
 C. your
 D. his

DIRECTIONS: Read the passage. From the drop-down list, choose the answer that **best** completes the sentence.

RICHARD'S BLOG

September 3:
Our Family Reunion

Since almost everyone in my family takes Labor Day off, my aunt and uncle decided to host a family reunion. The sun was shining, and the smell of burgers and hot dogs on the grill was making my mouth water. Who could have predicted that my wife and I would be ending [5. Drop-down 1] day in the emergency room?

Things started to go wrong when my aunt asked me to carry [5. Drop-down 2] prize-winning potato salad out to the patio. I forgot that the kids had been running in the hose earlier. You can guess what happened next. I slipped in the wet grass, and the potato salad flew everywhere. My wife ran over to check on me, and although I was trying to act cool, [5. Drop-down 3] ankle was really throbbing. She helped me up, and my uncle went for some ice. The kids thought it was like a slapstick routine and were really laughing!

The ice helped relieve the pain, but after an hour my ankle had swollen to the size of a softball. My cousin Dan volunteered to drive my wife and me to the hospital, and [5. Drop-down 4] offer. We arrived during an extremely busy time. Because my injury was not life-threatening, it took nearly three hours for me to see a doctor. As we were leaving, a nurse explained that holidays are often the busiest times of the year. "You'd never guess," she laughed, "how many family get-togethers end up here!"

Drop-Down Answer Options

5.1 A. ours
  B. our
  C. us
  D. we

5.2 A. their
  B. she
  C. his
  D. her

5.3 A. my
  B. her
  C. our
  D. we

5.4 A. we took up his
  B. us took up his
  C. we took up their
  D. us took up him

3 Basic Verb Tenses

Use with **Student Book** pp. 166–167

WRITING ASSESSMENT TARGET: V

1 Review the Skill

Basic verb tenses indicate whether an action or an event occurred in the **past**, occurs in the **present**, or will occur in the **future**. The past tense of regular verbs is formed by adding -d or -ed to the end of the verb. However, the past tense of many irregular verbs requires a change in spelling. The present tense of many verbs is formed by adding an -s to the main verb. The future tense of regular and irregular verbs is formed by placing the word *will* in front of the main verb.

2 Refine the Skill

By refining the skill of using basic verb tenses correctly, you will improve your writing and test-taking abilities, especially as they relate to the GED® Reasoning Through Language Arts test. Study the examples below. Then answer the questions that follow.

a You can find more information about regular and irregular verbs on pp. 282–283 and pp. 288–291 in this book.

▶ Study the chart below to review the formation of basic verb tenses for **regular verbs**.

Regular verbs	Formation	Example
Present tense	Add –s when the subject is any noun that can be substituted by *he, she,* or *it*.	He laughs at my jokes. It happens often.
Past tense	Add –d or –ed.	She managed.
Future tense	Use *will* before the verb.	She will cooperate.

b Many verbs in English are irregular and do not follow the indicated rules. To form verb tenses correctly, you will need to memorize irregular verb forms.

▶ Study the chart below to help you memorize some common **irregular verbs**.

Irregular Verb	Past Tense
to be	it was
to begin	she began
to take	I took
to have	he had
to give	we gave
to wear	you wore

1. **Next week, I traveled to Ohio, and I will visit my old friends.** Which correction should be made to the sentence?

   A. Replace traveled with will travel.
   B. Replace will visit with visited.
   C. Replace traveled with traveling.
   D. Replace will visit with visits.

2. **He always brushed his teeth before he goes to bed.** Which correction should be made to the sentence?

   A. Replace brushed with brush.
   B. Replace goes with will go.
   C. Replace brushed with brushes.
   D. Replace goes with go.

TEST-TAKING TIPS

Unless the action changes from past to present or from present to future, use the same tense in a sentence or when writing about an event or a topic. Keep tenses as consistent as possible.

★ Spotlighted Item: **DROP-DOWN**

DIRECTIONS: Read the passage. From the drop-down list, choose the answer that **best** completes the sentence.

Julie Harrison, Chair
Rosedale Neighborhood Association
4949 W. Sinclair Street
Arlen, TX 75709

Dear Ms. Harrison:

I am writing to follow up on the surveys that you distributed through your neighborhood association regarding our new restaurant. As you know, Kids' Eats is very sensitive about renovating the beloved Garcia's Hamburgers site, and we want our changes to reflect the wishes of the community.

The feedback we [3. Drop-down 1   ] from the surveys helped us reach these decisions:

- When we renovate the space in the coming months, we [3. Drop-down 2   ] as few cosmetic changes as possible. Although we will upgrade the building to make it more energy efficient, the twirly barstools, bouncy-horse seating, and period neon signs will remain.

- Your surveys request meals that are both healthy and kid friendly. In response, we are developing salads and fresh vegetable combos that will appeal to both kids and adults.

- Many of your surveys requested the addition of playscape facilities. You will be pleased to know that we will add an outdoor dining area that [3. Drop-down 3   ] a playscape.

Please tell your neighborhood association members how much we [3. Drop-down 4   ] their feedback, and encourage them to contact us with any additional concerns or suggestions. Kids' Eats is honored to be a part of the Rosedale neighborhood.

Sincerely,

Harmon Lamar

President, Kids' Eats, Inc.

Drop-Down Answer Options

3.1 A. received
B. receive
C. receives
D. will receive

3.2 A. made
B. make
C. will make
D. making

3.3 A. included
B. include
C. including
D. will include

3.4 A. will appreciate
B. appreciates
C. appreciating
D. appreciate

UNIT 4

Master the Skill

DIRECTIONS: Read the passage. From the drop-down list, choose the answer that **best** completes the sentence.

CHECKING YOUR OIL
GUIDELINES

It is important that you check the oil in your car often. Checking the oil [4. Drop-down 1] very easy and can keep you from having major repair bills. The first step is to park the car on a level surface, such as a driveway. Then turn off the engine, and open the hood. The engine should be warm.

Next, find the dipstick, a long, thin piece of metal with a loop at one end that [4. Drop-down 2] out of the engine. After you locate the dipstick, pull it out. Wipe the oil off the dipstick with a paper towel, and then replace the clean dipstick. Be sure that you push it all the way into the engine. Pull the dipstick out again, and look at the pointed end opposite the loop. If you look closely, you'll see a line of oil on the marked portion of the pointed end of the dipstick. This line indicates the oil level.

If the oil is below the line marked "full," you may need to add oil to your car. Always [4. Drop-down 3] your oil above the half-full mark, close to full. To add oil, you can use a funnel, but be sure not to add too much. Otherwise, your engine may flood. We recommend that you change the oil every 3,000 miles to ensure maximum performance of your automobile. You [4. Drop-down 4] improved gas mileage after you begin regular maintenance.

Drop-Down Answer Options

4.1 A. was
    B. will be
    C. are
    D. is

4.2 A. stick
    B. stuck
    C. sticks
    D. will stick

4.3 A. keep
    B. keeps
    C. kept
    D. keeping

4.4 A. noticed
    B. notices
    C. will notice
    D. notice

UNIT 4

DIRECTIONS: Read the passage. From the drop-down list, choose the answer that **best** completes the sentence.

MEMO

To: Fresh Foods Grocery Employees

From: Rachel Cabrino, President

Second quarter sales figures for Fresh Foods were $770,000, up 5 percent from the previous year's quarterly totals. Much of this increase can be traced to the success of our Farmers' Market Days and the increased traffic that those weekend events [5. Drop-down 1].

Despite static grocery store sales across the country, Fresh Foods increased sales in a number of areas, particularly organic dairy and produce selections. We believe that our current strengths in organic food sales [5. Drop-down 2] shoppers' confidence in the safety and purity of organic products.

Highlights of Fresh Foods' quarterly sales report [5. Drop-down 3]

- a 50 percent increase in the sales of competitively priced store-brand items,

- a 30 percent increase in locally grown and organic produce sales, and

- a 17 percent decrease in sales of prepared deli items.

On the basis of the information provided by department managers this quarter, we [5. Drop-down 4] the following changes beginning on the first of next month:

- increase the variety of store-brand products;

- advertise the Fresh Foods brand prominently in newspapers;

- continue to promote our local farmers and dairy suppliers; and

- decrease the selection of higher-priced deli items, substituting more "make at home" packages.

Drop-Down Answer Options

5.1 A. will generate
   B. generated
   C. generates
   D. generating

5.2 A. reflecting
   B. reflect
   C. reflects
   D. will reflect

5.3 A. will include
   B. includes
   C. include
   D. including

5.4 A. implemented
   B. implements
   C. implement
   D. will implement

UNIT 4

Verbs with Helping Verbs

Use with **Student Book** pp. 168–169

LESSON 4

1 Review the Skill

Helping verbs are combined with main verbs to help to show the time of an action. For example, adding *had* to the verb shows that an action in the past occurred before another action was started. Adding *has* or *have* to the main verb indicates that an action was started in the past and continues. Adding *will have* to the verb shows that an action will be completed at a specified time in the future.

The helping verbs *be, am, are, was,* and *were* plus the present participle (*-ing* form of a verb) indicate ongoing actions that are happening now, were happening in the past, or will be happening in the future.

2 Refine the Skill

By refining the skill of using verbs with helping verbs to show tenses, you will improve your writing and test-taking abilities, especially as they relate to the GED® Reasoning Through Language Arts test. Study the explanations and examples below. Then answer the questions that follow.

▶ Study the chart to review using helping verbs in different tenses.

a The **perfect tense** is formed by placing a form of the helping verb **have** in front of the past participle form of a verb, such as *finished* or *sung*. The helping verb indicates the tense; the participle never changes.

b The **progressive tense** requires a form of the helping verb **to be** in front of the present participle form of a verb. Present participles always end in *-ing*.

Past Perfect	An action that occurred before another past action was completed.	I had finished writing my essay before I started this project.
Present Perfect	An action that took place in the past and continues to take place in the present.	I have sung in this chorus for years.
Future Perfect	An action that is taking place now and will be finished in the future.	By the end of the day, I will have finished this work.
Present Progressive	An action that is ongoing in the present.	She is taking dance lessons.
Past Progressive	An action that was ongoing in the past.	They were earning money.
Future Progressive	An action that will be ongoing in the future.	He will be running in the next races.

USING LOGIC

Look for words that indicate the time of an action. Key words, such as *today, later, always, before, by,* and *then,* can help you determine the correct tense of the helping verb.

1. **By the end of tomorrow's trip, I had traveled more than 600 miles this week.** Which is the **best** way to write the underlined portion of the sentence?

   A. am traveling
   B. was traveling
   C. have traveled
   D. will have traveled

2. **Before he finally joined me, I will have run two miles.** Which correction should be made to the sentence?

   A. Replace will have run with have run.
   B. Replace will have run with will be running.
   C. Replace will have run with had run.
   D. Replace will have run with were running.

★ Spotlighted Item: **DROP-DOWN**

DIRECTIONS: Read the passage. From the drop-down list, choose the answer that **best** completes the sentence.

MODERN KITCHEN APPLIANCES
A COMPANY HISTORY

Our company [3. Drop-down 1] many lessons since opening 100 years ago. Modern Kitchen Appliances began in the late 1920s, a time of change for many American businesses. Electrical companies started to build power lines across the United States, and then telephones started to link homes and businesses. Many advances in kitchen appliances [3. Drop-down 2] at the time. For example, the refrigerator was just beginning to become popular in American kitchens.

As is the case with many other start-up businesses, the company's first product, the Homemaker's Helper, was a failure. A combination toaster and oven seemed like a good idea at the time, but it failed to excite consumers and had a number of performance problems. However, that failure was not the end of the company. We learned from the experience and went on to develop a range of other products that [3. Drop-down 3] exceptionally well over the years and continue to be popular in their newest versions.

At Modern Kitchen Appliances, we listen to our customers and strive to deliver the products they want and need. Over the past 100 years, our company has produced more than 150 successful and technologically innovative products. These include refrigerators and freezers, conventional and convection ovens, gas and electric ranges, dishwashers, and microwave ovens. Today, our products are used in millions of homes. We hope that by the time the company celebrates its next 100 years, millions more people [3. Drop-down 4] our products.

Drop-Down Answer Options

3.1 A. will have learned
B. had learned
C. is learning
D. has learned

3.2 A. have happened
B. were happening
C. will have happened
D. will be happening

3.3 A. had performed
B. will have performed
C. have performed
D. were performing

3.4 A. will have used
B. were using
C. had used
D. has used

UNIT 4

⭐ Spotlighted Item: **DROP-DOWN**

DIRECTIONS: Read the passage. From the drop-down list, choose the answer that **best** completes the sentence.

NO ATVS IN STATE PARKS

Dear Editor:

The *City Chronicle* has recently discovered that riders of ATVs (All-Terrain Vehicles) | 4. Drop-down 1 | a new bill in the state legislature. The bill would allow ATV enthusiasts to ride their vehicles in state parks. Many people are not aware that the bill is coming up for a vote next month, and it has important consequences for our state parks. It is important to stop this bill before it passes.

A recently conducted survey | 4. Drop-down 2 | that walkers and hikers in state parks outnumber potential ATV riders 5 to 1. Although I have nothing against ATVs, it is common knowledge that they are loud and cause damage to trails, even when people ride their ATVs responsibly. Over 70 percent of people surveyed expressed opposition to allowing ATVs in our state parks. These survey respondents cited legitimate concerns about excessive noise, damage to grassy areas and trails, and potential danger to walkers and hikers. People | 4. Drop-down 3 | it clear that they do not want to see ATVs in state parks!

Other places offer open spaces where people can ride. For example, thousands of acres of old coal mines in the southern part of the state | 4. Drop-down 4 | ATV riders from across the country. Also many outdoor areas have places where ATV riders can ride for small fees. These areas were designed for ATV riders and are more appropriate places for this activity. We should encourage our state's riders to use these areas rather than try to create new ones in our state parks.

Drop-Down Answer Options

4.1 A. were supporting
B. had supported
C. will have supported
D. are supporting

4.2 A. will have shown
B. had shown
C. has shown
D. was showing

4.3 A. is making
B. have made
C. will have made
D. had made

4.4 A. had attracted
B. will have attracted
C. has attracted
D. have attracted

UNIT 4

DIRECTIONS: Read the passage. From the drop-down list, choose the answer that **best** completes the sentence.

CHOOSING AND INSTALLING A CLOSET ORGANIZER

If you [5. Drop-down 1] from a cramped and messy closet, it may be time to install a closet organizer. There are a few things to consider once you [5. Drop-down 2] to buy and install a closet organizer. The most common types are wood (sometimes made of laminated particle board) and wire organizers. If appearance is not important, buy wire organizers, which usually cost less than the wooden variety. Wood organizers are generally sturdier and more attractive, although they can be harder to install. Whichever type you prefer, you can purchase the organizer at a hardware or home improvement store. Compare prices to get the best value for your money.

Remove everything from the closet, including the existing shelves and bars. If you remove the doors, you will find it easier to get the parts into the closet. Patch any holes with spackling compound or other fillers.

Assemble the closet organizer according to the manufacturer's instructions. Most organizers are put together with connecting bolts. You should not use a power screwdriver when assembling the organizer, but you may be able to use one when attaching it to the wall. After you [5. Drop-down 3] the organizer, measure and mark the wall to determine where to hang each part. Using appropriate fasteners, secure each part of the organizer to wall studs. It is important to ensure that screws are properly anchored to the wall.

After only a small investment of money and time, you [5. Drop-down 4] a whole new closet that will function much better than it did in the past!

Drop-Down Answer Options

5.1 A. will have suffered
B. had suffered
C. are suffering
D. was suffering

5.2 A. have decided
B. are deciding
C. had decided
D. will have decided

5.3 A. are constructing
B. had constructed
C. will have constructed
D. have constructed

5.4 A. had created
B. will have created
C. are creating
D. has created

Apostrophes

LESSON 5

Use with **Student Book** pp. 170–171

LANGUAGE ASSESSMENT TARGETS: L.1.1, L.2
WRITING ASSESSMENT TARGET: W.3

1 Review the Skill

You learned in Lesson 2 that possessive pronouns show that something belongs to someone or something else. Another way to show possession is to use an apostrophe to create a **possessive** noun. By adding an apostrophe and the letter *s* to the end of a singular noun, you show that something belongs to that noun. If a plural word ends with the letter *s*, then you add only the apostrophe to the end of the word.

Apostrophes also show **contractions**, or two words shortened into one word. When you form a contraction the apostrophe shows the place of the missing letter or letters.

2 Refine the Skill

By refining the skill of using apostrophes to show possession and contractions, you will improve your writing and test-taking abilities, especially as they relate to the GED® Reasoning Through Language Arts test. Study the explanations and examples below. Then answer the questions that follow.

▶ Remember to use an apostrophe to show possession (to whom or what something belongs). Also, use an apostrophe to combine two words to form a contraction.

Possession	Contractions
I borrowed the car of my friend. I borrowed my friend's car.	I should have spent more time studying for the test. I should've spent more time studying for the test.
The spouses of the officers always met on Sundays. The officers' spouses always met on Sundays.	We could not see the movie last night. We couldn't see the movie last night.

▶ Some possessives and contractions are frequently confused. Study the examples and explanations below.

Frequently Confused Possessives	Frequently Confused Contractions
Wrong: I read Dickens' novel. *Right:* I read Dickens's novel. Explanation: Add *'s* to singular nouns that end in *s*, including names.	*Wrong:* There coming to dinner. *Right:* They're coming to dinner. Explanation: *They're* is a contraction for *they are*.
Wrong: This store sells childrens' clothing. *Right:* This store sells children's clothing. Explanation: *Children* is plural and does not end in *s*, so the apostrophe comes before the *s*.	*Wrong:* You know its true. *Right:* You know it's true. Explanation: *Its* is a possesive. *It's* is a contraction for *it is*.

CONTENT TOPICS

A possessive word is usually followed by the thing it possesses: "Mia's yard" or "the tree's leaves." Sometimes, an adjective may come between the two words: "Mia's big yard" or "the tree's wet leaves."

1. **You should clean you're car before it's your turn to drive the car pool.** Which correction should be made to the sentence?

   A. Change you should to you'd.
   B. Change you're to your.
   C. Change it's to its.
   D. Change your to you're.

2. **Both boy's parents attended their children's concert.** Which correction should be made to the sentence?

   A. Change boy's to boys'.
   B. Change boy's to boys.
   C. Change children's to childrens'.
   D. Change children's to children.

UNIT 4

3 **Master the Skill**

★ Spotlighted Item: **DROP-DOWN**

DIRECTIONS: Read the passage. From the drop-down list, choose the answer that **best** completes the sentence.

From: josh_bowen23@xyz.com

Subject: Volunteer opportunities

Date: September 17, 2019 12:43 p.m. EDT

To: k.washington@parentsforpaws.org

Hi Kendra,

I was given your name by my neighbor, Dennis Trachtenberg. Dennis indicated that you are the contact person for volunteers at Parents for Paws. I'm sure that you are familiar with [3. Drop-down 1] volunteer work with your adoption program for dogs. As you know, he walks dogs two evenings a week and takes them to Sunday's riverfront market so that potential "new parents" can see the dogs and play with them.

I admire all of your [3. Drop-down 2] efforts in the community and hope I can join your team. I have always loved dogs, and I feel a special bond with them. I grew up with a household of wonderful dogs, and [3. Drop-down 3] had a dog most of my adult life. At the moment, I have one dog of my own, Sadie, that I adopted from a shelter. When I first got Sadie, she was about eight months old. She was skinny and scared, having been neglected and abused by her owners. With lots of love and attention, she's become a gentle, loving dog (as well as my best buddy). I feel very strongly about helping to give abandoned, abused, and unwanted dogs a loving home.

I am a teacher at Middlebury Junior High and coach the tennis team. As a teacher, I have a somewhat flexible schedule. I am available to walk dogs in the late afternoon or early evening. If I am not attending my [3. Drop-down 4] tennis matches, my weekends are usually free.

I look forward to hearing from you!

Drop-Down Answer Options

3.1 A. Dennis'
    B. Dennis
    C. Dennises
    D. Dennis's

3.2 A. volunteer's
    B. volunteers
    C. volunteers'
    D. volunteers's

3.3 A. Iv'e
    B. I've
    C. Ive'
    D. Ive

3.4 A. teams
    B. teams'
    C. team's
    D. teams's

UNIT 4

3 *Master the Skill*

★ Spotlighted Item: **DROP-DOWN**

DIRECTIONS: Read the passage. From the drop-down list, choose the answer that **best** completes the sentence.

JOB HUNTING TIPS

It was once fairly common for employees to work their entire careers at a single company. However, today's employees often work for a number of businesses throughout their careers. [4. Drop-down 1] a great deal of competition for the same job among people of different ages, backgrounds, and levels of experience. Given the intensity of the competition for high-paying jobs, [4. Drop-down 2] important that job seekers do not fall prey to common job-hunting mistakes.

Remember that the purpose of a good résumé is to secure an interview. Job [4. Drop-down 3] résumés should include contact information and a complete job history. Job hunters also should be prepared to explain any gaps in their job history or frequent job changes. Résumés should feature language that is varied but specific. Active words, such as *assisted, delivered, coordinated, prepared, organized, built,* or *managed,* provide the best description of work activities.

After job seekers land an interview, they must "sell" their abilities to potential employers. They should prepare for the interview so that they appear informed about the [4. Drop-down 4] history and ask intelligent questions. In return, employers want potential employees to be positive and consistent when answering questions. One way to impress a potential employer is to express career goals and explain how they match the goals of the company.

After the interview, many job seekers send a message thanking the people at the interview. The message usually contains further information or a brief statement about looking forward to hearing from them.

Drop-Down Answer Options

4.1 A. Their's
 B. Theirs
 C. There's
 D. There

4.2 A. it
 B. it's
 C. its
 D. it was

4.3 A. hunter's
 B. hunters
 C. hunters'
 D. hunters's

4.4 A. company's
 B. companies
 C. companies'
 D. companies's

UNIT 4

DIRECTIONS: Read the passage. From the drop-down list, choose the answer that **best** completes the sentence.

COOKING WITH FIRE!

As summer approaches, [5. Drop-down 1] time to start thinking about taking the grill out of storage, calling some friends, and having a cookout. However, before you fire up your grill, brush up on your grilling skills by observing a few simple tips:

- Clean the grill before and after you use it. Remaining food particles may become burnt onto the [5. Drop-down 2] grid and can alter the flavors of the next meats or vegetables that you cook on it. For example, particles left from grilled fish can give hamburgers an odd taste.

- [5. Drop-down 3] allow raw meat to touch food that you have already cooked. Keep uncooked and cooked meat on different plates or platters. Taking this precaution will prevent bacteria on the raw meat from contaminating the cooked food.

- Take the time to preheat the grill. This step will kill any bacteria on the grill and ensure you have reached the proper temperature before you start cooking.

- Good grilling requires a hot grill, but not too hot. The right temperature is usually in the range of 325°F to 400°F. A very high temperature can burn the outside of food while leaving the inside raw. On the other hand, if the temperature is too low, food will not sear properly and can become dry and bland.

If you follow these tips, [5. Drop-down 4] be able to cook a great meal on the grill and become the envy of other aspiring grill masters. From shrimp and fish to steaks and hamburgers, you're never far from a great meal when you fire up the grill.

Drop-Down Answer Options

5.1 A. it's
    B. its'
    C. its
    D. it was

5.2 A. grills'
    B. grills's
    C. grill's
    D. grills

5.3 A. Don't
    B. Dont
    C. Do'nt
    D. Dont'

5.4 A. you've
    B. you'll
    C. youw'll
    D. you

6 LESSON

Frequently Confused Words

Use with **Student Book** pp. 172–173

1 Review the Skill

As you learned in Lesson 5, some words sound the same but have different spellings and meanings. These words are called **homonyms**. For example, *knew* is the past tense of *know*, and *new* means "unused or recently created or purchased." Other words may have the same spellings but different meanings and may or may not have different pronunciations. The word *bat*, for example, may refer to a flying animal or to a stick for hitting a baseball. Finally, some words may sound almost the same but are spelled differently and have different meanings—for example, *accept* and *except*.

2 Refine the Skill

By refining the skill of using homonyms and frequently confused words correctly, you will improve your writing and test-taking abilities, especially as they relate to the GED® Reasoning Through Language Arts test. Study the explanations and examples below. Then answer the questions that follow.

▶ Use context clues to determine whether the correct homonym is used in a passage. Study the example.

| *Add* means to "combine numbers." | *Ad* is a short form of "advertisement." |

You should <u>add</u> the tax to be sure that the price in the <u>ad</u> is really a good deal.

▶ Study the words and their meanings in the table below. Also review the homonyms and frequently confused words discussed in the student book and listed in the appendix.

MORE COMMON HOMONYMS AND FREQUENTLY CONFUSED WORDS

accept	I <u>accept</u> your apology.	except	Everyone came <u>except</u> Sasha.
higher	The balloon rose <u>higher</u> and <u>higher</u> into the air.	hire	Our company will <u>hire</u> two new employees.
know	I <u>know</u> you wrecked the car.	no	When asked if I wrecked the car, I said <u>no</u>.
past	The story takes place many years in the <u>past</u>.	passed	The quarterback <u>passed</u> the football.
right	I had the <u>right</u> answer to the question.	write	I usually <u>write</u> e-mails instead of letters.
some	She gave me <u>some</u> money.	sum	The <u>sum</u> of two plus two equals four.

USING LOGIC

As you read, use clues from the passage to determine whether the correct word has been chosen and that its meaning is clear. If necessary, study the spellings and definitions of common homonyms.

1. **The weather caused this plane to fly hire than the others.** Which correction should be made to the sentence?

   A. Change <u>weather</u> to <u>whether</u>.
   B. Change <u>plane</u> to <u>plain</u>.
   C. Change <u>hire</u> to <u>higher</u>.
   D. Change <u>than</u> to <u>then</u>.

2. **I didn't know where to look for the knew watch I lost.** Which correction should be made to the sentence?

   A. Change <u>know</u> to <u>no</u>.
   B. Change <u>where</u> to <u>were</u>.
   C. Change <u>for</u> to <u>four</u>.
   D. Change <u>knew</u> to <u>new</u>.

UNIT 4

⭐ Spotlighted Item: **DROP-DOWN**

DIRECTIONS: Read the passage. From the drop-down list, choose the answer that **best** completes the sentence.

Dear Editor:

I read the latest issue of *Cooking with Flair Magazine* and was surprised by your article on Mexican food. I think the author, like many people, has the wrong idea about Mexican food. When many people think of Mexican food, the fast food and chain restaurants across the United States come [3. Drop-down 1]. Much of the food served at these restaurants is not authentic Mexican food. In fact, most restaurants have changed Mexican recipes or invented new ones to fit tastes "north of the border." These restaurants serve a type of food that is really Tex-Mex, a term that applies [3. Drop-down 2] dishes served in the restaurants that are typically called "Mexican" here in the United States.

Today, people who eat at Tex-Mex restaurants will find many dishes that appear to be Mexican but do not come from Mexico. Dishes such as chile con carne (chili with [3. Drop-down 3]), chile con queso (chili with cheese), and nachos are Tex-Mex dishes and not authentically Mexican. These dishes may have a distant connection to Mexican cuisine, but they are more or less regional recipes from the southwestern United States.

It would be nice to [3. Drop-down 4] an article that discusses real Mexican food. I expect a higher level of journalism from your magazine! If you want to write about Tex-Mex food, fine. However, you should call this type of food what it is and not confuse Tex-Mex with authentic Mexican cuisine.

Sincerely,

Filiberto Verdasco

Drop-Down Answer Options

3.1 A. to mine
    B. too mined
    C. two mined
    D. to mind

3.2 A. to
    B. too
    C. two
    D. do

3.3 A. mead
    B. meet
    C. meat
    D. mete

3.4 A. rede
    B. read
    C. reed
    D. red

UNIT 4

⭐ Spotlighted Item: **DROP-DOWN**

DIRECTIONS: Read the passage. From the drop-down list, choose the answer that **best** completes the sentence.

BOIL WATER ALERT
Rose Bud, Texas

The Rose Bud City Council has [4. Drop-down 1] out a boil water advisory for all residents of Rose Bud and some of the surrounding cities. The advisory will be in [4. Drop-down 2] until water samples tested through the state laboratory come back negative for bacteria.

This advisory has been issued because high levels of several types of bacteria have been identified in the city water supply. In response to this situation, city officials have added chlorine to the water. However, in the interest of safety, residents, particularly those whose ages are below 15 and above 65, should [4. Drop-down 3] to consume the water until the Department of Environmental Protection determines whether the water is safe to drink.

The City Council advises drinking bottled water if possible until the water can be determined to be safe. If it is necessary to consume water from your tap, the water should first be brought to a rolling boil for one minute. This action should kill harmful bacteria. Water can then be cooled and consumed. We ask all of our citizens to remember that safe water cannot always be identified by [4. Drop-down 4] or smell, so please follow the boil water advisory until you are informed that your water is safe to drink.

You can use tap water for cleaning. Disinfect dishes and cooking utensils by soaking them for at least one minute in clean tap water that contains one teaspoon of household bleach per gallon of water.

Drop-Down Answer Options

4.1 A. sent
    B. cent
    C. send
    D. scent

4.2 A. affect
    B. infect
    C. effect
    D. affected

4.3 A. wade
    B. wait
    C. way
    D. weight

4.4 A. site
    B. sight
    C. side
    D. cite

UNIT 4

DIRECTIONS: Read the passage. From the drop-down list, choose the answer that **best** completes the sentence.

LETTER FROM A CELL PHONE COMPANY

Dear Mr. Thompson:

Because you have been a valued USA Wireless customer for the [5. Drop-down 1] five years, we have an exciting deal just for you. If you extend your existing cell phone contract with us for another two years, you will be eligible to upgrade your current service plan to the Premium Members Plan for only an additional $10 a month. This change represents a savings of $240 a year for premium service—an offer that other cell phone providers can't match. You cannot pass up a deal like this!

The Premium Members Plan offers unlimited text messaging and unlimited data. In addition, if you extend your contract with us within [5. Drop-down 2] days of the date of this letter, you also will receive unlimited international calls for only $0.05 a minute for the first year of your new contract. For the second year of your contract, you will return to the standard international calling rate of $0.15 a minute.

If you ever wanted more from your cell phone without spending extra money to get premium services, now is the time to get the Premium Members Plan for a fraction of [5. Drop-down 3] usual cost. Simply call 1-123-555-0095 or [5. Drop-down 4] us an e-mail to let us know that you want to extend your contract.

Drop-Down Answer Options

5.1 A. pass
    B. past
    C. passed
    D. pasted

5.2 A. eighth
    B. ate
    C. aid
    D. eight

5.3 A. its
    B. they're
    C. it's
    D. their

5.4 A. right
    B. rite
    C. write
    D. ride

Basic Subject-Verb Agreement

Use with **Student Book** pp. 174–175

LANGUAGE ASSESSMENT TARGETS: L.1.2, L.

1 Review the Skill

Subject-verb agreement means that the verb in a sentence agrees with the subject in number. In other words, a singular subject takes a singular verb, and a plural subject takes a plural verb. Some sentences have two or more subjects. If the subjects are separated by the word *and,* they take a plural verb. If the subjects are separated by the word *or,* the verb must agree with the subject that is closest to the verb.

2 Refine the Skill

By refining the skill of using correct subject-verb agreement, you will improve your writing and test-taking abilities, especially as they relate to the GED® Reasoning Through Language Arts test. Study the explanations and examples below. Then answer the questions that follow.

▶ Study the chart below to review how to apply subject-verb agreement in your writing.

a Remember that when two subjects are joined by *or,* the verb agrees with the subject closer to the verb: for example, *The students or the teacher eats first.*

b The same rules apply to compound subjects that consist of more than two items. For example, *Christy, Antonio, and Ray drive to work every day.*

	Verb Agreement	Example
Singular subject	Singular verb	Christy drives to work every day.
Plural subject	Plural verb	Her friends drive to work every day.
Two subjects connected by *and*	Plural verb	Christy and Antonio drive to work every day.
Two subjects connected by *or* (singular subject)	Singular verb	Christy or Antonio drives to work every day.
Two subjects connected by *or* (plural subject)	Plural verb	Christy or her friends drive to work every day.

1. **My cousins live in Cleveland but roots for the Pittsburgh Steelers.** Which correction should be made to the sentence?

   A. Change <u>live</u> to <u>lives</u>.
   B. Change <u>live</u> to <u>living</u>.
   C. Change <u>roots</u> to <u>root</u>.
   D. Change <u>roots</u> to <u>rooting</u>

2. **Kendall or her sister drive us to get a snack after practice is over.** Which correction should be made to the sentence?

   A. Change <u>drive</u> to <u>drives</u>.
   B. Change <u>drive</u> to <u>driven</u>.
   C. Change <u>is</u> to <u>are</u>.
   D. Change <u>is</u> to <u>been</u>.

CONTENT TOPICS

Present-tense verbs ending in –s or –es are singular. The subject is always a singular noun or pronoun (for example, *Luke, the cat, it, he, she, Dr. Lee, science*). Do not assume that –s indicates a plural verb as it does a plural noun.

UNIT 4

Lesson 7 | Basic Subject-Verb Agreement

⭐ Spotlighted Item: **DROP-DOWN**

DIRECTIONS: Read the passage. From the drop-down list, choose the answer that **best** completes the sentence.

**DEEP SHADE TREE COMPANY:
WE'RE THERE FOR THE LIFE OF YOUR TREES**

Just like the decorations that you place inside your home, trees [3. Drop-down 1] the outside of your house personality and character. Not only do trees make your home more beautiful, they also provide you with cool, money-saving shade.

Deep Shade has been caring for trees for 25 years, working to increase their leafy beauty and lengthen their life spans. A certified arborist is on staff for consultations and diagnosis of tree diseases.

The services we offer include

- Pruning. Tree debris and dangerously overhanging limbs [3. Drop-down 2] siding and shingles. Our pruning service can save you thousands of dollars in construction repairs by removing small problem areas before they become bigger ones. In addition, debris can attract pests. For example, many homeowners discover that a possum or squirrel [3. Drop-down 3] the debris to gain access to its home.

- Tree maintenance. We offer deep fertilization, ball moss removal, and web-worm treatments. Our policy is to provide your trees with the nutrients they need to be healthy, not to provide chemical treatments that could harm children or pets.

- Removal of dead or dangerous trees. Our experienced staff members [3. Drop-down 4] the trees to see whether they pose a risk of falling.

Let us keep you in the shade. Contact us for an estimate at www.deepshadetrees.com or 123-555-TREE.

Drop-Down Answer Options

3.1 A. gave
 B. gives
 C. giving
 D. give

3.2 A. damage
 B. has damaged
 C. damages
 D. damaging

3.3 A. have used
 B. using
 C. has used
 D. use

3.4 A. has evaluated
 B. evaluate
 C. evaluates
 D. evaluated

UNIT 4

3 *Master the Skill*

★ Spotlighted Item: **DROP-DOWN**

DIRECTIONS: Read the passage. From the drop-down list, choose the answer that **best** completes the sentence.

To all my readers,

I want to thank you for reading my latest book, *All The Wrong Faces.* I [4. Drop-down 1] grateful for your time and the attention you pay to my works. Because of my travel schedule, I find it is often hard for me to connect with individual readers. It seems that many people would like to contact me, because they have often asked for my address. I am happy to announce that there is now a way for us to connect. You can e-mail your thoughts and comments about my work through my new Web site. Although I may not be able to respond to all e-mails personally, I can promise that I will respond to as many messages as possible. Your comments and feedback [4. Drop-down 2] very valuable to me.

News and information about my books are also going to be on my Web site, which also will offer links to other books that may interest you. Each month, I will recommend a book or two by some of my favorite authors. You will be able to buy these books directly from the Web site.

Thanks again for reading my newest book and all my others. Your support and your generosity [4. Drop-down 3] a lot to me. Please use my new Web site to write to me directly. I [4. Drop-down 4] forward to hearing from you!

Sincerely,

Shannon McConell

Drop-Down Answer Options

4.1 A. was
    B. were
    C. am
    D. are

4.2 A. was
    B. is
    C. being
    D. are

4.3 A. mean
    B. meaning
    C. means
    D. has meant

4.4 A. looked
    B. look
    C. are looking
    D. looks

DIRECTIONS: Read the passage. From the drop-down list, choose the answer that **best** completes the sentence.

PLEASE CUT THE COMMERCIALS!

I am writing this e-mail because I am concerned about the number of commercials being shown on your network during my favorite programs. While watching *The Nights of Our Lives* on Thursday evening, I counted no fewer than 50 commercials. There were eight separate program interruptions, and at least one of them included seven commercials. I think that six or seven commercials [5. Drop-down 1] more than I should have to watch!

To make matters worse, annoying pop-ups [5. Drop-down 2] throughout the program. These pop-ups usually fill about a third of the screen with announcements like this one: "An all-new episode of *Hall of Justice*, Monday night at 9:00 Eastern Time, 8:00 Central." This announcement is in addition to the four ads I saw for the show during the traditional commercial breaks.

Just how much does your network need to push its own programming? How many different people do you think are tuning in approximately every seven to eight minutes? Most people [5. Drop-down 3] a show all the way through. Do you expect the viewers at 15 minutes after the hour to be different from the viewers watching at five minutes after the hour?

There's a reason that more and more people are turning to streaming services. I can sit through an entire episode of *The Vampire's Girlfriend* without watching a single commercial. These constant commercial interruptions probably [5. Drop-down 4] viewers to stop buying your sponsors' products. You have no one to blame but yourselves.

Drop-Down Answer Options

5.1 A. is
    B. was
    C. has been
    D. are

5.2 A. was appearing
    B. appear
    C. appears
    D. appearing

5.3 A. watched
    B. watches
    C. watching
    D. watch

5.4 A. are causing
    B. is causing
    C. causes
    D. has caused

UNIT 4

Standard English

Use with *Student Book* pp. 176–177

LANGUAGE ASSESSMENT TARGET: L.

1 Review the Skill

Standard English refers to the agreed-upon form of the English language that is written and spoken by educated people. While many people use slang and other forms of informal language in casual speech, Standard English should be used in writing and formal speech. For example, in casual speech a person might say what sounds like *I could of done better* or *I coulda done better*. However, in Standard English, the correct sentence is written, *I could have done better*. Avoiding common Standard English mistakes will help you appear more educated and show that you have command of the language.

2 Refine the Skill

By refining the skill of using Standard English, you will improve your writing and test-taking abilities, especially as they relate to the GED® Reasoning Through Language Arts test. Study the explanations and examples below. Then answer the questions that follow.

Common Mistake	Standard English
He ain't very tall.	He isn't very tall.
Amy should of completed the application.	Amy should have completed the application.
I dunno how to ski.	I don't know how to ski.
Jake never goes nowhere.	Jake never goes anywhere.
My brother he is really smart.	My brother is really smart.
Angelo was suppose to be at work.	Angelo was supposed to be at work.
Try and call me this weekend if you have time.	Try to call me this weekend if you have time.
Before I hurt my knee, I use to jog every morning.	Before I hurt my knee, I used to jog every morning.
I don't see no sign.	I don't see a sign.

1. **I don't know nothing about astronomy.** Which correction should be made to the sentence?

   A. Change don't to not.
   B. Change nothing to anything.
   C. Change nothing to not anything.
   D. Add no before astronomy.

2. **I was suppose to take out the trash.** Which correction should be made to the sentence?

   A. Eliminate to.
   B. Change to to ta.
   C. Change suppose to supposed.
   D. Change suppose to supposed, and eliminate to.

USING LOGIC

Remember to avoid using two negatives when you are expressing a single negative thought. When you negate a negative word, you change the meaning to a positive. Use logic to test the meaning of your writing.

UNIT 4

★ Spotlighted Item: **DROP-DOWN**

DIRECTIONS: Read the passage. For each drop-down item, choose the option that **best** completes the sentence.

CITYGUIDE.COM MEMBER RESTAURANT REVIEW ★ ★ ★ ★

My wife and I took my sister and her husband to Carmelo's Family Style Ristorante last Saturday. My [3. Drop-down 1] celebrating her thirtieth birthday. It was our first time dining at Carmelo's since it opened last February. I can't believe we waited five months to go! We loved both the food and the atmosphere.

Although we [3. Drop-down 2] made a reservation, we didn't have to wait long for a table. While we waited, we enjoyed ourselves on the restaurant's back deck, where the restaurant offers jazz performances on Friday and Saturday nights. It was the perfect way to start our night. We [3. Drop-down 3] better than some live music before our dinner.

The restaurant is a beautiful space in an old warehouse with high ceilings, big windows overlooking downtown, wood floors, and several levels. We got a great booth on one of the upper levels that looked out over the space.

All of Carmelo's food is served family style. You order two or three different dishes for the table and then share them. This is a great idea when you have at least four people. We ordered lasagna, spaghetti with meatballs, and chicken piccata. The meatballs were fantastic! The chicken was tender and light with a delicious lemon sauce with just enough garlic.

I highly recommend Carmelo's. It is a great choice for a big dinner with lots of friends or for a special occasion with the whole family. In fact, I [3. Drop-down 4] else.

Drop-Down Answer Options

3.1 A. sister she was
    B. sister
    C. sister was
    D. sister she is

3.2 A. should have
    B. should a
    C. should of
    D. should

3.3 A. couldn't have asked for nothing
    B. couldn't have asked for no
    C. couldn't have asked for anything
    D. could have asked for anything

3.4 A. never want to go nowhere
    B. never want to go anywhere
    C. don't ever want to go nowhere
    D. don't never want to go anywhere

★ Spotlighted Item: **DROP-DOWN**

DIRECTIONS: Read the passage. For each drop-down item, choose the option that **best** completes the sentence.

APARTMENT BULLETIN BOARD NOTICE: NEVILLE'S DOG WALKING SERVICE

Is your dog suffering because you work long hours every day? Maybe your dog is getting older and is starting to have a few accidents. Do you [4. Drop-down 1] plan your schedule around whether you can rush home because Fido needs to go out?

Let me introduce myself: my name is Neville, and I just moved here from Chicago where I [4. Drop-down 2] work for a dog-walking service. Last week, when I saw how many people sped home from work at lunch, I decided this building needed a dog walker, and I would like to offer my services.

I'm hoping that many of you will be interested! I'd like to find at least twenty customers or else my business [4. Drop-down 3] chance of succeeding. I'll bet there are twice that many people in this building who would hire a dog walker if they knew one they could trust!

Here's how you can find out more about me and how I work. We will start with an interview. I will explain the professional techniques a dog walker uses to handle even the fussiest dogs. You, your dog, and I then will go on a walk together. I am confident that you will be impressed. I am even offering to walk your dog for a one-week trial period, and if you don't like my services after that, you don't [4. Drop-down 4] at all!

For more information, call 123-555-4321.

Drop-Down Answer Options

4.1 A. try and
    B. try
    C. try to
    D. try on

4.2 A. used
    B. used to
    C. use to
    D. used ta

4.3 A. won't have no
    B. will have no
    C. will not have no
    D. ain't got a

4.4 A. have to pay nothing
    B. have pay anything
    C. gotta pay nothing
    D. have to pay anything

DIRECTIONS: Read the passage. For each drop-down item, choose the option that **best** completes the sentence.

Dear State Insurance Commissioner:

I have been struggling with my insurance company for the last year. I called my congressional representative's office today and was told that you might be able to help.

For the last five years, I have been insured by Beneficial Network. I have always paid my premiums and until last year I
| 5. Drop-down 1 | doctor. Last August, however, I developed a severe pain in my wrist. The pain was so bad that I thought I might have to take time off from my job.

I went to my assigned doctor to have him look at my wrist, but he said that I | 5. Drop-down 2 | see another doctor who was a specialist. That same day the receptionist told me where to go to and even made my appointment for me later that week. The wrist doctor took some x-rays and gave me a cortisone shot. I came in two more times for shots, and I'm happy to say my wrist is better.

But two months later, my insurer sent me a bill for over $8,000! Apparently, those shots were considered "surgical procedures." In addition, this wrist doctor is "Out of Network," and she | 5. Drop-down 3 | covered by my insurance policy. I am very confused. My doctor (whom the insurance company assigned to me!) told me to go to the wrist doctor, and she took my insurance information and didn't tell me that I wasn't covered.

I don't have $8,000 and don't think I should have to pay this bill. I'm afraid if I don't | 5. Drop-down 4 | this soon, the insurance company will report me to the credit agencies.

Can you help me?

Sincerely,

Anita Jackson

Drop-Down Answer Options

5.1 A. didn't never see no
    B. ain't seen no
    C. never got to see no
    D. never had to see a

5.2 A. was opposing to
    B. was suppose to
    C. was supposed to
    D. was opposed a

5.3 A. ain't
    B. isn't
    C. weren't
    D. not

5.4 A. try and resolve
    B. try and resolving
    C. try to resolve
    D. try in resolve

9 LESSON

Capitalization

Use with **Student Book** pp. 178–179

1 Review the Skill

Capitalization helps readers identify **proper nouns** and **proper adjectives**. A proper noun is the name of a particular person (*Anna, Mr. Rivera*), place (*New York City*), or thing (*Hamlet*). Holidays, days of the week, and months of the year are proper nouns. A proper adjective is a descriptive word that comes from a proper noun: for example, the *Vietnamese* language.

People's titles, such as *Mr., Ms., Dr., Mrs.,* and *Miss* are capitalized. Titles of books, stories, songs, poems, newspapers and magazines and articles in them, plays, and movies are capitalized as well. However, prepositions and articles (*and, or,* and *but*) are not capitalized unless they are the first or last word in the title.

2 Refine the Skill

By refining the skill of using capitalization correctly, you will improve your writing and test-taking abilities, especially as they relate to the GED® Reasoning Through Language Arts test. Study the explanations and examples below. Then answer the questions that follow.

▶ Remember that capitalization identifies proper nouns and proper adjectives. Common nouns and adjectives should not be capitalized unless they are the first word of a sentence or part of a title.

a Capitalize major words in titles: for example, "In the Gloaming," *The English Patient*, "A Stay of Execution for the Wolves."

b *River* is capitalized in *the Nile River* because it is part of the name. This rule holds true for bodies of water or other geographical features like mountains or deserts.

	NOUNS		ADJECTIVES	
Common	**Proper**	**Common**	**Proper**
the doctor	Doctor Smith	dark chocolate	Belgian chocolate
the ocean	Pacific Ocean	national government	United States government
the river	the Nile River	tennis shoe	Mia's shoe
the judge	Judge Alex Roth	foreign accent	French accent

1. **Last saturday, Leo saw his friend's band play at the coffee shop on Main Street.** Which correction should be made to the sentence?

   A. Change <u>saturday</u> to <u>Saturday.</u>
   B. Change <u>friend's band</u> to <u>Friend's Band.</u>
   C. Change <u>coffee shop</u> to <u>Coffee Shop.</u>
   D. Change <u>Street</u> to <u>street.</u>

2. **The Mississippi River flows through several major american cities.** Which correction should be made to the sentence?

   A. Change <u>Mississippi</u> to <u>mississippi.</u>
   B. Change <u>River</u> to <u>river.</u>
   C. Change <u>american</u> to <u>American.</u>
   D. Change <u>cities</u> to <u>Cities.</u>

USING LOGIC

When referring to a place in general terms, such as *my favorite gym*, use lower-case letters. When using real names, such as *Actigym*, use capital letters. Logic can help you decide when to capitalize.

UNIT 4

3 *Master the Skill*

⭐ Spotlighted Item: **DROP-DOWN**

DIRECTIONS: Read the passage. From the drop-down list, choose the answer that **best** completes the sentence.

NET360 TIPS FOR KEEPING YOUR INTERNET USE SAFE

Welcome to the Net360 Internet experience! The Internet connects millions of people every day. Because of the Internet, a | 3. Drop-down 1 | can discuss with a fan in Australia what makes | 3. Drop-down 2 |.

Although using the Internet can be fun, it can also affect a person's life negatively if he or she is not careful. Net360 Internet users should follow a few simple guidelines to help keep their personal information safe.

Never open an e-mail attachment from a sender whom you do not know. Attachments may contain viruses or spyware that could infect your computer when you open them.

When posting to social media or other online sites, such as | 3. Drop-down 3 |, do not provide any information about yourself that you do not want everyone to know.

Never send your bank account, credit card, or | 3. Drop-down 4 | in an e-mail or post it online.

These are just a few tips to help protect your personal information while you are online. With knowledge of the dangers and a little common sense, you can have a safer, more enjoyable Internet experience.

Drop-Down Answer Options

3.1 A.   Beatles fan in botswana
    B.   beatles fan in Botswana
    C.   Beatles fan in Botswana
    D.   beatles fan in botswana

3.2 A.   *Rubber soul* a great Album
    B.   *Rubber Soul* a great Album
    C.   *Rubber Soul* a great album
    D.   *rubber soul* a great album

3.3 A.   Facebook or Craigslist
    B.   Facebook or craigslist
    C.   facebook or craigslist
    D.   facebook or Craigslist

3.4 A.   Social Security Number
    B.   Social Security number
    C.   Social security Number
    D.   social security number

UNIT 4

★ Spotlighted Item: **DROP-DOWN**

DIRECTIONS: Read the passage. From the drop-down list, choose the answer that **best** completes the sentence.

Garland County Hospital
Human Resources Department
855 Second Avenue
Hot Springs, AR 85196

To: All Employees

From: | 4. Drop-down 1 |

Subject: Workplace Technology Rules

In order to create a more productive working environment, please observe the following guidelines when using technology in the workplace.

Effective beginning | 4. Drop-down 2 | , set all cell phones to silent when entering any area of | 4. Drop-down 3 | . Vibrations, as well as ring tones, disrupt others who are working around you. In addition, do not use cell phones, headphones, or wireless earpieces in common areas, including restrooms. Again, these habits disrupt others who are using these areas. As much as possible, work-related telephone calls should occur at your desk or within your office. Personal phone calls should be limited and should not interfere with your work or interrupt the ability of others to work around you.

Finally, do not involve co-workers in | 4. Drop-down 4 | , including visual or text entries. While we understand that some co-workers may be your friends outside of work, please use caution and common sense in your interactions that can be seen, heard, or read by others. By keeping your work life and private life separate, you will avoid awkward situations at work that may damage people's reputations or careers.

Drop-Down Answer Options

4.1 A.   Lana Little, Human Resources Director
B.   Lana little, human resources Director
C.   Lana Little, Human Resources director
D.   Lana Little, Human resources director

4.2 A.   tuesday, February 20
B.   Tuesday, february 20
C.   tuesday, february 20
D.   Tuesday, February 20

4.3 A.   Garland County hospital
B.   Garland County Hospital
C.   Garland county hospital
D.   Garland county Hospital

4.4 A.   blogging or Social Networking
B.   blogging or social networking
C.   Blogging or Social Networking
D.   Blogging or social networking

DIRECTIONS: Read the passage. From the drop-down list, choose the answer that **best** completes the sentence.

IS FIGHTING NECESSARY IN HOCKEY?

Dear Editor:

Just as there are two sides to every hockey fight, there are two sides to the discussion of whether the [5. Drop-down 1] (NHL) should ban fighting. Both sides claim that their views have the longevity and popularity of the sport in mind. Like others, I've been torn on the issue.

Supporters of a ban argue that fighting puts players in too much danger. As an example, some people point to the death of Don Sanderson, who hit his head during a fight and died three weeks later. Supporters also argue that a ban on fighting would not only protect players but also encourage more families to attend games without exposing children to violence. As sports analyst [5. Drop-down 2] notes, a ban on fighting would increase the sport's popularity and bring in new fans.

However, supporters of fighting argue that some fans would stop watching the game if combat between players were banned. The article [5. Drop-down 3] suggests that fighting in the NHL brings in more fans than it keeps away. Also, some supporters believe that a ban would be ineffective. Other sports have banned fighting, but brawling continues.

While a ban might be ineffective, does it make sense to condone brawling? While I see both sides of the argument, I'm finding it hard to sit on the fence. I'm ready to commit to a ban. Is the NHL?

Sincerely,

Dwayne Leonard
[5. Drop-down 4]

Drop-Down Answer Options

5.1 A. National Hockey League
B. National Hockey league
C. national Hockey League
D. National hockey league

5.2 A. Elton Royce, jr.
B. elton royce, Jr.
C. Elton Royce, Jr.
D. elton royce, jr.

5.3 A. "A fight to the finish"
B. "A Fight to the Finish"
C. "a Fight to the Finish"
D. "A Fight To The Finish"

5.4 A. President, Leonard Sports Marketing
B. president, Leonard Sports Marketing
C. President, Leonard sports marketing
D. president, Leonard sports marketing

UNIT 4

Sentence Fragment Correction

Use with **Student Book** pp. 180–181

LANGUAGE ASSESSMENT TARGETS: L.2.1, L.2.2, L.

1 Review the Skill

A **complete sentence** has three components. First, it must have a subject that tells who or what the sentence is about. Next, it must have a verb that tells what the subject is doing or what the subject is. Finally, must represent a whole thought, or complete idea. Every sentence begins with a capital letter. The punctuatio at the end of a sentence depends on the sentence's purpose.

A **sentence fragment** may contain a subject or verb, or both, but it does not express a complete thought and cannot stand alone as a sentence. Sometimes, all you need to add is a subject or verb. For example, *was tired* becomes *I was tired.* You also can add a fragment to a complete sentence: for example, add *Although I was tired* to *I stayed up late: Although I was tired, I stayed up late.*

2 Refine the Skill

By refining the skill of recognizing sentence components and correcting sentence fragments, you will improve your writing and test-taking abilities, especially as they relate to the GED® Reasoning Through Language Arts test. Study the explanations and examples below. Then answer the questions that follow.

▶ These examples will help you understand that a sentence has a subject and verb and expresses a complete idea. Every sentence begins with a capital letter and ends with the correct punctuation.

SENTENCE COMPONENTS

Subject	Verb	Complete Idea	End Punctuation
My brother	drives	a sedan	. (statement)
We	won	the game	! (expresses excitement)
Who	has	the folder	? (asks a question)

▶ These examples show two ways of correcting a sentence fragment by combining it with a complete sentence.

Wrong: Before going to the store. I made a list of items to buy.
Right: Before going to the <u>store</u>, I made a list of items to buy.

Wrong: The hill was steep. But climbed it.
Right: The hill was <u>steep, but I</u> climbed it.

1. **Watched the game last night.** Which correction should be made?

   A. Insert a subject.
   B. Replace the period with an exclamation point.
   C. Insert a verb.
   D. Replace the period with a question mark.

2. **After my son came home from <u>school. I helped</u> him with his homework.** Which is the **best** way to write the underlined portion?

   A. school, helped
   B. school? I helped
   C. school, I helped
   D. school. Helped

 Spotlighted Item: **DROP-DOWN**

DIRECTIONS: Read the passage. From the drop-down list, choose the answer that **best** completes the sentence.

ENERGETIC ELECTRICAL DESIGN
Office Management
Corporate Headquarters

To: All Employees
From: Ray Burnice, Office Manager
Subject: Responding to Client Comments
Date: October 12, 2020

Effective immediately, we will implement a new procedure for responding to client comments on electrical design drawings. Each employee will be provided with an electronic "Review Comments" [**3. Drop-down 1**] accompany all revised drawings when such drawings are returned to the clients for review.

[**3. Drop-down 2**] the first column, you will note the drawing number or page number. In the second column, you will note the client comment number and whether you agree with the comment. In the third column, you will write the actual [**3. Drop-down 3**] an accurate summary. In the fourth column, you will write your response to the comment and record the action to be taken.

All sections of the form should be fully completed. The "action to be taken" column will serve as the basis for [**3. Drop-down 4**] are presented with the revised drawings. The project manager for each team will be responsible for ensuring that all planned actions have been addressed.

File a copy of this form in the project folder. Please see your supervisor to address any questions or concerns.

Drop-Down Answer Options

3.1 A. form. This form will
B. form. Will
C. form? This form will
D. form. this form will

3.2 A. Contains four clearly labeled columns. In
B. The form contains four columns. in
C. The form contains four columns. In
D. The form four clearly labeled columns. In

3.3 A. client comment. Or
B. client comment or
C. client comment? Or
D. client comment! or

3.4 A. follow up. when clients
B. follow up. When clients
C. follow up? When clients
D. follow up when clients

UNIT 4

⭐ Spotlighted Item: **DROP-DOWN**

DIRECTIONS: Read the passage. From the drop-down list, choose the answer that **best** completes the sentence.

Dear Prospective Contractor:

We are seeking proposals for an upcoming remodeling project in our home. We wish to remodel our master bathroom before the end of the year. This project will preserve the current layout of the room. Although the location of each fixture will remain the [4. Drop-down 1] plans do call for replacing several of the main fixtures in the bathroom.

We would like to replace the sink to create more counter space. The existing shower must be removed and a new, larger shower constructed in its place. We wish to add a medicine cabinet above [4. Drop-down 2] new light and exhaust fan. The existing linoleum should be torn out and replaced with tile flooring. The wallpaper also needs to be [4. Drop-down 3] walls and ceiling of the bathroom should be repainted.

We hope to use high-quality, yet affordable, materials and fixtures. The materials used should be moderately priced, attractive, and durable. To keep costs [4. Drop-down 4] hope to repurpose many items from the current bathroom. Our projected budget is approximately $7,000.

We look forward to reviewing your proposal. Please return your proposal to us by March 18, along with your earliest available start date for this project. We will inform you of our decision within 48 hours.

Sincerely,

Ricardo and Lisa Camacho

Drop-Down Answer Options

4.1 A. same. Our
    B. same. our
    C. same! Our
    D. same, our

4.2 A. the sink! As well as a
    B. the sink as well as a
    C. the sink. As well as a
    D. the sink. A

4.3 A. removed. the
    B. removed, and the
    C. removed? The
    D. removed!

4.4 A. down. We
    B. down. we
    C. down, we
    D. down! We

UNIT 4

DIRECTIONS: Read the passage. From the drop-down list, choose the answer that **best** completes the sentence.

JOIN OUR CITY YOUTH SOCCER LEAGUE!

Do you have a child under the age of 14 who might want to join a soccer [5. Drop-down 1] signing up members for this fall's Jamestown City Youth Soccer League.

[5. Drop-down 2] for young athletes. It involves physical skill and teamwork. Also, the rules don't have to be modified significantly for young players; the rules are easy to understand. Consider registering your children to play. Our league accepts children as young as four years old. You might also consider coaching a team or volunteering [5. Drop-down 3] nothing like a Saturday morning soccer game to bring families and communities together.

If you don't know much about soccer, it is simple to learn. Two teams of 11 players meet on a field with a goal at each end. Players move the ball toward the opposing team's goal with any part of their bodies except the arms or hands. Players score points by getting the ball into the opposing team's goal, past the goalie, or goalkeeper.

At the recreational level, players may assume any of three positions: fullback, midfielder (halfback), or forward (striker). Fullbacks are responsible [5. Drop-down 4] offense and defense. Forwards are responsible for scoring. Most young children figure out the game quickly, and it is well suited to children of many different ability levels.

We hope you consider joining the league. Registration is open until August 15 for our fall league.

Drop-Down Answer Options

5.1 A. league! We are currently
B. league. We currently
C. league? Currently
D. league? We are currently

5.2 A. Soccer is a great sport
B. Soccer, a great sport
C. Soccer a great and rewarding sport
D. Soccer really great

5.3 A. as a referee? There is
B. as a referee. There is
C. as a referee. There
D. as a referee. there is

5.4 A. for defense, assist with both
B. for defense. Midfielders with both
C. for defense. Midfielders assist with both
D. for defense. Assist with both

Commas

11 LESSON

Use with **Student Book** pp. 182–183

LANGUAGE ASSESSMENT TARGET: L.

1 Review the Skill

Commas divide sentences and sentence parts into meaningful units. Commas separate items in a series to clarify each item for readers, and commas separate two or more adjectives that describe the same noun. In addition, commas set off elements that introduce or interrupt a sentence, and commas are placed before a connecting word to combine two sentences. In dialogue, commas set off the speaker from the dialogue.

2 Refine the Skill

By refining the skill of using commas correctly, you will improve your writing and test-taking abilities, especially as they relate to the GED® Reasoning Through Language Arts test. Study the explanations and examples below. Then answer the questions that follow.

▶ Study the diagram to review the different uses for commas.

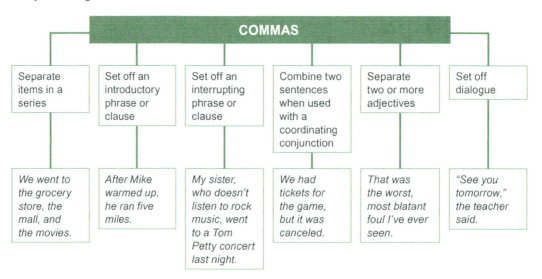

COMMAS

Separate items in a series	Set off an introductory phrase or clause	Set off an interrupting phrase or clause	Combine two sentences when used with a coordinating conjunction	Separate two or more adjectives	Set off dialogue
We went to the grocery store, the mall, and the movies.	*After Mike warmed up, he ran five miles.*	*My sister, who doesn't listen to rock music, went to a Tom Petty concert last night.*	*We had tickets for the game, but it was canceled.*	*That was the worst, most blatant foul I've ever seen.*	*"See you tomorrow," the teacher said.*

CONTENT TOPICS

In the sentence *I thank my parents, John and Martha*, it is clear that the parents are named John and Martha. Writing *I thank my parents, John, and Martha* indicates that additional people are thanked.

1. **As its name suggests, Seasons serves a seasonal menu that incorporates fresh wholesome products.** Which correction should be made to the sentence?

   A. Remove the comma after <u>suggests</u>.
   B. Insert a comma after <u>menu</u>.
   C. Insert a comma after <u>fresh</u>.
   D. Insert a comma after <u>wholesome</u>.

2. **"The salad, bread, and cheese are on the table" said Dan.** Which correction should be made to the sentence?

   A. Insert a comma after <u>table</u>.
   B. Remove the comma after <u>salad</u>.
   C. Remove the comma after <u>bread</u>.
   D. Insert a comma after <u>cheese</u>.

UNIT 4

★ Spotlighted Item: **DROP-DOWN**

DIRECTIONS: Read the passage. From the drop-down list, choose the answer that **best** completes the sentence.

LETTER FROM AN INTERNET PROVIDER

Dear Valued Customer:

This letter is to inform you that National Data will be updating its pricing plan this spring. Instead of [3. Drop-down 1] will now have the opportunity to pay by the amount of bandwidth you use each month.

Under the previous pricing plan, customers could choose among several Internet packages, including the Basic [3. Drop-down 2] the Supercharged High-Speed Plan. Although we were the first Internet service provider to offer customers a choice of high-speed options, we also were the first to realize that these options were not cost effective. Instead of raising the price of our Internet service options, we have decided to institute a pricing plan based on how much data you use.

With our consumption-based plan, all of our customers will have access to the Supercharged [3. Drop-down 3] they will have to pay only for the amount of bandwidth they use each month, up to a maximum fee equal to the current Supercharged High-Speed Plan rate. Now all National Data subscribers will have [3. Drop-down 4] access to the fastest Internet service in the area.

Drop-Down Answer Options

3.1 A. paying, a fixed rate, you
    B. paying a fixed rate you
    C. paying a fixed rate, you
    D. paying a fixed, rate you

3.2 A. Plan, the High-Speed
      Plan and,
    B. Plan, the High-Speed
      Plan, and
    C. Plan the High-Speed Plan
      and
    D. Plan the High-Speed
      Plan, and

3.3 A. High-Speed Plan but
    B. High-Speed, Plan but
    C. High-Speed Plan, but
    D. High-Speed Plan but,

3.4 A. convenient, affordable
    B. convenient affordable,
    C. convenient, affordable,
    D. convenient affordable

UNIT 4

★ Spotlighted Item: **DROP-DOWN**

DIRECTIONS: Read the passage. From the drop-down list, choose the answer that **best** completes the sentence.

Dear Mr. McMullen:

I recently stayed in your hotel during my extended business trip to Atlanta. I am writing to express my gratitude for a lovely experience. As I'm [**4. Drop-down 1**] difficult to be away from home. However, your facility and staff made this situation an enjoyable one.

To begin, my room was well stocked with supplies, including [**4. Drop-down 2**]. My coffee station even included cream and sugar. I also had a large supply of fresh towels each day.

The bed was [**4. Drop-down 3**] shower was easy to operate. Additionally, the housekeeping staff did a thorough job of cleaning my room each day. They were even gracious about coming back on the day I decided to sleep in.

Finally, the amenities at your hotel added to my overall experience. I was able to swim, exercise, and eat delicious meals, all without leaving the hotel. It's worth noting that the food was not typical of hotel fare. It was nutritious and elegantly plated.

[**4. Drop-down 4**] can promise you that I will recommend your hotel to my colleagues, and I will be back for a return visit!

Sincerely,

Rita Kennedy

Drop-Down Answer Options

4.1 A. sure ,you, understand it is
   B. sure you understand it is
   C. sure you understand, it is
   D. sure you understand it is,

4.2 A. soap, shampoo, drinking
      water, and coffee
   B. soap, shampoo, drinking
      water and, coffee
   C. soap shampoo, drinking
      water, and coffee
   D. soap shampoo drinking
      water and coffee

4.3 A. comfortable and the
      spacious,
   B. comfortable, and the
      spacious
   C. comfortable, and, the
      spacious
   D. comfortable and, the
      spacious

4.4 A. In closing, I
   B. In closing, I,
   C. In closing I
   D. In closing I,

DIRECTIONS: Read the passage. From the drop-down list, choose the answer that **best** completes the sentence.

SUMMONS FOR JURY DUTY:

THE VERDICT

After the witnesses finish their [5. Drop-down 1] will instruct you about the law regarding the case. You must base your decision on the judge's instructions about the law instead of your own ideas about what the law is or should be. You and other members of the jury then will go to the jury room. One jury member will be selected as the [5. Drop-down 2] of the jury. He or she will lead your discussions and bring your verdict into the court.

Your discussions in the jury room should include an honest expression of your opinions on the facts of the case and the testimony you have heard. Your discussions should also be tolerant and respectful of other people's opinions. In a civil case, you may have to decide whether there is any reason for the defendant to pay damages. If you find a reason to pay damages, you will determine how much the defendant should pay. If the jury cannot reach a unanimous verdict in a civil case within six hours, then a decision reached by 10 members of a 12-person jury is acceptable.

[5. Drop-down 3] discussions are finished when a unanimous verdict has been reached. If the [5. Drop-down 4] cannot reach a verdict, the foreperson must tell the judge. The jury has nothing to do with sentencing if it returns a guilty verdict. Sentencing is the judge's job.

Further information will be provided by the presiding judge if you are selected for jury duty.

Drop-Down Answer Options

5.1 A. testimonies the judge,
B. testimonies, the judge,
C. testimonies the judge
D. testimonies, the judge

5.2 A. foreperson the presiding member
B. foreperson the, presiding member
C. foreperson, the presiding member,
D. foreperson the presiding, member

5.3 A. In a criminal case jury
B. In a criminal case jury,
C. In a criminal, case jury
D. In a criminal case, jury

5.4 A. jury, after long discussions
B. jury, after long discussions,
C. jury after long discussions
D. jury after long discussions,

Sentence Combining

LANGUAGE ASSESSMENT TARGETS: L.1.6, L.1.8, L.1.9, L.2

1 Review the Skill

Writers often **combine sentences** to avoid using too many short sentences. Combining short, related sentences helps make writing smoother and easier to read. You can combine sentences with a connecting word, with a comma and a connecting word, with a semicolon, or with a semicolon and a signal word.

When you combine sentences you can eliminate repeated subjects, verbs, or objects. You can also clarify the relationship of one sentence to another sentence. For example, by combining sentences and adding word such as *when*, *because*, *after*, or *therefore*, you can show cause and effect, explain the sequence of events, o make comparisons.

2 Refine the Skill

By refining the skill of combining sentences correctly, you will improve your writing and test-taking abilities, especially as they relate to the GED® Reasoning Through Language Arts test. Study the explanations and examples below. Then answer the questions that follow.

▶ The ability to combine short, related sentences will help make your writing sound more fluid and sophisticated. Study the chart below to review ways of combining sentences:

a Repeating the subject, *Pedro,* in these two sentences sounds choppy.

b Words such as *as a result* help show the relationship of cause and effect between ideas. Combining sentences with words that signal relationships enhances the flow and clarity of writing.

	These sentences	Become one sentence
Combine repeated elements	Pedro drove to the store. Pedro bought a jacket.	Pedro drove to the store and bought a jacket.
Make compound sentences	Many people prefer texting to speaking in person. Communication skills may suffer because of this.	Many people prefer texting to speaking in person, and communication skills may suffer because of this.
Make complex sentences	Many people prefer texting to speaking in person. Communication skills may suffer because of this.	Because many people prefer texting to speaking in person, communication skills may suffer.
Show the relationsip of one idea to another	She was running very late. She missed the bus.	She was running very late; as a result, she missed the bus.

1. **Emma talked to Riley. Emma talked to Joan. Emma talked to Joan's mother.** Which is the **best** revision of the sentences?

   A. Emma talked to Riley. Emma talked to Joan and Joan's mother.
   B. Emma talked to Riley, Joan, and Joan's mother.
   C. Emma talked to Riley. Emma talked to Joan and her mother.
   D. Emma talked to Riley and Joan; Emma talked to Joan's mother.

2. **Carl made a sandwich. Carl was hungry.** Which is the **best** revision of the sentences?

   A. Carl made a sandwich; Carl was hungry.
   B. Carl made a sandwich and Carl was hungry.
   C. Carl made a sandwich because he was hungry.
   D. Carl made a sandwich; moreover, he was hungry.

 Spotlighted Item: **DROP-DOWN**

DIRECTIONS: Read the passage. From the drop-down list, choose the answer that **best** completes the sentence.

ADOPTING A CAT

In many cities, animal shelters are overcrowded with animals in need of homes. For many prospective pet owners, these shelters offer an inexpensive and ethical alternative to finding pets through expensive breeders or pet stores. For example, if you hope to adopt a cat, you may find that a shelter cat is the right pet for you.

If you identify a cat online that you might be interested in adopting, the next step is to visit the shelter and meet the animal. Many shelters will have pets on display for potential [3. Drop-down 1] may need to request to see a particular animal that you have identified online.

When you do meet your prospective pet, be sure to spend some time with it to get a sense of its personality and disposition. Some potential adopters may be looking for a laid-back lap [3. Drop-down 2] may be seeking an energetic playmate. Also consider how these cats interact with the other animals around them. A cat's temperament can prove especially important if you have other pets at [3. Drop-down 3] you might wish to have another pet in the future.

After you have selected your pet, shelter workers will ask you to fill out some paperwork. Often, these materials include a contract that requires you to provide for your pet and give it the necessary veterinary care. The shelter may require that a pet be spayed or neutered before it can be sent [3. Drop-down 4] be able to bring your new pet home on the same day as your visit.

Drop-Down Answer Options

3.1 A. adopters; similarly, you
B. adopters however, you
C. adopters; however, you
D. adopters, and you

3.2 A. cat. Other potential adopters
B. cat, but others
C. cat because others
D. cat; in addition, other potential adopters

3.3 A. home or if
B. home. A cat's temperament is important if
C. home, although
D. home; however,

3.4 A. home because you may
B. home, or you may
C. home. You may
D. home; you may

UNIT 4

★ Spotlighted Item: **DROP-DOWN**

DIRECTIONS: Read the passage. From the drop-down list, choose the answer that **best** completes the sentence.

SHANE'S BLOG

VOLUNTEERING AT MY COMMUNITY THEATER

A few months ago, I was looking for a way to get more involved in my community. Eventually, I searched online for volunteer opportunities. I found a local community theater seeking volunteers. At first, I was hesitant to check it

| 4. Drop-down 1 | to give it a try.

I went to a meeting for the theater group the next week. I quickly discovered there are many jobs for people to do behind the scenes that do not involve performing. For my first project, I helped construct the set for the performance of an upcoming play. The set was designed to resemble the interior of an apartment in the 1960s. Along with a crew of 10 people, I built

| 4. Drop-down 2 | and backdrops. It was hard work, yet I felt very proud of my contribution to the production.

Next, I assisted the lighting director as she prepared for the shows. She taught me the basics of lighting design. I learned that a play's mood, theme, and plot all contribute to a lighting director's decisions. The lighting director chooses which lights should be | 4. Drop-down 3 | how they should be arranged and operated. After we had completed the design, the director showed me how to enter it into the computer that controls the lighting. She marked a script with lighting cues so that I knew when to select the next lighting pattern on the computer.

For anyone looking for an exciting and rewarding volunteer opportunity, check out your local community theater. You will help your | 4. Drop-down 4 | learn some really cool stuff!

Drop-Down Answer Options

4.1 A. out, but I decided
    B. out; I decided
    C. out. Decided
    D. out, and I decided

4.2 A. platforms; I built doors
    B. platforms, but I also built doors
    C. platforms, doors,
    D. platforms. I built doors

4.3 A. used; she also chooses
    B. used and
    C. used, but she chooses
    D. used or chooses

4.4 A. community or
    B. community. You will
    C. community; however, you will
    D. community and

UNIT 4

DIRECTIONS: Read the passage. From the drop-down list, choose the answer that **best** completes the sentence.

JOB SHADOWING

Do you want to learn more about a possible

| 5. Drop-down 1 | If so, a job-shadow program may

be perfect for you. In a job-shadow situation, a potential employee observes the daily duties, responsibilities, and challenges of an actual employee.

Through such observations, you may determine whether you would like to pursue such a position as a temporary

| 5. Drop-down 2 | a career. The strategies outlined

below can help you enjoy a successful job-shadow experience.

First, identify a job that you have an interest in

| 5. Drop-down 3 | make arrangements for a visit.

Referrals from friends or family members, resources such as the Internet, or local workforce development contacts may help you identify the best person to contact. Even if you lack the training, qualifications, or degree to perform this job today, shadowing a person working in your field of interest may help you decide whether you want to pursue this work. After you have identified the job, you'll need to identify the name of a manager, supervisor, or human resources official who may be able to assist you in scheduling a job-shadow experience.

It may be difficult to arrange | 5. Drop-down 4 |

identified a job you want to shadow. Some businesses may be more open to offering job-shadow experiences than others. Issues of insurance, liability, and scheduling are all possible reasons for denials of job-shadow requests. As a result, you may need to call several companies before receiving permission to shadow one of their employees.

Drop-Down Answer Options

5.1 A. career. Do you want to experience a possible career firsthand?
B. career, but experience it firsthand?
C. career and experience it firsthand?
D. career in order to experience it firsthand?

5.2 A. job or even as
B. job, but even as
C. job; you may decide to pursue it as
D. job. You may decide to pursue it as

5.3 A. shadowing, or
B. shadowing; you need to
C. shadowing; however,
D. shadowing, and

5.4 A. to shadow an employee and you've
B. to shadow an employee after you've
C. shadowing, but you've
D. shadowing an employee. You've

Run-on Sentence Correction

Use with **Student Book** pp. 186–187

LANGUAGE ASSESSMENT TARGETS: L.2.2, L.

1 Review the Skill

A **run-on sentence** results when two or more sentences are combined without a connecting word and proper punctuation. In some run-on sentences, commas separate the sentences. These errors are comma splices. In other instances, the sentences are not separated at all. These errors are fused sentences. You can correct comma splices and fused sentences by adding the appropriate connecting word or words and punctuation (if needed) or by creating two sentences.

2 Refine the Skill

By refining the skill of correcting run-on sentences, you will improve your writing and test-taking abilities, especially as they relate to the GED® Reasoning Through Language Arts test. Study the explanations and examples below. Then answer the questions that follow.

▶ Remember that run-on sentences always express more than one idea. The key is to determine how best to combine the two ideas into one logical sentence or separate them in two sentences.

a Remember that some connecting words are *and*, *or*, *but*, *however*, *nor*, *yet*, *therefore*, and *so*. The correct choice is based on the content of the sentence.

Run-on Sentence	Correct by	Correct Sentence(s)
Wrong: The Warriors played a great game, they still lost.	adding a connecting word	*Right*: The Warriors played a great game, but they still lost.
Wrong: The TV cabinet came with assembly instructions it was not easy to put together.	adding a comma and a connecting word	*Right*: The TV cabinet came with assembly instructions, but it was not easy to put together.
Wrong: She is an excellent guitarist she probably practices a lot.	creating two sentences	*Right*: She is an excellent guitarist. She probably practices a lot.
Wrong: Sami plays soccer her brother plays tennis.	inserting a semicolon	*Right*: Sami plays soccer; her brother plays tennis.

1. **I knew my dad's baseball card collection had some value no one knew it was worth so much.** Which correction should be made to the sentence?

   A. Insert , but after <u>value</u>.
   B. Insert <u>and</u> after <u>value</u>.
   C. Insert a comma after <u>value</u>.
   D. Insert , so after <u>value</u>.

2. **The movie featured great acting and a clever script, I think it will win several awards.** Which correction should be made to the sentence?

   A. Insert <u>but</u> before <u>I</u>.
   B. Insert a comma after <u>acting</u>.
   C. Change <u>script,</u> to <u>script.</u>
   D. Remove the comma after <u>script</u>.

⭐ Spotlighted Item: **DROP-DOWN**

DIRECTIONS: Read the passage. From the drop-down list, choose the answer that **best** completes the sentence.

HEART DISEASE AND DIET
GUIDELINES FOR HEALTHIER EATING

Heart disease is a serious problem in the United States. Heart disease occurs as the result of fatty plaque deposits in the arteries that deliver blood to the [3. Drop-down 1] cause the arteries to become narrow and hard. This condition does not allow the heart to receive the blood it needs for healthy functioning. However, there is a simple way to reduce your risk of heart [3. Drop-down 2] involve medication. You may be able to eat your way to a healthy heart, avoiding the complications that come with heart disease such as chest pain, stroke, or heart attack.

Eating several types of food should keep your heart healthy. These foods include fruits, vegetables, grains, low-fat dairy products, fish, chicken, turkey, beans, and nuts. Moreover, you should eat polyunsaturated and monounsaturated [3. Drop-down 3] occur in vegetable oils, fish, and nuts. Examples of foods with "good" fats include walnuts, avocados, olive oil, almonds, cashews, and sesame seeds.

You should limit or avoid several food items to keep your heart healthy. These items include salt, sugar, processed foods that contain trans fat, and cholesterol found in some meats and fatty dairy products. You should also avoid saturated [3. Drop-down 4] "bad" fat is found in some meats and dairy products.

Drop-Down Answer Options

3.1 A. heart. These deposits
B. heart, these deposits
C. heart, so these deposits
D. heart, but these deposits

3.2 A. disease it doesn't
B. disease, it doesn't
C. disease, and it doesn't
D. disease. Doesn't

3.3 A. fats, these "good" fats
B. fats. These "good" fats
C. fats, but these "good" fats
D. fats, and these "good" fats

3.4 A. fat. This so-called
B. fat this so-called
C. fat, this so-called
D. fat and this so-called

UNIT 4

★ Spotlighted Item: **DROP-DOWN**

DIRECTIONS: Read the passage. From the drop-down list, choose the answer that **best** completes the sentence.

Orlando Suites Hotel & Conference Center
8970 International Drive
Orlando, FL 32819

Dear Sir or Madam:

I would like to obtain information about your hotel's ability to host the World Firefighters Association annual convention for 300 people from March 5 to March 9 of next year. I am the representative for members attending the convention from throughout [4. Drop-down 1] contacting several hotels for details about accommodations, guest services, and costs.

Please provide details regarding your hotel's ability to satisfy our group's room and meal needs. We will need two large meeting rooms for [4. Drop-down 2] only one room will need video projection capability. In addition, we want to reserve a block of 150 hotel rooms with double occupancy. Also, please provide details about your menu [4. Drop-down 3] menu choices are important to our members.

We would also like you to provide a complete breakdown of costs, including fees for any perks you can offer. Such perks may include airport transportation, on-site parking, and hospitality suites. Naturally, we are looking for the best deal [4. Drop-down 4] us about any special discounts or deals you can offer our group.

Thank you for your prompt attention to this request.

Sincerely,

Jacob Rinaldo

Drop-Down Answer Options

4.1 A. North America, I am
    B. North America I am
    C. North America, but I am
    D. North America, and I am

4.2 A. presentations so
    B. presentations, but
    C. presentations and
    D. presentations,

4.3 A. options. Heart-healthy
    B. options, heart-healthy
    C. options, and heart-healthy
    D. options and heart-healthy

4.4 A. possible, and please tell
    B. possible and please tell
    C. possible, so please tell
    D. possible so please tell

UNIT 4

DIRECTIONS: Read the passage. From the drop-down list, choose the answer that **best** completes the sentence.

MOVING TIME
PACKING TIPS

You made the decision to move. You've located a new place
| 5. Drop-down 1 | found a new job and made
arrangements to leave your old apartment. Now it's time to pack.
Packing, like any other job, is a task that requires the right tools.

The first and most important tool for packing your belongings
is boxes, of course. You can find good deals on boxes if you
| 5. Drop-down 2 | for the places with the best
prices. Internet companies may offer better deals than local
retailers. If you've hired a moving company, the company may
provide you with some boxes. You can also ask local businesses
such as liquor stores, grocery stores, or hair salons to save
boxes for you. Boxes can get very expensive if you buy them
| 5. Drop-down 3 | boxes can be free and help save
trees!

Next, you will need to seal and label the boxes after they're
packed. Use clear or brown packing tape in a dispenser rather
than masking tape to seal the | 5. Drop-down 4 |
sticks better than masking tape, particularly if the boxes may get
hot or cold during the move. Use colored permanent markers to
label every box with its contents, location in the new place, and
the name of the family member. You can also assign a different
color to each room for easy identification during the unloading
process.

The more organized you are when you pack, the easier time you
will have after you move and start unpacking!

Drop-Down Answer Options

5.1 A. to live, you've
    B. to live; you've
    C. to live you've
    D. to live, or you've

5.2 A. shop around look
    B. shop around so look
    C. shop around, but look
    D. shop around, so look

5.3 A. new and used
    B. new because used
    C. new, but used
    D. new, used

5.4 A. boxes, packing tape
    B. boxes, so packing tape
    C. boxes but packing tape
    D. boxes. Packing tape

14 LESSON

Modifiers

Use with *Student Book* pp. 188–189

LANGUAGE ASSESSMENT TARGET: L.

1 Review the Skill

A **modifier** is a word or phrase that describes, clarifies, and gives more detail about another word or word group. It should be placed as close as possible to the word it describes. A **misplaced modifier** is confusing because it is placed incorrectly and describes the wrong item. A **dangling modifier** describes a word that is missing from the sentence.

2 Refine the Skill

By refining the skill of using modifiers correctly, you will improve your writing and test-taking abilities, especially as they relate to the GED® Reasoning Through Language Arts test. Study the explanations and examples below. Then answer the questions that follow.

a Remember that a modifier can be an adjective, an adverb, or a prepositional phrase. A modifier can modify more than one word. For example, *She is **very** tall and thin.*

b Place an adverb after the direct object in a sentence with a verb and a direct object. For example, *Read the book carefully*, not *Read carefully the book.*

▶ Study the chart to review how to correct misplaced and dangling modifiers.

Misplaced Modifiers	Dangling Modifiers
Wrong: Kara **almost** ran two miles before feeling tired.	*Wrong:* Driving to work, two deer ran in front of my car.
To correct the sentence, ask yourself: *Which word should **almost** modify?*	To correct the sentence, ask yourself: **Who** *was driving to work?*
Right: Kara ran **almost** two miles before feeling tired.	*Right:* While driving to work, I saw two deer run in front of my car. *Right:* While I was driving to work, two deer ran in front of my car.

1. **Many people who plan their vacations overlook the cost of transportation often.** Which is the **best** revision of the sentence?

   A. Many people who often plan their vacations overlook the cost of transportation.
   B. Many people who plan their vacations overlook often the cost of transportation.
   C. Planning their vacations often, many people overlook the cost of transportation.
   D. Many people who plan their vacations often overlook the cost of transportation.

USING LOGIC

Introductory phrases beginning with ***to*** + **verb** or **verb** + ***ing*** often become dangling modifiers. To correct a dangling modifier, determine the intended subject of the sentence, and rewrite the sentence to include it.

2. **As you can see from my résumé, my experience almost meets all requirements for the position.** Which is the **best** revision of the sentence?

   A. As you can see from my résumé, almost all requirements for the position are met by my experience.
   B. As you can see from my résumé, my experience meets almost all requirements for the position.
   C. My experience almost meets all requirements for the position, as you can see from my résumé.
   D. My experience meets all requirements almost for the position, as you can see from my résumé.

UNIT 4

⭐ Spotlighted Item: **DROP-DOWN**

DIRECTIONS: Read the passage. From the drop-down list, choose the answer that **best** completes the sentence.

HOW TO PREPARE YOUR TAXES

The basic forms that most Americans use are the 1040, the 1040A, and the 1040EZ. Which form best suits your needs? Form 1040 is the standard tax form [3. Drop-down 1]. For simpler returns, you may use Form 1040A or the even more basic Form 1040EZ. Those in the military should refer to Publication 3, which details all tax-related scenarios for military personnel.

Before starting your taxes, [3. Drop-down 2]. This process may seem like a greater challenge than doing your taxes, but it shouldn't overwhelm you. The most important document is the W-2 form from your employer, which states both your annual wages and the taxes paid through the end of the tax year. You also will need proof of other sources of income, such as unemployment, Social Security benefits, state tax refunds, or alimony. Additionally, if you plan to itemize deductions, be sure that you have receipts for items such as medical or moving expenses and mortgage interest paid.

Now that you have all of your documentation in order, you are ready to fill out your forms. You can fill out paper forms or complete electronic forms. As you proceed, be sure [3. Drop-down 3]. Double-check your math.

Paper Forms: Put forms in sequential order. Doing so will make it easier for the IRS to read and review your return quickly. Also, remember to sign your return. The IRS says unsigned tax returns are one of the most common taxpayer mistakes. After completing your forms and making copies for your [3. Drop-down 4].

Electronic Forms: There are several options for electronic filing. You can use free fillable forms, a tax return preparation site, commercial software, or authorized e-file providers.

Drop-Down Answer Options

3.1 A. only used by people who itemize deductions
B. used only by people who itemize deductions
C. used by people only who itemize deductions
D. used by only people who itemize deductions

3.2 A. income and deduction documentation is gathered
B. you need to gather your income and deduction documentation
C. gathering of income and deduction documentation
D. income and deduction documentation will be gathered

3.3 A. you correctly fill out the forms completely
B. correctly you fill out the forms completely
C. you fill out the forms correctly and completely
D. you fill correctly and completely out the forms

3.4 A. files, it is time to mail your return
B. files, the return is ready to mail
C. files, you can mail your return
D. files, your return can be mailed

★ Spotlighted Item: **DROP-DOWN**

DIRECTIONS: Read the passage. From the drop-down list, choose the answer that **best** completes the sentence.

Dear Editor:

I am writing in response to the editorial about impulsive and reckless shopping. In my opinion, consumers must educate themselves about how stores try to manipulate and encourage their customers to buy more and spend more.

How many times have you entered a store for the [4. Drop-down 1] one thing, yet you left with many more items? This situation probably happens more times than you can count. To take advantage of this habit, [4. Drop-down 2] everywhere.

Product placement encourages people to buy impulsively. For example, by locating basic necessities such as milk and bread at the back of the store or in the middle of an aisle, [4. Drop-down 3] walk past additional items. Furthermore, grocery store designers intentionally place expensive items at eye level and make it difficult for shoppers to maneuver quickly by forcing frequent stops. They also are sure to place goodies, such as candy bars or magazines, near the checkout counter. In fact, retailers base their product placement on the assumption that you will buy what you see.

Shopping accessories make it easy to buy. After all, you always find plenty of oversized shopping carts near the front of a store, but you may have difficulty finding a hand-held basket. Helping customers shop, [4. Drop-down 4] on store shelves. Many stores offer specials and sales, which encourage shoppers to purchase even more items.

We need to see the strategies stores use so that we can make smart, educated decisions when we shop.

Sincerely,

Taylor Rattner

Drop-Down Answer Options

4.1
A. only purpose of buying
B. purpose of only buying
C. purpose only of buying
D. purpose of buying only

4.2
A. encouragement is
B. retailers encourage you
C. you are encouraged by retailers
D. encouragement can be found

4.3
A. grocery designers force you to
B. you are forced to
C. forcing you to
D. you

4.4
A. bright yellow sale stickers are placed
B. retailers place bright yellow sale stickers
C. by placing bright yellow sale stickers
D. shelves have bright yellow sale stickers

UNIT 4

DIRECTIONS: Read the passage. From the drop-down list, choose the answer that **best** completes the sentence.

TIPS FOR MODIFYING YOUR CAR

Modifying your car can be a great way to express [5. Drop-down 1]. Any automobile—from a classic muscle car to a brand-new pickup truck—can be outfitted with custom gear. Various options can make your vehicle [5. Drop-down 2]. However, when modifying your car, remember to do so within the laws governing vehicles and transportation.

For drivers looking to boost a vehicle's performance, a host of modifications to the engine can provide additional horsepower. Options for changing an auto's appearance include designer paint jobs, body kits and accessories, and custom tires and rims. Alterations can be made to shocks and springs to give the vehicle a desired lowrider look.

However you decide to modify your car, you will find it helpful to develop a step-by-step plan and budget for your modifications. Identifying the labor and cost involved for each modification will help you determine which items are absolutely necessary. Carrying a hefty price tag, [5. Drop-down 3] too expensive. Your plan will help you determine the order in which to make your modifications. For example, you should [5. Drop-down 4] new tires and rims. Finally, your plan will allow you to double-check each modification to ensure that it conforms to all laws.

Drop-Down Answer Options

5.1 A. yourself and add style to your vehicle creatively
   B. creatively yourself and add style to your vehicle
   C. yourself creatively and add style to your vehicle
   D. yourself and add creatively style to your vehicle

5.2 A. look and drive exactly as you wish
   B. exactly look and drive as you wish
   C. look exactly and drive as you wish
   D. look and drive as you wish exactly

5.3 A. you may find all modifications
   B. you may find some modifications
   C. some modifications may prove
   D. this can make some modifications

5.4 A. complete always bodywork before selecting
   B. complete bodywork always before selecting
   C. complete bodywork before selecting always
   D. always complete bodywork before selecting

# Advanced Pronoun Use

LESSON 15

Use with **Student Book** pp. 190–191

1 Review the Skill

As you learned in Lesson 2, <mark>subject pronouns</mark> do the action of a verb, and <mark>object pronouns</mark> receive the action of a verb or follow words such as *above*, *at*, *before*, *between*, *from*, *near*, *of*, and *to*. These rules apply to compound subjects and objects as well. You also learned that pronouns have antecedents, or words to which the pronouns refer. This rule is true for the pronouns *that*, *this*, and *which*. These pronouns should not refer to a sentence or an idea. For example, *The meeting was canceled. This cancellation ruined my day.*

2 Refine the Skill

By refining the skill of using pronouns correctly, you will improve your writing and test-taking abilities, especially as they relate to the GED® Reasoning Through Language Arts test. Read the information below. Then answer the questions that follow.

a When you pair the subject pronoun *I* or the object pronoun *me* with another noun or pronoun, *I* or *me* comes second. For example, *My sister and I often travel together.*

b Use *it* to replace a collective noun whose members act as a group. Use *they* or *them* to replace a collective noun whose members act individually. If the plural sounds odd, change the noun to a plural—for example, *jury members.*

Examples	Explanation
Wrong: Who did you call yesterday? *Right:* Whom did you call yesterday?	Whom is the **object** of *called*. You is the subject.
Wrong: I'm sure whomever they hire will do well. *Right:* I'm sure whoever they hire will do well.	Whoever is the subject of *will do*; they hire is an intervening expression that does not affect pronoun-antecedent agreement.
Wrong: Each student takes their place on line. *Right:* Each student takes his or her place on line.	Each is always singular and must take singular pronouns.
Wrong: Send your reply to my secretary and myself. *Right:* Send your reply to my secretary and me, and be sure to copy yourself on all correspondence.	Myself is an object pronoun used only when the subject and object are the same. Yourself is used correctly here.
Wrong: We hired an assistant. This will help reduce your workload. *Right:* We hired an assistant to help reduce your workload. *Right:* We hired an assistant. The new hire will help reduce your workload.	This must have an antecedent. The sentence can be corrected in a number of ways.
Wrong: Did you send this for Mitch and I? *Right:* Did you send this for Mitch and me?	Me is part of the compound object of *for*. I is a subject pronoun and is incorrect in this sentence.

1. **Write a letter to the new representative whom, after two recounts, finally was elected.** Which correction should be made to the sentence?

   A. Change <u>whom</u> to <u>whoever</u>.
   B. Change <u>whom</u> to <u>who</u>.
   C. Change <u>whom</u> to <u>whomever</u>.
   D. Change <u>whom</u> to <u>which</u>.

2. **Alex sent a copy to Vivian and I.** Which correction should be made to the sentence?

   A. Change <u>Vivian and I</u> to <u>I and Vivian</u>.
   B. Change <u>Vivian and I</u> to <u>she and me</u>.
   C. Change <u>Vivian and I</u> to <u>Vivian and me</u>.
   D. Change <u>Vivian and I</u> to <u>her and I</u>.

UNIT 4

★ Spotlighted Item: **DROP-DOWN**

DIRECTIONS: Read the passage. From the drop-down list, choose the answer that **best** completes the sentence.

CUSTOMER SERVICE POLICIES

As manager of California Auto Parts, Inc., I aim to provide the best value in replacement auto parts and installation services. Service team [3. Drop-down 1] want our customers to trust us and to come back for part replacement and installation. To ensure that customers receive the highest quality parts and service, we offer a three-part satisfaction guarantee.

1) Transparent Pricing On All Replacement Parts

When we deliver an estimate, we list the wholesale price of the part and the 10% stocking fee. If multiple options are available for a part, we will share the different prices, explain the options, and make recommendations that reflect the best value and choice for each situation.

2) Guaranteed Estimate Pricing

If the service costs exceed the estimate by more than 10 percent, we gladly complete the work [3. Drop-down 2], and the balance is free.

3) 90-Day Guarantee

All parts are guaranteed for 90 days. We want each customer to feel secure when [3. Drop-down 3] our garages. That's why, should a part break or malfunction within 90 days of installation, we will provide a replacement part and services at no cost. I personally ensure that we will stand behind any part we install.

If you have questions, ask anyone here, and [3. Drop-down 4] you speak to will be happy to provide more information. Choose our service personnel and mechanics to do the best job at the best price.

Ned Rainey
Manager

Drop-Down Answer Options

3.1 A. members and I
B. members and me
C. members and myself
D. members and us

3.2 A. ourself
B. by us
C. ourselves
D. themselves

3.3 A. they leave
B. him or her leaves
C. he or she leaves
D. them leave

3.4 A. whom
B. whoever
C. who
D. whichever

UNIT 4

⭐ Spotlighted Item: **DROP-DOWN**

DIRECTIONS: Read the passage. From the drop-down list, choose the answer that **best** completes the sentence.

Dear Mr. and Mrs. Cassedy:

For the past three years, I have had the pleasure of being part of the exceptional healthcare team at Manchester Pediatrics. I am sorry to inform you that as of November 15 of this year, I will no longer be with the practice.

My colleagues at Manchester Pediatrics, Dr. Felix Hernandez and Dr. Jordan Carol, are knowledgeable physicians skilled at working with young patients. At the beginning of November, the practice is also welcoming Dr. Tonya Smith,

| 4. Drop-down 1 | comes to the practice after her residency in pediatrics at the prestigious Marsh Clinic in Nashua. These accomplished and dedicated physicians have decades of pediatric experience among them. | 4. Drop-down 2 | should give you confidence in their expertise.

Please call the office to let the practice know the physician

| 4. Drop-down 3 | you would like as your child's pediatrician. We realize that your child may require urgent care before you have chosen a new doctor. Dr. Hernandez and I have spoken together, and | 4. Drop-down 4 | have agreed that he will see all children who require urgent care.

If you decide to take your child to another practice, please call the office to obtain a medical release form. Please also be aware that you might need to notify your health insurer of the change of physician.

Thank you for your confidence and trust. It has been a pleasure to work with you in providing healthcare for your child.

Sincerely,

Erica Johansen, MD

Drop-Down Answer Options

4.1 A. whomever
 B. who
 C. which
 D. whom

4.2 A. Which
 B. This
 C. Which combined experience
 D. This combined experience

4.3 A. which
 B. who
 C. whom
 D. whomever

4.4 A. he and I
 B. he and myself
 C. him and I
 D. me and him

DIRECTIONS: Read the passage. From the drop-down list, choose the answer that **best** completes the sentence.

Dear Editor:

I am writing today on behalf of the citizens and pedestrians of this town to remind the community that dogs—though they can be wonderful companions—are not people. Their rights are not violated by having to walk on a leash. Nor do we ask too much of their owners by insisting that they clean up after their pets.

On a recent stroll down Main Street, my wife and I met several dogs off their leashes and wandering far ahead of their owners. These dogs bounded up to [5. Drop-down 1]. What if one of us had a fear of dogs? There is an off-leash area in the local park. Every owner should keep [5. Drop-down 2] dog leashed outside of the park. The responsibility should be on owners to restrain their dogs, not on us to endure unleashed dogs.

In addition, I find that all too often, I must not so much walk down the sidewalk as tiptoe down it in an attempt to avoid dog droppings. Again, the responsibility lies with the dog owners. Anyone who can't stomach the thought of scooping up a dog's mess should not get a dog to begin with. It should not be up to pedestrians like [5. Drop-down 3] to sidestep a dog's mess.

I urge the dog owners of this town to demonstrate some consideration. The community should insist that police officers enforce fines for dog owners who don't keep dogs on leashes and who don't clean up after [5. Drop-down 4] against the law.

Drop-Down Answer Options

5.1 A. she and me
    B. my wife and I
    C. she and I
    D. my wife and me

5.2 A. them
    B. him or hers
    C. their
    D. his or her

5.3 A. I
    B. me
    C. myself
    D. we

5.4 A. them. These practices are
    B. them, which is
    C. them. This
    D. them, this is

Advanced Subject-Verb Agreement

LESSON

Use with **Student Book** pp. 192–193

LANGUAGE ASSESSMENT TARGET: L.

1 Review the Skill

Sometimes, sentence construction or certain pronouns can make **subject-verb agreement** more difficult t determine. Confusion in agreement can occur when sentences contain compound subjects, collective nouns, pronouns that can be singular or plural in different situations, asides (or intervening phrases between subject and verb), compound subjects joined by *nor*, and inverted constructions, such as sentences beginning with *there is* or *there are*.

2 Refine the Skill

By refining the skill of using complex subject-verb agreement correctly, you will improve your writing and test-taking abilities, especially as they relate to the GED® Reasoning Through Language Arts test. Read the explanations and examples below. Then answer the questions that follow.

Examples	Explanation
Wrong: Neither rain nor snow prevent the mail from being delivered. *Right*: Neither rain nor snow *prevents* the mail from being delivered.	When compound subjects are joined by *nor*, the verb agrees with the subject that is closer: *snow*
Wrong: My car, like my kitchen and my closets, are very messy. *Right*: My car, like my kitchen and my closets, *is* very messy.	The aside or intervening phrase, *like my kitchen and my closets*, does not make the subject plural. *My car* is singular.
Wrong: Although each of the movies are up for an award, only one will win. *Right*: Although each of the movies *is* up for an award, only one will win.	*Each* takes a singular verb.
Wrong: In the laundry basket is your shirt, jeans, and socks. *Right*: In the laundry basket *are* your shirt, jeans, and socks.	The subject—*shirt, jeans, and socks*—is plural and follows the verb. *Basket* is not the subject.
Wrong: The family go on vacation each year. *Right*: The family *goes* on vacation each year.	The family is acting as a whole, so it takes a singular verb.

1. **Each of my daughters are talented.** Which correction should be made to the sentence?

   A. Change <u>are</u> to <u>were</u>.
   B. Change <u>are</u> to <u>is</u>.
   C. Change <u>are</u> to <u>have been</u>.
   D. Change <u>are</u> to <u>is being</u>.

2. **Neither the cats nor the dog are allowed in the house.** Which correction should be made to the sentence?

   A. Change <u>are</u> to <u>being</u>.
   B. Change <u>are</u> to <u>is</u>.
   C. Change <u>are</u> to <u>have been</u>.
   D. Change <u>are</u> to <u>were</u>.

USING LOGIC

Find the subject closest to the verb in a neither/nor construction. If the subject is singular, use a singular verb. If it is plural, use a plural verb.

UNIT 4

3 **Master the Skill**

★ Spotlighted Item: **DROP-DOWN**

DIRECTIONS: Read the passage. For each drop-down item, choose the option that **best** completes the sentence.

HOW TO STAGE YOUR HOME

Experienced realtors know that staging a home before putting it on the market can dramatically increase the selling price. Staging involves enhancing the home's appearance so that it is appealing to the greatest number of potential buyers. A cluttered home that has been poorly maintained, as well as an empty home with no furniture or decorations, [3. Drop-down 1] to most buyers. Well-staged homes are furnished, but each of the rooms [3. Drop-down 2] free of clutter, and furniture is not crowded. Staging does not mean that homes should look bare! For example, you don't want a living room with only a sofa pushed against a wall opposite a TV. A seating arrangement that includes at least a sofa, an armchair, and a coffee table looks best.

Editing down, organizing, and getting rid of clutter [3. Drop-down 3] key to effective staging. You don't want too many knick-knacks or too many personal items. You want the potential buyers to see the home as theirs, not to be reminded of you and your family by seeing all of your photos and mementos. Clean the home as if you had guests coming to visit. Newspapers piled on tables or chairs don't make the best first impression to either guests or buyers! Tidy up bookcases, edit down how many objects are placed on tables, and clean out closets.

A fresh coat of paint in the interior rooms is almost always a good idea. No buyer likes to see scuffed or dirty walls. A number of buyers [3. Drop-down 4] neutral colors, so consider colors like tan, cream, and beige when painting. Try to avoid colors that are too bold or specific to your own tastes.

Drop-Down Answer Options

3.1 A. do not appeal
    B. are unappealing
    C. is unappealing
    D. are not appealing

3.2 A. is
    B. are
    C. were
    D. was

3.3 A. was
    B. is
    C. are
    D. were

3.4 A. is likely to prefer
    B. prefers
    C. prefer
    D. shows a preference for

UNIT 4

Master the Skill

★ Spotlighted Item: **DROP-DOWN**

DIRECTIONS: Read the passage. For each drop-down item, choose the option that **best** completes the sentence.

NEW CALLING SYSTEM

To all FabCo employees:

Last week, we finished updating our conference calling system. As of today, all of our employees [4. Drop-down 1] to use the new FabCo Messenger service.

The cost of maintaining telephone lines in all of the 45 countries with FabCo offices [4. Drop-down 2] enormous. The new FabCo Messenger software routes audio and video over the Internet, allowing us to forgo the expensive telecommunications infrastructure altogether. This transition is estimated to save thousands of dollars every month.

Every manager with team members in other offices, as well as managers working remotely from home, [4. Drop-down 3] to try the new videoconferencing features. Using them will enable you to spend valuable face time with your team while simultaneously allowing the company to save money by reducing travel costs.

You can obtain new headsets from your office's I.T. help desk. [4. Drop-down 4] a mono model and two stereo models available. Each model is available in wireless or wired versions. Employees working in remote locations can purchase their own headsets and submit receipts to the I.T. department for reimbursement up to $60.

FabCo Messenger includes several other new features, including personal voice mail and instant messaging, which we hope you'll find helpful.

Drop-Down Answer Options

4.1 A. required
B. require
C. is required
D. are required

4.2 A. are
B. is
C. were
D. have been

4.3 A. is encouraged
B. are encouraged
C. will have been encouraged
D. was encouraged

4.4 A. There is
B. There is both
C. There are
D. There were

DIRECTIONS: Read the passage. From the drop-down list, choose the answer that **best** completes the sentence.

NEW BADGE POLICY

To: WaveLength Team Members and Contractors
From: WaveLength Security Department
Date: November 9

Subject: New Badge Policy

Currently, a number of types of photo identification [5. Drop-down 1] by WaveLength employees and contractors to gain access to the buildings on the WaveLength campus. To avoid miscommunications and other security issues, the following badge policy will be in effect beginning November 15. WaveLength personnel on this campus [5. Drop-down 2] to comply with this policy. No exceptions will be made.

- All employees and contractors must wear their badges at all times while in the facility. Previous policy required that badges or IDs be shown only at point of entry.

- Badges must be clearly visible at all times. Clothing should not obstruct a clear view of the badge. Employees have customarily worn badges on shirt pockets where they are often obscured by jackets or sweaters.

- Employees and contractors must swipe their badges at each entry door, even if the door is already open. Too often these days, an employee enters a door with a group of people, including other employees or visitors to the facility, [5. Drop-down 3] the card to show security, and passes through. This method no longer will be permissible.

- Employees and contractors without badges must enter the building through the main doors to obtain a temporary badge. Neither department heads nor any other supervisor [5. Drop-down 4] to authorize a security guard to ignore this regulation.

Drop-Down Answer Options

5.1 A. is showed
 B. are showed
 C. is shown
 D. are shown

5.2 A. is required
 B. is require
 C. were required
 D. are required

5.3 A. held up
 B. hold up
 C. holds up
 D. was holding up

5.4 A. were allowed
 B. are allowed
 C. was allowed
 D. is allowed

UNIT 4

17 Parallelism

LESSON

Use with **Student Book** pp. 194–195

LANGUAGE ASSESSMENT TARGETS: L.1.6, L.

1 Review the Skill

A sentence has **parallel structure**, or parallelism, when it displays the same pattern to show that specific ideas have equal importance. Writers create parallelism by using the same word forms and sentence structure when stating their ideas. For example, verbs and verb forms should be written in a consistent form: *Browsing, comparing, and budgeting are important strategies for saving money.* Parallelism also helps eliminate wordiness.

2 Refine the Skill

By refining the skill of recognizing and creating parallelism, you will improve your writing and test-taking abilities, especially as they relate to the GED® Reasoning Through Language Arts test. Study the explanations and examples below. Then answer the questions that follow.

> ▶ A sentence has parallel structure if it displays a similar pattern to present ideas of equal importance.

a In the first example, using parallelism helps eliminate wordiness.

b In the second example, the incorrect sentence mixes a noun, *perseverance*; a gerund, *working*; and an infinitive, *to work*. The corrected sentence uses all nouns to show equal importance and provide clarity.

In the first example below, the positions played by Tommy are introduced in different ways. The correct sentence demonstrates parallelism. In the second example, the list of lessons learned should be written in a consistent form.

Awkward	Clear
Tommy plays both wide receiver and also is the team's cornerback.	Tommy plays both wide receiver and cornerback.
I learned many important lessons about working hard, perseverance, and to work as a team.	I learned many important lessons about hard work, perseverance, and teamwork.

1. **Chris set aside time to ride his bike and studying for the test.** Which correction should be made to the sentence?

   A. Replace <u>to ride</u> with <u>riding</u>.
   B. Replace <u>studying</u> with <u>to study</u>.
   C. Replace <u>studying</u> with <u>studies</u>.
   D. Replace <u>to ride</u> with <u>rode</u>.

2. **Coaching Little League provides an opportunity both to serve as a coach and acting as a role model for young people.** Which correction should be made to the sentence?

   A. Replace <u>provides</u> with <u>providing</u>.
   B. Replace <u>serve</u> with <u>serving</u>.
   C. Replace <u>model</u> with <u>modeling</u>.
   D. Replace <u>acting</u> with <u>to act</u>.

MAKING ASSUMPTIONS

If a sentence contains a connecting word such as *and*, *but*, or *or*, you can assume that the items or ideas in the sentence have equal importance.

UNIT 4

DIRECTIONS: Read the passage, read the questions, and choose the **best** answer.

FINDING AFFORDABLE CHILD CARE

1   Recent changes in the economy have made it increasingly difficult for people to stretch their earnings to cover their expenses. For people with children, the rising costs of child care have proven to be a particularly difficult expense to manage. As a result, many parents have begun to seek out or creating new types of reliable and affordable child care.

2   One affordable child care option involves enlisting friends, family members, or the people who live in their neighborhood to care for young children. These people may be willing to provide care at a rate that is far less expensive than what parents might find at an ordinary day care center. Some individuals may provide care in exchange for some other service that the parents can provide for them, such as yard work or house-sitting. Many parents also find security in knowing that their children are being supervised and cared for by a familiar adult.

3   Some parents trade babysitting duties with another family, or a co-op is formed by friends and neighbors. For example, five sets of parents might rotate responsibility for babysitting each other's children one day each week. Although there can be many children to babysit on their assigned day, the parents in the co-op gain four days in which they can go to work without having to pay for childcare.

4   An in-home babysitter for children who are school age may be another child care option that is affordable. Often, adolescents or college students from the neighborhood may be willing to look after young children in the family home. Because such work is flexible and can be done informally, many young people will take on babysitting work for a small fee.

3.   Which is the **best** way to write the underlined portion of this sentence? **As a result, many parents have begun to seek out or creating new types of reliable and affordable child care.**

A. to seek out or to creating
B. seeking out or to create
C. to seek out or to create
D. to seeking out, creating new types

4.   Which is the **best** way to write the underlined portion of this sentence? **One affordable child care option involves enlisting friends, family members, or the people who live in their neighborhood to care for young children.**

A. people who live near friends and family
B. friends who live in their neighborhood, family members who live in their neighborhood, or other people who live in their neighborhood
C. friends, family members, or neighbors
D. friends and family members, or people who live in their neighborhood

5.   Which is the **best** revision of this sentence? **Some parents trade babysitting duties with another family, or a co-op is formed by friends and neighbors.**

A. To trade babysitting with another family, some parents form a co-op with friends and neighbors.
B. Some parents trade babysitting duties with another family or form co-ops with friends and neighbors.
C. Some parents form a co-op with friends and neighbors or babysitting duties are traded with another family.
D. Some parents trade babysitting duties with another family or to form co-ops with friends and neighbors.

6.   Which is the **best** revision of this sentence? **An in-home babysitter for children who are school age may be another child care option that is affordable.**

A. A babysitter who is in-home may be another child care option that is affordable for children who are school age.
B. For school-age children, an in-home babysitter may be another child care option that is affordable.
C. Another child care option that is affordable for school-aged children is an in-home babysitter.
D. An in-home babysitter for school-age children may be another affordable child care option.

7.   Which correction should be made to this sentence? **Because such work is flexible and can be done informally, many young people will take on babysitting work for a small fee.**

A. Change can be done informally to informal.
B. Change flexible to not very flexible.
C. Change is flexible to offers flexibility.
D. Change can be done informally to informally.

UNIT 4

DIRECTIONS: Read the passage, read the questions, and choose the **best** answer.

YARD SALE ADVICE

1   People who spend every Saturday morning driving from yard sale to yard sale know something that you don't. They know you can find some fantastic used items at garage sales and yard sales, and sales that people have before they move are great, too. They also know that they can buy these items for a fraction of the cost of what they would pay if they bought them new at the store. Of course, sleeping late on Saturday is nice, but to keep a little extra money in your pocket is nice, too. Next weekend, maybe you should visit some yard sales. Keep your eyes open for some of these items.

2   Used books can be excellent yard sale deals. The retail markup on books is astronomical, and most people tire of them before the items wear out. Ask yourself this question: How many times will I realistically read this book? If the answer is only once, why spend $10 or $25 on a new copy? You can spend one dollar on the same book, used, and spending the other nine dollars on different items.

3   If you want to try out a new exercise routine, consider checking out equipment at local yard sales before you purchase something new. People often sell exercise equipment that they purchased for their homes and barely used. Exercise bikes, elliptical machines, and treadmills are routinely sold by owners who didn't stick to their well-intentioned exercise plans. Instead of paying hundreds or thousands of dollars for a new machine, buy one inexpensively at a yard sale.

4   You can also stock up on supplies for any upcoming home projects. Yard sales are great places to find used office furniture or non-electric tools. Why pay full price for items that are well made? A sturdy desk, an office chair, or a cabinet that is used for filing can last for years. A used hammer or screwdriver looks and functions the same as new ones.

8.   Which is the **best** way to write the underlined portion of this sentence? **They know you can find some fantastic used items at garage sales and yard sales, and sales that people have before they move are great, too.**

    A. garage sales, yard sales, and moving sales are great
    B. garage sales and yard sales before people move
    C. garage sales, yard sales, and moving sales
    D. garage, yard, moving sales

9.   Which is the **best** way to write the underlined portion this sentence? **Of course, sleeping late on Saturday is nice, but to keep a little extra money in your pocket is nice, too.**

    A. keeping a little extra money in your pocket is nice, too
    B. you should keep a little extra money in your pocket because it is nicer too
    C. also nice is to keep a little extra money in you pocket
    D. keeping a little extra money in your pocket

10.   Which is the **best** way to write the underlined portion of this sentence? **You can spend one dollar on the same book, used, and spending the other nine dollars on different items.**

    A. and ending up spending
    B. and spend
    C. and to spend
    D. and you end up spending

11.   Which correction should be made to the sentence **A sturdy desk, an office chair, or a cabinet that is used for filing can last for years.**

    A. Change a sturdy desk, an office chair to desk and chairs as well.
    B. Change a cabinet that is used for filing to a filing cabinet.
    C. Change a sturdy desk to a desk that is sturdy
    D. Change an office chair to a chair for an office.

★ Spotlighted Item: **DROP-DOWN**

DIRECTIONS: Read the passage. From the drop-down list, choose the answer that **best** completes the sentence.

HELP US HELP KIDS!

Dear Neighbors:

Next Saturday, the Westchester Youth Group is sponsoring a "Kids for Kids Day" in Oakbrook. Students from three Westchester County schools—Daley Junior High, Ryder Middle School, [12. Drop-down 1] Clifton Academy—will volunteer their time to help raise money for local kids in need. Events will include a car wash, a bake sale, a lawn-mowing service, and [12. Drop-down 2]. Funds raised at each of the events will benefit several area children's charities, including the Oakbrook Youth Crisis Center and the Westchester County Homeless Youth Support Agency. Money made at each event will go directly to these charities.

The members of the Westchester Youth Group need your support in making next Saturday a success! Prices will be irresistibly low on all items for sale and all services offered. For example, a full car wash and dry will cost you only $1. Or you can have your lawn mowed for as little as $5, depending on the size of your yard. The bake sale will have unbeatable prices. For example, you can buy four cookies [12. Drop-down 3] $1.

If you can help "Kids for Kids," head to one of our participating schools this Saturday, and take part in one of our events. You can buy great baked goods at Daley Junior High, get your car washed at Ryder Middle School, or [12. Drop-down 4] at Clifton Academy. Members who volunteer for lawn services will be driven to your home by adult sponsors who will supervise work and provide equipment.

Volunteers will be at all locations from 9 AM to 6 PM Saturday, September 7. We hope to see you then!

Drop-Down Answer Options

12.1 A. and
B. as well as
C. and students from
D. and students who go to

12.2 A. the pruning of trees
B. your trees can get pruned
C. pruning trees
D. a tree-pruning service

12.3 A. for $1 or a slice of pie will cost
B. or a slice of pie for
C. for $1, or even a slice of pie for
D. for $1 or a slice of pie for

12.4 A. there will be lawn service sign-up
B. signing up for lawn services
C. sign up for lawn services
D. lawn services will be available for purchase

UNIT 4

18 Transitions

Use with **Student Book** pp. 196–197

1 Review the Skill

Transitions connect ideas in writing. They can show the order of events, indicate a similarity or difference, or provide an example or explanation of a statement. Transitional words and phrases may occur within sentences, between sentences, between paragraphs, and between sections of text. Using transitions helps create logical and fluid writing.

2 Refine the Skill

By refining the skill of using transitions, you will improve your writing and test-taking abilities, especially as they relate to the GED® Reasoning Through Language Arts test. Study the explanations and examples below. Then answer the questions that follow.

▶ Remember that transitions show the relationship between two pieces of information. Use transitions within one sentence.

I like this <u>just as</u> **I like that.** = I like both items to the same degree.

I like this <u>although</u> **I do not like that.** = I like one thing but not the other.

I liked this; <u>subsequently,</u> **I liked that.** = After I liked one thing, I liked another related thing.

a Some transitions mean the same thing and are used interchangeably. For example, **nevertheless** and **nonetheless** both mean "in spite of." Depending on the sentence, **however**, **but**, and **yet** can have the same meaning.

▶ Use transitions between sentences.

I have a new cell phone. <u>However,</u> **it is difficult to use.** = Despite being new, the cell phone isn't easy to use.

I went swimming. <u>Then</u> **I ran to the store.** = After going swimming, I ran to the store.

I believe taxes are too high. <u>For example,</u> **sales tax is 8 percent.** = An 8 percent sales tax is an example of a tax that is too high.

b Remember that a comma often follows a transition when the word or phrase comes at the beginning of a sentence.

1. **I think the interest rate on my mortgage is too high. I do not qualify for a lower rate.** Which transition is the **most** effective to use at the beginning of the second sentence?

   A. Despite,
   B. However,
   C. Furthermore,
   D. For example,

CONTENT TOPICS

Transitions often show causal relationships: *I passed the GED® test. Therefore, I applied to college.* The word *therefore* explains that you applied to college because you passed the GED® test.

2. **He rarely** <u>drives. He</u> **has two cars.** Which is the **most** effective revision to the underlined portion of the sentences?

   A. drives. In contrast, he
   B. drives. In addition, he
   C. drives although he
   D. drives. Conversely, he

⭐ Spotlighted Item: **DROP-DOWN**

DIRECTIONS: Read the passage. From the drop-down list, choose the answer that **best** completes the sentence.

WRITING A RÉSUMÉ

A résumé has one primary function: to get you an interview. For some jobs, employers may receive hundreds of résumés. You want your résumé, which may end up among stacks of others, to grab the attention of a potential employer. You want the information to cause this tired, overworked employer to think, *I've got to meet this person.* | 3. Drop-down 1 | follow these tips to get your résumé to the top of the stack.

A résumé has two components: design and content. You want the design of your résumé to be clean, neat, and easy to read. Employers have little time to read each résumé. | 3. Drop-down 2 | you should choose the information that is most relevant to the particular job or career field for which you are applying. Make this information easily accessible through text features such as bullets, bold-faced type, headings, subheadings, and so on.

For the content of your résumé, use descriptive, clear language, especially verbs, to tell potential employers about your skills and qualifications. Point out how you will meet an employer's needs and how the employer will benefit by hiring you. Be thorough in describing your previous work | 3. Drop-down 3 | try to cram a résumé with everything you've ever thought, said, or done. | 3. Drop-down 4 | when writing your résumé, choose relevant information and present it in active, dynamic language in a design that is reader friendly and accessible.

Don't submit your resume by itself. Include a cover letter that addresses the specific job opportunity. A customized cover letter shows a potential employer that you have taken time with your application, and it will greatly enhance your chances of being noticed positively.

Drop-Down Answer Options

3.1 A. After that,
B. In the same way,
C. To begin,
D. Earlier,

3.2 A. What's more,
B. Consequently,
C. Next,
D. Furthermore,

3.3 A. experience. Moreover, don't
B. experience. For example, don't
C. experience, but don't
D. experience. In contrast,

3.4 A. Therefore,
B. Subsequently,
C. On the other hand,
D. First,

UNIT 4

★ Spotlighted Item: **DROP-DOWN**

DIRECTIONS: Read the passage. From the drop-down list, choose the answer that **best** completes the sentence.

Ms. Christine Churchman
Human Resources, Aspen Architecture
2323 Colorado Drive
Aspen, CO 81611

Dear Ms. Churchman:

I am responding to your listing with Aspen Architecture for a draftsperson. I believe that I would be an excellent fit for the position. I am currently a drafting and design student at Aspen Technical College, and I am looking for additional practical experience. [4. Drop-down 1] I am interested in beginning employment as an apprentice while finishing my education.

Prior to beginning my education, I worked in home and commercial construction. This experience has proved quite useful in drafting, as I understand the end result of my work. [4. Drop-down 2] I have real-world experience and understand how technical drawings are used by construction professionals. To illustrate my capabilities, I would like to share with you my portfolio of construction work.

I am a punctual, hardworking [4. Drop-down 3] you are likely to find that I am the first to arrive at the office in the morning and among the last to leave. My passion for and experience in this field will certainly benefit your company. [4. Drop-down 4] me for an interview at your earliest convenience.

I look forward to speaking with you.

Sincerely,

Darius Henson

Drop-Down Answer Options

4.1 A. For this reason,
    B. In the same way,
    C. Conversely,
    D. Still,

4.2 A. In contrast,
    B. However,
    C. Nevertheless,
    D. Moreover,

4.3 A. person, but
    B. person; however,
    C. person. Consequently,
    D. person. Nonetheless,

4.4 A. Please contact
    B. Similarly, please contact
    C. In addition, please contact
    D. Otherwise, please contact

DIRECTIONS: Read the passage. From the drop-down list, choose the answer that **best** completes the sentence.

LEASE AGREEMENT

Lessees agree to pay as rent the total sum of $9,000. This sum will be paid in 12 monthly installments of $750. The monthly rent is due on or before the first day of each month during the lease term. Rent received after the fifth day of the month will be subject to a $50 late charge, plus $10 per day after the fifth day of the month, until paid in full. [5. Drop-down 1] if rent is paid on the 10th of the month, the total amount due will be $750 plus $100 in late fees. All rent is to be paid by check or money order and made payable to Rosewood Apartments. Returned checks are subject to a $30 fee.

Lessees agree to provide a $750 security deposit to the Landlord before obtaining possession of the Premises. Lessees agree to submit to the Landlord a move-in checklist indicating the condition of the Premises within one week of obtaining possession. [5. Drop-down 2] the Landlord will have three days to repair all problems noted on the move-in checklist. [5. Drop-down 3] vacating, Lessees agree to submit to the Landlord a move-out checklist documenting the condition of the property. If necessary, the security deposit will be applied to unpaid utilities, unpaid rent, and re-rental expenses, as well as repair of damage to the Premises beyond normal wear and tear. Lessees understand that their liability for such damages is not limited to the amount of the security deposit.

Lessees agree that the Premises will not be assigned or sublet without written consent of the Landlord. Lessees agree that only those who have signed this document shall occupy the Premises. [5. Drop-down 4] Lessees agree to use the Premises only in the following ways. The Premises will be occupied for residential purposes only and will not be used for any commercial purposes or for any purpose deemed hazardous by the Landlord.

Drop-Down Answer Options

5.1 A. Nevertheless,
   B. In addition,
   C. For example,
   D. Conversely,

5.2 A. First,
   B. Earlier,
   C. At that time,
   D. Yesterday,

5.3 A. Consequently, upon
   B. Furthermore, upon
   C. In addition to
   D. As a result of

5.4 A. In addition,
   B. Nevertheless,
   C. After that,
   D. Similarly,

UNIT 4

19 Paragraph Organization

LESSON

Use with *Student Book* pp. 198–199

1 Review the Skill

LANGUAGE ASSESSMENT TARGET: L.
WRITING ASSESSMENT TARGET: W.2

A **paragraph** is logical and makes sense because it is *organized* in a specific way. The topic sentence introduces the subject, or main idea, of the paragraph and connects the ideas of the other sentences within the paragraph. The other sentences provide supporting details, which may include facts, statistics, explanations, examples, or analysis. Main ideas and topic sentences may be explicit or implicit.

2 Refine the Skill

By refining the skill of paragraph organization, you will improve your writing and test-taking abilities, especially as they relate to the GED® Reasoning Through Language Arts test. Study the diagram, and read the paragraph below. Then answer the questions that follow.

▶ Study the diagram below to understand the relationship between the topic sentence and the other sentences in a paragraph.

a The topic sentences of paragraphs may provide an outline of the main ideas of the passage.

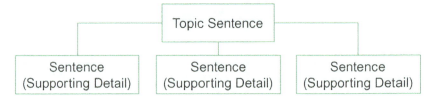

(1) If you suffer from allergies, you may find yourself making weekly visits to a doctor's office for an allergy shot. (2) These visits can be expensive. (3) Working out of St. Mary's Hospital in London in 1911, Leonard Noon and John Freeman experimented with the first allergy shots. (4) Noon and Freeman administered low doses of the extract through shots. (5) These researchers extracted pollen from grass and used the extract to treat people who had hay fever. (6) Patients received shots every three to four days. (7) Noon and Freeman gradually increased the extract dosage by delivering a series of shots. (8) Consequently, they found that they were able to relieve hay fever symptons.

1. Which is the **best** place for sentence 2? **These visits can be expensive.**

   A. Move sentence 2 to follow sentence 8.
   B. Remove sentence 2.
   C. Move sentence 2 to the beginning of the paragraph.
   D. Move sentence 2 to follow sentence 6.

2. Which is the **best** place for sentence 4? **Noon and Freeman administered low doses of the extract through shots.**

   A. Remove sentence 4.
   B. Move sentence 4 to follow sentence 1.
   C. Move sentence 4 to follow sentence 5.
   D. Move sentence 4 to follow sentence 7.

TEST-TAKING TIPS

To organize a paragraph effectively, examine the sentences within it, and identify their common theme. Ask: *How does each sentence relate to the main idea of the paragraph?*

UNIT 4

★ Spotlighted Item: **DRAG-AND-DROP**

DIRECTIONS: Read the passage and the question. Then use the drag-and-drop option to complete the first paragraph.

To: All Lehman Consulting Staff
From: Human Resources
Subject: New Travel Policies

A

Sentence 1
Sentence 2
Sentence 3
Sentence 4
Sentence 5

B

As a national consulting company, we understand that many of our employees travel regularly for work. As such, it is important that employees are comfortable when they travel, that travel does not take too much time from their work or home lives, and that travel is not a burden for those who spend much of their time on the road. We value our employees and believe that this new policy balances cost savings against the needs of our hard-working staff.

C

The centerpiece of the new policy is our company's new internal travel Web site, Travel Link. Beginning July 1, all travel must be booked through Travel Link. The site can be searched in the same way as commercial travel sites. Based on the locations and dates you provide, the site will offer options for plane tickets, car rentals, and hotels. You may select any of the three "best value" options listed for your criteria. You may select an option that is not a "best value" option only with approval from your manager. A manager must make an electronic approval in the system before an exception can be made. We are confident that travel booked through the site will provide convenient options and that you will find the new site efficient and easy to use.

3. The sentences below are part of the first paragraph of the memo. Drag and drop each sentence into its logical position on the chart.

A) The second goal was to ensure that employees were not unduly inconvenienced or penalized.
B) Before deciding on this policy, a team of employees was given two major goals in examining our current processes.
C) In an effort to control company costs and to establish a consistent process across our three locations, we are instituting a new travel policy for all staff.
D) Last week, the team made its final recommendation to company management, and the new policy was unanimously approved.
E) The first goal was to see how our travel policies might be improved in a way that would limit costs.

UNIT 4

DIRECTIONS: Read the passage, read each question, and choose the **best** answer.

TIPS FOR MAKING JEWELRY

A

(1) Today, many people enjoy making their own earrings and bracelets. (2) Making your own jewelry is easier than you might think. (3) All you really need to get started is the desire to be creative. (4) Now, a simple online search provides a variety of free instruction. (5) In the past, you had to take special classes to learn the correct technique.

B

(6) What does it take to get started making jewelry? (7) Beads come in a variety of shapes, colors, and sizes. (8) You will find the best selection of beads at hobby shops and craft stores. (9) For many people, the best materials to start with are beads. (10) Among the basic supplies that you will need are a bead tray, a bead board, beading needles, twisted wire needles, and beeswax. (11) You will also want to have tweezers, scissors, a beading awl, wire cutters, and flat-nose pliers.

C

(12) You can pick up the basic skills you need to get started making jewelry in several ways. (13) For example, you might go online and do a search for instructional videos and Web sites. (14) Also, you can get a book from the craft store or from a local library. (15) On the other hand, you may just decide to let your imagination run wild. (16) Some Web sites include great step-by-step demonstrations.

D

(17) It takes practice to develop the skill needed to become really good at jewelry-making. (18) As you start, however, a note of caution for beginners: keep your projects simple. (19) If you are patient, you will learn the necessary skills without making expensive mistakes. (20) Soon enough, you will be crafting your own earrings, bracelets, and necklaces. (21) You may even experiment with more expensive materials, such as semiprecious gemstones. (22) You will be able to create pieces of jewelry that are your own unique designs.

4. Which is the **best** place for sentence 4? **Now, a simple online search provides a variety of free instruction.**

   A. Move sentence 4 to follow sentence 5.
   B. Move sentence 4 to follow sentence 2.
   C. Remove sentence 4.
   D. Move sentence 4 to follow sentence 1.

5. Which is the **best** place for sentence 9? **For many people, the best materials to start with are beads.**

   A. Move sentence 9 to the beginning of paragraph B.
   B. Move sentence 9 to follow sentence 6.
   C. Move sentence 9 to follow sentence 7.
   D. Move sentence 9 to follow sentence 10.

6. Which is the **best** place for sentence 16? **Some Web sites include great step-by-step demonstrations.**

   A. Remove sentence 16.
   B. Move sentence 16 to follow sentence 14.
   C. Move sentence 16 to the beginning of paragraph C.
   D. Move sentence 16 to follow sentence 13.

7. Which is the **best** place for sentence 18? **As you start, however, a note of caution for beginners: keep your projects simple.**

   A. Move sentence 18 to follow sentence 19.
   B. Move sentence 18 to follow sentence 20.
   C. Move sentence 18 to follow sentence 21.
   D. Move sentence 18 to the beginning of paragraph D.

8. Which is the **best** place for sentence 22? **You will be able to create pieces of jewelry that are your own unique designs.**

   A. Move sentence 22 to the end of paragraph C.
   B. Move sentence 22 to the beginning of paragraph D.
   C. Move sentence 22 to follow sentence 20.
   D. Keep sentence 22 to where it is.

DIRECTIONS: Read the passage, read each question, and choose the **best** answer.

Dear Mr. Smith:

A

(1) You will be pleased to know that you are eligible for COBRA insurance benefits because you participated in a group health plan offered by your former employer. (2) COBRA can provide health benefits identical to those you had with your previous healthcare plan.

B

(3) You may find that the price of premiums is unmanageable. (4) The cost is so high because your former employer once paid for a large part of your insurance plan. (5) With COBRA coverage, you pay the entire amount. (6) Prudent Insurance Company is waiving its usual 2 percent administrative fee for customers who have recently lost their jobs. (7) If there is a downside to COBRA coverage, it is the cost to you.

C

(8) There are other positive aspects about COBRA that you should know. (9) For example, you can be covered from your last day of employment. (10) You may also qualify for a reduced COBRA premium. (11) This benefit means that you and your family will have insurance from the moment you leave your job, without a waiting period. (12) To qualify, you must have left your job after September 1, 2013.

D

(13) COBRA provides a safety net while you transition to your next job. (14) However, with COBRA, you are assured that you and your family will be taken care of in the event of illness or injury. (15) It offers you peace of mind. (16) Yes, the program is costly. (17) In the end, you will save money by participating in COBRA. (18) I believe it is worthwhile for your needs.

E

(19) Making a decision about your healthcare coverage is important. (20) Please feel free to contact me at any time. (21) Take the time to assess your needs. (22) Weigh all of the options available to you as you consider your choices.

9. Which is the **best** place for sentence 7? **If there is a downside to COBRA coverage, it is the cost to you.**

   A. Move sentence 7 to follow sentence 3.
   B. Move sentence 7 to follow sentence 4.
   C. Move sentence 7 to the beginning of paragraph B.
   D. Move sentence 7 to follow sentence 5.

10. Which is the **best** place for sentence 11? **This benefit means that you and your family will have insurance from the moment you leave your job, without a waiting period.**

    A. Remove sentence 11.
    B. Move sentence 11 to follow sentence 8.
    C. Move sentence 11 to follow sentence 12.
    D. Move sentence 11 to follow sentence 9.

11. Which is the **best** place for sentence 14? **However, with COBRA, you are assured that you and your family will be taken care of in the event of illness or injury.**

    A. Move sentence 14 to follow sentence 15.
    B. Move sentence 14 to the beginning of paragraph D.
    C. Move sentence 14 to follow sentence 19.
    D. Move sentence 14 to follow sentence 16.

12. Which is the **best** place for sentence 17? **In the end, you will save money by participating in COBRA.**

    A. Move sentence 17 to follow sentence 13.
    B. Remove sentence 17.
    C. Move sentence 17 to the beginning of paragraph D.
    D. Move sentence 17 to follow sentence 14.

13. Which is the **best** place for sentence 20? **Please feel free to contact me at any time.**

    A. Move sentence 20 to the beginning of paragraph E.
    B. Move sentence 20 to before sentence 22.
    C. Move sentence 20 to the end of paragraph E.
    D. Move sentence 20 to the end of paragraph D.

20 LESSON

Other Punctuation

Use with **Student Book** pp. 200–201

LANGUAGE ASSESSMENT TARGETS: L.2.2, L.2

1 Review the Skill

Punctuation makes written text easier to read. Like end marks and commas, other punctuation marks are meant to help clarify text. **Hyphens –** combine two modifiers. **Parentheses ( )** separate content that may not flow within the text. **Quotation marks " "** indicate the exact words that a person has spoken or written. **Colons :** introduce lists or examples, and **semicolons ;** connect two complete ideas.

2 Refine the Skill

By refining the skill of using punctuation correctly, you will improve your writing and test-taking abilities, especially as they relate to the GED® Reasoning Through Language Arts test. Study the explanations and examples below. Then answer the questions that follow.

▶ The sentences below show how punctuation can make texts easier to read.

Sentence Without Punctuation
This is a must win game we must do three things to win play tough defense force turnovers and put the ball in the end zone yelled the high strung coach.

Sentence With Punctuation
"This is a must-win game; we must do three things to win: play tough defense, force turnovers, and put the ball in the end zone!" yelled the high-strung coach.

a Remember to place the period in a sentence **outside** the close of the parenthesis. However, place the period **inside** the end quotation mark.

b When a question is part of a quotation, place the question mark inside the end quotation mark. When it is not, place the question mark outside the end quotation mark.

▶ Study the examples below.

Punctuation	Sentence
Hyphen	One of Harrison Ford's best-known roles is Indiana Jones.
Parentheses	Last winter, I reread *Catch-22* by Joseph Heller (my favorite author).
Quotation Marks	"Did you enjoy your holiday?" she asked.
Colon	Cindy has three pets: a dog, a cat, and a turtle.
Semicolon	Take an umbrella; rain is predicted for this evening.

1. **Will you join us for a barbecue on Labor Day?" she asked the new neighbor.** Which correction should be made to the sentence?

   A. Insert a comma after <u>Day</u>.
   B. Insert a quotation mark before <u>Will</u>.
   C. Remove the question mark after <u>Day</u>.
   D. Insert a hyphen after <u>new</u>.

2. **I am starting my diet <u>tomorrow "assuming I stick to my plan."</u>** Which is the **best** way to write the underlined portion of this sentence?

   A. <u>tomorrow, "assuming I stick to my plan."</u>
   B. <u>tomorrow: assuming I stick to my plan.</u>
   C. <u>tomorrow (assuming I stick to my plan).</u>
   D. <u>tomorrow; assuming I stick to my plan.</u>

UNIT 4

★ Spotlighted Item: **DROP-DOWN**

DIRECTIONS: Read the passage. From the drop-down list, choose the answer that **best** completes the sentence.

VOTE! A BASIC VOTING GUIDE

The Founders wrote the Constitution of the United States "to form a more perfect Union, establish Justice, [and] insure

| 3. Drop-down 1 | To help uphold these principles, every U.S. citizen over the age of 18 has the right and the responsibility to vote in local, state, and federal elections. Let's review some basic principles that every voter should follow before casting a ballot.

The first step in the voting process is to research the candidates and issues that will be on the next ballot;

| 3. Drop-down 2 | Months before Election Day, you will find summaries and opinions about the candidates and issues in newspapers, magazines, blogs, and Web sites. Be aware that a writer may have a certain agenda for or against a candidate or an | 3. Drop-down 3 | should read several sources to form a balanced point of view. As you gather information about the candidates and issues, determine which people and ideas align with your needs, values, and beliefs.

Another important step in the voting process is to find out where you will vote. After registering, you should receive a voter card in the mail that tells you where to vote. If you do not receive a card in the mail, call your state's board of elections to find out whether your registration has been recorded properly. When you arrive at your voting location on Election Day, be sure to have with you one of the following pieces of | 3. Drop-down 4 | a military identification card, or a utility bill.

Drop-Down Answer Options

3.1 A. domestic Tranquility.
B. domestic Tranquility."
C. domestic Tranquility".
D. "domestic Tranquility."

3.2 A. (a well informed voter is a good voter.
B. a well informed-voter is a good voter.
C. a well-informed voter is a good voter."
D. a well-informed voter is a good voter.

3.3 A. issue, therefore, you
B. issue; therefore, you
C. issue; therefore you
D. issue: therefore you

3.4 A. identification: a driver's license,
B. identification (a driver's license
C. identification; a driver's license
D. identification a driver's license

UNIT 4

★ Spotlighted Item: **DROP-DOWN**

DIRECTIONS: Read the passage. From the drop-down list, choose the answer that **best** completes the sentence.

HOW TO MAKE BARBECUE SAUCE

Even though you can find [4. Drop-down 1] sauce at the store, it's never quite as good as making it from scratch. Secret recipes for barbecue sauce have become the pride of barbecue masters in every state. If you're looking for a classic sauce that's easy to make, look no further. This recipe has the perfect balance of sweet, sour, and spicy.

You will need to set aside an hour or so to make your barbecue sauce. A good sauce requires time to cook so that the flavor is rich. First, add about two tablespoons of vegetable oil to a pan at medium heat. Add a chopped onion and three cloves of pressed garlic to the oil. Wait about five minutes, and then add the following [4. Drop-down 2] of ketchup, 1/2 cup of apple cider vinegar, 1/4 cup of Worcestershire sauce, 1/3 cup of dark brown sugar, and a tablespoon of chili powder. Depending on how spicy you like your sauce, add Tabasco sauce to taste. Then stir the ingredients slowly, allowing them to come to a low boil. Finally, reduce the heat and allow the sauce to simmer for about an hour.

While your sauce is simmering, fire up the barbecue, and prepare your favorite meats for grilling. This sauce is great on ribs, beef, chicken, and pork tenderloin. Serving one kind of meat surely will impress your [4. Drop-down 3] barbecue masters know to serve two or more kinds of meat. Brush the barbecue sauce on the meat near the end of cooking. If you apply the sauce too early, it will cause the sauce to burn instead of brown.

Now, you can tell your friends that you are a true barbecue master [4. Drop-down 4]

Drop-Down Answer Options

4.1 A. ready made-barbecue
   B. ready-made barbecue
   C. ready made barbecue
   D. ready, made barbecue

4.2 A. ingredients; 1 1/2 cups
   B. ingredients (1 1/2 cups
   C. ingredients: 1 1/2 cups
   D. ingredients, 1 1/2 cups

4.3 A. guests; however, the best
   B. guests, however, the best
   C. guests; however the best
   D. guests: however the best

4.4 A. (without giving away your secret recipe)
   B. "without giving away your secret recipe.
   C. without giving away your secret recipe.)
   D. (without giving away your secret recipe).

UNIT 4

DIRECTIONS: Read the passage. From the drop-down list, choose the answer that **best** completes the sentence.

HURRICANE AWARENESS WEEK

Ask yourself, [5. Drop-down 1] For those of us who live near the coast, [5. Drop-down 2] citizens is critical.

The Gulfport Emergency Response Agency is sponsoring Hurricane Awareness Week from June 21 through June 27. The purpose of this week is to help families respond to three important hurricane questions. The answers may save lives during a hurricane.

- Why is a hurricane dangerous?

- How might a hurricane affect me?

- What actions should I take in the event of a hurricane?

To answer these questions, participate in the following Hurricane Awareness Week activities:

Monday: Study famous hurricanes to learn about their causes and effects.

Tuesday: Help weather experts track hurricanes in the Atlantic, Caribbean, and Gulf of Mexico.

Wednesday: Learn about these hurricane [5. Drop-down 3] high winds, tornadoes, and flooding.

Thursday: Create a family safety plan.

Friday: Build a disaster [5. Drop-down 4]

All events are open to the public and will be held at the Gulfport Community Center.

Drop-Down Answer Options

5.1 A. "Am I prepared for a hurricane?"
B. Am I prepared for a hurricane?
C. "Am I prepared for a hurricane"?
D. "Am I prepared for a hurricane?

5.2 A. being "well prepared"
B. being well prepared
C. being well-prepared
D. (being well prepared)

5.3 A. hazards; storm surge,
B. hazards: storm surge,
C. hazards storm surge;
D. hazards, storm surge,

5.4 A. kit: including batteries, bottled water, and flashlights.
B. kit including (batteries, bottled-water, and flashlights).
C. kit; including batteries, bottled water, and flashlights.
D. kit (including batteries, bottled water, and flashlights).

Editing at Work

MARKETING, SALES, AND SERVICE

DIRECTIONS: Read the passage. From the drop-down list, choose the answer that **best** completes the sentence.

You are a telemarketer at a large cable company. You are editing a script that telemarketers will use when they speak to customers.

TELEMARKETING SCRIPT

Hello, [customer name], this is [your name], and I'm calling from Cost-Effective Cable Connections. Thank you for being a great customer. Am I calling at a good time?

[*Wait for the customer's response, and unless you get a firm "No,"*
| 1. Drop-down 1. | *to the next paragraph.*
*If customer gives a firm no, ask when a good time might
be to call again.*]

I'm calling today with a special promotion—you can start viewing the premium channel Sudsy today. With Sudsy, you will see all of the latest family dramas and romantic
| 1. Drop-down 2 | first! We can offer you this
channel free of charge for three months. Please note that this part of the call is being recorded. May I go ahead and add the channel to your package?

[*Wait for the customer's response. If Yes, say:*]

Great, and remember that for the next three months you can enjoy all of Sudsy's offerings free of charge. After that, you can continue using Sudsy for a charge of just $5.99 a month, which will be automatically added to
| 1. Drop-down 3 | bill, and you can cancel
the channel at any time.

[*Skip to last paragraph.*]

[*If No, say:*]

Are you sure you don't want to take advantage of this offer? Keep in mind that you won't lose any money by trying
| 1. Drop-down 4 | cancel at any time.

[*Wait for the customer's response. If Yes, go to paragraph 3,
above. If No, continue:*]

Thank you for taking the time to speak with me today. Cost-Effective Cable Company really appreciates your business!

Drop-Down Answer Options

1.1. A. will move
B. moving
C. moved
D. move

1.2. A. comedys
B. comedies
C. comedy's
D. comedies'

1.3. A. your
B. you're
C. yore
D. youre

1.4. A. it can
B. it you can
C. it, and you can
D. it, you can

UNIT 4

HOSPITALITY AND TOURISM

DIRECTIONS: Read the passage. From the drop-down list, choose the answer that **best** completes the sentence.

You are a travel agent working from home for a large firm. You are editing a memo that will be sent to all travel agents at the firm. The memo explains how to avoid Agency Debit Memos, which are expensive for the firm.

HOW TO AVOID AGENCY DEBIT MEMOS

Dear Travel Agent:

Now that you have been thoroughly trained in the Global Distribution System (GDS), you can book air travel for clients. However, because the GDS serves a number of different Central Reservation Systems (CRSs), you are dealing with a multitude of codes. A single mistake can result in our firm receiving an Agency Debit Memo (ADM). Airline carriers will fine our firm because of any mistakes you make.

Research from the Debit Memo Working Group (DMWG) shows that errors in taxes trigger a large number of ADMs. The rules for taxes are different for every country, so take [2. Drop-down 1].

Ticket exchanges and refunds [2. Drop-down 2] another trigger for ADMs. Try to avoid common mistakes. [2. Drop-down 3], agents often refund the entire price of a trip, only to learn afterward that taxes are non-refundable. Double check the exchange policy before entering the data.

Unfortunately, fraud is another source of problems resulting in ADMs. When identity thieves gain access to [2. Drop-down 4] purchase flights in bulk. They may then chargeback the cost of the flights, and the carrier will send an ADM for reimbursement by our firm. To avoid fraud, make sure to follow all verification procedures carefully.

Drop-Down Answer Options

2.1.
A. carefully the time to review them
B. the time to review them carefully
C. the carefully time to review them
D. the time to review carefully them

2.2.
A. was
B. were
C. is
D. are

2.3.
A. Subsequently
B. Consequently
C. For example
D. Although

2.4.
A. victims' credit cards, they may
B. victims', credit cards they may
C. victims' credit cards they may
D. victims' credit, cards they may

UNIT 4

Appendix

Glossary

Adjective: word that modifies or describes a noun or a pronoun

Adverb: word that modifies a verb, an adjective, or another adverb

Analogy: extended comparison to clarify an idea

Apostrophe: punctuation mark (') used to indicate possession or to form a contraction

Argument: statement expressing an opinion

Audience: readers of a text

Bias: not impartial; leaning to one side of an argument

Capitalization: *see Grammar Rules*

Categorize: to organize into groups based on specific criteria

Cause: action that makes another event happen

Character: person or being in a fictional work

Claim: statement about an issue or problem

Climax: part of the plot when the conflict is most intense

Collective noun: word that names a group of people, animals, or things

Colon: punctuation mark (:) used to introduce lists or examples

Combine sentences: *see Grammar Rules*

Comma: *see Grammar Rules*

Compare: to determine similarities

Complete sentence: *see Grammar Rules*

Complication: part of the plot that introduces conflicts the characters must confront and overcome; conflict

Conclusion (argumentative texts): statement that identifies what the author is trying to convince the readers of

Conclusion (extended response): final paragraph or sentence that summarizes the main ideas and details in order to confirm or prove the thesis

Conclusion (reading comprehension): broad inference based on smaller inferences

Connecting word: word that connects ideas or combines sentences

Connotation: emotional associations of a word that go beyond its definition

Context clue: detail that helps you figure out the meanings of unfamiliar words

Contraction: *see Grammar Rules*

Contrast: to determine differences

Counterclaim: objection to a claim or argument or expression of differing views about a topic

Dangling modifier: *see Grammar Rules–Modifier*

Data: any type of information, especially numbers and statistics

Denotation: word's dictionary definition or literal meaning

Draft: initial version of a writing

Effect: result of an action

Emotion (appeal to): persuasive appeal to feelings

Enumeration: listing details to emphasize an idea and/or create rhythm

Ethics (appeal to): persuasive appeal to credibility or sense of right and wrong

Evidence: facts, opinions, example, or other details that prove or disprove something. Valid evidence is accurate, reliable, complete, and relevant. Invalid evidence is inaccurate, unreliable, incomplete, or irrelevant. Relevant evidence is closely connected to the claims of the argument. Irrelevant evidence is not closely tied to the claims and may distract from the issue. Sufficient evidence is enough evidence to support an argument or claim. Insufficient evidence is not enough evidence to support an argument or claim.

Explanation: how or why evidence supports an argument or claim

Explicit: stated directly

Exposition: part of the plot that provides background information, introduces characters, and sets up events to come

Fact: detail that can be proven true

Falling action: part of the plot that occurs after the climax, when complications are being resolved

Faulty evidence: evidence that does not logically support a claim or that distorts information

Faulty reasoning: conclusion not supported by factual support

Figurative language: language that goes beyond its literal meaning

Format: method of organizing or presenting information. Information may be presented in text formats or in graphical formats, such as tables, charts, graphs, etc.

Future tense: *see Grammar Rules–Verb tense*

Generalization: broad statement that applies to entire groups of people, places, events, and so on

Genre: category of writing that has a particular form, content, or technique

Helping verb: *see Grammar Rules*

Homonyms: words that sound alike but have different meanings

Hyperbole: extreme exaggeration to achieve an effect

Hyphen: punctuation mark (-) used to combine two modifiers

Idiom: phrase with meaning that is unconnected to the underlying meaning of its component words

Imagery: language that appeals to the reader's senses to describe something

Implicit: unstated or implied

Inference: logical guess based on facts or evidence and prior knowledge

Insufficient: not enough

Introduction: first paragraph or sentence that gains readers' attention and introduces the thesis

Invalid: inaccurate, unreliable, incomplete, or irrelevant

Irony: expression of something that is different, and often the opposite, of its literal meaning

Irregular verb: *see Grammar Rules–Regular and irregular verbs*

Irrelevant: not tied closely to an idea, argument, or claim

Juxtaposition of ideas: placing opposing ideas together to emphasize contrast; also called antithesis

Logic (appeal to): persuasive appeal to reason

Main idea: most important idea in a paragraph or passage

Metaphor: direct comparison of two unlike things

Misplaced modifier: *see Grammar Rules–Modifier*

Modifier: *see Grammar Rules*

Narrator: observer or character who tells the story in fictional texts. A **first-person** narrator is a character in the story and can share only his or her own thoughts and feelings. First-person narrators use the pronoun *I* to tell the story. A **third-person** narrator is not a character in the story. A **limited** third-person narrator can share only one character's thoughts and feelings. An **omniscient** third-person narrator is all-knowing and can share the thoughts and feelings of all the characters. Third-person narrators use character names or the pronouns *he, she,* or *they,* to tell the story.

Noun: word that names a person, place, or thing

Object pronoun: pronoun that receives the action of a verb

Onomatopoeia: use of words that create the sounds they describe

Opinion: statement that reveals an author's viewpoint, judgement, or belief

Organizational structure: ordering of ideas in writing for a specific purpose

Organized: arranged so that details follow or lead to the topic sentence in a logical and orderly fashion

Paragraph: group of sentences that form a complete idea

Parallelism: repeating grammatically similar phrases to create rhythm or emphasize an idea

Parallel structure: *see Grammar Rules*

Parallelism: repeating grammatically similar phrases to create rhythm or emphasize an idea

Parentheses: punctuation marks ( ) that enclose information that is not critical to the meaning or structure of sentence

Past tense: *see Grammar Rules–Verb tenses*

Personification: giving human qualities to animals, inanimate objects, or elements in nature

Perspective: attitude toward a topic or subject

Persuade: to convince to do something or to think a certain way

Plot: series of events in a story. Plot consists of five stages: exposition, rising action, climax, falling action, and resolution.

Plural: indicates more than one

Point by point: structure that addresses a single point common to both subjects before moving to the next point

Point of view (fiction): *see Narrator*

Point of view (nonfiction): perspective and/or purpose with which an author writes a particular text

Position: author's point of view, stance, or attitude toward a topic

Possessive: *see Grammar Rules*

Premise: statement that leads to conclusion

Present tense: *see Grammar Rules–Verb tense*

Pronoun: *see Grammar Rules*

Pronoun-antecedent agreement: *see Grammar Rules–Pronoun*

Proper adjective: *see Grammar Rules–Capitalization*

Proper noun: *see Grammar Rules–Capitalization*

Punctuation: marks that provide structure within written text, such as periods (.), commas (,), question marks (?), and exclamation marks (!)

Purpose: reason an author writes a text. Common purposes include to describe, to inform, to persuade, and to entertain.

Qualifying statement: information that clarifies or highlights a point to make it more certain or that presents an exception to make it less certain

Quotation marks: punctuation marks (" ") that appear immediately before and after something that someone has said

Reasoning: process used to show that a conclusion is true

Regular verb: *see Grammar Rules–Regular and irregular verbs*

Relevant: tied closely to an idea, argument, or claim

Repetition: repeating words or phrases to create rhythm, emphasize an idea, or build to a climax

Resolution: part of the plot when conflicts are resolved and the story ends

Review: to read over writing to identify errors that can be corrected or to identify problems or weaknesses that can be improved

Revise: to make changes or corrections to improve writing

Rhetorical device: special way of using language to communicate a message effectively or to achieve a desired effect

Rising action: part of the plot that introduces complications, or conflicts

Run-on sentence: *see Grammar Rules*

Sarcasm: specific form of verbal irony that is intended to be satirical or hurtful

Semicolon: punctuation mark (;) used between two complete ideas

Sentence fragment: *see Grammar Rules*

Sequence: order in which events or steps occur

Setting: place and time in which events happen in fictional works

Signal word: word that shows how ideas are connected

Simile: comparison of two unlike things using the words *like* or *as*

Singular: indicates just one thing

Standard English: commonly agreed-upon form of the English language in writing and speaking. It includes rules of usage, spelling, grammar, pronunciation, vocabulary, and punctuation.

Structure: arrangement of ideas in a text

Style: way in which an author communicates thoughts or feelings

Subject by subject: structure that addresses one subject and all related points before moving to the next subject

Subject pronoun: pronoun that performs an action or is described

Subject: person or thing doing the action or being described in a sentence

Subject-verb agreement: *see Grammar Rules*

Sufficient: enough

Summary: restatement of the main points and important details in your own words

Supporting detail (extended response): detail that supports the topic sentence in a logical way

Supporting detail (reading comprehension): detail that provides more information about the main idea

Symbol: something that both stands for itself and represents something else

Synthesize: to combine ideas from one source or multiple sources to form a new idea

Textual evidence: details from the source texts that support your thesis

Theme: insight or general idea about life or human nature revealed by fictional works

Thesis: key statement or claim that answers the question posed by the prompt

Tone: author's attitude toward a topic as revealed through word choice

Topic sentence: sentence that explains the main idea of a paragraph; often the first sentence in a paragraph

Transition: word that shows connections or relationships between ideas

Transitional language: words or phrases that show how ideas are connected

Understatement: representing something as smaller or less intense to achieve an effect

Valid: accurate, reliable, complete, and relevant

Verb tense: *see Grammar Rules*

Verb: word that states an action or state of being

Visual: graphic representation of information

Grammar Rules

Capitalization: Proper nouns and proper adjectives, including titles, holidays, days of the week, and months of the year, are capitalized.

- ➤ **proper noun:** a name that identifies a particular person, place, or thing
  - the <u>C</u>leveland <u>C</u>avaliers
- ➤ **proper adjective:** a description based on a proper name
  - <u>G</u>erman sausages

Combine sentences: Short, related sentences can be combined to make writing more cohesive.

- ➤ **use connecting words:** I drove to the gas station. I drove to the mall.
  - I drove to the gas station *and* the mall.
- ➤ **create a list:** My son likes baseball. My son likes cars. My son likes ice cream.
  - My son likes baseball, cars, and ice cream.
- ➤ **use a semicolon:** They went to see a movie. It was a scary one.
  - They went to see a movie; it was a scary one.

Comma: A comma separates a sentence into meaningful units. It is used to represent a pause or to connect clauses or phrases.

- ➤ **to form a series:** I made roast chicken, mashed potatoes, and a salad for dinner.
- ➤ **after an introductory phrase:** To get to the restaurant, she had to take the bus.
- ➤ **to set off an interrupting or descriptive phrase:** My sister, who is in the Air Force, came home for Christmas.
- ➤ **to combine sentences:** We went to the game, and we stopped for burgers on the way home.
- ➤ **when using two or more adjectives:** She ran a long, hard race.

Complete sentence: A complete sentence must contain a subject, a verb, and appropriate end punctuation. A complete sentence will present a complete idea.

- ➤ Nick loved to skateboard.

Contraction: A contraction occurs when two words are shortened to one word by replacing a letter or letters with an apostrophe. Contractions are used in informal writing.

- ➤ Examples: they + have = they've, it + is = it's

Helping verb: A helping verb indicates that actions have occurred at various points in time.

- ➤ **past perfect tense:** used to indicate that an action took place in the past before another past action was completed. The word *had* appears before the main verb.
  - We *had driven* for more than three hours before we arrived at my aunt's house.

- ➤ **present perfect tense:** used to indicate that an action began in the past and continues into the present. The word *has* or *have* appears before the main verb.
  - He *has worked* there for more than a year.
- ➤ **future perfect tense:** used to indicate that an action will be completed at a specific time in the future. The words *will have* appear in front of the main verb.
  - By the end of the month, we *will have saved* enough money for a DVD player.

Modifier: A modifier describes, clarifies, or provides details about other words in a sentence. Avoid a **misplaced modifier,** which misleads readers by describing the wrong word in the sentence, or a **dangling modifier,** which does not apply logically to any word in the sentence.

- ➤ **misplaced modifier:** I only ran one mile. **correct:** I ran only one mile.
- ➤ **dangling modifier:** Running down the street, my long scarf blew across my face. **correct:** While I was running down the street, my long scarf blew across my face.

Parallel structure: A sentence with parallel structure displays the same pattern to indicate that two or more ideas are of equal importance.

- ➤ **wrong:** Both my sister's friend and the cousin of my friend work at the mall.
- ➤ **correct:** Both my sister's friend and my friend's cousin work at the mall.

Parentheses: Parentheses are used to separate text and often contain nonessential information—the sentence is intact without the parenthetical material.

- ➤ After work, Ryan drove to the gym (the one on Jefferson Road).

Plural noun: Often, a noun is made plural simply by the addition of *-s* or *-es*.

- ➤ add *-s* to most nouns: bottles, books
- ➤ add *-es* to nouns ending in *o*: tomatoes (tomato), heroes (hero)
- ➤ add *-es* to nouns ending in *ch, sh, ss, z,* or *x*: taxes (tax), churches (church)
- ➤ for nouns that end in *y* after a consonant, drop the *y* and add *-ies*: puppies (puppy), cities (city)
- ➤ for nouns that end in *f* or *fe*, drop the *f(e)* and add *-ves*: wives (wife), thieves (thief)
- ➤ some nouns change form: women (woman), teeth (tooth)
- ➤ some nouns don't change at all: fish, sheep

Possessive: Possessives show ownership. Possession is indicated by the use of an apostrophe and s ('s) or by an s followed by an apostrophe (s').

> for singular nouns, use an apostrophe and add s: **dog's** bone

> for most singular nouns ending in s, use an apostrophe and add s: **Mars's** moon

> for plural nouns ending in s, use only an apostrophe: **players'** meeting

Pronoun: A pronoun is a word that takes the place of a noun.

> **Examples:** *you, he, she, it, they, we, them, him, her, myself, whoever, whomever, each, somebody*

> The noun a pronoun replaces is called an antecedent. **Pronoun-antecedent agreement** occurs when pronouns agree in gender and number with their antecedents.

> • Sharon drove Keith home after work. **Replace nouns with pronouns**: *She* drove *him* home after work.

Regular and irregular verbs: Regular verbs indicate past, present, and future tenses when -*ed*, -*s*, or -*ing* is added to the base verb. Irregular verbs are less consistent; the spelling of such verbs often changes to indicate a particular tense.

Run-on sentence: A run-on sentence occurs when two or more sentences are joined incorrectly. A run-on sentence can be corrected by adding a connecting word, adding a comma and a connecting word, or creating two separate sentences.

> **wrong:** I met a friend at the movies we had a good time.

> **correct:** I met a friend at the movies, and we had a good time.

Sentence fragment: A sentence fragment does not express a complete idea.

> **Example:** Two days after it rained.

Subject-verb agreement: In a sentence, subjects and verbs must agree in person and number.

> **wrong:** Amber and I am going out to eat Friday.

> **right:** Amber and I *are* going out to eat Friday.

Verb tense: The three basic verb tenses are *past, present,* and *future.* Using the correct tense of the verb lets your readers know whether events have occurred in the past, are happening now, or will happen in the future. In the **past tense,** regular verbs end in -*d* or -*ed* (*walk* becomes *walked*). Irregular verbs often indicate the past tense by a spelling change (*eat* becomes *ate*). In the **present tense,** a regular verb maintains its root form (*make, walk, come*) or adds an -*s* (*makes, walks, comes*). In **future tense,** the helping verb *will* appears in front of the main verb (*move* becomes *will move*).

Frequently Confused Words

Some frequently confused words are homonyms. These are words that sound the same or nearly the same but are spelled differently and have different meanings. Sometimes the two words may be spelled alike but have different meanings. Below is a list of frequently confused words. Learn these words and you will be sure of using the right word every time.

accept: *to receive; to endure; to approve*
except: *to exclude; excluding*

affect: *to influence*
effect: *a result*

ate: *past tense of eat*
eight: *the number 8*

be: *to exist*
bee: *an insect*

beat: *to strike or hit*
beet: *a type of root vegetable*

board: *a piece of wood*
bored: *uninterested*

brake: *to stop*
break: *to damage or destroy; a rest period*

buy: *to get by paying money*
by: *near; according to*

capital: *city that is the seat of government; money to invest; very important*
capitol: *building in which the legislature meets*

cell: *a small room, as in a prison*
sell: *to offer for sale*

cent: *a penny*
scent: *to smell*
sent: *caused to go; transmitted*

close: *to shut; to finish; near*
clothes: *something to wear on the body, usually made of cloth*

complement: *to go with; to make whole*
compliment: *flattering words*

coarse: *rough or harsh*
course: *a path or track; part of a meal*

dear: *much loved; sweet*
deer: *an animal*

desert: *a dry, barren, sandy region*
dessert: *the final, usually sweet, course of a meal*

feat: *an accomplishment*
feet: *plural of foot*

flour: *ground grain used in making bread*
flower: *the bloom or blossom on a plant*

for: *to be used as; meant to belong to*
four: *the number 4*

grate: *to shred*
great: *very good*

hear: *to listen*
here: *in this place*

hole: *opening*
whole: *entire*

hour: *60 minutes*
our: *belonging to us*

its: *possessive of it*
it's: *contraction of it is*

knew: *was certain of*
new: *modern; recent*

know: *to have information*
no: *not at all; opposite of yes*

lessen: *to decrease*
lesson: *something that is taught*

leave: *to go away*
let: *to allow*

loose: *not tight*
lose: *to fail to keep or win*

made: *created*
maid: *a person who cleans*

mail: *letters or packages delivered by the post office*
male: *man or boy; the opposite of female*

main: *most important*
mane: *the hair of a horse or lion*

meat: *animal flesh that is eaten*
meet: *to get together*

one: *the number 1*
won: *past tense of win*

pail: *a bucket or tub*
pale: *light in color*

pain: *soreness, aching*
pane: *the glass in a window*

passed: *went by*
past: *a time before; opposite of future*

patience: *ability to wait*
patients: *plural of patient*

peace: *freedom from war; harmony; calm*
piece: *a part of something*

plain: *ordinary; simple*
plane: *airplane; a flat surface*

pole: *a long piece of wood or metal*
poll: *a listing of people; a vote*

principal: *first in rank; the head of a school*
principle: *a rule or belief*

quiet: *silent; still*
quite: *completely; really; positively*

right: *correct; opposite of <u>left</u>*
write: *to form visible words*

road: *a path or street*
rode: *past tense of the verb <u>ride</u>*

role: *a part played*
roll: *to turn over; a type of bread*

scene: *a view; part of a play or movie*
seen: *past participle of <u>see</u>*

sea: *the ocean*
see: *to look at*

set: *to put or lay something in a place*
sit: *to rest oneself on a chair or perch*

sight: *the ability to see*
site: *a place or location*

some: *a few*
sum: *the total amount*

stake: *a pointed piece of metal or wood for driving into the ground*
steak: *a slice of beef or fish for cooking*

steal: *to take dishonestly or unlawfully*
steel: *a hard, tough metal*

than: *a conjunction used to compare two things, as in <u>larger than</u> or <u>more than</u>*
then: *an adverb meaning at that time, next, or after*

their: *belonging to them*
there: *at or in that place*
they're: *a contraction of the words <u>they are</u>*

threw: *past tense of <u>throw</u>*
through: *in one side and out the other side*

to: *in the direction of*
too: *in addition; very*
two: *the number <u>2</u>*

wait: *to stay until something happens; to serve food at a meal*
weight: *how heavy something is*

weak: *opposite of <u>strong</u>*
week: *seven days*

wear: *to have clothing on the body*
where: *referring to a place*

weather: *the climate*
whether: *in case; in either case*

who's: *contraction of <u>who is</u> or <u>who has</u>*
whose: *possessive of <u>who</u>*

wood: *what trees are made of*
would: *helping verb; also, the past tense of <u>will</u>*

you're: *contraction of <u>you are</u>*
your: *belonging to you*

Frequently Misspelled Words

Although most word processing programs include a spell-checker, you won't be able to count on that feature when you write your essay for the GED® Reasoning Through Language Arts test. Below is a list of some commonly misspelled words for you to study.

A

a lot
absence
accept
accident
achieve (*When in doubt, think i before e, except after c, and words that say "hey!" as in neighbor and weigh.*)
accommodate
address
again
against
agree
all right
almost
already
although
always
appear
approach
argue
attention
August
author
awful
awkward

B

balloon
beautiful
because
beginning
being
believe
benefit
between
bicycle
borrow
business

C

calendar
captain
career
cereal
chief
coffee
college
congratulate
curiosity

D

daily
daughter
definitely
delicious
describe
difference
different

discover
disease
distance
dollar
doubt

E

easy
education
effect
eight
either
embarrass
emergency
English (The *E* is always capitalized.)
enough
environment
equipment
especially
excellent
except
exercise
extreme

F

familiar
February
financial
forehead
foreign
former
fourteen
fourth
friend
further

G

gallon
general
genius
government
governor
grammar
grateful
great
grocery
guard
guess

H

half
happiness
healthy
heard
heavy
height
heroes
holiday
hopeless

hospital
hurrying

I

immediately
increase
independence
independent
innocence
instead
interrupt
invitation
island

J

January
jealous

K

kitchen
knowledge

L

language
laugh
library
license
light
likely
losing
loyal

M

maintenance
marriage
mathematics
measure
medicine
million
muscle
mystery

N

natural
necessary
neighbor
neither
niece
night

O

o'clock
occasion
ocean
often
operate
opinion

P

parallel
particular
patience
people
perfect
perform
perhaps
permanent
personal
personality
picture
piece
poison
political
positive
possess
potatoes
prepare
prescription
probably
produce
professional
profit
promise
pronounce

Q

quality
quiet
quite

R

raise
realize
reason
receipt
receive
recipe
recognize
recommend
relieve
responsible
restaurant
rhythm
ridiculous
right
roommate

S

sandwich
scene
schedule
science
season
secretary
sense
separate
service
sight
signal
similar
since
soldier
sophomore
soul
source
special
stomach
strength
stretch
succeed
successful
supposedly
surprise

sweat
sympathy

T

technical
though
through
together
tomorrow
tongue
toward
tragedy
tries
twelfth
twelve

U

unnecessary
unusual
usual

V

vacuum
valuable
variety
vegetable
view
voice
volume

W

weather
Wednesday
weird
whether
which
while

Verb Conjugation Tables

to be	past	present	future	past perfect	present perfect	future perfect
I	was	am	will be	had been	have been	will have been
you	were	are	will be	had been	have been	will have been
he/she/it	was	is	will be	had been	has been	will have been
we	were	are	will be	had been	have been	will have been
they	were	are	will be	had been	have been	will have been

to say	past	present	future	past perfect	present perfect	future perfect
I	said	say	will say	had said	have said	will have said
you	said	say	will say	had said	have said	will have said
he/she/it	said	says	will say	had said	has said	will have said
we	said	say	will say	had said	have said	will have said
they	said	say	will say	had said	have said	will have said

to make	past	present	future	past perfect	present perfect	future perfect
I	made	make	will make	had made	have made	will have made
you	made	make	will make	had made	have made	will have made
he/she/it	made	makes	will make	had made	has made	will have made
we	made	make	will make	had made	have made	will have made
they	made	make	will make	had made	have made	will have made

to become	past	present	future	past perfect	present perfect	future perfect
I	became	become	will become	had become	have become	will have become
you	became	become	will become	had become	have become	will have become
he/she/it	became	becomes	will become	had become	has become	will have become
we	became	become	will become	had become	have become	will have become
they	became	become	will become	had become	have become	will have become

to come	past	present	future	past perfect	present perfect	future perfect
I	came	come	will come	had come	have come	will have come
you	came	come	will come	had come	have come	will have come
he/she/it	came	comes	will come	had come	has come	will have come
we	came	come	will come	had come	have come	will have come
they	came	come	will come	had come	have come	will have come

to live	past	present	future	past perfect	present perfect	future perfect
I	lived	live	will live	had lived	have lived	will have lived
you	lived	live	will live	had lived	have lived	will have lived
he/she/it	lived	lives	will live	had lived	has lived	will have lived
we	lived	live	will live	had lived	have lived	will have lived
they	lived	live	will live	had lived	have lived	will have lived

to have	past	present	future	past perfect	present perfect	future perfect
I	had	have	will have	had had	have had	will have had
you	had	have	will have	had had	have had	will have had
he/she/it	had	has	will have	had had	has had	will have had
we	had	have	will have	had had	have had	will have had
they	had	have	will have	had had	have had	will have had

to read	past	present	future	past perfect	present perfect	future perfect
I	read	read	will read	had read	have read	will have read
you	read	read	will read	had read	have read	will have read
he/she/it	read	reads	will read	had read	has read	will have read
we	read	read	will read	had read	have read	will have read
they	read	read	will read	had read	have read	will have read

to bring	past	present	future	past perfect	present perfect	future perfect
I	brought	bring	will bring	had brought	have brought	will have brought
you	brought	bring	will bring	had brought	have brought	will have brought
he/she/it	brought	brings	will bring	had brought	has brought	will have brought
we	brought	bring	will bring	had brought	have brought	will have brought
they	brought	bring	will bring	had brought	have brought	will have brought

to write	past	present	future	past perfect	present perfect	future perfect
I	wrote	write	will write	had written	have written	will have written
you	wrote	write	will write	had written	have written	will have written
he/she/it	wrote	writes	will write	had written	has written	will have written
we	wrote	write	will write	had written	have written	will have written
they	wrote	write	will write	had written	have written	will have written

to begin	past	present	future	past perfect	present perfect	future perfect
I	began	begin	will begin	had begun	have begun	will have begun
you	began	begin	will begin	had begun	have begun	will have begun
he/she/it	began	begins	will begin	had begun	has begun	will have begun
we	began	begin	will begin	had begun	have begun	will have begun
they	began	begin	will begin	had begun	have begun	will have begun

to take	past	present	future	past perfect	present perfect	future perfect
I	took	take	will take	had taken	have taken	will have taken
you	took	take	will take	had taken	have taken	will have taken
he/she/it	took	takes	will take	had taken	has taken	will have taken
we	took	take	will take	had taken	have taken	will have taken
they	took	take	will take	had taken	have taken	will have taken

to lay	past	present	future	past perfect	present perfect	future perfect
I	laid	lay	will lay	had laid	have laid	will have laid
you	laid	lay	will lay	had laid	have laid	will have laid
he/she/it	laid	lays	will lay	had laid	has laid	will have laid
we	laid	lay	will lay	had laid	have laid	will have laid
they	laid	lay	will lay	had laid	have laid	will have laid

to sell	past	present	future	past perfect	present perfect	future perfect
I	sold	sell	will sell	had sold	have sold	will have sold
you	sold	sell	will sell	had sold	have sold	will have sold
he/she/it	sold	sells	will sell	had sold	has sold	will have sold
we	sold	sell	will sell	had sold	have sold	will have sold
they	sold	sell	will sell	had sold	have sold	will have sold

to leave	past	present	future	past perfect	present perfect	future perfect
I	left	leave	will leave	had left	have left	will have left
you	left	leave	will leave	had left	have left	will have left
he/she/it	left	leaves	will leave	had left	has left	will have left
we	left	leave	will leave	had left	have left	will have left
they	left	leave	will leave	had left	have left	will have left

to run	past	present	future	past perfect	present perfect	future perfect
I	ran	run	will run	had run	have run	will have run
you	ran	run	will run	had run	have run	will have run
he/she/it	ran	runs	will run	had run	has run	will have run
we	ran	run	will run	had run	have run	will have run
they	ran	run	will run	had run	have run	will have run

to sit	past	present	future	past perfect	present perfect	future perfect
I	sat	sit	will sit	had sat	have sat	will have sat
you	sat	sit	will sit	had sat	have sat	will have sat
he/she/it	sat	sits	will sit	had sat	has sat	will have sat
we	sat	sit	will sit	had sat	have sat	will have sat
they	sat	sit	will sit	had sat	have sat	will have sat

to lose	past	present	future	past perfect	present perfect	future perfect
I	lost	lose	will lose	had lost	have lost	will have lost
you	lost	lose	will lose	had lost	have lost	will have lost
he/she/it	lost	loses	will lose	had lost	has lost	will have lost
we	lost	lose	will lose	had lost	have lost	will have lost
they	lost	lose	will lose	had lost	have lost	will have lost

to know	past	present	future	past perfect	present perfect	future perfect
I	knew	know	will know	had known	have known	will have known
you	knew	know	will know	had known	have known	will have known
he/she/it	knew	knows	will know	had known	has known	will have known
we	knew	know	will know	had known	have known	will have known
they	knew	know	will know	had known	have known	will have known

Extended Response Scoring Rubrics

Score	Description
	Trait 1: Creation of Arguments and Use of Evidence
2	• Generates text-based argument(s) and establishes a purpose that is connected to the prompt • Cites relevant and specific evidence from source text(s) to support argument (may include few irrelevant pieces of evidence or unsupported claims) • Analyzes the issue and/or evaluates the validity of the argumentation within the source texts (e.g., distinguishes between supported and unsupported claims, makes reasonable inferences about underlying premises or assumptions, identifies fallacious reasoning, evaluates the credibility of sources, etc.)
1	• Generates an argument and demonstrates some connection to the prompt • Cites some evidence from source text(s) to support argument (may include a mix of relevant and irrelevant citations or a mix of textual and non-textual references) • Partially analyzes the issue and/or evaluates the validity of the argumentation within the source texts; may be simplistic, limited, or inaccurate
0	• May attempt to create an argument or lacks purpose or connection to the prompt or does neither • Cites minimal or no evidence from source text(s) (sections of text may be copied from source) • Minimally analyzes the issue and/or evaluates the validity of the argumentation within the source texts; may completely lack analysis or demonstrate minimal or no understanding of the given argument(s)

Non-scorable Responses (Score of 0/Condition Codes)
- Response exclusively contains text copied from source text(s) or prompt
- Response shows no evidence that test-taker has read the prompt or is off-topic
- Response is incomprehensible
- Response is not in English
- Response has not been attempted (blank)

Courtesy of the GED® Testing Service

Score	Description
	Trait 2: Development of Ideas and Organizational Structure
2	• Contains ideas that are well developed and generally logical; most ideas are elaborated upon • Contains a sensible progression of ideas with clear connections between details and main points • Establishes an organizational structure that conveys the message and purpose of the response; applies transitional devices appropriately • Establishes and maintains a formal style and appropriate tone that demonstrate awareness of the audience and purpose of the task • Chooses specific words to express ideas clearly
1	• Contains ideas that are inconsistently developed and/or may reflect simplistic or vague reasoning; some ideas are elaborated upon • Demonstrates some evidence of a progression of ideas, but details may be disjointed or lacking connection to main ideas • Establishes an organization structure that may inconsistently group ideas or is partially effective at conveying the message of the task; uses transitional devices inconsistently • May inconsistently maintain a formal style and appropriate tone to demonstrate an awareness of the audience and purpose of the task • May occasionally misuse words and/or choose words that express ideas in vague terms
0	• Contains ideas that are insufficiently or illogically developed, with minimal or no elaboration on main ideas • Contains an unclear or no progression of ideas; details may be absent or irrelevant to the main ideas • Establishes an ineffective or no discernable organizational structure; does not apply transitional devices, or does so inappropriately • Uses an informal style and/or inappropriate tone that demonstrates limited or no awareness of audience and purpose • May frequently misuse words, overuse slang or express ideas in a vague or repetitious manner

Non-scorable Responses (Score of 0/Condition Codes)
- Response exclusively contains text copied from source text(s) or prompt
- Response shows no evidence that test-taker has read the prompt or is off-topic
- Response is incomprehensible
- Response is not in English
- Response has not been attempted (blank)

Courtesy of the GED® Testing Service

APPENDIX

Score	Description
	Trait 3: Clarity and Command of Standard English Conventions
2	• Demonstrates largely correct sentence structure and a general fluency that enhances clarity with specific regard to the following skills: 1) varied sentence structure within a paragraph or paragraphs 2) correct subordination, coordination and parallelism 3) avoidance of wordiness and awkward sentence structures 4) usage of transitional words, conjunctive adverbs and other words that support logic and clarity 5) avoidance of run-on sentences, fused sentences, or sentence fragments • Demonstrates competent application of conventions with specific regard to the following skills: 1) frequently confused words and homonyms, including contractions 2) subject-verb agreement 3) pronoun usage, including pronoun antecedent agreement, unclear pronoun references, and pronoun case 4) placement of modifiers and correct word order 5) capitalization (e.g., proper nouns, titles, and beginnings of sentences) 6) use of apostrophes with possessive nouns 7) use of punctuation (e.g., commas in a series or in appositives and other non-essential elements, end marks, and appropriate punctuation for clause separation) • May contain some errors in mechanics and conventions, but they do not interfere with comprehension; overall, standard usage is at a level appropriate for on-demand draft writing.
1	• Demonstrates inconsistent sentence structure; may contain some repetitive, choppy, rambling, or awkward sentences that may detract from clarity; demonstrates inconsistent control over skills 1–5 as listed in the first bullet under Trait 3, Score Point 2 above • Demonstrates inconsistent control of basic conventions with specific regard to skills 1–7 as listed in the second bullet under Trait 3, Score Point 2 above • May contain frequent errors in mechanics and conventions that occasionally interfere with comprehension; standard usage is at a minimally acceptable level of appropriateness for on-demand draft writing.
0	• Demonstrates consistently flawed sentence structure such that meaning may be obscured; demonstrates minimal control over skills 1–5 as listed in the first bullet under Trait 3, Score Point 2 above • Demonstrates minimal control of basic conventions with specific regard to skills 1–7 as listed in the second bullet under Trait 3, Score Point 2 above • Contains severe and frequent errors in mechanics and conventions that interfere with comprehension; overall, standard usage is at an unacceptable level for on-demand draft writing OR • Response is insufficient to demonstrate level of mastery over conventions and usage

Non-scorable Responses (Score of 0/Condition Codes)
• Response exclusively contains text copied from source text(s) or prompt
• Response shows no evidence that test-taker has read the prompt or is off-topic
• Response is incomprehensible
• Response is not in English
• Response has not been attempted (blank)

Courtesy of the GED® Testing Service

Answer Key

UNIT 1 READING COMPREHENSION

LESSON 1, pp. 2–5

1. **C; DOK Level: 2; Reading Assessment Target:** R.2.1. The main idea of the passage is that older adults receive great benefits from exercise. Answers A, B, and D are details provided to support the main idea.

2. **A; DOK Level: 2; Reading Assessment Targets:** R.2.5, R.3.5, R.5.2. The second paragraph develops the main idea by providing a more detailed explanation of the four types of exercises and their benefits to older adults, so answer A is correct. Answers B, C, and D focus on specific details in the second paragraph, not on the second paragraph as a whole.

3. **D; DOK Level: 2; Reading Assessment Target:** R.2.1. The detail that people spend more than half of their day sitting or being inactive supports the main idea that people should move more instead of kicking back and relaxing. Answers A, B, and C are not main ideas; they are details that provide examples of what people are doing instead of moving.

4. **B; DOK Level: 2; Reading Assessment Targets:** R.2.1, R.2.5, R.5.1, R.5.2. The information in paragraph 3 supports the main idea that being inactive has negative effects. The passage does not state that the effects of sitting all day can be reversed nor that there are any long-term benefits of being sedentary. This paragraph does not discuss the effects of being active.

5. **A; DOK Level: 2; Reading Assessment Target:** R.2.1. The main idea of paragraph 2 is that studies have found you improve your chance for good health when you move. The other answer options provide details about the research results cited.

6. **C; DOK Level: 2; Reading Assessment Targets:** R.2.1, R.2.5, R.3.5. The passage's reference to the fact that when metabolism slows, you burn fewer calories and boost the chance that extra energy will be stored as fat provides a supporting detail in paragraph 6. This information explains and supports the main idea of paragraph 6. This statement is not an implicit or explicit main idea of the passage or a topic sentence for paragraph 6.

7. **C; DOK Level: 2; Reading Assessment Target:** R.2.1 The author clearly believes that all wildlife, especially birds, should be protected from harm. President Roosevelt likely would support the statement in answer A, but he does not mention people protecting nature, nor does he address a specific group. Answer B states his feelings about birds and supports his main idea, but it is not the main idea itself. Answer D incorrectly restricts the scope of possible legislation.

8. **B; DOK Level: 2; Reading Assessment Target:** R.2.1. Although the paragraph begins with a mention of the seasons, this statement is a detail of the main idea, which appears in the statement "I only wish that besides protecting the songsters, the birds of the grove, the orchard, the garden and the meadow, we could also protect the birds of the sea shore and of the wilderness." Therefore, answer A is incorrect, and answer B is correct. Answer C is incorrect because the author does not indicate the level of danger. Answer D summarizes a detail about the beauty of birds in different seasons and is, therefore, not the main idea.

9. **C; DOK Level: 2; Reading Assessment Targets:** R.2.1, R.2.5. Answer C best supports the main idea that laws must be made to protect birds. This detail specifically references legislation to protect birds. While all of the other answers support the main idea, answer C is the most explicit.

10. **B; DOK Level: 2; Reading Assessment Targets:** R.2.5, R.3.5, R.5.1, R.5.4. The author's comparison of the loss of pigeons with the possible loss of the Catskill Mountains extends his theme that birds deserve protection even though they may not seem as grand or important as other features of nature, such as mountains. Answer A is incorrect because Roosevelt does not state that the Catskills are endangered but asks the reader to imagine that they might be. Answers C and D are incorrect; although pigeons and the mountains are wild things and cannot protect themselves, these claims do not reflect the author's purpose in the comparison.

11. **A; DOK Level: 2, Reading Assessment Target:** R.2.4. Answer A is correct because the author compares the loss of a species with such losses. Answer B is a detail about the loss of a species of forest bird. Answer C is only a part of the main idea and may be misread as the main idea because it appears at the end of the paragraph. Answer D is a detail that supports the main idea.

12. **C; DOK Level: 2; Reading Assessment Target:** R.2.1. Answer C is correct: Segregation deprives minority children of an equal chance for a good education, as indicated in paragraphs 2, 3, and 4. The passage does state that every child needs a good education to succeed. It also states that education is perhaps the most important function of state and local governments. But neither of these is a statement of the main idea. Therefore, answers A and D are incorrect. Answer B is incorrect because the claim is not supported in this passage and would be a supporting detail if it were.

13. **A; DOK Level: 2; Reading Assessment Targets:** R.2.1, R.2.5, R.5.1, R.5.2. The information in paragraph 3 supports the conclusion that segregation in schools creates feelings of inferiority in black children, thus lowering their self-esteem. The passage does not state that most white people want to send their children to segregated schools. The effect of segregation on white children is also not explained. Answer D is incorrect because the passage discusses at length the possible effect of segregation on black children.

14. **D; DOK Level:** 2; **Reading Assessment Targets:** R.2.4, R.2.5. Answer D is correct because it is the only one that directly addresses the roots of racial prejudice at the base of the practice of segregation. Answers A, B, and C address the sense of inferiority some children feel or address the impact of the policy and lack of benefits to black children under this system, but they do not address the racial prejudice at its core.

15. **A; DOK Level:** 2; **Reading Assessment Targets:** R.2.1, R.2.5, R.5.1, R.5.2. Answer A supports the main idea because the sense of inferiority that affects motivation is a barrier to obtaining a good education. Answer B is incorrect because white children's achievement in segregated schools is not mentioned in the passage. Answers C and D are irrelevant generalizations.

LESSON 2, *pp. 6–9*

1. **C; DOK Level:** 2; **Reading Assessment Target:** R.2.2. Answer C is the best summary because it reproduces the general conclusion of the article: In a food chain, energy flows from the sun to producers and then to the consumers. Answers A, B, and D are details and do not cover the most important information of the passage as a whole.

2. **D; DOK Level:** 2; **Reading Assessment Targets:** R.2.2, R.5.1. This sentence explains the function of the food chain in terms of energy flow from producers to consumers and thus summarizes the passage (answer D). The sentence does not provide additional information about consumers or producers, so answers A and B are incorrect. The second paragraph is about consumers, not food chains, so answer C is incorrect.

3. **B; DOK Level:** 2; **Reading Assessment Target:** R.2.2. Answer B is the most inclusive statement about the findings of the study. Answer A is also a finding; however, it explains only part of the findings and does not mention that fewer arrests were made, nor does it consider other factors. The decreased percentage (answer C) is a detail supporting the main idea, which is about the overall result of the study. Answer D misstates an opinion of criminologists; it is not a result of the study.

4. **B; DOK Level:** 2; **Reading Assessment Target:** R.2.2. Answer B summarizes the most important information in the paragraph. Answer A is the first sentence in the paragraph, but it does not provide much information about these results. In addition, the writer of the summary has inserted his or her opinion. Answer C is partly correct, but it does not indicate the need for therapy, which is the key point in the paragraph. Answer D is an extension of what the paragraph indicates; nothing is mentioned about jobs.

5. **D; DOK Level:** 2; **Reading Assessment Targets:** R.2.1, R.2.2. Answer D states the most important information in the paragraph. Answer A introduces the information, but it is not as specific as answer D. Answers B and C provide additional information about the main idea.

6. **C; DOK Level:** 2; **Reading Assessment Targets:** R.5.1, R.5.2, R.5.3. Although the last paragraph often summarizes the entire passage, it does not do so in this case. Therefore, answer A is incorrect. The clear clue word, *Another*, indicates that the paragraph will include more information rather than summarize what comes before it (answer C). Answer B is incorrect as well, as the information in the paragraph reflects another aspect of the study not discussed in the previous paragraph. Answer D is incorrect because the study reveals more than one negative result.

7. **D; DOK Level:** 2; **Reading Assessment Target:** R.2.2. The main point of the first paragraph is that Johnson has come to ask for the support, or help, of all Americans. Answers A, B, and C are ideas that he conveys in the paragraph, but they do not express the main idea.

8. **B; DOK Level:** 2; **Reading Assessment Target:** R.2.2. Answer B is correct because it is the most thorough summary of the paragraph. Johnson does say that Kennedy's death was a terrible event, but he says more in the paragraph than just a reference to the assassination. Although Johnson urges Government to act decisively, the passage does not mention that the country is paralyzed. Answer D has less information than answer B and, therefore, is not the best choice.

9. **A; DOK Level:** 2; **Reading Assessment Targets:** R.2.2, R.5.1, R.5.2, R.5.4. Paragraph 3 summarizes the key points of Johnson's presidential agenda. He is asking support for specific programs and policies and lists several in the paragraph. These are a continuation of Kennedy's plans, although not necessarily Kennedy's past accomplishments. They are not Johnson's past achievements but rather his goals for the future.

10. **C; DOK Level:** 2; **Reading Assessment Targets:** R.2.2, R.5.1, R.6.4. The final words, "let us continue," refer to the desire to continue Kennedy's policies and programs. Johnson adapts Kennedy's statement, "let us begin." He seeks support to continue in the direction that Kennedy began. He does not wish to start over but rather to continue. Although Johnson may hope that Kennedy is not forgotten, that is not his point here. Although Johnson earlier mentioned the burden of his presidency, he is not referring to a burden in this statement.

11. **D; DOK Level:** 2; **Reading Assessment Targets:** R.2.1, R.2.2. The author's main point is that the Muselmanner are tragic because they are unaware of who and where they are. He repeats this idea by saying that they "felt nothing" and "were dead and did not know it." Although it is true that they are prisoners in Auschwitz, their situation as prisoners is not what makes them most tragic. Answer C is incorrect because the author states the opposite: they feel no hunger, thirst, or pain. The tragedy is more than merely where they are.

12. **A; DOK Level:** 2; **Reading Assessment Target:** R.2.2. The author says "anger can be creative," but indifference "is never creative." He also says that indifference "elicits no response." The best summary is answer A. The author does not suggest that anger and hatred go away quickly, nor does he say that anger and hatred are simpler emotions than indifference.

13. **C; DOK Level:** 2; **Reading Assessment Target:** R.2.2. The author says that indifference is an "end" as a way of saying that nothing comes after it; indifference does not lead to any action by people or result in a response to human suffering. He does not say that indifference occurs after anger and hatred but instead compares indifference with them. He compares indifference with a living death but does not indicate that it is the last step before death, even though it could be. Therefore, B is not the best answer. Although indifference does hurt people, he does not say that it is a goal of people who aim to hurt others.

UNIT 1 *(continued)*

14. D; DOK Level: 2; Reading Assessment Targets: R.2.2, R.5.1, R.6.4. The correct answer is D because the author believes strongly that the offense of indifference is so great that its impact is felt on many levels, it is both wrong and destructive to the self. Answer A is incorrect because that is not implied in this passage. Answer B is incorrect because the author shows in this sentence that the impact on the indifferent is extremely damaging. While answer C is true, it is not the main focus of this statement.

15. A; DOK Level: 2; Reading Assessment Targets: R.2.2, R.6.1. The author's primary point in the passage is that indifference is a punishment because it denies people their humanity. People are left with "no hope" and are exiled "from human memory." The best summary is answer A. Indifference is not good; the author calls it "evil." Indifference is not equal to hatred; it is worse than hatred because hatred can be productive. Although the author might agree that indifference should be fought, this idea is a conclusion one might make from the passage, not the best summary of it.

LESSON 3, *pp. 10–13*

1. B; DOK Level: 1; Reading Assessment Target: R.3.1. The text states that Identification Order 1 was created in December of 1919 and the Ten Most Wanted List was created in 1950. Therefore, using subtraction, the correct answer is 31 years.

2. DOK Level: 1; Reading Assessment Targets: R.3.1, R.5.3. This is the correct sequence for the flowchart: 1) **Powell serves as National Security Advisor.** 2) **Powell serves as Chairman of Joint Chiefs of Staff.** 3) **Powell founds America's Promise.** 4) **George W. Bush appoints Powell as Secretary of State.** The sequence reflects the order in which important events in Powell's life occurred. In biographes, events may be presented out of chronological order, so proper sequencing requires careful attention to dates and signal words, such as *after* and *during*.

3. DOK Level: 1; Reading Assessment Target: R.3.1. The correct order of the timeline is as follows: January 1, 1777: **Dr. Waldo joins the First Connecticut Infantry Regiment.** November 10, 1777: **Dr. Waldo begins journaling at Valley Forge.** December 8, 1777: **Dr. Waldo's regiment is called to gather in front of the Washington barracks.** October 1, 1779: **Dr. Albigence Waldo resigns from service.**

4. DOK Level: 1; Reading Assessment Targets: R.3.1, R.5.3. 1) **The bill is referred to committee.** 2) **The committee holds hearings on the bill.** 3) **The committee votes to report the bill.** 4) **The House votes to pass the bill.** 5) **The Senate votes to pass the bill.** 6) **The President signs the bill into law.** The sequence of steps is clearly presented in the passage.

HIGH IMPACT LESSON: SEQUENCE OF EVENTS, *pp. 14–15*

1. C; DOK Level: 2; Reading Assessment Targets: R.3.1. The text states that the previous step is: "The server receives the request and interprets it." Answer A includes information about a different type of server, so it is incorrect. Answers B and D both show steps that occur *after* the web server assembles the content, so they are incorrect.

2. A; DOK Level: 2; Reading Assessment Targets: R.3.1. According to the passage, the music's volume levels adjusted as the last part of Step 1. Answers B, C, and D all include information about steps that happen after the music's volume levels are adjusted, so they are incorrect.

3. D; DOK Level: 2; Reading Assessment Targets: R.3.1. According to the passage, in Step 2 "The lathe cuts grooves into an aluminum disc." Mixing equipment is used to add or remove vocals, instruments, and other elements, so answer A is incorrect. Although it is not specifically stated in the passage, printers are generally used to create adhesive labels, so answer B is incorrect. According to the passage, electroplating requires a tank of liquid with dissolved nickel, so answer C is incorrect.

4. B; DOK Level: 2; Reading Assessment Targets: R.3.1. The chemical coating on the master disc appears in Step 3, which provides information on the electroplating process that fuses the nickel to the silver. The passage does not say that chemical coating is needed for the music editing, lathing, or extruding processes, so answers A, C, and D are incorrect.

5. D; DOK Level: 2; Reading Assessment Targets: R.3.1. Step 5 tells readers that the adhesive labels need to be placed on the plastic biscuits before they are pressed. After the metal stamper presses the biscuits into finished records would be too late to create the labels. Recording and mixing the music, creating the metal stamper, and loading the PVC pellets all occur before this step, so answers A, B, and C are incorrect.

6. C; DOK Level: 2; Reading Assessment Targets: R.3.1. According to the passage, the records are trimmed before they are packaged. Creating the labels, pressing the biscuits, and loading the PVC pellets are all steps that happen much earlier in the process, so answers A, B, and D are incorrect.

LESSON 4, *pp. 16–19*

1. B; DOK Level: 1; Reading Assessment Target: R. 2.1. In this passage, the author makes a connection between the age of a voter and the voter's mobility. Older voters have less mobility and, therefore, are more likely to be registered and more likely to vote. Where a voter lives is relevant to the author's point, but the relevance relates to the idea of mobility, not specific location. The author does not discuss a voter's free time or interest in politics.

2. C; DOK Level: 2; Reading Assessment Targets: R.5.1, R.5.2. The second paragraph provides additional explanation for the connection between a voter's age and mobility as they relate to voting and voter registration. Answer A is incorrect; although the author does mention registration, it is not discussed in detail nor is it the purpose of the paragraph. Answer B is incorrect because the author mentions only younger voters and mobility. No other categories are mentioned. Answer D is incorrect because the author does not discuss how age is defined.

3. DOK Level: 1; Reading Assessment Target: R.2.1, R.2.5. The web should contain these minerals: **calcium**, **arsenic**, **zinc**, and **iron**.

4. **D; DOK Level: 1; Reading Assessment Target:** R.2.1. The author states that "where plants and factories had closed down, they found empty main streets." These towns have a lack of industry in common. Although Wagner discusses Forest City, Iowa, she does not say that the towns visited were all in or near Iowa. The vibrant towns with proud employees are those towns with successful industry, not those that lack it. No ties to farming are mentioned in the passage.

5. **A; DOK Level: 1; Reading Assessment Target:** R.2.1. Forest City, Iowa, is offered as an example of a type of town with a vibrant community and a successful factory, where employees take pride in their work. It is not a town with fading industry. Answer B is incorrect because the Winnebago factory is not a service industry. A factory produces a product; it does not provide a service. Although tourists may visit the factory, the town thrives because of the industry itself, not the tourists. Forest City may be a thriving community in Iowa, and Iowa may have other such communities, but the author does not limit these communities to a single state (as indicated in paragraph 1).

6. **B; DOK Level: 3; Reading Assessment Targets:** R.2.4, R.2.5, R.2.7, R.2.8. The author does not explicitly describe a conscious consumer but refers to "conscious consumerism" in paragraph 4. Although the author refers to conscious consumerism in this instance as buying American products, it is a narrow definition of the term. The best description is "someone who cares about how and where a product is made." This description requires readers to synthesize key points made throughout the passage about why Sarah Wagner wants to buy American. Key points include references both to employees of companies who take "pride in their work" and to the importance of supporting American companies because they help keep American communities vibrant. Answers A and D are details of answer B. Flexibility in answer C may in fact apply to answer B, but flexibility may apply as well to anything involving shopping. Therefore, the answer is too broad a statement.

7. **A; DOK Level: 3; Reading Assessment Targets:** R.2.3, R.2.7. Answer A is correct. In paragraph 5 the writer specifically calls out gift giving as a way to support American-made products. While the other answers may be correct, they are not in the text.

8. **A; DOK Level: 2; Reading Assessment Target:** R.2.5. A realist, according to the passage, is someone who does not expect to buy American-made products all the time but tries to do so when feasible. The passage contains no comparisons between the quality of American-made products and imported products; the purchase of American products is to keep American industry in business. The passage does not mention the expense of American-made products. The fact that Wagner has the time and the commitment to look for American-made products (answer D) might be a sub-category, but it does not explain the idea of what a realist is.

9. **B; DOK Level: 3; Reading Assessment Targets:** R.2.3, R.2.4, R.2.7. The author implicitly defines a heritage brand as "American-made clothing and accessories." The reference to "style" blogs suggests that this category is related to clothing or fashion. The word *heritage* implies a long-standing brand. The best answer is that a sweater made in the United States by a long-standing American brand would be categorized as a heritage brand. Answer A states that the computer is made in China. Answer C states that the shirt is made in Italy. Answer D does not specify where the jeans are made.

10. **D; DOK Level: 2; Reading Assessment Targets:** R.5.1, R.5.4. Paragraph 3 mentions Apple as an example of a company that is responding to the demand for more American-made products. Therefore, answer D is correct. Although paragraph 3 may explain something about a niche market, its purpose is to provide an example, not to explain a term. Therefore, answer A is not the best choice. Answer B is incorrect because there is a contradiction of ideas. Answer C is incorrect because paragraph 3 does not refer to style blogs, nor has it anything to do with clothing. This information appears in paragraph 2.

11. **A; DOK Level: 2; Reading Assessment Targets:** R.2.5, R.5.1. The author states that manufacturing "benefits other sectors that support its operations," making the point that manufacturing helps create jobs in many other industries. The other answer options are statements made in the passage but do not directly relate to how manufacturing as a category of industry affects the creation of American jobs.

12. **C; DOK Level: 3; Reading Assessment Targets:** R.2.3, R.2.7. In paragraph 6, American-made electronics and appliances are identified as categories of products that are difficult to find. Therefore, a digital camera would be most difficult to find. The other answer choices are examples of categories that are easier to find.

LESSON 5, *pp. 20–23*

1. **D; DOK Level: 2; Reading Assessment Targets:** R.2.1, R.2.5. The passage states the remains of plants and animals contain carbon and that when left on the ground, these remains become a source of energy for microbes in soil. Answer A describes photosynthesis, not decomposition. Answer B describes respiration, not decomposition. Answer C relates to plant and animal remains that are "safe from microbes" and become fossil fuels.

2. **B; DOK Level: 1; Reading Assessment Targets:** R.2.1, R.2.5. The passage indicates that tissues and bones are destroyed. Answer A is incorrect because the passage does not mention infection. Answer C is incorrect because the remains sink to the bottom of the ocean before they are compressed. Answer D is incorrect because carbon, not tissue and bone, are released into the atmosphere.

3. **A; DOK Level: 2; Reading Assessment Target:** R.2.1. The first four lines of the passage indicate that both parties "screamed government waste," suggesting they believed $90 million was too much to spend, so answer A is correct. Answer B is incorrect because nothing is mentioned about new solutions. Answer C is incorrect because both parties agreed that the topic is important. The results of the study were published in the same month in which the passage was published. Answer D misstates the information in paragraph 1.

4. **C; DOK Level: 1; Reading Assessment Target:** R.2.1. Paragraph 3 clearly states the result of Kieffer's conclusion: that violent video games increased short-term hostility. Therefore, answer C is correct. Answers A, B, and D are incorrect because they misstate or contradict information in the passage.

5. **B; DOK Level:** 3; **Reading Assessment Targets:** R.3.4, R.5.2. The author cites the court case as consistent with public opinion that violent video games do not cause long-term violent effects; therefore, watching a violent video cannot be a defense for murder because a murder would suggest more than a momentary effect. The study found that the effects were only short term. The age of the defendant was not relevant to the question or the jury's verdict.

6. **DOK Level:** 1; Reading Assessment Targets: R.2.1, R.2.5. The possible effects of hyperthermia are **heat edema**, **malfunctioning organs**, and **brain damage**, as indicated in paragraphs 4 and 5. Lowered body temperature and sweating prevent hyperthermia. Sensitivity to extreme heat could cause someone to be susceptible to hyperthermia. Leg pain is not mentioned in the passage.

7. **B; DOK Level:** 1; **Reading Assessment Target:** R.2.1. Answer B is correct, as stated in paragraph 2. Answer A may be close, but not all three-leafed plants are poison ivy. Because poison ivy comes from direct contact with urushiol, blisters do not contain the substance and thus do not cause the reaction. Answer D may seem plausible, but the words in the answer choice do not state specifically that the poison ivy plant is being burned, and the passage indicates that inhalation may cause lung damage rather than a rash.

8. **D; DOK Level:** 2; **Reading Assessment Target:** R.2.1. Answer D is correct because this information appears in paragraph 4. Answer A contradicts information in the passage; urushiol causes the allergic reaction; it does not protect against it. Infection is caused by bacteria from the fingernails; urushiol does not decrease susceptibility to infection. More urushiol makes the case more severe, but nothing in the passage distinguishes between the severity of individual symptoms; therefore, answer C is incorrect.

9. **C; DOK Level:** 1; **Reading Assessment Target:** R.2.1. Answer C is the only possible choice because only urushiol causes the spread of the rash. Answers A and D contradict information in the passage. Answer B might seem plausible, but nothing is mentioned about urushiol on the animal's fur.

10. **B; DOK Level:** 2; **Reading Assessment Target:** R.2.1. Paragraph 4 specifically states that a cause of blisters appearing in a straight line could be from the plant brushing against the skin in a straight line. The other options are not explanations provided in the text.

11. **B; DOK Level:** 1; **Reading Assessment Target:** R.2.1. Answer B is the only possible choice, as the information is stated in paragraph 6. Answers A, C, and D are incorrect because the blisters do not contain urushiol, which is the only substance that causes the rash to appear and to spread, nor does scratching the rash affect the lungs and nasal passages.

12. **A; DOK Level:** 3; **Reading Assessment Targets:** R.2.7, R.3.4. Answer A is correct. Washing might get rid of urushiol. Answers B, C, and D may be true, but the information has nothing to do with poison ivy.

1. **B; DOK Level:** 2; **Reading Assessment Targets:** R.2.1, R.3.4. The passage indicates that Lincoln and Radical Republicans in Congress had differing views about how the nation should be rebuilt and lists aspects of each side's plan. By analyzing the examples provided for each plan, you can determine that Lincoln's objective was to bring together the northern and southern states in a cohesive whole and that the Radical Republicans intended to diminish the role of the Confederates in the restored nation. The passage does not address timelines for the plans or provide information about how much responsibility for Reconstruction either plan delegated to state governments. The plans did not call for similar treatment of the Confederate states; only the Radical Republicans' plan imposed harsh penalties on the Confederacy.

2. **A; DOK Level:** 2; **Reading Assessment Targets:** R.2.1, R.3.2, R.3.4. The information in the passage indicates that Lincoln hoped to rebuild the nation and keep peace by extending forgiveness to the Confederates, whereas the Radical Republicans believed that the Confederates should be punished severely. Both plans may have been considered bold or ambitious, although the passage does not provide enough information to make this determination.

3. **B; DOK Level:** 2; **Reading Assessment Targets:** R.3.4, R.5.2. In paragraph 3, the author says that Dr. Smith-Spangler wanted to answer the question of whether there were benefits to eating organic food and thus introduces the elements that will be compared: organic and non-organic produce, as specified in paragraph 4. Answer A is incorrect because the first two paragraphs give a reason for buying organic food. Although answer C may seem possible, the quotations are not explained; rather, the answers to the questions are introduced. Answer D is incorrect because this conclusion appears later in the passage.

4. **D; DOK Level:** 2; **Reading Assessment Targets:** R.3.4, R.5.2. Answer D is correct because organic farms do not use synthetic fertilizers and pesticides, whereas conventional farms often do. Answer A is incorrect because it would seem that organic farms treat animals better, even though a value judgment is not made in the passage. Conventional farms may use synthetic fertilizers; organic farms are not permitted to use synthetic fertilizer, but this ban does not extend to natural fertilizers. Answer C is a misreading of the text. Organic farms do not give antibiotics to animals, but conventional farms often do. The comparison is incorrect because conventional farms do both, and organic farms do neither.

5. **A; DOK Level:** 1; **Reading Assessment Target:** R.2.1. Dr. Smith-Spangler found that both organic and non-organic plant and animal products had the same amount of vitamin content. Nothing is mentioned about the taste of food before or after cooking. The level of antibiotic-resistant bacteria varied, and more phosphorus appeared in organic products.

6. **B; DOK Level:** 2; **Reading Assessment Targets:** R.2.5, R.3.4, R.3.5, R.5.1. Although conventional farms may or may not be careful with pesticides, care in using them does not affect the outcome. Pesticide levels were considerably higher in non-organic food, so if pesticides are considered unhealthful and thus to be avoided, the correct answer is B. All organic meat is not mentioned, only pork and chicken. In addition, the statement is an exaggeration of the text, which mentions the lower likelihood of containing the bacteria. The author does mention the slightly higher level of phosphorus but treats it as less significant than the pesticide level.

7. DOK Level: 2; Reading Assessment Targets: R.3.4. Saturated Fats: **Raises LDL, Increases heart disease;** Unsaturated Fats: **Mostly plant sources, Reduces heart disease;** Both: **Provides energy, Helps vitamin absorption**

8. C; DOK; Level: 2; Reading Assessment Targets: R.2.1, R.2.4, R.2.8, R.3.4. Both documents were created to govern the states. When the Articles of Confederation proved insufficient, American leaders had to establish another kind of government. Answer A is incorrect because all states ratified the Articles of Confederation, but only nine states were needed to ratify the original Constitution. Answer B is incorrect because *55* refers to the number of delegates who attended the Constitutional Convention, not the number of signatures on either document. Answer D is a misreading of the passage. Paragraph 2 mentions the Northwest Ordinance in relation to the creation of new states. Neither the Articles of Confederation nor the U.S. Constitution is part of that document.

9. B; DOK Level: 2; Reading Assessment Targets: R.2.1, R.2.2, R.2.4, R.3.4. The reason for creating the U.S. Constitution was the failure of the Articles of Confederation to provide a strong national government. Therefore, answer B is correct. Answer A is incorrect because both documents provided plans for admitting new states. The U.S. Constitution, not the Articles of Confederation, established three branches of government. Answer D is incorrect because the Bill of Rights was added to the Constitution; nothing is mentioned in the passage about the Articles of Confederation's containing a Bill of Rights.

10. D; DOK Level: 2; Reading Assessment Targets: R.2.1, R.2.2, R.2.5. Answer D is correct, according to the information in paragraph 3 which mentions both legislatures. Answer A has the information reversed. Answer B is incorrect because the Constitution established the presidency and Supreme Court. Nothing is mentioned in the passage about these specific provisions in the Articles of Confederation. Answer C is incorrect because the Articles provided for one legislative branch, not three, whereas the U.S. Constitution provided for two.

11. D; DOK Level: 3; Reading Assessment Target: R.2.7. Only answer D would have been possible because under the Articles of Confederation, states collected taxes. The U.S. Constitution gave this power to the national government. Answer A is incorrect; Congress could not collect taxes. Answer B is incorrect because all states had to ratify a constitutional amendment. Answer C is incorrect because under the Articles of Confederation, each state had a single representative.

12. B; DOK Level: 2; Reading Assessment Targets: R.2.1, R.2.2, R.3.4. Because the states had more power than the national government, they could function individually by levying taxes and coining money. The stronger national government provided by the Constitution removed much power from the states. Answer A is incorrect because nothing in the passage states or implies that the Articles listed individual rights or responsibilities. Nothing is mentioned about patterning the documents on French or British models. Answer D is a misreading of the passage. The Articles were written after the colonies became independent, and the framers of the U.S. Constitution deliberately created a strong national government.

1. C; DOK Level: 2; **Reading Assessment Target:** R.5.3. The word *Although* is used to contrast the benefits of clusters (shared resources) with the drawbacks (increased competition). Answer A is incorrect because the sentence does not show a cause-and-effect relationship. While "shared resources" is an example of a benefit, the word *Although* is not used to merely give an example of a benefit, so answer B is incorrect. Since the sentence gives a drawback and a benefit, answer D is incorrect.

2. A; DOK Level: 2; **Reading Assessment Target:** R.5.3. The word *However* is used to make a contrast between the sentence's two ideas that "infectious disease rates have dropped" and that "the rates of noncommunicable diseases—specifically, chronic diet-related diseases—have risen." Since infectious diseases have decreased, answers B, C, and D are incorrect.

3. C; DOK Level: 2; **Reading Assessment Target:** R.5.3. The phrase *due in part to* shows a cause-and-effect relationship. Changes in lifestyle behaviors are partly the cause of the rising "rates of noncommunicable diseases—specifically, chronic diet-related diseases." Answer A is incorrect. Lifestyle behaviors is not an example of chronic diet-related disease. The sentence does not compare or contrast chronic diet-related diseases and lifestyle behaviors, so answers B and D are incorrect.

4. D; DOK Level: 2; **Reading Assessment Target:** R.5.3. The first sentence describes how a "history of poor eating and physical activity patterns" have increased with time. The second sentence describes how these same behaviors have contributed "to significant health challenges that now face the U.S. population." Answers A, B, and C each include phrases from these sentences but do not describe the behaviors set out in the first sentence. They are incorrect.

5. D; DOK Level: 2; **Reading Assessment Target:** R.5.3. The last sentence in paragraph 2 lists examples that support the previous sentence. The phrase *These include* signals this relationship. Answers A and B are incorrect. The phrase does not show a comparison or create a sequence. Answer C is incorrect. The phrase does not create a contrast.

6. B; DOK Level: 2; **Reading Assessment Target:** R.5.3. The phrase *not to mention* is used to add information about the results of these conditions (high rates of overweight and obesity). While the sentence details two specific effects caused by these results, the phrase *not to mention* does not show this cause-and-effect relationship, so answer A is incorrect. Answer C is incorrect because the sentence does not provide any benefits to these conditions. While the sentence does note two different results of these conditions, it does not compare them.

ANSWER KEY

LESSON 7, *pp. 30–33*

1. **A; DOK Level:** 2; **Reading Assessment Target:** R.6.1. The author's point of view is that alternative energy sources will only gain widespread use when their cost is competitive with existing sources of energy, such as oil and gas. Answers B, C, and D are not supported by the passage.

2. **C; DOK Level:** 2; **Reading Assessment Targets:** R.4.3/L.4.3, R.5.1, R.5.2, R.6.1, R.6.4. The author uses the word *utopia* to advance his point of view that alternative energy is not yet in widespread use. Conaway says that "we will get there," so answer A is incorrect. Conaway does not dismiss alternative energy outright, so answers B and D are incorrect.

3. **DOK Level:** 3; **Reading Assessment Targets:** R.2.3, R.6.1, R.6.3. The completed chart should include **freedom of speech**, **traditional American ideals**, **thoughtful political debate** in the Smith supports column and **special treatment for political leaders**, **thought control**, and **making unsupported claims** in the Smith opposes column. The author indicates her support of traditional American ideals and freedom of speech when she discusses and lists the basic principles of Americanism. Her speech itself is part of a thoughtful political debate, so she clearly supports such discussions. She criticizes senators for engaging in character assassination, so she opposes making unsupported claims. She is critical of senators' inability to take the same type of criticism they are delivering; therefore, she does not believe in special treatment for political leaders. She refers specifically to thought control in the last sentence as a dangerous consequence of curtailed freedoms; her opposition to thought control, therefore, is clear.

4. **A; DOK Level:** 2; **Reading Assessment Targets:** R.4.3/L.4.3, R.6.1. Words such as *rejected* and *second-rate* indicate the author's point of view about foreign medical schools. Answers B, C, and D are incorrect because they contradict what the author states in paragraph 1.

5. **C; DOK Level:** 2; **Reading Assessment Targets:** R.6.1, R.6.2. The author agrees with the statement in answer C, as indicated by the situations addressed in the passage. Although students receiving foreign training will benefit from the proposal, answer A does not reflect the author's point of view about this statement. If the proposal offered a good compromise, it would not cause bitter controversy. Therefore, answer B is incorrect. The author makes no comment about whether the proposal has or lacks reasoning.

6. **B; DOK Level:** 2; **Reading Assessment Targets:** R.6.1, R.6.2. Answer A is incorrect because it may allow students to do clinical training in the United States, which is what the parents would like. Therefore, answer B is correct because the proposal does address this concern. The proposal does not fully agree with the parents' viewpoint because the proposal mentions rating the schools—this is not on the parents' agenda, according to the passage. The proposal does not fully agree or disagree with the parents' viewpoint about returning students.

7. **D; DOK Level:** 2; **Reading Assessment Targets:** R.2.7, R.6.1, R.6.2. The author is aligned with the Association of American Medical Colleges in questioning the quality of training received in foreign medical schools and in permitting students enrolled in them to return to the United States for clinical training in American hospitals. Even the title of the editorial emphasizes the author's disapproval. Answers A and B are incorrect because the New York Board of Regents, not medical educators, has addressed parents' concerns. Answer C is incorrect because the points of view of the students themselves have not been mentioned.

8. **C; DOK Level:** 2; **Reading Assessment Targets:** R.3.5, R.6.1. The editorial reflects considerable knowledge about the actions of the Fish and Wildlife Service; state laws in Wyoming, Montana, and Idaho; statistics about the killing of wolves; and Judge Molloy's recent decision. Answer A is incorrect because the author seems to have considerable information at hand. Answer B is incorrect because nothing is mentioned about the judge's previous decisions. Although the author may be opposed to hunting, nothing is stated in the passage. If there is an implication that the author opposes hunting, the answer nonetheless is not as clear as answer C, and thus is not the best answer.

9. **C; DOK Level:** 2; **Reading Assessment Targets:** R.4.3/L.4.3, R.6.1. The use of the word *slaughter* to discuss the need to maintain protections for gray wolves demonstrate the author's support for protecting them. While the other options support the protections, they do not share the strong language used in answer C.

10. **B; DOK Level:** 2; **Reading Assessment Targets:** R.4.3/L.4.3, R.6.1. Judge Molloy is irritated, if not angry, with the Fish and Wildlife Service, as evidenced in his decision to restore federal protection for gray wolves, in the language he used ("flip-flopped"), and by the author's reference to the judge's being annoyed at the agency's failure to explain its actions. The judge is definitely not pleased, nor indifferent. On the contrary, he seems quite familiar with the actions of the Fish and Wildlife Service, as indicated in his findings and in the agency's failures.

11. **D; DOK Level:** 2; **Reading Assessment Target:** R.6.1. The author is writing an editorial, the purpose of which is to comment on a situation or event; it is not merely to inform or to advise that people inform themselves. Considering the strong language in the editorial, the author likely agrees with Judge Molloy. The author gives no indication of favoring any animal over another. By supporting Judge Molloy's rulings, the author demonstrates disagreement with the Wyoming, Montana, and Idaho relaxation of protection. Therefore, answer D is correct because the author most likely believes that the wolves should be protected.

12. **A; DOK Level:** 2; **Reading Assessment Targets:** R.3.4, R.3.5, R.6.1. By lifting the protections of the act, the Fish and Wildlife Service indicated its point of view that gray wolves were no longer endangered. Answer B is incorrect because the Service agreed with the Wyoming law and lifted protection for gray wolves. Conservation groups suing the Fish and Wildlife Service hope that the Service will be forced to present a better plan; doing so is not the Service's point of view on the subject of protecting gray wolves. Answer D is contrary to the lifted protection of gray wolves; the Fish and Wildlife Service does not seek to limit hunting.

1. **B; DOK Level:** 3; **Reading Assessment Targets:** R.2.4. The paragraph states that laser surgery for cosmetic purposes will not be covered. The reader can infer that medically necessary laser surgery will be covered.

2. **B; DOK Level:** 2; **Reading Assessment Targets:** R.2.3, R.4.3/L.4.3, R.5.1. Answers A, C, and D may be logical and accurate statements, but they do not reflect the best inference to make from the author's exact words, which imply that he is thinking about both the present circumstances of the land and its likely forgotten past. Answer B is correct because it implies that he is looking at a single place and perceiving it through different lenses, in this case the past and the present.

3. **D; DOK Level:** 2; **Reading Assessment Targets:** R.2.3, R.4.1 /L.4.1. Thoreau mentions the Musketaquid, a Native American people who lived in the area around Concord, Massachusetts. The relics mentioned are those left by the Musketaquid. Nothing in the paragraph relates to the author's family, his neighbors, or settlers.

4. **B; DOK Level:** 2; **Reading Assessment Targets:** R.2.3, R.4.1/L.4.1, R.4.3/L.4.3. The passage is about Thoreau and the Native Americans who inhabited the land; it is not about the author's direct ancestors. Thoreau implies that everything he does to the land erases memories of the Musketaquid. Although Thoreau does mention that others worked the land before him, the implication is explained in answer B and goes beyond the statement in answer C. No claims on the land are mentioned or implied.

5. **C; DOK Level:** 3; **Reading Assessment Targets:** R.2.3, R.2.4, R.4.1/L/4.1. The author suggests that decayed wood is part of an eternal cycle of life. The end of one piece of a tree's life is the beginning of life for "mosses and fungi." Generations have come before the decayed tree and generations will come after it. Although decay is a natural process, this information is not the author's suggestion in the paragraph. He does not imply that there are older forms of wood, but rather that this is a stage in an eternal cycle. Mosses and fungi are not older than decayed wood; instead they are the next stage in the cycle.

6. **C; DOK Level:** 3; **Reading Assessment Targets:** R.2.3, R.2.4, R.2.5, R.3.5. In the first sentence of paragraph 3, the author points out that nature has both "russet hues as well as green." Russet hues would represent dying plants while green hues would represent thriving plants. The author notes that the same thing can be considered both old and new at the same time, depending on how one looks at it.

7. **D; DOK Level:** 2; **Reading Assessment Targets:** R.2.3, R.2.4. In paragraph 1, the author explains that Alfred Nobel was "shaken by this condemnation" (being labeled "The Merchant of Death"), which implies he did not want to be known as that. Answer A is incorrect because the prize was for peace, not to credit the invention of dynamite. Answer B is incorrect because Nobel wanted more than to simply be remembered. Answer C is incorrect because nothing implies that he wanted to encourage people to invent things.

8. **B; DOK Level:** 2; **Reading Assessment Targets:** R.2.3, R.4.3/L.4.3. To answer this question, it helps to know that Al Gore lost the 2000 presidential election and was Vice President of the United States from 1992–2000. However, if you do not know this, you can assume that Gore's political hopes "died" in 2000 (see byline). Answer A is incorrect because no reference is made to an event occurring in 1992. Answer C is incorrect because the obituary has nothing to do with Gore's friend. Answer D is incorrect because the obituary mentioned in paragraph 1 is a mistaken obituary for Alfred Nobel, and Gore's "political obituary" is a figurative, not a literal, expression, meaning the end of Gore's political career.

9. **A; DOK Level:** 2; **Reading Assessment Targets:** R.2.3, R.2.4, R.4.3/L.4.3. The author states that the problem is not temporary and will not fix itself. The author implies that people need to take action to fix the problem. Answer B is incorrect because the author indicates that "we must make it right," which implies that something can be done to fix the problem. The author does not mention force, so answer C is incorrect. Answer D contradicts the author's statement, so it is incorrect.

10. **B; DOK Level:** 2; **Reading Assessment Targets:** R.2.3, R.2.4, R.4.3/L.4.3, R.5.1, R.6.4. Answer B is correct; it is the author's call to action, which extends the analogy: that people have caused the "disease" of global warming and now must do something about it. Answer A is incorrect because it misinterprets the author's analogy of global warming and disease; the author does not mean literally that people are sick. The author does not mention punishment; he believes that people—that is, the human race—have caused global warming and need to correct the situation, not be punished for having caused it. Answer D is incorrect because second opinions are mentioned in the paragraph as part of the analogy; the last sentence does not specifically refer to them.

11. **A; DOK Level:** 2; **Reading Assessment Targets:** R.2.3, R.2.4. In paragraph 1, Faulkner indirectly states that fear is causing writers to forget what is most important about writing. Answers B, C, and D do not address or result from fear; all are unrelated in this passage.

12. **D; DOK Level:** 2; **Reading Assessment Targets:** R.2.3, R.4.1/L.4.1, R.4.3/L.4.3, R.5.1. Answer D is correct because "problems of the human heart in conflict with itself" involve human emotions. Answer A is not addressed in the passage. Answer B may be plausible but does not interpret the author's words as precisely as answer D. Readers' interests are not mentioned or implied in the passage.

13. **C; DOK Level:** 2; **Reading Assessment Targets:** R.2.3, R.2.4, R.5.1, R.6.3. Answer C is the best answer because it encompasses all of what Faulkner explains: writing that is based on fear and that ignores essential human nature or emotions is worthless and superficial. The other answer choices may or may not apply to the writing he is discussing, but superficiality applies to all.

14. **A; DOK Level:** 2; **Reading Assessment Targets:** R.2.3, R.2.4, R.5.1, R.5.4, R.6.1, R.6.3. Answer A reflects the author's view that man is immortal "because he has a soul, a spirit capable of compassion and sacrifice and endurance." Answers B and C are true but are not what Faulkner implies. Answer D is the opposite of what Faulkner states.

15. **B; DOK Level: 2; Reading Assessment Targets:** R.2.3, R.2.4, R.5.1, R.5.4, R.6.1, R.6.3. The author states, "The poet's voice ... can be one of the props, the pillars to help him endure and prevail." Faulkner believes that the poet and the writer have a duty to write and share their gifts of compassion and endurance. He uses structural imagery to imply that poets and writers can provide necessary support for society. The other answer choices might explain part of the function of poets and writers, but they do not express the entire implication in Faulkner's terms.

LESSON 9, pp. 38–41

1. **C; DOK Level: 2; Reading Assessment Target:** R.4.2/L.4.2. The term *politician* has all the negative connotations of "back room dealings" and general corruption. By using the term *public servant*, the author removes these connotations and presents elected officials as those who serve their communities—a more positive view. Therefore, answer C is correct. Answer A would describe a politician more than a public servant. Answers B and D are not supported by the text.

2. **A; DOK Level: 2; Reading Assessment Target:** R.4.3/L.4.3. The author uses expressions that call for all citizens, including elected officials, to shape a common future, to unite, to participate, to work for the common good. Answer C is not completely incorrect, but if her tone were completely upbeat, she would most likely say how good things are rather than urge people to work harder to make corrections. Therefore, A is a better answer than C. Answer B is incorrect, as the speaker seems to care very much. No sarcasm is shown in the speech, so answer D is incorrect.

3. **B; DOK Level: 2; Reading Assessment Target:** R.4.3/L.4.3. The tone is one of hope and triumph. Biden uses both of these words in the first paragraph to describe the results of the election. Answers A, C, and D are not supported by the passage.

4. **B; DOK Level: 2; Reading Assessment Targets:** R.4.3/L.4.3, R.5.2. Paragraph 6 uses a mix of complete sentences and fragments (the final two sentences), whereas paragraph 7 uses complete sentences. Answers A, C, and D do not accurately reflect the structure of the two paragraphs.

5. **A; DOK Level 2; Reading Assessment Targets:** R.4.1/L.4.1, R.4.3/L.4.3. Biden thanks his predecessors and emphasizes that he is part of "We the People." Both of these actions are humble in nature. Answers B, C, and D are not supported by the passage.

6. **DOK Level: 2; Reading Assessment Targets:** R.4.1/L.4.1, R.4.3/L4.3. The completed web should include these words: **artsy, exhaustive,** and **devise**. These words all have connotative meanings that contribute to the subjective and descriptive tone of the passage. Here, *artsy* has the connotation of pretense at artistic work; *exhaustive* has the connotation of excess; and *devise* has the connotation of making up something to fit the circumstances.

7. **C; DOK Level: 2; Reading Assessment Targets:** R.4.1/L.4.1, R.5.1. The use of *hard* suggests that these sciences are based more in reality, whereas psychology is more "fantasy." Although *hard* can mean "rigid" or "difficult," these are not the implications here.

8. **A; DOK Level: 3; Reading Assessment Targets:** R.4.3/L.4.3, R.5.1, R.5.2. In paragraph 2, the author provides examples of personality testing that seem ridiculous and thus support her viewpoint in paragraph 1. Therefore, answer B is incorrect; she has not changed her mind. The tone is not more emotional; in fact, it seems more controlled and less judgmental even though the point of view remains the same. The author's historical examples have nothing to do with her and are, therefore, not personal.

9. **C; DOK Level: 2; Reading Assessment Target:** R.4.3/L.4.3. The author's style could best be called anecdotal. She tells a story about her own experiences of making mistakes. Her writing is open and honest, not mysterious. She is not argumentative or emotional.

10. **D; DOK Level: 2; Reading Assessment Target:** R.4.3/L.4.3. The author's statement demonstrates that she is humble, open, and honest. The author does not see herself as below the people she addresses. She has experience with science. She is confident in her message.

11. **B; DOK Level: 2; Reading Assessment Targets:** R.4.1/L.4.1, R.4.2/L.4.2. The word *demeaning* means "damaging to one's reputation." If mistakes were demeaning, she would be more concerned with making mistakes. Answer A describes the effect of the word *humbling*, so it is incorrect. *Demeaning* is not sarcastic, nor is it less formal than *humbling*.

LESSON 10, pp. 42–45

1. **A; DOK Level: 2; Reading Assessment Target:** R.2.8. Paragraph 2 states that Florida is the country's leading producer of sugarcane and that the southern part of the state "has rich soil and long growing seasons." Paragraph 1 states that sugarcane grows in warm, rainy climates, so answer B is incorrect. Paragraph 2 describes how in Louisiana and Texas sugarcane is grown mostly along the Mississippi and Rio Grande rivers, so answer C is incorrect. Answer D is incorrect because the passage does not provide employment information.

2. **D; DOK Level: 2; Reading Assessment Target:** R.2.8. Paragraph 1 states U.S. sugarcane production is limited to three states, implying the remaining 47 states are largely unsuitable for growing it. Answer A is incorrect because the passage does not provide employment information. Since the United States is ranked 10th in the world for production and sugarcane plantations are limited to a small area of the country, it is not reasonable to conclude answer B is correct. Nothing in the passage discusses sugarcane imports, so answer C is incorrect.

3. **DOK Level: 2; Reading Assessment Target:** R.2.8. The passage states that the benefits of a work-from-home economy include the following: **Attract workers from many locations, Flexible work hours, Decreased commuting,** and **Inclusive hiring practices**. Challenges of a work-from-home economy include the following: **Some people do not have reliable Internet** and **Lack of dedicated work space**.

4. **C; DOK Level: 2; Reading Assessment Target:** R.2.8. Paragraph 1 states that more women are earning degrees in STEM-related fields; however, the gap remains. It is reasonable to conclude answer C is correct. Nothing in the passage supports answer A. Paragraph 1 states both women and men are increasingly earning STEM degrees, so answer B is incorrect. Paragraph 1 also states that women "account for less than 30 percent of the jobs in these fields," showing this gap can be measured, so answer D is incorrect.

5. **B; DOK Level: 2; Reading Assessment Target:** R.2.8. Although the author does not specifically cite a cause for the gender gap, the passage discusses both "social obstacles" and "workplace discrimination," so it is reasonable to conclude answer B is correct. Paragraph 1 states more men are getting STEM degrees, so answer A is incorrect. Answer C is incorrect since the author highlights several ways to close the gender gap. Although paragraph 5 discusses ways "women who already work in these fields" can help other women, nothing suggests they are the only people who can eliminate the gap, so answer D is incorrect.

6. **A; DOK Level: 2; Reading Assessment Target:** R.2.8. Paragraph 5 states these groups "increase women's standing in these organizations and decrease the sense of isolation many women feel," which reasonably can benefit those who are starting their careers in STEM fields. The passage does not connect the utility of these groups to different stages in women's careers, and it is reasonable to conclude they help women who are already in leadership positions; answer B is incorrect. The author indicates that these groups can reduce the gender gap, so answer C is incorrect. Answer D is incorrect, since these groups can be designed to decrease the sense of isolation.

7. **D; DOK Level: 2; Reading Assessment Target:** R.2.8. The passage discusses the gender gap and ways experts suggest it can be closed, so answer D is a reasonable conclusion. The passage states that women already make significant contributions in STEM-related careers; however, this is not the author's overall point of view, so answer A is incorrect. The author's inclusion of several solutions implies the gap can eventually be closed, so answer B is incorrect. Although the passage states workplace discrimination and hostility contribute to the gap, this is not the focus of the passage, so answer C is incorrect.

8. **A; DOK Level: 3; Reading Assessment Targets:** R.2.4, R.2.8, R.3.3, R.3.5, R.4.3/L.4.3. Answer A is the most logical conclusion because the use of the word *cement* implies that the pieces are already in place and that "cementing" them means keeping them as they are. Whether or not this situation is historically accurate is not the issue, as historical accuracy is not being questioned. Nothing in the passage leads to the conclusion in answer B. Answer C is incorrect because it is the opposite of what the author feels. Although the author might wish for the situation in answer D, he has not yet reached that point.

9. **C; DOK Level: 2; Reading Assessment Targets:** R.2.8, R.3.2. Although the author mentions the word *remember* more than once, evidence does not indicate that he has forgotten anything significant. The evidence indicates that he was awed by the attention he had received. The author shows no indication of pessimism; in fact, he seems optimistic about the future and about his role in shaping it. The author seems humbled by the attention he receives; therefore, answer D is incorrect.

10. **D; DOK Level: 2; Reading Assessment Targets:** R.2.5, R.2.8, R.3.2, R.5.1. Answer D includes the fact that Washington is surprised by the recognition he is receiving, which implies that he is humble. The other answer choices do not lead to such a conclusion.

11. **B; DOK Level: 2; Reading Assessment Targets:** R.2.8, R.3.4. The entire passage addresses the success of the author's speech. The passage contains no indication that the speech amused anyone nor that it caused debate or created racial unrest. Answer B is the only possible choice.

1. **C; DOK Level: 2; Reading Assessment Target:** R.2.7. Moving back home is a wise choice for adult children because it reduces expenses and helps them save money. This generalization is the author's main idea in the passage. The author does not claim that moving back home allows people to work only part-time, pursue interests, or have parents take on more expenses as a result. The author's point is that young adults who move back home can save more of the money they earn and reduce expenses by sharing them with the family. Parents will not necessarily pay for more things; rather, expenses will be pooled by everyone.

2. **A; DOK Level: 3; Reading Assessment Targets:** R.2.7, R.8.3. The author does not provide support for the generalization that the cost of living is high "throughout the nation." Some support for the fact that it is high everywhere in the nation would add validity. A definition of the cost of living would not support the claim because it would not address the issue of high costs as widespread. Similarly, an example of what something costs would not support the idea that costs are high everywhere. Instead, prices would need to be compared in several places.

3. **D; DOK Level: 2; Reading Assessment Target:** R.2.8. Paragraph 1 states the generalization that "employers do not understand what behaviors are prohibited." Although many employers may not understand what is prohibited, many other employers have legal departments that study and understand the issues. Answers A, B, and C are incorrect because these statements are not generalizations.

4. **A; DOK Level: 2; Reading Assessment Target:** R.2.8. Paragraph 2 discusses racial discrimination in the workplace. Paragraph 3 provides other examples of workplace stereotyping and discrimination based on sex, gender, sexual preferences, or gender identity. Paragraph 3 does not make generalizations about men or women, so answers B and C are incorrect. Also, the passage states that "Sex-related discrimination also extends to employees who are treated unfairly because of their sexual preference or gender identity," so answer D is incorrect.

5. **A. DOK Level: 2; Reading Assessment Target:** R.2.8. Paragraphs 4 and 5 provide information on illegal employer actions and on state and federal laws that protect employees. This supports answer A. The passage does not include information about whether gender-based discrimination occurs more often than racial discrimination, so answer B is incorrect. The passage states: "Employees should at the very least become familiar" with discrimination laws, so answer C is incorrect. Although reporting discrimination may result in retaliation, there is not enough information to consider this an accurate generalization, so answer D is incorrect.

6. **D; DOK Level: 2; Reading Assessment Target:** R.2.8. Consulting an expert is generally a good idea since discrimination and other legal issues may require special knowledge. Paragraph 6 states that employees should document and report events, so answer A is incorrect. The passage notes that employers may not know what is prohibited, but there is no discussion of training, so answer B is incorrect. The passage does not discuss the emotional damage of discrimination, and instead mentions legal issues in paragraph 5, so answer C is incorrect.

7. B; DOK Level: 2; Reading Assessment Target: R.2.7. The author states "Custody proceedings are often brutal and adversarial." Based on this statement, a generalization can be made that custody battles are combative. The information in this paragraph supports this answer choice and not the others.

8. B; DOK Level: 2; Reading Assessment Target: R.2.7. Paragraph 2 states that stereotypes "ensure that Mom becomes the primary custodian." Answers A, C, and D are not supported by the text.

9. D; DOK Level: 2; Reading Assessment Target: R.2.7. Answer D is correct because custody decisions are based on the stereotype of male aggression. Answers A and C are incorrect because the evidence in the passage contradicts the statements: men are often unhappy about custody arrangements and challenge them in court, usually wanting more or equal custody. Answer B is incorrect because nothing is mentioned in the passage about men's careers.

10. C; DOK Level: 2; Reading Assessment Target: R.2.7. According to the author, enjoying violent movies does not make a man a worse or less reliable father. The stereotype about men and violence is misinterpreted in answer A. Although studies may show a connection between violence and watching violent movies, that information is not part of the passage. Answer B is incorrect because it too misinterprets information in the passage. Answer D is irrelevant and not addressed in the passage.

11. B; DOK Level: 2; Reading Assessment Target: R.2.7. Answer B best reflects the author's ideas about men and child custody, stating that men often have unfair custodial arrangements. There is no indication in the passage that all custody arrangements should be the same, and some circumstances might make the decision unwise. Answer C is incorrect because the laws favor women, not men. If men are looked on more favorably since the year in which the passage was written, that fact is outside the scope of the passage and is, therefore, irrelevant. Although staying married might solve custody problems, this solution is not suggested in the passage.

12. DOK Level: 2; Reading Assessment Target: R.2.7. The correctly completed chart appears below. These generalizations are made from information in the text. The author mentions that young children are exposed to television, from which they learn much that is not academic. The author emphasizes the role of testing and its influence in determining a student's intelligence. Such tracking places demands on students accordingly. College seems to be the portal to graduate school. Graduate school is the place that turns out fierce competitors, who have survived and mastered the system. Note that this passage is ironic, or tongue in cheek.

Stage of Education	Generalization
Preschool Years	This group learns a great deal from exposure to media.
The Twelve Years of Formal Education	Students are labeled by test scores, which determine their formal education.
College	Students impress teachers to move to the next level of education.
Graduate School	Students must be shrewd and do what it takes to achieve more than their classmates.

LESSON 12, *pp. 50–53*

1. B; DOK Level: 3; Reading Assessment Targets: R.2.7, R.2.8, R.4.3/L.4.3, R.9.1/R.7.1, R.9.2. The analogy that describes both situations best is a bridge that goes halfway across a river. Lincoln describes a country in which half the states allow slavery, and half do not. He argues that the situation cannot continue in this in-between place, without one resolution for all states in the Union. Similarly, a bridge cannot function if it goes only halfway across a river. Johnson describes progress since the Emancipation Proclamation as unfinished and "unfulfilled." Progress is best compared with a bridge that extends only halfway across a river. The other answer options do not adequately describe both situations. A person waking up in the morning or who is blind suddenly seeing would indicate new insights or revelations. A phone unanswered might be closer but gives more indication of ignoring a problem than it does of incompletion.

2. D; DOK Level: 3; Reading Assessment Targets: R.2.7, R.2.8. Paragraph 3 states the WHO declared a global influenza pandemic on June 11, 2009. Synthesizing the information in paragraphs 1-3 allows readers to deduce that answer D is the most logical conclusion. Confirming the spread of a new virus does not speed up the process for creating a vaccine, lessen the infection rate, or prevent healthcare systems from being overwhelmed.

3. A; DOK Level: 3; Reading Assessment Targets: R.2.7, R.2.8. Paragraph 6 discusses IRAT which "assesses the potential pandemic risk posed by influenza A viruses currently circulating in animals." This implies that animal viruses can spread to humans. Answers B, C, and D are not supported by the passage.

4. C; DOK Level: 3; Reading Assessment Targets: R.2.7, R.2.8. Shelter-in-place orders would cause the most social disruption. Answers A, B, and D may cause some social disruption but not as much as a shelter-in-place order.

5. B; DOK Level: 2; Reading Assessment Targets: R.2.8. Paragraph 3 states electric rickshaws "have not been as affordable as diesel rickshaws," so it is reasonable to conclude diesel rickshaws are purchased because of their lower prices. Although electric rickshaws create less pollution, this is not reason enough for rickshaw owners to prefer them, so answer A is incorrect. Diesel fuel costs more than electricity, so answer C is incorrect. There is nothing to indicate electric rickshaws are ubiquitous, or everywhere, in India, so answer D is incorrect.

6. C; DOK Level: 2; Reading Assessment Targets: R.2.8. Paragraph 4 shows that cheaper electricity is a reason for buying an electric rickshaw. If diesel fuel becomes more expensive, and this disparity increases, that would likely increase the sales of electric rickshaws. A change in the cost of diesel fuel changes the cost of owning a diesel rickshaw, which in turn affects the sales of electric rickshaws, so answers A and D are incorrect. Cheaper diesel fuel would likely increase sales of diesel rickshaws, relative to electric rickshaws, which would likely decrease, so answer B is incorrect.

7. A. DOK Level: 2; Reading Assessment Targets: R.2.8. In paragraph 3 critics note the country has an unreliable electrical infrastructure. To fuel these new vehicles, the power grid needs to be more reliable. Although more fuel-efficient diesel engines would reduce air pollution, the government's plan is to increase electric rickshaw use, so answer B is incorrect. Although rickshaws use the roads, there is nothing in the article to suggest it is necessary for the government to repair or construct roads, so answer C is incorrect. Although it might be helpful to remind people that diesel rickshaws are discouraged, education spending is not necessary, so answer D is incorrect.

8. B; DOK Level: 2; Reading Assessment Targets: R.2.8. Although it is not explicitly state, it is reasonable to infer that Amazon's decision was related to the government's announcement. Because of this, answer A is incorrect. The government announced its plan before Amazon's decision, so answer C is incorrect. Since Amazon's decision conforms to the government's plan, answer D is unlikely and incorrect.

9. D; DOK Level: 2; Reading Assessment Targets: R.2.7, R.2.8, R.3.4, R.9.2. The first passage explains that smells are processed more quickly than other sensory information. The second passage explains that smells are linked to emotional memories. Based on both ideas, the reader can generalize that a smell can create strong responses even before a person recognizes what smell it is. Answer D is correct. Neither passage suggests that smells create less of an emotional response as people age. Answer B is incorrect because repeated exposure to scents intensifies the memory. Answer C is incorrect because smells and emotions are stuck together in memory, and neither passage suggests that these factors change over time.

10. B; DOK Level: 2; Reading Assessment Targets: R.2.7, R.2.8, R.3.4, R.9.2. Viewing a photo involves the sense of sight; hearing the notes of a song involves the sense of hearing. Neither of these senses is processed as quickly as smell. Answer C does involve smell, but it is an initial experience with a new smell and will not likely cause the emotional response triggered by a smell associated with a previous powerful emotion (such as being reminded of the feelings for a "first love").

11. C; DOK Level: 3; Reading Assessment Targets: R.2.7, R.2.8, R.3.4, R.9.1/R.7.1, R.9.2. The passages explain that the sense of smell triggers memories of powerful emotional experiences in which a memory and smell are associated. The question indicates that the smell of chlorine will trigger an experience in which a person smelled chlorine and associated the smell with a positive event. Answers A and B are incorrect because looking at a photo of a pool or hearing about a water park does not include the actual experience of smelling chlorine. Answer D does involve smell, but disinfectant covering hospital odors is most likely not associated with a happy event. Answer C is correct because the emotional experience of enjoying summer days at a pool is connected to the actual experience of the smell of chlorine experienced at the time the memory was formed.

12. B; DOK Level: 2; Reading Assessment Targets: R.2.8, R.9.1/R.7.1, R.9.2. The first passage explains that smells are experienced more quickly than other senses because the sense of smell does not pass through the thalamus. Therefore, smells are processed more quickly. The smell of jet fuel may trigger an immediate memory because of this factor. That the smell of jet fuel is stronger than other fuels is not relevant to the speed at which it triggers a memory. Answer C is not supported by the passages. Answer D is incorrect because neither passage suggests that the brain processes smell more accurately, only that it processes it faster.

LESSON 13, pp. 54–57

1. A; DOK Level: 2; Reading Assessment Target: R.4.1/L.4.1. The word *din* appears as part of the description of noisy Fleet Street. *Muddy* is most likely a word that readers will know as not having anything to do with noise. Answers C and D appear in contexts of calm and quiet. This question is best answered by a process of elimination.

2. C; DOK Level: 3; Reading Assessment Target: R.4.1/L.4.1. Throughout the passage, the author contrasts a noisy place with a quiet, shaded, peaceful place. An oasis is a cool spot with water in a desert. Answer C best fits the author's reference to oases, with which he compares the Paradise of Bachelors. Answer A indicates no quiet or peace. Answer B indicates no shade, and answer D indicates a geographical location that may or may not be peaceful, quiet, or shady.

3. D; DOK Level: 2; Reading Assessment Target: R.4.1/L.4.1. The narrator and her teacher have been outside since the morning and are returning home, which indicates that they were out for a walk. A vacation in a faraway place would have taken longer than a morning, so answer A is incorrect. While *ramble* can mean "a story or discussion that is aimless or long-winded," that meaning does not make sense in this context, so answers B and C are incorrect.

4. B; DOK Level: 2; Reading Assessment Target: R.4.1/L.4.1. When the weather is sultry, it is hot and humid. Therefore, the weather is unpleasant. The storm has not yet happened, so answer A is incorrect. The author contrasts the warm and sultry weather of noon with "fine" morning weather, so answers C and D are incorrect.

5. A; DOK Level: 2; Reading Assessment Target: R.4.2/L.4.2. The word *sinister* means "dark and evil." Using the word *worrisome* softens the connotation or threatening tone of the sentence. It would not make the tone of the sentence more threatening or humorous, so answers B and C are incorrect. The sentence does not have a humorous tone, so answer D is incorrect.

6. D; DOK Level: 2; Reading Assessment Targets: R.4.1/L.4.1, R.4.3/L.4.3. The author uses the personification to illustrate that the tree is shaking in the strong winds of the storm. The word *shiver* reinforces that the narrator is afraid of the storm. Later in the paragraph, the narrator says "terror held me fast," so she is not lonely, excited, or cold when the storm hits.

7. C; DOK Level: 2; Reading Assessment Target: R.4.2/L.4.2. The word *emaciated* means "very thin" or "starved." *Slender* means "stylishly thin" and thus "healthy." If the man were slender instead of emancipated, it would suggest that the "sallow" and "sickly looking" description is due to recent developments. The word *slender* does not imply "well-groomed," so answer A is incorrect. The words *sallow* and *sickly* would still make the man appear to be unwell, so answer B is incorrect. Answer D gives the meaning of the sentence with the word *emaciated*, so it is incorrect.

8. D; DOK Level: 2; Reading Assessment Target: R.4.1/L.4.1. The expression *middle term of life* is a way of saying that someone is middle-aged. This man is described as beyond middle-aged. Answers A and C are incorrect because the passage indicates that the gardener has gray hair. There is no indication that he looked older than his actual age, so answer B is incorrect.

9. **B; DOK Level:** 2; **Reading Assessment Target:** R.4.1/L.4.1. *Redundant* means "unnecessary" or "repetitious." In this context it means having more health, beauty, and energy than needed. The girl appears like a flower in fullest bloom. The context clue is "a bloom so deep and vivid that one shade more would have been too much." Answers A, C, and D are not supported by the passage.

10. **A; DOK Level:** 2; **Reading Assessment Target:** R.4.1/L.4.1. The expression *grown morbid* means "has become sick or diseased." The narrator uses the term metaphorically to describe Giovanni's reaction as he watches the girl enter the garden. He views her as a flower that should be touched only while wearing a mask or a glove. Answers B, C, and D are not supported by the passage.

11. **B; DOK Level:** 1; **Reading Assessment Target:** R.4.1/L.4.1. The term is defined in paragraph 1 as the equivalent of *Mr.* While others are referred to as *brethren*, Zelig is not, so answer A is incorrect. The iron Zelig uses is for clothing, so answer C is incorrect. While Zelig works in a cloakshop, the passage does not indicate that he has a title related to his work, so answer D is incorrect.

12. **C; DOK Level:** 2; **Reading Assessment Target:** R.4.1/L.4.1. According to the excerpt, you can assume that a stave is something required to keep a barrel together or whole. The phrase *a barrel with a stave missing* indicates that the neighbors think Zelig is not entirely whole or not mentally stable or competent or "not all there." Answers A, B, and D are not supported by the details in the passage.

13. **A; DOK Level:** 2; **Reading Assessment Target:** R.4.1/L.4.1. The narrator describes Zelig as someone who does not fit in with other people. From this context, you can assume that the word *alien* means "different or strange." Answers B, C, and D are not supported by the passage.

14. **D; DOK Level:** 2; **Reading Assessment Target:** R.4.1/L.4.1. Cast-iron is known to be strong and sturdy. Zelig is described this way, implying that despite looking a mess, his physique is strong and sturdy. Details in the excerpt do not imply that Zelig is quick to lose his temper, stubborn and unyielding, or loud and opinionated.

15. **B; DOK Level:** 2; **Reading Assessment Target:** R.4.1/L.4.1. The most common synonyms are *messy* and *unkempt*. You learn that Zelig's hair is long and that his clothes are shabby and hang loosely on him. On the basis of these clues, you can assume that Zelig's grooming habits are not very good. While Zelig is tall, *disheveled* does not refer to his size, so answer A is incorrect. His appearance is the opposite of neat, so answer C is incorrect. He is not described as clumsy, so answer D is incorrect.

HIGH IMPACT LESSON: CONNOTATIVE MEANINGS, pp. 58–59

1. **A; DOK Level:** 2; **Reading Assessment Targets:** R.4.1/L.4.1. Context clues tell readers the contrasting "victories" were significant; the initial reverse was extreme and overwhelming. The verb *stagger* also means to move from side to side, cause hesitation, or alternate in a pattern. However, these meanings do not fit the context of the passage, so answers B, C, and D are incorrect.

2. **B; DOK Level:** 2; **Reading Assessment Targets:** R.4.1/L.4.1. The passage says David was "struck" by a fact, or idea. In this context, the fact does not physically hit him, but occur in his thoughts. Although answers A, C, and D are synonyms for "struck," they do not fit the context of the passage, so they are incorrect.

3. **D; DOK Level:** 2; **Reading Assessment Targets:** R.4.1/L.4.1. The word *phenomenon* implies that the event was unusual and significant, while the word *fact* implies an ordinary event. Answers A and B are incorrect because David "liked the difference," which implies he enjoys being able to ask questions and thinks the teachers are sincere. Answer C describes the current meaning, so it is incorrect.

4. **A; DOK Level:** 2; **Reading Assessment Targets:** R.4.1/L.4.1. Lightning, a bright flash of electricity, is often associated with intelligence and the ability to learn quickly. The passage does not discuss supernatural powers, so answer B is incorrect. Answers C and D are incorrect because the passage does not indicate the teachers are fearful or that David is temperamental.

5. **C; DOK Level:** 2; **Reading Assessment Targets:** R.4.1/L.4.1. The context indicates the teachers consider grammar and arithmetic separate studies, and if David were to teach them *instead*, he would unite or combine. Answers A and B do not fix the context of the passage. Answer D would have the opposite meaning and is incorrect.

6. **B; DOK Level:** 2; **Reading Assessment Targets:** R.4.1/L.4.1. In this context, *formulate* implies that David is asking the questions as soon as he can put his thoughts into words. He is not asking questions without thought, in an insulting way, or in a meek way.

LESSON 14, pp. 60–63

1. **C; DOK Level:** 2; **Reading Assessment Targets:** R.3.2, R.3.4. John wants things "put down in figures" because he is "practical in the extreme," according to the way the narrator views him. As such, the reader can assume that John looks for the concrete and quantifiable. Answers A and C are other effects of John's practicality, not an overall cause. The fact that John is a physician might relate to his practicality, but this fact is not part of the cause-and-effect relationship that the author sets up.

2. **B; DOK Level:** 2; **Reading Assessment Targets:** R.3.2, R.3.4. The reader can assume that the narrator feels powerless because her husband and her brother, both physicians, do not believe she is really sick. The narrator asks, "And what can one do?" about the fact that her husband "does not believe" she is sick. The narrator does not know what action to take and feels trapped by the opinions of her husband and brother. The narrator disagrees with the judgment that nothing is really the matter with her and implies that her condition is more than the temporary nervous depression that her husband calls it. There is no suggestion that she is receiving treatment.

3. DOK Level: 2; Reading Assessment Targets: R.2.5, R.3.2, R.3.4. The completed chart should include in the first box: **Mathilde was unhappy with her lack of wealth.** The passage indicates that Mathilde stopped visiting her wealthy friend because Mathilde was sad when she returned home from a visit. In the second box: **Mathilde's husband gave her money to buy a dress.** Mathilde's husband agrees to give her money for a dress so they can attend the ball. In the third box: **Mathilde borrowed a necklace from Jeanne Forestier.** Mathilde borrows jewelry from her friend because Mathilde worried people will think she is poor if she does not wear jewelry to the ball.

4. C; DOK Level: 2; Reading Assessment Target: R.2.1. The information appears in paragraph 3. In this passage, the guest does not leave, nor does he pay for lodging. Answer B is incorrect because the grandmother scolds Sylvia; she does not encourage her to do anything but wants the child to reveal the location of the white heron. Nothing in the passage indicates what the guest will do on his own.

5. D; DOK Level: 2; Reading Assessment Targets: R.2.5, R.3.2, R.3.4. Sylvia's inability to speak is caused by her reluctance to reveal the location of the white heron, so answer A is incorrect. Her torn dress indicates poverty. The text makes no mention of the grandmother's confession, so answer C is incorrect. Answer D is correct because the guest notices "the way the shy little girl looked."

6. B; DOK Level: 2; Reading Assessment Targets: R.3.2, R.3.4. Answer B is correct because the family is poor, and the grandmother's actions indicate that she would like to have the money. Answer A is incorrect because Sylvia is shy, and nothing is mentioned about her entertaining guests. The grandmother seems to have no interest in the bird except as a means of receiving money. Nothing is mentioned about Sylvia's knowledge of birds, only her knowledge of the heron's location.

7. B; DOK Level: 2; Reading Assessment Targets: R.3.2, R.3.4. B is correct because Sylvia's thoughts of the heron and the happiness the memories bring her while she is being questioned about its location show she does not want the sportsman to find it. She wants it to remain free as it is in this memory. A is incorrect because there is no indication from the text that she wants to help her grandmother in this situation. While C and D may be true, they are incorrect because they are not supported by the text.

8. D; DOK Level: 2; Reading Assessment Targets: R.3.2, R.3.4. Answer D is correct because the passage indicates her attachment to the bird and the fact that the guest is a hunter (sportsman). Answer A is incorrect because it contradicts the information in the passage; Sylvia does know the location. Although Sylvia is shy, her silence is not caused by trouble speaking to strangers. Answer C is incorrect because Sylvia is more concerned about the bird than about money and does not ask her grandmother to request a larger amount.

9. C; DOK Level: 3; Reading Assessment Targets: R.2.7, R.3.2, R.3.4. As a result of Sylvia's silence, the grandmother most likely will not get money from the guest and not become rich. Answer B is incorrect because the passage does not indicate that he will find the bird. Sylvia's grandmother most likely will not praise her because Sylvia has not told the guest where to find the bird and has thus prevented the grandmother from receiving payment for the information. Answer C is the most likely result.

10. B; DOK Level: 2; Reading Assessment Targets: R.3.2, R.3.4. Although the woman is an experienced traveler, nothing is mentioned about the time at which she arrives at the airport, nor is anything mentioned about delays. She may be experienced, but she is unsure about the duration of the flight. Therefore, B is the best answer.

11. D; DOK Level: 2; Reading Assessment Targets: R.3.2, R.4.3/L.4.3. The reader can assume that the narrator describes Miami as "so wrong" because the city looks more like a "real-estate advertisement" than like a typical American city. The author suggests that there is something both beautiful and unreal about the look of the city. Although the author describes wind blowing a palm tree, the reference points out the tropical appearance more than danger from weather. There is no clear indication that the woman dislikes Miami.

12. C; DOK Level: 2; Reading Assessment Targets: R.3.2, R.3.3, R.3.4, R.3.5. Answer C is correct even though the woman would have preferred the seat to herself. Answer A is incorrect because the woman does not want to speak. Answer B is incorrect because there is no indication that the woman is or wishes to be rude. Answer D is incorrect because she looks out of the window briefly and does not want to do so again.

13. A; DOK Level: 3; Reading Assessment Targets: R.2.7, R.2.8. The woman's actions all have indicated that she is ignoring the man. If she continues to behave as she has behaved, she will ignore him. They will not have a conversation. She is not likely to change her seat immediately because she has selected the seat she is in knowing that it is more spacious than others, so answer C is incorrect. The woman is concerned about the man's snoring; nothing indicates that she will snore, so answer D is incorrect.

14. B; DOK Level: 3; Reading Assessment Targets: R.2.7, R.2.8. Answer A is incorrect because all the woman's actions indicate that she wishes to sleep and not be bothered by or meet anyone. Therefore, answer B is correct. There is no indication that the woman enjoys looking at scenery because she implies that she does not want to look out of the window; when she does briefly, she does not like what she sees. She does not enjoy airplane travel, as she does not trust planes. Although she may enjoy other methods of travel, answer D would not be the best choice.

15. A; DOK Level: 2; Reading Assessment Targets: R.3.2, R.3.4. Answer A is correct because much of the text describes how she handled her flight experience. She did not look at the man when she responded, but moved over and hoped he would not snore, allowing her to easily ignore him. While B and D could have happened, the text does not provide support for these conclusions. C is incorrect, because there is not evidence to support the idea that she may have been lonely.

LESSON 15, pp. 64–67

1. B; DOK Level: 2; Reading Assessment Targets: R.2.1, R.3.4. When the narrator compares Jo to a colt, she wants to highlight her "long limbs" that she never seemed to know what to do with. This description implies that Jo is not very graceful. Therefore, answer B is correct. Answer A is incorrect because Jo is not graceful. While Jo does have the features described in answers C and D, these features are not related to the comparison.

2. **B; DOK Level:** 2; **Reading Assessment Targets:** R.3.3, R.3.4. Margaret is described as "very pretty" and vain about her hands, while Jo's description reveals that she is not as pretty and a bit awkward. Jo's hair is her "one beauty," which implies that she is not as pretty. She is also described as having an "uncomfortable appearance," which suggests that she is a bit awkward. Therefore, the correct answer is B. Answers A, C, and D contradict information in the passage. Jo is not described as beautiful or shy, and she is tan and has gray eyes.

3. **A; DOK Level:** 2; **Reading Assessment Target:** R.3.2. Although the information is not stated, the children clearly go to the same school because the Kelvey girls know to stay away from the Burnell girls. Paragraph 2 supports the inference by explaining why the Burnell girls go to this school. Answer B is incorrect because the Kelvey girls do not seem to play with other children. Answer C is incorrect because nothing is mentioned about wildflowers other than that Lil Kelvey brought a bunch to the teacher. Answer D is incorrect because the Burnells are not shunned.

4. **A; DOK Level:** 2; **Reading Assessment Targets:** R.3.2, R.3.4. The exclusion of the girls shows a difference in status. If the reader does not already know that the Kelvey girls are shunned because of their family situation and lack of money, they are designated here as not belonging to the group. Nothing is mentioned about ages or sizes, nor does it appear that anyone dislikes Isabel. In fact, all except the Kelveys want to be her friend.

5. **C; DOK Level:** 3; **Reading Assessment Targets:** R.2.7, R.3.3, R.3.4. The author implies that the Burnell children are from a well-to-do family and of a higher social class than the Kelveys. The suggestion is that if the Burnell parents had a choice, they would send their children to a school that admitted students only from a similar social class. The quality of the school's education is never discussed. The distance from their home is not the criticism being made of the school. The idea of abolishing social class distinction would be opposite to the Burnells' way of thinking.

6. **B; DOK Level:** 2; **Reading Assessment Targets:** R.3.2, R.3.4. Answer B is correct because the Kelveys are at the bottom of the social and economic scale, according to the passage. Answers A and C are misreadings of the text. In answer A, fashion is not used to mean clothing, although these families most likely are more fashionably dressed. Although nothing is mentioned specifically about education level, the implication is that the Kelveys are less educated than the others.

7. **D; DOK Level:** 2; **Reading Assessment Targets:** R.3.2, R.3.4, R.4.3/L.4.3, R.5.3. The word *even* includes the teacher, perhaps least expected to be in the category, with the others who shun the Kelveys. Although a teacher is expected to treat all students equally, her special voice implies that she does not treat the Kelveys well. Therefore, answer A is incorrect. Answer B is incorrect because there is no indication that she feels sorry for the girls. Answer C is incorrect because the teacher is like, not unlike, the others.

8. **C; DOK Level:** 1; **Reading Assessment Target:** R.3.3. The narrator describes Mr. Bingley as "good-looking" and Mr. Darcy as "handsome," so both men are handsome. Mr. Bingley is also described as "pleasant," "lively," and "amiable," while Mr. Darcy is described as "disagreeable," "forbidding," and "unworthy." Mr. Darcy is the intense and standoffish character, so answer A is incorrect. Mr. Darcy does not dance because he is shy or reserved; he does not dance because the women are "not handsome enough to tempt" him, so answer B is wrong. Answer D is correct based on people's initial reaction to the men, but people soon found Mr. Darcy's attitude and manners lacking as the ball progressed.

9. **D; DOK Level:** 2; **Reading Assessment Targets:** R.2.1, R.2.5, R.3.3, R.3.4. The conversation shows that Mr. Bingley is enjoying the company of the people at the ball while Mr. Darcy thinks that the women are "not handsome enough to tempt" him to dance. The conversation confirms the narrator's description of both characters. Answers A, B, and C are not supported by the conversation.

10. **A; DOK Level:** 2; **Reading Assessment Targets:** R.3.3, R.3.4, R.3.5. The house in the meadow could have provided a dwelling for a family before the war but is now torn apart, revealing the difference between pre-war and post-war conditions (answer A). The well may have contained water before or after the battles began, so the fact that it may contain water for the soldiers does not exhibit a contrast in pre-war and post-war conditions (answer B). That the soldiers bicker may indicate that they are under stress rather than that they have become close by knowing one another for a while, so this detail is not the best emphasis of pre-war and post-war conditions (answer C). The idea of military leaders consulting each other rather than consulting the soldiers reflects a common scenario in war but does not exhibit a contrast in pre-war and post-war conditions (answer D).

11. **C; DOK Level:** 2; **Reading Assessment Targets:** R.3.3, R.3.5. Collins and the other soldiers use incorrect grammar, making them seem uneducated (answer C). The other soldiers are goading Collins into endangering his life, so they are not concerned with his welfare (answer A). None of the soldiers display resentment toward the captain and the colonel (answer B). Collins is the only soldier who shows a willingness to take a big risk (answer D).

12. **B; DOK Level:** 2; **Reading Assessment Targets:** R.3.2, R.3.3, R.3.4. Collins displays naïve and impulsive behavior when he decides to endanger his life for a drink of water; the captain and the colonel show experience and caution in responding to Collins's request (answer B). Collins's actions are not motivated by hope, and the captain and the colonel do not exhibit a lack of hope (answer A). Collins's actions are ill-advised, not brave and fearless, and the captain and the colonel seem confident rather than anxious and self-doubting (answer C). Collins is straightforward, rather than cunning, so answer D is incorrect.

13. **D; DOK Level:** 3; **Reading Assessment Targets:** R.2.2, R.2.6, R.2.8, R.3.3, R.3.4, R.3.5. The author uses language such as "grass was rippling gently" and "green and beautiful calm" to emphasize the peaceful quality of the natural setting and language such as "terrible onslaught," "monstrous," and "massacre" to emphasize the violent wartime activity. This contrast highlights and emphasizes the destructive nature of war (answer D). The author portrays nature as innocent and fragile, rather than powerful, so answer A is incorrect. The author does not indicate that wartime will end soon, so answer B is incorrect. The author does not provide details to emphasize complex battle tactics, so answer C is incorrect.

1. **D; DOK Level:** 2; **Reading Assessment Targets:** R.5.3. This phrase shows the first in a sequence of decisions the narrator makes. *Together* indicates that the narrator took only money and jewels with him, so answer A is incorrect. *Now* indicates the current time and that the narrator is still in Geneva, so answer B is incorrect. *When I was happy and beloved* provides a contrast to the present time; it does not indicate a flashback, so answer C is incorrect.

2. **B; DOK Level:** 2; **Reading Assessment Targets:** R.5.3. The paragraph begins the morning of one day and ends that night. There is no indication that the paragraph takes place over the course of one year, three months, or three days.

3. **A; DOK Level:** 2; **Reading Assessment Targets:** R.5.3. This is one of several phrases throughout the passage that shows the passage of time throughout the day, from morning to night. Although the sentence's description of the sky's changing color might be interpreted as a change in weather, this is not the purpose of the transition, so answer B is incorrect. The phrase does not set up a transition to a different location or point of view, so answers C and D are incorrect.

4. **B; DOK Level:** 2; **Reading Assessment Targets:** R.5.3. The change to darkness shows both passing time and the building of tension associated with nighttime. This passage does not have a flashback, so answer A is incorrect. The phrase *to the right and left and rear* implies that the men are surrounded by wolves, so answers C and D are both incorrect.

5. **A; DOK Level:** 3; **Reading Assessment Targets:** R.5.3. The word *when* connects the previous idea of Henry adding ice to the beans to the following idea, which is Henry being startled. The other answer options do not signal an unexpected turn of events.

LESSON 16, *pp. 70–73*

1. **D; DOK Level:** 2; **Reading Assessment Target:** R.3.2. Answer D is correct. It is stated in the passage, but readers must identify it as a conflict. Answer A is incorrect; the aunt mentions nothing about regaining her youth, only memories of it. She wants her niece to remember with her, to pass down her memories, but nothing is mentioned about writing them. Therefore, answer B is incorrect. The aunt knows she is old and will die before long, but nothing is mentioned about her fear of dying alone. Therefore, answer C is incorrect.

2. **B; DOK Level:** 2; **Reading Assessment Targets:** R.3.2, R.3.4. Answer B is the best choice, as indicated by the last sentence. The aunt's conflict is resolved. Answer A is incorrect because Aunt Margaret wants her memories and her past kept alive, not hidden. Answer C is incorrect because nothing specific is mentioned about photo albums. Rather, the implication is that Anna and her aunt will talk and that Anna will remember, with images in her mind. Answer D is incorrect because the implication is that Anna already lives with her aunt. Nothing is mentioned about moving.

3. **D; DOK Level:** 3; **Reading Assessment Targets:** R.2.7, R.3.2, R.3.3. Answer D is the most logical choice. The women's discussion of the canary and of Mrs. Wright's fondness for it implies that the women found it dead and infer that John Wright had killed it. Although answer A mentions the canary, there is no indication that the women stole it. Answer B is incorrect because Mr. Peters is the sheriff. Answer C is incorrect because nothing is mentioned about the women's being questioned earlier in the story.

4. **A; DOK Level:** 2; **Reading Assessment Targets:** R.3.2, R.3.3. The sound of a knob turning is a complication because the women now have very little time to act without being seen. This complication leads directly to the climax. The other answers are incorrect because the knob turning is an action in the story, not exposition about previous events or situations. Answer C is incorrect because falling action is after the climax, which is yet to occur. Answer D is incorrect because the resolution has not yet occurred.

5. **C; DOK Level:** 2; **Reading Assessment Targets:** R.3.2, R.3.3. The climax of the story occurs when Martha Hale snatches the box and puts it in her pocket. This action occurs just before the men return to the room and see the box, at which point the tension shifts from the events themselves and toward their resolution. This moment stated in answer C is the point of highest tension because there is no time to waste. The other answers do not indicate moments of highest tension, although they may be tense.

6. **B; DOK Level:** 3; **Reading Assessment Targets:** R.2.7, R.2.8, R.3.2, R.3.3. The reader can assume that the sheriff and county attorney will remain unaware of the canary and the box. It is clear that the women want to keep the existence of the canary a secret. There is no evidence that Mrs. Peters will tell, since they had gazed at each other "without flinching." There is no reason to suspect that the sheriff or county attorney will notice the box.

7. **A; DOK Level:** 2; **Reading Assessment Target:** R.3.2. The information provides background information and is, therefore, part of the exposition. Because of its content, it cannot be a conflict (although it might introduce one), climax, or resolution.

8. **C; DOK Level:** 2; **Reading Assessment Targets:** R.3.2, R.3.3. Answer C is the best choice. The implication is confirmed in paragraph 7. Answer A is incorrect because Mary's actions contradict the statement. She would not behave as indifferently as she does if she loved Stephen. The passage states, too, that he was an unsuccessful suitor. Although answer B seems to be correct for a brief moment in the story, Mary is mistaken when she hears Stephen's story. She has misinterpreted his haste to visit her. Answer D is incorrect because Stephen's mother tells him that Mary's husband has died; there is no indication that she has been gossiping about Mary.

9. **C; DOK Level:** 2; **Reading Assessment Targets:** R.3.2, R.3.3, R.3.5. Answer A is incorrect because Stephen tells his news after Mary says that she is disappointed. Mary has no idea that Stephen has news of her husband, as Stephen does not say anything at first. Answer B is incorrect because Mary does not mention the time, only that it was at night and that she did not want to disturb her sister. Answer C is correct because Mary misinterprets Stephen's reference to "comforting her," thinking it is romantic and disrespectful rather than good news about her husband. Answer D is incorrect because Mary never mentions anything about Stephen's mother.

UNIT 1 *(continued)*

10. **B; DOK Level:** 3; **Reading Assessment Targets:** R.2.7, R.3.2, R.3.3. Although all answers could be possible, the most likely answer, based on story events, is answer B: that Mary's husband will return. Answer A is incorrect because at this point Mary's husband is alive, and Stephen has indicated concern, not romantic interest in Mary. There is no indication that Mary will leave her husband, as she is overcome with joy on finding out he is alive; therefore, answer C is incorrect. Stephen has told Mary that he saw her husband, who had already been rescued, so answer D is incorrect.

11. **D; DOK Level:** 2; **Reading Assessment Target:** R.3.2. The statement provides background information about Mrs. Mallard, so it is part of the exposition. The information about Mrs. Mallard's weak heart is important because it establishes that she is vulnerable to a heart attack, which she has at the end of the story. This information is not part of the resolution, climax, or conflict.

12. **C. DOK Level:** 2; **Reading Assessment Targets:** R.3.2, R.3.3. The story's climax occurs when Mrs. Mallard sits in her room and suddenly realizes that she is "free, free, free!" Answers A and B are part of the exposition and occur before the climax. Answer D is part of the falling action and occurs after the climax.

13. **A; DOK Level:** 2; **Reading Assessment Targets:** R.3.2, R.3.3, R.3.4, R.5.1, R.5.4. In paragraphs 3, 4, and 5, Mrs. Mallard realizes that she is free. She has "triumph in her eyes" and carries "herself like a goddess of Victory." These descriptions show that she is happy to be free of her husband. So, when her husband appears, she dies of disappointment, not joy. Mrs. Mallard was not scared of her husband or terrified of being alone. While Mrs. Mallard will "weep again" when she see her husband's body, she is not too saddened by the news.

HIGH IMPACT LESSON: SEQUENCE AND PLOT, *pp. 74–75*

1. **B; DOK Level:** 3; **Reading Assessment Targets:** R.3.1. The second sentence tells us when the prince became silent, the mob left him alone. Answers A and C both reverse the cause-and-effect relationship between events, so they are incorrect. Answer D is incorrect because these two events are unrelated.

2. **D; DOK Level:** 2; **Reading Assessment Targets:** R.3.1. The first sentence in the passage tells use Robert talked a good deal about himself. Answer A is incorrect because this is the second event that is described. Answer B is perhaps the earliest chronological event described in the passage, but it is not the first action in the plot, so it is incorrect. Robert discussed future plans to travel to Mexico, but had not yet been there, so answer C is incorrect.

3. **B; DOK Level:** 2; **Reading Assessment Targets:** R.3.1. The phrase *In former times* transitions readers to Robert remembering when the house was his family's summer home. Although answers A, C, and D provide additional details, none of this is information presented specifically out of chronological order.

4. **A; DOK Level:** 2; **Reading Assessment Targets:** R.3.1. The third sentence tells readers Mrs. Pontellier read the letter. The following sentence tells readers Robert was interested in learning more. The passage says Mrs. Pontellier's sister had moved East, not Robert, so answer B is incorrect. Mrs. Pontellier had talked about her father's Mississippi plantation, but that was before she read the letter, so answer C is incorrect. Answer D is incorrect because it was Mrs. Pontellier's sister who was engaged to be married, not Mrs. Pontellier.

5. **C; DOK Level:** 3; **Reading Assessment Targets:** R.3.1. Paragraph 4 is the most direct information about Mrs. Pontellier putting away the letter. Although answers A and B are related to Mrs. Pontellier reading the letter, there is nothing to indicate either was the reason for her putting the letter away, so they are incorrect. Although Mrs. Pontellier noted Leonce had not returned after she put away the letter, there is nothing to indicate this was the reason for putting the letter away, so answer D is incorrect.

6. **D; DOK Level:** 3; **Reading Assessment Targets:** R.3.1. Mrs. Pontellier talked a little bit about herself in paragraph 1, and she read the letter in paragraph 3. Although Leonce did disappear, there is nothing to indicate he returned for dinner, so answer A is incorrect. Although Robert did work in a mercantile house, he did not go to Mexico, so answer B is incorrect. Although Madame Lebrun did maintain a comfortable existence, it was Mrs. Pontellier who talked about her father's plantation in Mississippi, so answer C is incorrect.

LESSON 17, *pp. 76–79*

1. **B; DOK Level:** 2; **Reading Assessment Targets:** R.3.2, R.3.5. Answer B is correct because Mr. Hooper's slow, quiet walk, his tidy appearance, and the lack of anything remarkable about him suggest that he is neat and reserved. Although he may be awkward and strange, these details do not suggest these attributes, so answer A is incorrect. His easy walk and quiet manner do not suggest that he is troubled or self-conscious.

2. **C; DOK Level:** 2; **Reading Assessment Targets:** R.3.2, R.3.5. Answer C is correct because the passage indicates that the parishioners are "so wonder-struck" that they do not return his greeting. This detail and the use of the word *gloomy* suggest that the veil gives the minister a chilling appearance. Answers A and D do not suggest anything chilling or sinister about the minister. Although concealment of the eyes may seem chilling, it is not as much proof as is the response of the other characters to the minister's appearance.

3. **DOK Level:** 2; **Reading Assessment Targets:** R.3.2, R.3.3, R.3.5. The completed character web should include the following descriptions: **He looks like a surgeon when he works. He is a wizard at driving. His behavior is selfish. He makes no effort with women.** These characteristics contribute to Nick's surprising appeal. The author suggests that women are drawn to qualities in Nick that are alluring but are not normally positive qualities. Women are drawn to his swagger, confidence, and seeming disregard for their affections. He is a "bad boy" who is a powerful draw, even if he should not be so by intellectual or logical standards.

4. **C; DOK Level:** 2; **Reading Assessment Targets:** R.3.2, R.3.5. The narrator states that he had nothing to fear when there was knocking at the door. He at this point feels confident that he will not be found out. Answers A and B imply that he thought he might be found out, which is not the case in paragraph 1. There is no text evidence to support answer D.

5. D; DOK Level: 2; Reading Assessment Targets: R.3.3, R.3.5, R.4.3/L.4.3. Although the narrator makes claims about feeling lighthearted and triumphant, he gives himself away in paragraph 3 by indicating that he was truly at ease only after he was sure he had convinced the police officers that no wrongdoing had occurred. The narrator's explanations about the shriek and the old man's whereabouts are lies he offers to cover up the murder; they do not provide clues as to how he feels about the success of the cover-up. His overly accommodating response to the police officers is part of his act to convince them that all is well; he may be nervous as they tour the house, but his statements do not reveal such a feeling, and his actions suggest confidence that the police officers will find no evidence against him.

6. A; DOK Level: 2; Reading Assessment Targets: R.3.2, R.3.5. The police officers' relaxed actions suggest that they do not suspect foul play and that, in fact, they trust the narrator's explanation of the shriek. On the other hand, nothing about their actions suggests that they are apologetic about disturbing the narrator to address the complaint lodged by the neighbor. If the police officers were thorough, they would not be satisfied by the lack of noticeable evidence and would continue to question the narrator about the events of the night.

7. B; DOK Level: 2; Reading Assessment Targets: R.3.2, R.3.5. Because the narrator has killed someone, it can be inferred that the narrator's headache, ear ringing, and paleness are signs of guilt. He is not murderous while he sits with the officers. Although he has fooled the officers and chats with them cheerily at first, he soon begins to have a headache, ear ringing, and paleness and wishes that the officers would leave, so his confidence and cheerfulness have waned.

8. C; DOK Level: 2; Reading Assessment Targets: R.3.2, R.3.3, R.3.4, R.3.5. Because the behavior of the police officers never changes, it is likely that they do not hear the noise and are not aware of the narrator's headache or concerned about his talkativeness. The relaxed attitudes of the officers and their willingness to engage in mundane conversation indicate that they no longer are trying to obtain evidence.

9. D; DOK Level: 2; Reading Assessment Targets: R.3.2, R.3.3, R.3.4, R.3.5. The narrator confesses because his mental illness leads him to believe that the sound of the dead man's heartbeat is not in his ears but can be heard in the room. He does not think the house is alive; he thinks the dead man's heart has come to life. His accusations in paragraph 4 indicate his beliefs that the police officers are villains and are trying to trick him, but these beliefs are further symptoms of his madness; neither is the primary reason for his confession.

10. C. DOK Level: 2; Reading Assessment Targets: R.3.2, R.3.5. Answer C is correct; the details of the first two sentences of paragraph 1 reveal that Ethan Frome was most likely a lonely and sensitive man. In those first two sentences Ethan Frome is not described as a tireless traveler, a cheerful and sociable man, or a serious professional. In fact, it is mentioned that his studies were unfinished. Therefore, answers A, B, and D are wrong.

11. D; DOK Level: 2; Reading Assessment Targets: R.3.2, R.3.3, R.3.4. Answer D is correct; Ethan felt that his affinity to nature was a heavy burden. In this regard, he wonders if he will be the "sole victim of this mournful privilege." The word victim implies that his affinity brings him neither happiness nor enjoyment. The word sole indicates that he does not share this characteristic with friends.

12. B; DOK Level: 2; Reading Assessment Targets: R.3.2, R.3.5. The correct answer is B. The word that best describes Ethan's feelings about Mattie is fascination. This can be inferred from the words "Then he learned that one other spirit had trembled with the same touch of wonder." Nothing in the paragraph implies that he felt bitterness, annoyance, or boredom. Therefore, answers A, C, and D are wrong.

13. C; DOK Level: 2; Reading Assessment Targets: R.3.2, R.3.5, R.4.3 /L.4.3. Answer C is correct. From the information on Mattie in the last paragraphs, readers can infer that she is enthusiastic and sensitive. Mattie is amazed at what Ethan teaches her and sees beauty in a sunset. Nothing in the last paragraphs implies that Mattie is serious or controlling. While Mattie could be cunning and efficient, or cheerful and jovial, the text gives no evidence of this and instead describes her sensitivity and enthusiasm for knowledge and nature.

14. D; DOK Level: 2; Reading Assessment Targets: R.3.2, R.3.4, R.3.5. Answer D is correct. From the details in paragraph 3, readers can infer that Ethan will probably feel increasingly drawn to Mattie. The text mentions that he feels "other sensations, less definable but more exquisite, which drew them together with a shock of silent joy." Answer A contradicts what is implied in the paragraph. Nothing indicates that Ethan wants to find new friends or convince Mattie to start painting. Therefore, answers B and C are incorrect.

15. D; DOK Level: 2; Reading Assessment Targets: R.3.3, R.3.5, R.4.3/L.4.3. Answer D is correct. This is the only option that demonstrates a shift from Ethan's sadness and loneliness to profound joy. Mattie's demonstrated interest in the things that bring joy to Ethan transforms his mood. A, B, and C are incorrect as they focus on what is missing from Ethan's life and his feelings of isolation from others, as they cannot relate to the things that matter to him.

16. A; DOK Level: 2; Reading Assessment Targets: R.3.2, R.3.5. Answer A is correct. Ethan is clearly touched by Mattie's reaction to his knowledge and sense of wonder, making this the only correct option. Answer B is not supported by this paragraph. Answers C and D take a negative view of Ethan's response to Mattie, which is incorrect. This paragraph portrays positivity on Ethan's part.

LESSON 18, pp. 80–83

1. A; DOK Level: 3; Reading Assessment Targets: R.3.2, R.3.3, R.3.5, R.4.1/RL.4.1, R.4.3/L.4.3. Details such as "low-hanging heavens," "air was heavy," and "ribboned shadows" reveal an oppressive environment that is squeezing in on the characters. Answer B is incorrect because the farming operation is rural, not modern. Answer C is incorrect because the sweetness is oppressive, not a positive description of the land. Answer D is incorrect because the narrator creates a feeling of oppression, not love of agriculture.

2. C; DOK Level: 3; Reading Assessment Targets: R.3.2, R.3.3, R.3.5. Answer C is the only logical answer. The low-hanging and oppressive environment combined with the fact that the sweetness in the air "drenches" the town and the men, suggests that the men feel trapped. Answers A, B, and D are part of the description of the setting and, therefore, do not explain it.

3. **D; DOK Level:** 1; **Reading Assessment Target:** R.2.1, R.3.2. Answer D is correct because the landscape looks the same on three sides only, as stated in paragraph 1. The west is different. Answer A is incorrect because grass is described as "rust-red" and cannot be seen to the west. Answer B is incorrect because mud is mentioned only in describing the stream. Answer C misinterprets information in the passage; there is a stream, but no river, which is on the western side.

4. **A; DOK Level:** 2; **Reading Assessment Target:** R.3.2. Answer A is correct because the narrator states in paragraph 1 that Canute would have shot himself except for the trees. Answer B is incorrect because the implication is that Canute does not enjoy much about life, nor does the narrator say or imply anything that shows Canute's feelings about the wind. Answer C is incorrect because he is deeply depressed; although he built his house by himself, nothing is stated or implied about his attachment to or feelings about it. Answer D is incorrect because nothing is mentioned about Canute's earlier life.

5. **A; DOK Level:** 2; **Reading Assessment Target:** R.3.2. The landscape is described in paragraph 1. The wigwam is situated at "the base of some irregularly ascending hills. A footpath wound its way gently down the sloping land till it reached the broad river bottom. . . ." Therefore, answer A is correct. Answer B is incorrect because the landscape is the opposite. Answer C is incorrect because no farms are mentioned. Answer D is incorrect because there is a path to the river.

6. **C; DOK Level:** 2; **Reading Assessment Target:** R.3.2. Answer C is correct because the girl's buckskin slip and moccasins and her wigwam home reflect the dress and living quarters of many Native American people living in the Midwest at the time in which the story takes place. Answer A is incorrect for two reasons: there is no indication of a small town, just the wigwam, and *Missouri* names the river, not the state. Although the date is plausible, answer B is incorrect because no big cities are mentioned. Answer D may be plausible, but it does not answer the question about the girl's clothing and home.

7. **C; DOK Level:** 2; **Reading Assessment Targets:** R.3.2, R.3.3, R.3.4. Answer C is correct because the girl is described as being as free as the wind and as spirited as the deer. Answer A states the opposite of the correct answer; the girl is at one with the outdoors. Nothing is mentioned about her enjoyment of reading. Answer B is incorrect because her mother pays close attention to her and encourages her spirit. Answer D is incorrect because the girl is shown as wild and free, not calm.

8. **B; DOK Level:** 2; **Reading Assessment Targets:** R.3.2, R.3.5. Answer B is the best description. The setting describes a neighborhood in a city. The neighborhood is populated with "outcasts." The neighborhood is clearly not rural or wealthy. It is most likely not residential, as the text indicates that it comprises mostly wholesale stores.

9. **C; DOK Level:** 2; **Reading Assessment Targets:** R.3.2, R.3.5. Answer C is correct. The personification of the echo in the text gives the sense of complete silence and stillness on the street, that even the slightest noise would disturb it. While the sadness and fear may be part of the mood of the passage, the focus of this text is the silence. Answer D is incorrect because despite the silence, the mood in the text is not peaceful.

10. **D; DOK Level:** 2; **Reading Assessment Targets:** R.3.2, R.3.5. The description of the rain in paragraph 2 and the description of the neighborhood create a gloomy and forbidding feeling. Answers A and B are incorrect because nothing in the description of the rain, the bleak neighborhood, and huddled figures in a bread line suggests these feelings. Answer C may be more likely than A and B, but the setting is very worldly and not distant.

11. **A; DOK: Level:** 3; **Reading Assessment Targets:** R.2.7, R.3.2, R.3.5. Readers can infer that he is homeless. On the basis of this assumption, and that Sam is tired and cold, a shelter would be the most likely place a person in his position would go. Answer B is incorrect because the weather is too bad for staying outdoors. Answer C might be correct if the restaurant were distributing food, but no mention is made of this. Answer D, too, would be logical if another bakery were mentioned, but neither answer choice indicates a more likely decision.

12. **A; DOK: Level:** 2; **Reading Assessment Targets:** R.3.2, R.3.5. The description of the desertion and the iron-shuttered fronts of the wholesale stores makes answer A the best choice. The area is not upscale, judging by the residents, nor does anything indicate that it features warehouses. The South Side of Chicago is not suburban, nor is there evidence that the area is a performing arts district.

13. **C; DOK Level:** 2; **Reading Assessment Targets:** R.3.2, R.3.3, R.3.4, R.3.5. Most people would not want to stand outside in line late on a cold night to wait for food, so the characters already would be uncomfortable. The weather, "a fine drizzle that pervaded the air," emphasizes the characters' discomfort. The rain would have no effect on the characters' gratitude, so answer A is incorrect. No connection is mentioned between rain and making bread, so answer B is incorrect. Answer D is incorrect because the rain would emphasize the gloom, not contrast with it.

14. **D; DOK Level:** 2; **Reading Assessment Target:** R.3.2. The first sentence of paragraph 1 suggests that the protagonist felt depressed. The sentence says ". . . was not calculated to raise the spirits of the young surgeon, or to dispel any feeling of anxiety or depression." Therefore, answer D is correct. Answers A and B contradict information in the first sentence. There is no indication that the protagonist is afraid, so answer C is incorrect.

15. **C; DOK Level:** 2; **Reading Assessment Targets:** R.3.2, R.3.5. The setting is most likely that of a poor suburb—there are neglected houses and signs of poverty. Therefore, answer C is correct. Answer A is the opposite of the correct choice. Answers B and D are incorrect because the author describes "irregular lanes" with cottages and people.

16. **C; DOK Level:** 2; **Reading Assessment Targets:** R.3.2, R.3.5. The description of the woman in paragraph 2 adds to the dreariness of the setting. The description of her and her actions are part of the setting; therefore, answer C is correct. Answer A is incorrect, as the text does not lay blame for the circumstances on the characters. Answers B and D are not demonstrated in the text.

17. B; DOK Level: 2; **Reading Assessment Targets:** R.3.2, R.3.3, R.3.5. The first sentence of paragraph 3 suggests that the way home was unpleasant and complicated. He says: "After plodding wearily through the mud and mire; making many inquiries for the place to which he had been directed; and receiving as many contradictory and unsatisfactory replies in return; the young man at length arrived before the house which had been pointed out to him as the object of his destination." Therefore, the correct answer is B. Answer A contradicts the information in the first sentence. Answer C is incorrect because the doctor did reach his destination. Answer D is incorrect because while the doctor asked people for directions, there is no indication that people delayed him along the way.

18. B; DOK Level: 2; **Reading Assessment Targets:** R.3.2, R.3.5, R.4.3/L.4.3. The sensation that the protagonist most likely had when he saw the house was despair. The author describes the house as having ". . . even a more desolate and unpromising exterior than any he had yet passed." Therefore, answer B is correct. Nothing in the passage suggests that the protagonist was happy, angry, or jealous.

LESSON 19, *pp. 84–87*

1. A; DOK Level: 2; **Reading Assessment Target:** R.4.3/L.4.3. Answer A is correct because Dencombe's life is compared with a glass that measures medicine dosage. Answers B and D are misinterpretations of the comparison, as they are narrow interpretations that do not logically reflect a synthesis of the two elements being compared. The glass is scored like a thermometer; it is not an actual thermometer. Answer C is incorrect because it is not part of this comparison.

2. B; DOK Level: 2; **Reading Assessment Target:** R.4.3/L.4.3. Answer A may be correct in terms of the passage, but it does not reflect the actual comparison: the depth of the human spirit with the depth of the ocean (answer B). Answers C and D contradict the comparison, which indicates that the human spirit is deeper than the ocean, and thus not superficial and shallow.

3. C; DOK Level: 2; **Reading Assessment Target:** R.4.1/L.4.1. The story uses personification to give human qualities to inanimate objects. A leaf is given the human ability to be persistent and tap. "[T]apped hurriedly, persistently" is not a metaphor, hyperbole, or onomatopoeia.

4. B; DOK Level: 2; **Reading Assessment Target:** R.4.3/L.4.3. *Gurgling*, *bubbling*, and *squeaking* imitate the sounds the water makes and are examples of onomatopoeia. Answers A, C, and D do not contain any words that imitate sounds.

5. B; DOK Level: 2; **Reading Assessment Target:** R.4.2/L.4.2. Answer B is correct because the simile uses the qualities of a cat to emphasize that Rebecca is walking quickly and quietly. Answer A is incorrect because cats do not move loudly. Answers C and D might emphasize the qualities of a cat, but the comparisons do not fit the context of the sentence.

6. D; DOK Level: 3; **Reading Assessment Targets:** R.2.7, R.4.3/L.4.3. The wind displays human qualities by *raging* and *wrenching* at the window fastenings. Therefore, D is the correct answer. Answer A is incorrect because it uses sensory language, not personification, to describe the light. Answers B and C are incorrect because the daddy-long-legs and the wind are not given human qualities.

7. B; DOK Level: 2; **Reading Assessment Targets:** R.4.3/L.4.3, R.5.2. Answer B is correct because the metaphor indicates that hugging and kissing the bride might cause wrinkles, or "crumples," in her dress. Meg welcomes such wrinkles, as she states in paragraph 2, as signs of love. Answer A is incorrect because it implies indifference, not love. Answer C is a misreading of the passage. Amy says that Meg looks like herself but "so sweet and lovely." Answer D is unsupported by the text. Although Meg may be nervous or somewhat sad about leaving, nothing suggests that she would prefer not to get married.

8. D; DOK Level: 2; **Reading Assessment Target:** R.4.3/L.4.3. Answer D is correct, suggesting the term *empty nest*. Parents often feel mixed emotions at a son's or daughter's wedding. Answers A and C are unsupported by the text. Nothing indicates disapproval or concern about finances. Answer B is a misinterpretation of the reference to a bird's nest; the meaning is figurative, not literal, nor does it indicate that Meg attends to the birds.

9. A; DOK Level: 3; **Reading Assessment Targets:** R.4.3/L.4.3, R.5.1. Answer A best explains the two examples of hyperbole in the sentence. The first example emphasizes that the Professor's kindness has a positive effect on many boys. The second emphasizes that Jo has an extremely forgiving nature. Answer B is incorrect because the descriptions of the Professor and Jo show kindness and patience, not strictness or academic rigor. Answer C may seem plausible, but these descriptions suggest a negative atmosphere. *Permissiveness* has connotations of "too much freedom," which the author does not mean to convey, given that Jo is happy and the boys do well. Nothing is mentioned about academic standards. Therefore, answer A is a better choice. Answer D is incorrect because nothing is mentioned about academic training. The number of times Jo forgives a boy expresses her patient and forgiving nature, not the loss of it.

10. C; DOK Level: 2; **Reading Assessment Target:** R.4.3/L.4.3. Answer C is the best choice because a whirlpool moves in circles and suggests constant motion. Although boys at the beach might see whirlpools, the metaphor does not suggest a beach setting. The boys are at the school, not at the shore. Answer B is not the best choice because nothing is suggested about studying the movement of water. The boys themselves, not their studies, are the subject of the comparison. Answer D seems more plausible but is not as good a choice as answer C because it omits mentioning the boys and brings in additional objects—a top and a toy.

11. A; DOK Level: 2; **Reading Assessment Target:** R.4.3/L.4.3. Answer A indicates that the boys are growing spontaneously and naturally. Answers B and D are incorrect because they reflect too literal an interpretation of parts of the simile, which compares the boys' growth to that of dandelions in spring. The comparison is about growth, not about lawns or gardens. Answer C is incorrect because it has nothing to do with growth or spontaneity, even though the boys may well enjoy outdoor activity.

12. **C; DOK Level:** 2; **Reading Assessment Target:** R.4.3/L.4.3. Before using the words *hum* and *burr*, the narrator explains that he felt his senses leaving him and that the last distinct words he heard were those of his death sentence. So the onomatopoeic words *hum* and *burr* that describe the voices of the Inquisition judges emphasize that the narrator cannot distinguish individual sounds. The narrator states that he is losing his sense of hearing but does not indicate that he has ringing in his ears. He hears the voices of the Inquisition judges as indistinct sound (a hum or a burr), not as musical notes, which are mentioned later in the passage in another context. The narrator uses the phrase "burr of a mill wheel" to represent the voices of the Inquisition judges, not as a literal clue about his location.

13. **C; DOK Level:** 2; **Reading Assessment Targets:** R.3.2, R.3.5, R.4.3/L.4.3. In comparing the candles with charitable angels who might save him, the narrator indicates that he has hope. The comparison of the candles with angels likely does not represent warmth or regret because nothing about the narrator's circumstances suggests this sensation or emotion. Although the narrator may feel fear, a view of candles as charitable angels is more likely to represent the positive emotion of hope than the negative emotion of fear.

14. **A; DOK Level:** 2; **Reading Assessment Targets:** R.3.2, R.3.5, R.4.3/L.4.3. The narrator connects the sensation of touching a battery wire with feelings of nausea and hopelessness, indicating that dread about his future is causing him physical discomfort. He feels terrified of death, not excited to be alive. The account of feeling as though every fiber in his being had touched the wire of a battery is a figurative description of how he feels, not a literal description related to his sentence; there is no evidence in the passage that the judges have sentenced him to be electrocuted. The sensation of touching the wire of a battery is not related to being unbound because the narrator's captors have unbound him before he has this feeling.

15. **B; DOK Level:** 2; **Reading Assessment Targets:** R.3.2, R.3.5, R.4.3/L.4.3. In the rest of the sentence the narrator says, "… what sweet rest there must be in the grave." Therefore, answer B is correct because it confirms the thought that death would be restful and welcome as an end to the narrator's suffering, as music brings pleasure to a listener. Rest implies peace and calm, so answer A is incorrect. Answer C has no context, as nothing is mentioned about understanding. Answer D is a misinterpretation of the simile; the musical note brings pleasure rather than contemplation of musical creativity.

16. **B; DOK Level:** 2; **Reading Assessment Targets:** R.3.5, R.4.3/L.4.3. The image of a soul's descent into Hades represents a desperate situation, and other details in the passage indicate that the narrator is facing a desperate situation. No other details in the passage suggest that the narrator deserves to be condemned or meets a fiery death. The image of a soul's descent into Hades could suggest that the Inquisition judges are or seem like demons; however, the simile describes the narrator's fainting spell, so it more likely represents his circumstances than the literal or figurative characters of the judges.

HIGH IMPACT LESSON: FIGURATIVE MEANINGS, *pp. 88–89*

1. **C; DOK Level:** 2; **Reading Assessment Targets:** R.4.1/L.4.1. The phrases "the breaking down of men" and "what happened to them afterward" provide context clues that the most likely answer is C. *Creeping* suggests movement, the opposite of freezing, so answer A is incorrect. Although the text indicates Jurgis laughed, this is in contrast to the meaning of the phrase, so answer B is incorrect. Although the phrase indicates movement of the body, nothing in the passage indicates flinching with pain, so answer D is incorrect.

2. **B; DOK Level:** 2; **Reading Assessment Targets:** R.4.1/L.4.1. The author refers to the city as *she* and describes several actions—"peering out," "toiled," and "turned." These are human-like actions that help readers better relate to Atlanta. The city peers out into "the promise of the future," so answer A is incorrect. Answer C is incorrect because the city later wakes. Answer D is incorrect because Atlanta also "toiled for her daily bread."

3. **D; DOK Level:** 2; **Reading Assessment Targets:** R.4.1/L.4.1. The phrase uses auditory imagery to create an expressive tone; less descriptive language would make the passage plain. Answer A is incorrect because the passage's tone is serious. Answer B is incorrect because simpler language would be less descriptive. Although the phrase describes noises, the tone of the passage itself is neither noisy nor quiet, so answer C is incorrect.

4. **A; DOK Level:** 2; **Reading Assessment Targets:** R.4.1/L.4.1. A *widow* is a woman who survives the death of her spouse; here, the word collectively describes the people of Atlanta who survived the war. Although in American culture widows are depicted as wearing black and mourning, this passage shows them returning to work, so answer B is incorrect. While the verb *rose* can indicate an increase in elevation, the context does not support that meaning here, so answer C is incorrect. Answer D is incorrect, since the passage does not indicate the city opened itself up after the war.

5. **D; DOK Level:** 3; **Reading Assessment Targets:** R.4.1/L.4.1. Paragraph 3 describes a complicated and unsettling emotion the author feels about Atlanta after the war. The *ghost* in this context is a memory, and the *untrue dream* describes an idea that was incorrect or not true. Although the passage mentions ashes, nothing indicates this phrase is meant to describe the survivors or the remains of the burned buildings, so answers A and B are incorrect. Also, this is not a story about supernatural occurrences, so answer C is incorrect.

6. **C; DOK Level:** 3; **Reading Assessment Targets:** R.4.1/L.4.1. The phrase is followed by the contrasting idea "they of Atlanta turned resolutely toward the future," showing the strength of the city's population. The passage does not use sarcasm, and repeatedly supports its main idea that the people of Atlanta are strong, so answers A and B are incorrect. Answer D is incorrect because the passage focuses on the strength of Atlanta rebuilding after the war.

1. **D; DOK Level:** 2; **Reading Assessment Targets:** R.3.2, R.3.5. Answer D is the only possible answer. The narrator describes the scene, nothing else. Answers A, B, and C are incorrect because nothing is mentioned about what characters are thinking, how they are feeling, or why events are taking place.

2. **B; DOK Level:** 3; **Reading Assessment Targets:** R.2.7, R.3.2. If the man were the narrator, he would tell the story in first-person point of view and would reveal his own thoughts and feelings. Therefore, answers A, C, and D are incorrect.

3. **C; DOK Level:** 2; **Reading Assessment Targets:** R.2.8, R.3.5. The narrator refers to Jo and Meg by name, so the narrator is neither of these characters. The narrator does not use first-person pronouns, so the author did not write this passage in first-person point of view. The narrator does give readers insight into memories and thoughts that Jo and Meg have, so the narrator is omniscient.

4. **A; DOK Level:** 2; **Reading Assessment Target:** R.3.2. It is the narrator's perspective that Meg has "small vanities." This is offered in the third-person narration, and there is no indication in the passage that any of the other girls or Meg's mother has this perspective.

5. **D; DOK Level:** 2; **Reading Assessment Targets:** R.3.3, R.6.3. In fiction, point of view indicates how the story is told; therefore, answer D is correct. Answers A, B, and C might be better answers if the story were not fiction and did not have a narrator. The story is not about reading habits but about a family. Although the girls' reactions to their gifts are being discussed, the author's purpose for this point of view is not to analyze the reactions. Jo's despair could be described by Jo herself, if she were the narrator, so answer C is incorrect.

6. **C; DOK Level:** 3; **Reading Assessment Targets:** R.3.3, R.5.1, R.6.3. The narrator describes Meg as sweet and pious, and Meg's statement demonstrates sweetness and piety. She says that she will read her book (presumably the Bible) every day and that it will do her good. This behavior does not show her as vain. It is Jo who is described as disappointed at not seeing presents in her stocking. It is also Jo who is described as feeling that the book was a true guidebook for any pilgrim. Meg also may feel this way, but the narrator says this of Jo.

7. **A; DOK Level:** 2; **Reading Assessment Target:** R.3.2. In this passage, the narrator provides information only about Dexter's thoughts and feelings. The narrator does not share the thoughts and feelings of the girl, Hilda, or Mr. Jones.

8. **D; DOK Level:** 2; **Reading Assessment Target:** R.3.2. It is the narrator's perspective that the girl is "beautifully ugly." Dexter is only 14, so it is unlikely he would have enough life experiences to make this observation. This is offered in the third-person narration, and there is no indication in the passage that any of the characters has this perspective.

9. **B; DOK Level:** 2; **Reading Assessment Target:** R.3.2. The narrator knows what the girl is thinking because she is described as blatantly artificial, yet convincing. Answer A is incorrect because the nurse's thoughts or intentions are not mentioned, even though she is observed and quoted. Answer C is incorrect because the narrator describes more than mere actions. The narrator's descriptions indicate the girl's thoughts or intentions. Answer D is incorrect because the narrator may or may not describe the girl sympathetically. Indeed, the description of her smile is ambiguous.

10. **C; DOK Level:** 3; **Reading Assessment Targets:** R.3.2, R.3.3. As the narrator and a character in the story, Dexter would use *I* to describe his feelings as a first-person narrator would. Answers A and D would not depend upon the point of view. A first-person narrator may or may not overhear a conversation. Answer B is incorrect because a third-person narrator who is not part of the story uses these pronouns.

11. **A; DOK Level:** 2; **Reading Assessment Target:** R.3.2. Answer A is correct. The use of the word *I* indicates a first-person perspective. The other options are incorrect.

12. **D; DOK Level:** 2; **Reading Assessment Target:** R.3.2. The narrator, Nick, describes Jordan Baker's motivations and actions as he sees, assumes, or understands them. Answer A is incorrect because there are no interactions with other characters in this excerpt. Jordan Baker is being described; she is not describing herself, so answer B is incorrect. While the narrator mentions Daisy's party, Daisy is not describing Jordan, so answer C is incorrect.

13. **C; DOK Level:** 3; **Reading Assessment Target:** R.3.3. The statement indicates that the narrator does not like to lie to others. He wants to end his current long-distance relationship before acting on his feelings for Jordan. He states that he does not mind that Jordan is dishonest, so answer A is incorrect. He says that he is slow to act on his feelings, so answer B is incorrect. He considers himself an honest person, so answer D is incorrect.

14. **A; DOK Level:** 2; **Reading Assessment Targets:** R.3.2, R.3.5. The narrator emphasizes his honesty by stating that he is honest and by sharing his desire to end his long-distance relationship. Answers B, C, and D are not supported by the passage.

1. **A; DOK Level:** 2; **Reading Assessment Targets:** R.3.2, R.3.3, R.3.4. Answer A is correct because after describing the run-down condition of the room, Sarah mentions that it is the room in which Nanny entertains her friends and in which she eventually will be married. Answer B is incorrect because Sarah mentions the lack of a carpet as a detail in the description of the room's condition; she does not indicate that the exposed floor makes her feel the cold. Answer C is incorrect because her husband is unwilling to discuss the matter and has not wanted to spend money on improvements. Answer D contradicts information in the passage; the implication is that Sarah has neither complained nor spoken directly about the condition of the room.

2. B; DOK Level: 2; Reading Assessment Targets: R.3.2, R.3.3, R.3.5. Answer B is correct because Sarah mentions the price of the wallpaper she put up ten years ago, indicating that the paper was cheap and that her labor cost her husband nothing. She also states that other families with less money have nicer homes. Answer A is incorrect because her daughter, not her husband, entertains or will want to entertain friends. Answer C is incorrect because Sarah implies that the family has more than enough money and states that families with less money live more comfortably. Answer D is incorrect because Sarah's husband refuses to engage in discussion, as shown in the last two sentences of the passage.

3. A; DOK Level: 2; Reading Assessment Target: R.3.2. Answer A is correct; the text indicates that she "lifted from England to California." Answer B is incorrect; she ends up in California, and her speech pattern is described as British English. She may or may not like tea, but she serves it to the children. There is no indication of her liking or disliking it herself. Answer D is incorrect because she seems to like children as she has made them feel grown up and comfortable.

4. B; DOK Level: 2; Reading Assessment Target: R.3.2. Answer B is correct because the author states, "Being handed cups of tea, no matter how reduced by milk, made them believe that they had grown up overnight." The children clearly perceived tea as an adult activity and being invited to tea meant they were being treated as mature individuals. While the other answers might be true, the text does not support them.

5. C; DOK Level: 2; Reading Assessment Target: R.3.2. Answers A and B reflect a misinterpretation of the text. Edie has moved from England; Mrs. Ransom has neither gone to England, nor abandoned her children. The implication is that she has died in childbirth, as the narrator mentions that the twins are responsible for their mother's death. Answer D is incorrect because Mr. Ransom is referred to as a widower, not a divorced man.

6. D; DOK Level: 2; Reading Assessment Target: R.3.2. Answer A is incorrect because Edie does not seem desperate for attention. On the contrary, she invites the children for tea and pays attention to them. Even if she had wanted attention, nothing in the passage indicates that she is desperate. Answer B is incorrect because the evidence in the passage supports the idea of her being pleasant and attentive rather than annoyed and bored. Answer C is a misreading of the passage. Mr. Ransom is grieving, not Edie.

7. C; DOK Level: 2; Reading Assessment Target: R.3.2. Edie is most likely a governess who has been hired to help raise the children. She is English, whereas the family can be assumed to be American. This information makes it less likely that she is a relation of the family. It is doubtful that she is the new wife, since Mr. Ransom appears to be a very recent widower.

8. B; DOK Level: 2; Reading Assessment Target: R.3.2. Answer B is the best choice because Mr. Ransom "aches" for his wife. Answer A may be logical because it seems that Mr. Ransom does not sleep well, but nothing is mentioned about Mr. Ransom's being exhausted by the children. Answer C is incorrect because nothing is mentioned about new responsibilities, although he may have them. Without a reference in the passage, you cannot make a logical inference. He does not seem comforted by dreams.

9. D; DOK Level: 3; Reading Assessment Targets: R.2.7, R.3.2, R.3.5. Answer A is incorrect because Edie has not arrived for a visit. She is most likely not a family member and is there solely to care for the children. Answer B is incorrect because Edie is there to work by caring for the children. There is no family bond, and she is not there to go to school or merely to reside with relatives. Answer C is incorrect because there is no teaching taking place, nor does learning enter into the passage, nor is the grandfather likely to be paid, as Edie is. Answer D is the best parallel because the grandmother comes to help care for a child.

10. B; DOK Level: 2; Reading Assessment Targets: R.3.2, R.3.3. Before this scene, no one can remember seeing a Znaeym and a von Gradwitz talking in friendship. Therefore, the most logical answer choice is B—that Ulrich and Georg and their families have been enemies. Answer A is incorrect because they have become friends during this experience. Nothing in the passage indicates that the families are or were business associates nor that Ulrich and Georg have had adventures together.

11. C; DOK Level: 2; Reading Assessment Targets: R.3.2, R.3.3, R.3.5. Because the two are waiting for help and they shout for help, they are most likely injured and cannot get out of the forest on their own. Answer A is incorrect because the cold would not keep them from leaving the forest. Answers B and D are incorrect because nothing indicates that they are hunting, and they already have ended their feud.

12. D; DOK Level: 2; Reading Assessment Targets: R.3.2, R.3.3. Despite their predicament, the men expect to be rescued so that they may have peace among their people. Although they know they are in a dangerous situation, they believe their men are arriving and show no indication of annoyance. Therefore, answer A is incorrect. Although they may be thankful for their new friendship, it is because of the peace it will bring to their people. Therefore, answer B is incorrect. Answer C is incorrect because they have ended the feud.

13. B; DOK Level: 2; Reading Assessment Targets: R.2.7, R.3.2, R.3.3. The men are injured and helpless, and wolves are advancing on them. Answers A and C are incorrect because nothing indicates that either man plans to break the pact of friendship or that either will feud with forester folk. Answer D is incorrect because Ulrich and Georg are likely to be killed before they freeze to death.

14. A; DOK Level: 3; Reading Assessment Targets: R.3.2, R.3.3, R.3.4, R.3.5. Shortly after believing that he saw rescuers in the distance, Ulrich realizes that the figures are wolves. This realization changes the joy of new friendship to fear. Answer B is incorrect because Georg's men are not to be seen. Answer C is plausible, but not the best choice because Ulrich is more concerned with wolves than with dangers of walking alone in the forest. Answer D is incorrect because Georg does not know about the wolves until Ulrich tells him at the very end of the passage. At that point, Georg's thoughts are unknown.

15. B; DOK Level: 1; Reading Assessment Target: R.2.1. The first paragraph indicates that "the only way I know she's there at all is because the dog points in the living room." The narrator does note that Pauline makes a board creak, smokes a cigarette, and coughs, but those are not what alert the narrator that Pauline is on her porch.

16. **C; DOK Level: 2; Reading Assessment Target:** R.3.2. It is reasonable to assume this information indicates that Pauline is younger than the narrator. The narrator invites Pauline inside, which indicates that Pauline does not annoy the narrator. Pauline is lying when she claims to be "passing by," but there is no indication that she is lying at the end of the passage. Pauline seems to be nervous and unsure of herself, so answer D is incorrect.

17. **D; DOK Level: 2; Reading Assessment Target:** R.3.2. Konrad is the ex-husband of the narrator and current husband of Pauline. The narrator mentions her "husband's new wife," says that Pauline lives in the city with Konrad, and speaks of "their" flat. Stray is the narrator's dog, and there is no mention of a neighbor or brother.

18. **A; DOK Level: 3; Reading Assessment Targets:** R.3.3, R.3.4. The narrator seems concerned. The narrator wishes she could do something about the visits, but she is also willing to invite Pauline into the house. She feels some bond with Pauline, saying "lies are the least of our problems." There is no indication that the narrator is jealous of, amused by, or angry at Pauline.

19. **D; DOK Level: 2; Reading Assessment Targets:** R.3.2, R.3.4. Pauline seems unsure of herself and nervous about angering her husband. Pauline says that she must get back home because "You know how he is," implying that he is demanding, someone who worries, or is difficult in some way. The actions of the narrator and Pauline imply they both have negative feelings about Konrad, so answers A, B, and C are incorrect.

20. **C; DOK Level: 3; Reading Assessment Targets:** R.3.2, R.3.3, R.3.4. In paragraph 3, the words *Sometimes, Today,* and *same* indicate that Pauline has visited before. Answer B is not supported by the details in the passage. This scene takes place when the "afternoon light" is bright, so answers A and D are incorrect.

LESSON 22, *pp. 98–101*

1. **A; DOK Level: 2; Reading Assessment Target:** R.2.6. The narrator describes the different ways in which the children entertain themselves, so a logical theme would be the statement in answer A. Nothing is said about the effect of cold air on gardens nor about the effect of winter on city dwellers. Nor is anything implied about danger when the children hide from the narrator's uncle.

2. **C; DOK Level: 2; Reading Assessment Target:** R.2.6. The best choice is answer C because the word *glowed* has positive connotations regarding the children's playing. They seem exhilarated by the sting of the cold and enjoy themselves to the fullest. Answers A and B have no relevance to the theme. Answer D has no relevance to the theme unless the theme was misinterpreted in the previous question.

3. **C; DOK Level: 2; Reading Assessment Target:** R.2.6. Answer C is correct because evidence in the passage shows Ray as disappointed in life, and he runs after Hal to prevent Hal from making the same mistake that Ray believes led to his own disappointment. Answer A is incorrect because nothing is mentioned about how Ray is treated. Answer B is incorrect because the passage implies that marriage may lead to disappointment, not to tragedy. Answer D seems possible, but it is incorrect because it is not known whether Ray and Hal are good friends, nor has Hal done anything that helps Ray. In addition, no "problem" is mentioned in the passage.

4. **A; DOK Level: 2; Reading Assessment Targets:** R.2.6, R.3.3. Answer A is correct because Ray feels burdened by marriage and children. He is not protesting against his work (answer B) as much as the fact that he is tied to it because of family responsibilities. His torn overcoat may be a symbol of his life, but he is not protesting against it. Nothing is known about the extent of his friendship with Hal.

5. **B; DOK Level: 2; Reading Assessment Target:** R.2.6. Answer B is correct because he wants to prevent Hal from making the same mistake as he (Ray) made. This action supports the theme of the passage. Answer A may reflect the beginning of Ray's decision but not the action itself. Answer C is not part of the theme. Answer D reflects Ray's status and perhaps his disappointment with life but is not as closely related thematically as his action is.

6. **C; DOK Level: 2; Reading Assessment Targets:** R.2.6, R.5.1, R.5.4. The fact that Ray will not share his thoughts with Hal is most closely related to the theme, based on the details in paragraph 1. Answer A is incorrect because Ray's thoughts and feelings are not summarized in paragraph 3. Answer B is incorrect because the landscape, other than dark fields, is not described, nor does it relate to the theme. Answer D is incorrect because Hal's clothing is not directly related to the theme nor to anything mentioned in paragraph 1.

7. **A; DOK Level: 2; Reading Assessment Targets:** R.2.6. Ray is trying to keep Hal from being as disappointed as he was, but Hal is not following Ray's advice, so answer A is correct. The other options are not supported by the text and offer explanations that do not support the theme.

8. **D; DOK Level: 2; Reading Assessment Target:** R.2.6. The stranger leaves the money to test the town's honesty. Hadleyburg has become too sure of itself as an upright community, and such moral certainty, or self-righteousness, can create a dangerous situation. The townspeople have not been corrupted yet, so answer A is incorrect. The stranger spends a year planning his revenge, so answer B is incorrect. The stranger seems to understand the town's reputation, so answer C is incorrect.

9. **B; DOK Level: 3; Reading Assessment Targets:** R.2.6, R.5.1. The old woman's first thought on reading that the sack contains gold is that the door is not locked. This detail brings into question the underlying honesty of both the woman and the people of Hadleyburg. She is afraid either that people will find out about the gold or that they might steal it. The woman is not distrustful of the stranger, so answer A is incorrect. Answers C and D are not supported by the passage.

10. **A; DOK Level: 1; Reading Assessment Target:** R.2.1. Paragraph 2 indicates that "Hadleyburg had the ill luck to offend a passing stranger" who was bitter and revengeful. Answers B, C, and D are not supported by the passage.

11. **B; DOK Level: 2; Reading Assessment Target:** R.2.6. Harvey says the idea is well-meaning, but it might not succeed in practice. He expresses doubt, so answer A is not correct. He says they are "well meaning," so answer C is incorrect. He is unsure whether they will succeed or fail, so answer D is incorrect.

12. **C; DOK Level: 2; Reading Assessment Target:** R.2.5. Paragraphs 7–9 describe how the boys put holes in the dustbin, splashed red ink on the Association building, and pretended that the soldiers had killed or captured the girls. They use the toys, so answers A and D are incorrect. They do not use them for their intended purpose, so answer B is incorrect.

UNIT 1 (continued)

13. **A; DOK Level:** 2; **Reading Assessment Target:** R.2.4. Eleanor likes the idea of peace toys because they go along with her idea that parents can use toys to influence their children's thoughts and ideas. While she does ask Harvey to bring the toys at Easter, there is no indication that B is true. She believes that some toys can teach life skills, so answer C is incorrect. She wants her children to have the peace toys, so answer D is incorrect.

14. **D; DOK Level:** 3; **Reading Assessment Target:** R.2.6. The boys did not change the way they play with toys. The events in the passage do not support answers A, B, or C.

LESSON 23, pp. 102–105

1. **B; DOK Level:** 2; **Reading Assessment Targets:** R.2.8, R.3.5. The most logical conclusion that can be drawn from the passage is that Rip Van Winkle and his wife struggle financially. The narrator indicates that Rip Van Winkle "would rather starve on a penny than work for a pound." Therefore, the correct answer is B. Answer A is incorrect because Rip Van Winkle and his wife do not appear to have a happy marriage. Answer C is incorrect because his wife would not criticize him if they held similar values. There is no evidence that answer D is correct.

2. **A; DOK Level:** 2; **Reading Assessment Targets:** R.2.8, R.3.2, R.3.5. The most logical conclusion that can be drawn about Rip Van Winkle is that he is a man with little motivation to work. Therefore, answer A is correct. While he may feel relaxed at home, he would not feel that comfortable considering his wife continually criticizes him. Therefore, answer B is incorrect. The passage indicates that Rip Van Winkle does not argue with his wife, so answer C is incorrect. Answer D is contradicted by the last sentence of the passage, which indicates that he leaves the house to get away from his wife.

3. **D; DOK Level:** 2; **Reading Assessment Targets:** R.2.8, R.3.2, R.3.3. Answer D is the best answer because Angela's leaving gifts shows consideration for her friends, and her arrangements show organization. Although nothing is mentioned about how Angela treated Sissy Miller, details in the passage indicate that Angela probably treated her well. Answer B is incorrect because nothing is mentioned about the value of Angela's jewelry, although most pieces are likely to have more sentimental than monetary value, according to details in the passage. Answer C is incorrect because nothing is mentioned about Angela's wealth or fame. Although employing a secretary may indicate that Angela was busy and needed an assistant, having an assistant is not enough evidence on which to conclude that Angela was rich and famous.

4. **D; DOK Level:** 2; **Reading Assessment Targets:** R.2.8, R.3.3, R.3.5. The narrator says that Angela's death was sudden; however, she had time to label each object and tell her husband to whom it should go. This information implies that Angela planned her own death. Answer A is incorrect because nothing in the passage indicates whether she told her secrets to Sissy Miller. Answer B is incorrect because she did not forget her husband. He has the diaries. Answer C is incorrect because Angela was not ill.

5. **A; DOK Level:** 2; **Reading Assessment Targets:** R.2.8, R.3.3, R.3.5. From the statement and the information in the passage, you can conclude that the diary discusses problems with her marriage. The narrator suggests that Gilbert Clandon did not know his wife as well as he thought, nor was their marriage as solid as he thought. Although he may have been curious about what she was writing, it is unlikely that this was the gift he would most cherish. It is also unlikely that the diary contained love poems. There is no indication that Angela hoped the diary would be published.

6. **C; DOK Level:** 2; **Reading Assessment Targets:** R.2.8, R.3.3, R.4.3/L.4.3, R.5.1. Answer C is correct because Gilbert seems to be unaware of the extent of his wife's unhappiness and that she took her own life. Answer A is incorrect because Angela's refusal to share the diary with Gilbert while she was alive caused problems. Although answer B may be an accurate statement about life, it is not a specific conclusion drawn from the evidence in the passage. Answer D is incorrect because diaries and jewelry have nothing to do with each other. If the diary was a cause of friction, Angela's jewelry was not. In fact, Gilbert had bought some objects, and no indication of friction exists about them.

7. **A; DOK Level:** 2; **Reading Assessment Targets:** R.2.8, R.3.3. Based on this statement, answer A is the only logical conclusion among the answer choices. If he believed she would outlive him, then he believed he would never read the diary. While answer B may be true, it is not indicated by the text in the question. There is no text evidence provided to support the conclusions in answers C and D.

8. **A; DOK Level:** 3; **Reading Assessment Target:** R.2.8. His comment that other farmer houses do not have dirty roller towels can lead the reader to conclude that he thinks the other wives can keep a clean kitchen. He makes no indication that he dislikes roller towels, so answer B is incorrect. He knows how roller towels work, so answer C is incorrect. There is no indication that he disagrees about the amount of work on a farm, so answer D is incorrect.

9. **C; DOK Level:** 3; **Reading Assessment Target:** R.2.8. From his questioning, he seems to be most interested in the Wrights' relationship because he was quick to ask if the Wrights got along with each other. He is not "quick to ask" the other questions.

10. **C; DOK Level:** 3; **Reading Assessment Target:** R.2.8. Mrs. Hale's comment, "I don't think a place would be any the cheerfuller for John Wright's bein' in it" leads the reader to conclude that he was a difficult person to live with. Answers A, B, and D are not supported by the passage.

11. **D; DOK Level:** 2; **Reading Assessment Targets:** R.2.8, R.3.3, R.3.5. From the conversation in the passage, it is reasonable to conclude that Laird attempts to be open and honest with his mother. He brings up the issue of his father's leaving quickly after dinner and also says that he thinks his father does not like being around him. Although Laird uses humor, he does not avoid uncomfortable topics; in fact, he addresses one. He is not cautious about opening up to his mother. Laird may be angry with his father, but he is not angry with his mother.

12. B; DOK Level: 2; Reading Assessment Targets: R.2.8, R.3.3, R.4.3/L.4.3. Answer B is the most logical conclusion because a distant father and a son who feels as though he has consistently disappointed his father most probably do not get along well. Answers A and C contradict the evidence in the passage. Answer D is too strong a statement on the basis of the information in the passage.

13. B; DOK Level: 2; Reading Assessment Targets: R.2.8, R.4.3/L.4.3, R.5.1. Laird's mother loves him and cherishes the time she still has with him. She believes that Martin is losing the joy of spending time with their dying son and of getting to know him better. Answer A is incorrect because it states the opposite of what Laird's mother believes. Answer C is a misreading of the passage. She does not love her husband more than her son. Answer D is incorrect because the passage indicates that she shares Laird's sense of humor and that she does not think Laird is disrespectful. If anything, she would most likely think that Martin was the one showing disrespect.

14. C; DOK Level: 2; Reading Assessment Targets: R.2.8, R.3.2, R.3.3, R.3.5. From the mother's references to Martin's obsession with his work and absence from home (whether physical or emotional), answer C is the most logical conclusion. Answer A may seem correct, but Laird has not always been ill. Answers B and D misstate information in the passage. Martin has not disciplined Laird, nor have the parents shared equally in raising him, given Martin's distance from the family.

LESSON 24, pp. 106–109

1. B; DOK Level: 3; Reading Assessment Targets: R.2.8, R.3.2. Answer B is correct because the passage indicates that Paul's nerves were steady and that he gave an acceptable reason for his holiday request. His behavior, therefore, attracted no unusual attention. Answers A, C, and D indicate unusual behavior and thus contradict information in the passage.

2. D; DOK Level: 3; Reading Assessment Targets: R.2.7, R.2.8. You can predict that things will probably end badly for Paul once his crime is discovered. He is using stolen money to run away from his problems. It would be unlikely that he could return to his job. There is no indication that he has a plan for the future or for avoiding capture. It is unlikely that he will return and admit what he has done or that he will use the money to live honestly in New York. His actions appear impulsive with little regard for the consequences.

3. C; DOK Level: 3; Reading Assessment Targets: R.2.7, R.2.8, R.3.3, R.3.4. The narrator refers to her mother's "weathered beauty" and points out that unlike other women, her mother's actions match her words. Answers A, B, and D are not supported by the passage.

4. D; DOK Level: 3; Reading Assessment Targets: R.2.7, R.3.2, R.4.3/L.4.3. Answer A is incorrect because the parallel would be with a person who is flashy and pays attention to fashion and appearances. Margaret's mother is portrayed as someone who is sensible and practical—neither trait aligning with a sports car. Answer B is more plausible but not as good a choice as D because environmental or budgetary concerns are not mentioned or implied. Answer C is incorrect because this kind of car would align with someone who was trying to look as though she were younger by means of "restoration." Answer D is the best choice because it is cared for, practical, and not a flashy showpiece.

5. B; DOK Level: 2; Reading Assessment Targets: R.2.7, R.3.2, R.4.1/L.4.1, R.4.3/L.4.3. Answer A is incorrect because nothing indicates that Margaret is old fashioned. She was a beauty in the 1940s but has accepted her age and the present; she seems neither quaint nor out of touch with reality. Answer C is incorrect because nothing in her behavior indicates arrogance. Answer D is incorrect because she claims she does not want to be considered "pathetic" by submitting to plastic surgery or other methods to make her appear younger. Answer B is correct because she accepts who she is and lives accordingly.

6. A; DOK Level: 3; Reading Assessment Targets: R.2.7, R.3.3. Answer A is the best choice because the narrator characterizes her mother as practical, sensible, and aging gracefully. Someone who eats sensibly would fit this description. Answer B would probably be an exaggeration; if Margaret goes to a gym for health reasons, she would not overdo exercise. Answer C is incorrect because the passage does not indicate anything about Margaret's social preferences; however, it is unlikely that she would enjoy such events. Answer D contradicts the detail in paragraph 1 that Margaret would not buy a dress merely because it is on sale.

7. C; DOK Level: 3; Reading Assessment Targets: R.2.7, R.3.3. Answer C is correct because Margaret is not interested in beauty products. Answers A and D indicate interest and thus contradict the information in the passage. Answer B is incorrect because no money problems are indicated in the passage.

8. C; DOK Level: 3; Reading Assessment Targets: R.2.7, R.2.8. C is the correct answer because the passage makes it clear that she has no regrets and no intention of trying to change who he has become. Because she is not longing to change herself or for the past, the other options are incorrect.

9. DOK Level: 3; Reading Assessment Targets: R.2.7, R.2.8, R.3.3. Based on the passage, Flora's governess enjoys her position and looks forward to taking care of Flora. Flora's governess would **take great care of Flora** and **try to make Flora happy**. Flora's governess would not **neglect her duties** or **resent having so much responsibility**.

10. A; DOK Level: 3; Reading Assessment Target: R.2.7. Answer A is the closest parallel because both show individuals taking a moment from work to admire something around them. Answer B is incorrect because the band manager is working, not taking a moment to do something else. Answer C is incorrect because the gardener is not stopping work and probably would not appreciate the child's removing the flower. Answer D is incorrect because the worker's lunch hour is most likely free time, and the wording of the answer choice does not state that he enjoys or appreciates the surroundings.

11. C; DOK Level: 3; Reading Assessment Targets: R.2.7, R.3.3. Answer C is correct because Laura comes from a wealthy family and, according to the passage, spends time with the leisured class, whom you might find at a country club. Answers A, B, and D are incorrect because nothing indicates that Laura works in an office or would like to work, whether on a farm or in a garden supply store, despite the appeal of the workmen.

UNIT 1 *(continued)*

12. **C; DOK Level: 3; Reading Assessment Targets:** R.2.7, R.2.8, R.3.3. Laura would most likely make excuses for the workmen if they did a poor job. From the information in the excerpt, Laura seems hesitant about confrontation and upsetting the workmen. She is unlikely to refuse to pay them or to demand that they complete the job to her satisfaction. She notices things, but her interpretations are romanticized. She finds the workmen appealing, and she is likely to make excuses for them. She is likely to notice but equally likely to avoid confrontation.

13. **B; DOK Level: 3; Reading Assessment Targets:** R.2.7, R.3.3, R.3.5. Answer B is correct because it is mentioned several times; it is emphasized and supported by Laura's interest in the workman who smells the lavender. The other three options are mentioned only in relation to the workmen.

READING COMPREHENSION AT WORK, *pp. 110–111*

MARKETING, SALES, AND SERVICE

1. **A; DOK Level: 2; Reading Assessment Target:** R.2.1. The sentence "Sales receipts are an essential part of the sales process" is the topic sentence of paragraph 1. It states the main idea. Answers B, C, and D are incorrect. They are supporting details that help explain why sales receipts are important.

2. **C; DOK Level: 2; Reading Assessment Target:** R.2.2. The first sentence of paragraph 2, "Every sale requires a sales receipt," is the topic sentence. Answer C summarizes this main idea. Answers A and B are incorrect. They are details that support the main idea. While the paragraph discusses completing receipts by hand, it implies most receipts are generated by the store's point-of-sale system, so answer D is incorrect.

3. **B; DOK Level: 2; Reading Assessment Target:** R.2.8. Paragraph 3 describes the five components of the sales receipt form. The most logical conclusion is that "Sales associates need to complete all five of the components listed." Answer A is incorrect. The paragraph advises associates to write the customer account numbers but does not indicate that the numbers should be memorized. Answer C is incorrect because receipt form has other sections that need to be completed. Answer D is incorrect. The instructions state to check the correct box for the form of payment, which implies sales receipt forms need to be completed for items bought using cash, a check, or a credit card.

4. **D; DOK Level: 2; Reading Assessment Target:** R.4.2. The word *memorize* means to commit to memory, which has a much stronger connotation than the phrase *become familiar with*. Because of this stronger connotation, answers A and C are incorrect. Also, although paragraph 2 states that failing to complete a sales receipt might result in disciplinary action, there is no reason to believe that forgetting to complete a sales receipt would lead to getting fired. Therefore, answer D is incorrect.

HEALTH SCIENCE

5. **D; DOK Level: 2; Reading Assessment Target:** R.4.1. Paragraph 2 explains that aspiration systems reduce or eliminate *cross contamination*. It then describes how the system decreases the microbial cloud so its radius is less than the average distance between the patient and the dental professional. The most logical conclusion is that cross contamination is the transfer of bacteria between patients and dental professionals. Although the microbial cloud can cause cross contamination, it is not the definition of the phrase, so answer A is incorrect. Answer B is incorrect. The collection of this material describes what the aspiration systems do. Answer C is incorrect. It describes the purpose of the aspiration systems, which is to prevent cross contamination.

6. **C; DOK Level: 2; Reading Assessment Target:** R.5.4. Paragraph 3 explains systems "that separate the liquid from the air in the engine room are called wet suction. Systems that separate the liquid in the dental equipment are called dry suction." Although the excerpt mentions other groups of categories, the text does not describe these as types of aspiration systems, so answers A, B, and D are incorrect.

7. **A; DOK Level: 2; Reading Assessment Target:** R.5.3. The transition word *Because* signals a cause-and-effect relationship described in the first sentence of paragraph 4. It does not show a direct relationship between the information in paragraph 4 and the previous paragraphs, so answers B, C, and D are incorrect.

8. **D; DOK Level: 2; Reading Assessment Target:** R.5.2. Paragraph 4 states the equipment "should be disinfected every day to avoid unpleasant odors and prevent system clogs." The next sentence states, "This involves disassembling, or taking apart, certain sections of the system." The most logical conclusion is that the equipment is taken apart first, and then it is cleaned. Although the text mentions the "volume of patients," it is not associated with system clogs, so answer A is incorrect. Answer B is incorrect. It reverses the sequence of disassembling and cleaning. Answer C is incorrect. The sections of equipment are taken apart to be cleaned because they collect bacteria while assembled.

UNIT 2 ARGUMENT ANALYSIS AND TEXT COMPARISON

LESSON 1, *pp. 112–115*

1. **A; DOK Level: 2; Reading Assessment Target:** R.2.7, R.6.1. The authors' purpose is to educate a general audience about getting the flu vaccine. As a result, the authors do not include a lot of specialized vocabulary that might be difficult for general readers. If the authors were writing for doctors, they might include medical terms. Therefore, answer A is correct. A funny story, information about what to expect when getting a shot, and information about the cost of flu shots would all be interesting or useful for a general rather than a specific audience.

2. **D; DOK Level: 2; Reading Assessment Targets:** R.6.1, R.6.3 In addition to general details about the flu vaccine, the authors include details that encourage readers to get a flu shot. These include the information that people who get a vaccine are about half as likely to get sick and that they are likely to be less sick if they do get the flu. Answers A and B provide information about the CDC and flu vaccine, but they do not provide reasons for getting the flu shot. Answer C is not stated in the passage and would not help persuade someone to get a vaccine.

3. **A; DOK Level: 1; Reading Assessment Targets:** R.2.1, R.6.1. The letter is written by W. T. Sherman, a general who commanded the Union Army. Sherman is writing to J. B. Hood, who was a general in the Confederate Army. Hood's information is in paragraph 1. Sherman's information is given in the attribution that appears at the end. The fact that they are enemies, on opposing sides, is clear from the contents of the letter and is stated in paragraph 4.

4. **C; DOK Level: 1; Reading Assessment Target:** R.6.1. In the first paragraph, the author states that he wants to confirm the plans for evacuating Atlanta. Answers A, B, and D are implicit purposes, so they are incorrect.

5. **B; DOK Level: 2; Reading Assessment Targets:** R.5.1, R.5.4, R.6.1, R.6.2, R.6.3, R.8.2. Sherman defends himself against the accusation of heartless cruelty. There is no indication that General Hood accused Sherman of pity or bravery, so answers A and B are incorrect. General Sherman implies that General Hood is hypocritical, so answer D is incorrect.

6. **C; DOK Level: 2; Reading Assessment Target:** R.6.1. The passage discusses the increasing desire for possessions, for which people create needs, thus confusing what they want with what they need. Therefore, answer C best explains the author's overall purpose. The author uses the example of a house to illustrate his main point, but the house itself is an example. The author continues to use the example of a house in describing animals' housing needs and continues it again in discussing the increasing need for more "necessities." Answer choices other than C relate to the example of houses, not to the author's main purpose.

7. **A; DOK Level: 2; Reading Assessment Targets:** R.6.1, R.6.4. The author offers examples of how and why people spend money on items they do not need and presents these spending habits in a negative light, thus supporting the author's purpose. While the other options may be true, they are not supported by the text.

8. **A; DOK Level: 3; Reading Assessment Targets:** R.4.3/L.4.3, R.6.1, R.6.4. In contrasting the tyranny of things with oppression by another person, the author notes that when people are oppressed by others, people are quick to react to protect their freedom. The tyranny of things happens slowly, and people are willing participants. People realize only gradually that they have given up their freedoms to their things. Although the passage begins by discussing how people see conveniences and luxuries as necessities (answer B), the contrast does not support this point. The passage does not discuss how common oppression is (answer C) or state that humans often destroy themselves (answer D).

9. **C; DOK Level: 3; Reading Assessment Targets:** R.2.7, R.6.1, R.6.3. The author makes the argument that things can oppress people in much the same way as tyrants and that people come to view luxury or convenience items as necessities. The author writes, "Our opulent friends are constantly demonstrating by example how indispensably convenient the modern necessities are, and we keep buying such things until we either exceed our incomes or miss the higher concerns of life." This statement suggests that the author's implied purpose is to persuade readers to be more thoughtful about the things they purchase. Answer C best expresses this idea. The author's position is not so extreme that he would encourage readers to give up all material possessions, as stated in answer A. Although the author talks about oppression by others, he does not suggest overthrowing the government (answer B). The author uses nature as an example to show how humans far exceed their needs when they build, but the purpose of the article is not to encourage readers to study nature (answer D).

10. **B; DOK Level: 3; Reading Assessment Targets:** R.5.4, R.6.4. The second-to-last sentence states that a person "goes on having things and imagining that he is richer for owning them." The last sentence reverses this wording to state, "it is the things that own him." This reversal emphasizes the way things can come to dominate a person's life, limiting that person's freedom as he or she must work to pay for and maintain the things. Answer B best expresses this idea. The last sentence does not summarize the quotations in the sentence before (answer A), nor does it paraphrase the sentence before to make a statement about tyranny (answer C). The last sentence does not add details emphasizing that people want to live lifestyles they cannot afford (answer D).

11. **A; DOK Level: 1; Reading Assessment Target:** R.6.1. The purpose, summarized in answer A, appears in the first paragraph. Perhaps more people will take the deduction because it is easier to document, but this is not the explicit purpose. The dimensions of a home office give taxpayers information about what they can deduct, but this information is not the IRS's explicit purpose. Taxpayers who work from home comprise part of the audience and already work from home, so answer D is incorrect.

12. **B; DOK Level: 2; Reading Assessment Targets:** R.4.3/L.4.3, R.6.3. The passage notes that the change to the home office tax deduction is "part of ongoing efforts by the Administration" and then uses favorable language to explain these efforts, such as "reduce paperwork burdens," "streamline and simplify," and "make interacting with the federal government easier and more efficient for businesses of all sizes." This positive language is intended to encourage support for the changed deduction and the Administration, which enacted it. Answer B best expresses this implicit purpose. The passage does not go into detail about which tax forms readers should file (answer A), nor does it tell a story about a specific, successful home business (answer D). The passage describes a single change to the way one deduction is calculated. It does not describe broader proposed changes to the tax code (answer C).

13. **C; DOK Level: 2; Reading Assessment Targets:** R.2.5, R.3.5, R.8.2. The evidence in answer C best supports the claim because it indicates that a significant percentage of the workforce owns or works for small businesses. Although the government is trying to simplify the tax code for small business (answer A), this information does not indicate the importance of small businesses in the economy. Likewise, the information in answers B and D does not relate to the role small businesses play in the economy.

14. **C; DOK Level: 3; Reading Assessment Targets:** R.2.7, R.3.5. General readers are unlikely to need to see a sample calculation of the deduction, but owners of home businesses would likely benefit from such information. An explanation of how the IRS determined the new calculation method (answer A) would likely provide more information than even an owner of a home business would need. An estimate of how many people failed to claim the old deduction (answer B) would not add to a home-business owner's understanding of the revised deduction. An address to which taxpayers can send comments about the tax code (answer D) would benefit general readers as well as owners of home businesses.

15. **A; DOK Level: 3; Reading Assessment Targets:** R.2.7, R.2.8, R.3.2, R.3.5. At the end of the passage, the authors note that many businesses are going virtual and hiring employees who might live far away. These employees use technology to work from home. This situation implies that the authors believe employees must be flexible (answer A) because they may not work in a traditional office setting. Members of the 21st Century workforce must master technology and work in nontraditional settings, so answer B is incorrect. Although 21st-century workers might be organized and loyal (answers C and D), no details in the passage indicate that the authors think of them this way.

LESSON 2, *pp. 116–119*

1. **B; DOK Level: 2; Reading Assessment Targets:** R.6.1, R.8.2. Answer B is correct because the detail explains that freight rail has low fuel consumption. Low fuel consumption indicates that rail does not require a lot of oil. The fuel consumption does not relate to the cost of building rail (answer A), nor does it relate to the amount of land railroads require (answer C). Although using little fuel is efficient, the detail does not explain the importance of such efficiencies nor why they should not be ignored (answer D).

2. **A; DOK Level: 3; Reading Assessment Targets:** R.2.7, R.6.1. This fact is most likely to appeal to environmentalists, who would appreciate the benefits of taking trucks off the road (answer A). The other groups mentioned—politicians (answer B), truck drivers (answer C), and police officers (answer D)—would likely have mixed or negative opinions about taking trucks off the roads.

3. **DOK Level: 2; Reading Assessment Targets:** R.5.1, R.8.1, R.8.2. **Claim:** It ought to be possible, in short, for every American to enjoy the privileges of being American without regard to his race or his color. **Evidence:** The Negro baby born in America today … has about one-half as much chance of completing a high school as a white baby. **Evidence:** The Negro baby born in America today … [has] twice as much chance of becoming unemployed. **Evidence:** Difficulties over segregation and discrimination exist in every city, in every State of the Union. **Conclusion:** One hundred years of delay have passed since President Lincoln freed the slaves, yet their heirs, their grandsons, are not fully free.

The claim is the main idea of the passage, and the conclusion asks the audience to think in a certain way. The evidence cited supports the main claim.

4. **C; DOK Level: 2; Reading Assessment Targets:** R.5.2, R.5.4. The author's main purpose is to persuade readers that funding tuberculosis research is critical to fight AIDS. To this end, the second paragraph highlights the number of HIV patients who die as a result of tuberculosis and the threat that multi-drug resistant tuberculosis could reverse the progress made against HIV/AIDS. Therefore, answer C is correct. Answer A is incorrect because while the author does mention HIV, tuberculosis, and malaria, the author does not explain symptoms of these diseases. Answer B is incorrect because the author does not inform readers about treatments for HIV. While the third and fourth paragraph sets out the intentions of the Global Fund, this information is not the focus of the passage; therefore, answer D is incorrect.

5. **C; DOK Level: 2; Reading Assessment Targets:** R.6.2, R.8.1. The quote from Secretary Kerry indicates that "TB is curable" and can be eliminated. This quote supports the author's claim that the goal of ending TB deaths in our lifetime is within our reach. The quote does not support the claims presented in answers A, B, and D.

6. **C; DOK Level: 2; Reading Assessment Targets:** R.6.2, R.8.1. The author claims that if the progression of multi-drug resistant tuberculosis is not controlled, all the gains made in the fight against HIV/AIDS could be lost; therefore, answer C is correct. Answer A is incorrect because the author does not mention that there are still many patients dying of HIV/AIDS, nor does she say that progress in the fight against this disease should not be celebrated. Answer B is incorrect because the passage indicates that one in four people with the HIV virus dies from tuberculosis. Answer D is incorrect because the passage indicates that the Global Fund is an opportunity for donor countries to increase their commitments to eradicate these diseases from some of the most marginalized populations, but the article does not say that they have not done enough.

7. **C; DOK Level: 2; Reading Assessment Target:** R.8.6. The information provided in the second paragraph focuses on the relationship between TB and HIV. To support the claim that TB and HIV are a deadly combination, the author states that TB is the leading cause of death of people with HIV and accounts for one in four HIV-related deaths. Answer C is correct. Answers A and B are incorrect because they do not focus on the relationship between HIV and TB. While answer D is related to the relationship between HIV and TB, it does not explain how the combination of TB and HIV is deadly.

8. **B; DOK Level: 2; Reading Assessment Targets:** R.5.1, R.5.4. Paragraph 1 provides background information to help readers better understand Roberts's decision and argument. Although paragraph 1 does explain the government's claim, the rest of the passage does not give evidence to support it (answer A). Paragraph 1 does not provide evidence to support Roberts's claim, which appears in paragraph 4 (answer C). Paragraph 1 does explain the position of those opposed to the act, but the rest of the passage does not counter this position—the passage supports it. Answer D is incorrect.

9. **D; DOK Level: 2; Reading Assessment Target:** R.5.3. Answer A indicates a choice and its classification as a transition word is questionable. Answer B indicates an opposing or contrasting idea. Answer C indicates additional information or ideas. The word *consequently* indicates a causal relationship—the consequence, or result, of a cause.

10. **A; DOK Level: 2; Reading Assessment Target:** R.5.3. The word *therefore* indicates a cause-and-effect relationship. In this passage, *therefore* shows how Roberts's understanding of the Commerce Clause led him to believe that the individual mandate is unconstitutional (answer A). The other answer choices are inaccurate because they do not relate to details connected in a cause-and-effect relationship by the word *therefore*. Answer C is also incorrect because it relates to information not included in the passage.

11. **C; DOK Level: 2; Reading Assessment Targets:** R.2.2, R.3.1, R.8.1. Answer C best summarizes the steps of Roberts's argument. Answer A is incorrect because Roberts was making a decision about the individual mandate, not the act as a whole, and because Roberts decided the individual mandate was unconstitutional under the Commerce Clause. Answer B is incorrect because it does not relate to Roberts's decision. Likewise, answer D is incorrect because it does not relate to Roberts's argument.

LESSON 3, *pp. 120–123*

1. **D; DOK Level: 2; Reading Assessment Targets:** R.4.3/L.4.3, R.6.1, R.8.2. Language such as **significant health risk** and **critical** appeal to readers' emotions and make readers fearful about the dangers of e-cigarettes. This language does not show that the author is a credible source, so answer A is incorrect. Language indicating a credible source would be an appeal to ethics. The author does not attempt to mislead readers, so answer B is incorrect. This language does not relate to e-cigarette use, so answer C is incorrect.

2. **C; DOK Level: 2; Reading Assessment Target:** R.8.2. Answer C is correct because an appeal to ethics involves credibility. Answer A relates to a logical appeal. Answer B would add information, but it would not relate to the authors' credibility. Answer D relates to an argument, not to credibility, even if the differing opinions are two credible sources.

3. **DOK Level: 2; Reading Assessment Target:** R.8.2. Logical: **Each electoral vote in Alaska is equivalent to approximately 112,000 people. Each electoral vote in New York is equivalent to approximately 404,000 eligible people.** The detail is logical because it can be proved or disproved and thus is considered an appeal to reason. Emotional: **Defecting electors in a close race could cause a crisis of confidence in our electoral system. In a nation where voting rights are grounded in the one person, one vote principle, the electoral college is a hopeless anachronism.** Both details considered emotional have strong language that could arouse readers' feelings of fear ("crisis of confidence") and need for change ("hopeless anachronism"). Ethical: **I am pleased to be here today to express the League's support for a constitutional amendment.** The ethical appeal is the speaker's identification as the League's representative, which lends authority.

4. **A; DOK Level: 2; Reading Assessment Targets:** R.8.2, R.8.3. The authors appeal to ethics by quoting a credible source, an NIH expert on teen driving. Although the authors cite the number of death caused by car accidents in 2018 and provide examples of distractions, these details are not appeals to ethics. Answer D is incorrect because the author does not use particularly strong language to discuss keeping your eyes on the road.

5. **B; DOK Level: 2; Reading Assessment Targets:** R.5.2, R.8.2. Answer B is correct because paragraph 10 restates this claim by providing a quote from an expert. Answer A is incorrect because the paragraph does not provide data from the study it mentions. Answer C is incorrect because the paragraph does not counter the claim. Answer D is incorrect because the paragraph does not broaden the claim.

6. **A; DOK Level: 2; Reading Assessment Target:** R.8.2. Answer A is correct because the statement cannot be proved true or false. On the other hand, the information in answers B, C, and D can be investigated and verified as accurate or inaccurate.

7. **C; DOK Level: 2; Reading Assessment Targets:** R.8.2, R.8.3. Answer C is correct because the authors appeal to logic and reason by providing data. The statement is not an appeal to ethics, emotion, or values.

8. **D; DOK Level: 2; Reading Assessment Targets:** R.2.4, R.2.5, R.6.3 The author's implicit claim is that red wolves need the help of humans in order to survive and no longer be on the endangered species list. Although red wolves eat a variety of small animals, the evidence does not suggest that they contribute to these animals being endangered, so answer A is incorrect. Answers B and C are facts the author states directly and thus cannot be implied claims.

9. **A; DOK Level: 2; Reading Assessment Target:** R.8.2 This opinion is supported by the fact that wildlife enthusiasts, such as hikers and hunters, will want to visit or live in communities that support and/or sustain the red wolf. Answer C addresses how the local communities can aid in the protection of the red wolf but does not address how the red wolf contributes to local economies. The facts in answers B and D are not related to the opinion.

10. **B; DOK Level: 2; Reading Assessment Targets:** R.5.1, R.8.2 The statement uses strong language to describe the red wolf in the past and why the red wolf is in danger now, and thus appeals to the emotion of preserving the animal. Answer A and D are incorrect because the information does not include data. Answer C might seem plausible but the information does not contain an opinion.

11. **C; DOK Level: 2; Reading Assessment Target: R.8.4**
Answer C states a claim not supported by evidence in the passage. The brochure does not discuss the cost of protection efforts and does not consider them unsuccessful. The claims expressed in other answer choices are supported by evidence in the passage. Evidence supporting answer A appears in the bulleted list in paragraph 3. Evidence supporting answer B appears in paragraph 2. Evidence supporting answer D appears in paragraph 1.

HIGH IMPACT LESSON: PREMISE OF AN ARGUMENT, *pp. 124–125*

1. **D; DOK Level: 2; Reading Assessment Target: R.8.6.**
The writer assumes that women will want to improve their working conditions in industry and will therefore want to have the vote. Answers A, B, and C are all stated within the text and are therefore not implicit premises.

2. **B; DOK Level: 2; Reading Assessment Target: R.8.6.**
Hull's explicit premise is that children are more in demand for work outside the home because machines do not demand strength or skill. She does not believe factories should employ children. She says that weaving in the past required strength, so that only now, with machines, can children do the job. She does not say that the Industrial Age is an improvement on other eras.

3. **D; DOK Level: 2; Reading Assessment Target: R.8.6.**
Hull has as an explicit premise that child labor "pauperizes the community," and also hurts its morals. Although Hull does not want children to work in factories, she does not insist that readers do. She makes the point that she hopes "we" the readers are not too indolent, or lazy, to stop child labor, but she does not state that we are too lazy. She does not believe that cheap cotton is more important than a child's development, but that accepting child labor confuses our moral sense so that we may start to think this way.

4. **A; DOK Level: 2; Reading Assessment Target: R.8.6.** The implicit premise is that pauperism is something people want to avoid. Hull states explicitly that child labor is "bringing on premature old age" for the children. She also states that child labor "debauches our moral sentiment, it confuses our sense of values." She does not state that aging prematurely is worth it if children are gainfully employed, and it is not an implicit assumption.

5. **C; DOK Level: 2; Reading Assessment Target: R.8.6.**
The conclusion of the argument is what all the premises lead to. In this case, it is clear that Hull believes that child labor should be stopped. While she does explain that machines make it easier for children to work outside the home, that is not the conclusion of her argument. Hull also explains that child labor confuses our moral sensibilities so that we may start to think that cheap cotton is more important than raising a child correctly. That child labor makes cotton cheaper, though, is not the conclusion of her argument. Hull does mention that it is an industrial epoch; however, that is not the argument's conclusion.

6. **D; DOK Level: 2; Reading Assessment Target: R.8.6.**
Grievous and *pauperizes* are both emotional words, so "also, the grievous charge is true that it pauperizes the community itself" is the correct answer. The other answers do not include overly emotional language.

LESSON 4, *pp. 126–129*

1. **C; DOK Level: 2; Reading Assessment Targets: R.6.2, R.7.2, R.7.4.** The graph shows that a dramatic decline in measles cases began after the introduction of the vaccine, so answer C is correct. The graph does not compare the effectiveness of cleanliness and nutrition with that of vaccinations (answer A). Neither the graph nor the text gives information about diseases other than measles (answer B). The graph does show that numbers of cases of measles rose and fell before the vaccine was introduced (answer D), but that information does not relate to the viewpoint that diseases such as measles were declining before the introduction of the vaccine.

2. **D; DOK Level: 2; Reading Assessment Targets: R.6.1, R.7.2, R.7.4.** The year the vaccine was licensed is indicated on the graph to show that the introduction of the vaccine led to the decline of measles (answer D). The line on the graph, not the indication about the vaccine license, shows how quickly cases declined, so answer A is incorrect. Similarly, the line shows when the decline began (answer B). The graph does not prove that cleanliness and nutrition are unimportant (answer C) but that the vaccine was what brought about the dramatic and permanent decline of the disease.

3. **B; DOK Level: 3; Reading Assessment Targets: R.6.3, R.7.2.** The passage states that the executive order removing Japanese Americans was "a fundamental setback of American principles," and the picture shows the Japanese Americans having been removed from their homes and waiting in front of barracks. Together, the passage and photograph imply that the civil rights of Japanese Americans were violated by the removal order because much of the Japanese Americans' freedom was taken away. Therefore, answer B is correct. Answer A is incorrect because the photo itself does not suggest that Japanese Americans feared the reissue of the removal order. Answer C is incorrect because although the passage notes that Japanese Americans made contributions on the battlefield, neither the passage nor the photo suggests that Americans are likely to forget this. Neither the passage nor the photo suggests that the War Relocation Authority provided inadequate food, so answer D is incorrect.

4. **A; DOK Level: 3; Reading Assessment Target: R.7.2.** The photograph shows an aspect of what life was like at Tanforan Assembly Center—in this instance, waiting in front of the mess hall. The photograph does not show how many Japanese Americans stayed at the center (answer B) nor how Japanese Americans contributed on the battlefield (answer C). The photo gives no indication about how Americans' views about World War II may have changed (answer D).

5. **C; DOK Level: 3; Reading Assessment Targets: R.6.3, R.7.2, R.8.2.** The purpose of the photograph is to arouse sympathy and understanding for Japanese Americans removed during the war. Although the photograph may inform readers about an important moment in American history (answer A), this is not its primary purpose, which is to appeal to readers' emotions. There is no indication of doubt about the existence of the camps, so answer B is incorrect. Answer D is incorrect because the photograph could reflect, not necessarily add to, the anger of Japanese Americans who experienced removal. Nor is anger necessarily the emotion felt by those who experienced removal.

6. **A; DOK Level:** 2; **Reading Assessment Targets:** R.6.3, R.7.2. The photograph shows rough barracks and Japanese Americans waiting in line to eat, suggesting that conditions were uncomfortable and that Japanese Americans did not enjoy the same freedoms they had at home (answer A). Answers B and C are incorrect because readers could reach these conclusions without seeing the photograph. Answer D is incorrect because neither the passage nor the photograph suggests that Japanese Americans were separated from their friends and families at the camp.

7. **B; DOK Level:** 2; **Reading Assessment Targets:** R.3.5, R.7.2, R.7.4. The graph does not provide the number of people that are fed by farmers. The graph supports the claim that fewer farmers are more efficient because the number of farms has decreased, so answer A is incorrect. Answers C and D correspond to the numerical data shown in the graph.

8. **B; DOK Level:** 3; **Reading Assessment Targets:** R.2.8, R.7.2, R.7.4. The graph shows a sharp decrease in farms between 1940 and 1980. The text explains that farms are fewer and more efficient because of technology. From this evidence, you can draw the conclusion that advances in farming technology have greatly increased at that time, so answer B is correct. The conclusion in answer A contradicts the text. Answer C is not a logical conclusion because the number of farms decreased in 1950. Answer D is not implied in the text or the graph.

9. **D; DOK Level:** 2; **Reading Assessment Targets:** R.6.3, R.7.2, R.7.4. The graph clearly shows the number of farms declining over the last century. The graph does not indicate how many people are fed per farmer, so answer A is incorrect. Although the graph shows the number of farms in 1900, this is not the overall purpose of the graph. The graph is not relevant to the information in answer C.

10. **A; DOK Level:** 3; **Reading Assessment Targets:** R.2.8, R.7.2, R.7.4. The graph shows a sharp decline in the number of farms when compared to the early 1900s. The number or percentage of farmers is not shown, only the number of farms, so answer B is incorrect. The claims in answers C and D are not represented in the graph.

11. **D; DOK Level:** 2; **Reading Assessment Targets:** R.7.2, R.7.4. The data cited in the question indicate that number of jobs requiring STEM workers will rise more quickly than other jobs. Therefore, STEM workers will be in demand and less likely than other workers to experience joblessness. The percentages given are related to the likelihood of experience joblessness, so answers A and B are incorrect. The data does not support answer C.

12. **B; DOK Level:** 3; **Reading Assessment Targets:** R.7.2, R.7.4. The table shows that in each category STEM workers earn more than NON-STEM workers. The data do not support answer A. The largest difference in earnings occurs between STEM and non-STEM workers with a high school diploma or less, so answer C is incorrect. The data does not identify how many workers have a high school diploma or less, so answer D is incorrect.

LESSON 5, *pp. 130–133*

1. **C; DOK Level:** 2; **Reading Assessment Targets:** R.8.3, R.8.5. Answer C is correct. The author presents only one point of view in this argument—that gluten-free diets are a worthless fad. The fact that the author does not address opposing viewpoints or evidence suggests bias. Answer A is incorrect because the author does not include testimonials and notes that celebrities are not nutrition experts. The author does not use strong language to frighten readers (answer B), nor does the author support the claim with a false cause-and-effect relationship (answer D).

2. **C; DOK Level:** 2; **Reading Assessment Targets:** R.8.2, R.8.5. Answer C is correct because the detail suggests that readers should be part of a particular group. The other answers are incorrect because they list details that do not relate to people's need to fit in.

3. **C; DOK Level:** 2; **Reading Assessment Target:** R.8.5. The correct answer is C because the author states that voters (the worker, the businessman, the housewife) chose to get rid of liquor agents to have more money for "children's education" and "older citizens." This suggests an inaccurate either/or relationship between liquor agents and funding for schools and seniors. The author does not suggest a cause-and-effect relationship between his election and successful factories (answer A). The author discusses liquor agents in paragraph 1, so the information is relevant (answer B). The author does not make a bandwagon appeal to encourage voters to support his policies (answer D).

4. **A; DOK Level:** 3; **Reading Assessment Targets:** R.3.2, R.4.3/L.4.3, R.6.4, R.8.5. The author makes a connection to previous generations to make the audience, composed mostly of his supporters in Alabama, feel patriotic and proud. The audience would not likely feel the emotions mentioned in answers B and D. Although the audience of Wallace supporters might feel satisfied and optimistic at Wallace's victory, these words do not arouse satisfaction and optimism for the future as much as they do patriotism and pride in the past.

5. **B; DOK Level:** 2; **Reading Assessment Targets:** R.4.3/L.4.3, R.6.4, R.8.5. The author uses this fiery language to arouse the audience's anger about desegregation (answer B). This language is not intended to arouse tolerance (answer A) or to make the audience feel regret about segregation (answer D). This language does not appeal to the audience's sense of shame (answer C).

6. **A; DOK Level:** 2; **Reading Assessment Targets:** R.4.3/L.4.3, R.6.4, R.8.3, R.8.5. Answer A is correct because the author uses exaggeration—comparing walking in Washington, D.C., with flying a B-29 bomber during World War II. He does not provide facts and data, so answer B is incorrect. Although he refers to a personal experience, he does so for the sake of exaggeration, so answer C is incorrect. The author does not cite an example of how desegregation has influenced violence (answer D).

7. **B; DOK Level:** 2; **Reading Assessment Targets:** R.4.3/L.4.3, R.6.1, R.8.6. Answer B best describes the tone and its effect on readers. The tone is not bullying, so answer A is incorrect. Answer C is incorrect because the tone is not threatening, and the effect does not make readers fearful of buying American products. Answer D is incorrect because the tone is not lighthearted, and the purpose of the passage is to show that the source of products is important.

8. **C; DOK Level:** 2; **Reading Assessment Targets:** R.2.5, R.3.2, R.5.1, R.8.5. The detail that would most likely make readers fearful of buying foreign goods is that poisonous levels of lead are in tens of millions of toys shipped to the United States (answer C). Although readers might feel guilty or upset about foreign labor standards, this detail is unlikely to make readers fearful, so answer A is incorrect. Answer B is likely to make readers feel positive about buying American goods, but it is unlikely to make readers fearful about foreign goods. Answer D might make readers feel anxious about the future, but this detail is unlikely to make readers fearful about foreign products.

9. **D; DOK Level:** 2; **Reading Assessment Targets:** R.8.2, R.8.5. The author suggests that if readers do not buy American products, there will be far fewer jobs for Americans. This suggestion creates an inaccurate either/or situation because many factors affect unemployment in the United States. Answer D is correct. The author does not suggest that the United States will fall behind technologically, so answer A is incorrect. Answer B is incorrect because although the author suggests that foreign products could harm children, he does not suggest that either readers buy American or their children will be hurt by their toys. Answer C is incorrect because the author does not suggest that either readers buy American products or conditions will never improve for foreign workers.

10. **C; DOK Level:** 2; **Reading Assessment Targets:** R.8.2, R.8.5. The author appeals to readers' fears about the American position of leadership by suggesting that the lack of American ability to manufacture products is strategically unsound (answer C). The other answer choices do not relate to U.S. leadership.

11. **D; DOK Level:** 2; **Reading Assessment Target:** R.8.5. The correct answer is D because the author begins by pointing out that women lack the power to enforce laws. A and C are incorrect because the author does not discuss the economy or women's intelligence in paragraph 1. Answer B is incorrect because while the author states that immunity from service would make women irresponsible voters, the author does not state that they have not earned the right to vote.

12. **D; DOK Level:** 3; **Reading Assessment Targets:** R.8.4, R.8.5, R.8.6. It is not sound reasoning to predict effects on the basis of something that did not happen, which is what the statement does. Answer D best expresses why the reasoning in the statement is faulty. The statement responds to the argument that women should have the right to vote, which suggests that women want the vote in order to advance morally, intellectually, and economically; therefore, answer A is incorrect. The authors do not use threatening language, so answer B is incorrect. Answer C is incorrect because the statement is a response to the argument that women should have the right to vote.

13. **A; DOK Level:** 3; **Reading Assessment Target:** R.8.5. This statement is faulty reasoning because it suggests that to do any good, it must do every good (be a "cure-all for existing evils"). The author does not suggest that evils have resulted from the right to vote, only that the vote has not cured all "existing evils," so answer B is incorrect. Answer C is incorrect because the statement is not an appeal to popularity or readers' need to fit in. Answer D is incorrect because the author does not suggest that the right to vote led to evils among men.

14. **B; DOK Level:** 3; **Reading Assessment Target:** R.8.5. The evidence does not address specific reasons women might want suffrage. A more effective argument would respond to the evidence of opposing viewpoints. Therefore, answer B is correct. The authors do not share personal stories, so answer A is incorrect. Answer C is incorrect because the authors do not include testimonials. The author does not use patriotic language, so answer D is incorrect.

LESSON 6, pp. 134–137

1. **D; DOK Level:** 2; **Reading Assessment Targets:** R.8.2, R.8.3. The author claims that the problems of wind power outweigh the benefits. Answer D is correct because it is an example of one of the problems of wind power. Answer A is not valid because it is not relevant to the claim. Whether environmentalists support wind power has no bearing on how well wind power works and whether development of wind power should be subsidized. Answer B similarly states irrelevant information. Answer C is incorrect because the author does not provide specific information to show that wind power is an immature technology.

2. **C; DOK Level:** 3; **Reading Assessment Targets:** R.8.3, R.8.4. Additional data showing the high cost of constructing wind farms (answer C) would provide further evidence of the financial drawbacks of wind farms. Although examples of some of the benefits of wind power might help the author to show balance, it would not strengthen the claim about the drawbacks of wind power (answer A). Answer B is not relevant to the claim. Stories from people who have to rely on wind power would not strengthen the claim as much as responses to the perceived benefits of wind power. Answer D is incorrect.

3. **C; DOK Level:** 2; **Reading Assessment Targets:** R.8.3, R.8.6. Dr. Feng is a transplant surgeon, and, because of her profession, the reader assumes that she has expertise about organ transplantation. Answer A is incorrect because Dr. Feng does not describe several surgeries. Answers B and D are incorrect because including statistics or providing facts from different sources may enhance the overall validity of the argument, but they are not provided in Dr. Feng's quotations.

4. **B; DOK Level:** 2; **Reading Assessment Targets:** R.8.2, R.8.3, R.8.5. Answer B is correct because indicating your decision to be an organ donor while you are alive is a gift to your family so they do not have to make that decision for you. This removes the burden of making that decision from the family. The other answers present information that is not relevant to the claim.

5. **C; DOK Level:** 2; **Reading Assessment Targets:** R.8.2, R.8.5. Answer C is correct because data showing the types of risks resulting from organ donor surgery and their survival rates would be strong support for the claim that donating certain organs requires major surgery, which carries risks. Quotations from researchers about family members applying to become organ donors (answer A) do not relate directly to the risks from surgery. Answer B is incorrect because the length of major surgeries does not relate specifically to organ donor surgery. Answer D is incorrect because stories from family members who donated organs to other family members would represent only a small sample of the types of risks.

6. **D; DOK Level:** 2; **Reading Assessment Targets:** R.4.3/L.4.3, R.6.3, R.6.4, R.8.3, R.8.5. Answer D uses emotional language ("gift," "major impact," "remembered," and "gratitude") to encourage organ donation. Answers A and B are incorrect because they do not include emotional language. Answer C uses data, not emotional language, for encouragement.

7. **A; DOK Level:** 2; **Reading Assessment Target:** R.8.3. This is an example of incomplete evidence because the authors do not include data about overall reduction in crashes. Answer B is incorrect because the Insurance Institute for Highway Safety is a relevant source on the issue. Answer C is incorrect because the paragraph does mention the speed of vehicles. Answer D is incorrect because the statement is relevant to the claim.

8. **D; DOK Level:** 3; **Reading Assessment Targets:** R.5.1, R.5.4, R.8.2, R.8.3. The cost of a roundabout is irrelevant to the claim that roundabouts are safer. Answers A, B, and C are relevant to the claim.

9. **C; DOK Level:** 2; **Reading Assessment Targets:** R.5.1, R.5.4, R.8.2, R.8.4. The information from the Federal Highway Administration supports the claim that roundabouts are safer. The information does not support the claims listed answers A, B, and D.

10. **B; DOK Level:** 3; **Reading Assessment Targets:** R.2.8, R.6.3, R.8.3, R.8.4. The authors include information about how quickly film decays and how few early films survive. This evidence indicates that the need to preserve early films is urgent. Answer A is incorrect because the evidence does not suggest that film is the most effective way to capture history. Answer C is incorrect because although the authors state that Hollywood films are generally not in danger, they do not suggest that Hollywood is contributing to the loss of films. Answer D is incorrect because the evidence does not suggest that saving orphan films could bring financial rewards.

11. **D; DOK Level:** 2; **Reading Assessment Targets:** R.5.1, R.8.3, R.8.5. Paragraph 1 refers to American inventor Thomas Edison and contains emotional and patriotic language ("generations of Americans," "dreamed," "save a century of history") to persuade readers. This emotional language is not valid evidence. Answer A is incorrect because the authors do list familiar ways in which film is used. Answer B is incorrect because although the authors do not present opposing viewpoints, this answer is not the best explanation of why some of the evidence is invalid. Answer C is incorrect because the paragraph does not include a testimonial from Thomas Edison.

12. **A; DOK Level:** 2; **Reading Assessment Targets:** R.8.2, R.8.3, R.8.5. Answer A is correct because the Library of Congress is a reliable source, and the information is directly relevant to the article's claim that the need to preserve early films is urgent. Answers B, C, and D are incorrect because these are not accurate descriptions of the evidence and its purpose.

13. **C; DOK Level:** 3; **Reading Assessment Targets:** R.8.2, R.8.3, R.8.4. Answer C is correct because a chart comparing resources spent preserving Hollywood films and orphan films would strengthen the claim that orphan films are in greater need of preservation. Such a chart would likely show that far less is spent preserving orphan films. Answers A and D would not supply evidence relevant to the claim. A film history professor would be a reliable source, but a statement about the importance of orphan films would not be relevant to the claim, which is about contrasting resources spent preserving Hollywood films versus orphan films.

HIGH IMPACT LESSON: EVALUATE SUPPORT AND EVIDENCE, *pp. 138–139*

1. **D; DOK Level:** 2; **Reading Assessment Target:** R.8.3. Inhofe uses the snowball to support his argument that global warming is not real, but it is insufficient evidence because global warming refers to a trend over time and cannot be judged by one event. Inhofe is not arguing that global warming is real or causes unprecedented snowstorms, so answer A and B are incorrect. While Inhofe implies that global warming is based on hysteria, a snowball is not sufficient evidence to support this claim, so answer C is incorrect.

2. **A; DOK Level:** 2; **Reading Assessment Target:** R.8.3. Inhofe uses the phrase "Siberian Express" to describe the current weather. Again, he is trying to show that global warming cannot be real since it is currently cold. There is nothing in the speech to suggest that global warming causes surprising weather conditions. Inhofe is not suggesting that outlets are trying to scare Americans about the cold weather (he accuses Obama of trying to scare Americans about global warming). There is nothing in the speech to suggest that Inhofe thinks America's weather is becoming too much like Russia's.

3. **B; DOK Level:** 2; **Reading Assessment Target:** R.8.3. With the phrase "extreme climate agenda," Inhofe uses emotional language and shows that he and his argument may be biased. The language is not effectively persuasive. It is not factual language; it shows the speaker's opinion. It does not appeal to listeners' sense of justice; it appeals to their emotions.

4. **D; DOK Level:** 2; **Reading Assessment Target:** R.8.3. Inhofe emphasizes his belief that Obama's views on climate change are unreasonable by pointing out that Obama says that climate change is more of a risk than terrorism. This argument rests on the assumption that terrorism is a terrible, immediate threat to Americans. Inhofe does not believe that Obama is insufficiently worried about climate change. He does mention several attacks carried out by terrorists, but those serve as evidence for the idea that terrorism is a grave threat. Inhofe does state that Obama is detached from realities Americans face, but that does not tell why his views on climate change are unreasonable.

5. **A; DOK Level:** 2; **Reading Assessment Target:** R.8.3. Inhofe includes the list of terrorist attacks to support his point that terrorism is more of a threat to Americans than climate change. He gives no evidence for the idea that terrorism attacks increase because of climate change. He does not believe that Obama is right about climate change, and so that is not why he includes the list. Inhofe is critical of Obama, but the list on its own does not support the idea that Obama is afraid to deal with the threat of terrorism.

6. **B; DOK Level:** 2; **Reading Assessment Target:** R.8.3. The best evaluation is that the list of attacks is insufficient evidence to prove that the threat of terrorism is greater than the threat of climate change. To prove that, Inhofe would have to address the current and future dangers of climate change, which he does not do here. Though the list is sufficient to show that Americans face danger from terrorism, it does not fully address Inhofe's main argument—that Obama is wrong to think that climate change is a greater threat than terrorism. The list of attacks is not relevant to the claim that Obama is detached from reality; the attacks could occur no matter how engaged Obama was. Answer D is incorrect because the list of attacks is relevant to the idea that terrorism poses a threat to Americans. However, that is not Inhofe's main argument.

UNIT 2 *(continued)*

1. A; DOK Level: 2; **Reading Assessment Targets:** R.5.2, R.5.3. The transition word *however* indicates contrast. In this case, the contrast is between the benefits and drawbacks of paying students (answer A). Although the author notes a connection between payment and test scores (answer B), *however* does not signal a cause-and-effect relationship. The author's viewpoint is that paying students has positives and negatives, so the information introduced by *however* is not evidence that contradicts the author's viewpoint; therefore, answer C is incorrect. The author does not present alternative strategies to paying students, so answer D is incorrect.

2. D; DOK Level: 2; **Reading Assessment Targets:** R.5.4, R.6.1, R.8.1. The author wishes to acknowledge some of the drawbacks associated with paying students for achievement, and using a pro/con structure is the most effective way for the author to do so. Answer D is correct. The passage does not include a call to action, so answer A is incorrect. The passage begins with background information and a statement of the claim, not with supporting evidence; therefore, answer B is incorrect. The author's claim is not based on showing that another claim is wrong, so answer C is incorrect.

3. C; DOK Level: 2; **Reading Assessment Targets:** R.5.1, R.8.1, R.8.2, R.8.3, R.8.5. The National Research Council is a reliable source, so one reason the author includes the reference is to show that the example is from a reliable source (answer C). Answer A is incorrect because the author does not suggest that the evidence from the National Research Council is incorrect. Answer B is incorrect because the passage does not include information about the range of studies the National Research Council conducts nor its purpose. Answer D is incorrect because the author does not suggest that most research is done by government organizations.

4. D; DOK Level: 2; **Reading Assessment Targets:** R.5.2, R.8.1, R.8.3. The author includes the information about murder rates in Canada to show further evidence that murder rates are not related to the use of the death penalty. Answer D is correct. Answer A is incorrect; although Canada does not use the death penalty, the author does not include the example to show this difference. Answer B is incorrect because the example does not show that the death penalty is unnecessary in Canada. Answer C is incorrect because the claim is that the death penalty is ineffective.

5. B; DOK Level: 2; **Reading Assessment Targets:** R.5.1, R.5.4, R.8.1. In paragraph 9, the author provides an explanation for why the murder rate in the United States has declined (the decline resulting from actions other than the death penalty). Answer B is correct. Answer A is incorrect because the author is not providing further evidence that the death penalty is ineffective. Answer C is incorrect because paragraph 9 does not include a personal story. Answer D is incorrect because the paragraph does not identify who provided the author with information about murder rates.

6. A; DOK Level: 3; **Reading Assessment Targets:** R.5.4, R.6.1, R.6.2, R.8.1. In this passage, the author makes the claim that those who argue that the death penalty deters crime are incorrect. This claim is based on showing that another point of view is inaccurate, so a refutation/proof structure is an effective format. The author is not listing positives and negatives of using the death penalty, so answer B is incorrect. Answer C is incorrect because the author presents evidence of equal strength. Answer D is incorrect because the passage begins by presenting the viewpoint that the author wishes to refute.

7. A; DOK Level: 2; **Reading Assessment Targets:** R.5.2, R.5.4, R.6.2, R.8.1. Answer A is correct because the author uses a refutation/proof structure. Answer B is incorrect because Anthony does not offer pros and cons on the question of whether women have the right to vote; in fact, for Anthony there is no con. Answer C is incorrect because she does not use a sandwich structure for her argument. D is incorrect because Anthony does not begin with the strongest evidence for her argument. She begins by summarizing her conclusion and then presents the arguments that support it.

8. D; DOK Level: 2; **Reading Assessment Targets:** R.5.1, R.8.1. Answer D is correct because the excerpt from the preamble helps Anthony establish that the rights of citizens, including the right to vote, were conferred upon all of the people of the United States, including women, in the Constitution. Answer A is incorrect because the excerpt does not discuss women or specific rights belonging to them directly. Answers B and C are incorrect because the passage neither explains the meaning of the U.S. Constitution nor discusses the division between state and federal powers.

9. B; DOK Level: 2; **Reading Assessment Targets:** R.4.3/L.4.3, R.5.1, R.5.2, R.5.4, R.8.1. Answer B is correct because Anthony uses this paragraph to establish that a person within the United States who has certain rights is a citizen and that citizens have the right to vote. This definition sets up the argument in the next paragraph, in which Anthony states that because no one can deny that women are "persons" in the United States with certain privileges, they are citizens and, therefore, are entitled to vote. Answer A is incorrect because the paragraph explains that "persons" are citizens; the connection with women appears outside this paragraph. Answer C is incorrect because the paragraph confirms the definitions provided by Webster, Worcester, and Bouvier. Answer D is incorrect; although the paragraph helps set up the argument for a woman's right to vote, it does not specifically mention the U.S. Constitution or women.

10. C; DOK Level: 2; **Reading Assessment Targets:** R.5.1, R.6.1, R.6.3 In paragraph 1, the author offers facts and opinions about the negative effects of alcohol abuse, and thus gives evidence and an appeal to reason. In paragraph 2, the author explicitly states that the prevention of initial abusive drinking patterns will lessen the "costs" of alcoholism and alcohol abuse. Answer C is correct. The passage does not present benefits, so answer A is incorrect. The author's claim is not implied, so answer B is incorrect. The author does not share a personal story in paragraph 1; therefore, answer D is incorrect.

11. **D; DOK Level: 2; Reading Assessment Targets:** R.5.3, R.8.1. The words *for example* indicate that specific evidence is forthcoming, so answer D is correct. *For example* does not indicate differences or cause/effect, so answers A and B are incorrect. Answer C is incorrect because the second sentence does not discuss the negative side of an argument.

12. **B; DOK Level: 2; Reading Assessment Targets:** R.5.4, R.8.1. Answer B best describes the structure of the argument. Answer A is incorrect because the passage does not discuss pros and cons related to a claim. Answer C is incorrect because although the author ends paragraph 1 with the claim, he does not order the evidence strongest to weakest. Answer D is incorrect because the author does not tell a personal story.

LESSON 8, *pp. 144–147*

1. **C; DOK Level: 2; Reading Assessment Target:** R.6.4. The juxtaposition of opposites emphasizes the importance of the soldiers who "gave their lives" for the good of the nation. Answer C is correct. Answers A and B are incorrect because the juxtaposition does not refer to violence or the soldiers' loved ones. Answer D is incorrect because the author does not refer to how many soldiers died and because the purpose of the juxtaposition is not to emphasize numbers.

2. **A; DOK Level: 2; Reading Assessment Target:** R.6.4. The parallelism centers around the idea that the government will persevere in the war and in fact ends the sentence that states this determination. Therefore, the parallelism emphasizes Lincoln's determination to persevere through the war. The language Lincoln uses does not convey sadness or anger, so answers B and C are incorrect. Although answer D seems plausible, Lincoln does not refer to the U.S. Constitution, so it is not the best choice.

3. **D; DOK Level: 2; Reading Assessment Target:** R.6.4. By using the same structure but reversing the order of the phrases, the author emphasizes the connection between women's rights and human rights. Answer D is correct. Answer A is incorrect because the purpose of the sentence is not to say that human rights are worth fighting for but that women's rights and human rights are one and the same. Similarly, the author's statement is not that she has respect for women's rights but that women's rights are human rights. Answer B is incorrect. Answer C is incorrect because the statement does not imply that most women are denied human rights.

4. **B; DOK Level: 2; Reading Assessment Targets:** R.6.1, R.6.3, R.6.4. The purpose of the qualifying statement in paragraph 4 is to suggest that not letting women participate fully in the conference is as bad as not letting them attend (answer B). The sentence begins by stating that it is indefensible that many women were not allowed to attend the conference. The qualifying statement adds women who are not allowed to participate fully to the characterization. Answer A is incorrect because the qualifying statement does not celebrate that so many women were able to attend. Answer C is incorrect because the statement is much stronger than noting that the conference is incomplete. Answer D is incorrect because the statement is about women who were not able to attend, not women who overcame challenges to attend.

5. **C; DOK Level: 3; Reading Assessment Targets:** R.6.1, R.6.3, R.6.4. The author clarifies that freedom has clear definitions that do not change depending on who a person is or where a person lives. Answer C is correct. Answer A is incorrect because the purpose of the enumeration is not to show how the rights of women have changed, despite references to the past. Answer B is incorrect because the purpose of the enumeration is not to show that the author has studied the work of civil rights leaders; civil rights leaders are not mentioned. Answer D is incorrect because the purpose of the enumeration is not to suggest that people do not understand what freedom really is.

6. **A; DOK Level: 2; Reading Assessment Target:** R.6.4. The author states "We have also been reminded, in V-J Day observances last weekend, of the good that comes when men and women join together to combat the forces of tyranny and build a better world." Comparing the fight for women's rights to V-J Day is an example of an analogy.

7. **A; DOK Level: 2; Reading Assessment Targets:** R.4.3/L.4.3, R.6.1, R.6.4. The sailors on the lost ship do not realize that fresh water is available. The author suggests that, similarly, African Americans may not realize that opportunities exist in the communities where they live. Answer B is incorrect because the author is not encouraging African Americans to leave the South but to stay and take advantage of opportunities where they are. Answer C is incorrect because the author uses a sea voyage as an analogy; he does not offer advice about sailing. Answer D is incorrect because the analogy and the rest of the paragraph suggest that Americans of all races should be friends.

8. **D; DOK Level: 2; Reading Assessment Targets:** R.5.1, R.6.4. The enumeration introduces the paragraph, which is about the variety of work African Americans can pursue. Answer D is correct. Answer A is incorrect because the enumeration does not contradict the rest of the paragraph. Answer B is incorrect because the enumeration is not part of a build-up of information. Answer C is incorrect because although the list begins with a reference to the analogy of the previous paragraph, the purpose of the enumeration is to introduce the rest of the paragraph.

9. **B; DOK Level: 2; Reading Assessment Targets:** R.4.3/L.4.3, R.5.1, R.5.2, R.6.3, R.6.4. Answer B is correct because the author includes a call to action in both paragraphs 1 and 2. The phrase emphasizes the call and unifies the passage by continuing the forceful wording of the analogy. Although the author specifically mentions occupations in paragraph 2, the analogy itself is not applicable to those occupations. The author refers to labor, but not as part of the analogy. Answer D is incorrect because future prosperity will come as a result of action and is thus a step removed from the language of the analogy and the call to action.

10. **A; DOK Level: 2; Reading Assessment Targets:** R.4.3/L.4.3, R.6.4. The author uses this juxtaposition of opposites to say that everyone must work his or her way up. Answer A is correct. Answers B, C, and D are incorrect interpretations of the juxtaposition of opposites.

11. **D; DOK Level: 2; Reading Assessment Target:** R.6.4. When the author says "We observe today not a victory of party, but a celebration of freedom—symbolizing an end, as well as a beginning—signifying renewal, as well as change," he uses grammatically similar phrases to make his point.

12. **C; DOK Level:** 2; **Reading Assessment Target:** R.6.4. By juxtaposing *human poverty* and *human life* as things that humans have the power to abolish, the author emphasizes the best and worst parts of human resourcefulness. Answer C is correct. Answer A is incorrect because the juxtaposition does relate to human advancement, but it does not illustrate how technologically advanced humans have become, nor does it indicate lagging "behind." Answer B is incorrect because the juxtaposition is meant to suggest that there are few problems beyond the scope of human inventiveness. Answer D is incorrect because the juxtaposition does not suggest anything about the position of the President.

13. **A; DOK Level:** 2; **Reading Assessment Target:** R.6.4. Answer A is correct because the author refers to the American Revolution to make the audience feel proud and connected to history. Answer B is incorrect because the author makes no indication that liberty is threatened. Answer C is incorrect because the purpose of the reference is not to make the audience feel disappointed. Answer D is incorrect because the intent of the reference is not to make the audience feel excited and hopeful, although the audience may react with these emotions elsewhere in the speech.

14. **A; DOK Level:** 2; **Reading Assessment Targets:** R.4.3/L.4.3, R.6.4. The list of characteristics makes the "new generation of Americans" sound steadfast and determined. The tone of the enumeration is hopeful (answer A). Although the characteristics and overall tone of the speech indicate sincerity (answer B), the wording is more focused on hope for the future, so answer A is more specific. Answers C and D are incorrect because fear and doubt do not reflect the tone.

15. **C; DOK Level:** 2; **Reading Assessment Target:** R.6.4. The author repeats the phrases and includes the word *any* to emphasize that there is no challenge the United States cannot overcome. Nothing specific is mentioned, but the repetition evokes patriotism and a sense of unity. The purpose of the repetition is not to emphasize threats (answer A) or to emphasize the victories of the United States (answer B), neither of which are mentioned here. The author does not refer to how far the United States has come in the past century (answer D).

LESSON 9, *pp. 148–151*

1. **D; DOK Level:** 3; **Reading Assessment Targets:** R.9.1/R.7.1, R.9.2 Freeman suggest parents who can't make the transition from spectator to parent could have a negative impact on their children, and Torres discusses how "overzealous sports parents" negatively affect their children, so answer D is correct. Freeman does not suggest that overbearing parents are misunderstood, and Torres expresses frustration toward "overzealous sports parents." Neither author says that athletes need passionate sports parents to succeed. Freeman does not suggest that successful athletes have pushy sports parents, and Torres does not mention the frequency with which she sees pushy sports parents.

2. **A; DOK Level:** 2; **Reading Assessment Target:** R.6.1. Freeman explains how passionate and well-meaning parents' actions during and after sports games may have a negative impact on children because "staying off the field may be easier." Freeman does not provide entertaining stories. Freeman does not mention college athletes directly. Freeman does not mention athlete and parent discussions.

3. **D; DOK Level:** 3; **Reading Assessment Targets:** R.9.1/R.7.1, R.9.2 Freeman describes parents as "well-meaning" and "passionate" while Torres became upset during his child's game, despite his best intentions. Freeman suggests that parents consider their level of involvement but does not suggest that coaches facilitate this, and Torres does not speak to this point, so answer A is incorrect. Neither author states or implies that youth sports culture cannot change, so answer B is incorrect. Neither author directly discusses the effects of parents who "berate" other people's children during games, so answer C is incorrect.

4. **B; DOK Level:** 3; **Reading Assessment Targets:** R.9.1/R.7.1, R.9.2 Freeman provides logical reasoning for her assertion that passionate and well-meaning sports parents negatively affect children, and Torres provides an engaging personal narrative that includes emotional appeals. Freeman's language is straightforward, and Torres is colorful and personal, so answers A and C are incorrect. Freeman does not include engaging anecdotes, so answer D is incorrect.

5. **D; DOK Level:** 2; **Reading Assessment Targets:** R.2.2, R.6.1. Riley says that artists "forge connections between the past and the present" and "envision the future." Riley does not mention the stimulation of dialogue. She suggests that arts cross boundaries, not the reverse. She does not suggest emotional bonds among generations of students.

6. **C; DOK Level:** 2; **Reading Assessment Targets:** R.6.1. Iyo says, "Every community needs the arts and theater is communal. Thriving theaters will bring excitement and help nearby businesses," so answer C is correct. Iyo emphasizes that the arts are economically beneficial to communities, so answer A is incorrect. Iyo never states that theater will prevent war, so answer B is incorrect. Answer D is incorrect because Iyo does not state that the social benefits of the arts would suffer if people focused on economic benefits and, in fact, stresses economic benefits of the arts as positive.

7. **A; DOK Level:** 1; **Reading Assessment Targets:** R.2.1, R.6.1. Riley writes in opposition to the school board's decision to close the school; she writes to persuade the board to reconsider its decision. Her purpose is not to entertain readers with biographical details, as there are none. She briefly suggests a contrast between traditional and alternative high schools in support of a larger claim, but this comparison is not her main focus. She explains the role of the school in the neighborhood in support of a larger claim.

8. **B; DOK Level:** 2; **Reading Assessment Targets:** R.6.3. Iyo makes the argument that contributing to theater companies is important for helping the companies produce innovative work and for helping the community, so answer B is correct. Iyo mentions a well-known company, but it is not the main focus, so answer A is incorrect. Iyo mentions the Royal Shakespeare Company, but it is not part of the main purpose of the letter, so answer C is incorrect. Answer D is incorrect because Iyo does not promote specific fundraising opportunities.

9. **A; DOK Level:** 2; **Reading Assessment Targets:** R.2.2. Iyo believes that contributing to theaters will help make theaters successful, which in turn will have artistic and economic benefits; therefore, answer A is correct, and answer B is incorrect. Answers C and D are incorrect because Iyo does not emphasize the general importance of charitable giving for businesses, nor does he mention anything about benefits for local government.

10. B; DOK Level: 2; Reading Assessment Targets: R.2.1, R.5.1, R.5.4, R.6.1. Riley lists several reasons in support of her claim, including a list of reasons explaining why students need flexibility. Answer A is incorrect because Riley says that a combined school is unacceptable. Economics is a logical appeal, not an emotional one or an ethical one. Riley mentions nothing about repurposing the school.

11. C; DOK Level: 3; Reading Assessment Targets: R.7.4, R.9.1/R.7.1. Answer C is correct because both authors emphasize that businesses such as hotels and restaurants that are near cultural or arts centers profit economically. Nothing is mentioned about government support for the arts, so answers A and D are incorrect. Nothing is mentioned about ticket prices, so answer B is incorrect as well.

12. D; DOK Level: 3; Reading Assessment Targets: R.7.4, R.9.1/R.7.1. Answer D is correct because Riley mentions professionals who attended an arts-focused high school that helped prepare them for their careers; Iyo mentions artists as examples of those who could perfect their craft in successful theaters before becoming famous. Answer A is incorrect because Riley does not mention knowing any of the artists, nor does Iyo focus on heritage. Riley does mention that young artists need instruction but does not mention what it should be; Iyo most likely believes that artists learn from each other, both young and old. Although Riley implies that the Board's decision about the school will affect students negatively, she does not state that people do not appreciate young artists. The specific artists Iyo mentions are not named as supporters of the theater, but as actors in the theater.

13. D; DOK Level: 3; Reading Assessment Targets: R.9.1/R.7.1, R.9.2. Both authors hold the arts in high regard, so answer D is the best choice. Both authors feel strongly about the importance and relevance of art, so neither author's tone is ironic, negative, or resigned.

LESSON 10, pp. 152–155

1. D; DOK Level: 3; Reading Assessment Targets: R.7.2, R.7.3, R.9.1/R.7.1. Both the article and the table show that the moon has useful resources. Answer A is incorrect because cost efficiency is not mentioned in the table. Answer B is incorrect because neither text states or implies that any of these minerals are not found on Earth. Answer C is incorrect because moon mining is not mentioned in the table.

2. Both, Passage, Passage DOK Level: 3; Reading Assessment Targets: R.7.2, R.7.3, R.7.4, R.9.1/R.7.1. The table and the passage mention the minimum age. Only the passage includes information about term lengths and the number of senators.

3. A; DOK Level: 2; Reading Assessment Targets: R.5.1, R.5.4. Although the article is specifically about Jefferson's gardening, the author admires Jefferson's talents, accomplishments, and varied interests. Paragraph 1 emphasizes this aspect of Jefferson: despite all he did as a political leader, he had time for more accomplishments. Answer B is incorrect because paragraph 2 introduces Jefferson's gardening as experimental. Answer C is incorrect because Jefferson's motives for gardening are not explained in paragraph 1. Answer D is incorrect because the main idea of the article is not that gardening is full of failure or difficulty, nor does paragraph 1 mention failure.

4. C; DOK Level: 2; Reading Assessment Targets: R.5.1, R.6.3, R.6.4. The author quotes Jefferson to illustrate that Jefferson faced failure as well as success in his experimental gardening. Answer A is incorrect because the quotations are excerpts from Jefferson's journal; they are not anecdotes. Answer B may be plausible, but it does not reflect the author's purpose as much as answer C does. Answer D is incorrect because the quotations in paragraph 3 indicate failure; the final quotation in paragraph 4, however, shows optimism.

5. A; DOK Level: 3; Reading Assessment Targets: R.7.3, R.9.1/R.7.1. Answer A is correct as Jefferson's detailed notes are a hint that he approached his gardening as one would approach work in a laboratory. Answer B is incorrect as paragraph 2 supports the idea that he viewed his gardening as a laboratory. Answers C and D are not supported by the text in paragraph 2.

6. A; DOK Level: 2; Reading Assessment Target: R.5.4. The garden notes are characteristic of journal entries because Jefferson makes mechanical errors in his writing; writes in a personal shorthand, using incomplete sentences and abbreviations; and lists entries by date. Answer B does not apply to journal writing. Answers C and D may or may not apply to journal writing.

7. D; DOK Level: 3; Reading Assessment Targets: R.5.4, R.6.3. The garden notes effectively maintain information about Jefferson's garden for his own reference because they are clear, concise, and are organized by date. Answer A is incorrect because the text contains no traditional transitions. Answer B is incorrect because few headers appear in the garden notes. Answer C is incorrect because the numbers indicate dates, not steps in a process.

8. B; DOK Level: 3; Reading Assessment Targets: R.7.3, R.9.1/R.7.1. Both the article and the garden notes show that gardening, while rewarding, can be a difficult endeavor that presents both failure and success. Answer A is incorrect because nothing is mentioned or implied about the importance of taking notes. Answer C is incorrect because Jefferson's notes do not mention exotic crops. Answer D is incorrect because only the article addresses Jefferson's belief that introducing useful plants to one's culture is a great service.

9. C; DOK Level: 3; Reading Assessment Targets: R.7.3, R.9.1/R.7.1. The purpose of the article is to inform readers about Jefferson's experimentation with gardening, whereas the garden notes were written by Jefferson himself to maintain records of his garden, based on his observations, for his own reference. Answer A is incorrect because the notes do not provide instruction. Answer B is incorrect because the article and the notes address his failures as well as his successes. Answer D is incorrect because neither passage is instructive for someone learning to or trying to garden.

10. A; DOK Level: 3; Reading Assessment Targets: R.7.3, R.9.1/R.7.1. The article is written for a general audience, but the garden notes were written by Jefferson for his own use. Answer B is incorrect because "visitors to Jefferson's garden" is too narrow an audience. Answer C is incorrect because anyone might find the article interesting, and the garden notes were intended for Jefferson's own use. Answer D is incorrect because neither text offers enough information to show readers how to garden.

11. **B; DOK Level:** 3; **Reading Assessment Targets:** R.7.4, R.9.1/R.7.1. Both texts reveal that Jefferson was organized, patient, and eager to learn. He kept meticulous notes on his gardening observations, enjoyed experimenting with new plants, and was willing to accept failure as well as success. Answer A is incorrect because the article indicates that Jefferson was a busy man. Answer C is incorrect because nothing in either text implies that Jefferson was quiet or uncomfortable around others. Answer D is incorrect because although he was intelligent and a keen observer, nothing in either text indicates that he was impractical.

LESSON 11, *pp. 156–159*

1. **A; DOK Level:** 3; **Reading Assessment Targets:** R.9.1/R.7.1, R.9.2. Reagan associates the Great Society with high poverty rates, which he attributes to the great expansion of government programs. Through this association, readers can determine that Reagan associates the Great Society with an intrusive government; therefore, answer A is correct. He does not associate it with economic progress (answer B), great American wealth (answer C), or the dangers of social progress (answer D). Johnson's descriptions depict the Great Society positively, associating it with engagement in a large community (answer A), not a local community (answer D) or an individual approach (answer C). Although Johnson mentions commerce, he does not focus on it, so answer B is incorrect.

2. **D; DOK Level:** 2; **Reading Assessment Targets:** R.6.1, R.6.3. Reagan provides reasons and examples to persuade his audience why big government is problematic, so answer D is correct. Reagan's main purpose is not to inform, so answers A and C are incorrect. Reagan uses examples of federal spending to show why big government programs are problematic, not to persuade that more government oversight is needed, so answer B is incorrect.

3. **B; DOK Level:** 2; **Reading Assessment Targets:** R.5.1, R.5.2. Reagan uses examples to show how too much taxing and spending can be problematic, so answer B is correct. Reagan does not give examples of inflation, so answer A is incorrect. Reagan does not focus on economic principles, so answer C is incorrect. Reagan does not focus on interest rates, so answer D is incorrect.

4. **A; DOK Level:** 2; **Reading Assessment Targets:** R.4.3/L.4.3, R.5.1, R.6.1. The language in the first paragraph contains metaphors, so answer A is correct. Johnson does not use specific examples in his text, so answer B is incorrect. The language is eloquent and metaphoric, not simple and direct or informal and conversational, so answers C and D are incorrect.

5. **C; DOK Level:** 3; **Reading Assessment Targets:** R.9.1/R.7.1, R.9.2. Reagan is critical of opposing viewpoints and policies throughout the text (answer C). Johnson uses inspiring language and ideas throughout his text, so his tone reflects optimism (answer C). Reagan is not sentimental, and, although Johnson is positive, he is not joyful, so answer A is incorrect. Reagan is passionate, so he is not indifferent; although Johnson may show pride, both parts of the answer must be correct, which they are not in answer B. Reagan is not mournful, and Johnson is not ironic, so answer D is incorrect.

6. **D; Level:** 3; **Reading Assessment Targets:** R.2.7, R.9.1/R.7.1, R.9.2. Answer D is correct because Reagan is opposed to a big federal government and would not advocate another big spending plan. Johnson states in paragraph 3 that the "solution to these problems does not rest on a massive program in Washington." Answer A is incorrect because Johnson does not mention the private sector. Neither author supports local governments' assuming more control. Reagan opposes government regulation of the economy, and Johnson indicates that local governments have limited resources. Reagan would agree with answer C, but Johnson most likely would not.

7. **A; DOK Level:** 2; **Reading Assessment Target:** R.5.3. Answer A is correct because the word *But* indicates that the author is providing evidence that stand-alone renewable energy systems benefit not only people living in remote areas; people near energy grids use stand-alone systems to help protect the environment and to avoid dealing with power companies. The author does not show disagreement with the traditional practice of getting power from a power provider, so answer B is incorrect. The author suggests that stand-alone renewable energy systems are cost effective, so answer C is incorrect. *But* does not indicate agreement, so answer D is incorrect as well.

8. **D; DOK Level:** 2; **Reading Assessment Targets:** R.6.1, R.6.3. The author shows that those living far from energy grids, as well as those living near them, can benefit from using stand-alone renewable energy systems, so answer D is correct. The author does not indicate that stand-alone systems are costly, inconvenient, or unreliable, so answers A and C are incorrect. The author never indicates that the stand-alone systems are underrated, so answer B is incorrect.

9. **B; DOK Level:** 2; **Reading Assessment Targets:** R.6.1, R.6.3. The author explains why consumers would want a stand-alone renewable energy system, why such a system is beneficial, how it works, and what is needed for it to work; therefore, answer B is correct. The author is not persuasive, merely informative; therefore, answers A and C are incorrect. The author's focus is on stand-alone renewable energy systems, not on reducing energy costs and minimizing inconvenience, so answer D is incorrect.

10. **C; DOK Level:** 2; **Reading Assessment Targets:** R.6.1, R.6.3. Answer C is correct because the author explains how a grid-connected renewable energy system works, how such a system can save money, and what is needed for it to work. The author is not persuasive, merely informative; therefore, answers B and D are incorrect. Although the author does mention that power providers have grid-connection requirements, the author does not provide great detail and does not focus solely on the matter.

11. **D; DOK Level:** 3; **Reading Assessment Targets:** R.9.1/R.7.1, R.9.2. Answer D is correct because both authors indicate that renewable energy systems help save money, energy, and the environment. Answer A is incorrect because neither author indicates that consumers should do the work of switching energy systems themselves. Answer B is incorrect because the authors do not explain a switch to renewable energy systems as costly or inconvenient. Answer C is incorrect because the author of the second passage states the benefits of having access to power grids.

12. **A; DOK Level: 3; Reading Assessment Targets:** R.9.1/R.7.1, R.9.2. Answer A is correct; the author of the second passage addresses energy systems that obtain power from both renewable energy sources and a grid. The first passage addresses only stand-alone renewable energy systems. Answer B is incorrect because both passages address environmentally friendly systems. Answer C is incorrect because both passages list what consumers need to purchase. Answer D is incorrect because both passages indicate when each renewable energy system makes sense.

13. **B; DOK Level: 3; Reading Assessment Targets:** R.9.1/R.7.1, R.9.2. Both authors use straightforward language and factual evidence, such as specific details and examples, so answer B is correct. Neither author uses an aggressive tone or cautionary language, so answer A is incorrect. Neither uses emotional or figurative language, so answer C is incorrect. Neither author includes anecdotes, so answer D is incorrect.

14. **C; DOK Level: 3; Reading Assessment Target:** R.9.1/R.7.1. Answer C is correct; both authors explain the benefits of using renewable energy systems and mention them as making sense for small businesses as they save in costs. Answers A, B, and D are incorrect because nothing about the authors' professions, homes, or businesses is implied in the passages.

15. **D; DOK Level: 3; Reading Assessment Target:** R.9.1/R.7.1. Answer D is correct; the information from both passages suggests that a frugal homeowner dealing with unpredictable seasons would best benefit from a grid-connected system so that he or she could rely on the power grid when wind, water, or solar power were not available. Answers A and B are incorrect because a homeowner who cares about the environment or lives far from a power grid would most likely choose the stand-alone system. Answer C is incorrect because the first passage explains that those choosing to live independently of power providers would also prefer the stand-alone system.

LESSON 12, *pp. 160–163*

1. **A; DOK Level: 3; Reading Assessment Targets:** R.7.3, R.7.4. Obama's speech indicates that Parks's actions "defied injustice" and had a profound impact on the world. The FAQ text reveals that Parks refused to give up her seat to a white person and was arrested as a consequence. The FAQ text also provides information about the events that followed her action. The conclusion may be drawn that Parks's act helped others follow her example because it precipitated a "change" in the world. Answers B, C, and D are incorrect because nothing in either passage indicates that Parks caused other public disturbances, that she was already acting as part of a protest, or that her actions were out of character. Remember that answer choices must come from the texts, not solely from prior knowledge. Therefore, even if you know that Parks's actions were not spontaneous, the information in these passages does not support this information.

2. **DOK Level: 2; Reading Assessment Target:** R.7.3. President Obama Honors Rosa Parks: **An act of civil disobedience changed a nation. Courageous acts by ordinary people lead to change.** Rosa Parks FAQ: **People should believe in themselves and their ideals. All people deserve the same opportunities.** These statements are paraphrases from both passages.

3. **D; DOK Level: 2; Reading Assessment Target:** R.6.1. The purpose of the memoir is to entertain readers with an interesting story about chicken soup. Answer A is incorrect because the narrator does not attempt to encourage readers to make their own chicken soup. Answer B is incorrect because the memoir never mentions store-bought chicken soup. Answer C is incorrect because the narrator does not explain how to make the soup but only mentions some of the soup's ingredients.

4. **B; DOK Level: 3; Reading Assessment Target:** R.7.3. Although the memoir makes a reference to a chicken soup recipe, it does not provide a list of steps in a process. The memoir is written in paragraph form, but the recipe lists numbered steps so that readers can follow it. Answer A is incorrect because the memoir does not appear as a list of steps, and the recipe does not suggest that one idea is more important than another. Answer C is incorrect because the memoir does not make comparisons and contrasts, and the recipe appears as a list of steps. Answer D is incorrect because the memoir is not based on cause-and-effect relationships.

5. **C; DOK Level: 2 Reading Assessment Targets:** R.5.1, R.5.3. The word *consequently* signals a cause-and-effect relationship—what follows the word is a result, or consequence, of information that precedes it. Answer A is incorrect because a signal of contradiction might be *however* or *on the other hand*. Answer B is incorrect because a transition always relates to information coming before and/or after it. Answer D is incorrect because a word indicating sequence could be *next* or *finally*.

6. **B; DOK Level: 3; Reading Assessment Target:** R.7.3. Although the memoir mentions some of the ingredients that the author's grandmother used and describes some of the process, the recipe covers the entire process in greater detail so that the reader can actually follow instructions to prepare the syrup. Answer A is incorrect because the recipe shows no gaps in information. Answer C is incorrect because the recipe does explain how the syrup is used. Answer D is incorrect because both passages give an introduction and context to the remedy.

7. **A; DOK Level: 3; Reading Assessment Targets:** R.4.3/L.4.3, R.7.3. Although this answer is actually an opinion, it is the one that best answers the question. The informality and direct writing style make both passages entertaining and easy to follow, including the actual syrup recipe. Answer B is incorrect; although illness is mentioned, neither the context nor the tone is gloomy, and the remedies seem useful and not unpleasant. Although the author cautions readers at the end of the recipe, the tone of neither passage is cautionary; therefore, answer C is incorrect. Answer D is incorrect because no specific research is included, except for a reference in the memoir, nor does the author of either passage attempt to persuade readers to use these remedies.

8. **C; DOK Level: 2; Reading Assessment Targets:** R.2.8, R.6.1, R.6.3. Answer C is correct because the author's attitude toward the grandmother's old ways seems to assume that readers, too, will dismiss old-world superstitions. Answer A is incorrect because nothing suggests that the author expects readers to know how to make the soup. The purpose is not to provide a recipe. Answer B is incorrect because the author's explanations of Greek words and practices reflect the assumption that readers are unfamiliar with Greek culture. Answer D is incorrect because, if anything, the author assumes that readers treat viral illnesses with over-the-counter medicines.

9. **A; DOK Level:** 3; **Reading Assessment Target:** R.7.3. Although the memoir does explain that the chicken soup boosts the immune system, it does not explain why natural remedies are healthier alternatives to over-the-counter cold and flu remedies as the recipe does. Answer B is incorrect because the memoir does not mention the ease of making chicken soup. Answer C is incorrect because the memoir indicates nothing about safety measures. Answer D is incorrect because the author of the memoir mentions unusual ingredients.

10. **B; DOK Level:** 3; **Reading Assessment Target:** R.7.3. Both passages point out that natural remedies can be as effective as modern medicines in treating viral infections. Answer A is incorrect because neither passage mentions consulting a doctor before using the remedy—except in the case of checking children's dosage for the syrup. Answer C is incorrect because neither passage compares the home remedy with the same remedy bought in stores. Answer D is incorrect because the memoir does not mention the lack of safety in using over-the-counter medications.

11. **B; DOK Level:** 3; **Reading Assessment Targets:** R.2.7, R.7.4. On the basis of the grandmother's ideas and practices, she most likely would use elderberry syrup as a preventive measure. Answer A is incorrect because she favors home remedies. Answer C is incorrect because nothing is mentioned or implied about her reliance on doctors for all illnesses. Although answer D may seem correct—and is close to correct—it is not the best answer. The author states that the *kako mati* is to ward off others' envy, not illness directly.

LESSON 13, *pp. 164–167*

1. **D; DOK Level:** 3; **Reading Assessment Target:** R.7.4. The article indicates that a person can earn an income and maintain ties to the workforce. You can thus assume that the recipient should accept the position and continue his search for a full-time, permanent position. Answer A is incorrect because the letter says that the recipient will not get benefits. Answer B is incorrect because the letter implies that the recipient has some editorial skills and experience, so editing is not a new field. Answer C is incorrect because nothing in the letter indicates gaps in his résumé.

2. **DOK Level:** 3; **Reading Assessment Targets:** R.7.4, R.9.1/R.7.1. Provides: **experience in desired field, acquisition of professional contacts, leads to letters of recommendation**; Does Not Provide: **insurance benefits, high pay, paid vacation.** The article encourages readers to accept part-time positions to gain more experience in their field of interest, to gain professional contacts through work, and have more people from whom to request letters of recommendation, all of which will help job seekers gain employment. The letter indicates that a part-time job may not include benefits, high pay, or paid vacation.

3. **C; DOK Level:** 3; **Reading Assessment Targets:** R.7.4, R.9.1/R.7.1. Answer C is correct because wild rice is mentioned as being a whole grain. Answers A and D are incorrect because the products may or may not be made with whole grains. Answer B is incorrect because neither text equates *organic* with *whole grain*. There is no indication that the chips are made with whole grains.

4. **B; DOK Level:** 3; **Reading Assessment Targets:** R.7.3, R.9.1/.R.7.1. Both passages are written to inform readers that food labels can be misleading and to provide information about how to read them correctly. Answer A is incorrect because nothing is mentioned about growing food or the benefits of organic products. No anecdotes are provided in either text, so answer C is incorrect. Although answer D is plausible, the passages focus on labeling rather than health values. The fact that refining strips away the most nutritious portions of the grain is mentioned once, and its implication is clear; however, it is not either author's purpose to compare nutritional values.

5. **A; DOK Level:** 3; **Reading Assessment Targets:** R.7.3, R.7.4. Both passages indicate that food labels use misleading and confusing language and, therefore, cannot be trusted. Answer B is incorrect because the first passage indicates that not all labels are regulated and that terms are legally defined. Answer C is incorrect because food labels do not always tell people what they need to know and, therefore, can be misleading. Answer D is incorrect because food labels are not necessarily honest, according to the passages.

6. **C; DOK Level:** 3; **Reading Assessment Targets:** R.7.3, R.7.4. Both the first passage and the table explain the meanings of terms commonly used on food labels so that consumers can make better choices. Answer A is incorrect because neither the first passage nor the table addresses consumers' skepticism. Answer B is incorrect because the first passage does not mention the Whole Grain Stamp. Answer D is incorrect because foods labeled as "natural grain" products are not necessarily better than foods labeled as "multigrain."

7. **B; DOK Level:** 3; **Reading Assessment Target:** R.7.4. A loaf of organic whole grain bread would be the most nutritious choice. According to the first passage and the table, the choices in answers A, C, and D would have preservatives or would be missing the beneficial nutrients of whole grain products.

8. **C; DOK Level:** 3; **Reading Assessment Targets:** R.7.3, R.7.4. Both the first passage and table indicate that refined grains lose their beneficial nutrients. Answers A and B are incorrect because refined grains do not necessarily contain preservatives, unnatural substances, or food dyes. Answer D is incorrect because corn syrup is not reserved for refined grains alone.

9. **D; DOK Level:** 3; **Reading Assessment Target:** R.7.4. On the basis of the content and source of both passages, answer D is the most likely choice. The audience of the first passage is not limited to farmers; according to the source reference of the second passage, the author is likely a member of the Whole Grain Council, but nothing suggests that he or she helped create the stamp. Therefore, answer A is incorrect. Some of the information in answers B and C may be accurate, but it is based on generalizations or conclusions that do not have enough support in the passages.

10. **A; DOK Level:** 3; **Reading Assessment Target:** R.7.4. Answer A is the best choice. The article and table indicate that food producers are willing to use deception on food labels to get people to buy foods by marketing them as healthful. Answer B is incorrect because the table does not discuss regulation. Answer C is incorrect because neither text discusses the food industries' interest in its consumers. Answer D is not the best choice because neither text specifically discusses organic growers or whole-food advocates and their opinion about the Whole Grain Stamp.

11. **B; DOK Level: 3; Reading Assessment Target:** R.7.4. Answer B is correct because oatmeal is a whole grain. The foods mentioned in answers A, C, and D are not whole grain products, according to food labeling and the information in the passages.

12. **C; DOK Level: 3; Reading Assessment Target:** R.7.4. Answer C is correct because both passages address inaccurate or deceptive labeling. Answer A is incorrect because it contradicts the views of both authors. Answer B is incorrect because the first passage mentions deceptive labeling in other kinds of food. Answer D is incorrect because of the generalization that all organic or all natural products are mislabeled. Although some, or even many, may be, not all are.

UNIT 3 EXTENDED RESPONSE

LESSON 1, *pp. 170–173*

1. **A; DOK Level: 3; Reading Assessment Targets:** R.9.2, R.9.3. Answer A is correct because Clemmitt mentions the claim that social media have been changing "how people think and learn," while Leung argues that social media have positive effects on literacy and communication. Answer B is incorrect because Clemmitt merely indicates change; it is still not completely clear that her claim will be negative. Leung, on the other hand, claims that social media are positively changing how people communicate. Answer C is incorrect because Leung, not Clemmitt, mentions the positive effects of social media; Leung mentions annoyance as part of a statement supporting her claim. The evidence says that texting is about more than annoying others. Answer D is incorrect because Clemmitt makes no positive statement about social media, whereas Leung claims that social media have a positive, not negative, effect on learning.

2. **B; DOK Level: 3; Reading Assessment Targets:** R.9.2, R.9.3. Answer B is correct because Clemmitt cites a research study that focuses on the effects of social media on brain function, while Leung cites a research study that focuses on the effects of social media on communication. Answer A is incorrect because only Clemmitt cites a study that focuses on the brain. Answer C is incorrect because only Leung cites a study that focuses on social interactions. Answer D is incorrect because the study cited by Leung focuses on social interactions, not emotions.

3. **D; DOK Level: 3; Reading Assessment Targets:** R.9.2, R.9.3. Answer D is correct because Clemmitt quotes a researcher who says that constant attention shifts caused by social media add to stress, while Leung quotes a teacher who says that texting notifications can help relieve students' stress. Answer A is incorrect because only Clemmitt claims that social media can add to stress. Answer B is incorrect because it is Clemmitt who claims that social media add to stress, while Leung claims that social media relieve stress. Answer C is incorrect because only Leung claims that social media relieve stress.

Chart; DOK Level: 2; Reading Assessment Targets: R.5.1, R.5.3, R.5.4, R.6.1, R.6.2, R.6.4.
Clemmitt
Author's Point of View: "Some believe that . . . social media . . . may already be [changing] how people think and learn." The author's claim is that social media have negative effects on the brain.
Acknowledgment and Response to Conflicting Viewpoint or Counterclaim: "When electronic devices were first becoming [popular], some hoped they would teach a new generation how to multitask better than previous generations did. But research [shows] that people who grew up with electronic devices 'really can't multitask' either, says . . . Larry Rosen, a professor of psychology at California State University, Dominguez Hills." The author acknowledges that some people hoped technology would improve multitasking, but she counters that research does not support this hope.
Rhetorical Strategy: Qualifying Statement: "While the long-term effects of such behavior are unknown, research has shown that 'frequent sleep interruptions make it harder for the brain to consolidate the day's learning and memories,' she says." The introductory clause qualifies, or weakens, the information that follows.
Supporting Reason or Key Idea: "The sleep disruptions that [go along with] social technology may help account for [mental] changes, says . . . Kaveri Subrahmanyam, a professor of psychology at California State University, Los Angeles. . . ." The effect of sleep deprivation on the brain as a result of social media is one of the author's reasons for claiming that social media negatively affect the brain.
Transitional Language or Signal Words That Indicate Relationships: Cause and Effect: "As a result, the typical technology-obsessed person now gives 'continuous partial attention' to just about everything and full attention to almost nothing." The phrase *As a result* signals a cause-and-effect relationship between ideas.

Chart; DOK Level: 2; Reading Assessment Targets: R.5.1, R.5.3, R.5.4, R.6.1, R.6.2, R.6.4.
Leung
Author's Point of View: "Some studies have shown that texting improves communication skills." The author's claim is that texting improves communication.
Acknowledgment and Response to Conflicting Viewpoint or Counterclaim: "Recent criticisms that text language, including abbreviations and contractions, for example, may begin to appear in formal writing have not proven true. Dr. Plester concludes that text language follows the general rules of language and that people 'have a sophisticated understanding of the appropriate use of words.'" The author acknowledges criticisms and then says that the criticisms are not valid based on research. **Rhetorical Strategy: Bandwagon:** "A study by the Pew Research Center found that on average, older teenagers send about 60 texts per day and use texting as their 'dominant daily mode of communication.' Their adult counterparts are not far behind in this rising trend. Perhaps the next time it's time to call the family to dinner, it might be more efficient to send a group text." The author cites a statistic that shows the popularity of texting and then suggests that readers join the trend.
Supporting Reason or Key Idea: "In reality, texters may be improving their literacy skills." This reason supports the author's claim that texting improves communication.
Transitional Language or Signal Words That Indicate Relationships: Addition: "Furthermore, texting is a fast and convenient way to communicate with others." The word *Furthermore* is a transition word that shows an addition to a previous idea.

UNIT 3 (continued)

1. **D; DOK Level:** 3; **Reading Assessment Targets:** R.9.2, R.9.3; **Writing Assessment Targets:** W.1, W.2. The prompt asks which article's position is better supported. So you must decide which article has a stronger overall argument. Simply stating that the two arguments are equally supported or equally weak (answers A and C) does not address the prompt. Stating that Clemmitt fails to address the benefits of social media (answer B) also does not address the prompt, although it may be a valid point for the body of your response. The best response is answer D.

Chart; **DOK Level:** 2; **Reading Assessment Targets:** R.8.1, R.8.2.
Claim: Social media may be changing how people think and learn.
Reason 1: More multitasking
Evidence: Quotations based on research study by psychology professor Larry Rosen
Reason 2: Sleep disruptions cause mental changes
Evidence: Quotations from psychology professor Kaveri Subrahmanyam

Chart; **DOK Level:** 2; **Reading Assessment Targets:** R.8.1, R.8.2.
Claim: Texting improves communication skills.
Reason 1: Literacy
Evidence: Quotations based on research study by Dr. Beverly Plester
Reason 2: Speed and convenience
Evidence: Quotation from reading-language arts teacher Elsa Turner

2. **DOK Level:** 3; **Reading Assessment Target:** R.8.3. Possible response: One strength of Clemmitt's argument is that she supports it with evidence based on research. One weakness of her argument is that some of the research evidence is qualified, indicating uncertainty. For example, "social media . . . may already be [changing] how people think and learn" and "long-term effects of such behavior are unknown."

3. **DOK Level:** 3; **Reading Assessment Target:** R.8.3. Possible response: One strength of Leung's argument is that she provides evidence based on research and practical experience. One weakness of her argument is that she uses bandwagon rhetoric in her conclusion.

Text Mark-Up; DOK Level: 2; **Reading Assessment Targets:** R.5.3, R.6.2, R.6.4, R.8.1, R.8.2, R.9.3. You should correctly mark one example of each text element in each passage. Examples from the Leung passage appear in the chart on page 176; you should try to locate secondary examples, when possible, in the passage. Examples of markups from the Clemmitt passage follow:
Claim (put in brackets): Some believe that . . . social media . . . may already be [changing] how people think and learn.

Reason 1 (circle and number): Multitask
Evidence (underline): The very nature of the brain seems to decree that, for many activities, people simply can't do two or more tasks at once. In addition, while the brain can switch rapidly from task to task, doing so takes more time to do the tasks.
Rhetorical Techniques (box text and label the technique: in this case, a juxtaposition of opposites and a qualifying statement: (juxtaposition of opposites) The typical technology-obsessed person now gives "continuous partial attention" to just about everything and full attention to almost nothing; (qualifying statement) While

the long-term effects of such behavior are unknown . . .
Opposing Viewpoint (use wavy underline): But research [shows] that people who grew up with electronic devices "really can't multitask" either, says . . . Larry Rosen, a professor of psychology at California State University, Dominguez Hills.
Relationship (place triangle around "As a result"): As a result, the typical technology-obsessed person now gives "continuous partial attention" to just about everything and full attention to almost nothing. "You never do anything in depth," he says.

Web diagram; DOK Level: 3; **Writing Assessment Targets:** W.1, W.2.
Possible responses:
Clemmitt supports her argument better than Leung supports her argument because Clemmitt persuades readers to think about the subject of social media in a new way.
Leung makes a stronger argument than Clemmitt because she presents a variety of evidence.
While Leung argues that social media are beneficial, Clemmitt makes a better argument against social media because she cites credible scientists and their research.
Leung better supports her claim because she does not qualify the uncertainty in her evidence as Clemmitt does.

1. **A; DOK Level:** 3; **Reading Assessment Targets:** R.5.3, R.9.2; **Writing Assessment Targets:** W.1, W.2. Answer A is correct because transitional language is another common point between the two passages. Both authors use transitional language to advance their arguments. Multitasking (answer B) and sleep disruption (answer D) are reasons given by Clemmitt, but not Leung. Literacy (answer C) is a reason given by Leung, but not Clemmitt.

Graphic Organizer; DOK Level: 3; **Reading Assessment Targets:** R.9.2, R.9.3; **Writing Assessment Targets:** W.1, W.2. Be sure that you have listed three logical points of comparison and that you have selected relevant, specific, and sufficient text evidence for each point from each passage. For example, you may choose **Claim/Point of View**, **Reasons**, and **Tone** for your three points of comparison/contrast. Under **Claim/Point of View**, you may write that Clemmitt's claim is that social media may be changing the way users think and learn, while Leung's claim is that texting may help improve literacy. Under **Reasons**, you may write that Clemmitt lists reasons such as multitasking and sleep disruption to support her claim, while Leung lists exposure to written words and ease of communication. Under **Tone**, you may note that Clemmitt's tone is apprehensive and cautionary, while Leung's tone is friendly and casual.

Graphic Organizer; DOK Level: 3; **Reading Assessment Targets:** R.9.2, R.9.3; **Writing Assessment Targets**: W.1, W.2. Be sure that you have listed three additional logical points of comparison and that you have selected relevant, specific, and sufficient text evidence for each point from each passage. For example, you may choose **Purpose**, **Counterargument**, and **Evidence** for your three points of comparison/contrast. Under **Purpose**, you may note that Clemmitt's purpose is to warn readers about the potential negative mental effects on social media users, while Leung's purpose is to inform readers about the literacy benefits of texting. Under **Counterargument**, you may write that Clemmitt and Leung both use direct quotations from experts to refute their respective counterarguments (in Clemmitt's case, the argument that social media teach multitasking; in Leung's, the criticism that texting does not follow the standard conventions of English). Under **Evidence**, you may note that Clemmitt and Leung both use quotations by experts to support their claims, and that Leung also cites statistics from a Pew Research Center study.

2. **DOK Level:** 3; **Writing Assessment Targets:** W.1, W.2. Be sure you have selected three of the six points from the graphic organizers on the two preceding pages.

3. **DOK Level:** 3; **Writing Assessment Targets:** W.1, W.2. Be sure you offer valid and logical explanations for your choices by focusing on the relationships among the points and their relation to your chosen thesis statement.

4. **DOK Level:** 3; **Writing Assessment Targets:** W.1, W.2. Be sure you offer valid and logical explanations for your eliminations by focusing on the relationships among the points and their relation to your chosen thesis statement.

LESSON 4, *pp. 182–185*

1. **C; DOK Level:** 3; **Writing Assessment Targets:** W.1, W.2. In a subject-by-subject structure, after introducing a point about rhetorical strategy, you would provide evidence from the first subject (in this case, the Clemmitt passage), so answer C is correct. You would provide evidence from both passages only if you were using a point-by-point structure, so answer B is incorrect. In addition, you would not introduce or explain additional points until evidence for the first point has been provided, so answers A and D are incorrect.

Web diagram; DOK Level: 2; **Writing Assessment Targets:** W.1, W.2. Answers will vary. Be sure you have correctly copied the three points of comparison or contrast you defined in Unit 3, Lesson 3, and that you have used numbers to rank the points from most important to least important. For example, if your points were **Claim/Point of View**, **Reasons**, and **Tone**, you might rank **Claim/Point of View** as most important (1), **Reasons** as next most important (2), and **Tone** as least important (3).

2. **DOK Level:** 3; **Writing Assessment Targets:** W.1, W.2. Answers will vary. Be sure you have explained why this point will be most convincing in support of your thesis statement. For example, if you have chosen **Claim/Point of View** as the most important point of comparison, mention that the author's point of view is most important because it makes up the central argument of each passage.

3. **DOK Level:** 3; **Writing Assessment Targets:** W.1, W.2. Answers will vary. Be sure you have explained why this point will be convincing in support of your thesis statement. For example, if you have chosen **Reasons** as the second most important point of comparison, mention that the reasons are the individual arguments that support each author's central claim.

4. **DOK Level:** 3; **Writing Assessment Targets:** W.1, W.2. Answers will vary. Be sure you have explained why this point may be least convincing in support of your thesis statement. For example, if you have chosen **Tone** as the least important point of comparison, explain that tone is a stylistic element of writing and is not as persuasive as hard evidence.

5. **DOK Level:** 3; **Writing Assessment Targets:** W.1, W.2. Answers will vary. You may choose **most important to least important** because your purpose is to persuade readers with a sound logical argument, not lose their attention or anger them by putting the most important point last.

Organizational Flowchart; DOK Level: 3; **Writing Assessment Targets:** W.1, W.2.
Answers will vary. Review your plan for the purposeful, logical progression of ideas with evidence closely tied to your main points. Be sure you have chosen an effective organizational structure that is well suited to your thesis statement and purpose for writing.

An example of the subject-by-subject organizer would be
Subject/Passage 1: Clemmitt
Point 1: Claim/Point of View; **Evidence:** Clemmitt's claim is that social media may be changing the way users think and learn.
Point 2: Reasons; **Evidence:** Clemmitt lists reasons such as multitasking and sleep disruption to support her claim.
Point 3: Tone; **Evidence:** Clemmitt's tone is apprehensive and cautionary.
Subject/Passage 2: Leung
Point 1: Claim/Point of View; **Evidence:** Leung's claim is that texting may help improve literacy.
Point 2: Reasons; **Evidence:** Leung lists reasons such as exposure to written words and ease of communication to support her claim.
Point 3: Tone; **Evidence:** Leung's tone is friendly and casual.

Organizational Flowchart; DOK Level: 3; **Writing Assessment Targets:** W.1, W.2. Answers will vary. Review your plan for the purposeful, logical progression of ideas with evidence closely tied to your main points. Be sure you have chosen an effective organizational structure that is well suited to your thesis statement and purpose for writing.

An example of the point-by-point chart would be
Point 1: Claim/Point of View; **Evidence from Subject/Passage 1:** Clemmitt's claim is that social media may be changing the way users think and learn; **Evidence from Subject/Passage 2:** Leung's claim is that texting may help improve literacy.
Point 2: Reasons; **Evidence from Subject/Passage 1:** Clemmitt lists multitasking and sleep disruption to support her claim; **Evidence from Subject/Passage 2:** Leung lists exposure to written words and ease of communication to support her claim.
Point 3: Tone; **Evidence from Subject/Passage 1:** Clemmitt's tone is apprehensive and cautionary; **Evidence from Subject/Passage 2:** Leung's tone is friendly and casual.

UNIT 3 (continued)

LESSON 5, pp. 186–189

1. **B; DOK Level: 2; Reading Assessment Target:** R.5.1; **Writing Assessment Targets:** W.1, W.2. Answer B is an example of concluding with a surprising fact or statistic, because it gives numerical data (60 texts per day) about the texting habits of teenagers. Answers A and D are examples of the connection strategy, in which the final thought of the conclusion connects the topic of the essay to the lives of the readers. Answer C, which describes a dinner scene in the Martinez household, is an example of concluding with an anecdote.

Introduction Chart; DOK Level: 2; Reading Assessment Target: R.5.4; **Writing Assessment Targets:** W.1, W.2.
Action: "You call your son, daughter, or spouse to dinner." *To call* is a physical action, not a mental one, so this introduction is an action lead. Note that although this introduction does contain dialogue, it technically leads with the action.
Dialogue/Quotation: "'Right now, with social networks and other tools on the Internet, . . . 500 million people have a way to say what they're thinking and have their voice be heard,' says Mark Zuckerberg, founder of Facebook." This introduction leads with a tagged quotation by Facebook founder Mark Zuckerberg, so it is a Dialogue/Quotation lead.
Reaction: "The [appeal] of socializing online has created a nation of mobile device [fans] . . ." An *appeal* is something that is processed by the brain, so this introduction is an example of a reaction lead. Note that it is neither a physical action (action lead) nor an example of speech (dialogue/quotation lead).

Conclusion Chart; DOK Level: 2; Reading Assessment Target: R.5.4; **Writing Assessment Targets:** W.1, W.2
Anecdote: "During dinner time at the Martinez house, family members sit at the table and text friends and coworkers." The author concludes with a short story, or scenario, about dinner time at the Martinez household, so this conclusion is an anecdote.
Connection: "Perhaps the next time it's time to call the family to dinner, it might be more efficient to send a group text." The author gives readers a suggestion that connects the topic of the passage to their own lives. She does not offer a fact or tell a story.
Fact/Statistic: "While the long-term effects of such behavior are unknown, research has shown that . . ." The reference to research suggests that this concluding thought is a fact, not a connection or an anecdote.

2. **DOK Level: 3; Writing Assessment Targets:** W.1, W.2, W.3; **Language Assessment Target:** L.1.9. Answers will vary. Be sure to use active verbs in your lead.

3. **DOK Level: 3; Writing Assessment Targets:** W.1, W.2, W.3; **Language Assessment Target:** L.2.4. Answers will vary. Be sure to use quotation marks and speaker tags correctly in your lead.

4. **DOK Level: 3; Writing Assessment Targets:** W.1, W.2, W.3; **Language Assessment Target:** L.1.9. Answers will vary. Be sure to use reactive verbs, such as *think, wonder,* or *dream,* in your lead.

5. **DOK Level: 3; Writing Assessment Targets:** W.1, W.2, W.3; **Language Assessment Target:** L.1.9. Answers will vary. Be sure to select appropriate transitional language that connects the lead you selected to your thesis statement.

6. **DOK Level: 2; Writing Assessment Targets:** W.1, W.2, W.3; **Language Assessment Target:** L.1.9. Answers will vary. Be sure to retrieve your thesis statement from Unit 3, Lesson 2. You may revise your statement here for clarity and flow.

7. **DOK Level: 2; Writing Assessment Targets:** W.2, W.3; **Language Assessment Target:** L.1.9. Answers will vary. Some examples of concluding transitions include *In summary, To conclude,* and *Finally.*

8. **DOK Level: 3; Writing Assessment Targets:** W.1, W.2, W.3. Answers will vary. Be sure your summary includes only the most important points and evidence. Use different wording from what you previously used in your planning charts in Unit 3, Lessons 3 and 4.

9. **DOK Level: 3; Writing Assessment Targets:** W.1, W.2, W.3. Answers will vary. Be sure to refer to real or imagined characters and events in your anecdote.

10. **DOK Level: 3; Writing Assessment Targets:** W.1, W.2, W.3. Answers will vary. Be sure to connect your topic to the lives of your readers in some way.

11. **DOK Level: 3; Writing Assessment Targets:** W.1, W.2, W.3. Answers will vary. Because you will not have the ability to conduct separate research during a test, you may use a fact or statistic from one of the passages and then comment on it.

12. **DOK Level: 3; Writing Assessment Targets:** W.1, W.2. Answers will vary. Be sure to circle one of the concluding thoughts you wrote for items 9–11.

LESSON 6, pp. 190–193

1. **B; DOK Level: 2; Reading Assessment Target:** R.5.3; **Writing Assessment Targets:** W.2, W.3; **Language Assessment Target:** L.1.9. Item V in the outline marks the transition from the first subject (Clemmitt's passage) to the second subject (Leung's passage). Both authors address social media, but their ideas on the topic are contrasting. Therefore, the transition *on the other hand* (answer B) best introduces Leung's ideas and shows that they differ from Clemmitt's. Answer A shows a contrast but does not use a transition. Answer C implies that the two authors agree with each other. Answer D uses the wrong transition (*in addition*) to show contrast.

Frame; DOK Level: 3; Writing Assessment Targets: W.1, W.2, W.3; **Language Assessment Target:** L.1.9. Use the GED® Reasoning Through Language Arts Extended Response Scoring Rubric for Trait 1 (Creation of Arguments and Use of Evidence) and Trait 2 (Development of Ideas and Organizational Structure) to review your draft. You can find these rubrics on pages 295–297. You may also consult the annotated sample extended response for Unit 3, Lesson 7.

LESSON 7, pp. 194–197

1. **D; DOK Level: 2; Writing Assessment Targets:** W.1, W.2, W.3; **Language Assessment Target:** L.1.4. Answer D is correct because *soda, coffee, and high-fat foods* is a more specific and formal phrase than *bad things.* In addition, it establishes a connection to the word *diet* in the next sentence, creating a logical parallel between bad eating habits and bad technological habits. The remaining answer choices—*unhealthful things, foods and drinks,* and *stuff that is harmful for them*—are more general phrases that lack the strength and specificity of answer D.

Revision Chart; DOK Level: 2; **Writing Assessment Targets:** W.2, W.3; **Language Assessment Targets:** L.1.4, L.1.8, L.1.9. Use the GED® Reasoning Through Language Arts Extended Response Scoring Rubric for Trait 2 (Development of Ideas and Organizational Structure) and Trait 3 (Clarity and Command of Standard English Conventions) to assess your chart. You can find these rubrics on pages 295–297. You may also consult the annotated corrected sample extended response below.

Revision Chart; DOK Level: 2; **Writing Assessment Targets:** W.2, W.3; **Language Assessment Targets:** L.1.6, L.1.8, L.1.9, L.2.2. Use the GED® Reasoning Through Language Arts Extended Response Scoring Rubric for Trait 2 (Development of Ideas and Organizational Structure) and Trait 3 (Clarity and Command of Standard English Conventions) to assess your chart. You can find these rubrics on pages 295–297. You may also consult the annotated corrected sample extended response below.

Revision Chart; DOK Level: 2; **Writing Assessment Targets:** W.2, W.3; **Language Assessment Targets:** L.1.1, L.1.2, L.1.3, L.1.5, L.1.7, L.2.1, L.2.3, L.2.4. Use the GED® Reasoning Through Language Arts Extended Response Scoring Rubric for Trait 2 (Development of Ideas and Organizational Structure) and Trait 3 (Clarity and Command of Standard English Conventions) to assess your chart. You can find these rubrics on pages 295–297. You may also consult the annotated corrected sample extended response below.

UNIT 3 *(continued)*

1 The writer uses an action strategy to attract the attention of readers and introduce the thesis statement.

4 The writer establishes a point-by-point organizational structure and uses transitions to show the logical relationships among ideas.

6 The writer correctly applies standard English conventions by using an apostrophe with a singular possessive noun and correct capitalization.

7 The writer shows a logical progression and development of ideas closely tied to the thesis.

10 The writer integrates text evidence with fluidity.

1 You've grabbed five items for purchase in the grocery store. You're in a hurry to get home, so you choose the speedy checkout line. There are two customers ahead of you. **2** The cashier finishes with the first person, but the second fails to move forward. He is texting! If this scenario seems familiar to you, you're not alone. People everywhere are multitasking and not doing it well. **3** Although authors such as Kristine Leung sing the praises of social media, Marcia Clemmitt makes a stronger argument against social media in her article "Social Media Becoming a Distraction."

4 While Leung and Clemmitt support their points of view with clear evidence, Clemmitt's evidence is based in science. She cites research from two reputable psychology professors. **5** California State University psychology professor Larry Rosen explains that social media interfere with the ability of the brain to focus. California State University psychology professor Kaveri Subrahmanyam proposes that social media interrupt sleep patterns and compromise the brain's ability to process learning and memory. In contrast, Leung cites evidence regarding the effects of social media on literacy. Coventry University researcher Dr. Beverly Plester says that exposure to written words makes one more literate, which is likely true, but sources for the written word are not limited to social media. **6** Leung's evidence regarding the speed and convenience of social media comes from a classroom teacher and is anecdotal, not scientific.

7 Both authors respond to counterarguments, but once again, Clemmitt does so more effectively. Clemmitt acknowledges the hope of a technological generation: the increased ability to multitask. She **8** refutes this claim with Rosen's research. Multiple distractions and interruptions from social media actually compromise a person's ability to do any one thing well. **9** Conversely, Leung acknowledges a social fear that texting language may begin to appear in formal writing. She refutes this claim by denying it, but she does not offer evidence to support this denial. Instead, she provides Dr. Plester's conclusion, but not the research findings on which the conclusion is based.

Finally, each author employs rhetorical strategies to convince readers of her point of view. **10** Clemmitt uses qualifying statements, such as, "the long-term effects of such behavior (sleeping with cell phones) are unknown." This strategy is effective because brain research with regard to social media is new and ongoing. Researchers, such as Subrahmanyam, do not claim to know everything, but they are sharing current findings. On the other hand, Leung uses a cheap bandwagon strategy in her conclusion, "the next time it's time to call the family to dinner, it might be more efficient to send a group text." In essence, she seems to say that social media must be good because everyone is using it, a statement demonstrating faulty logic.

In conclusion, Clemmitt makes a stronger case against social media by citing credible scientific evidence from Rosen and Subrahmanyam about the disturbing effects of social media on the brain, including their disruption of sleep patterns and the brain's ability to focus. Leung's anecdotal evidence from a reading-language arts teacher pales in comparison. **11** While people may be charmed by the convenience of social media, they must resist the technological dumbing down of modern culture while they still have the brain power to do so.

2 The writer demonstrates varied sentence structure with this compound sentence. This variety creates fluency throughout the response.

3 The writer's thesis makes a text-based argument, establishes a purpose that is connected to the prompt, and shows an awareness of the audience.

5 The writer cites relevant, specific, and sufficient evidence to support the thesis and points.

8 The writer shows purposeful word choice and advanced vocabulary.

9 The writer assesses the validity of a passage.

11 After summarizing the main ideas, the writer leaves readers with a final thought.

ANSWER KEY

UNIT 4 EDITING

1. **D; DOK Level: 1; Writing Assessment Target:** W.3. *Countys* should be changed to *counties*. To form the plural of a word that ends with the letter *y* after a consonant, remove the *y* and add *–ies*. Answers A and B are incorrect because words that are not proper nouns are capitalized. Answer C introduces an incorrect spelling.

2. **B; DOK Level: 1; Writing Assessment Target:** W.3. The plural of *calf* is formed by dropping the *f* and adding *–ves*. *Calfs* should be replaced with *calves*. Answers A and D introduce incorrect spellings. *Spring* is not capitalized.

3.1 **D; DOK Level: 1; Language Assessment Target:** L.2.1. The name of a college is a proper noun and should be capitalized. The correct answer is *Warner College*. The other answers do not reflect proper capitalization.

3.2 **C; DOK Level: 1; Writing Assessment Target:** W.3. The plural of *tornado* is formed by adding *–es*. The correct answer is *tornadoes*. The other answer options are misspelled.

3.3 **A; DOK Level: 1; Writing Assessment Target:** W.3. *Members* is plural, but *student body* remains singular because there is only one student body at the college. *Student body* is a collective noun; *members* are acting individually.

3.4 **C; DOK Level: 1; Language Assessment Target:** L.2.1. The phrase *campus police officers* is not a proper noun because it is a general description. Therefore, no words should be capitalized. The other options contain incorrect capitalization of common nouns.

4.1 **A; DOK Level: 1; Writing Assessment Targets:** W.3, L.2.1. The common noun *government* should not be capitalized nor should it be plural because the writer is referring to one government—the one responsible for the trial. Also, the plural options would not agree with the singular verb and are spelled incorrectly.

4.2 **B; DOK Level: 1; Language Assessment Target:** L.2.1. These are proper nouns. Always capitalize any reference to the *Constitution of the United States*, even if you say *United States Constitution* or *the Constitution*. *United States* is always capitalized. Therefore, B is the only correct answer.

4.3 **D; DOK Level: 1; Writing Assessment Target:** W.3. The noun *juries* is incorrect because there is only one jury in the passage. In addition, the plural is spelled incorrectly in answer C. *Jury* is a collective noun because it is a group made up of more than one person and acts as a single unit: *The jury makes its decision based on the facts in a case.*

4.4 **C; DOK Level: 1; Language Assessment Target:** L.2.1. Both first and last names are proper nouns and both must be capitalized. Answer C is the only correct choice.

5.1 **C; DOK Level: 1; Writing Assessment Target:** W.3. The plural of *quantity* is formed by dropping the *y* and adding *–ies*. The correct answer is *quantities*.

5.2 **A; DOK Level: 1; Writing Assessment Target:** W.3. The singular and plural forms of *fish* are the same. The correct plural of *batch* is *batches* because the word ends in *ch*. Answer A is the only one in which both spellings are correct.

5.3 **D; DOK Level: 1; Writing Assessment Target:** W.3. The plural of *shelf* is formed by dropping the *f* and adding *–ves*. The plural of *item* is formed by adding *–s*. Therefore, the correct answer is *shelves and items*.

5.4 **A; DOK Level 1; Writing Assessment Target:** W.3. The plural of *peach* is formed by adding *–es*. The plural of *strawberry* is formed by dropping the *y* and adding *–ies*. Therefore, the correct answer is *peaches and strawberries*.

1. **C; DOK Level: 1; Language Assessment Target:** L.1.3. *Tony and I* should be replaced with the plural subject pronoun *we*. Answer A is awkward and repetitious and puts the first-person pronoun in the wrong place (as does answer D). *Us* is an object pronoun. *Me and Tony* is incorrect because *me* is an object pronoun; in addition, when using *me* or *I* as part of a compound, these pronouns come last: for example, *Tony and I* is correct, not *I and Tony*.

2. **D; DOK Level: 1; Language Assessment Target:** L.1.3. *Jennifer's* should be replaced with the possessive pronoun *her*. Answer A is incorrect because the pronoun is not replacing two nouns. *She* is incorrect because it is a subject pronoun, not a possessive. *His* does not agree in gender with *Jennifer*.

3.1 **A; DOK Level: 1; Language Assessment Target:** L.1.3. The plural subject pronoun *they* should be used. *They* replaces *satellite communication, social media, communication apps, and the Internet*. *It* is singular and cannot replace a compound subject. *We* refers to people, not things. *Them* is an object pronoun and cannot be the subject of a sentence.

3.2 **D; DOK Level: 1; Language Assessment Target:** L.1.3. The singular *person* must take *his or her* as a bias-free singular possessive pronoun. *He* is a subject pronoun and not bias free. *Their* is plural, thus incorrect. *Him or her* is an object pronoun and therefore incorrect.

3.3 **D; DOK Level: 1; Language Assessment Target:** L.1.3. The possessive pronoun *their* is the best choice because *their* agrees with the subject of the sentence, *they*. *Your* does not agree with the subject. *Them* is an object pronoun. *Us* is an object pronoun and does not agree with the subject.

3.4 **B; DOK Level: 1; Language Assessment Target:** L.1.3. The possessive pronoun *its* agrees with the singular subject of the sentence, the collective noun *society*. *Their* and *it* do not agree with the subject. *It's* is a contraction meaning "it is" and not a possessive pronoun, even though it may look like one.

4.1 **A; DOK Level: 1; Language Assessment Target:** L.1.3. The subject pronoun *you* is the best selection because it agrees with *you* in the previous sentence and maintains consistency. The other subject pronoun options in answers B and C do not agree with *you,* and *them* (answer D) is an object pronoun.

4.2 **D; DOK Level: 1; Language Assessment Target:** L.1.3. Because the gender of the supervisor is not specified, the singular object pronoun *him or her* is the best selection. *Them* and *us* are plural object pronouns. *She or he* is a subject pronoun.

4.3 **C; DOK Level: 1; Language Assessment Target:** L.1.3. A possessive pronoun is required, and the possessive pronoun *your* agrees with the subject pronoun *you*. *Their* and *its* do not agree with *you*. Answer B is incorrect as well because *you* is not a possessive pronoun.

UNIT 4 *(continued)*

4.4 B; DOK Level: 1; Language Assessment Target: L.1.3. The subject, *employees*, is plural and, therefore, takes a plural possessive pronoun. If the antecedent were singular and not gender specific, answer A would be correct. *Your* and *his* do not agree with *employees*.

5.1 B; DOK Level: 1; Language Assessment Target: L.1.3. The correct answer is *our* because the pronoun must be a possessive. *Ours* is incorrect because it does not take the place of two nouns or pronouns. The other answer choices are not possessive pronouns.

5.2 D; DOK Level: 1; Language Assessment Target: L.1.3. The object pronoun *her* is correct because *her* agrees with the gender of the subject, *aunt*. According to the context, the reader assumes that the potato salad is the aunt's, making *his* and *their* incorrect. *She* is a subject pronoun and does not show possession.

5.3 A; DOK Level: 1; Language Assessment Target: L.1.3. The context indicates that the writer has hurt his ankle, so the possessive pronoun *my* is the correct choice. *Her* and *our* do not fit the context, and *we* is not a possessive pronoun.

5.4 A; DOK Level: 1; Language Assessment Target: L.1.3. The correct answer is *we took up his* because the antecedent of *we* is *my wife and I*, and the offer is *Dan's* (or *his*). Answer B is incorrect because *us* is an object pronoun. Answer C is incorrect because *their* is plural. Answer D is incorrect because it uses the object pronouns instead of the subject and possessive pronouns.

LESSON 3, *pp. 206–209*

1. A; DOK Level: 1; Writing Assessment Target: W.3. The sentence indicates that the travel will occur next week, so the future tense verb *will travel* should replace *traveled*. *Will travel* also is consistent with the future tense verb *will visit* in the sentence.

2. C; DOK Level: 1; Writing Assessment Target: W.3. The sentence indicates that the brushing of teeth before bed happens in the present, so the present tense verb *brushes* is correct. *Brushes* also is consistent with the present tense verb *goes* in the sentence. The other answer choices reflect the wrong tense or verb form.

3.1 A; DOK Level: 1; Writing Assessment Target: W.3. Receiving feedback occurred in the past, so *received* is correct. *Received* is consistent with the tense of the verb *helped* in the sentence. The other answer choices are not past-tense verbs.

3.2 C; DOK Level: 1; Writing Assessment Target: W.3. The renovation will occur in the future, so *will make* is correct. *Will make* is consistent with the tense of the verb *will upgrade* in the next sentence. Answers A and B are the wrong tenses, and answer D is incomplete.

3.3 D; DOK Level: 1; Writing Assessment Target: W.3. The outdoor dining area will be built in the future, so *will include* is correct. *Will include* is consistent with the verb *will add* earlier in the sentence. Answers A and B are the wrong tenses, and answer C is incomplete.

3.4 D; DOK Level 1; Writing Assessment Target: W.3. The writer indicates that his appreciation is in the present. Although it could be in the past, when he received the feedback, the past tense is not a choice. Therefore, answer D is correct. Answer B is the present tense, but it does not agree with the subject.

4.1 D; DOK Level: 1; Writing Assessment Target: W.3. This construction requires the present tense verb *is*. The other tenses make no sense because the passage is written in the present tense. Although answer C is present tense, it is the incorrect verb form.

4.2 C; DOK Level: 1; Writing Assessment Target: W.3. This construction also requires the present tense to remain consistent with the passage. Therefore, *sticks* is correct. Although answer A is present tense, it is the incorrect verb form.

4.3 A; DOK Level: 1; Writing Assessment Target: W.3. This construction also requires the present tense to remain consistent with the passage. Therefore, *keep* is correct. Although answer B is present tense, it is the incorrect verb form.

4.4 C; DOK Level: 1; Writing Assessment Target: W.3. This event takes place in the future, after readers begin regular oil changes, so the verb must be in the future tense. Answer C is the only correct option.

5.1 B; DOK Level: 1; Writing Assessment Target: W.3. The success of the Farmers' Market Days already has occurred, so the past tense verb *generated* is correct. The other answer choices are not past-tense forms.

5.2 B; DOK Level: 1; Writing Assessment Target: W.3. The sentence indicates that strengths are current, so the present tense verb *reflect* is correct. *Reflects* is present tense but the incorrect verb form.

5.3 C; DOK Level: 1; Writing Assessment Target: W.3. The text of the report is current, so the present tense is correct. *Includes* is present tense but the wrong verb form.

5.4 D; DOK Level: 1; Writing Assessment Target: W.3. The changes at the grocery store will occur in the future (next month), so the future tense verb *will implement* is correct. The other answer choices are not future-tense verbs.

LESSON 4, *pp. 210–213*

1. D; DOK Level: 1; Writing Assessment Target: W.3. The sentence describes an action that will be completed at a specific time in the future: *By the end of tomorrow's trip*. Therefore, the future perfect *will have traveled* is the only correct response.

2. C; DOK Level: 1; Writing Assessment Target: W.3. The action (*he joined me*) took place in the past but after another past action was completed. The past perfect *had run* is the only correct choice. First he ran, and then he joined.

3.1 D; DOK Level: 1; Writing Assessment Target: W.3. The company's learning began in the past and is current, or continues, into the present. The present perfect *has learned* is correct. Using the present progressive tense, *is learning*, ignores the connection to the past, which is the learning that has continued for more than 100 years. Answer A is incorrect because it indicates that the learning is finished. Answer B does not fit the context of the sentence.

3.2 B; DOK Level: 1; Writing Assessment Target: W.3. The passage describes the advances that were happening in the late 1920s. These advances continued over a period of time. Therefore, the past progressive *were happening* is correct. The other answers do not fit the context of the sentence.

3.3 **C; DOK Level:** 1; **Writing Assessment Target:** W.3. The products began performing well in the past and continue to perform well. Therefore, the present perfect *have performed* is correct. *Have performed* also is consistent with the tense of *have been embraced* in the sentence. The other answers are not in the correct tense.

3.4 **A; DOK Level:** 1; **Writing Assessment Target:** W.3. The passage expresses a hope that by a specific point in the future (100 years), the company's products will have been used by millions more people. Therefore, the future perfect tense *will have used* is correct.

4.1 **D; DOK Level:** 1; **Writing Assessment Target:** W.3. The bill is a new bill that is currently under consideration and is being supported on an ongoing basis by riders of ATVs. Therefore, the present progressive *are supporting* is correct. Although answer A is correct grammatically, answer D is a better fit for the context of the passage because it indicates that the action is current.

4.2 **C; DOK Level:** 1; **Writing Assessment Target:** W.3. The recently conducted survey was conducted in the past, and the survey results are still current and relevant. Therefore, the present perfect *has shown* is correct.

4.3 **B; DOK Level:** 1; **Writing Assessment Target:** W.3. The writer says that people have already expressed disapproval of ATVs in state parks, and this disapproval continues into the present. Therefore, the present perfect *have made* is correct.

4.4 **D; DOK Level:** 1; **Writing Assessment Target:** W.3. The acres of coal mines began attracting ATV riders in the past and continue to attract ATV riders in the present. Therefore, the present perfect *have attracted* is correct. The other present perfect verb form, *has attracted*, is incorrect because it needs a singular, not a plural, subject.

5.1 **C; DOK Level:** 1; **Writing Assessment Target:** W.3. The sentence refers to the possible ongoing suffering of people with disorganized closets. Therefore, the present progressive *are suffering* is correct.

5.2 **A; DOK Level:** 1; **Writing Assessment Target:** W.3. The decision to purchase a closet organizer happened in the past and continues into the present. Therefore, the present perfect *have decided* is correct and the only answer that makes sense in the sentence.

5.3 **D; DOK Level:** 1; **Writing Assessment Target:** W.3. The construction of the closet organizer has already happened, and the work on the closet continues into the present with the measuring. Therefore, the present perfect *have constructed* is correct. The other answer choices do not make sense in the context of the passage.

5.4 **B; DOK Level:** 1; **Writing Assessment Target:** W.3. After the future action of "only a small investment of money and time" has been completed, the customer will have created the result of a whole new closet. Therefore, the future perfect *will have created* is correct.

1. **B; DOK Level:** 1; **Language Assessment Target:** L.1.1. *Your* is the correct form of the possessive. The possessive is required to show that the car belongs to *you*. *It's* is the correct form of the contraction for *it is*. *Your turn* is the correct form of the possessive. *You'd* is a contraction for *you would*. *You'd* does not make sense in the context of the sentence.

2. **A; DOK Level:** 1; **Language Assessment Target:** L.2.3. The sentence indicates that there are two boys *(both boys)*. The possessive is required to show that the parents belong to the boys. Because *boys* is a plural noun, the possessive is formed by adding an apostrophe after the *s*. *Children's* is the correct form of the plural possessive. It is a plural noun that does not end in *s*.

3.1 **D; DOK Level:** 1; **Language Assessment Target:** L.2.3. The first name *Dennis* is a singular noun. The possessive is formed by adding an apostrophe and an *s*: *Dennis's* volunteer work. Answer A omits the *s*, answer B is not a possessive, and answer C is a plural.

3.2 **C; DOK Level:** 1; **Language Assessment Target:** L.2.3. *Volunteers* is a plural noun (the sentence refers to "all of them"). The possessive is formed by adding an apostrophe after the *s*: *volunteers' efforts*. Answer A is the singular possessive noun, answer B is the plural noun, and answer D reflects an incorrect construction of the plural possessive noun.

3.3 **B; DOK Level:** 1; **Writing Assessment Target:** W.3. *I've* is the only correct form of the contraction for *I have*. The apostrophe shows where the letters *ha* have been omitted.

3.4 **C; DOK Level:** 1; **Language Assessment Target:** L.2.3. *Team* is a singular collective noun. The writer coaches one team. The sentence refers to the tennis matches of the team. The possessive is formed by adding an apostrophe and *–s*: *team's tennis matches*. Although *teams'* would be grammatically correct for a plural construction, the context indicates only one team. Answer A shows no possession, and answer D is written incorrectly.

4.1 **C; DOK Level:** 1; **Language Assessment Target:** L.1.1. *There's* is the correct form of the contraction for *there is*: *there's a great deal of competition*. *Theirs* is a possessive and is incorrect. *There* is grammatically incorrect because the verb *is* is missing.

4.2 **B; DOK Level:** 1; **Language Assessment Target:** L.1.1. *It's* is the correct from of the contraction for *it is*: *it's important*. *Its* is a possessive and is incorrect. *It* is missing the verb *is*. *It was* is the wrong tense.

4.3 **C; DOK Level:** 1; **Language Assessment Target:** L.2.3. *Hunters'* is the correct form of the plural possessive. The possessive is required to show that the résumés belong to them. Answer A is incorrect because it is a singular possessive. Answer B is incorrect because it is a plural, not a possessive plural. Answer D is incorrect because it adds an extra *s* after the apostrophe.

4.4 **A; DOK Level:** 1; **Language Assessment Target:** L.2.3. The possessive is required (job hunters should know the "history of the company" at which they interview). The sentence refers to one company, so the singular form of the noun *company* should be used. *Company's history* is correct. The other answer choices are not the singular possessive form of the word.

UNIT 4 *(continued)*

5.1 A; DOK Level: 1; Language Assessment Targets:
L.1.1, L.2.3. *It's* is the correct form of the contraction for *it is: it's time to start. Its'* is a misspelling of the contraction. *Its* is a possessive and is incorrect. *It was* is in the wrong tense because summer is approaching.

5.2 C; DOK Level: 1; Language Assessment Target:
L.2.3. The possessive should be used to show that the grid belongs to the grill. *Grill* is a singular noun, and the possessive is formed by adding an apostrophe and *s: grill's grid.*

5.3 A; DOK Level: 1; Writing Assessment Target: W.3.
Don't is the correct contraction of *do not.* The apostrophe takes the place of the missing letter *o.* The other answer choices are incorrect because the apostrophe is either missing or in the wrong place.

5.4 B; DOK Level: 1; Writing Assessment Target: W.3.
You'll is the correct form of the contraction for *you will. You've* does not make sense in the sentence. *Youw'll* is a misspelling of the contraction. *You* is incorrect because the phrase *you be able* is not grammatically correct.

LESSON 6, *pp. 218–221*

1. C; DOK Level 1; Language Assessment Target: L.1.1.
The homonym *hire* should be changed to *higher,* meaning that the plane goes farther up in the air than other planes. *Hire* means to "employ or engage." The other frequently confused words are correct in this sentence.

2. D; DOK Level 1; Language Assessment Target: L.1.1.
Knew should be changed to *new,* meaning that the speaker did not know where to look for the watch that was recently purchased. The other frequently confused words are correct in this sentence.

3.1 D; DOK Level: 1; Language Assessment Target: L.1.1.
The expression *come to mind* means to "think of something," so *to mind* is the correct answer. The homonym *mined* is the past tense of the verb *to mine,* as in "to mine for coal." *Too* means "also," and *two* is the number.

3.2 A; DOK Level: 1; Language Assessment Target:
L.1.1. *To* is a preposition that means "in the direction of." The term *Tex-Mex* applies *to* the dishes. The homonym *too* means "also" or "excessively"; the homonym *two* refers to the number. *Do* makes no sense in the context of the sentence.

3.3 C; DOK Level: 1; Language Assessment Target:
L.1.1. Chili con carne is defined as chile with *meat,* meaning "flesh that is eaten." The homonym *meet* means "get together." The homonym *mete* means "give out" or "distribute." *Mead* makes no sense in context.

3.4 B; DOK Level: 1; Language Assessment Target:
L.1.1. The correct word is *read,* the homonym of *reed,* which is a kind of tall grass. *Rede* is a misspelling, and *red* is a homonym of the past tense of *read.*

4.1 A; DOK Level: 1; Language Assessment Target: L.1.1.
The council *sent* out the alert, meaning the council "caused the alert to be transmitted." The homonym *scent* refers to a smell; the homonym *cent* means a "penny." *Send* is the wrong tense.

4.2 C; DOK Level: 1; Language Assessment Target:
L.1.1. The advisory will be in *effect* until the water is safe, meaning that the advisory will remain in place until that time. The verb *affect* means to "influence." The verb *infect* means to "cause illness or contamination."

4.3 B; DOK Level: 1; Language Assessment Target:
L.1.1. The young and elderly should *wait* to consume the water, meaning they should "delay action" until then. The homonym *weight* refers to how heavy something is. *Way* refers to a direction, as in "go that way." *Wade* means to "walk in very shallow water."

4.4 B; DOK Level: 1; Language Assessment Target:
L.1.1. Safe water cannot always be identified by *sight,* meaning that it cannot always be seen to be safe. The homonym *site* refers to a place; the homonym *cite* means "quote" or "refer to something that someone has said or written." *Side,* which sounds somewhat similar, makes no sense in context.

5.1 B; DOK Level: 1; Language Assessment Target: L.1.1.
Mr. Thompson has been a loyal customer for five years before now, so *past* is the correct answer. The homonym *passed* means "went by" or "moved," as in "he passed through towns." *Pass* and *pasted* do not make sense in this context.

5.2 D; DOK Level: 1; Language Assessment Target:
L.1.1. *Eight* refers to the number, as in eight (8) days. The homonym *ate* is the past tense of the verb *to eat.* The other answer choices make no sense in context.

5.3 A; DOK Level: 1; Language Assessment Targets:
L.1.1, L.1.3. The customer can get the plan for a fraction of *its* usual cost. *Its* is a possessive pronoun meaning "the plan's" in this context. *It's* is a contraction for *it is. Their* is incorrect because *their* does not agree with the singular *plan.*

5.4 C; DOK Level: 1; Language Assessment Target:
L.1.1. You *write* an e-mail, meaning that you form visible words. The homonym *right* means "correct." The homonym *rite* is a ritual or ceremony. *Ride* makes no sense in context.

LESSON 7, *pp. 222–225*

1. C; DOK Level: 1; Language Assessment Target: L.1.2.
The subject is plural (*My cousins*) and takes a plural verb. Answer A changes the correct plural to singular and, therefore, is incorrect. Answer B is not a complete verb form. Answer D is an incorrect verb form.

2. A; DOK Level 1; Language Assessment Target: L.1.7.
Drives agrees with the singular *her sister.* When two subjects (*Kendall or her sister*) are connected by *or,* the verb agrees with the subject closer to the verb. In this case, both subjects are singular. The present tense is correct because the action occurs in the present. The other subject and verb in the sentence agree.

3.1 D; DOK Level: 1; Language Assessment Target:
L.1.2. The verb *give* agrees with *trees,* the plural subject of the sentence. The present tense is correct because the action occurs in the present, and the present tense is used in the next sentence. *Gave* is past tense. *Giving* is the wrong form of the verb.

3.2 A; DOK Level: 1; Language Assessment Target:
L.1.7. The compound subject of the sentence, *debris and limbs,* takes the plural verb *damage. Damages* and *has damaged* are singular. *Damaging* is the wrong form of the verb.

3.3 **C; DOK Level: 1; Language Assessment Target:** L.1.7. *Has used* agrees with the singular *squirrel*. When two subjects (*a possum or squirrel*) are connected by *or*, the verb agrees with the subject closer to the verb. In this case, both subjects are singular. *Have used* and *use* are plural forms of the verb. *Using* is the wrong form of the verb.

3.4 **B; DOK Level: 1; Language Assessment Target:** L.1.2. *Evaluate* agrees with the plural subject *members*. *Has evaluated* and *evaluates* are singular forms of the verb. *Evaluated* is the wrong tense because the action is not in the past.

4.1 **C; DOK Level: 1; Language Assessment Target:** L.1.2. The singular *am* agrees with *I*, the subject of the sentence. *Are* and *were* are plural forms of the verb *to be*. The author is still grateful, so the past tense *was* does not make sense in the sentence.

4.2 **D; DOK Level: 1; Language Assessment Target:** L.1.7. The compound subject *comments and feedback* takes the plural verb *are*. *Is* and *was* are singular. *Being* is the wrong form of the verb.

4.3 **A; DOK Level: 1; Language Assessment Target:** L.1.7. The compound subject *support and generosity* takes the plural verb *mean*. *Means* and *has meant* are singular forms of the verb. *Meaning* is the wrong form of the verb.

4.4 **B; DOK Level: 1; Language Assessment Target:** L.1.2. The singular *look* agrees with *I*, the subject of the sentence. *Looks* does not agree with the first-person singular subject, *I*, and *are looking* is a plural form of the verb. The past tense *looked* does not make sense in the sentence because the author is not referring to a past action.

5.1 **D; DOK Level: 1; Language Assessment Target:** L.1.2. *Are* agrees with the plural *commercials*. The other answer options are singular forms of the verb. Do not be confused by the adjective phrase, *six or seven*; its presence does not affect the verb.

5.2 **B; DOK Level: 1; Language Assessment Target:** L.1.2. The subject *pop-ups* is plural and agrees with the plural form of the verb, *appear*. *Was appearing* and *appears* are singular. *Appearing* is the wrong form of the verb.

5.3 **D; DOK Level: 1; Language Assessment Target:** L.1.2. *Most people* is a plural subject and takes the plural form of the verb, *watch*. *Watches* is singular. The past tense, *watched*, does not make sense in the sentence. *Watching* is the wrong form of the verb.

5.4 **A; DOK Level: 1; Language Assessment Target:** L.1.2. *These constant commercial interruptions* is the plural subject and takes the plural form of the verb, *are causing*. Answers B, C, and D are all singular.

LESSON 8, pp. 226–229

1. **B; DOK Level: 1; Language Assessment Target:** L.1.4. Change *nothing* to *anything* to eliminate the double negative. Answer A is incorrect because *not* does not correct the double negative. *Not anything* introduces a double negative. Adding *no* before *astronomy* creates an additional negative and is grammatically incorrect.

2. **C; DOK Level: 1; Language Assessment Target:** L.1.4. Change *suppose* to *supposed*. *Supposed to* is the correct construction for the expression meaning "should" or "should have." When used this way, *supposed* must be followed by *to*. *Ta* is not a standard English word.

3.1 **C; DOK Level: 1; Language Assessment Target:** L.1.4. Writing *sister was* avoids the incorrect repetition of the pronoun in answers A and D. Answer B incorrectly omits the verb.

3.2 **A; DOK Level: 1; Language Assessment Target:** L.1.4. *Have* follows the helping verb *should* in this construction. *Should of* and *should a* sound similar when spoken but are not correct. Using *should* alone is grammatically incorrect.

3.3 **C; DOK Level: 1; Language Assessment Target:** L.1.4. Writing *couldn't have asked for anything* avoids a double negative. Answers A and B do not correct the double negative. Answer D does not make sense in the context of the sentence.

3.4 **B; DOK Level: 1; Language Assessment Target:** L.1.4. Answer B is the only choice that does not create a double negative and is thus correct.

4.1 **C; DOK Level: 1; Language Assessment Target:** L.1.4. *Try to* is the correct construction for the expression. Answer A does not reflect standard English. Answers B and D make no sense in context.

4.2 **B; DOK Level: 1; Language Assessment Target:** L.1.4. *Used to* is the proper form. The other options are grammatically incorrect.

4.3 **B; DOK Level: 1; Language Assessment Target:** L.1.4. *Will have no* is the grammatically correct option. *Won't have no* and *will not have no* are the same (*won't* is a contraction of *will not*), and both are improper forms of the negative. Answer D is not considered standard English.

4.4 **D; DOK Level: 1; Language Assessment Target:** L.1.4. Writing *have to pay anything* avoids the use of a double negative after *don't*. The other answer options are grammatically incorrect.

5.1 **D; DOK Level: 1; Language Assessment Target:** L.1.4. Writing *never had to see a* is correct. This phrase avoids a double negative construction. The other options create a double negative and are grammatically incorrect.

5.2 **C; DOK Level: 1; Language Assessment Target:** L.1.4. *Was supposed to* is the correct construction for the expression meaning "should have." When used this way, *supposed* must be followed by *to*. *Opposing* and *opposed* are the wrong words, even though they sounds similar in spoken English.

5.3 **B; DOK Level: 1; Language Assessment Target:** L.1.4. *Isn't* is the correct answer. *Ain't* is slang. *Weren't* does not agree with the subject of the sentence and is the wrong tense. *Not* is an incorrect use of a negative.

5.4 **C; DOK Level: 1; Language Assessment Target:** L.1.4. The correct construction is *try to resolve*. Although *try and resolve* and *try in resolve* sound similar when spoken, they are grammatically incorrect. *Try and resolving* is also grammatically incorrect.

LESSON 9, pp. 230–233

1. **A; DOK Level: 1; Language Assessment Target:** L.2.1. The days of the week are proper nouns, so *saturday* should be changed to *Saturday*. *Friend's band* and *coffee shop* are not proper nouns or proper adjectives and are not capitalized. *Main Street* is the name of a street and is capitalized.

2. **C; DOK Level: 1; Language Assessment Target:** L.2.1. *American* is a proper adjective and should be capitalized. *Mississippi River* is the name of a river and should be capitalized. *Cities* is a common noun and is not capitalized.

UNIT 4 (continued)

3.1 C; DOK Level: 1; Language Assessment Target: L.2.1. *The Beatles* is the name of a rock band and is capitalized. *Botswana* is a proper noun naming the country and is capitalized: *Beatles fan in Botswana.*

3.2 C; DOK Level: 1; Language Assessment Target: L.2.1. *Rubber Soul* is the title of the album. It is a proper noun. *Album* is a general noun, not part of the title, and is not capitalized.

3.3 A; DOK Level: 1; Language Assessment Target: L.2.1. *Facebook* and *Craigslist* are the titles of Web sites and are proper nouns. They are both capitalized.

3.4 B; DOK Level: 1; Language Assessment Target: L.2.1. *Social Security* is the name of a government program and is capitalized. *Number* is a common noun and is not capitalized.

4.1 A; DOK Level: 1; Language Assessment Target: L.2.1. *Lana Little* is a specific woman's name and thus capitalized as a proper noun. *Human Resources Director* is a title, so it should be capitalized. Each initial letter in the title is capitalized: *Lana Little, Human Resources Director.*

4.2 D; DOK Level: 1; Language Assessment Target: L.2.1. Days of the week and months of the year are capitalized, so both *Tuesday* and *February* should be capitalized: *Tuesday, February 20.*

4.3 B; DOK Level: 1; Language Assessment Target: L.2.1. *Garland County Hospital* is the name of the hospital and is a proper noun. Each initial letter should be capitalized.

4.4 B; DOK Level: 1; Language Assessment Target: L.2.1. Answer B is correct because the common nouns are not capitalized. *Blogging* and *social networking* are not proper nouns. They describe general types of activities. Neither should be capitalized.

5.1 A; DOK Level: 1; Language Assessment Target: L.2.1. The *National Hockey League* is a proper noun and should be capitalized: *the National Hockey League. League* is part of the title; the league is a specific one.

5.2 C; DOK Level: 1; Language Assessment Target: L.2.1. As part of a person's name, *Jr.* should be capitalized. *Elton Royce* is a proper noun, so both names should be capitalized. *Elton Royce, Jr.* is correct.

5.3 B; DOK Level: 1; Language Assessment Target: L.2.1. The title of the article is "A Fight to the Finish." The first and last words should be capitalized. Major words in the title also should be capitalized; *to* and *the* should be lowercase. They would be capitalized if, like *a*, they were the first or last word of the title.

5.4 A; DOK Level: 1; Language Assessment Target: L.2.1. *President* is a title and is capitalized when it appears with a specific name *(Dwayne Leonard). Leonard Sports Marketing* is the name of a company and is capitalized. Each initial letter in the name of the organization is capitalized.

LESSON 10, pp. 234–237

1. A; DOK Level: 1; Language Assessment Target: L.2.2. The sentence has a verb and ends with the correct punctuation, but it does not have a subject that tells who watched the game. Adding a subject, such as *Rudy* or *we*, corrects the fragment.

2. C; DOK Level: 1; Language Assessment Targets: L.2.2, L.2.4. The first sentence is a fragment and should be combined with the second. Answer C combines the two sentences correctly and gets rid of the fragment. Answer A is missing a subject in the second part of the sentence. Answer B uses incorrect end punctuation. Answer D does not correct the fragment and introduces a second fragment.

3.1 A; DOK Level: 1; Language Assessment Targets: L.2.1, L.2.2, L.2.4. The first sentence makes a statement rather than poses a question or expresses excitement. Therefore, a period belongs at the end of the sentence rather than a question mark or an exclamation point. The first letter of the second sentence should be capitalized. Answer B is incorrect because the second sentence is missing a subject.

3.2 C; DOK Level: 1; Language Assessment Targets: L.2.2. L.2.4. *Contains four columns* is a fragment. It does not specify what contains four columns. You need to add a subject: *The form. In* starts the next sentence. A period is required to separate the two sentences. The correct answer should read: *The form contains four columns. In . . .*

3.3 B; DOK Level: 1; Language Assessment Targets: L.2.2, L.2.4. The two parts of this sentence should be combined so that the second is not a fragment. Answer B is the only choice that eliminates the fragment. The other answers keep the fragment and end with incorrect punctuation.

3.4 D; DOK Level: 1; Language Assessment Target: L.2.2. The sentence is complete and correct without dividing it into two or inserting punctuation. The correct answer should read: *. . . follow up when clients . . . .* Dividing the sentence creates two fragments.

4.1 D; DOK Level: 1; Language Assessment Targets: L.2.2. L.2.4. *Although the location of each fixture will remain the same* is an introductory clause that should be separated from the rest of the sentence with a comma. Separating the clause with a period or an exclamation point makes it a fragment. The correct answer should read: *Although the location of each fixture will remain the same, our plans do call . . . .*

4.2 B; DOK Level: 1; Language Assessment Target: L.2.2. Answer B is the only choice that does not create a fragment and is, therefore, correct.

4.3 B; DOK Level: 1; Language Assessment Targets: L.2.1, L.2.2, L.2.4. Answer B is correct because it creates a compound sentence by joining the two parts with a comma and the word *and*. Although answers A and C create two sentences, the capitalization in answer A and punctuation in answer C are incorrect. Both are incorrect in answer D.

4.4 C; DOK Level: 1; Language Assessment Targets: L.2.1, L.2.2, L.2.4. Answer C is correct because it corrects a fragment by combining it with a complete sentence. Answers A, B, and D do not correct the fragment, and answers B and D demonstrate other errors in capitalization and punctuation.

5.1 D; DOK Level 1; Language Assessment Targets: L.2.2, L.2.4. The first sentence should end with a question mark because it asks the reader a question. The second sentence requires a subject, *We.* Answer A incorrectly uses an exclamation point to end the first sentence. Answer B incorrectly uses a period. Answer C omits the subject of the second sentence. The correct answer should read *. . . league? We are currently . . . .*

5.2 A; DOK Level: 1; Language Assessment Target: L.2.2 . The sentence should read: *Soccer is a great sport for young athletes.* Answers C and D omit the verb, *is,* which would make the sentence complete. Adding descriptive words does not make the sentence complete. Answer B inserts a comma incorrectly and also lacks the verb.

5.3 B; DOK Level: 1; Language Assessment Targets:
L.2.1, L.2.2, L.2.4. *You might also consider coaching a team or volunteering as a referee* forms a complete sentence and should end with a period because it is a statement, not a question. The second sentence should begin with a capital letter and must include a verb, *is.* Answer C omits the verb. Answer D does not capitalize the first word in the sentence. The correct answer should read . . . *as a referee. There is* . . . .

5.4 C; DOK Level: 1; Language Assessment Targets:
L.2.2, L.2.4. The correct answer should be written as two separate sentences: . . . *defense. Midfielders assist with both* . . . . The second sentence should include the subject, *Midfielders,* and the verb, *assist.* Answer A omits the subject and uses incorrect punctuation. Answer B omits the verb. Answer D omits the subject.

LESSON 11, *pp. 238–241*

1. C; DOK Level: 1; Language Assessment Target: L.2.4.
When two or more adjectives describe the same noun, a comma usually separates them. A comma should be inserted between the two adjectives *fresh* and *wholesome,* which describe the noun *products.* The comma remains after *suggests* because it is part of an introductory clause. The other punctuation in the sentence is correct.

2. A; DOK Level: 1; Language Assessment Target: L.2.4.
A comma should be placed after *table* at the end of the quotation to set off the dialogue from the speaker: *"The salad, bread, and cheese are on the table," said Dan.* The other commas are placed correctly to separate items in a series.

3.1 C; DOK Level: 1; Language Assessment Target:
L.2.4. The sentence begins with an introductory phrase (*Instead of paying a fixed rate*) after which a comma should appear. Answer A has an additional, incorrectly placed comma inserted. Answer B omits the necessary comma. The comma is placed incorrectly in answer D.

3.2 B; DOK Level: 1; Language Assessment Target:
L.2.4. Commas separate items in a series: *including the Basic Plan, the High-Speed Plan, and the Supercharged High-Speed Plan.* Answer A omits the final comma in the series and adds an incorrect one after *and.* Answer C omits all necessary commas. Answer D omits the first comma in the series.

3.3 C; DOK Level: 1; Language Assessment Target:
L.2.4. The sentence is made up of two clauses. Its two parts are connected by the connecting word *but.* A comma should be placed after the words *High-Speed Plan* because they appear before the connecting word. Answer A omits the necessary comma. The comma is placed incorrectly in answers B and D.

3.4 A; DOK Level: 1; Language Assessment Target:
L.2.4. When two or more adjectives describe the same noun, a comma usually separates them. In this sentence, the adjectives *convenient* and *affordable* modify the noun *access,* so a comma should be placed between the two adjectives. Answer B inserts the comma incorrectly. Answer C inserts an unnecessary comma after *affordable.* Answer D omits the necessary comma.

4.1 C; DOK Level: 1; Language Assessment Target:
L.2.4. The sentence begins with an introductory clause, *As I'm sure you understand.* A comma should be placed after this clause to separate it from the rest of the sentence. Answer A includes two incorrectly placed commas. Answer B omits the necessary comma. The comma is incorrectly placed in answer D.

4.2 A; DOK Level: 1; Language Assessment Target:
L.2.4. Commas separate items in a series. The sentence lists four different items the writer found in her hotel room. Commas should be placed after the first three items to indicate that four items make up the series: *including soap, shampoo, drinking water, and coffee.* Answer B omits the final comma and has an incorrectly placed comma after *and.* Answer C omits the first comma. Answer D omits all necessary commas.

4.3 B; DOK Level: 1; Language Assessment Target:
L.2.4. Answer B is correct because a comma is needed before the connecting word *and.* No other commas are needed. The other answer options insert commas incorrectly.

4.4 A; DOK Level: 1; Language Assessment Target: L.2.4.
The sentence begins with the introductory phrase *In closing.* A comma is required after *closing.* Answer B incorrectly includes a comma after *I.* Answer D inserts the comma in the wrong place. Answer C omits the necessary comma.

5.1 D; DOK Level: 1; Language Assessment Target:
L.2.4. The sentence begins with the introductory clause, *After the witnesses finish their testimonies.* A comma is required after *testimonies.* Answer A omits the necessary comma and incorrectly places a comma after *judge.* Answer B includes an incorrect comma after *judge.* Answer C omits the necessary comma.

5.2 C; DOK Level: 1; Language Assessment Target:
L.2.4. The sentence includes a descriptive phrase (an appositive) and requires a comma after *foreperson* and after *member.* The phrase *the presiding member* should be set off because it renames and defines *foreperson.* Answer A omits both necessary commas. Answers B and D insert the comma incorrectly.

5.3 D; DOK Level: 1; Language Assessment Target:
L.2.4. The sentence begins with an introductory phrase, *In a criminal case.* A comma is required after *case.* Answer A omits the comma. Answers B and C insert the comma in the wrong place.

5.4 B; DOK Level: 1; Language Assessment Target:
L.2.4. The phrase *after long discussions* interrupts the sentence and should be set off by placing a comma after *jury* and a comma after *discussions.* Answer A omits the second comma. Answer C omits both commas. Answer D omits the first comma.

LESSON 12, *pp. 242–245*

1. B; DOK Level: 2; Language Assessment Targets:
L.1.6, L.1.8. Answer B eliminates the wordiness caused by the repetition of the subject and verb in the three sentences. The other answer options contain repetition of the subject. Answer C uses a pronoun unclearly because the reader does not know whether the mother is Joan's or Emma's.

UNIT 4 (continued)

2. C; DOK Level: 2; Language Assessment Targets:
L.1.6, L.1.8, L.1.9. Answer C connects the ideas in the two sentences by explaining that Carl's hunger motivated him to make a sandwich: *Carl made a sandwich because he was hungry.* Answer A does not connect the two ideas. The conjunction *and* in Answer B does not establish a cause-and-effect relationship. Answer D separates the two ideas with the use of the semicolon and the word *moreover,* which does not make sense in the context of the sentences.

3.1 C; DOK Level: 2; Language Assessment Targets: L.1.6, L.1.9. Answer C establishes the logical connection between the two ideas (although you saw a cat online, you still may need to ask to see it at the shelter because it may not be on display). Answer B omits the needed semicolon before *however.* Answer A suggests a comparative relationship that does not make sense in the sentence. The use of *and* in answer D does not properly connect the two ideas.

3.2 B; DOK Level: 2; Language Assessment Targets:
L.1.6, L.1.9. Answer B establishes the correct relationship between the two ideas: some people want a laid back lap cat, *but* others want an energetic playmate. Answer A does not combine the two ideas and repeats the subject needlessly. Answers C and D do not make the correct connection between the two ideas, and the combined sentences do not make sense.

3.3 A; DOK Level: 2; Language Assessment Targets:
L.1.6, L.1.8, L.1.9. Answer A best connects the two ideas, providing two reasons that a cat's temperament can be important. Answer B is wordy and repeats the subject. Answers C and D do not provide logical connections between the ideas.

3.4 B; DOK Level: 2; Language Assessment Targets:
L.1.6, L.1.8, L.1.9. Answer B creates a compound sentence that logically connects the two ideas by providing the two options of what might occur. Answer A incorrectly sets up a causal relationship. Answers C and D do not connect the two ideas and do not create good flow.

4.1 A; DOK Level: 2; Language Assessment Targets:
L.1.6., L.1.8. Answer A uses a comma and the conjunction *but* to create a compound sentence and establish the logical relationship between the two ideas. Answer B does not make any connection between the ideas, and the combined sentence is choppy and awkward. Answer C creates a fragment. Answer D does not use a logical connecting word, and the combined sentence does not make sense in context.

4.2 C; DOK Level: 2; Language Assessment Targets: L.1.6, L.1.8. Answer C eliminates wordiness by placing the related words in a series. Parallel structure is created by using commas and the word *and.* Answers A and D repeat the subject and verb needlessly and are wordy. Answer B is wordy and uses a conjunction, *but,* that does not make sense in the sentence.

4.3 B; DOK Level: 2; Language Assessment Targets:
L.1.6, L.1.9. Answer B eliminates wordiness and properly joins the two ideas with the conjunction *and.* Answer A is wordy because the subject and verb are repeated. Answers C and D use conjunctions that do not make sense in the sentence.

4.4 D; DOK Level: 2; Language Assessment Targets:
L.1.6, L.1.8. Answer D eliminates wordiness by not repeating the subject and verb: *You will help your community and learn some really cool stuff!* Answers A and C do not make the proper connection between the ideas. Answer B is wordy because it repeats the subject and verb.

5.1 C; DOK Level: 2; Language Assessment Targets: L.1.6, L.1.8, L.1.9. Answer C eliminates wordiness and makes the logical connection between the two ideas. The question asks whether the reader wants to do two things: learn about a career and experience it firsthand. Answer A needlessly repeats the subject and verb. Moreover, the first sentence ends with a period instead of a question mark. Answers B and D do not make a logical connection between the two ideas.

5.2 A; DOK Level: 2; Language Assessment Targets:
L.1.6, L.1.8. Answer A is the least wordy and combines the ideas logically. The use of *but* does not make sense in the sentence in answer B. Answers C and D needlessly repeat the subject and verb.

5.3 D; DOK Level: 2; Language Assessment Targets:
L.1.6, L.1.8, L.1.9. Answer D avoids repeating the subject and verb and connects the ideas logically: both actions should be taken, not one or the other. Answer A suggests that one or the other should be done. Answer B repeats the subject and the verb unnecessarily. Answer C does not logically combine the ideas.

5.4 B; DOK Level: 2; Language Assessment Targets:
L.1.6, L.1.9. Answer B shows the logical sequential relationship between the ideas: *It may be difficult to arrange to shadow an employee after you've identified a job you want to shadow.* Although the sentence may seem wordy, all words are needed for clarity. Answers A and C do not connect the ideas logically. Answer D does not make any connection between the ideas, and the two sentences do not flow.

<hr/>

LESSON 13, pp. 246–249

1. A; DOK Level: 2; Language Assessment Targets:
L.2.2, L.2.4. Two complete sentences combined make this sentence a run-on. To correct the error, add a comma and a connecting word between the two sentences: *I knew my dad's baseball card collection had some value, but no one knew it was worth so much.* Inserting only a comma or only a connecting word does not correct the run-on. Although answer D does include a comma and a connecting word, the connecting word does not make sense in the sentence.

2. C; DOK Level: 2; Language Assessment Targets:
L.2.2, L.2.4.The sentence is a run-on because the two ideas are connected with only a comma. The best correction is to make each idea its own sentence: *The movie featured great acting and a clever script. I think it will win several awards.* Connecting the two ideas with a comma and the word *but* is grammatically correct but does not make logical sense. Adding a comma after *acting* does not correct the run-on and creates a comma error in the sentence. Answer D creates a fused sentence.

3.1 A; DOK Level: 2; Language Assessment Targets:
L.2.2, L.2.4. Each idea should be its own sentence: *Heart disease occurs as the result of fatty plaque deposits in the arteries that deliver blood to the heart. These deposits cause the arteries to become narrow and hard.* Combining the two ideas with only a comma creates a run-on sentence. Although a comma and a connecting word could be used, answers C and D use connecting words that do not make sense in the sentence.

3.2 C; DOK Level: 2; Language Assessment Targets: L.2.2, L.2.4. These sentences can be written as one sentence by using a comma and the word *and*: *However, there is a simple way to reduce your risk of heart disease, and it doesn't involve medication.* Inserting only a comma creates a run-on sentence, as does using no punctuation. Answer D creates a fragment because the second sentence has no subject.

3.3 B; DOK Level: 2; Language Assessment Targets: L.2.2, L.2.4. Make each idea its own sentence: *You should also eat polyunsaturated and monounsaturated fats. These "good" fats occur in vegetable oils, fish, and nuts.* Combining the two ideas with only a comma creates a run-on sentence. Combining the ideas with a connecting word and a comma does not work well in this situation. Answer C uses a connecting word that does not make sense in context. Answer D uses a connecting word that sounds awkward.

3.4 A; DOK Level: 2; Language Assessment Targets: L.2.2, L.2.4. Make each idea its own sentence: *You should also avoid saturated fat. This so-called "bad" fat is found in some meats and dairy products.* Connecting the two ideas with only a comma, with only *and*, or with no punctuation creates a run-on.

4.1 D; DOK Level: 2; Language Assessment Targets: L.2.2, L.2.4. The best way to write the two ideas is to combine them with a comma and *and*: *I am the representative for members attending the convention from throughout North America, and I am contacting several hotels for details about accommodations, guest services, and costs.* Answer A omits the connecting word *and*, creating a run-on sentence. Answer B has no connecting word or punctuation and is a run-on. Answer C uses a connecting word that does not make sense in the sentence.

4.2 B; DOK Level: 2; Language Assessment Targets: L.2.2, L.2.4. The best way to write the two ideas is to combine them with a comma and *but*: *We will need two large meeting rooms for presentations, but only one room will need video projection capability.* Answers A and C omit the comma. Answer D omits the connecting word and creates a run-on.

4.3 A; DOK Level: 2; Language Assessment Targets: L.2.2, L.2.4. Each idea should be its own sentence: *Also, please provide details about your menu options. Heart-healthy menu choices are important to our members.* Combining the two ideas with only a comma creates a run-on sentence. While a comma and a connecting word could be used, answer C does not make sense in the sentence. Answer D omits the necessary comma.

4.4 C; DOK Level: 2; Language Assessment Targets: L.2.2, L.2.4. The best way to write the two ideas is to combine them with a comma and *so*: *Naturally, we are looking for the best deal possible, so please tell us about any special discounts or deals you can offer our group.* Answer A uses a connecting word that does not work well in the sentence. Answers B and D omit the comma.

5.1 B; DOK Level: 2; Language Assessment Targets: L.2.2, L.2.4. The best answer is B, connecting the sentences with a semicolon: *You've located a new place to live; you've found a new job. …* Combining the two ideas with only a comma or with no punctuation creates a run-on sentence. While a comma and a connecting word could be used, answer D does not make sense in the sentence.

5.2 D; DOK Level: 2; Language Assessment Targets: L.2.2, L.2.4. The best way to write the two ideas is to combine them with a comma and *so: You can find good deals on boxes if you shop around, so look for the places with the best prices.* Answers A and B omit the comma, and A creates a run-on sentence. Answer C uses a conjunction that does not make sense in the sentence.

5.3 C; DOK Level: 2; Language Assessment Targets: L.2.2, L.2.4. The best way to write the two ideas is to combine them with a comma and *but: Boxes can get very expensive if you buy them new, but used boxes can be free and help save trees!* Answer A omits the comma. Answer B establishes an incorrect cause-and-effect relationship. Answer D omits the connecting word and creates a run-on.

5.4 D; DOK Level: 2; Language Assessment Targets: L.2.2, L.2.4. Each idea works best as its own sentence: *Use clear or brown packing tape in a dispenser rather than masking tape to seal the boxes. Packing tape sticks better than masking tape, particularly if the boxes may get hot or cold during the move.* Combining the two ideas with only a comma or with no punctuation creates an error. While a comma and a connecting word could be used, answer B does not make sense in the sentence.

LESSON 14, *pp. 250–253*

1. D; DOK Level: 2; Reading Assessment Target: L.1.5. The word *often* is a misplaced modifier in the sentence. It describes the verb *overlook* and should be moved before it in the sentence. The modifier is misplaced in the other answer options, confusing the meaning of the sentence.

2. B; DOK Level: 2; Reading Assessment Target: L.1.5. The word *almost* belongs near the word it modifies: *all.* Answer B is correct because it is clear that the writer's experience, as indicated on the résumé, meets *almost all* of the requirements for the position. *All* does not modify the verb *meet*, nor does the introductory part of the sentence (a clause) cause a dangling modifier.

3.1 B; DOK Level: 2; Reading Assessment Target: L.1.5. Answer B is correct because *only* modifies *people who itemize deductions*, meaning that no other people use this form. Answer A is incorrect because *only* modifies *used*, not *people*, and misstates the meaning of the sentence. Answers C and D incorrectly place the modifier in awkward positions that change the meaning of the sentence.

3.2 B; DOK Level: 2; Reading Assessment Target: L.1.5. To avoid a dangling modifier, place the subject *you* after the introductory phrase. Answer B is correct: *Before starting your taxes, you need to gather your income and deduction documentation.* The other answer options do not have a word that the introductory phrase modifies.

3.3 C; DOK Level: 2; Reading Assessment Target: L.1.5. The adverbs *correctly* and *completely* both modify the verb phrase *fill out.* The adverb should be placed after the direct object, *the forms.* Answer C is correct: *As you proceed, be sure you fill out the forms correctly and completely.* In the other answer options, the modifiers are misplaced, creating confusing sentences.

3.4 C; DOK Level: 2; Reading Assessment Target: L.1.5. Answer C is correct because it avoids a dangling modifier. *You* are the person who has completed the forms and made copies for your files. The other answer choices do not have a subject that the introductory phrase modifies.

4.1 D; DOK Level: 2; Reading Assessment Target: L.1.5. Answer D is correct because *only* modifies *one* and belongs in front of it to avoid confusion. *Only* does not modify *buying.* Although *only* could modify *purpose,* meaning that the consumer's one purpose is to buy one thing, the structure of the sentence makes such an interpretation less apparent and the answer choices not as clearly correct as answer D.

4.2 B; DOK Level: 2; Reading Assessment Target: L.1.5. To avoid a dangling modifier, place the subject *retailers* after the introductory phrase. Answer B is correct: *To take advantage of this habit, retailers encourage you everywhere.* In this sentence, retailers are the people who take advantage. The other answer options do not have a subject that is modified by the introductory phrase.

4.3 A; DOK Level: 2; Reading Assessment Target: L.1.5. Answer A is correct because it includes the correct subject that the long introductory phrase modifies. Answers B and D have *you* as the incorrect subject because *grocery designers,* not *you,* placed these items as indicated in the passage. Answer C is missing the subject and creates a sentence fragment.

4.4 B; DOK Level: 2; Reading Assessment Target: L.1.5. To avoid a dangling modifier, place the subject, *retailers,* after the introductory phrase. Answer B is correct: *Helping customers shop, retailers place bright yellow sale stickers on store shelves.* Answers A and B do not have a *subject* that the introductory phrase modifies. Answer D is incorrect because, as written, the introductory phrase modifies *shelves,* and these do not help people shop.

5.1 C; DOK Level: 2; Reading Assessment Target: L.1.5. The adverb *creatively* modifies the verb *express. Creatively* belongs after the direct object *yourself.* The correct answer is C: *Modifying your car can be a great way to express yourself creatively and add extra style to your vehicle.* In the other answer options, *creatively* is a misplaced modifier.

5.2 A; DOK Level: 2; Reading Assessment Target: L.1.5. The adverb *exactly* modifies the phrase *as you wish. Exactly* belongs before the phrase: *Various options can make your vehicle look and drive exactly as you wish.* In the other answer options, *exactly* is a misplaced modifier.

5.3 C; DOK Level: 2; Reading Assessment Target: L.1.5. To avoid a dangling modifier, the subject of the sentence should be *modifications.* In this sentence, *modifications* has its own modifier, *some. Some* is placed before *modifications.* Answer C is correct: *Carrying a hefty price tag, some modifications may prove too expensive.* The other answer options do not have a subject that agrees with the introductory phrase.

5.4 D; DOK Level: 2; Reading Assessment Target: L.1.5. The adverb *always* modifies the main verb *complete.* Place *always* before *complete* in the sentence: *For example, you should always complete bodywork before selecting new tires and rims.* In the other answer options, *always* is a misplaced modifier.

1. B; DOK Level: 2; Language Assessment Target: L.1.7. Answer B is correct because *whom* should be replaced with the subject pronoun *who.* The pronoun *who* introduces a part of the sentence that tells more about the representative but is separated from the verb by the phrase *after two recounts by the board of elections.* Answer A is incorrect because the person is known. Answer C is incorrect because the person is known, and the changed pronoun is still an object pronoun. Answer D is incorrect because *which* does not refer to people.

2. C; DOK Level: 1; Language Assessment Target: L.1.7. Answer C is correct because the subject pronoun *I* should be replaced by the object pronoun *me* and because the pronoun should follow the noun. Answer A is incorrect because the subject pronoun *I* should be replaced by the object pronoun *me.* Answer B is incorrect because *she* is a subject pronoun. Answer D is incorrect because the subject pronoun *I* should be replaced by the object pronoun *me.*

3.1 A; DOK Level: 1; Language Assessment Target: L.1.7. The subject pronoun *I* correctly completes this sentence. Answer B is incorrect because *me* is an object pronoun. Answer C is incorrect because a subject pronoun is needed when the pronoun is part of the subject. Answer D is a plural object pronoun, when a singular subject pronoun is needed.

3.2 C; DOK Level: 1; Language Assessment Target: L.1.3. Answer C is correct because the subject pronoun *we* is the same person(s) as the object of *by* (unstated), which is *ourselves.* Answer A is incorrect because *ourself* is not a word. Answer B is awkward and not used in standard English. The pronoun in answer D does not agree with its antecedent, *we,* and is, therefore, incorrect.

3.3 C; DOK Level: 2; Language Assessment Target: L.1.3. Answer C is correct because the pronoun refers to the singular subject *Each person,* which takes a singular verb (*leaves*) and singular pronoun. The subject pronoun is needed because it is the subject of *leaves.* Answer A is incorrect because both the pronoun and verb are plural. Answer B is incorrect because the pronoun case is wrong; the pronouns must be subject pronouns, not object pronouns. Answer D is incorrect because the pronoun is the wrong case and number, and the verb is plural.

3.4 B; DOK Level: 2; Language Assessment Target: L.1.7. The pronoun *whoever* completes this sentence because the sentence requires a subject pronoun and because the author refers to someone unknown (*anyone*). The subject pronoun *whoever* is the subject of the verb *will be.* The interceding element *you speak to* does not affect the pronoun-antecedent agreement. Answer A is incorrect because *whom* is an object pronoun. Answer C is incorrect because *who* does not make sense in context. Answer D is incorrect because *whichever* is not used for references to people.

4.1 B; DOK Level: 2; Language Assessment Target: L.1.3. Answer B is correct because *who* is the subject of *comes.* Answers A and D are incorrect because they are object pronouns, and answer A makes no sense in context. Answer C is incorrect because *which* is not used for people.

4.2 D; DOK Level: 2; Language Assessment Target:
L.1.3. Answer D is correct because the word *this* is not left without an antecedent. Answers A and B do not refer correctly to an antecedent, and answers A and C create sentence fragments.

4.3 C; DOK Level: 2; Language Assessment Target:
L.1.7. Answer C is correct because *whom* is the object of *would like*. The subject of *would like* is *you*. Answer A is incorrect because *which* is not used for people. Answer B is incorrect because an object pronoun, not a subject pronoun, is needed. Answer D is incorrect because the person is known—one of the doctors.

4.4 A; DOK Level: 2; Language Assessment Target:
L.1.7. Answer A is correct because in this sentence, the author refers to herself and Dr. Hernandez. Because the author and Dr. Hernandez are doing the action (agreeing), the subject pronouns *he* and *I* are correct. The other answer choices do not contain subject pronouns.

5.1 D; DOK Level: 1; Language Assessment Target: L.1.7.
Answer D is correct. In this sentence, the author refers to himself and his wife. Because the noun and pronoun follow the word *to*, the object pronoun *me* is correct. Answer A is incorrect because *she* is a subject pronoun. Answer B is incorrect because *I* is a subject pronoun. Answer C is incorrect because *she* and *I* are subject pronouns.

5.2 D; DOK Level: 1; Language Assessment Target:
L.1.3. Answer D is correct because *every owner* is singular and needs a singular pronoun. Answer A is incorrect because it is a plural object pronoun, not a possessive pronoun. Answer B is incorrect because *him* and *hers* are object and possessive pronouns. Answer C is incorrect because the possessive pronoun must be singular.

5.3 B; DOK Level: 1; Language Assessment Target:
L.1.7. Answer B is correct because the author compares others with himself. An object pronoun always follows the word *like* when it indicates a comparison. Answers A and D are subject pronouns. Answer C is incorrect because the subject (*pedestrians*) and object are not the same person (even though they may be part of the same group).

5.4 A; DOK Level: 2; Language Assessment Target:
L.1.3. Answer A is correct because *These practices* becomes the subject of the sentence. The pronouns in answers B and C have no specific antecedents. Answer D is incorrect because *this* has no specific antecedent, and the comma after *them* creates a comma splice.

LESSON 16, *pp. 258–261*

1. B; DOK Level: 1; Language Assessment Target: L.1.7.
The subject *each* always takes a singular verb. *Were* and *have been* are plural, so answers A and C are incorrect. The change in answer D creates a grammatically incorrect sentence.

2. B; DOK Level: 1; Language Assessment Target: L.1.7.
The verb is closer to the singular subject, *dog*, so the singular verb *is* should be used. Answer A creates a grammatically incorrect sentence. Answers C and D are plural forms.

3.1 C; DOK Level: 1; Language Assessment Target: L.1.7.
The subject, *a cluttered home*, is singular and takes a singular verb: *is*. The long aside and the word *decorations* next to the verb should be ignored. The other options are plural verbs.

3.2 A; DOK Level: 1; Language Assessment Target:
L.1.7. The subject is *each*, which takes a singular verb. Answers B and C are plural verbs. Answer D changes the tense to the past, and although the agreement is correct, the tense shift is not. Therefore, A is the best answer choice.

3.3 C; DOK Level: 1; Language Assessment Target:
L.1.7. The subject is compound and takes a plural verb. Context requires that the sentence be in the present tense. *Are* is correct because it is plural and present tense. Answer A is singular and past tense. Answer B is singular. Answer D is past tense.

3.4 C; DOK Level: 1; Language Assessment Target:
L.1.7. The subject, *a number*, takes the plural verb *prefer*. The other options are singular.

4.1 D; DOK Level: 1; Language Assessment Target: L.1.7.
The subject, *all*, is plural in its reference to *employees*. Answers A and B are grammatically incorrect because they are not in the passive voice. Answer C is singular.

4.2 B; DOK Level: 1; Language Assessment Target:
L.1.7. *The cost* is a singular subject and takes a singular verb. The words between the subject and verb do not affect the subject-verb relationship. The other options all are plural.

4.3 A; DOK Level: 1; Language Assessment Target:
L.1.7. The subject, *every manager*, is singular and takes the singular verb *is encouraged*. The aside does not affect subject-verb agreement. Answer B is plural. Answers C and D are in the wrong tense.

4.4 C; DOK Level: 1; Language Assessment Target:
L.1.7. The subject, *mono model and two stereo models*, is compound and takes the plural form, *there are*. In this situation the subject follows the verb. *There were* is the wrong tense for the context. Answers A and B are singular.

5.1 D; DOK Level: 1; Language Assessment Target: L.1.7.
The subject, *a number*, takes a plural form of the verb. The present tense should be used because the sentence says "currently." Answers A and B are not grammatically correct. Answer C is singular.

5.2 D; DOK Level: 1; Language Assessment Target:
L.1.7. The subject, *personnel*, takes a plural verb. The word *personnel* is always plural. Answer A is singular. The context of the sentence requires present tense. Answer B is grammatically incorrect. Answer C is past tense.

5.3 C; DOK Level: 1; Language Assessment Target:
L.1.7. The subject, *an employee*, is singular and takes a singular verb; *holds up* is correct. The present tense should be used because the sentence says "these days." Answers A and D are past-tense forms. Answer B is plural.

5.4 D; DOK Level: 1; Language Assessment Target:
L.1.7. In this compound subject construction using neither/nor, *any other supervisor* is closer to the verb and is singular; *is allowed* is correct. Answers A and B are plural. Answer C is the wrong tense.

LESSON 17, *pp. 262–265*

1. B; DOK Level: 2; Language Assessment Target: L.1.6.
As written, the sentence does not display parallelism. *Studying* must be changed to *to study* to match the form of the verb *to ride: Chris set aside time to ride his bike and to study for the test.* The other answer options are neither parallel nor grammatically correct.

2. **D; DOK Level: 2; Language Assessment Target:** L.1.6. The sentence mentions the opportunity to do two things: serve as a coach and act as a role model. To give these two opportunities parallel structure, replace *acting* with *to act*. The revised sentence should read: *Coaching Little League provides an opportunity both to serve as a coach and to act as a role model for young people.* The other answer options are neither parallel nor grammatically correct.

3. **C; DOK Level: 2; Language Assessment Target:** L.1.6. To maintain parallelism, the forms of *seek* and *create* should be parallel—either both gerunds (*seeking* and *creating*) or both infinitives (*to seek* and *to create*). The correct sentence should read *As a result, many parents have begun to seek out or to create new types of reliable and affordable child care.* Answers A and B do not have parallel verb forms. Answer D is neither grammatically correct nor parallel.

4. **C; DOK Level: 2; Language Assessment Targets:** L.1.6, L.1.8. The sentence requires parallelism to describe the three types of people that parents have enlisted for child care. To create this parallelism, you must revise the third category—*people who live in their neighborhood*—to match the other two items, *friends* and *family members*. The best way to revise this portion is to replace it with the word *neighbors: One affordable child care option involves enlisting friends, family members, or neighbors to care for young children.* In addition to creating parallelism, the revision eliminates wordiness. The meaning of the sentence is changed in answer A. Answer B suggests that all of the people live in the neighborhood, which the original sentence does not state. Answer D is not parallel.

5. **B; DOK Level: 2; Language Assessment Targets:** L.1.6, L.1.8. The sentence is not parallel because different forms of the verbs are used. The correct form of the sentence should read *Some parents trade babysitting duties with another family or form co-ops with friends and neighbors.* The meaning of the sentence is changed in answer A. Answers C and D are not parallel.

6. **D; DOK Level: 2; Language Assessment Targets:** L.1.6, L.1.8. The sentence is not parallel because it has a mix of adjectives and adjective clauses. The correct form of the sentence should read *An in-home babysitter for school-age children may be another affordable child care option.* Answer A uses adjective clauses throughout but changes the meaning of the sentence and creates wordiness. Answers B and C do not have parallel structure and do not have the same meaning.

7. **A; DOK Level: 2; Language Assessment Targets:** L.1.6, L.1.8. The words modifying the noun *work* (*flexible* and *can be done informally*) are not parallel. Substituting the single adjective *informal* for the phrase *can be done informally* creates parallelism and eliminates wordiness: *Because such work is flexible and informal, many young people will take on babysitting work for a small fee.* The other answer options do not create parallelism.

8. **C; DOK Level: 2; Language Assessment Targets:** L.1.6, L.1.8. Answer C is correct because it is the clearest statement, and the three types of sales are stated in parallel structure in a series. Answer A is not parallel. Answer B changes the meaning of the sentence. Answer D leaves out too much; although it cuts out repeated words, these words are needed for clarity.

9. **A; DOK Level: 2; Language Assessment Targets:** L.1.6, L.1.8. The two equal ideas presented in the sentence are (1) sleeping late on Saturday is nice and (2) to keep a little extra money in your pocket is nice. They are not presented in parallel structure because the gerund verb form *sleeping* and the infinitive verb form *to keep* do not match. Answer A eliminates wordiness and creates parallel structure. *Sleeping late on Saturday is nice, but keeping a little extra money in your pocket is nice, too.* Answers B and C are wordy and not parallel. Answer D does not make sense.

10. **B; DOK Level: 2; Language Assessment Target:** L.1.6. In this sentence, the two equal ideas are (1) you can spend, and (2) spending. They are not presented in parallel structure because the verb forms *spend* and *spending* do not match. To correct this sentence, change the second idea to match the first: *You can spend one dollar on the same book, used, and spend the other nine dollars on different items.* The other answer options are not parallel.

11. **B; DOK Level: 2; Language Assessment Targets:** L.1.6, L.1.8. Although *A sturdy desk, an office chair,* and *a cabinet that is used for filing* are almost parallel, a better version would replace the third item in the series with *filing cabinet*, which is closer to the other terms and less wordy: *A sturdy desk, an office chair, or a filing cabinet can last for years.* The other answer options are not parallel or are wordier than the original.

12.1 **A; DOK Level: 2; Language Assessment Targets:** L.1.6, L.1.8. The list of the schools in the sentence should be kept parallel by connecting *Clifton Academy* to the rest of the schools with a comma followed by *and: Students from three Westchester County schools—Daley Junior High, Ryder Middle School, and Clifton Academy—will volunteer their time to help raise money for local kids in need.* Answer B is incorrect because using *as well as* breaks the parallel structure of the series. Answers C and D are needlessly wordy and not parallel.

12.2 **D; DOK Level: 2; Language Assessment Target:** L.1.6. The fundraising events are listed in parallel structure: *a car wash, a bake sale, a lawn-mowing service.* Therefore, to maintain parallel structure, the final event should be written in the same form: *a tree-pruning service.* The other answer options are not parallel.

12.3 **B; DOK Level: 2; Language Assessment Targets:** L.1.6, L.1.8. Either four cookies or one slice of pie will cost $1. To make the sentence parallel and avoid wordiness, the sentence should read *For example, you can buy four cookies or a slice of pie for $1.* The other answer options are not parallel and needlessly wordy.

12.4 **C; DOK Level: 2; Language Assessment Target:** L.1.6. The sentence mentions something that you can do at each school on the day of the fundraiser. These activities should be written in the same way: *You can buy great baked goods at Daley Junior High, get your car washed at Ryder Middle School, or sign up for lawn services at Clifton Academy.* The other answer options do not reflect parallelism.

1. **B; DOK Level:** 1; **Language Assessment Target:** L.1.9. Because the two sentences show a contrast, the best transition to use is *however*. This word expresses what the person thinks. On one hand, the person believes that the interest rate on the mortgage is too high. On the other hand, the person does not qualify for a lower rate. *Despite* also indicates a contrast, but you would need to add more than just the word *despite* for the sentence to make sense. *Furthermore* and *for example* do not indicate a contrast.

2. **C; DOK Level:** 1; **Language Assessment Target:** L.1.9. The sentences show a contrast between having two cars and not driving often. The best transition is *although* because it shows that there is a difference between the two ideas. *Although* helps explain that even though he has two cars, surprisingly, he does not drive often. *In contrast* and *conversely* also show contrast but sound awkward in the context of the sentences. *In addition* does not show contrast.

3.1 **C; DOK Level:** 1; **Language Assessment Target:** L.1.9. The transitional phrase *to begin* provides a logical transition between sentences. It means "here is where to start the process" and indicates a transition between the content of paragraphs 1 and 2: *To begin, follow these tips to get your résumé to the top of the stack.* The time transitions *earlier* and *after that* do not make sense in the context. *In the same way* does not make sense because no similarity is described.

3.2 **B; DOK Level:** 1; **Language Assessment Target:** L.1.9. The transition word *consequently* fits best. Because "employers have little time to read each résumé," "you should choose the information that is most relevant." The other answer options do not help show the cause-and-effect relationship as well as *consequently*.

3.3 **C; DOK Level:** 1; **Language Assessment Target:** L.1.9. The transition word *but* fits best in this context because it helps warn the reader about a potential mistake. The reader is encouraged to provide information but not to provide too much: *Be thorough in describing your previous work experience, but don't try to cram a résumé with everything you've ever thought, said, or done.* The other answer options do not make the relationship between the two statements clear.

3.4 **A; DOK Level:** 1; **Language Assessment Target:** L.1.9. The transition word *therefore* summarizes what has already been said and fits perfectly at the beginning of the final sentence in this paragraph. The other answer options do not make sense in the context of the paragraph.

4.1 **A; DOK Level:** 1; **Language Assessment Target:** L.1.9. The transition *For this reason* explains why the writer is interested in beginning employment as an apprentice (because he wants practical experience). The other answer options do not make sense in the context of the paragraph.

4.2 **D; DOK Level:** 1; **Language Assessment Target:** L.1.9. The transition word *moreover* works best because the applicant is providing additional information: *Moreover, I have real-world experience and understand how technical drawings are used by construction professionals.* The other answer options include transition words that make a contrast to the previous sentence rather than add to its claim.

4.3 **C; DOK Level:** 1; **Language Assessment Target:** L.1.9. The transition word *consequently* is a clue that the remaining information in the sentence should be the result of something in a previous sentence. The information *I am a punctual, hardworking person* in the preceding sentence best fits these criteria. The other answer options include transition words that make a contrast rather than indicate a result.

4.4 **A; DOK Level:** 1; **Language Assessment Target:** L.1.9. No transition word or phrase is needed in the sentence. The correct answer should read: *Please contact me for an interview at your earliest convenience.* The transition words provided in answers B, C, and D do not help the flow of the paragraph or work within the context.

5.1 **C; DOK Level:** 1; **Language Assessment Target:** L.1.9. The transitional phrase *For example* establishes the connection to the description of late fees; the sentence that follows provides supporting detail for how late fees will be calculated. The transition words *nevertheless* and *conversely* show contrast, not support. The transitional phrase *in addition* introduces a new idea, not an example.

5.2 **C; DOK Level:** 1; **Language Assessment Target:** L.1.9. The transitional phrase *At that time* works best because it helps make the connection to what happens at the time that the checklist is submitted: *At that time, the Landlord will have three days to repair all problems noted on the move-in checklist.* The other transition words refer to times that do not make sense in the context of the paragraph.

5.3 **B; DOK Level:** 1; **Language Assessment Target:** L.1.9. The transitional phrase *Furthermore, upon vacating* works best because it makes the connection to what happens when the lessees move out and adds to the responsibility of the move-in list: *Furthermore, upon vacating, Lessees agree to submit to the Landlord a move-out checklist documenting the condition of the property.* The other transition words do not make the connection to additional responsibility and time, nor do they make sense in context.

5.4 **A; DOK Level:** 1; **Language Assessment Target:** L.1.9. The transition *In addition* works best because it indicates that the lease agreement is introducing another topic (in this case, a group of policies in the lease): *In addition, Lessees agree to use the Premises only in the following ways.* *Nevertheless* shows contrast, not an additional idea. *Similarly* shows that two ideas are alike. *After that* shows a time sequence.

1. **B; DOK Level:** 2; **Writing Assessment Target:** W.2; **Language Assessment Target:** L.1.9. Remove sentence 2 because it is off the topic. Sentence 2 comments on the expense of visiting a doctor for allergy shots, but the topic of the paragraph is the development of the allergy shot. Sentence 2 interrupts the flow and breaks the connection between sentence 1 and sentence 3, thus destroying the unity of the paragraph. Moving it elsewhere does not improve the paragraph.

UNIT 4 (continued)

2. **C; DOK Level: 2; Writing Assessment Target:** W.2; **Language Assessment Target:** L.1.9. Sentence 4 should follow sentence 5 because sentence 5 discusses the extraction of pollen. Logically, this step comes first in the sequence described in the paragraph. Administering the extract cannot occur until after it has been extracted. Moving sentence 4 corrects the sequence in the paragraph.

3. **DOK Level: 2; Writing Assessment Target:** W.2; **Language Assessment Target:** L.1.9. Sentence 1: **Sentence C** introduces the topic of the memo and the paragraph: a new travel policy has been instituted to control company costs.

Sentence 2: **Sentence B** is the second sentence because it supports the topic sentence by providing background for the new policy. Sentence B introduces the idea that a team was formed to study the travel policy issue. The word *this* indicates that the policy already has been mentioned, so sentence B cannot be the first sentence.

Sentence 3: **Sentence E** is the logical choice because sentence B indicates two goals of the study. The transition *first goal* and the content of the sentence indicate that this is the first of the goals.

Sentence 4: **Sentence A** is the logical choice because it is the second goal, indicated by the content and the transition *second goal*.

Sentence 5: **Sentence D** is a concluding sentence in the paragraph because it explains the result of the team's work: that a recommendation was made and that the company approved the recommendation. The sequence of ideas in the paragraph requires that this sentence come after the other sentences. Furthermore, this sentence provides a logical conclusion to the paragraph.

4. **A; DOK Level: 2; Writing Assessment Target:** W.2; **Language Assessment Target:** L.1.9. Sentence 5 explains what happened *in the past,* and sentence 4 tells what happens *now*. The logical sequence is to place sentence 4 after sentence 5 because the transition word *now* needs a point of contrast: *now* as opposed to *the past*. The flow of the paragraph is less logical if the order of the sentences is not reversed. No other place makes sense in the paragraph, and there is no reason to delete the sentence.

5. **B; DOK Level: 2; Writing Assessment Target:** W.2; **Language Assessment Target:** L.1.9. Sentence 9 is the topic sentence because it introduces beads as the best material to use when starting to make jewelry. Although it is the topic sentence, it does not belong at the very beginning of the paragraph because it provides the answer to the question asked in sentence 6. No other place in the paragraph is logical for sentence 9.

6. **D; DOK Level: 2; Writing Assessment Target:** W.2; **Language Assessment Target:** L.1.9. Sentence 16 follows sentence 13 because it is part of an example of the information you will find when you look on Web sites for information about how to make jewelry. The transition *for example* in sentence 13 gives you a clue, and the sentences explaining the example belong together. Sentence 16 is closely related to the information in the paragraph and should not be removed.

7. **D; DOK Level: 2; Writing Assessment Target:** W.2; **Language Assessment Target:** L.1.9. Sentence 18 is the topic sentence because it introduces the topic of keeping projects simple when a person begins making jewelry. The other sentences continue the idea of keeping projects simple and progressing to more difficult ones as the person gains more experience.

8. **C; DOK Level: 2; Writing Assessment Target:** W.2; **Language Assessment Target:** L.1.9. Sentence 22 should be placed after sentence 20, as it follows up on and expands on the subject of sentence 20. It is not connected to the previous paragraph, so choice A is incorrect. Answer D is not the best location for this sentence as it is more connected to the idea that comes before. Answer B is incorrect because it does not flow with the natural progression of the paragraph and the patience needed to reach the skill mentioned in the sentence.

9. **C; DOK Level: 2; Writing Assessment Target:** W.2; **Language Assessment Target:** L.1.9. Sentence 7 is the topic sentence because it introduces the high cost of COBRA coverage and logically belongs at the beginning of the paragraph. Without it, the paragraph is difficult to understand.

10. **D; DOK Level: 2; Writing Assessment Target:** W.2; **Language Assessment Target:** L.1.9. Sentence 11 follows sentence 9 because it provides additional explanation about the eligibility date of COBRA coverage. No other placement makes logical sense. The sentence should not be removed because it provides important and relevant information.

11. **D; DOK Level: 2; Writing Assessment Target:** W.2; **Language Assessment Target:** L.1.9. Sentence 14 should follow sentence 16 because it explains that the benefits of the plan are worthwhile, even though the plan is costly.

12. **B; DOK Level: 2; Writing Assessment Target:** W.2; **Language Assessment Target:** L.1.9. Sentence 17 should be removed from paragraph D. The content of the paragraph and the passage does not say that COBRA saves money in the end. In fact, the paragraph says that COBRA is costly. The advantage to COBRA is not financial saving but rather "peace of mind."

13. **C; DOK Level: 2; Writing Assessment Target:** W.2; **Language Assessment Target:** L.1.9. Sentence 20 should be placed at the end of paragraph E, as it is the final thought. After all of the information given, if the addressee still needs assistance, he should reach out to the writer of the letter. The other locations do not make sense, as the addressee is given more information after each of those locations.

LESSON 20, *pp. 274–277*

1. **B; DOK Level: 1; Language Assessment Targets:** L.2.2, L.2.4. The quotation is missing the initial quotation mark; therefore, answer B is correct. Answer A is incorrect because no comma is needed after *Day*. The existing punctuation is correct. Answer C is incorrect because the question mark is needed as the end mark of the quoted question. Answer D is incorrect because there is no reason to add a hyphen, which indicates a compound. *New* and *neighbor* makes no sense as a compound. *New* is the only word that modifies *neighbor*.

2. **C; DOK Level: 1; Language Assessment Target:** L.2.4. Writers often use parentheses to set aside parts of a sentence that are not necessary for understanding the meaning but that provide extra information. In this sentence, the phrase *assuming I stick to my plan* is extra information and needs to be separated from the rest of the sentence. The corrected sentence should read: *I am starting my diet tomorrow (assuming I stick to my plan)*. The phrase should not be quoted because the writer is not quoting someone else (the writer is speaking in the first person). Using a colon or a semicolon is not the correct way to separate the phrase.

3.1 B; DOK Level: 1; **Language Assessment Target:** L.2.4. The words *domestic Tranquility* are part of a quotation from the U.S. Constitution and should be placed in quotation marks. The period belongs inside the final quotation mark. The sentence includes the initial quotation mark beginning the quotation. It must have a final quotation mark to close the quotation. The correct sentence should read: *The Founders wrote the Constitution of the United States "to form a more perfect Union, establish Justice, [and] insure domestic Tranquility."*

3.2 D; DOK Level: 1; **Language Assessment Target:** L.2.4. The modifiers *well* and *informed* should be hyphenated because they form a combined idea. The correct sentence should read: *The first step in the voting process is to research the candidates and issues that will be on the next ballot; a well-informed voter is a good voter.* The hyphen is omitted from answer A and misplaced in answer B. Answer C has an incorrect end quotation mark.

3.3 B; DOK Level: 1; **Language Assessment Targets:** L.2.2, L.2.4. A semicolon should combine the two sentences and be placed before the transition word *therefore.* A comma must follow *therefore.* The correct sentence should read: *Be aware that a writer may have a certain agenda for or against a candidate or an issue; therefore, you should read several sources to form a balanced point of view.* Answer A creates a run-on sentence. Answer C omits the comma, and answer D uses a colon instead of a semicolon.

3.4 A; DOK Level: 1; **Language Assessment Target:** L.2.4. A colon is used to introduce a list. In this sentence, three pieces of identification are listed. The correct sentence should read: *When you arrive at your voting location on Election Day, be sure to have with you one of the following pieces of identification: a driver's license, a military identification card, or a utility bill.* Answers B and C have incorrect punctuation. Answer D omits the correct punctuation.

4.1 B; DOK Level: 1; **Language Assessment Target:** L.2.4. The modifier *ready-made* should be hyphenated because the words form a combined idea. The correct sentence should read: *Even though you can find ready-made barbecue sauce at the store, it's never quite as good as making it from scratch.* The hyphen is misplaced in answer A and omitted in answer C. Answer D includes incorrect comma use.

4.2 C; DOK Level: 1; **Language Assessment Target:** L.2.4. A colon introduces a list. In this sentence, a series of ingredients is listed. The correct sentence should read: *Wait about five minutes, and then add the following ingredients: 1 1/2 cups of ketchup, 1/2 cup of apple cider vinegar, 1/4 cup of Worcestershire sauce, 1/3 cup of dark brown sugar, and a tablespoon of chili powder.* The other answer options use incorrect punctuation.

4.3 A; DOK Level: 1; **Language Assessment Target:** L.2.4. A semicolon should combine the two sentences. The semicolon belongs before the transition word *however.* A comma must follow *however.* The correct sentence should read: *Serving one type of meat surely will impress your guests; however, the best barbecue masters know to serve two or more types of meat.* Answers B, C, and D have incorrect punctuation.

4.4 D; DOK Level: 1; **Language Assessment Target:** L.2.4. Answer D is correct because the parentheses are complete and placed correctly. Answer A is missing the end punctuation. Answer B uses only an introductory quotation mark, so even if quotation marks were needed, the answer would be incorrect. Answer C is missing the introductory parenthesis and places the period inside the end parenthesis.

5.1 A; DOK Level: 1; **Language Assessment Target:** L.2.4. The question is phrased as a direct quotation and should have quotation marks around it. The question mark belongs inside the closing quotation mark. The correct sentence should read: *Ask yourself, "Am I prepared for a hurricane?"* Quotation marks are omitted in answer B. The question mark is placed in the wrong position in answer C. The final quotation mark is not included in answer D.

5.2 C; DOK Level: 1; **Language Assessment Target:** L.2.4. The modifier *well-prepared* should be hyphenated because the words form a combined idea. The correct sentence should read: *For those of us who live near the coast, being well-prepared citizens is critical.* The hyphen is missing from answer B. The other answer options have incorrect punctuation.

5.3 B; DOK Level: 1; **Language Assessment Target:** L.2.4. A colon introduces a list. In this sentence, the list contains four hurricane hazards. The correct sentence should read: *Learn about hurricane hazards: storm surge, high winds, tornadoes, and flooding.* The semicolon in answer A is incorrect because it should not separate a complete statement and a list. Answer C is missing the colon, and the first comma in answer D is incorrect.

5.4 D; DOK Level: 1; **Language Assessment Target:** L.2.4. Writers often use parentheses to set aside parts of a sentence that are not necessary for understanding its meaning but provide extra information. In this sentence, it is not necessary for the reader to know the items in the disaster kit. This is additional information. The correct sentence should read: *Build a disaster kit (including batteries, bottled water, and flashlights).* The other answer options have incorrect punctuation.

EDITING AT WORK, *pp. 278–279*

MARKETING, SALES, AND SERVICE

1.1 D; DOK Level: 1; **Writing Assessment Target:** W.3 The sentence is giving information about what to do in the present, so the present-tense *move* is required. *Will move* and *moved* are the wrong tense, and *moving* is the wrong form.

1.2 B; DOK Level: 1; **Writing Assessment Target:** W.3 The word *comedies* is correct in this context. *Comedys* is an incorrect spelling of *comedies.* There is no need for possessive, so *comedy's* and *comedies'* are incorrect.

1.3 A; DOK Level: 1; **Language Assessment Targets:** L.1.1, L.1.3 The possessive pronoun *your* is correct. *You're* is the contraction for *you are*, which does not make sense in this context. *Yore* and *youre* are incorrect because they misspell *your.*

1.4 C; DOK Level: 2; **Language Assessment Targets:** L.2.2, L.2.4 These clauses can be combined by using a comma and the word *and. Keep in mind that you won't lose any money by trying it, and you can cancel at any time. It can* does not make sense in context. Using *it you can* creates a run-on sentence. Answers B and D create a run-on sentence. Using a comma by itself creates a run-on sentence.

HOSPITALITY AND TOURISM

2.1 **B; DOK Level:** 2; **Language Assessment Target:**
L.1.5. *Carefully* modifies the infinitive *to review.* The adverb should be placed after the object *them. The rules for taxes are different for every country, so take the time to review them carefully.* In the other answer options, *carefully* is a misplaced modifier.

2.2 **D; DOK Level:** 2; **Language Assessment Target:**
L.1.7. The subject is compound and takes a plural verb. Context requires that it be in the present tense. *Are* is correct. *Was* is incorrect because it is singular and past tense. *Were* is past tense, and *is* is singular.

2.3 **C; DOK Level:** 1; **Language Assessment Target:**
L.1.9. The transitional phrase *For example* establishes the connection to common mistakes. Refunding the entire cost of a trip when taxes are non-refundable is an example of a common mistake. *Subsequently* indicates that the refund will happen after common mistakes. *Consequently* indicates that the refund will happen as a result of common mistakes. *Although* indicates a contrast between the two ideas.

2.4 **A; DOK Level:** 1; **Language Assessment Target:**
L.2.4. The sentence begins with an introductory phrase—*When identity thieves gain access to victims' credit cards*—after which a comma should be placed. Placing the comma after *victims'* or *credit* is incorrect. Omitting the comma is also incorrect.

Index

A

Action strategy, 186
Adjectives
  function of, 250–253
  hyphenated, 274
  proper adjectives, 230
  separated by commas, 197, 238–251
Adverbs, 196, 250–253, 274
Ain't, 83, 99, 226, 229
Analogies, 50, 84, 144
Analysis as supporting detail, 270
Anecdotes, 170, 176, 186–187, 189
Antecedents, 197, 202, 254
Antithesis, 144
Apostrophes, 197, 214–217
Appeals
  to emotions, 30, 120–121, 126, 130
  to ethics, 120–121
  to logic, 120–121
  to patriotism, 38
Argument analysis
  analyzing elements of persuasion,
    116–119
  analyzing rhetorical devices, 144–147
  analyzing structure, 140–143
  analyzing visuals and data, 126–129
  classifying valid and invalid evidence,
    134–137
  determining author's purpose, 112–115
  identifying evidence, 120–123
  identifying faulty evidence, 130–133
  premise, 124–125
Article titles, 230–233
Asides, 258–261
At Work
  Editing at Work, 278–279
  Reading Comprehension at Work,
    110–111
Audience
  determining genre, 160
  identifying to understand author's
    purpose, 112
  style appropriate to, 38
Author's perspective, 148, 156
Author's point of view, 30–34, 46
Author's purpose
  determining, 42, 112–115, 156
  determining genre, 160
  style appropriate to, 38

B

Biased arguments, 134
Book titles, 230–233
Brainstorming, 178
But, 266

C

Call to action, 186
Capitalization, 197, 230–234

Categorizing, 16–19
Cause and effect
  evaluating, 130
  identifying in fiction, 60–63
  identifying in nonfiction, 20–23
  showing in combined sentences, 242
  transitions showing, 172, 266
Characters
  actions, thoughts, dialogue affecting
    events, 60
  analyzing, 76–79, 106
  making inferences about, 94
  relationship to setting, 80
Charts, 126
Claims
  developing, 174–177
  support of, 116, 120, 134, 140, 170
  understanding to evaluate evidence,
    134
Clauses, 196–197, 238–241
Climax, 70, 144
Closer Look at Items
  context clues in passages, 54
  drag-and-drop items, 120
  fill-in-the-blank questions, 70
  signal words for cause-and-effect
    questions, 20
  skills demonstrated, 130
Collective nouns, 198–201, 254,
  258–261
Colons, 274–277
Commas
  checking for proper placement,
    196–197
  in complex sentences, 242
  in compound sentences, 238, 242
  in dialogue and quotations, 238–241
  following transition words, 246
  function of, 274–277
  separating adjectives, 238–241
  in series, 238–241
Comma splices, 246
Common nouns, 230
Comparing and contrasting
  analogies, 144
  in fiction, 64–67
  in nonfiction, 24–27
  opposing arguments, 170–173
  showing in combined sentences, 242
  texts, 148–151
  texts with different formats, 152–155
  texts with different genres, 160–163
  texts with similar genres, 156–159
  using Venn diagrams, 178
Complete idea, 234–237, 274
Complex sentences, 196, 242
Complications in plot, 70
Compound sentences, 196, 238, 242
Compound subjects, 222, 254, 258
Computer Tips, electronic highlighting,
  116, 144
Conclusion, 140, 186–189
Conclusions, drawing
  drawing in fiction, 102–105
  drawing from multiple texts, 164–167
  drawing in nonfiction, 42–45, 50

  in persuasive texts, 140
  writing, 186–189
Conflict, 70
Conjunctions
  combining sentences with, 196,
    242–265, 266
  connecting parts of subjects, 242,
    258–261
Connecting words, 242–245, 246
  See also **Conjunctions**
Connection strategy, 186
Connotations, 38, 54, 58–59
Content Practices, vii
Content Topics, vii
  figurative language in nonfiction, 84
  interrupting phrases/clauses, 238
  plural nouns, 198
  possessive words, 214
  singular present-tense verbs, 222
  transitions showing causal
    relationships, 266
  using reflexive pronouns, 254
Context clues, using, 34, 54–57, 218
Contractions, 195, 214–217
Contrasting. *See* **Comparing and
  contrasting**
Coulda, 226
Counterclaims, 116, 172–173, 176

D

Dangling modifiers, 250
Data, analyzing, 126–129
Defining points for extended response,
  178–181
Depth of Knowledge (DOK), vi
Descriptions, 2
Diagrams, 152
Dialogue, 186–188, 238–241, 274–277
Double negatives, 226
Drafting extended response, 190–193
Dunno, 226

E

Editing
  apostrophes, 197, 214–217
  capitalization, 197, 230–233
  commas, 196, 197, 238–242, 246, 266,
    274
  frequently confused words, 197, 218–221
  modifiers, 197, 250–253. *See also*
  **Adjective; Adverbs; Prepositional
  phrases**
  nouns, 194, 197–202, 214–217, 222,
    230, 238, 254, 258–261
  paragraph organization, 270–273
  parallelism, 144, 176, 196, 262–265
  pronouns, 197, 202–205, 214, 222,
    226, 254–257, 258
  punctuation, 196–197, 214–217, 234,
    238–249, 266, 274–277

INDEX

S

Sandwich structure, 140
Semicolons, 196, 242, 274–277
Sentences
  combining, 238–241, 242–245, 274–277
  components of, 234
  correcting fragments, 234–237
  correcting run-ons, 246–249
  inverted construction, 258–261
  making corrections, 196
  parallel structure, 262–265
  punctuation of, 234, 238–241, 274–277
  topic sentences, 2, 270–273
Sequence, 6, 10–13, 14–15, 74–75, 182, 242
Series, 238–241
Setting
  analyzing, 80–83
  making inferences about, 94
Should of, 226
Signal words
  for cause and effect, 20, 60, 172–174
  combining sentences with, 242
  for comparisons and contrasts, 16, 24, 84
  for conclusions, 140
  for generalizations, 46
  for sequences, 6, 10
Similes, 84
Singular nouns, 198–201
Singular subjects, 197, 222
Singular verbs, 197, 222
Song titles, 230–233
Sources, reliability of, 134
Speeches, 160
Spotlighted Items
  drag-and-drop, 11–12, 17, 22, 26, 31, 40, 43, 49, 61, 77, 108, 117, 120–121, 153, 161, 165, 172–173, 187, 271
  drop-down, 198–277
  extended response, 170–197
Standard English, 226–229
Statistics, 2, 170, 176, 270
Steck-Vaughn Test Preparation for GED® Test, x–xi
Stereotypes, 46
Stories. *See* Fiction Story titles, 230–233
Structure of extended response, 182–185
Study skills, xv
Style and tone
  analyzing, 38–41
  in different genres, 160
  use of rhetorical devices, 144
Subject areas on GED® test, vi
Subject-by-subject structure, 182–185, 190
Subject of sentence, 234
Subject-verb agreement, 197, 222–225, 258–261
Subordinating conjunctions, 196
Summarizing, 6–9
Summaries, 6
Supporting details, 2, 126, 130, 270
Suppose to, 226
Synthesizing information, 50–53, 164–167

T

Tables, 126, 129, 152, 153
Tenses, 206–209
Test-Taking Tips, xiv
  answering questions about two passages, 50
  consistent tenses, 206
  details revealing theme, 98
  determining author's purpose, 38
  evaluating evidence, 134
  examining visuals, 126
  finding information in texts, 24
  hyphens, 274
  identifying author's perspective, 148
  identifying cause and effect, 60
  making inferences, 34, 94, 112
  multiple-choice questions, 156
  paragraph organization, 270
  pronouns indicating point of view, 90
  questions about paired passages, 160
  relating paragraphs to main idea, 16
  response to other points of view, 170
  topic sentences, 2
  word choice, 194
Text comparison
  comparing and contrasting texts, 148–151
  of different formats, 152–155
  in different genres, 160–163
  gaining information from multiple texts, 164–167
  in similar genres, 156–159
Text structure
  of arguments, 140–143
  comparing, 156
  of extended response, 182–185, 190
Theme, identifying, 98–101
There is/There are, 258–261
Thesis of extended response
  developing, 174–177
  gathering supporting points and evidence, 178–181
  introduction and restatement of, 186
Thesis statement for extended response, 174, 177, 181, 186, 188, 190–191
Timelines, 10, 12, 152
Titles
  of articles, 152
  capitalization of, 230–233
  clues to main idea in, 2
  of graphs and tables, 126, 152
Tone
  analyzing, 38–41
  comparing, 156
  making inferences from, 34
  use of rhetorical devices, 144
Topic, 30, 38, 42, 116, 182, 186, 206
Topic sentences, 2, 270–273
Transitions, 28–29, 68–69, 140, 172–174, 176, 186, 188–195, 266–269. *See also* Signal words

U

Usage, 194-195
Use to, 226

Using Logic
  brainstorming argument points, 178
  combining sentences, 242
  common and proper nouns, 230
  considering audience, 182
  dangling modifiers, 250
  double negatives, 226
  drawing conclusions, 42, 102
  elements of setting, 80
  fill-in-the-blank questions, 174
  identifying fragments, 234
  identifying run-on sentences, 246
  key words for time, 210
  over-generalization, 46
  pronoun-antecedent agreement, 202
  subject-verb agreement with *neither/nor*, 258
  summaries, 6
  titles of text and tables, 152
  transitions, 140, 186
  using a frame for body of paragraphs, 190
  using context clues, 218
  viewpoint of editorials and opinion pieces, 30

V

Vague language, 194
Valid evidence, 134
Valid generalizations, 46
Venn diagrams, 178
Verbals, 262
Verbs
  agreement with subject, 197, 222–225, 258–260
  basic tenses, 206–209
  with helping verbs, 210–213
  as part of sentences, 234–237
  perfect tenses, 210–213
  progressive tenses, 210–213
  regular and irregular verbs, 206–209
  vague verbs, 194
Viewpoint. *See* Author's point of view; Narrative point of view, determining; Point of view
Visuals, analyzing, 126–129

W

Will, 210
Word choice, 38, 156, 194–195
Wordiness, 195, 262

Y

Yet, 24, 266